THE SWORD AND THE FLAME

Selections from Heinrich Heine's Prose

THE SWORD AND THE FLAME

Selections from Heinrich Heine's Prose

EDITED WITH AN INTRODUCTION BY
ALFRED WERNER

NEW YORK · THOMAS YOSELOFF · LONDON

© 1960 by A. S. Barnes and Company, Inc.

Library of Congress Catalog Card Number : 59—946r

Thomas Yoseloff, *Publisher*
11 East 36th Street
New York 16, N.Y.

*

Thomas Yoseloff Ltd.
123 New Bond Street
London W.1, England

*The selections from Heine's prose are based on
the translation by Charles Godfrey Leland.*

Printed in the United States of America

FOR JUDITH

Hymn

I am the sword, I am the flame.

I brought light into your darkness, and when the battle began, I fought in your van, in the first row.

Round about me lie the corpses of my friends, but we have conquered. We have conquered, but the corpses of my friends are lying all around us. In the midst of the jubilant triumphal chants, there sound the dirges of the funeral. But we have time neither for rejoicing nor for mourning. Once more the trumpets sound, a new battle begins.

I am the sword, I am the flame.

Translated by Sophie Wilkins

Contents

Introduction

Heine's Puzzling Character

Heine, the clarion of all brains which seethe
With bright revolt and swift iconoclasm . . .
MICHAEL WILLIAM ROSSETTI

IN 1837 THE POET HEINRICH HEINE WROTE TO HIS BROTHER
MAXIMILIAN:

How shall I fare in my old age? Frankly speaking, I do not care to
think of it. I presume that I shall increase the number of noble and
great Germans who go to their graves with broken hearts and torn
coats. Presumably the city of Duesseldorf will erect me a monument.

The first part of the prophecy came true in 1856. But Heine was
in his grave ninety-seven years before his native city finally erected
a monument in his honor. There had been monuments in Frankfurt-
on-Main and in Hamburg, but they were removed in 1933, that
miserable year in which " Die Lorelei " appeared in German school
textbooks with the laconic remark: " Author unknown." Heine
would have been mildly amused by the spectacle of educators, in
a fit of Nazi-dictated amnesia, forgetting the name of the author of
that poem about the maiden combing her golden hair on a cliff
by the River Rhine.

Yet he would have laughed out loud upon hearing the disputes
still raging about his personality and work. His unsurpassed irony
would have been titillated by this battle of conflicting opinions.
For some still go along with Thomas Carlyle who called Heine a
" blackguard " (and, to substantiate this verdict, they can cite passages in his writings that reveal Heine full of vengeance and spite).
Others claim, with equal justification, that he was vindictive only
when provoked, and that he could be the most loyal and generous
of men. When, in 1956, the Heine Centenary called forth the publication of a dozen volumes, the new biographers once more asked
the same questions that had been raised before by two or three
generations of writers:

Was Heine really sympathetic to the hardships of people, or

11

was he, who calmly pocketed a pension from a reactionary ruler, merely an opportunist, in love with nobody but himself? Was he essentially an improvident poet who produced potboilers to ward off bankruptcy, or was he merely a skillful journalist who, in rare moments of inspiration, wrote a few immortal songs? Was he honest in what he wrote and did?

After having read these biographies, one is inclined to think that, whatever answers may have been attempted, there are as many Heines as there are books about him. Nevertheless, one fact should emerge with clarity: plagued by doubts though he was, Heine was basically honest. If he contradicted himself, it was not because, as his enemies claimed, he lacked conviction, but because a human being changes constantly. The cocky Heine of twenty-five, emboldened by his early success, was not the same Heine as the stricken man of fifty-five, waiting for death to end his pain yet at the same time stubbornly clinging to life, still ironic yet full of wisdom.

It was the aging Heine that Ferdinand Lassalle knew and pitied as a man " hated and bespattered with mud by the mindless multitude, thrust out and betrayed by the baseness of his own family of shopkeepers . . . the very picture of genius done to death by the sledge hammer blows of mediocrity." Heine's recent biographer, Elizabeth M. Butler, is less dramatic in her expressions, but she, too, refuses to criticize him as venal, mercenary, or simply irresponsible. Equally far from hero worship as from the Philistines' petty criticism, she wrote:

It is sometimes difficult to come to terms with Heine, because it is difficult to come to terms with life. Life, like Heine, can be disquieting, life also destroys what it creates. Like Heine, life questions our human values and often gives unacceptable answers.

One need not, then, overlook certain unpretty episodes in Heine's life in order to maintain that, among other things, he epitomizes the tragedy of modern man struggling in an age of transition, the genius in distress, fighting for sheer physical survival. He himself did not feel very comfortable about his " Byronic dividedness," yet he managed to explain and even excuse it with a very persuasive argument:

Oh, dear reader, if you feel like complaining about that "divided-ness," you should rather complain that the world itself has been torn neatly in half. For since the poet's heart is the center of the world, it follows that he must now be grievously divided. Whoever claims that his heart has remained whole is only confessing that he has a prosaic, remotely provincial, small-town heart. But through mine the great rift of the world has passed, and for that very reason I know that the mighty gods have granted me high favor above many others and thought me worthy of the martyrdom of poets.

When he wrote this, Heine was only thirty-four, had acquired fame, and was still far, very far away from that real martyrdom that was to corrode the last eight years of his life. But one suspects that this melodramatic swagger served to conceal a genuine concern for public opinion. The satanic amorality displayed by some of his confreres was alien to this scion of a proper middle-class family who liked to talk grandiosely but, amorous escapades not-withstanding, lived a life essentially of work, reading, writing, attending exhibitions and the theater, and permitted himself few opportunities to play Cagliostro or Casanova. In fact, he winced at the verdict hurled at him from the start of his career: "*Ein Talent, doch kein Charakter.*" Revenging himself on his denigrators, he reversed this indictment when penning the epitaph for his respect-able, yet very mediocre, hero, the dancing-bear Atta Troll: "*Kein Talent, doch ein Charakter!*" Was mediocrity all that the public demanded?

Were it not for the fact that this "no character" accusation kept some of the public from the full enjoyment of Heine's never-aging, subtle, yet virile, poetry and the joyous cascades of his vivacious prose, we might not be concerned here with the charge. Heine knew what the world thought of him as a person. He did not enjoy the ill repute, and he was sure he did not deserve it. He once wrote: "Wit is bearable only when it rests on a serious foundation." He was a serious and, on the whole, ethical person who hurt himself more by his tendency to conceal his sensitive nature behind outbursts of self-deflating humor than by his careless deeds, of which he had no more than his quota.

He developed this protective device at an early age, for when he was only twenty-two a close friend felt that Heine needed defense: "He is one of the best-hearted and most faithful persons I have ever known, but he acts as though ashamed of his affability, and shows himself in the worst possible light."

At the height of his career Heine boasted of his venality to the priggish publicist Ludwig Boerne (who was the wrong confidant). Yet, as August Lewald wrote, despite his often difficult financial situation, "Heine avoided all contact with corruption; I have myself seen him refuse the proposals of publishers which did not seem to him quite above suspicion."

Many people who met him were deceived by his mannerisms; for years he cultivated not only the Byronic pose but also the satanic expression that denotes a genius given to reckless living. But he could not mislead Robert Schumann. The composer (who was to set to music "The Two Grenadiers" and other poems) understood that Heine was neither misanthrope nor nihilist: "About his mouth lay a bitter, ironic smile, but it was a smile only for the pettiness of life, and a scorn only for petty people."

It might be better still to hear what Heine said about himself, for Heine is "known" to too many people by what others have said rather than from what he himself has written. Heine was both myth and mystery, yet so little Olympian, so disarmingly frank most of the time, that only evil intention or gross ignorance of human nature has created the distorted image still haunting his name.

The many-faceted character of a poet offers sharp edges to the grasp. Heine self-consciously gloried in these contradictions: "I am a Jew, a Christian; I am tragedy, I am comedy—Heraclitus and Democritus in one; a Greek, a Hebrew; an adorer of despotism as incarnate in Napoleon; an admirer of communism as embodied in Proudhon; a Latin, a Teuton; a beast, a devil, a god."

Among German writers of the past only Goethe was as complicated, as "contradictory," as Heine. But the son of a patrician and

14

the cabinet minister of a German prince could get away with many a bold statement and a most unorthodox way of life, whereas Heine, the son of a simple Jewish tradesman, a free-lance writer without status and regular income, could not. Goethe's affairs of the heart are noted in textbooks for German secondary schools, and the pupils are required to memorize the names of the women he loved. No one castigated Goethe for his *Venetian Epigrams*, although they are as frankly sexual as the most daring verse Heine wrote ; Goethe's outspokenly anti-Christian utterances and his admiration for Napoleon, the enslaver of the Germans, did not prevent him from becoming the god of German literature.

For a profligate, atheist, and political mountebank (for that is what he represented to the solid German citizen of his time), Heine started out with unusually serious principles : " Be severe with yourself, that is the artist's foremost law." There were not many young men at the universities of Bonn, Goettingen, and Berlin as earnest as he ; and Heine, while he loathed the study of law, which had been forced upon him by his rich uncle Salomon, absorbed an enormous amount of knowledge in history, literature, and philosophy that was to be useful in later years in the writing of his great prose works, *The Romantic School* and *History of Religion and Philosophy in Germany*. As a student he shunned the drinking bouts of his fellows. He wooed such respectable young ladies as his lovely but haughty cousins : first Amalie, then Therese. We might speculate what turn his life would have taken had one of these daughters of the millionaire Salomon Heine accepted the poet as a husband. Surely his life would have run differently — but would he have lived more happily with one of these pampered, spoiled creatures than with the childish, lazy, and ignorant, yet also cheerful and feminine, Parisian shopgirl he did marry ? Whatever the answer, this much can be said — that while Heine would always have been Heine, his life and work would have been different had he not in his twenties contracted syphilis[1] (which, before Ehrlich's

---

[1] It is now generally believed that Heine's illness was caused by a syphilitic infection ; some biographers, however, still maintain that his illness was a progressive muscular atrophy, and thus not connected with a venereal disease.

discovery of salvarsan, was incurable) ; and if, instead of a life of unceasing financial anxiety, he could have realized his ardent dream of a professorship at a German university, or at least obtained some other steady and respectable position.

It is curious that only he of all the children of Betty van Geldern and Samson Heine did not achieve social success. Charlotte married a rich Hamburg merchant ; Max was appointed a physician to the Czar's court at St. Petersburg ; Gustav became editor of the most conservative Viennese paper and was rewarded with the title of Baron. Heine was an aristocrat of a different kind. While still a fairly young man, he was made aware — at first very unhappily — of an abyss between himself and the world. In a letter, he wrote :

A fearful delusion possesses me : I am beginning to believe myself that I am differently organized spiritually from other people and that I have more depth. Somber wrath lies like a burning mantle of snow over my soul. I long for eternal night . . . so much that is baleful oppresses my heart.

Oddly enough, the one member of his family to whom he felt the closest kinship was the renowned banker Salomon Heine, a poorly educated man with neither taste nor higher desires, but a genius nevertheless. For nearly a quarter of a century the poet fenced with his uncle, begging for money and more money — now jabbing at the millionaire with his poisoned wit, now swallowing his pride and once again begging for money. He was fascinated by this curious man who dominated his life and who sought first to turn him into a cloth dealer (Harry Heine & Co. went into bankruptcy in the first year!), then granted him funds for university study, but only for the study of law. Sending a copy of a new poem to a friend, Heine asked : " But, really . . . after you have read this song do you still really believe that I shall become a lawyer?"

In 1825, the year in which he was baptized into the Lutheran faith and received his Doctor of Law degree, he wrote to a lady about himself and his uncle :

We are . . . similar in manner and character : the same stubborn, bold incredible softness of heart and incalculable madness, only that

16

fortune has made of him a millionaire and of me the contrary, I mean a poet, and has thus developed us along entirely different lines in viewpoint and mode of living.

A poet! Many of the people who have written about Heine have missed this significant point. They no more understood what it means to be a poet than the banker whose sole comment on his nephew's fame was: " If the boy had only learned something he would not be driven to write books." The honest but limited Boerne thought he dealt his young colleague a deathblow when he declared: " All that he loves in Truth is the beautiful." Yet an artist's approach to Truth is different from that of a philosopher, or of a political thinker like Boerne. A poet reacts to the world not with his intellect alone, but with his excitable nerve-ends as well. His impressionability, his extreme susceptibility to both beauty and its opposite, his sensualism, often make him a poor reporter, and an even worse historian, for the artistic effect is more important to him than accuracy. When a friend, reading the manuscript of *History of Religion and Philosophy in Germany* objected, with reason, to certain passages, Heine reacted like a poet: " But isn't it well expressed?"

That a poet's communication with the world takes place on a different level from that of other men ; that his perceptual method (non-rational, non-logical) obtains results as valuable as those based on conceptual thinking ; that the knowledge acquired by poetic intuition is comparable to that of a mystic whose emotion penetrates the world more deeply than does Reason — all this Heine's great adversary, Ludwig Boerne, was unable to understand. One could have expected that these two men, with so much common background and experience, should have got along very well. Both loathed the narrow ghetto milieu in which they grew up. Both were hampered by anti-Semitism and embraced Lutheranism to remove an obstacle to their careers. Both emigrated to France after the Revolution of 1830, lured by the prospect of living under a regime so joyfully different (as it first appeared) from the oppressive government of the kings and princes of Germany.

They met in Paris in 1831. Boerne almost immediately began to

17

dislike and suspect the younger man. While naturally kindhearted, he just could not tolerate anyone who did not fully share his puritan and republican views: " Heine has no soul. . . . He cares only for the aesthetic or sensual element." Politically, Heine (whose great gifts he could not deny) seemed to him continually to waver from the left to the right and back, without ever entirely embracing any interest. He was correct in saying that Heine cared overmuch for the aesthetic element. Aesthetics played no role in Boerne's life and work: he had no heart for poetry, no eye for the arts, no ear for music. As a drama critic, he was mainly concerned with the political stand of the playwrights. Throughout his life Boerne energetically attacked Goethe for what he considered political sins, whereas Heine, though snubbed by Goethe and annoyed by the Olympian's alliance with the existing powers, did not permit his anger with the reactionary to diminish his boundless admiration for the poet.

In his unfortunate book about Boerne — unfortunate because it contained, apart from justifiable attacks on the journalist's personality and political principles, a number of petty remarks aimed at the late Boerne's private life — he declared:

No doubt Boerne meant it metaphorically when he said that if a king were to shake his hand he would put it in the fire afterwards to cleanse it; but I mean it not in the least metaphorically but quite literally when I say that if the people shook mine I should want to wash it.

With his preference for the delicate, the refined, the lovely, and his loathing of everything clumsy and coarse, Heine might have belonged to the *ancien régime*.

But Heine was nevertheless aware that he was living in the nineteenth century, the era of revolution, of emancipation. He perceived that the tragedy of Europe lay in the opposition between the elite and the multitude, the one suffering from a decadent slackness, the other from the uncouth and primitive quality of its vigor. Heine clearly sensed the contradictoriness of human nature, the impossibility of redeeming Man by means of a single political prescription, and so could not very well go along with the revolutionary Boerne. These dogmatic thinkers believed they had sure-fire nostrums for all ills. Meditating on the kaleidoscopic variety of the human soul, with its still uncharted configurations, the poet hated the rigidity of all systems, all organized philosophy. Referring to the " inconsistency " which made Heine say that he favored a republic governed by monarchists, or a monarchy governed by republicans, the biographer H. G. Atkins explained:

This very inconsistency is often only a higher degree of poetic and aesthetic truth. He responded to every impulse, uncontrolled by the usual restraints of common sense and expediency. He was the artist who reflected every changing aspect of life, and was, for his very indifference to contradictions, the more faithful recorder of passing moods. He was the more true to the impression of the moment, because he did not feel the necessity of making all he said conform to some preconceived and consistent philosophy of life.

Heine had a mind large enough to provide room for both thesis and anti-thesis, and it was the misfortune of this ardent disciple of Hegel that he was never able to achieve the synthesis. But who on earth has really done so? Little minds with one idea may believe that, after a life of search and work, a good man can close his eyes with a feeling of true satisfaction. Such individuals would, of course, never understand the outburst of bitterness and frustration from the dying Heine:

> Holy parables discarding,
>   Hypothetical and pious,
> Our accursed questions answer,
>   And with truth direct supply us.

> Tell us plainly why the good men
>   'Neath a heavy cross should bleed,
> While the wicked man rides proudly
>   Like a conqueror on his steed.

> Whose the fault ? Is God in Heaven
>   Not Almighty after all ?
> Is He wrong of His contriving ?
>   That were surely base and small.

So we ask and ask unceasing
Till a handful of old clay
Stops our mouths and we are silenced.
But is that an answer, pray ?

(Translated by Margaret Armour)

Among his contemporaries there were three poets of importance whom fate treated as unkindly. These were the Austrian Lenau, who was to die in a lunatic asylum, the Italian Leopardi, invalided by a spinal disease, and Heine's French translator, Nerval, who committed suicide. But their lyre had only one string, and it sounded a note of hopeless pessimism. Heine's moods ranged from a buoyant optimism to a pessimism which nevertheless stubbornly affirmed life. He had moods of despair as a young man with life before him, and as a *moribond spirituel* he voiced the gayest witticism at a time when he knew that he had perhaps only a few more days to live.

No poet understood better than he what Ecclesiastes meant in saying a living dog was better than a dead lion. Heine was madly, frantically in love with life. He sympathized with Achilles, who, in his roguish poem, " Der Scheidende " (The Parting One), would rather be the " smallest living Philistine at Stuttgart on the Neckar " (a city the poet especially despised) than a hero in the world of the dead. Asceticism as presented by the church was loathsome to him, and his abhorrence of the self-denial and self-mortification demanded by Christianity impelled him to the clever but not altogether convincing division of mankind into Nazarenes and Hellenes, spiritualists and sensualists ; Heine naturally considered himself one of the latter.

But, again, he was too complex a being to subscribe without reservation to any one party for any length of time. Irresponsibly he had lumped together Jewish rabbis and Christian priests as the destroyers of antiquity's *joie de vivre*, as those who had invented a next world as a compensation for this Vale of Tribulation. (Actually, asceticism, holding as sinful the desires of the flesh, is alien to Judaism.) And he erred—though not for long—in believing he had found the creed for himself in Saint-Simonism, which recognised in the sensual nature of Man an aspect of the manifestations of God. Heine, toward the end of his life, turned to the religion of the Jewish community. Again, total acceptance of the new-old faith was not for Heine the skeptic. In a long ecstatic poem, written for his last love, *La Mouche* (Camille Selden), the conviction is expressed that the strife between truth and beauty, between Nazarenes and Hellenes, would never cease, and that there was no final answer on earth.

If we follow Heine's distinction between men who are striving for a goal (as exemplified by Boerne) and those who enjoy life to its capacity (like himself, or, rather, as he would have liked to be), we must conclude that there was as much in him of the Nazarene as of the Hellene. He himself was a Boerne — but one with the poetic power, the magnificent insight into the machinery of Man, that was so sadly lacking in the political journalist from Frankfort-on-Main. Had he been a mere " hedonist " his work would have been too shallow, too egocentric, to survive a full century. Had he written only political essays, like those of Boerne's, his work would have been of little interest to the future.

To deceive people about his true nature he boasted about his physical prowess, made exaggerated claims to importance, and spoke lightly about subjects that were most holy to him, and this not only to trusted friends but even to strangers whom he felt obliged to amuse and entertain with his sprightly wit. In the first years after his death a whole library was written by men and women who knew him and remembered his conversations — many a charming but not always authentic flippancy received more credence than what he himself wrote deliberately and with great care. His *aperçus*, his *bon mots*, are, of course, part of Heine, but only the smooth epidermis beneath which there was an intricate network of hair-triggered nerves. Beneath the thin veneer of faked cynicism his heart was forever wrung by the plight of people, not only of individuals like the poet's wife and mother, but also of groups of people like the starving Silesian weavers, the Negro slaves in America, and the persecuted Jews in Damascus. Late in life he said that he could joke about everything except his sickness and his work ; this, too, was a jocular remark. But it is an established fact that for a professed hedonist he took astonishing pains with his work, especially his poems, subjecting every line, every word, to a severe scrutiny and constantly battling with publishers and censors who cut and garbled his creations.

Whether he knew it or not, whether he wished to admit it or not, it was the constant clash of the " Nazarene " and " Hellene " within him which produced a rift in his soul. In order to be " a complete man . . . an absolute man, in whom spirit and matter were not separated " (for him the most desirable accomplishment, and the way he characterized Martin Luther), Heine could not help being at once animal and god. The one-sided men, the fanatics of party or religion, could not understand this. And even the sensitive poet Gérard de Nerval, who knew him well, saw only contradictions in Heine, whom he characterized as " both hard and soft, cruel and tender, cynical and gullible, prosaic and lyrical, impassioned and reserved, an ancient and a modern." Neither he nor some of the poet's biographers were aware of the astonishing personal integration the poet ultimately achieved, the maturity of outlook that made it possible for him to remark, toward the end, that his life had been " beautiful."

What there may have been of the " animal " in Heine was felt only by those who had been foolhardy enough to aim at his vulnerable and sensitive spots. Heine had one weakness, one that cost him dearly because it involved him throughout his life in countless unsavory struggles : his vengefulness. His confidant, Alfred Meissner, related how the invalid Heine pointed to a little box near him which contained his Memoirs. In them he had drawn many most unflattering portraits of individuals who had wronged him, especially the relatives who had worked against his interests in the fight for his inheritance from uncle Salomon Heine. " There are many who know of the box, and tremble lest I should open it," Heine remarked with glee. (Most of these Memoirs seem to have been destroyed by some members of the family years after Heine's death, so that all that has come to us are the initial pages dealing with Heine's boyhood.) Meissner thereupon commented : " So he could hate, intensely, furiously, with an energy which I have never witnessed in any other man ; but it was only because he could also love. His heart was good ; while his heart belonged only to his friends, his hate was for his enemies."

Heine did not disown this trait:

My nature is the most peaceful in the world. All I ask for is a simple cottage, a decent bed, good food, some flowers in front of my window, and a few trees beside my door. Then, if God wanted to make me completely happy, He would let me enjoy the spectacle of six or seven of my enemies dangling from those trees. I would forgive them all the wrongs they had done me—forgive them from the bottom of my heart, for we must forgive our enemies. But not until they are hanged.

This was, of course, a piece of Heinesque irony ; his cruelty was only skin-deep, and in his later life he sincerely regretted the meanness of his attacks on the homosexual Count von Platen, and on Boerne. Heine enjoying the sight of torture — what an absurd concept! In reality, he could not stand cruelty. On the island of Norderney he once went hunting, but did not enjoy it, and actually shot into the air to warn the birds ; he was shocked when, by accident, he killed a young seagull. " When one's ancestors in ages beyond recollection killed stags," he philosophized, " the descendant still finds pleasure in this legitimate occupation. But my ancestors do not belong to the hunters so much as to the hunted."

He loved his mother dearly, and in his tragic last years went to great lengths to deceive the old lady in Germany about the state of his health. " My mother believes me to be as well and sound as when I last saw her," he told Meissner. " I write to her often, as well as I can in a cheerful humor, and tell her of my wife and how happy I am. If she notices that only the signature is mine, the explanation is that I have pains in the eyes which will soon pass off. And thus she is content. For the rest, that a son should be as sick and wretched as I am, no mother would believe."

He was suspiciously self-sacrificing in his relations with Mathilde (as he renamed Crescentia Eugenie), with whom he lived for more than twenty years ; he may have been unfaithful in the seven years she was his mistress, but when she became his wife their bourgeois marriage was as correct and proper as any other respectable union. He knew that she was vain, egotistical, irresponsible. Yet he protected her, wrote her the tenderest letters when he was away, tried desperately to raise her in the esteem of others (who, nevertheless, saw in her only the garrulous, plump fishwife), and took great care to see that she would be well provided for after his death. " I have an excellent wife," he told the writer Fanny Lewald, " whom I have loved beyond words and for thirteen years have called my own without hesitating a minute, without a moment in which I loved her less, without jealousy, in unchanging mutual understanding and in the fullness of freedom. Even now I am often terrified during my sleepless nights by the memory of that happiness, I thrill with rapture at the thought of this fullness of happiness."

Did he cover up his unhappiness? Those who remember the stories about the unprovoked scenes Mathilde made, about her lack of housewifely virtues, about her callous indifference to the pains of the mortally sick man, might be inclined to think that Heine protested too much. But whatever the source of his attraction to this woman may have been, he did love her profoundly, as several verses she inspired testify without doubt. (One can lie in prose, but not in poetry.) There is one which starts, most tenderly,

> O little lamb, I was assigned
> to be thy shepherd true and kind . . .

in which he begs the Lord to take care of Mathilde when the game was " o'er " :

> O God, then in Thy hands once more
> I lay the crook, and do Thou keep
> My little lamb, when I to sleep
> Am laid . . .

(Translated by Margaret Armour)

In another poem, more Heinesque in tone, he warns her not to catch cold at his funeral, since the Paris streets and the cemeteries, especially, were always so wet. But Heine did not need to worry a bit ; Madame Heine was not among the mourners who followed his coffin !

Biographers who should have known better have described him as one who, with all his gifts, lacked " charity." Barker Fairley, who categorically denied that Heine was an introvert, saw him as merely an observer, a commentator, a social writer only in the broadest sense of the term, " just as social, in fact, as a variety theater, a vaudeville, a revue." After a thorough perusal of Heine's work, it is hard to see how one can miss the man, young or aging, passionately in love with women ; the thinker deeply penetrating art, literature, philosophy, and religion ; the political analyst sincerely concerned with " the defense of the individual," with accomplishing " a cordial understanding between Germany and France."

Heine, were he to read the books written about him, especially in the last fifty years, would smile with that same sad yet understanding smile that greets us from his portraits. He would be puzzled particularly by the works of those who claim to be his admirers — and try to pull him into any one camp. Heine the patriotic German, Heine the ardent Jew, Heine the Communist, Heine the staunch conservative, Heine the romantic, Heine the anti-romantic, Heine the outstanding poet whose prose was plain journalism, Heine the great prose writer whose poetry, with a few exceptions, has become obsolete — which of them is the real Heine ? Each of them, we think, and none !

But the quarrel about him did not start with his death. He must have known what was coming, for he had been in the limelight ever since 1821, when his first collection of poetry was published. He often smarted under the attacks that punctuated his life, particularly since some of them had been provoked by his own indiscretion, naïveté, or carelessness. He had the rare distinction of having the Bundestag (the Diet of the Deutscher Bund — thirty-five sovereign German states and four city republics) occupy itself with his writings, and to proscribe not only all the books he had written but even those that he might write thereafter !

Fortunately not even Death or the fears of it could silence Heine,

25

who, though weak and perhaps even cowardly in small matters, showed great fortitude in the face of unbearable pain. In 1835 death was still two decades away, but as a reminder he had a partial paralysis of his left hand, a limping gait, and constant headaches. Needing money very badly, he kept on writing and writing desperately.

The story about his last walk is widely known. On a lovely spring day in 1848 he was a haggard, gray-bearded man dragging himself along the boulevards with the aid of a cane and looking much older than his fifty years. He suddenly encountered wild revolutionary crowds, singing the " Marseillaise." Whether or not the poet's story — that he fled and reached the Louvre to collapse before the statue of the Venus of Milo — is an exaggeration of what actually happened, this was his final stroll through the city that he loved so dearly. For eight years he endured pain so severe as to tempt a man to suicide. Yet in these years, the paralyzed, near-blind Heine dictated some exquisite prose and wrote long, passionate poems that have hardly been matched in world literature.

He did not even lose his sense of humor, that humor which, as the philosopher Schopenhauer recognized clearly, was based on a deep seriousness too shy for direct expression. Whimsically, he talked of competing for the gold medal in the capacity to suffer, should such a prize be offered at the Paris Exhibition of 1855. He mocked his literary fame : " What good does it do me that young men and women put laurels on my marble bust, while an old horny-handed nurse rubs my actual head with cantharides."

He talked flippantly about his recent return to religion, sincere though it was : " When I cannot stand the pain I take morphine ; when I am unable to take care of my affairs, I hand them over to God. . . ."

But in his platonic passion for Camille Selden there was nothing but the candor and romance of dramatic poetry.

It was to her that he confessed how anxious he was to continue to live, even under the circumstances : " I feel I must cling to life, even if all I cling to is only a rotting beam."

To the faithful Théophile Gautier, himself an outstanding poet, we owe an unforgettable description of Heine in his last weeks:

Illness had attenuated, emaciated, dissected him at will, and with the unwearied patience of an artist of the Middle Ages; from the statue of a Greek God it had shaped a Christ gaunt as a skeleton, in which the nerves, the tendons, and the veins were revealed. Thus ravaged, he was still beautiful. When he raised his heavy eyelid, a flash shot from his half-blinded pupil. Genius resuscitated this dead face. Lazarus came forth from his grave for a few minutes.

On the thirteenth of February, 1856, Heine worked for six hours, explaining to the protesting nurse that he had only four more days to work. To Camille Selden he said: " Take your hat off, that I may see you better." According to the nurse, his last words were: " Write—paper—pencil." Of his colleagues, only two escorted him to the place of his last rest—Gautier and Alexandre Dumas *père*. On the marble slab at the Montmartre Cemetery only ten letters were incised: HENRI HEINE.

It was only decades later that an imposing tombstone, topped by a marble bust of the poet (by Louis Hasselriis) was erected. Engraved on this tombstone is the poet's name and " Frau Heine " (Mathilde died in 1883), and the short poem " Wo?", which begins:

> Where shall I, of wandering weary,
> Find my resting-place at last?

The poet's niece, the Princess della Rocca, wondered why not even a *Requiescat in pace* had been added. But he was not to sleep in peace. His wit, as sharp as the flashes of lightning that pierce a sultry night, has continued to keep the nations from lethargy and smugness.

The Artist Heine

Whoever does not go as far as his heart commands
and his reason allows him to go, is a coward ; whoever advances further, is a slave.

HEINE, in *The Salon*, 1833

LIKE MANY A POET, HEINE HAD ONE FAVORITE SUBJECT — HIMSELF :
the amours, the hatreds, the desires and frustrations of the student,
later Doctor of Law, later celebrated writer, finally " martyr,"
Heinrich Heine. He has often been equated with Lord Byron, but
there was actually a wide gap between the two, between the
swashbuckling English aristocrat who went to Greece as a soldier
in the cause of freedom, and the German Jew who attacked in-
justices no less effectively from the safety of his fireside. Still, Heine
patterned himself on the earlier poet, admiring his contempt for
conventional morality and his affirmation of a poet's right to live
a life suiting his temperament. Not only did Heine translate the
poem " Fare Thee Well " and passages from *Manfred* and *Childe
Harold*, but he also imitated Byron in dress and coiffure : " He is
the only man with whom I feel an affinity."

Actually, the appellation of " the German Byron," given him by
admirers when his first verses appeared, does him an injustice, as it
covers only a few early manifestations of his genius. Heine was
unique in nineteenth-century European literature. He was the first
modern Jew to write poetry of note in a language other than
Hebrew, and he enriched the German language despite the fact
that, at the start, he had been no master of it at all and often committed curious grammatical errors. (In his parental home a Rhineland dialect interspersed with Yiddish terms was spoken.) He was
the first German poet to live (and with what difficulty !) as a free-
lance writer ; the men before him either sought and found the
patronage of a prince or eked out livings as librarians, university
professors, or private tutors. He dared to be a journalist at a time

28

when, at least in Germany, many people did not consider journalism an occupation worthy of a gentleman. He dabbled in every kind of writing ; he turned out, apart from his poetry, two verse-plays, fiction, political reports, lengthy essays on religion and philosophy, scenarios for ballets, and reviews of theater, concerts, and art exhibitions. As early as 1826 he remarked to a friend that it was " a matter of indifference " to him what he wrote about : " It is all God's world and deserving of observation. And what I do not read out of things, I read into them." He much later confessed : " I have, God forgive me, tried out everything in literature." Nor did he ever worry that, one day, he might exhaust his golden lode of subject matter. For he wrote : " So long as my heart is filled with love, and my neighbor's head filled with folly, I shall never lack material to write on."

In honesty it must be admitted that some of his pieces were potboilers. He often ventured opinions on subjects he had not studied thoroughly and occasionally risked statements that could easily be refuted. He contradicted himself frequently, though he was frank enough to admit former mistakes. But even in his second-rate pieces there is at least a clever line, a brilliant phrase, an inspired coinage, that earns him forgiveness. *Nihil tetigit quod non ornavit* can be applied to Heine, for on each of the thousands of pages he left us there is an inimitable flourish lifting even newspaper dispatches into the realm of art.

In a letter that the young Heine wrote, in 1822, to his colleague Carl Immermann, he referred to his poems as " the passkey to the sickroom of my feelings." The subject of all his poems is himself : Heine, rejected by his lovely but unsympathetic cousins, by his rich uncle, by a fatherland that had no sinecure for him ; Heine, worrying about the primitive and selfish wife whom he loved though he was fully aware of her shortcomings ; Heine, using his pen dipped in bitter satire to hurt all who were guilty, or were believed guilty, of *lèse-majesté* toward him ; Heine, raging against the insufferable physical pains he endured on what he called his mattress grave ; Heine, mortally ill, yet in the face of death singing of his love to the young woman who daily visited and comforted the tortured man.

He identified his own emotional experiences with the universe at large. " I sense the sweet pain of existence, I feel all the joys and agonies of the world," he wrote in *Journey from Munich to Genoa*. " I suffer for the salvation of the entire human race. I atone for its sins, but I also enjoy them." In this he was a typical romantic poet.

In his younger years he used every sort of prop in staging his feelings — nightingales, roses, violets, moonlight, stars — and some-times he was so eager to furbish the settings that the genuine emotion that initially inspired him was lost. At such times he sounds artificial and false. But he gradually dispensed with such props and confined himself to the essentials. He learned to condense his thoughts, to employ an epigrammatic style entirely new in German poetry. A poet by the grace of God, he had an unerring ear for the rhythm and melody of words. He knew how to combine the simplicity of a folk song with the terseness achieved only through merciless, uncompromising revision. One may be repelled by an occasional excess of exhibitionism, annoyed by outbursts of depravity, irritated by a cheap joke, but yet will find the artfulness of this master compelling.

" In art the form is everything, the substance nothing," Heine once asserted. Years after Heine's death the French critic Victor Cousin minted the phrase *L'art pour l'art*. Heine had announced this concept long before in a letter : " My motto remains : Art is the purpose of art, as love is the purpose of love, and even as life itself is the purpose of life."

Similarly he declared in one of the essays collected in *The Salon* : " I am for the autonomy of art. It is not to be regarded as the handmaiden of religion or politics ; it is its own definite justifica-tion, just as the world is." And in *Lutetia*, the last great prose work to appear before his death, he defined the " supreme consideration of art as the self-conscious freedom of the spirit."

Whatever limitations fettered Heine the man, he was free in the kingdom of poetry. Except for his beginnings, he never used traditional literary forms without adapting them to his own pur-pose. Still he did not think that naturalness should be sacrificed at

30

the altar of frostily perfect form. When engaging in his notorious dispute with Count von Platen, he qualified his own statement that form was everything. Platen, he maintained, stood for the cultivation of formal beauty in verse, for the excessive preoccupation with metrical problems. Heine was appalled by the unnaturalness of Platen's poetry :

The deeper notes of nature, as we find them in folk songs, in children and in other poets have never burst forth from the soul of Platen . . . . The anxious compulsion which he has to impose upon himself in order to say anything, he calls " a great deed in words "—so utterly unknown to him is the very nature of poetry that he does not understand that the Word is a " deed " only with the rhetorician, and that with the poet it is an " event. " Language has never become the master in him as it has in the real poet ; on the contrary it is he who has become master in language or rather of language, like a virtuoso on his instrument. The greater the advance he made in the direction of technical skill, the greater was the opinion he had of his virtuosity ; his skill extended over every form, he could versify the most difficult passages, he often, one may say, wrote poems on the G string.

Heine was not the first German to use free verse ; Goethe's early dithyrambic odes were written a half-century before Heine's *North Sea*. But he was the first to write poems of unrestrained fancy — not Pindaric ecstasies but real poetry composed in ordinary, everyday language. Goethe was little moved by his first sight of the ocean, and on the rare occasions he sang of it, praised the peacefulness of the quiet sea. Heine, however, was thrilled by the sight of the wild North Sea, mirroring as it did the turbulence in his own heart. This was genuine infatuation :

I love the sea, even as my own soul. Often do I fancy that the sea is in truth my very soul ; and as in the sea there are hidden waterplants that only swim up to the surface at the moment of their bloom and sink down again at the moment of their decay, even so do wondrous flower-pictures swim up out of the depth of my soul, spread their light and fragrance, and again vanish.

After having published the *North Sea* cycle, Heine wrote to a

fellow-poet expressing doubts that it would suit the public taste :
" The unusual irregular meter may possibly make ordinary sugar-
and-water readers seasick."

Heine's fears were justified, and it took many years before lovers
of poetry were ready for this unusual work. The Danish critic
Georg Brandes wrote in *Main Currents in Nineteenth Century
Literature* : " In Heine's *North Sea* poems we hear, for the first time
in German poetry, the roar of the ocean, with all its freshness and
in all its might. Here for the first time we have shells in the sand
beneath our feet, and seagulls in the air above us."

In these poems Heine made use of a device known as *Stim-
mungsbrechung*, that sudden and exaggerated turn that has baffled
many a reader, that rapid and inexplicable change from sweet to
bitter or from sublime to ridiculous. In " A Sea-Ghost " the poet,
gazing into the ocean, seeing there the face of his beloved, is ready
to plunge into the water :

> But just at the proper moment
> The captain seized me by the foot,
> From ship's edge dragged me,
> and cried, peevishly laughing,
> " Doctor, are you demented ? "

(Translated by Frederic T. Wood)

Heine did not invent this " romantic irony," though he was one
of its most successful practitioners. The doctrine of romantic irony
had grown out of nineteenth-century man's disillusionment with
the world, which he wanted to grasp completely only to find that
there were limits to human understanding. It was thus a symbol of
despair, the release from tension of an individual without belief,
without hope. This device has frequently been misunderstood, and
critics have charged that with it the poet aims at the innocent souls
who take him seriously and whom he wants to feel his own intellectual superiority. Actually, the pointed punch line is a dagger
thrust into the poet's own ego! Heine is here the jester, the man
who once called himself " a nightingale nestling in the wig of a
Voltaire "—basically serious and conscientious but holding a mask
before the face that would betray his constant suffering.

Conditions in his native country worried him deeply ; his concern expressed itself in satire. Revisiting Germany in the winter of 1843 - 44, he saw that nothing had changed in a dozen years. Back in Paris he aired his anger in a long mock-epic poem, " Germany, A Winter's Tale " :

> Still the same wooden, pedantic folk,
> Still every move a complete
> Right angle and still in every face
> The hard, frozen-in conceit.
>
> And still they stalk as stiffly about
> As pokers : straight and slick,
> As though, once beaten well with it,
> They ended by swallowing the stick.

And what about the French ? Though Heine had married a French girl and had been widely and generously accepted by the Parisian intelligentsia who, unlike those in Germany, harbored no anti-Semitic sin, he was not blind to disquieting phenomena in his adopted country. In the same poem he complains, half-humorously, that the French were not French any more :

> They all philosophize and talk
> Of Hegel, of *Fischte*, and Kant.
> They smoke tobacco, they all drink beer,
> Like us, they bowl nine-pins and rant.
>
> They're all Philistines now, like us,
> In fact, they go farther, for fair ;
> They're eager to follow Hengstenberg,
> They've quite forgotten Voltaire.
>
> *(Translated by Herman Salinger)*

(" Fischte " is, of course, the German philosopher, whose name Fichte comes clumsily to the Gallic tongue ; Hengstenberg was a reactionary Lutheran theologian.)

In 1848 paralysis set in. The invalid no longer had heart for the masquerade ; hence the deeply moving poems he wrote in his last years are devoid not only of the sugary sentimentality of his earliest lyrics but also of the buffoonery and occasional vulgarity of the

33

verses he wrote in his middle period. Today, connoisseurs of poetry treasure far above the *Book of Songs* (1827) the *Romancero* of 1851, though in the time of our grandparents and parents the former was the one book invariably found next to the Bible on the shelves of a German household. Even the sharpest critics of Heine, among them the Viennese satirist Karl Kraus, who felt an annoying element of artificiality in Heine's earlier work, were compelled to concede that here Heine was utterly sincere.

In the *Romancero* there is, perhaps, nothing more touching than the cycle of " Lazarus " poems, to which belongs the " Appendix to Lazarus," published posthumously. The dying poet speaks :

> How slowly Time, the horrid snail,
> Seems on his tardy way to crawl,
> While I, a prisoner of one spot,
> Languish and cannot move at all !
>
> No sunbeam, not a ray of hope
> Reaches my cell to pierce the gloom :
> I know that for the grave alone
> I shall exchange this hateful room . . .
>
> *(Translated by Margaret Armour)*

A few weeks before his death, Heine wrote the long poem " La Mouche," inspired, of course, by Camille Selden. The old conflicts that haunted and bewildered him throughout his life, fancy and fact, matter and spirit, truth and beauty, Nazarenes and Hellenes, recur in his dream, and no bridge between these dichotomies appears to the dying man :

> Does the old superstition haunt my bier,
> And are the marble phantoms still debating ?
> Is sylvan Pan, with his loud cry of fear,
> The anathemas of Moses emulating ?
>
> Oh, well I know they never will agree ;
> Beauty and truth will always be at variance.
> The army of mankind will always be
> Split in two camps : the Hellenes and Barbarians . . .
>
> *(Translated by Margaret Armour)*

Heine did not exaggerate when he himself called the *Romancero* " horribly beautiful," words that might be applied to most of the poems he wrote in his last years. " It is," wrote Heine, " like a lamentation from the grave ; in it somebody buried alive is crying out in the night . . . the German lyric has never heard such tones, and could not, in fact, for never was a poet in such a position."

Heine knew full well that he had revolutionized German poetry by making it European. One should not be misled by his remark that poetry to him had always been merely a " divine plaything," and that he would rather wish to be remembered as a " soldier in the war for the liberation of mankind." Matthew Arnold — whose mission was to shock the Victorians out of their smug lethargy — was one of the few to prefer Heine for his discontent, for his feud with Philistinism, rather than for his poetry. But Arnold's view is one-sided and does not indicate Heine's importance in the realm of German poetry, an importance which cannot be stressed too strongly. For Heine replaced the spiritual reticence and subtle twilight effects peculiar to the poetry of the Romantics by " a bold concrete imagery which seems to drag the most feeling emotions into the unequivocal glare of daylight," as one of his biographers put it. The boldness of his metaphors, the directness of his approach, the simplicity of expression, lift his work far above that of most of his contemporaries. He was the first to give stark expression to the dissonance between romantic ideals and the hard facts of life. He spoke the truth when he declared : " With me the old school of lyrical poetry comes to an end ; with me the modern German lyric begins."

The philosopher Nietzsche, to whom Heine was " the highest conception of a lyrical poet," called his poetry " sweet and passionate music." A German himself, Nietzsche had the privilege of enjoying Heine in the original. Unfortunately, any but a full knowledge of German is not enough for the subtlety of his innuendoes, the diabolic cleverness of his jests, though a fair knowledge of the language may suffice to perceive the rhythm and melody of the words he chose. Indeed, only when a great poet is stimulated by great work in another tongue to write his own version, does poetry survive translation—*vide* Shelley's inspired transmutation of the prologue to Goethe's *Faust* as compared with Longfellow's more literal translations of Goethe. Heine had no Shelley. But Longfellow did translate him, and so did Emma Lazarus, Elizabeth Barrett Browning, Havelock Ellis, Thomas Hardy, Francis Turner Palgrave, Ernest Rhys, John Addington Symonds, and Humbert Wolfe, among the better known. More recently, the Americans Louis Untermeyer and Aaron Kramer undertook the arduous task of rendering large segments of Heine's poetic work into acceptable English.

Yet despite the existence of dozens of English versions, Heine's poetry remains a sealed book to those not thoroughly familiar with German. Those who read him in English can only be disappointed. Heine himself discouraged translators of his poems when he dismissed French renderings of his verses as moonbeams packed in straw. He warningly wrote: " Poetry . . . hardly bears the process of exportation. To be rightly esteemed it needs to be enjoyed in the land of its birth, like certain tropical fruits." What a reviewer of Theodore Martin's translations wrote some sixty years ago still holds true, with a few notable exceptions, of the efforts made thereafter :

Heine's verses dance and sway like the nixies he loved. Their every motion seems informed with the perfect suavity and spontaneity of pure nature. They tinkle down the air like sunset bells, they float like clouds, they wave like flowers, they twitter like skylarks, they have in them something of the swiftness and the certainty of exquisite physical sensations. In such a transcript as Sir Theodore's all this is lost ; Heine becomes a mere prentice-metrist ; he sets the teeth on edge as surely as Browning himself ; the verse that recalled a dance of naiads suggests a springless cart on a highland road ; Terpsichore is made to prance a hobnailed breakdown. The poem disappears, and in its place you have an indifferent copy of verse.[1]

---

[1] Heine was one of the very few Germans to leave a mark on English and American poetry. It has often been pointed out how closely the form of A. E. Housman resembles Heine's. A modern poet, Louise Bogan, made the following poignant comment :
Housman took over not only Heine's simplicity and directness of language but Heine's wit, which could be warm and cold in turn. Many of Heine's songs, in

Nor is Heine's prose easy to translate, for at its best it is as terse, as epigrammatic, as pungent as the poetry ; yet the obstacles are not insurmountable, and a good portion of the prose is available in fair translation. His prose far outweighs his poetry in quantity, though not necessarily in quality. He wrote poetry when driven by an inner urge, while his prose was not always inspired by creative imagination. In Paris, the extravagance of his wife, his poor judgment in money matters, and eventually the vast expenses of his sickness forced him to undertake many a task that was no more than hack writing. But even in these, in spite of hurry and distaste, his genius broke through now and then, and his fantastic skill reveals itself even in his most trifling work. Rarely is there a dull line in his prose, never a heavy Teutonic passage, though he often discussed weighty and difficult subjects.

Even those who did not agree with him on every subject admitted that he was a catalytic agent, that he brought an entirely new note into German prose. Julian Schmidt, the literary historian, describes the impression made by *Hartz Journey*, Heine's first work in prose, a romantic satire aimed at the Philistine :

Seldom has a book in Germany elicited such loud and universal interest. Differences of rank and age vanished before the mighty impression. Forward-striving youth was inspired by its drunken dithyrambics, and gray Diplomacy sipped with secret delight the sweet poison whose hurtful effects it did not for a moment forget. It was the first free breath that followed a heavy, sultry atmosphere. A bold harlequin had leaped into their midst, brandished his wooden sword right and left, and by his antics excited the people to that merriment that could alone dispel their gloom.

Heine's prose often sounds like the most casual talk. Like a brilliant conversationalist, he holds us spellbound to the end, what-

---

spite of their seeming casualness, are epigrams in the classic manner ; even effects of pathos are brought off by the very neatness of balance of the syntax, and a brilliant pointedness and condensation are everywhere evident. Auden, MacNiece, and, currently, John Betjeman have profited from Heine's example. At the moment, however, the tendency of the contemporary lyricist is to break away from Heine's miniatures into larger frames. Out of their great sorrows, modern poets tend to make more and more elaborate and extensive songs.

ever he may discuss. This skilled interpreter mastered the art of producing images, of appealing to the senses no less than to the intellect, and he attributed this ability to the fact that he was primarily a poet:

For the writing of perfect prose there is requisite, among other things, a great mastery over metrical forms. Without such mastery a prose writer will be deficient in a certain tact, he will let escape him certain word combinations, expressions, caesurae and phrases, that are admissible only in poetry, and the result will be a secret discordance, which may offend a few, but these very delicate, ears.

Heine always remained the cool master of his style. He was unmatched in his technique of conveying a thought in a few words which, though uttered quite casually, penetrate deeply into the very substance of an institution or a personality. " The aristocracy," he once said, " is composed chiefly of asses — asses that talk about horses." About the poet Alfred de Musset: " Vanity is one of his four Achilles' heels." About a handsome scribbler of verse: " All women love him — all except the Muses." Asked whether his terrible illness was incurable, he replied: " Of course not — I shall die of it some day." The quip, " God will forgive me, that is His profession," which he is said to have made a short while before his death, may have been falsely attributed to him, but *si non è vero, è ben trovato.*

He could be tenderly lyrical, as when he described his journey through the Hartz mountains: " The blue silk coverlet of the sky was so transparent that one could look deep into it right into the Holy of Holies, where the angels sit at the feet of God, and in the features of His countenance study Thorough Bass."

He could be as seductive as the Italian women he praised:

I love these pale, elegiac countenances from which great black eyes shed forth their love-pain. I love the dark tints of those proud necks; their first love was Phoebus, who kissed them brown. I love even that overripe bust with its purple points, as if amorous birds had been pecking at it. But, above all, I love that genial gait, that dumb music of the body, those limbs that move in sweetest rhythm, voluptuous, pliant, with divine enticement.

When he treated a difficult subject, how different he was from the German professors who often spoke ponderously, as if every word were worth an ounce of gold. Mark how Heine introduced Spinoza:

In reading Spinoza"s work we become conscious of a feeling like that which pervades us at the sight of great Nature herself in her most lifelike state of repose. We behold a forest of heaven-reaching thoughts whose blossoming topmost boughs are tossing like the waves of the sea, whilst their immovable stems are rooted in the eternal earth. There is a peculiar indescribable fragrance about the writings of Spinoza. We seem to breathe in them the air of the future.

There is little in nineteenth-century German prose that has either the crystal lucidity or the flexibility of Heine. To find a comparable spirit one has to look beyond the boundaries of Germany — to Voltaire perhaps, who, like his pupil Heine, is never tedious, rhetorical, or obscure ; or to Anatole France, who admitted being indebted to Heine. But Heine had limitations, and like every good artist, he knew them. After his two failures at writing plays (*Almansor* and *Ratcliff*), he never again attempted drama ; his novel *The Rabbi of Bacherach* remained a fragment — he realized that he was incapable of designing works of larger scope with balanced architecture.

He was able to bow before those whose greatness he would never match. He was an unswerving admirer of Goethe. " I love you," he wrote to the septuagenarian, sending him his first poems. " I kiss the hallowed hand which has pointed out to me and the whole of the German people the road to the kingdom of heaven." Goethe did not deign to reply. A meeting, three years later, between the old and the young poet was brief and unsatisfactory. Goethe at that time (1824) was loathed by the young German liberals as a reactionary who always sided with the princes against the people and as an unpatriotic partisan of Napoleon. But Heine, too, had been fascinated by the Emperor at one time, and was not sure whether he did not prefer the sophisticated German aristocrats to the uncouth German plebeians. At any rate, even while he attacked Goethe's anti-national aloofness and personal egotism, he never failed to recognize the greatness of the Olympian. In a letter to Varnhagen he paid tribute to the old man whom, in an angry mood, he had assailed as a weak decrepit god, a lackey of aristocrats: " We who are, most of us, sick men, are far too firmly rooted in our sickly, discordant, romantic feelings to see instantly how sane, harmonious and plastic Goethe shows himself in his works."

As an artist, Heine was able to write, and write astonishingly well, even on subjects to which he brought no special technical training, namely art and music. In Paris, as a foreign correspondent working for German newspapers, he was assigned to review several Salons, those large-scale annual exhibitions of contemporary art. Heine was not really equipped for the task, but, like Goethe, he was an *Augenmensch*: he had been born with an eye for form and color. His criticisms of the visual arts were no more " professional " than his views on music. Yet, since he was a sensitive poet, his intuition often broke through the wall of his limitations and pierced through to the core of artistic experience. At a time when Delacroix and his fellow Romantic painters were far from general acceptance, Heine, echoing the efforts of these men, emphasized that it was the painter's primary task not to copy nature but to express feeling and passion. " In art," he wrote in a review of the Salon of 1831, " I am a supernaturalist. I believe the artist cannot find all his types in Nature, but that the most significant types are simultaneously revealed in his soul as the inborn symbolism of inborn ideas."

As a music critic, he extolled the wild talent of the still struggling Hector Berlioz. He erred, overrating some composers and under-estimating others, but was, on the whole, most perceptive. The composer Ferdinand Hiller tried to explain how Heine, despite his lack of practical musical training, managed so well as a critic: " Because of his imaginative and penetrating mind, he divined more in music than many so-called musical people."

He was truly, above anything else, imaginative and penetrating. Those who complained that he was superficial had in all likelihood never approached him with receptiveness, with that compassion and sense of proportion that would help them to push aside the gaily decorated screen behind which there is a door to the inner sanctum of a great poet. Or they were weak souls, shaken by his irony, that barbed fence by which the poet might ward off those whose company he desired not, either during his lifetime or even fifty or a hundred years after his death.

Those who at one time or another admired him were a strangely assorted crowd. Among the Germans they included not only Nietzsche and Thomas Mann but even Bismarck, whose Junker background should have made him a foe of Heine's. Among the giants who paid tribute to him were Ibsen, Tolstoy, Dostoevsky, and Whitman. English writers who admired him included Robert Louis Stevenson, Matthew Arnold, and Lafcadio Hearn. There are the millions all over the world who have heard him in *lieder* by Schubert, Schumann, and Brahms without necessarily realizing that it was his divine stanzas that inspired these composers to write their songs. And, to end on a Heinesque note, after 1933 many a German boy and girl continued to sing " Die Lorelei " without knowing who the poet was.

The Sword and the Flame

The golden age is not in the past. It is in the future.

HENRI DE SAINT-SIMON

THERE ARE TWO WAYS TO READ HEINRICH HEINE'S POLITICAL POETRY
and prose, which comprise three-fourths of his total work. You can
focus on those passages that seem to support your own philosophy,
or you can take Heine as he was in reality: a man born at the end
of the Age of Enlightenment, who matured in the Romantic Age
and was fated to die on the threshold of a new era; a poet and
thinker who strove to understand the events of his time, who saw
the problems as insoluble and no particular doctrine as entirely
effective; a free spirit who acknowledged his own prejudices and
endeavored to be honest with himself.

The first way to read Heine is the easier one. Anyone, even a
Communist or a Fascist, can quote Heine on his side. Had not Heine
been a Jew, the Nazis might have interpreted him as a protagonist
of Teutonic chauvinism. For Heine did indeed write: " All of
Europe, the whole world, will become German! Of this mission and
this universal domination of Europe I often dream when walking
under oak trees."

However, what he actually desired was not a " Greater Germany " but a victory of the idealistic philosophy of Kant, Fichte,
and Hegel. At the same time, he was not sure whether German
philosophy might not deteriorate into a tool of ferocious imperialism and aggression. In 1870, and again in 1914 and 1940, the
French had reason to recall the warning Heine uttered in his work
on modern German civilization (first published in 1834 in *Revue
des Deux Mondes*):

The German revolution will not be milder and gentler because it
was preceded by Kant's *Critique*, by Fichte's transcendental idealism,
and even by the philosophy of nature. These doctrines have developed
revolutionary forces that wait only for the day when they erupt and

fill the world with terror and admiration. There will be Kantians forthcoming who will hear nothing of poetry in the visible world, either, and with sword and axe will mercilessly churn the soul of our European life, to exterminate the very last roots of the past. Armed Fichteans will enter the lists, whose fanaticism of will can be curbed neither by fear nor by self-interest. . . . Christianity has—and that is its fairest merit—somewhat mitigated that brutal German lust for battle. But it cannot destroy it ; and once the taming talisman, the Cross, is broken, the savagery of the old battlers will flare up again. . . . That talisman is brittle. The day will come when it will collapse pitiably. The old stone gods will rise from forgotten rubble and rub the dust of a thousand years from their eyes, and Thor will leap up and with his giant hammer start smashing Gothic cathedrals. . . .

One can well understand why the Prussian censor of 1835 blue-penciled these sentences when the articles appeared in book form!

Nothing was more repugnant to Heine than a glorification of a *Vaterland* turned into one huge military barracks and imposing its will on other nations through gunpowder and lead. What he wanted he made quite clear when he addressed his definition of patriotism to his former countrymen :

Calm yourselves, I will honor and esteem your colors when they are no longer an idle and a servile mummery. Plant the black-red-and-gold banner upon the heights of German thought. Make it the standard of free humanity and I will give my best heart's blood for it. Calm yourselves. I love the Fatherland as much as you do. Because of this love I have passed thirteen years of my life in exile. . . .

Nor would Heine have approved of Bolshevism, with its regime of terror, with its drab and depressing uniformity and standardization of cultural expression. The *Great Soviet Encyclopedia* hails him as the one German poet who came close to understanding the mission of the working class ; it states that Heine's *Book of Songs* was the only German volume that Lenin took into his Siberian exile. But a Soviet critic, writing an introduction to a recent popular Heine edition published in Leipzig, noted with a sigh that Heine, though a friend of Marx, " did not succeed in becoming a real Marxist."

He certainly never wished to become one. His 1855 preface to *Lutetia*, cited by the extreme left as documentary " proof " that Heine had " seen the light," proves nothing more than that the invalid of Avenue Matignon, fed up with both the reactionary France of Napoleon III and the aggressive Prussia of Friedrich Wilhelm IV, recognized the growing importance of the proletariat as a political power. His position was akin to that of many desperate liberals in the 1930's who were willing to side with Moscow simply because any foe of the Nazis had to be considered an ally. Above everything, the dying Heine hated and feared the Teutomaniacs whom he had fought with his pen for more than thirty years. Thus he said : " Out of hatred to the champions of Nationalism I could almost turn to loving the Communists."

Mark the " almost " — which makes all the difference! Heine was no novice in politics. He who would wash his hand, if the people shook it, did not fall for the myth of the " noble proletarian." Fearing what he called " the great herd of mankind," he was not the man of the people Walt Whitman was. He was aware of his prejudice : " Most dangerous to me is that brutal, aristocratic pride that is rooted in my heart . . . which whispers to me so much contempt against industry and could mislead me into the most distinguished wickedness." Heine's biographer, Max Brod, once defined the poet's formula : " All for justice and all for the proletariat, but not by the proletariat."

Heine wanted to be a poet — and nothing but a poet. " They have forced me to take to the sword," he sighed in 1826. " My position never favored my development into a singer of soft love ballads."

His targets were those who kept his native land in the fetters of reaction, the Philistines — *Die Philister, die beschraenkten, diese geistig eingeengten* " — who, limited and intellectually confined, not only had debased poetry and music and had no sense of humor, but also hated and feared progress and were against any change in the *status quo* : that same German middle class which, in Heine's lifetime, out of fear of the radical movements, backed the thirty-six German rulers and their absolutism, and which, in 1933, would vote for Hitler merely because he had promised protection from the threat of Communism.

What Heine strove for, a country rid of feudalism and clericalism and led by an aristocracy of brains, was anathema to the so-called non-political German, whose immaturity and inertia enabled a Metternich to become master of Central Europe during the long night between 1815 and 1848. Heine wrote bitterly:

I am weary of political bickering, and long for peace, at least for a condition of affairs in which I can give myself freely to my own natural inclination, to my dreamy way of living, to my imagination and brooding thoughts. What irony of fate that I, who am so fain to sleep on the pillow of . . . silent contemplation, should be marked out to whip my fellow-Germans out of their torpor!

That was jotted down during a vacation on the island of Heligoland in June, 1830. But a few weeks later he learned of the Revolution in France, the one that unseated the reactionary Bourbon, Charles X, a king who, as a historian put it, " had all the qualities necessary for gaily losing a battle or for gracefully ruining a dynasty." Heine was jubilant, even expecting that the Revolution might spill over the borders and rouse the indolent minds of the German Philistines:

Gone is my yearning for rest. I know now what I will, what I shall, what I must do. . . . I am the son of the Revolution and I again take up the charmed weapons upon which my mother breathed her magic words of blessing. Give me my lyre that I may sing a battle-song. I am all joy and song, all sword and flame!

How can we explain this sudden change of mood? Heine had the impressionable character of a true poet, and he approached politics not with the stern single-mindedness of a Boerne or a Marx, but with the same illogical passion which might be roused in him by the sight of a beautiful woman. Primarily a poet, he had the misfortune to have been born into a period in which, as Napoleon said to Goethe, politics was fate. The first half of the nineteenth century saw the development of nationalism and socialism, the strife for a parliamentary democracy, the emancipation of the Jew. Heine was willy-nilly drawn into the whirlpool.

Perhaps the most devastating comment on Heine's inability to serve a political cause without reservation and without wavering has come from Boerne, who had once wanted the younger and more famous man as his ally in the struggle against German reaction:

Heine, with his sybaritic nature, is so effeminate that the fall of a rose leaf disturbs his sleep: how, then, shall he rest comfortably on the knotty bed of freedom? Where is there any beauty without a fault? Where is there any good thing without its ridiculous side? Nature is seldom a poet and never rhymes; let him whom her rhymeless prose cannot please, turn to poetry.

Heine, the poet, with his hatred of all systems and all organized philosophy, was incapable of appreciating the ardent German patriot and unflinching liberal. In the book on Boerne he had over-simplified matters as much as his antagonist. There would be a substantial element of truth in his division of mankind into Hellenes and Nazarenes had not Heine clearly phrased it in such a way as to place the " Nazarenes " in an unfavorable light:

Boerne was entirely a Nazarene; his antipathy to Goethe came directly from his Nazarene spirit; his later political exaltation was grounded in that sharp asceticism, that thirst for martyrdom, that is found everywhere among the republicans which they call republican virtue and which is so little different from the passionate longing of the earlier Christians.

To repeat: Heine was both Nazarene and Hellene. The emancipation of mankind could not be achieved, he felt, before each individual had been made free to enjoy the beauty of life. It is true that he was dominated by emotion rather than by reason, that he lacked Marx's theoretical insight into the workings of society; true, too, that, compared to Boerne, with his one-track mind and sure-fire solutions, Heine seems inconsistent in his political views to the point of irresponsibility. Yet, is it not also true that he is to be credited for revising his opinions, for admitting mistakes, and for risking accusations of being a turncoat?

One ought to remember that Heine's life began when the first

Napoleon rose to power, and that another Napoleon was firmly entrenched in power at the time of Heine's death. Heine was a boy of seven when Bonaparte took the crown from the hands of the Pope and set it on his own head. He was nine when the Emperor's army occupied Duesseldorf. Like all Jews of the Rhineland, the precocious lad admired Napoleon, who had brought the Jews emancipation from medieval restrictions. The poet's admiration for the Emperor can be felt in his great ballad " The Two Grenadiers," and in his reminiscences of Napoleon's riding through the Palace gardens of Duesseldorf (" What it was to me when I saw him, I myself, with thrice blessed eyes, his very self ! Hosannah ! The Emperor !"). In Heine's writings we see nevertheless a slow process of decanonization. The admiration became mixed with misgivings, and after a while Napoleon appears as " the representative of colossal will, but at the same time a warning example of the ephemeral effect of unbounded will." Eventually, Heine saw him as the one who betrayed freedom itself by his *coup d'état* of the eighteenth of Brumaire, and he even commended the French liberals for having withheld support from the " liberticide " Emperor in his last desperate struggle.

If Heine retained to his very end at least a modicum of admiration for the glamorous figure of the first Napoleon, he had little love for Louis Napoleon, who through the *coup d'état* of December, 1851, made himself the ruler of France and was proclaimed Emperor Napoleon III after a period of ruthless and bloody oppression of the opposition. Read the satirical poem, " Die Wahlesel," about the donkeys who had elected the greater donkey (Napoleon III) as their emperor, and also the shrewd and accurate forecast of 1840 that the Bonapartist party was merely " a very convenient transition party." Both Frenchmen and Germans, seeing the Second Empire crumble under the Prussian hammer blows in 1870, had an opportunity to reread the pages wherein Heine conjectured that, should the Bonapartists attain supremacy, their regime would not last very long, and would, like the earlier Napoleonic government, merely " form a short intermediary period."

He was not a bit impressed by the new Napoleon :

The beautiful ideals of political morality, legality, civic virtue, freedom and equality, the roseate morning dreams of the eighteenth century, for the sake of which our fathers met their death so bravely, and which we, no less eager for the martyr's crown, dreamt together with them—now lie at our feet, broken, scattered potsherds.

It took Heine many years to decide that he did not, indeed could not, belong to any one narrowly circumscribed political party, that his was an eclectic humanism that defied definition and dogma. After seeing his demigod, Napoleon, dethroned and exiled, he had embraced German nationalism. Joining one of the German *Burschenschaften*, the fraternities of university students, he believed he was fighting on the side of progress because the students were against the regime of Metternich and his allies, the German princes, and were suffering persecution by the police.

Soon, however, Heine was to find that the fraternities were no less reactionary in spirit than the oppressive rulers and that the ideals of liberty and equality were often ignored or even disowned for the sake of the only good that seemed to matter—national unity. At the university of Goettingen he realized that the followers of Friedrich Ludwig Jahn, the patriot leader who wanted the German nation to recuperate and gain strength through calisthenics, were narrow-minded chauvinists, engaged in preparing proscription lists:

Anyone who was descended, even seven generations back, from a Frenchman, a Jew, or a Slav was to be condemned to exile. Anybody who had ever written anything against Jahn or the absurdities of the Old Germans themselves might expect the death penalty, carried out, of course, with the axe and not by the French invention, the guillotine.

Quickly Heine understood that he could never tolerate the German brand of nationalism, which makes the German's heart " shrink like leather in the cold, until he loathes all that is foreign, until he abandons all claim to be a citizen of the world or even a European, and desires only to be a German, narrow and limited."

It is not surprising that Heine felt little at ease in a Germany where the alternative to a most unenlightened eighteenth-century absolutism seemed to lie in a philosophy anticipating many features of twentieth-century National Socialism. Heine's characterization of the spiritual ancestors of Hitler, Goebbels, and Streicher is unmatched in accuracy:

Their fanaticism, carried on with all the fervor of a religion, exceeds in energy the enthusiasm which reason alone can command. In addition, they have at their service all the slogans which are most effective with an ignorant people. Words like " Fatherland," " Germany," and " faith of our ancestors " will always galvanize the masses more than " humanity," " citizen of the world," " spirit of youth," or " truth. " I mean to say by this that the representatives of the nationalist idea have their roots more deeply sunk in German soil than the representatives of cosmopolitanism, and that we shall always be beaten by them unless we swiftly forestall them—with the help of the guillotine.

Heine was one of thousands of German liberals who decided that life was unbearable in the *Vaterland*, that France was the only place where their ideas and ideals would be appreciated and from which they could work for the destruction of the evil forces in Central Europe. The news of the July Revolution turned the poet into an ardent Francophile:

Liberty is the new religion . . . the French are the chosen people of that religion, for in their tongue are written its first gospels and its dogmas. Paris is the new Jerusalem, and the Rhine is the Jordan which separates the holy land of liberty from the country of the Philistines.

Unfortunately Paris failed to become the New Jerusalem the exile had expected. The Revolution had merely replaced a reactionary Bourbon with a " citizen king " who permitted the real power to be seized by the bankers and merchants from the hands of the counts and bishops. The new France gave only lip service to democracy, and when the more courageous of those republicans who had overthrown Charles X became restive, Louis Philippe ordered the troops to take the most drastic measures against the malcontents. According to Heine, who wrote as a foreign correspondent for German papers, sixty thousand men were defending Louis Philippe's *Juste-Milieu* against a handful of rebels:

The heroism of these daredevils is being praised unanimously ; they are said to have accomplished miracles of valor. They constantly called *Vive la République !* and found no echo in the breasts of the people. . . . God knows I am no republican. I know that if the republicans conquer they will cut my throat because I will not also admire everything they admire ; but still the tears rose in my eyes today when I stepped on places still wet with their blood.

The climax of this long report incidentally is a typically Heinesque bit of irony : " A tailor, who, this morning on the Place Vendôme dared mention the republicans' good intentions, was beaten up by a strong woman who probably was his wife. That is the counter-revolution."

Personally, Heine did not suffer from any restrictions in France ; in fact, he was cordially received by the intelligentsia as a distinguished foreigner, and, whatever curbs on freedom were invoked after 1830, France was a paradise of liberty compared to the German lands. It was in France that Heine was able to explore the philosophical and political systems that had their roots there. Claude, Comte de Saint-Simon, had died six years before Heine's arrival, but his teachings continued to have influence. In 1830 the Saint-Simonists issued a manifesto demanding the abolition of individual inheritance rights, communal control of the means of production, and the enfranchisement of women. Dissensions between the two disciples of the founder of the sect, Bazard and Enfantin, were among the factors that led to a dissolution of the group.

A study of Saint-Simonism helped to prepare Heine for a movement of greater importance to him and of the greatest significance to the world — Socialism. Heine had much contact with some of the leaders of Socialism, especially with those ardent young men, Marx and Lassalle. But by no stretch of the imagination can Heine be called a Socialist in the strict sense. At the time of his death (1856), Socialism was far from being a political force ; Marx was a poverty-stricken exile in London and Lassalle still a long way from founding the General Union of German Workers. Still, there are countless passages in his poetry and prose which prove that Heine strongly sympathized with the underdog and that he considered the existing social order unsatisfactory. When news of the revolt of the Silesian weavers reached him, he wrote a poem angrily assailing those responsible for the starvation and humiliation of the workingmen :

> A curse to the Fatherland, whose face is
> Covered with filth and foul disgraces ;
> Where the bud is crushed before it can seed,
> And the worm grows fat on corruption and greed.

(Translated by Louis Untermeyer)

His general Credo was the same, whether expressed in verse.

> Oh, let us here on earth be glad,
> We're tired of want and pain,
> The lazy belly shall not consume
> What toiling fingers gain.

(Translated by Herman Salinger)

or in prose :

I believe in progress. I believe that mankind is destined for happiness, and I have a better opinion of the deity than those pious souls who imagine that He created man only for suffering. Yes, here on earth I would establish by means of the blessings of free political and industrial institutions that beatific state which according to the opinions of the pious will be realized only on the Day of Judgment—and in Heaven.

Heine held that every human being should live under decent conditions ; he also wished to see wars abolished, but he did not stop there. He dreamed of a great federation of peoples — " the Holy Alliance of Nations " — and of a time when " we shall no longer need to sustain standing armies of many hundreds of thousands of murderers because of mutual distrust. We shall use our swords and horses to plow with, and we shall win peace, prosperity, and freedom."

But he did not speculate *how* this " beatific state " might be achieved, and, moreover, he shunned any kind of political action. Ludolf Wienbarg, one of the leaders of the Junges Deutschland movement with which Heine's name was linked, was not unfair to the poet when he said:

If it had depended upon Heine to destroy the established order of society to change the face of the world and, with one stroke of his pen, establish a regime to all appearances perfect, he would certainly have hesitated. Life and the world gave him material for his satire, for his vivid descriptive writing and his poetical outpourings; he had strongly pronounced sympathies and antipathies; he was capable of great enthusiasm for great characters and for great historic forces; but an abyss separated him from the struggling masses and from their leaders in action.

Heine was perhaps too sensitive, too soft-hearted, for a world in which it seemed changes could be made only by force and with the shedding of much blood. His fear of brutality, of violence, his abhorrence of the rule of insipid mediocrity, made it impossible for him to participate in change.

The Communism to which he refers in his writings was, of course, not of the Russian variety which was to shake the world six decades after the poet's death. He was a follower—as much as he could "follow" any man—of the "Communist" Proudhon, that moral reformer for whom justice was the basis of all human relationships and revolution's goal the achievement of justice.

He was afraid of what he saw coming and honest enough to admit that this new force was likely to stay. In the aforementioned 1855 preface to the French version of *Lutetia*, he summed up all his fears. He feared the dark iconoclasts who, once they had gained power, might heartlessly smash the marble statues of beauty, destroy the fantastic toys and spangles of art, cut down the grove of laurels and plant potatoes instead. In the new order, he foresaw that the lilies that neither toil nor spin would no more be allowed to exist, and that his own *Book of Songs* would provide the grocer with paper for little bags.

It must be pointed out that many writers have omitted the continuation of this thought in order to put a special emphasis on Heine's opposition to Communism. For Heine went on to say: " Blessed be the grocer who shall one day use the pages of my poems as paper-bags for the coffee and snuff of poor old women, who in this present world of injustice too often have to go without that solace."

And Heine, who had the fatal gift of seeing the two sides of a problem, ended with a desperate "*Fiat justitia, pereat mundus !*" He was not pleased to think that the world in which he had grown up, however faulty it was, would be replaced by one of *Gleichschaltung* and rigid rule.

He forecast in *Lutetia*: "The future smells of Russian leather, blood, godlessness, and much flogging. I advise our grandsons to be born with a very thick hide on their backs."

Heine was terribly fearful of what José Ortega y Gasset later was to call "the Revolt of the Masses." He was shocked by the alliance of atheism and Communism. Having repudiated the former, he also abhorred the latter, not as a man fearing the loss of his material gains, but as an artist and scholar apprehensive that a victory of Communism might destroy the fruits of man's noblest achievements:

The emancipation of the people was the great effort of our life, and we have struggled for it and borne nameless misery, at home as in exile ; but the pure, sensitive nature of the poet opposes itself to every personal close contact with the people, and even more do we shrink with horror at the thought of their caresses, from which God protect us.

It is impossible to cast Heine as a political leader, for he did not have the clear, unalterable concepts expected of one, and his witticisms are of little help as political guidance. He was a puzzle to all simple souls. His fellow-emigrés in Paris complained that Heine was not above selling out liberty, but they simply failed to understand him. Boerne, despite his wit, could only view as a natural enemy the poet who arrayed himself against all systems, whose fatherland was not Germany but the world. Inquiring where Heine had first gone after his arrival in Paris, Boerne expected to hear an enthusiastic " to the ruins of the Bastille." He was deeply shocked when Heine candidly admitted that his first visit had been to the Bibliothèque Nationale to look at an old manuscript of Walter von de Vogelweide, the medieval Minnesinger.

Boerne was right — Heine did love the beautiful ; but he did not love it merely for himself. He wanted, not a drab mass-civilization, not a proletarian society, but a world of beauty and satisfaction for everyone. George Eliot understood that dream of his when she hailed him as " a lover of freedom, who has spoken wise and brave words on behalf of his fellow-men " ; so did Matthew Arnold, to whom Heine was " a brilliant, and most effective soldier in the Liberation War of humanity." Havelock Ellis envisaged the poet as a new Moses, gazing from the vulgar Pisgah of his day into a promised land that he would never enter. Today, more than a century after the poet's death, we have not as yet entered that promised land. We are searching still, and the " irresponsible hedonist," Heinrich Heine, is among those who may help us in our search for the right path.

Heine and the Absolute

> I was never a great metaphysician.
>
> *Confessions*
>
> My mind has never sympathised with any religious creed!
>
> *Last Will*, 1848.

HEINE'S RETURN TO GOD ANTICIPATES THAT OF ANOTHER FAMOUS nineteenth-century literary figure, Count Leo Tolstoy. Having completed *Anna Karenina*, Tolstoy began to question his mode of living. After a seemingly peaceful and contented life, he decided, about 1881, that true happiness could be found only by returning to primitive Christianity. If his contemporaries were startled by the Russian novelist's new morality, which turned against his former life, Heinrich Heine's " return to God " was, perhaps, an even more baffling event, since the German-Jewish poet had earned a reputation as an ardent enemy of religion. The poetess Elizabeth Barrett Browning was one of the thousands who were deeply moved by his change of heart. In a letter of 1854 she wrote:

You know how that brilliant, witty, true poet Heine, who was an atheist (as much as a man can pretend to be), has made a public profession of a change of opinion which was pathetic to my eyes and heart the other day as I read it. He has joined no church, but simply (to use his own words) has " returned home to God like the prodigal soon after a long tending of the swine. " It is delightful to go home to God, even after a tending of the swine. Poor Heine has lived a sort of living death for years, quite deprived by his limbs, and suffering tortures to boot, I understand.

For more than a century, Heine's " recantation " has puzzled both freethinkers and believers. Did this mocker and desecrator really mean all he said and wrote in his grievous last eight years? Had he recovered completely from his terrible illness, would he not have explained away, wittily and persuasively, his much-advertised " conversion," as earlier he had explained away his infatuation with paganism? If Heine was a genuine *Baal Teshubah*

55

(the Hebrew for penitent), his merit was, of course, greater than that of a perfectly religious man who had never sinned — but could he be considered one since his change of philosophy was not in the direction of any religious orthodoxy?

To do justice to Heine one has to bear in mind the fortuitous character of his development as a thinker, and also his milieu, molded by the doctrines of eighteenth-century French materialism. The truth is that, like many great men, Heine was profoundly religious without ever being willing to immerse himself completely in one creed or to accept a dogma without questioning. Moreover, he was too honest to pretend that he believed. Throughout his life he was preoccupied with religion, examining the tenets of every faith, at one time adopting atheism as a sort of *ersatz* religion. Now and then he let his arrows loose against all religions, and even denied the very existence of God, yet he always returned to one spring or another to quench his metaphysical thirst. His philosophical unrest was increased by the skepticism that prevailed in the post-Napoleonic world: the power of the church, if not broken, at least had been shaken, and there was a tremendous rise in the number of young men attending universities, traveling the widening world, and discovering new and revolutionary ideas in books.

The father, Samson Heine, seems to have been pious, but not out of deep conviction. If he objected to his first-born's boldly anti-religious ideas, he did so, as he confessed in a letter to " Harry " (as the poet was originally named), mainly because he feared that his son's careless talk might antagonize and alienate customers of his dress-goods shop. But neither he nor his wife Betty were opposed to their son's conversion. And the same Harry Heine who, as a nine-year-old, refused to help put out a fire on a *Shabbes*, shortly found out that the strict law could be interpreted in a manner to outwit the Law-giver. Thus on a Saturday he bit off grapes one by one from a vine. " Red-headed Harry, what are you doing?" his shocked Jewish schoolmates asked. " We are forbidden to pluck them with our hands," Harry explained, " but the Law does not say anything about biting and eating."

The instruction in Judaism he received as a child in the local *heder* (religious school) impressed him far less than what he learned subsequently at the Lyceum, a secondary school staffed with members of a suppressed Roman Catholic order. It is significant that these Catholics were to a large extent skeptics themselves, thus leading the precocious boy into a state of religious indifference. For a time he was utterly confused. The same boy who devoutly kissed the hand of every clergyman whom he encountered—and Catholic Duesseldorf swarmed with them—made the curious mistake of repeatedly answering the question of his professor at the Lyceum, " Henri, what is *de Glaube* (faith) in French?" with " It is *le crédit.*" Eventually the examiner shouted angrily, " It is *la religion!*" and beat Heine mercilessly while his classmates laughed. Was Henri's answer prompted by ignorance or malice? Heine, retrospectively, added this comment to the episode:

From that minute I have never been able to pronounce the word religion but that my back has turned blue with fear, and my cheeks red with shame. And I candidly confess, *le crédit* has been a greater help throughout my life than *la religion.*

It may not be true, as Heine recalled late in life, that the director of the Lyceum tried to convince Frau Heine that her son should go to a Catholic seminary in Rome. But there can be no doubt that the poet was in his youth strongly attracted by the ritual and lore of Catholicism. In a letter written in 1816, the young man, after having been rebuffed by his cousin Amalie, wrote to his friend Christian Sethe:

In a religious matter I may soon have to tell you something very strange. You will exclaim: Has Heine gone mad? But I *must* have a Madonna. Will the heavenly one be a substitute for the one of this earth? I can drown my endless pain only in the endless depth of mysticism.

Heine must have played with the notion of becoming a Catholic. Only one who was deeply drawn to the mystic beauty of Catholicism would have written " The Pilgrimage to Keevlar," which, with other poems of a near-Catholic tendency, appeared in his first volume of poetry, issued in 1822. (The number of Jewish-born writers attracted by Catholicism is large ; in our time they include the late Franz Werfel, and Ilya Ehrenburg, whose early poetry is colored by Catholic-mystical leanings and who once even considered joining a Benedictine order.) In *Confessions* the aging Heine recalled :

I too was frequently enthusiastic for the highly glorified Queen of Heaven, out of the legends of Her grace and goodness I made delicate verses, and my first published poems contain traces of this Madonna period, traces which I carefully and foolishly removed from later editions.

There came, however, the shattering influence of Hegel, whose iconoclastic lectures Heine attended in Berlin in 1821. Hegel replaced God by the Absolute Idea. In *Confessions* there is this interesting passage about Heine's relationship with the philosopher :

One fine starlit evening, as we stood looking out from the window, I, a young man of twenty-five, having just dined well and drunk my coffee, spoke enthusiastically concerning the stars, and called them the home of departed spirits. " The stars, hum, hum, " muttered Hegel. " The stars are only a brilliant leprosy in heaven's face. " " In God's name, then, " I exclaimed, " is there no place of bliss above, where virtue meets with its reward after death ? " But he, the master, glaring at me with his pale eyes, said sharply, " So ! You want a bonus for having taken care of your sick mother, and refrained from poisoning your worthy brother ? "

Were it possible to have no religion, Heine had none when, on June 28, 1825, he had himself baptized. Significantly, he chose Lutheranism, the most conservative form of Protestantism, because it was the one most acceptable to the rulers in the Prussia of Friedrich Wilhelm III. Since a lot of nonsense has been written about the baptism, a few facts might well be given.

It was impossible for a Jew in the Germany of the 1820's to enter any profession unless he embraced Christianity. Even Eduard Gans, the vice-president of the Society for the Science of Judaism, to which Heine belonged for a while, became a Christian merely to be able to pursue a career in law. Gabriel Riesser, a champion of

Jewish emancipation who spurned baptism, had to wait for many years until an ordinance was passed in Hamburg admitting two Jewish notaries to practice. Although Heine's family did not object to a changing of religion, he himself loathed the act for purely personal reasons. In a letter to Moser he expressed the opinion that as a Christian he might be able to do more in behalf of his " unfortunate racial brethren." He considered it, nevertheless, " beneath my dignity," and " a blot on my honor " to become a convert in order to obtain office. The letter ends in a pessimistic mood:

We live in a sad time. Scoundrels are considered the best people, and the best must become scoundrels. I very well understand the words of the Psalmist : O Lord, give me my daily bread, lest I blaspheme your name !

Even Leopold Zunz, president of the defunct Society, was pessimistic. " Seeing that I was preaching in the wilderness, I ceased to preach," the eminent Jewish scholar admitted, " but not to become faithless to what I proclaimed." Zunz, of course, remained a practicing Jew. Heine lacked this strength of conviction and, a few weeks before obtaining the Doctor of Law Degree at Goettingen, yielded to expediency. He was not the only one to succumb to a reactionary society. Gustav Karpeles reports that for the years between 1816 and 1843 no fewer than 3,273 German Jews (out of one hundred thousand) are recorded as having converted to Protestantism, an average of 121 annually. This does not take into account a large number of conversions to Catholicism.

In a poem Heine chided Gans for having done just what he himself had done. A half-year after his own conversion he referred, in a letter to his confidant, Moses Moser, to the rumor that Gans was already preaching Christianity and trying to convert Jews : " If this is conviction, he is a fool ; if hypocrisy, a knave. . . . I confess that I should have been better pleased to hear that Gans had been stealing silver spoons." He returned in the letter to the same metaphor : " I should be sorry if my own baptism were to strike you more favorably. I give you my word of honor — if our laws allowed stealing silver spoons, I should not have been baptized."

An anthology of utterances by Heine, deploring or ridiculing his step and assailing baptized Jews in general, could fill a volume. Here are a few barbed samples:

" No Jew can ever believe in the divinity of any other Jews."

" I have become a typical Christian ; I sponge on the rich Jews."

" Last Saturday I went to the Temple and I was pleased to hear Dr. Solomon pillory the converted Jews and scorn those who had deserted the religion of their fathers for dubious benefits."

" I want to become a Japanese. They abominate nothing as they do the Cross."

Finally, a statement made many years later : " You can't change your religion. You can only renounce the one from which you are estranged for another to which you will never belong. I am baptized — but I am not converted."

He spoke the truth ; he was never truly a Christian. On the other hand, despite his lifelong attachment to the Jewish people, the poet never fully endorsed Judaism as a religion either — not even after the celebrated and much-publicized return to God on the " mattress grave." Yet in the four decades of his adult life he always felt an emptiness, a vacuum he was impelled to fill with some creed. Had the neo-orthodoxy of Samson Raphael Hirsch, that revival of Orthodox Judaism in a modernized and aesthetic form, come earlier, it might have attracted Heine, at least for a while. But the watered-down version of Judaism, as propounded by the earliest protagonists of Reform Judaism, only annoyed him. (" They make themselves a *tallis* from the wool of God's lamb," he wrote to friend Emmanuel Wohlwill in 1823, " a jacket from the feathers of the dove, and underpants from Christian love. Then they go bankrupt and their scions call themselves, God. Christ and Company.")

It is safe to say that Heine found a solace neither in dialectic philosophy, nor in atheism, nor in a rather artificial worship of the Greek gods. Since Christianity starved his senses and paganism his soul, where was his haven of refuge? About 1831 he believed he had found what he needed in the form of Saint-Simonism, an ersatz religion whose headquarters were in Paris, that city to which

Heine escaped from German anti-Semitism and reaction. Both Christianity and Judaism had, in the poet's opinion, something in common that he found impossible to accept : a repudiation of the flesh and its desires.

But Judaism is not an ascetic religion. Nor was Heine correct in assuming that Judaism was averse to beauty. The Jews do not worship it in the manner of the Greeks. But it is significant that the pious Jew is expected to recite certain benedictions on viewing objects of beauty, thus thanking God for having created them for men to enjoy. According to Judaism, the world is good, and the very forces which apparently work for evil will finally result in good ; the desires of the flesh are not sinful *per se*, but they must not reach the point of excess. A trenchant legend tells us that the exiles who returned from Babylon were so holy that they were granted the privilege of annihilating the power of the greatest temptation of Israel—sexual passion. But to their great dismay they discovered that no children were born and that even the hens would not lay eggs. The holy men were forced to decide that passions are necessary and good.

Claude Henri, Comte de Saint-Simon, creator of what he called the New Christianity, had been dead for several years by 1831, but his propaganda was carried on by his pupils, Bazard and Enfantin. These two proclaimed: " The world was waiting for a savior — Saint-Simon appeared. In him, Moses and Jesus are united."

Briefly, Saint-Simonism combined a sort of technocratic Socialism with vaguely pantheistic and sensualistic ideas. It stressed just what Heine stood for : internationalism, world peace, social justice, love of the flesh, and the holiness of beauty. The movement gave to Heine what he completely lacked in the last years of his residence in Germany: a belief in a superior being, minus the restrictions imposed on the believer by the positive religions.

In *History of Religion and Philosophy in Germany* Heine endeavored to link Spinoza's pantheism with the ideas of Saint-Simonism, for which he had become a spokesman. He stressed both its democratic character and its opposition to the materialism that had driven the men of 1789:

We [the Saint-Simonians] promote the well-being of matter, the material happiness of nations, not because, like the materialists, we despise the spirit, but because we know that the divinity of man manifests itself also in his bodily appearance and that misery destroys and degrades the body, the image of God, and that thereby the spirit, too, perishes . . . . We have no desire to be *sansculottes*, nor frugal citizens, nor cheap presidents. We are founding a democracy of gods equal in power, holiness and felicity. You [the sons of the French Revolution] are asking for simplicity in dress, frugal living and sobriety in pleasures ; we, however, demand nectar and ambrosia, purple cloaks, costly perfumes, delights and luxury, dancing of laughing nymphs, music and comedies. Let this not displease you, oh virtuous republicans ! Our reply to your censorious reproaches is what the fool in Shakespeare said : " Dost thou think because thou art virtuous, there shall be no more cakes and ale ? "

Heine adored Spinoza as the one philosopher who showed a road beyond Christianity, Judaism and Deism :

The Jews represent God as a tyrant thunder-clad ; the Christians as a loving father ; the God of the Deist is above the world and rules it from on high. But the God of pantheism is in the world, for pantheism identifies God and the world.

Freely interpreting Spinozism as a hedonistic philosophy, he grouped the Dutch-Jewish thinker among the " Hellenes," as distinguished from the ascetic and iconoclastic " Nazarenes." For Heine, anticipating Nietzsche, looked askance at any philosophy or creed that preached self-denial and self-mortification. He loathed the dualism of orthodox Christianity, with its dichotomy of good and evil wherein the body, with its appetites, is regarded as the evil part to be subdued. Hence, he had high regard for Martin Luther who, with his sound earthiness, had challenged this old asceticism :

He [Luther] could lose himself in the depths of pure spirituality, and yet he knew very well the glories of this world and valued them . . . he was a complete man, I might say an absolute man, in whom spirit and matter were not separated. "

So, incidentally, was Shakespeare :

62

Shakespeare is a Jew and a Greek at the same time ; or rather, both elements, spiritualism and art, have been reconciled in him and have permeated each other to such a degree that they have evolved into a higher unity. Is perhaps such harmonious blending of both elements the task of all European civilization ? We are still a great distance away from such an accomplishment.

At one point he asserted that there was no need for religion in the industrial age : If in the dreary past the poor needed the consolation of religion, this could be dispensed with now, since " the development of industry and economics makes it possible for the material burden to be lifted from man's shoulders and opens the possibility of happiness for all in this world."

Heine's hedonistic outlook on life was badly shaken as the terrible disease from which he suffered began to take its toll. By 1837 he was plagued with shattering headaches, inflamation of the eyes, and partial paralysis of the left arm and foot. By 1846 he was in such bad shape that, when a young poet invited him to have a glass of wine at a café, the older writer refused for reasons of health : " Am I not regarded in Germany as the great hedonist, the apostle of the emancipation of the flesh? And now, behold me ! A poor, water-drinking paragon of virtue, a world-forsaker, a perfect Trappist !"

The great change, described (and overstressed) in every report on Heine, came later, in the early spring of 1848. Heine recognized that " the blessed Goddess of Beauty, the Dear Lady of Milo " was no more able to come to his aid than any other of the pagan idols. Fated to be confined to bed for the remaining eight years — years of pain hardly any other poet has ever endured — he sought a *rapprochement* with the God, not of his father (for his father was a primitive little man devoid of religion), but of his forefathers. To his brother Maximilian he wrote that in his sleepless nights of torture he was composing beautiful prayers addressed to the God of the Jews, and in a subsequent letter he closed with a sincere " Glory and Honor to the Lord in Heaven !"

He even publicly demonstrated his renunciation of his former beliefs in a manifesto that appeared in a German paper, *Allgemeine*

Zeitung, in 1849, in which he declared :

I am no longer the Great Heathen Number Two [Number One being Goethe]. . . . I am no longer what I used to be : a happy and rather plump Hellene, physically vigorous, smiling down on the melancholy Nazarene. I am now only a thin etching of misery, an unhappy man, a poor, sick Jew.

For the past hundred years religionists of all camps have rejoiced in the conversion of that impudent mocker Heine as a shining victory of the church over militant atheism. But this is an over-simplification. In the first place, Heine was an atheist in the true sense of the term for a short time only ; secondly, Heine " returned" with scores of mental reservations.

Below are a few excerpts documenting the meanderings of the ailing Heine in the realm of belief. In a postscript to the collection of poetry, *Romancero* (1851), he admitted having returned to God like the Prodigal Son, after having for many years tended the swine among the Hegelians (*vide* Elizabeth Barrett Browning's letter). What caused the return? " *Das himmlische Heimweh* " is the simple answer — the nostalgia for heaven. This phrase, by the way, appeared in the same touching story which mentioned his dis-appointment in Venus' helplessness.

There is a more detailed report to be found in the 1852 preface to the second edition of *History of Religion and Philosophy in Germany*, where he explained :

What sent me on the way to salvation was no vision, no seraphic ecstasy, no heavenly voice, no transcendental dream, nor any other miracle. My enlightenment came to me just from the reading of a book. A book ? Yes, it is an old simple book, modest as nature and as natural, a book which looks unassuming and workaday, like the sun which warms us, like the bread which nourishes us. A book which gazes at us with a homely look, which is like a kindly benediction, such as might come from an old granny who reads daily in this book with dear, trembling lip and spectacles on her nose. And this book is called, *tout court*, the Bible. Rightly, it is named the Holy Scripture. He who has lost his God can find Him again in this book.

Anyone else would have stopped there. Not so Heine, who hated to see the fundamentalists, the reactionary theologians, use his conversion as an argument in their favor. Hence, he made it absolutely clear in the epilogue to *Romancero* that, while he had gone back to a personal God, he remained outside the official church:

I must expressly contradict the report that my backsliding has carried me so far as even to the threshold of a Church, and that I have been received into her bosom. No, my religious convictions and views are still untainted by any tincture of ecclesiasticism; no chime of bells has allured me, no altar candles have dazzled me, I have dallied with no dogma, and have not utterly renounced my reason.

Similarly, in the preface to *Lutetia* he pours cold water upon those who believed he had returned to religion like a simple, unsophisticated creature:

Pious souls seem anxious to be cheated by me, with the tale of some miracle, and they have a desire to know whether, like Saul, I had seen the light on my way to Damascus. No, ye faithful believers, I never journeyed to Damascus . . .

The elucidating contribution to an understanding of Heine's religious feelings can be found, however, in his *Confessions* of 1854, in which he sums up the errors and quests of his whole life by stating:

How strange! After whirling round all my life in all the dirty mazes of philosophy, after rioting in all the orgies of intellect, and coquetting with every possible system without finding satisfaction, like Messalina after a night of dissipation, I now find myself suddenly at the same standpoint as Uncle Tom, the Bible, and I kneel beside my black brother in the same spirit of devotion.

In his last years Heine, who as a celebrity was visited by curious people, was frequently asked to give his views on God and religion. It was a long way he had journeyed from that height of hostility, as expressed in *The Baths of Lucca* (1830), where he made Hirsch Hyacinth say that the Jewish religion was not a religion but a misfortune, and that he would not wish it on his worst enemy. To Adolf Stahr he remarked that, while with his intellect he could not believe that there was existence after death, he could not grasp this with his emotion. He also said to Ludwig Kalisch:

I do not make a secret of my Jewish allegiance, to which I have never returned, because I never abjured it. I was not baptized from aversion to Judaism, and my professions of atheism were never quite serious. My former friends, the Hegelians, have turned out scamps. Human misery is too great for men to die without faith.

Those who know Heine only as the eternal joker who could never pass up a good pun may be puzzled by the dead-seriousness of his second *Last Will* (of 1851), which contains this moving passage:

I die in the belief in one God, Creator of heaven and earth, whose mercy I supplicate in behalf of my immortal soul. I regret that in my writings I sometimes spoke of sacred things with levity, due not so much to my own inclination, as to the spirit of my age. If unwittingly I have offended against good usage and morality, which constitute the true essence of all monotheistic religions, may God and men forgive me.

In the same spirit is the letter to his publisher, Campe, referring to a bonfire to which the dying man condemned earlier blasphemous manuscripts:

When the paper was crackling in the flames, a kind of curious feeling came over me. I wondered whether I had acted like a hero or like a madman, and near me I heard the voice of some Mephistopheles whispering: The Lord will pay you a much better fee for that than Campe, and besides you need not bother yourself about printing, nor will you have the trouble of bargaining with Campe about the manuscripts as you would about a pair of old trousers.

But the fear that he might be misunderstood, a fear that caused him to reject the last rites of all creeds, dictated these additional lines:

Do not believe the rumour in circulation that I have lately become a pious lambkin. The real change which I have undergone is only a spiritual one, and the consequence of an act of thinking rather than of sweet sentimentalism, and my sickbed is not the cause of it, of that I am sure. Great, lofty thoughts, full of awe, have come over me.

But they were mental sparks of lightning and not phosphorous vapors . . .

Almost to his last breath Heine retained his clear intellect, and for this great gift alone he might have been grateful to the Lord he had rediscovered. But there was no letup of his pain, and as we turn the pages toward the end of his life, we find, little by little, the old irony returning. When *La Mouche* asked him whether he had not found Saint Augustine's *Confessions* interesting, he replied, in a mocking voice: " Certainly, charming up to the moment when he converts himself."

In which camp, then, was the dying Heine? The answer can be found in a short sentence of only five words, contained in his last prose work, *Confessions*. Curiously, it has been overlooked by practically all who have written on the subject, although it indicates how close the poet came intuitively to a basic tenet of Judaism. " *Gutsein ist besser denn Schoenheit,*" he wrote — to be good is better than to be beautiful. This idea was expressed more than two thousand years earlier in the thirtieth verse of the last chapter of Proverbs, in which the fear of God is held to be superior to " favor " and " beauty."

Ethics has precedence over aesthetics, Heine conceded, and in the blaze of this declaration all that is dubious and even sordid in Heine's life and work evaporates, vanishing into nothingness. Besides, while he remained a *Freigeist*, an irreverent jester to his end, talking about God, Heaven, and the immortality of the soul with the irony of a Voltaire, in one particular Heine adhered to the Mosaic ethics throughout his life, without interruption, and without mental reservations: in his profound interest in the social struggles of his day. Whether he attacked those responsible for the frightful pogroms in Damascus or those who permitted the shameless exploitation of the weavers of Silesia, he aided the attempts of the oppressed to throw off their oppressors.

In *Confessions*, he talks of " Israel's love of freedom " which flourished " while slavery was legal and thriving not in the vicinity alone but among all nations of antiquity, including the philosophical Greeks." These following sentences convey not only the gist of Heine's social philosophy, but also the quality of Heine's prose. Heine called Moses a Socialist, yet one who, as a practical man, was a reformer rather than a revolutionary :

Instead of wrestling with the impossible, instead of hot-headedly decreeing the abolition of property, Moses only strove for its moral reform. He sought to establish harmony between property and morality, the true law of reason, and effected it by introducing the " Year of Jubilee, " when every alienated heritage . . . reverted to the original owner, no matter in what way it had passed from his hands . . .

Moses did not want to abolish property. Rather, he wanted everybody to own some, so that poverty should make of no man a serf with servile thoughts. Freedom always was the great emancipator's final idea ; it flames and breathes in all his laws on pauperism. Slavery itself he hated beyond measure, almost grimly, but he could not quite destroy this inhumanity either ; it was still too deeply rooted in the life of that primitive age, and he had to restrict himself to legal alleviation of the slaves' fate, to making the purchase of their freedom easier and limiting the period of their service. If, however, a slave whom the law finally set free refused absolutely to leave his master's house, Moses ordered the incorrigible servile wretch to be nailed by his ear to the house's gate-post, and after this shameful exhibition be condemned to servitude for life. O Moses, our teacher—Moshe Rabbenu, august fighter against slavery—hand me hammer and nails, that I may nail our peaceful, black-red-and-gold liveried slaves [the Germans] by their long ears to the Brandenburg Gate !

Heine's Judaism

A man doomed never to belong . . . The curse that had fallen on him in the cradle ; he could not *belong*.

LEWIS BROWNE, on Heine

SEVERAL MONTHS AFTER HIS CONVERSION TO LUTHERANISM IN JUNE 1825, Heine wrote to a friend : " Is it not foolish : hardly am I baptized, when I am decried as a Jew ? "

Had he been born a hundred years earlier he could have slipped quietly into the mainstream of a Christian world that made no distinction as to race or nationality amongst people who had accepted the tenets of Christendom. In the eighteenth century, even a professing Jew (like Moses Mendelssohn) might be welcomed into the ranks of the intelligentsia. For this was the era of humanism and universalism highlighted by Kant, Lessing, Wieland, and their counterparts outside Germany. Lessing and Mendelssohn were close friends. The poet Wieland strongly doubted the possibility of German nationhood, and even dreaded the idea for fear that such a nation would eradicate liberty and intellectual life in Germany. To the philosopher Kant, Germany appeared as *das Land der Welt-buerger*, the country of cosmopolitans, whose task it was " to gather the good of all nations and to harmonize it, and to accept all of them equally willingly."

About the time of Heine's birth (1797), religious discrimination was on the wane, anti-Semitism in the racial sense did not exist and the term itself was not to be coined before the 1870's. Nevertheless, the nineteenth century was to be the age of an aggressive nationalism. In 1819 Hartwig Hundt, in his *Judenspiegel*, advocated that Jewish men should be castrated, Jewish women placed in houses of prostitution, and Jewish children sold to planters in the West Indies to take the place of colored slaves. University professors, in a frenzy of Teutonic enthusiasm, voiced opinions foreshadowing the ruthless Judeophobia of Rosenberg and Streicher. In the same year pogroms erupted throughout Franconia. A decade later synagogues as well as Jewish-owned shops and homes were raided by mobs in the enlightened and liberal city of Hamburg, where Heine's uncle, the famous banker Salomon Heine was living.

It is not likely that Heine would ever have been stirred by Jewish nationalist feelings had it not been that the outside world forced upon him the concept of the *nie abzuwaschende Jude*, the Jew who cannot wash away his Jewishness with baptismal water. Even if religion had played a more important role in the Heine household at Duesseldorf, it is unlikely that an individual as skeptical as Heine would have accepted Judaism without question. Had not German nationalism, in the process of severing its link with the humanism of old, introduced a " racialism " that ignored baptismal certificates, Heine might have lingered in its camp a little longer than he actually did ; in the end, however, his searching and critical mind would inevitably have rejected the narrowness and bigotry of the Teutonic world. For any kind of nationalism was as repugnant to Heine as it was to his fellow-expatriate and rival, Ludwig Boerne, who wrote : " *Ich hasse jede Gesellschaft, die kleiner ist als die menschliche* " (I hate every kind of society smaller than humanity).

But Heine, unlike the very rational Boerne, could be impressed by non-rational factors at the peril of his sound judgment. As a student, he succumbed to the lure of the German *Burschenschaften*, seduced by their flamboyant talk about an ideal " Holy German Empire " that would replace the weak and disunited post-Napoleonic Germany. He joined a fraternity, got mixed up in jingoistic activities, and seriously subscribed, as some of his early poems indicate, to the ardent nationalism that inflamed German academic youth. But disillusionment came to the son of Samson Heine when he realized that the *Burschenschaften* were basically reactionary and anti-Jewish, and that his interest in German culture was shared by few. At Goettingen, for instance, he was one of a handful of students attending the lectures on Old German : " There are only nine who care about the language, the mind, and the spirit of their forefathers ! "

His early enthusiasm for everything German, for the pageantry, poetry, and folklore of the Middle Ages, soon turned to a revulsion which found its expression in a strongly worded letter (April, 1822) to a friend, Christian Sethe : " Everything German is odious to me, and unfortunately you are a German. Everything German affects me like an emetic. The German language rends my ears. At times my own poems nauseate me, when I see they are written in German." And he added in French a wild attack on the Germans, " *une race si ennuyante et malicieuse*," expressing the wish to go to Arabia to compose Arabic poetry.

The break with German nationalism left him temporarily without a cause — he who always needed a cause to champion, though never whole-heartedly and never for long. After a while, in the *Verein fuer Kultur und Wissenschaft des Judentums*, newly formed in Berlin by a band of young intellectuals, Heine, the secular Jew, believed he had found exactly what he wanted.

The purpose of this learned society, as Heine put it later (in an essay on Ludwig Marcus, 1844), was " none other than the adjustment of historic Judaism to modern science." Heine did not, as Louis Untermeyer claims, contribute to the society's journal, *Zeitschrift fuer die Wissenschaft des Judentums*. But for a short time he was its recording secretary, and he taught Jewish history three hours weekly to boys at the school established by the *Verein*.

By the time he became a member, in August, 1822, the poet already had finished his play in blank verse, *Almansor*. This is not one of his outstanding works, but one of considerable biographical interest, for it reveals, under thin disguise, sympathy with his fellow-Jews and fury with their oppressors. Almansor, the brave young Moorish prince, who, with his girl in his arms, leaps to his death to avoid surrender to the Spanish knights, is Heine as he fancied himself. The cruel Spaniards obviously represent the German nationalists.

If Spaniards and Moors used swords to decide whether Christianity or Islam was superior, most of the ideological battles in the last century were fought with pen and ink, and the *Verein*, indeed, used up quantities of both. Heine's role in the *Verein* has been exaggerated by some of his biographers. Since he left Berlin in May, 1823, his active participation was limited to a period of less than ten months. It is true that for many years thereafter he continued to correspond with fellow-members, but that was all ; anyway, the *Verein* itself disintegrated in 1824. The poet did profit greatly from his contacts with such scholarly men as Ludwig Marcus and Leopold Zunz, and several important poems, as well as *The Rabbi of Bacherach*, would not have been written but for Heine's experience as a member of the *Verein*.

But the only major work Heine actually finished in the *Verein* period of an essay, *Ueber Polen*, the fruit of a journey he made through Posen, a part of Poland annexed by Prussia. About one-tenth of the essay deals with the local Jews. Reared among Jews who in dress, speech, and thinking could in no way be distinguished from their Gentile neighbors, Heine for the first time encountered Jews of a different kind :

The social position of the Jews in Poland is somewhere between the peasant and the nobleman. They compose more than a quarter of the population and are engaged in all the trades and, therefore, entitled to be called the third estate of Poland . . . .

In the part of Poland that now belongs to Prussia, no Jew can obtain employment by the state, unless he permits himself to be baptized ; in the Russian part of Poland, on the contrary, the Jews are admitted to all public offices because that is deemed expedient . . . .

It would be desirable for our government to try to inspire the Jew of the Grand Duchy [i.e., Posen] with more love for agriculture, as there are said to be few Jewish farmers. There are many of them in Russian Poland. The Polish Jew is supposed to have acquired his dislike for the plough while witnessing the wretched state of the serfs. As soon as the humiliating status of the peasant will have been abolished, the Jew also will reach for the plough . . . .

With few exceptions all the taverns in Poland are in the hands of the Jews, and their many liquor distilleries do much harm to the country, as they tempt the peasant to debauchery. But the drinking of alcohol is necessary to the peasant's happiness . . . .

Every nobleman has a Jew in the village or in the town whom he calls " Faktor " and who handles all his commissions, does his buying and selling, provides him with information and so on. A peculiar

institution, fully demonstrating the indolence of the Polish nobleman . . . .

The exterior of the Polish Jew is horrible. I shudder when I recall the
impression I had when, for the first time I saw a Polish village, chiefly
inhabited by Jews . . . . Yet this aversion soon gave way to pity when
I observed more closely the state of these people and noticed their
sheds, which look like pigsties, where they live, pray, bargain and—
suffer. Their language is a German mixed with Hebrew and modeled
after the Polish. In previous times they had fled persecution in Germany
because in religious matters Poland has always distinguished herself by
her tolerance . . . . The Jews were the first to bring craftsmanship and
trade to Poland and were favored by Casimir the Great with important
privileges. They seem to have been nearer to the nobility than to the
peasantry ; for according to an old law a Jew, by the mere fact of
conversion to Christianity, was raised to the nobility. I do not know if
and why this law has fallen into oblivion.

In these early days, however, the Jews were certainly much superior
in culture and mental equipment to the noblemen, who were skilled
only in the art of fighting and still lacked French refinements. The
Jews at least were interested in their Hebrew scholarly and religious
books, for the sake of which they have left their homeland and the
comforts of life. But apparently they have not kept pace with the
advancement of European culture, and their spiritual world has sunk
into an unpleasant superstition which a hair-splitting scholasticism has
molded into thousands of queer shapes . . . . Still, despite the barbarian
fur cap which covers his head, and the even more barbarian ideas that
fill it, I prefer the Polish Jew, smelling of garlic, with his dirty fur coat,
his beard, and his queer speech, to many a German Jew in all the glory
of his government bonds.

It was through the *Verein* that Heine learned of Mordecai
Manuel Noah's fantastic plan to found a Jewish state on Grand
Island in the Niagara River ; by a letter, dated January 1, 1822, this
society had notified Major Noah of his election as honorary member. But Heine's references to Noah were written after his connection with the *Verein* had become merely theoretical and his
enthusiasm for a renaissance of Jewish culture and for Jewish
nationalism was already waning. From Lueneburg he wrote mockingly to his friend Moses Moser in Berlin (May, 1823) :

When, some day, Ganstown [Eduard Gans was vice-president of the *Verein*] is built and a happier generation will *bensh lulav* and ,chew *matzoth* on the Mississippi [he meant Niagara], and a new Jewish literature starts to flourish—then our present commercial slang will be a part of the poetic language, and little Marcus' lyrical grandson will sing, in *tallit* and *teffilin*, before the whole *kehillah* of Ganstown : They sat by the waters of the Spree [the river flowing through Berlin] and counted treasury-bills, when there their enemies came and demanded : Deliver unto us your London bills—high is their rate of exchange !

In a letter of April 23, 1826, Heine sarcastically referred to the debacle of Noah's grandiose scheme. He told Moser of a dream in which he saw Noah performing the miracle of silencing the loquacious Gans. Writing to Leopold Zung (May, 1826), he asked his friend, ironically, to place a volume of his (Heine's) latest book in the library of the long-defunct *Verein*, or, should the library have been transferred to Ararat, to place the same book in Frau Zunz' kitchen.

Heine was obviously disappointed in the *Verein*, whose goals were both unclear and unrealistic, whose leadership was — notwithstanding the gifts of a Zunz, Gans, Moser, and Marcus — incompetent, and whose program lacked support. Zunz and Gans, president and vice-president, outspokenly criticized their indifferent co-religionists. Seeing the *Verein* swamped by material difficulties because the wealthy Jews refused to give any help, Gans declared in a report : " The only link which unites the Jews is that of fear ; the only higher interest for which they are willing to part with some portion of their worldly goods is that of charity."

Zunz found the German Jews to be " adrift and without discipline or principles, turning to Christianity because they have nothing else to turn to : one section still sunk in the squalor of past ages, despised by Europe, another rustling papers in minor Government offices, rich or bankrupt, persecuted or tolerated in turn." Heine did not fit this description, yet he, too, lacked the strength of conviction. His identification with the Jewish group was (like that of Disraeli, who became a member of the Church of England) a matter of pride, not of religious affiliation, Besides, Heine's determination to endure the fate of a Jew surrounded by hostile Christians often wavered. Here are a few excerpts from letters sent to relatives and friends after his departure from Berlin:

To Immanuel Wohlwill (April 1, 1823): " I do not have the courage to wear the traditional beard, to hear myself called ' dirty Jew,' to fast, etc."

To Moritz Embden (May 3, 1823): " My attachment to Judaism has its roots solely in a profound antipathy to Christianity. I who have no use for any dogmatic religion, shall perhaps one day become converted to the most orthodox rabbinism, because I consider it a good antidote."

To Moses Moser (August 23, 1823): " I have rid you of the illusion that I was enthusiastic about the Jewish religion. I admit that I shall never cease to bestir myself on behalf of the rights of Jews to equal citizenship, and when troublous times come, as I feel sure they will come, from their drinking-halls to their palaces, the German mob will hear my voice resound."

Once more to Moser (January 9, 1824): " You give me no news about the *Verein*. If you think the cause of our brethren is not as close to my heart as it used to be you are much mistaken. ' May my right hand wither, if I forget thee, Yerusholayim.' "

To the same (June 25, 1824): " I am studying the chronicles thoroughly and especially much *historia judaica*, the latter on account of its connection with the Rabbi [*The Rabbi of Bacherach*] and perhaps, also, from inner necessity. As I turn the pages of those sad annals, very strange feelings pervade me, an abundance of instruction and suffering. The spirit of Jewish history reveals itself to me ever more gradually, and this spiritual armor will certainly be of assistance to me later."

But this " spiritual armor " proved to be of no help in Heine's struggle for physical survival. Conversion to Lutheranism did not improve matters, either. In July, 1826, only a year after the baptism, Heine confessed to Moser his desire to say farewell to the German fatherland. His endeavors to find himself any position that would guarantee him a regular income, be it that of an editor, a college professor, or even a town clerk in Hamburg, were all in vain ; nor could he live on the royalties received on his books, and he was loath to depend on his rich uncle's charity. Hence, the news of the July Revolution in France stirred him with enthusiasm, and when, in 1831, he moved to Paris for good, his decision to settle in France was prompted as much by the wish to live under what seemed to him a liberal, progressive regime as by the prospect of leaving behind the *nie abzuwaschende Jude*.

In Paris Heine was extremely happy, relishing the courtesy and respect of the Parisians, who treated him as a distinguished foreigner, so happy that he wrote to a friend in Germany : " If anyone asks you how I feel, tell him, ' Like a fish in water,' or rather, tell people that when one fish in the sea asks another how he feels, the reply is, ' Like Heine in Paris.' "

He felt himself to be neither a German nor a Jew, but a cosmopolite whose task it was to work for a reconciliation of those great nations, the French and the German, whose hostility had already sparked many conflagrations. His second task — as important as the first — was to work for the emancipation of mankind. As he formulated it as early as 1828 : " not simply the emancipation of the Irish, the Greeks, Frankfurt Jews, West Indian blacks, and all such oppressed people, but the emancipation of the whole world, and especially of Europe, which has now come of age, and is tearing itself loose from the apron-strings of the privileged classes, the aristocracy " (*Journey from Munich to Genoa.*)

In his principal works of that period — *French Affairs*, the three volumes of *The Salon*, his contributions to the *Augsburger Allgemeine Zeitung* — there are only occasional references to Jews and Judaism (for instance, in the wonderful pen portraits of Spinoza and Moses Mendelssohn). Elsewhere there are beautiful passages on Shylock and on the Bible. In the memorial to Ludwig Marcus the poet recalled the optimistic days of fight, twenty years before, when both he and the little hunchbacked scholar firmly believed in the mission of the *Verein*. While acknowledging the pure intentions, the glorious idealism of the membership, Heine could not, in retrospect, conceal his opinion that the Society's goals had from the beginning been much too limited, that anyone working for it could not go beyond " searching the battlefields of the past for the bones of the champion that had preceded him."

This first Parisian period produced also the third and final chapter of *The Rabbi of Bacherach*. We have only to compare the first two chapters, written in 1825 by the erstwhile member of the *Verein*, with Chapter Three, added a decade and a half later, to see that the sentimental naïveté is entirely gone. The romantic poetry of the fragment's early parts was written in the hope that, as the poet told his confidant Moser, the finished novel would be " an immortal book, an eternal lamp in God's cathedral." In fact, the farcical third chapter has nothing in common with the tender legend of medieval persecution and flight. The Spanish Cavalier who talks so facetiously to Rabbi Abraham and his beautiful wife Sarah is nobody but the nineteenth century mocker, Henri Heine of Paris:

"Thou hast never loved us, Don Isaac," Rabbi Abraham reproached the Marrano.

"Well," replied the Spaniard, "I like your cookery much better than your creed—which wants the right sauce. I really never could rightly digest you . . . . Yes, I am a heathen, and the melancholy self-tormenting Nazarenes are quite as little to my taste as the dry and joyless Hebrews. But . . . do not look at me with disdain. My nose is not a renegade. When I once by chance came at dinnertime into this street, and the well-known savory odors of the Jewish kitchen rose to my nose, I was seized by the same yearning which our fathers felt for the fleshpots of Egypt, pleasant-tasting memories of youth came unto me."

And this continues for several pages, until the reader is relieved by the final statement: " The conclusion and the chapters which follow are lost, not from any fault of the author."

Yet, when the occasion required seriousness, Heine, the jocular, the vain and irreverent " Don Isaac," was adept at transforming his light pen into a sharp sword. Such an occasion offered itself in the year 1840. In February of that year, in far-away Damascus, a Capuchin friar suddenly disappeared, whereupon the Capuchins spread the rumor that the local Jews had slain him in order to use his blood in *matzoth*. In the course of an investigation undertaken by the Turkish Governor, many Jews were thrown into jail and tortured there, and some never came out alive. Only through the intervention of Austria and England, and through the efforts of such Jewish leaders as Isaac Adolphe Cremieux and Moses Montefiore, was the Governor finally compelled to release the surviving Jewish prisoners and put an end to the outrageous investigation.

Since France was divided over the Damascus Affair almost as it was to be, more than fifty years later, over the Dreyfus Case, the reports Heine sent from Paris to the *Allgemeine Zeitung* of Augsburg are of considerable historical interest. Though written from the standpoint of a liberal, unprejudiced Christian (Heine speaks of " our Christian brothers "), these newspaper articles reveal the Jew in Heine. One recalls Theodor Herzl's dispatches about the trial of Captain Dreyfus to the *Neue Freie Presse*, though Heine's anger was more marked, his language even less bridled by reason. Among other things, Heine wrote with irony about certain German papers which exaggerated the interest taken by French Jewry in the cruel fate of their religionists in Damascus :

In fact, we would rather praise than blame the Jews of Paris *if* they, as the North German journals like to put it, showed such great zeal and pity for their unfortunate brothers in the faith of Damascus, and shunned no pecuniary sacrifice for the honorable rescue of their slandered religion. But such is not the case . . . .

The interest which the Jews here take in the tragedy of Damascus reduces itself to very minute manifestations. The Israelitic *Consistorium* assembled and deliberated in the lukewarm fashion of all such bodies, and the only result of its deliberations was the opinion that the legal documents of the trial should be published . . . .

One of the most highly prized members of the religious community here . . . would not give a hundred francs should any one ask him to contribute to a fund for rescuing his great race, It is an old, a lamentable, and yet not a worn-out discovery, that the meanest and most sordid motives are ascribed to every one who raises his voice in vindication of the Jews ; but I do not believe that Israel ever gave money, save when its teeth were drawn by force . . . .

In his morning audience M. Thiers [the French Premier] assures his hearers with the air of deepest conviction that it is perfectly settled that the Jews drank Christian blood at the Passover feast, *chacun à son gout ;* all the reports of witnesses confirm the fact that the Rabbis of Damascus butchered Pater Thomas and drank his blood . . . in which we could behold a sad superstition, a religious fanaticism which still prevails in the East, while the Jews of the West have become much more humane and enlightened . . . as, for instance, M. de Rothschild who, it is true, has not gone over to the Christian Church, but all the more zealously to the Christian kitchen . . . .

The old system of extirpating races is gradually becoming extinct in the East, through European influence. The right of individuals to exist is also receiving there a higher recognition, and the cruelties of torture are slowly vanishing before a milder system of criminal jurisprudence. The bloody story of Damascus will conduce to this result ; and in reference to this, the journey of M. Cremieux to Alexandria [to see Mehemet Ali, ruler of Egypt and suzerain of Syria] is one of the most important events in the annals of humanity.

Yet while he loathed the idea of people being wronged solely because they belonged to a particular national (or religious) group, Heine did not permit his abhorrence of what now is called " genocide " to turn him into a protagonist of nationalism either. He made it clear that it does not suit a poet to play the part of a nationalist, that the poet is by nature a cosmopolite. When, in 1835, his picture was included in an anthology, *Gallerie der ausgezeichnetsten Israeliten aller Jahrhunderte*, Heine, in a Parisian paper, announced that this was a mistake, since he belonged to the Lutheran faith. (Simultaneously, Gabriel Riesser, the great champion of Jewish emancipation, deplored the inclusion of the picture of this convert to Christianity.) [1]

---

[1] The novelist Berthold Auerbach also felt that Heine was a burden rather than a boon for the Jews. Heine found, however, a staunch defender in the historian Heinrich Graetz. Jewish nationalists are divided on the question whether Heine's poems can be included in Jewish national literature. Ahad Ha'am refused to include him because he wrote in German : " The national literature of any nation is only that which is written in its own language. " In 1956 a square at Haifa, Israel, was named after the poet, against the frantic opposition of the religious groups who held his " conversion " against him. A new Hebrew translation of " Princess Sabbath " could not be published in Israel : the editor did not wish to risk offending the Hebrew reader by offering him a poem in which the Almighty conveys to Moses on Mount Sinai, along with the Ten Commandments, the art of cooking *tchalent*.

79

Notwithstanding the cosmopolitanism of the mature Heine, and whatever his religious belief, or lack of it, may have been, however many nasty jabs he took at the Jews, the man who could give us such a glowing description of the Passover celebration (in *The Rabbi of Bacherach*) or of the Sabbath glory (in " Princess Sabbath "), the man who created one of the tenderest portraits of a humble Jewish peddler (Moses Lump, in *The Baths of Lucca*), did have an affinity to the people from whom he sprang. It is often held that it took a horrible illness to bring Heine back to his brethren, to lead him to refer to himself as a " poor Jew, sick to death " (as he did in 1849). This is erroneous. One can trace a direct line from the passage in *Ludwig Boerne, eine Denkschrift* (1840), referring to the Jews as " the dough from which gods are kneaded," to that statement in *Gestaendnisse* (1854), extolling the Bible and Moses, the greatest artist of all times. Here the moribund author declared himself proud " that his ancestors came of the noble house of Israel," and that he was " a descendant of the martyrs who gave a god and a moral code to the world, and who have fought and suffered on every battlefield of thought." [2]

It was not lack of reverence for the Eternal Power that made the invalid of the Rue d'Amsterdam say to the faithful Alfred

---

[2] Of Heine's numerous biographers, Max Brod is most concerned with what he considers to be the *Jewish* aspects in Heine's life and work. Undoubtedly, George Eliot exaggerated and over-simplified when she said : " Heine and his ancestors spent their youth in German air, and were reared on Wurst and Sauerkraut, so that he is as much German as a pheasant is an English bird, or a potato an Irish vegetable. " But it is also hard to prove that, as Max Brod sees it, Heine presents " Jewish Spirit working in an alien material. "

I, for one, cannot notice any " sound Jewish instincts " nor discover any " manly Jewish bearing " in Heine who had very little Jewish knowledge, and was encouraged rather than dissuaded by his family to embrace Christianity to adapt himself to the prevailing winds. His political enemies often unfairly pointed at what they considered loathsome " Jewish " traits in his make-up. But Heine viewed himself as a German even after his " return " to his ancestral faith. Only once did he refer to himself as a Jewish poet, and this in bitter jest. But he was not joking when, in a moment of justified pride, he exclaimed :

> *I am a German poet,*
> *In Germany I'm famed :*
> *When the best names are mentioned,*
> *My name is also named.*

Meissner that if he were once again well enough to walk without crutches he would go not to a church but straight to the nearest dance hall. It was reverence for life, cruel, egotistical, pleasure-seeking, unprincipled as it might be, that made him speak thus. His temple was the world, his nation was mankind. " It would be in bad taste and petty of me," he explained to Meissner, " ever to be ashamed — as my slanderers have accused me — of being a Jew, but it would be equally ridiculous to claim that I am one." When Heine asserted that in his writings he had, time and again, defended the Jews, this was not an empty boast but the full truth. Still, " I could never immolate myself completely for their sake, like Herr Riesser and some others. I can lose myself in no party, neither Republican nor Patriot, Christian nor Jew."

"If I Think of Germany . . ."

IN 1831 HEINE LEFT GERMANY, WHERE LIFE SEEMED UNBEARABLE to him, in order to reside in France. Writing in German, however, he needed a German audience, and he continued working for German newspapers and selling his major works to the Hamburg publisher Julius Campe. He was one of the most widely read authors in Central Europe when, in 1835, he suffered a staggering blow: first, the Prussian Diet and thereafter the Bundestag, the Federal Diet, proscribed all the past and future writings of the group called Young Germany, whose most eminent representative was Heine.[1]

As usual, when bad news reached him, he parried the blow with a quip:

I had taken such pains over the German language, with its accusative and dative, and knew well how to string the words together beautifully, like pearls. I had found such pleasure in that occupation, for it shortened the long winter evening of my exile . . . and made me almost imagine I was home with my mother . . . . And now I have been forbidden to write!

He did not take the blow passively. In a declaration curiously foreshadowing Zola's famous *J'Accuse* letter on the Dreyfus case, he proclaimed:

I lay my charge against the authors of this document and accuse them of having abused the people's trust; I accuse them of having insulted the majesty of the people; I accuse them of high treason against the German nation. I accuse!

But this strong language could hardly be expected to bring about

---

[1] The Bundestag banned these writers because "they attacked the Christian religion in the most insolent manner, in literary works accessible to all classes, debased the existing social relationships and destroyed all discipline and morality." But the authors against whom this decree was directed constituted no united group; they were rivals rather than confederates, although they had a common enemy and a common ground of discontent.

a change in the hearts and minds of the German authorities. The edicts were not revoked, and they threatened to rob him not only of his public but also of his income. He was driven to accept one of the pensions France gave to distinguished yet needy emigrés. (When, after the French Revolution of 1848, it became known that he had been the recipient of such a grant, the same Germans who had not had the meanest position for him, now loudly, and without foundation, asserted that this pension had bought his silence on the faults of the French regime.) This predicament also drove him to make the most extravagant concessions to Campe (who outwitted the German government by transferring his press to Danish territory and smuggling the " radical " works by Heine and others back into the German lands under every kind of ruse).

In 1843 and 1844 he visited his native country, the second time accompanied by his French wife. Refused a Prussian visa, he had to journey by ship from Amsterdam to Hamburg to avoid crossing Prussian territory, where he would have risked arrest. He cut short his second stay in the free city of Hamburg after a warning that he might not be quite safe there, since the Prussian government was not above kidnapping. " My legs do not have the talent to bear iron rings of the sort Weitling bore," he wrote to Karl Marx in Paris, referring to the Socialist agitator who had been placed in chains in a Magdeburg jail. The Prussians believed him to be more closely connected with Marx' paper, *Vorwaerts*, than he really was (he had merely contributed a few poems.) When, two years later, he wanted to go to Berlin to consult a famous physician about his rapidly increasing illness, he was informed that should he ever be found on Prussian soil he would be arrested and imprisoned for *lèse-majesté*.

He died without having once more visited his homeland. But his writings continued to be read wherever German was spoken, and every singer knew by heart his lyrics that were set to music by Schubert, Schumann, Mendelssohn, and Brahms. His most bitter enemy in Germany, Wolfgang Menzel, died in 1873,[2] but new foes

---

[2] Menzel had dubbed the Young Germany group " Young Palestine, " although it included only two Jews, Boerne and Heine. He who began as a staunch liberal

had been born. They had their day three decades after Heine's death when some of his admirers wondered why Germany, which had honored second- and third-rate poets with monuments, had not erected a single one to Heine.[3]

There is no need now to relate in detail the refusal of one city after another to honor Heine with a monument, or to repeat the insidious slanders by self-styled patriots against the dead poet. It is true that he also had powerful defenders, among them Chancellor Bismarck, who considered him Goethe's poetic equal. Was Heine really wrong, Bismarck wondered, when he demanded that the claws of the Hohenzollern eagle be cut for having snatched up so much booty? Had not Frederick the Great annexed Silesia without any justification? As for the charge that Heine had glorified Napoleon, the Prussian Junker Bismarck, who was hardly a philo-Semite, had this to say:

I cannot blame him for that, for, had I been in his shoes, I would hardly have reacted differently. Had I, like Heine, been born a Jew, would I have liked having the gates of the Ghetto locked at eight o'clock in the evening, or the subjection of my people to the toughest

---

ended as an arch-reactionary who stood for imperialism, for strict censorship, for corporal and capital punishment. Long before Hitler was born, Menzel decried the mingling of races (the superior race was, of course, the noble and heroic Indo-Caucasian). He assailed the church (which stabbed nations in the back) and derided parliamentarism (the Frankfort parliament of 1848 was packed with professors and Jews).

[3] What infuriated the German Michel was not so much the vigor of Heine's harangues as the fact that they came from one who had just emerged from the Ghetto. The Critic Alfred Kerr noted that the Swabian poet, Friedrich Hoelderlin, was honoured by a memorial tablet at his birthplace although he had expressed himself about Germany in language a hundred times more corrosive than Heine ever used. In the novel, *Hyperion*, Hoelderlin had his hero say this about Germany and the Germans:

Barbarians from old, grown only more barbaric through industry and science and even religion, quite incapable of any divine feeling, utterly disqualified for the boon of the sacred graces, offensive to any generous soul through exaggerated pettiness of every degree, dull and inharmonious as the fragments of a discarded vessel . . . . I cannot imagine any people more divided than the Germans. You see craftsmen but no men, thinkers but no men, priests but no men, masters and servants, the young and the mature, but no men—is it not like a battlefield where hands and arms and shattered limbs lie around in confusion while streams of blood soak into the sand?

special legislation ? It was inevitable that a Heine had to praise as a redeemer from a torturous yoke the man who introduced French law in the Rhineland and abolished discriminatory laws.

Among the most ardent admirers of Heine was Elizabeth, Empress of Austria. In 1887 she summoned the German sculptor Ernst Herter to Vienna and commissioned him to design a monument to be donated by her to the city of Duesseldorf. Herter made three different models, but the German city rejected them one after another, for reasons more closely connected with prejudice than aesthetics. Mayence did not want a monument either. Dismayed, the Empress dropped the plan and ordered the Danish sculptor Louis Hasselriis to make a statue for her estate at Corfu. It was a seated study in marble of the aging poet, bearded and emaciated, in his hand a page on which is written the first verse of the poem, *" Was will die einsame Traene."* Shipped to her Corfu palace, Achilleon, the Heine statue sat there for several quiet years on an elevation facing the blue sea. But in 1898 the Empress was assassinated, and when the German Emperor, William II, acquired Achilleon he had no use for the monument. It was purchased by a descendant of Heine's publisher, Campe, and offered to the city of Hamburg. A heated controversy followed, as a result of which Hasselriis' work was dumped into a warehouse. Eventually, the statue was liberated from its prison and in 1927 placed in the Donnerspark. But in 1933 the Nazis removed it, and it would have been lost had not Campe's daughter, who had married a Frenchman, taken it to Toulon. The city fathers accepted the gift of the statue, but did nothing with it until in 1955 Hamburg approached Toulon requesting its return. No, said Toulon, we shall keep it, and it was placed in a public garden.

Despite Treitschke and Bartels, to name the leading opponents of Heine at the turn of this century, one must not forget the many excellent unbiased German scholars who wrote detailed Heine biographies and painstakingly edited his works. Neither professor Treitschke, who held that Heine, as an " Oriental," was incapable of drinking heavily in the Teuton manner, nor Adolf Bartels, who insulted the dead poet in a manner anticipating Nazi criticism,

could counteract the publication of Ernst Elster's superbly annotated edition of Heine's *Saemtliche Werke*, of *Conversations with
Heine* (edited by Heinrich Hubert Houben), and of the substantial
biography by Max J. Wolff. The listing of German doctoral
dissertations, monographs, and major articles on Heine written
between 1856 and 1933 and again after 1945 would fill a book.

During the short life of the Weimar Republic, a Heine monument
by the sculptor Hugo Lederer was erected in Hamburg. Certain
stanzas, suppressed in the Kaiserreich because of their critical attitude toward the Hohenzollerns, could be printed again. A Heinrich
Heine society was founded by the Hamburg book dealer and
antiquarian Carl Henry Hoym. A manifesto of the society urged all
" intellectually alert individuals who see in Heine not only a great
poet but also a fighter for freedom, humanity, and the reconciliation
of nations " to " unite in a thinking action group."

But in 1933 all this came to an end. In his drama, *Almansor*,
which he wrote as a young man, Heine had lashed out against book
burnings : when Almansor, horrified, remarks that the Koran had
been burned in the market-place at Granada, the Moor Hassan says
that this was but a prologue–where books are burned, men, too,
are burned in the end. How catastrophically true this proved to be !
Likewise, in Shakespeare's *Girls and Women* he had forecast a
devilish civilization in which the sufferings of the Jews would be
much greater than they were in the Middle Ages : " If Satan . . .
should conquer, there will fall on the heads of the poor Jews a
tempest of persecution which will far surpass their previous sufferings."

While men like Treitschke and Bartels could, at least, plead
before the Supreme Court of history that their attitudes toward
Heine had not changed perceptibly in their long careers, there is
no excuse for Dietrich Eckart, who in 1893, editing a volume of
Heine's poetry, had lavished full praise on the poet (" the chords
of his lyre are of the purest gold " he wrote: " not a single dissonance disturbs the divine harmony of his songs "), but who ended
as a detractor of Heine and a mentor of Adolf Hitler. Some of the
men who in 1932 signed an appeal for funds for the establishment

of a Heine monument at Duesseldorf joined the book burners only
a year later. The limit of impudence and idiocy was reached by
that Nazi writer who demanded that " Aryans " write new verses
to replace the Heine lyrics set to music by German composers.
This suggestion was, of course, as unsuccessful as a similar one,
the demand that Mendelssohn's incidental music to *Midsummer
Night's Dream* be rewritten by an Aryan composer.

In Frankfort-on-Main, Heine lovers were quick enough to spirit
away the Heine monument before the Nazis could seize it. Concealed for twelve long years after the fall of the Nazi regime, it
was ceremoniously restored to its old place in one of the city parks.
The work of Georg Kolbe, it shows a bronze youth and maiden,
with a profile of the poet at the base. Lederer's monument, which
stood in the Hamburg Stadtpark, the Commons, has disappeared
completely, but a bronze cast was made from a model discovered
in a private collection and presented to the Europa College in the
same city. In 1953, Duesseldorf at last got its monument, consisting of a female figure by the famous French sculptor, Aristide
Maillol, and, at its base, a profile relief of the poet's head, the work
of Ivo Beucker. It is located in the Hofgarten, on Napoleon Hill,
where Heine as a young boy saw the Emperor ride by on horseback.

Heine himself, on the subject of monuments, exercised his
typical ironic wit. When in 1852 Maximilian Heine, the Russian
privy councilor and physician to the court at St. Petersburg, visited
his sick brother and prophesied that Duesseldorf would be the first
German city to erect him a monument, Heine interrupted with a
mocking smile : " I have one already in Hamburg. . . . If you turn
to the left beyond the Boersenplatz, you will see a large, beautiful
house, belonging to . . . Herr Julius Campe. It is a gorgeous monument of stone gratefully commemorating the many and large
editions of my *Book of Songs*." (While the first edition of *Book of
Songs* did not sell out for ten years, with a changing taste of 1837
the book became a best-seller, and by Heine's death in 1856 no
fewer than thirteen large editions had been sold.)

Like every writer, however, he wondered : was he understood

in his native country? All that he could find out was that he was widely read. Unfortunately, many volumes of Heine were destroyed during the Nazi period or otherwise lost to Germany. To replace these, both West and East Germany have brought out, in the last fifteen years, numerous one-volume Heine anthologies or reprints of individual works ; while there are now new editions of *Ausgewaehlte Werke*, no publisher has yet ventured upon the most urgent task : a new, up-to-date, annotated, and final edition of *Saemtliche Werke* to replace the seven-volume Meyers Klassiker and the eleven-volume Insel-Verlag Heine, long out of print and almost unavailable.

The major events in post-war Germany to the Heine reader abroad were not the celebrations of the anniversary—in which the reorganized Heine Society played a prominent part—but two literary events. One was the completion by Friedrich Hirth of the monumental six-volume edition of Heine's letters, half of the text being scholarly comments.

The second event was the acquisition in 1956 by the city of Duesseldorf of the Strauss Collection, the largest known collection of Heine's original manuscripts. After the death of Mathilde Heine in 1883, these manuscripts were scattered all over the world. Some of them were later acquired by the Municipal Library of Duesseldorf, others formed the nucleus of the collection assembled after World War I by the German bankers Carl and Albert Strauss. Emigrating to the United States in 1939, the owners succeeded in smuggling these treasures out of Germany under the guise of business papers. For seventeen years the collection lay in the vaults of a New York bank until it was sought by Duesseldorf and incorporated into its Heine Archives. These archives boast of more than 3,500 volumes by and about Heine. While the Duesseldorf archives fortunately survived Nazism and war, the poet's birthplace on Bolkerstrasse was bombed in 1943. Self-mockingly, Heine related how he told its owner, an old lady, that " on pain of her life " she must not sell it :

For the whole house she would get so much as the tip that the green-veiled, gentle Englishwomen give to the maid when she shows them the room where I first saw the light of the world, and the hencoop in which my father used to confine me when I had stolen grapes, and the brown door on which my mother taught me to write the letters of the alphabet with chalk. Heavens, dear lady, if I have become a famous writer, it cost my poor mother trouble enough !

Despite the speeches of February, 1956, the issuance of a Heine stamp, the unveiling of plaques on houses where Heine resided, Heine is no longer sufficiently read in his native country.[4] The older generation claims to have read him when they were young ; the young ones barely know his name. But those who make the effort to read him will find that nearly all of his prose and a good part of his poetry is as much alive today as it was a hundred years ago.

A restless seeker, tortured by doubt, swinging from one extreme to the other, and finding no way of reconciling the hedonism of the Greeks with the spiritualism of the Jews, he lacked the quality of leadership. Vacillating between love and reason, beauty and truth, Heine does not belong in the rank of the great, such as Lao-tse, Plato, Moses, the Church Fathers, Thomas Aquinas, or Goethe, who found a way to harmonize conflicting forces. He died believing that the conflict was insoluble.

The Germans of today need not accept all of his opinions. In one respect, though, a thorough acquaintance with Heine will profit the new Germans in their attempts to rid themselves of that depressing heritage of the past called chauvinism. Whatever else he may have been, Heine was a dedicated anti-chauvinist. In one of his early writings, the poet related that at a masked ball in Berlin a super-patriot chided him for speaking French. Reassuring his public that he, too, loved Germany and the Germans, the poet added : " But I love no less the inhabitants of the rest of the earth

---

[4] Literary criticism *à la* Treitschke and Bartels, which concentrated not on a writer's qualities but on his origins, has not yet disappeared in post-war Germany. (Or has it returned after several years of cautious restraint ?) A history of German poetry, published in 1954, attacks Heine largely because he was a Jew. Here is a typical sentence, describing the economic and cultural rise of German Jewry in the last century : " From the shady usurers often came the rich ennobled speculator and the virtuoso of rhyme. "

who are forty times more numerous than those of Germany. . . .
I am therefore forty times more worthy than those who are unable
to extract themselves from the morass of national egotism."

Heine in America

In the near future, the world will either be an American
Republic or a Russian Universal Monarchy.

Lutetia, 1840

THE WEATHER WAS AS DREARY AND DRIZZLY IN NEW YORK ON
February 17, 1956, when American admirers of Heine gathered
around the Lorelei Fountain in the Bronx, as the weather had
been when the poet was laid to rest in Montmartre Cemetery a
hundred years earlier. This time speeches were made by representatives of the Federal Republic of Germany, the City of New
York, and the Carl Schurz Memorial Foundation. Wreaths of
flowers were placed at the base of the monument, on which is
carved a low-relief portrait of Heinrich Heine.

After the ceremonies were over, two park attendants who had
been watching from a distance, came over to me.

" That Heine, he was a great poet, wasn't he?" one asked.

" No, he was a philosopher—like Sir Francis Bacon!" the other
man insisted.

" He was both," I said. And I thought: how significant that the
mention of Heine could again start an argument, even in an
obscure park in the Bronx!

It seemed to me ironic, too, that the earliest public monument honoring Heine stands in America,[1] for Heine wrote more
barbed phrases than praise about a country he knew only from
hearsay. The story goes back to 1893 when, learning of the
rejection by Duesseldorf and Mayence of the Heine monument,
Americans of German origin organized a committee that commissioned its sculptor, Ernst Herter, to make a monument for
America, but one not identical with the one that, in all three

---

[1] There is a Heine bust, by Kurt Harold Isenstein, in Cleveland's German
Garden, which is a link in the chain of eighteen cultural gardens, a section of
the huge Rockefeller Park. Sponsored by various nationality groups, the
Gardens were created to show that in America there is " peace, understanding,
and co-operation among the peoples of all nations. "

versions, had been rejected by the Rhineland cities. This fourth version was, indeed, accepted by the committee. But now the trouble began. It took the donations of thousands to pay for the execution of the monument in white Tyrolean marble. The Lorelei Fountain was en route when the committee began to find it more difficult than it had expected to obtain the proper site in New York. They had hoped to place it in Central Park, but the city fathers, turning to the New York Sculpture Society for advice, were told that, since the three Rhine maidens were nude and the Lorelei herself not " decent " either, this plan could not be recommended. Opposition arose on another front: some German-Americans, echoing the anti-Heine sentiments of the *Vaterland*, began a protest against the very idea of a monument to Heine. Several locations offered by New York were rejected by the committee as totally unacceptable.

After twenty months in a New York warehouse, Lorelei and the Rhine maidens were finally permitted to make the second, much shorter stage of their journey. This one was to the Bronx where, in July, 1899, in the presence of the sculptor, who had come from Europe, the fountain was solemnly unveiled. The fountain carries no inscription other than the words " Heinrich Heine " beneath the portrait on the base. Only the initiated will understand the subtle irony in one of the two other reliefs: the youth (Heine!) about to kill a dragon, holds a pen instead of a spear, and the monster wears a wig to symbolize the German bureaucrat.

Many comments on America can be found in Heine's works, his correspondence, and his conversations. As a young man teaching in the *Verein* in Berlin, he often talked about a subject close to his heart—tolerance and freedom of worship. As one of his students recalled, he advised them to emigrate to America, or, at least, to England: " In those countries it does not occur to anyone to ask: What do you, or what don't you believe? In these countries, everybody can be happy after his own fashion " (H. H. Houben, *Gespraeche mit Heine*).

His own *Hartz Journey* was, unquestionably, influenced by

92

Washington Irving's *Tales of a Traveler*. Heine himself, in a letter to Ludwig Robert (March 4, 1825), noted in it a tinge of " Washington Irving's *Beobachtung* " (observation *à la* Washington Irving). About that time, and even later, he flirted with the idea of leaving decrepit Europe, with its prejudices and its feudalism, and of emigrating to the New World. In *Journey from Munich to Genoa* (1828) one finds a sentence pointing to the United States as a haven of refuge for all lovers of liberty : " Even if all Europe became one dungeon, there would now be still another hole for escape ; this is America, and, thank God! that hole is even bigger than the dungeon itself."

In the *English Fragments* of the same year he coined the term *europamuede* (tired of Europe).

In an introduction to Robert Wesselhoeft's pamphlet, *Kahldorf ueber den Adel* (1831), Heine again referred to the New World, as he praised " Lafayette, the hero of two hemispheres and two centuries, who with the Argonauts of Liberty returned from America, whence he brought to Europe the golden fleece, the idea of a free constitution."

But written reports from America, or perhaps talks with the *Amerikamuede* who had returned, seem to have convinced Heine that the United States was not the paradise he had believed it. Blasts against America can be found in *Ludwig Boerne, a Memorial*, namely in passages from letters written by the poet in the summer of 1830 while he was vacationing on the island of Heligoland in the North Sea. At that time he felt that he could not carry on in the police state of Germany much longer. Should he go to Italy ? To England ?

. . . or shall I betake myself to America, to that huge region of free men, where the invisible fetters would be more galling to me than the visible ones at home ; and where the most odious of all tyrants—the mob—exercises its brutal authority. And yet my vocation as liberator compels me publicly to praise and extol this country ! Oh, you good German peasants, go to America ! You will there find neither princes nor nobles ; all men are alike there ; all are equally churls, except, indeed, a few millions whose skins are black and brown, and who are treated like dogs.

At the same time, these Americans are zealous churchgoers:
This hypocrisy they have learned from the English, who have
bequeathed to them their worst characteristics. Material pursuits are
their true religion ; money is their God, their only almighty God. Of
course, there may be many noble souls who in secret deprecate this
universal self-seeking and injustice. But if they attack it, they expose
themselves to martyrdom, the like of which is inconceivable in Europe.

He was fortunately mistaken in his pessimism concerning the
future development of the United States, since he believed that
sooner or later the governors of the states would become sovereigns,
an event which would spell the end of American republicanism.
Here is his characterization of America in the late poem, "Whither
Now?":

> I have more than once been tempted
> By America's renown,
> Where, in Freedom's mighty stable
> Stalled alike is every clown.
>
> But I fear a land where skittles
> Can be played without a king,
> Where the natives chew tobacco
> And spittoons are not the thing.
>
> *(Translated by Margaret Armour).*

Yet were not the Abolitionists and other critics in antebellum
America, whose knowledge was first-hand, equally worried about
the state of civilization in the young republic? Just because he was
not easily satisfied, Heine was an ideal critic of the contemporary
scene, one who wished nothing more than to see all men happy,
well-fed, well-clothed, well-housed.[2]

Heine had no chance to judge for himself whether his opinions
of America were well founded or not. Toward the end of his life,
he had reason to mention the New World with a feeling of gratitude. Talking to his Boswell, the writer Alfred Meissner, in 1854,

---

[2] An avid reader, Heine was, of course, familiar with the best-seller of the
eighteen-fifties, Harriet Beecher Stowe's *Uncle Tom's Cabin*, to which he once
refers in his *Confessions* when he speaks about his own return to religion.

he compared the malicious treatment of his work in the Germany he loved so much to the praise he received in France, and to the facts that his works were being reprinted in North America and lectures given about him in New York and Albany. The following year he learned of the English translation (by the American, Leland) of the *Reisebilder*, and wrote to his French publisher, Calmann-Levy:

A piece of good news that I forgot to communicate to you the other day. An English translation of the *Reisebilder* which has appeared in New York [actually, in Philadelphia] has met with an enormous success, according to a correspondent in the *Augsburger Zeitung* (which does not love me enough to invent successes for me).

It was in the same year that a Philadelphia publisher of a pirated German edition, J. Weik, asked Heine to write a foreword. The fear that the financially hard-pressed poet might be tempted to violate his old contract by such an offer sent his German publisher, Julius Campe, to Paris, where he persuaded Heine to decline. The *Saemtliche Werke*, first published in six volumes (1855), appeared without a preface by Heine.

American readers differed in their reactions to Heine's life and works. Although Longfellow appreciated Heine's lyrical gift and translated some of the poems, he had nothing in common with Heine's spirit. In *Graham's Magazine* (1842) he described the poet as " the leader of the new school in Germany which is seeking to establish a religion of sensuality, and to build a palace of pleasure on the ruins of the church." Objecting to " the fierce implacable hatred " with which Heine pursued his foe, Long-fellow also declared that Heine combined " the recklessness of Byron " with " the sentimentality of Sterne." Years later he found " Deutschland, ein Wintermaerchen " " a sneering, sarcastic, in parts beautiful, in parts, indecent, poem." Referring in 1854 to *Romancero*, the poems Heine wrote on his sickbed, Longfellow was not reconciled, as they were " witty and wicked as ever."

Walt Whitman was much closer to Heine in his thinking, and agreed fully with Matthew Arnold's essay which hailed Heine as an enemy of Philistinism. To his confidant, Horace Traubel (according to the latter's *With Walt Whitman in Camden*, 1906), Whitman expressed his approval of the Briton's essay, which he had read " with zest," and continued :

Heine ! Oh, how great ! The more you stop to look, to examine, the deeper seem the roots ; the broader and higher the umbrage. And Heine was free—was one of the men who win by degrees. He was a master of pregnant sarcasm : he brought down a hundred humbuggeries if he brought down two. At times he plays with you with a deliberate, baffling sportiveness.

Among American devotees of Heine was Emma Lazarus, a protege of the philosopher Emerson and a poet. She was only sixteen in 1866 when she published *Poems and Translations*, which included some of the finest English renderings of Heine's poetry. In her own sonnet, " The Venus of the Louvre," she referred to Heine's last stroll through Paris when he collapsed beside the Greek statue :

> . . . But at her feet a pale, death-stricken Jew,
> Her life-adorer, sobbed farewell to love.
> Here Heine wept ! Here still he weeps anew,
> Nor ever shall his shadow lift or move
> While mourns one ardent heart, one poet-brain
> For vanished Hellas and Hebraic pain.

Among Heine's American translators was, oddly enough, Mark Twain. In *A Tramp Abroad* (1880) he yielded to the temptation to render " Die Lorelei " into English stanzas. He conceded that his version might not be a good one (" for poetry isn't my line ") but hoped that it would serve his purpose, namely, " to give the un-German young girl a jingle of words to hang the tune on until she can get hold of a good version."

Louis Untermeyer was the most ambitious of all American translators, tackling a greater number of songs, hymns, and ballads than anyone else had dared. He is also the author of a widely read Heine biography.

A Heine admirer was the American statesman of German birth, Carl Schurz. A Rhinelander like the poet, he was a student at the

Jesuit Gymnasium in Cologne. In his *Reminiscences*, Schurz wrote:

This was to me like a revelation. I felt almost as if I had never before read a lyric poem; and yet many of Heine's songs sounded to me as if I had always known them, as if the fairies had sung them to me at my cradle. All the verses that I myself had written until then [Schurz was then about sixteen], which were mostly of the declamatory kind, went at once into the fire and I saw them burn with genuine relief. The reading and the rereading of the *Book of Songs* was to me an indescribable revelry. Then I read the *Pictures of Travel*, the various political poems, and *Atta Troll*, with its acrid political satire, the wit of which did not good to the heart, but sharply turned one's thoughts upon the condition of the fatherland.

When they laid Heine to his last rest in the Montmartre cemetery, Walt Whitman had just rung in a new era of poetry with his *Leaves of Grass*, and Abraham Lincoln was just emerging from obscurity, envisaging a new kind of democracy, one entirely unknown in the Old World. But the nineteenth century did not belong to Whitman and Lincoln alone. Subtle and, at times, imperceptible though the influence of Heine on modern man may have been, there can be no doubt that he loosened the tongues of many who might otherwise have remained silent. He gave the stamp of legitimacy to the *freie Schriftsteller* (a term more adequately translated by " free writer " than free-lance writer), who fights for his ideals with allegiance only to his own conscience. Heine demonstrated, through his own triumph over illness, financial worry, and official hostility that the mind can gloriously overcome obstacles through the freedom of the will, man's most precious possession.

Selections from Heinrich Heine's Prose

Florentine Nights

IN THE ANTE-ROOM MAXIMILIAN FOUND THE PHYSICIAN, WHO WAS
drawing on his black gloves. " I am in a great hurry," said the latter
hastily ; " Signora Maria has not slept all day, and only just now
has fallen into a little nap. I need not tell you that she must not be
disturbed by any noise, and when she wakens she must not speak
for her life! She must lie still, not move in the least — the only
movement permitted her is that of a mental nature. I beg you —
tell her all or any kind of fanciful stories, so that she will only
listen quietly."

" Rest assured, doctor," replied Maximilian, with a mournful
smile. " I have trained myself for a talker, and will not let her
speak. And I will tell her fantastic stuff enough — as much as you
will. But how long will she live ?"

" I am in a great hurry," replied the physician, and disappeared.

Black Deborah with her acute ear had quickly recognized the
step of the newcomer, and softly opened for him the door. At his
nod she as quietly left the chamber, and Maximilian found himself
alone by his friend. The chamber was dimly lit by a single lamp,
which cast half fearful, half inquisitive gleams on the face of the
beautiful woman who, clad entirely in white muslin, lay sleeping
calmly on a green-silk sofa.

Silent, with folded arms, Maximilian stood a while before the
sleeper and regarded the beautiful limbs, which the light garb
rather revealed than hid, and every time when a strip of light fell
on the pale face his heart throbbed: " In God's name!" he murmured, "*what* is that? What memory is it that wakes in me?
Ah, I know now — this white form on the green ground — yes —
now "——

At that instant the invalid awoke, and as if gazing from the
depth of a dream, the soft dark violet eyes looked questioning —
praying, on the friend. " Of what were you thinking just now,

Maximilian?" she said, with that terrible, soft voice, such as is heard from those who suffer from lung disease, and in which we seem to hear the prattle of a child, the chirping of a bird, and the death-rattle. " Of what were you thinking?" she repeated, and raised her head so hastily that the long locks curled about it like gold serpents frightened up.

" For God's sake," cried Maximilian, as he softly pressed her back again on the sofa, " remain quiet, say nothing ; I will tell you all that I think or feel—yes, even what I don't know.

" In fact," he continued, " I do not know exactly what I just now thought and felt. Pictures from childhood swept like twilight dreams through my soul. I thought of my mother's chateau—of its garden run wild, of the beautiful marble statue which lay in the green grass. I called it my mother's chateau, but I beg you, on my life, do not understand by that anything magnificent or grand. I have always been accustomed to hear it so called. My father laid a curious emphasis on ' the castle,' and smiled oddly as he said it. It was not till a later time that I learned the meaning of this smile —when I, a boy of twelve, went with my mother to the chateau. It was my first journey. We drove all day through a thick forest, whose dark thrills I shall never forget, and it was not till twilight that we first paused at a long cross-bar which separated us from a great meadow. We were obliged to wait almost half-an-hour before a ' boy ' came from a mud hut close by, who pushed away the barrier and let us in. I say ' boy,' because old Martha always called her forty-year-old nephew by this term. This youth, in order to receive ' the gracious quality,' had donned the old livery of his late uncle, and we had been obliged to wait until he had brushed it clean. Could he have had more time he would have also put on his stockings ; but, as it was, his long bare legs were in good keeping with his scarlet coat. Whether he wore breeches under it I do not know. Our servant John, who, like me, had often heard of ' the chateau,' made a very strange face when the ' boy ' led us to the little broken building where the late Herr had dwelt. But he was startled indeed when my mother bade him bring in the beds. How could he suppose there were no beds at ' the chateau '? And the order of my mother to provide sleeping comforts he had either never heard or neglected it as superfluous trouble.

" The little dwelling, just one story high, which had not boasted in its best days more than five inhabitable rooms, was now a pitiful picture of the passed away. Wrecked furniture, ragged hangings and carpets, not one window-pane unbroken, the floor torn up here and there, and everywhere ugly traces of the most outrageous acts of the soldiery.

" ' Those who were quartered on us amused themselves very much at our expense,' said the ' boy,' with a stupid smile. My mother made a sign to him that we would gladly be alone, and while he busied himself with John, I went to see the garden, which also wore the most inconsolable air of ruin. The great trees were partly hacked away, partly felled, and spiteful, sneering parasites rose over the fallen trunks. Here and there one could recognize the way amid the box-bushes growing wildly out of trim. Here and there too stood statues, the most of which had lost their heads or at least their noses. I remember a Diana whose nether limbs were overgrown with dark ivy in a comical fashion, and also of a goddess of plenty from whose cornucopia flowed rank, poisonous weeds. One statue only had been spared — God knows how — from the mischief of man and Time. It had indeed been hurled from its pedestal into the high grass, but it lay there uninjured — a marble goddess, with the most exquisitely pure features, and with a finely chiseled noble breast which gleamed up from the high grass like a Greek Apocalypse. I was almost terrified at the sight ; this statue inspired in me a strange, close, feverish terror, and a secret bashfulness kept me from gazing long at its lovely mien.

" When I returned to my mother she stood by the window, lost in thought, her head resting on her right hand, while tears ran without ceasing down her cheeks. I had never seen her weep like this. She embraced me hastily and tenderly, and made excuse that owing to John's neglect I could not have a proper bed. ' Old Martha,' she said, ' is very ill, and cannot give up her bed for you, my dear child. But John can arrange the cushions from the coach so that you can sleep on them, and you may take his cloak for covering.

I will sleep here on straw ; this was the bedroom of my late father
— it looked far better once than it now does. Leave me alone.' And
the tears ran more irrepressibly from her eyes.

" Whether it was the not being used to such a bed, or to my
excited feelings, I could not sleep. The moon shone so directly at
me through the broken panes, that it seemed as if it would lure me
out into the clear summer night. Whether I turned to the right side
or the left, whether I opened or impatiently shut my eyes, I could
think of nothing but the beautiful marble statue which I had seen
in the grass. I could not understand the bashfulness which seized
me when I first saw it ; I felt vexed at this childish feeling, and said
to myself, ' Tomorrow I will kiss thee, thou beautiful marble face ;
kiss thee on the lovely corner of the mouth where the lips melt
into such a charming dimple!' And then an impatience such as I
had never before felt rippled through all my limbs, I could not
resist the strange impulse, and at last I jumped up boldly and said :
' What does it matter if I kiss thee even now, beautiful form!'

" I stole softly from the house, lest my mother should hear,
which was all the easier because the entrance, though it bore a great
coat-of-arms, had no door, and hastily wound my way through the
shrubbery of the wasted garden. There was not a sound — all rested
silently and solemnly in the calm moonshine. The shadows of the
trees seemed to be nailed to the ground. There in the green grass lay
the beautiful goddess, as immovable as all around ; but her lovely
limbs seemed to be fettered, not by petrifying death, but by quiet
slumber, and as I drew near I almost feared lest she might be
wakened by the lightest sound. I held my breath as I bent over to
behold her beautiful face ; a shuddering, troubled fear seemed to
repel me from, and a youthful lustyhood to attract me to her ;
my heart beat as if I were about to commit a murder, and at last I
kissed the beautiful goddess with a passion, a tenderness, and a
desperation such as I never felt in my life from any kiss. Nor can I
ever forget the grimly sweet emotion which ran through all my
soul as the comforting, blessing coldness of those marble lips
touched mine. . . . And so, Maria, as I just now stood before you
and I saw you lying in your white muslin dress on the green sofa,

your appearance reminded me of the white marble image in the green grass. Had you slept longer my lips could not have resisted "
——

" Max! Max!" cried the woman from the depths of her soul. " Terrible! You know that a kiss from your mouth "——
" Ah—only be silent ; I know that would be something terrible to you! Do not look at me so imploringly! I do not doubt your feelings, although their deepest ground lies hidden from me. I have never dared to press my lips to yours "——

But Maria did not allow him to conclude. She had grasped his hand, covered it with earnest kisses, and said, smiling : " Pardon! pardon! But go on and tell me more of your amour. How long did you love the marble beauty whom you kissed in the garden of your mother's chateau?"

" We left the next day," replied Maximilian, " and I never saw its beautiful form again. But a strange passion for marble statues ever afterwards inspired me, and I felt even today its irresistible power. I came from the Lorenzo, the library of the Medici, and found myself, I know not how, in the chapel where that most magnificent of the races of Italy has built itself a resting-place of gems, and lies in peace. A full hour I remained absorbed in gazing at the marble image of a woman whose powerful frame attests the bold skill of Michael Angelo, while the whole form is inspired with an ethereal sweetness such as we are not accustomed to expect in that master. All the realm of dreams, with all its silent blisses, is enchanted into this marble ; a tender repose dwells in the beautiful limbs, a soothing moonlight courses through its veins : it is the *Night* of Michael Angelo Buonarotti. Oh! how gladly would I sleep in the arms of this Night!

" The painted forms of women," continued Maximilian, after a pause, " have never interested me so deeply as statues. I was only once in love with a picture. It was a wonderfully beautiful Madonna in a church in Cologne. I was at that time a zealous church-goer, and all my soul was sunk in the mysticism of Catholicism. I would then, like the Spanish cavalier, have gladly fought every day for the Immaculate Conception of Mary, the Queen of the Angels, the fairest lady of heaven and of earth. I interested myself in the whole Holy Family, and took off my hat with special friendliness before any image of Saint Joseph. But this state did not last long, and I left the Virgin almost without ceremony as soon as I became acquainted in a gallery of antiquities with a Greek nymph who kept me long a captive in her marble fetters."

" And you always loved only chiseled or painted women?" tittered Maria.

" No! I have loved dead women too," replied Maximilian, as a very grave expression came over his features. He did not observe that as he said this Maria seemed to shrink as if terrified, and he continued in a calm voice—

" Yes, it is very strange how I once fell in love with a girl after she had been dead for seven years. When I first became acquainted with little Very, I was extremely pleased with her. For three days I was deeply interested in her, and took the greatest pleasure in all that she did and said, and in every expression of her piquant, exquisite self, without being in the least sentimentally inclined. Nor was I indeed moved to any extravagant grief when I learned, some months later, that she had suddenly died in consequence of a nervous fever. I forgot her entirely, and I am sure that for years I never thought once about her.

" Seven years had passed away, and I found myself in Potsdam, determined to enjoy the whole beautiful summer in undisturbed solitude. I did not associate with any one ; my only company was the statues which are in the garden of Sans Souci.

" It happened one day that certain features, and a strangely winsome voice and gesture, suddenly recurred to me, without my being able to identify the person whom they characterized. Nothing is more annoying than such stumbling about among old memories, and I was therefore surprised as with joy when I, after a few days, all at once recalled little Very, and found that it was *her* charming and forgotten form which had so strangely moved me. Indeed I rejoiced over this discovery like one who has quite unexpectedly found again his most intimate friend. The faded lines gradually took color, and at last the sweet little one seemed to be again before me

—smiling, pouting, witty, and more beautiful than ever. From this time the darling image would not leave me, it filled all my soul ; wherever I went or stayed, stayed or went, it was by my side— spoke with me, laughed with me, always pleasantly and gently, yet without any special tenderness. But I was every day more and more enchanted by this form, which ever became more and more *real* to me. It is easy to call spirits, but hard to send them again to their dark Nothing—they look at us then so pitifully and imploringly that our hearts cannot resist such earnest prayers. And as I could not tear myself away, the end was that I fell in love with little Very, after she had been dead for seven years.

" So I lived for six months in Potsdam, completely absorbed in this love. I avoided more carefully than ever any touch with the outer world, so that even if any one in the street came too near me I felt a most uncomfortable sensation. I had, as regards any rencounter with people, such a repulsion as night-wandering spirits feel, for it is said that when they meet a living human being they are as much terrified as the one who sees them. By chance there came through Potsdam a traveler whom I could not avoid—my brother. At seeing him, and hearing from him the last news of the day, I awoke as from a deep dream, and, as if shrinking with alarm, I suddenly felt in what a horrible solitude I had so long been living. I had during this time not even remarked the course of the seasons, and I regarded with amazement the trees, which, having long lost their leaves, were now covered with autumnal hoar-frost. I soon left Potsdam and little Very, and in another city, where important business awaited me, I was, by means of sharp pressure and urgent circumstance, soon driven into harsh reality.

" Ah, heaven !" continued Maximilian, while a painful smile moved his upper lip, " how the living women with whom I then came into unavoidable contact tormented me—delicately tormented me—with their pouting, jealousing, and gasping ! In how many balls was I obliged to trot around with them, in how much gossiping scandal must I be mingled ? What restless variety, what joy in lying, what kissing-treachery and poisoned flowers ! Those ladies knew how to utterly spoil for me all joy and happiness and love, so that for a time I became a woman-hater, who damned the whole sex. It was with me something as it was with the French officer who, during the Russian campaign, was rescued with trouble from the icy trenches of the Beresina, but who from that time had such an antipathy for everything frozen that he repelled with horror even the sweetest and most delicious ices at Tortoni's. Yes, the memory of the Beresina of love which I then passed made for a time detestable the daintiest dames — women like angels, girls like vanilla-sherbet "——

" I beg you," cried Maria, " do not abuse women ! That is the way of speaking among men — mere chaff and cant. After all, to be happy you must have women."

" Oh ! " sighed Maximilian, " that is true, of course. But women have but one way to make men happy, and thirty thousand to torment them."

" Dear friend," replied Maria, while she suppressed a smile, " I speak of the harmony of two souls in tune. Have you never felt this happiness ? But I see a strange blush on your cheeks — speak Max ! "

" It is true, Maria ; I feel like a boy at confessing to you the fortunate love which once made me infinitely happy. Its memory is not lost to me, and my soul often retreats to its cool shade when the burning dust and noonday heat of life become intolerable. But I am not in condition to give you a clear idea of this loved one. She was of such ethereal nature that she could only appear to me in dreams. I think, Maria, that you have no commonplace prejudice against dreams, for these nightly phenomena have as much reality as those rougher images of the day which we can handle, and with which we are often defiled. Yes, it was in dreams that I saw that dear and lovely being, who, above all others, helped to make life happy. I can tell you little as to her appearance. I really cannot accurately describe her features. Her face was unlike anything which I ever saw before or since. So far as I can remember it was not white and rosy, but all of one tone — a softly crimsoned pale brunette, and transparent as crystal. The charm of this face consisted neither in absolutely perfect symmetry nor in interesting liveliness ; its character lay far more in an enchanting yet terrible truthfulness. It was a face full of conscious love and graceful goodness ; it was more a soul than a face, and therefore I have never been quite able to visualize it. The eyes were soft as flowers ; the lips somewhat pale, but winsomely curved. She wore a silk dressing-gown of cornflower blue — this was all her dress. The neck and feet were bare, and the delicate tenderness of the limbs often peeped as if stealthily through the slight, soft garment. Nor can I clearly set forth the words which we spoke ; I can only remember that we bound ourselves to one another, and that we caressed and comforted one another, joyfully and happily, frankly and confidingly, like bridegroom and bride, or almost like brother and sister. And we often did not talk at all, but gazed into each other's eyes, and in this blissful beholding we remained for eternities. How I *awoke* I know not, but I long reveled in the after-feelings of this happy love. I was long intoxicated with unheard-of-delight ; the yearning depth of my heart was full of happiness ; a joy before unknown seemed to spread over all my feelings, and I remained glad and gay, though I never again saw the loved one of my dreams. But had I not enjoyed whole eternities in her glance? And she indeed knew me too well not to know also that I love no repetitions."

"Truly," cried Maria, " you are *un homme à bonne fortune.* But tell me, was Mademoiselle Laurence a marble statue or a picture, a dear girl, or a dream?"

" Perhaps all together," replied Maximilian, very seriously.

" I can well believe, dear friend, that this love was of a rather doubtful substance. And when will you tell me this story?"

" Tomorrow. It is long, and I am tired today. I have been at the opera, and have too much music in my ears."

" You go a great deal to the opera, Max, and I believe that it is more to see than to hear."

" You are quite right, Maria ; I really go to the opera to see the faces of the beautiful Italian women. True, they are pretty enough even outside the theatre, and an investigator into history could, from the ideality of their features, easily trace the influence of the formative arts on the forms of the Italian people. Here Nature has taken back from the artists the capital which she once lent; and lo !

it has, in the most enrapturing manner, paid compound interest.
The sense of the Beautiful has penetrated all the people ; and as
the flesh once acted on the spirit, so the spirit now works upon the
flesh. And the devotions before those beautiful Madonnas, those
lovely altar-pieces, which as Madonnas sink into the soul of the
bridegroom while the bride is sensuously impressed by a handsome
saint, are not in vain. From such elective affinities a race of human
beings has sprung which is even more beautiful than the charming
soil on which it springs, or the sunny heaven which flashes round
it like a golden frame. The men do not interest me much unless
they are painted or sculptured, and I leave to you, Maria, all
possible enthusiasm for those handsome, supple Italians who have
such wild black beards and noble aquiline noses, and such soft,
crafty eyes. They say the Lombards are the finest men. I have never
investigated them very closely ; I have only earnestly studied the
Lombard women, and these I declare are really as beautiful as they
are famed to be. But they must even in the Middle Ages have been
fairly fair. It is said that the beauty of the ladies of Milan was the
reason of the secret impulse which sent Francis the First on his
Italian campaign. The knightly king was doubtless desirous of
knowing whether his spiritual little cousins, the kinsfolk of his god-
mothers, were as beautiful as he had heard boasted. Poor rogue ! he
paid dearly at Pavia for his curiosity.

" But the full beauty of these Italian women is first seen when
their faces are lighted up by music. I say *lighted up*, because the
effect of music, as I have seen it in the opera, on the faces of
beautiful women, is quite like those effects of light and shadow
which astonish us when we see statues in the night by torchlight.
Such marble images then reveal in the terrifying truth their in-
dwelling spirit and awful silent secrets. In like manner the whole
life of the beautiful Italians shows itself to us when we see them in
the opera ; the varying melodies then waken in their souls an array
of feelings, memories, wishes, and woes, which at once speak out
in the movements of their features, in their blushing, their paleness,
and even in their eyes. He who can read may then read in their
beautiful faces many sweet and interesting things, stories as strange

as the novels of Boccaccio, feelings as tender as the sonnets of Petrarch, whims as odd as the *Ottaverime* of Ariosto—often enough, too, frightful treachery and sublime evil as poetic as the Hell of Dante. Yes, it is worth while to look up at the boxes. If the men would only not meanwhile express their inspiration with such frightful noise. This insane applause in an Italian theatre becomes annoying. But music is the soul of these people, their life, their national cause. In other countries there are certainly musicians who equal the greatest Italian celebrities, but there is no musical multitude like this. Music is represented here in Italy, not by individuals, but reveals itself in the whole population ; it has become *the people* itself. Among us in the North it is quite otherwise ; there music has become individual, and is called Mozart or Meyerbeer. And, more than that, when we closely examine the best which such Northern musicians offer us, we find in it Italian sunshine and orange perfume which belong much more to beautiful Italy, the home of music, than to our Germany. Yes, Italy will ever be the home of music, even if its great Maestri sink into the grave or grow silent, even though Bellini die and Rossini is mute."

" True," said Maria, " Rossini has long been still ; if I am not mistaken, for ten years."

" That is perhaps a jest of his," replied Maximilian. " He wishes to show that the name of the ' Swan of Pesaro,' which has been given him, is utterly inappropriate. Swans sing at the end of their lives, but Rossini has become silent in the middle of his. And I think that there he did well, and proved himself to be a genius. An artist who has only talent feels to the end of his life the impulse to work it out ; he is goaded by ambition ; he feels that he is always short of perfection, and he is impelled to attain to the highest. But genius has already given us his highest possible work ; he is content ; he scorns the world and petty ambition, and goes home as Shakespeare did, or promenades, smiling and jesting, on the Boulevard des Italiens in Paris, like Joachim Rossini. If the genius enjoys fair physical health he may live in this fashion a long time after he has completed his masterpieces, or, as people say, has fulfilled his mission. It is a mere prejudice or fancy for men to imagine that

genius must die young. I think that from thirty to forty years is
believed to be the fatal limit of such lives. How often I have teased
poor Bellini with this, and prophesied that he in his quality as
genius must die as soon as he should attain the dangerous age.
Strange, in spite of my jesting tone, he tormented himself over this
prophecy ; he called me his *jettatore,*[1] and always made the sign of
the *jettatura*. He wished so much to live ; he had such a passionate
antipathy to death that he would not hear it mentioned. He was
afraid of it as a child who fears to sleep in the dark. He was a good,
dear child himself, sometimes rather naughty ; but one only need
threaten him with his early death, and he became at once whimpering and praying, and made the *jettatura* with his two uplifted
fingers. . . . Poor Bellini ! "

" Then you knew him personally ? Was he handsome ? "

" He was not plain. You see that we men also cannot answer
affirmatively when such a question is put to us regarding one of our
own sex. He was of tall, slender form, as one who had suddenly
shot up, who moved and gestured daintily, I might say coquettishly,
always *à quatre épingles ;*[2] regular features, rather long and pale ;
light blonde, almost golden hair, *friséd* in little locks ; a very high
and noble forehead, a straight nose, very light blue eyes, a beautifully proportioned mouth, and round chin. His traits had in them
something vague, devoid of character or milk-like, and in this milk
face there often curled sweet-sourly an expression of pain. This
anguished look supplied in Bellini's face the want of wit and spirit,
but it was a pain without depth ; it shone dimly and without poetry
in his eyes, and quivered without passion on his lips. This flat,
insipid suffering seemed to be affected by the young maestro after
a bygone fashion. His hair was curled in such a dreamy-visionary,
melancholy manner, his clothes fitted his dainty form so yearningly
and sentimentally, he carried his little bamboo cane so idyllically,
that he always reminded me of those young, old-fashioned lovers

---

[1] *Jettatore.* One who has the evil eye, and casts (*jetta*) its influence on
others.

[2] *Tiré à quatre épingles.* Said of one who has taken extreme pains to be
well or showily dressed.

whom we see in rococo-shepherd plays acting affectedly with rib-
boned crooks and light-colored jackets and beautiful little breeches!
And his gait was so maidenly, so elegant, so ethereal! The whole
man looked like a sighing swain *en escarpins.* The ladies doted on
him, but I doubt whether he ever inspired a great passion. To me
his personal appearance always had in it something drolly unpleasant, the real reason for which was perhaps his manner of
speaking French. For though he had lived several years in France,
he spoke its language so badly that its like was not to be heard even
in England. I will not say that he spoke it *badly.* for the word *bad*
would here be entirely too good. One must say outrageously,
incestuously, world-destroyingly — as a cataclysm. Yes, when one
was in society with him, and he like a public executioner broke the
poor French words on the wheel, and without sign or trembling
dealt out a tremendous *coq à l'âne,* one felt as if the very world
must split as with a thunder-crack. A deathly stillness then spread
over the entire hall, for death himself seemed to be painting terror
on every face with chalk and cinnabar ; ladies knew not whether
they should faint or fly ; men looked in sudden amazement at
their breeches to realise that they really wore such things ; and,
what was worst of all, this horror awoke at the same time a convulsive, maddening desire to laugh which could hardly be repressed.
Therefore if any one sat by Bellini in society, his neighborhood
inspired a certain anxious apprehension which was sure to excite
a horrible interest at once attractive and repulsive. Very often his
unconscious puns were simply amusing, and in their monkey-like
unmeaningness reminded one of the castle of his fellow-countryman, the Prince of Pallagonia, which is described by Goethe in his
Italian journey as a museum of baroque eccentricities and rubbishy
monstrosities, huddled together without rhyme or reason. As Bellini
always believed on such occasions that he had said something quite
harmless and serious, his face formed the drollest contrast with his
words. Then it was that that which was unpleasing in his expression came out most cuttingly. Yet what I did not like in it was not,
however, of such a kind that it could be described as a defect,
and it certainly was not unpleasing to ladies. Bellini's face, like

his whole physique, had that physical freshness, that blooming sensuousness, that rose-color which makes on *me* a disagreeable impression—on me, I say, because I like much better that which is death-like and of marble. It was not till a later time, when I began to know Bellini, that I felt a liking for him. This came from observing that his character was perfectly noble and good. His soul is certainly pure, and has remained unspotted by contact with vile things. Nor was there wanting in him that harmless good-nature, or the childlike, such as is never wanting in *genial* men, even if they do not show it to every one.

" Yes, I remember," continued Maximilian, as he sank on the seat by which he had so far stood upright, leaning on the arm. " I remember a single instant during which Bellini appeared to me in such a charming light that I regarded him with pleasure, and determined to learn to know him more intimately. But it was unfortunately the last time I was destined to see him in this life. This was one evening after supper in the house of a great lady, who had the smallest foot in Paris, and when he had become merry, and the sweetest melodies rang from the pianoforte. I can see him now, the good Bellini, when, exhausted by the many mad Bellinisms which he had chattered, he sat on a seat—it was very low, almost like a footstool, so that he found himself at the feet of a fair lady who had reclined opposite him on a sofa, and with sweet mischievousness looked down on him, while he toiled away to entertain her with a few French phrases, getting ever deeper into difficulties, commenting in his Sicilian jargon in order to prove that what he said was not foolish, but, on the contrary, the most refined flattery. I do not think that the beautiful lady paid much attention to Bellini's phrases. She had taken his little cane, wherewith he often helped himself out of weak places in rhetoric, and calmly used it to dis-arrange the elaborate arrangement of the hair on both temples of the young maestro. This caprice well became the smile which gave her features an expression such as I have never seen on a living human face. It was one of those which belong far more to the dream-realm of poetry than to the rough reality of life—contours recalling Da Vinci, that noble soul!—with the naive dimples in the chin, and the sentimental pointed-out bending chin of the Lombard school. The color was rather of a Roman softness, a mother-of-pearl gleam, aristocratic paleness — morbidezza. In short, it was such a face as can only be found in old Italian portraits, in which the masters of the sixteenth century depicted as a master-work the portraits of great ladies whom they loved — such as poets sang when they sang for immortality, and such as German and French heroes yearned for when they girded on their swords, and seeking great deeds rushed over the Alps. Yes, yes, it was such a face, in which there played a smile of sweetest mischief and of aristocratic waywardness, while she, the fair lady, disarranged the blonde locks of good Bellini with the bamboo cane. At that instant Bellini seemed to be transfigured to some utterly strange apparition, and all at once he became allied to my heart. His face shone in the reflected light of that smile ; it was perhaps the goldenest moment of his life. I shall never forget him. Fourteen days after I read in the newspapers that Italy had lost one of her most famous sons.

" Strangely enough the death of Paganini was announced at the same time. I did not doubt this in the least, because the old faded Paganini always looked like a dying man, but the death of the young and rosy Bellini seemed incredible. And yet the announcement of the death of the first was simply an error of the press. Paganini is alive and well at Genoa, and Bellini lies in his grave in Paris."

" Do you like Paganini ?" asked Maria.

" This man," exclaimed Maximilian, " is a glory to his country, and certainly deserves the most distinguished mention if one will speak of the musical notabilities of Italy."

" I have never seen him," said Maria, " but according to report his exterior does not perfectly set forth the beautiful—— I have seen portraits of him "——

" None of which were like him," said Maximilian. " They all make him too ugly, or else flatter him, and do not give his true character. I think that only one man ever succeeded in putting the true physiognomy of Paganini on paper. He who did it is a deaf painter named Leyser, who, in his inspired frolicking, hit off with a few pencil strokes the head of Paganini so well that one laughs and is frightened at the truth of the portrait. ' The devil guided my hand,' said the artist to me. mysteriously laughing low, and nodding his head with good-natured irony as he was wont to do in his till eulen spiegel aspects ? ? ? This painter was always a queer owl. In spite of his deafness he loved music enthusiastically, and he really understood it when he was near enough to the orchestra to read the music in the faces of the musicians, and judge of the more or less successful execution by the fingering ; and, in fact, he wrote criticisms of the operas for a distinguished journal in Hamburg. What is there wonderful in that? The deaf painter could, in the visible signature of the playing, *see the tones*. Are there not men to whom tones themselves are only invisible signatures in which they hear colors and forms?"

" Such a man are *you !*" cried Maria.

" I am sorry that I no longer possess the little drawing by Leyser ; it would perhaps give you an idea of Paganini's appearance. It was only in harsh, black, fleeting strokes that one could set forth those unearthly traits which seemed to belong rather to the sulphurous realm of shadows than to the sunny world of life. ' Truly the devil guided my hand,' asserted the deaf painter, as we stood by Alster pavilion in Hamburg on the day when Paganini gave his first concert there. ' Yes, my friend, it is true, what the whole world declares, that he has given himself over to the devil, body and soul, in order to become the best violinist in the world, and fiddle millions of money, and finally to get away from the damned galleys where he had suffered many years. For, you see, friend, when he was leader of the orchestra in Lucca, he fell in love with a theatrical princess, became jealous of a little abbé, was perhaps made *cocu*, stabbed his untrue Amata in good Italian fashion, went for that to the galleys in Genoa, and at last sold himself to the devil to be delivered and to become the greatest violin-player, and be able to get out of us a tribute — of two thalers. . . . But, look! " Speak of the Devil!" there he comes in the Avenue with his ambiguous *famulus !* '

" In fact it was Paganini himself whom I beheld. He wore a

116

dark-grey overcoat, which came to his feet, making him appear extremely tall. His long black hair fell in tangled locks on his shoulders, forming a dark frame for the pale, corpse-like countenance, in which care, genius, and hell combined had graved their ineffaceable signs. By him capered along a short, comfortable-looking figure, commonplace, showy in dress, with a rosy wrinkled face, light-grey short coat with steel buttons, greeting right and left with irresistible amiability, but all the time squinting sideways with anxious apprehension at the dark form which, serious and reflecting, walked by his side. It recalled the picture by Retzsch, in which Faust is walking with Wagner before the gate of Leipzig. The deaf artist commented on both figures in his wild fashion, and bade me observe carefully the measured long step of Paganini. ' Is it not,' he said, ' as if he still had the iron cross rod between his legs? He has got the convict step and can never lose it. See how contemptuously and ironically he often looks down at his companion when he bores him with *his* commonplace questions ; — and yet he cannot get rid of him — a bloody contract binds him to that servant, who is Satan himself. Ignorant people think, of course, that this companion is the writer of comedies and anecdotes, Harrys of Hanover, whom Paganini takes with him as business-manager for his concerts ; but the multitude does not know that the devil took the form of Mr. George Harrys, the soul he keeps locked up with other rubbish in a chest in Hanover, where it will remain till the devil restores its proper fleshly envelope, when he will probably accompany his master, Paganini, through the world in the more befitting form of a black poodle.'

" But if Paganini seemed to me sufficiently incredible and wonderful as I saw him walking under the green leaves of the Hamburg Jungfernsteig, what were my impressions of his fearfully eccentric apparition that evening in the concert! This was given in the Comedy Theatre of Hamburg, and the art-loving public had assembled so early and in such numbers that it was with difficulty that I conquered a place by the orchestra. Though it was post-day I saw in the balcony-boxes the whole refined and cultured business world — a whole Olympus of bankers and similar millionaires, the gods of coffee and sugar, with their plump wife-goddesses, Junos of the Wandrahm and Aphrodites of Dreckwall.[3] There was a holy quiet in all the hall. Every eye was turned to the stage, every ear prepared to hear. My neighbor, an old huckster in furs, took the cotton from his ears, the better to take in the expensive tones, which cost two dollars entrance-money. At last there appeared on the stage a dark figure, which seemed to have risen from the under-world. It was Paganini, in his black dress suit ; the black evening coat and black waistcoat, of an appalling cut, were probably such as are pre-scribed by infernal etiquette at the court of Proserpine, while the loose trousers flapped vexatiously on the thin legs of the maestro. His long arms seemed to grow yet longer, as he held the violin in one hand, the bow down in the other, and almost bowed to the ground as he bestowed on the public his unheardof reverence. In the angular bending of his body there was a fearful woodenness, and at the same time something foolishly brute-like, which would have caused laughter at his salutation ; but his *fáce*, which, in the strong orchestral illumination, seemed more corpse-like than ever, had in it something so bashfully modest that a shuddering pity sup-pressed our desire to laugh. Had he learned those bows from an automaton or a dog? Was that imploring look that of one in deathly illness, or was there lurking behind it the mockery of a crafty money-grubber? Was that a living man, who knows that he is about to perish and who will delight the public in the arena of art, like a dying gladiator with his convulsions or a dead man risen from the grave, a vampire with a violin, who, if he does not suck blood from our hearts, will, come what may, draw the money from our pockets?

" Such questions crossed one another flitting in our heads while Paganini made his unceasing compliments in gesture, but all such thoughts flitted afar when the wondrous master set his violin to his chin and began to play. As for me, you know well my musical second sight — my gift of seeing with every note which I hear its corresponding figure of sound ; and so it came that Paganini, with

---

[3] Red light districts of Hamburg.

every stroke of his bow, brought visible forms and facts before my eyes ; that he told me in a musical picture-writing all kinds of startling stories ; that he juggled before me at the same time a show of colored Chinese shadows, in all of which he with his violin was chief actor. Even with the first note from his bow the scene changed ; he stood all at once with his music-desk in a cheerful hall, which was gaily and irrgularly decorated with curved and twining furniture in the Pompadour style, everywhere little mirrors, gilt cupids, Chinese porcelain, an exquisitely charming chaos of ribbons, flower garlands, white gloves, torn laces, false pearls, diadems of gilt sheet metal, and similar celestial theatrical properties, such as one sees in the sanctum of a prima donna. Paganini's external appearance had also changed, very much indeed to his advantage ; he wore knee-breeches of lilac satin, a silver embroidered white waistcoat, a coat of light-blue satin with buttons wound with gold ; and little locks of carefully curled hair played round his face, which bloomed with the roses of youth and gleamed with sweetest tenderness, when he eyed the pretty little dames who stood round his music-desk while he played his violin.

" Indeed I saw by his side a pretty young creature, in old-fashioned dress of white satin puffed out on the hips, the waist seeming for that all the more piquantly narrow, the powdered hair friséed aloft, the pretty round face flashing out all the more freely with its dazzling eyes, its rouged cheeks, court plaster beauty-patches, and impertinent sweet little nose. She held in her hand a white scroll of paper, and by the movements of her lips, and the coquettish movements of her form, seemed to be singing, but I could not hear one of her trills, and it was only by the playing of the violin with which the youthful Paganini accompanied the charming child that I could imagine what she sang, and what he himself felt in his soul while she sang. Ah! those were melodies such as the nightingale flutes in the twilight, when the perfume of the rose intoxicates her sympathetic heart, inspired by Spring with deepest longing. Ah! that was a melting, voluptuous, deep-desiring happiness! There were tones which kissed, and then, pouting, turned away, and again laughing, embraced and melted together, and then lost, enraptured, intoxicated, died away in one. Yes, the tones mingled in gay sport, like butterflies when one in jest flies from another, hides itself behind a flower, is found and hunted out, and finally, light-hearted and trifling, flutters up with the other —up into the golden sunlight. But a spider—a vile spider—can bring about a dire tragedy for such enamored butterflies. Did the young heart divine aught like *that*? A long melancholy sighing tone, like the premonition of a coming evil, slid slowly through the most enrapturing melodies which flashed from Paganini's playing ; his eyes became moist ; worshipping he knelt before his Amata —but oh! as he bowed to kiss her feet he saw beneath the bed—a little abbé! I do not know what he had against the poor man, but the Genoese became pale as death ; he grappled in rage the little fellow, gave him boxes on the ear and not a few kicks, hurled him headlong out of doors, and then, drawing a stiletto from his pocket, plunged it into the breast of the young beauty.

" At that instant cries of ' Bravo! Bravo!' rang from every side. Hamburg's inspired men and women paid their tribute of the most roaring applause to the great artist, who had ended the first part of his concert, and who with more angles and contortions than before bowed before them. It seemed to me that in his face was a more imploring humility than ever, but in his eyes flickered a tormenting fear like a wretched sinner's.

" ' Divine!' cried my neighbor, the fur-dealer ; ' that piece alone was well worth two thalers.'

" When Paganini began to play again it seemed to be dark before my eyes. The tones did not change as before into bright shapes and hues ; the form of the Master wrapped itself in gloomy shadows, from whose depth his music came wailing in the most cutting accents of sorrow. Only from time to time, as a little lamp which hung over him cast a feeble light on his features, could I see his pallid countenance, which still retained traces of youth. His garb was strange indeed—divided in two parts, one red, one yellow. Heavy fetters hung to his feet. Behind him grimaced a face whose physiognomy indicated a jovial, he-goat nature ; and I saw long, hairy hands which seemed to belong to it, moving now and then on the strings of the violin which Paganini played, often guiding his hand, while a floating, applauding laugh accompanied the tones which welled forth more painfully, and as if bleeding, from the violin. They were tones like the song of the fallen angels who had wooed and wantoned with the daughters of Earth, and been banished from the kingdom of the blest, and fallen, with cheeks burning with shame, into the under-world : tones in whose bottomless abyss there was neither comfort nor hope. Should the holy in heaven hear such music the praise of God would be mute on their pale lips, and they, weeping, would hide their pious heads. Ever and anon, when in the melodious torments of this piece the *obligato* goat-laughter came bleating in, I saw in the background a multitude of little female figures, who, in malicious glee, nodded their horrible heads and rubbed their breasts in mocking mischief. Then there came in hurried crowds from the violin sounds of pain, and a terrible sighing and gasping, such as no one ever heard on earth before, and perhaps will never hear again, unless it shall be in the Vale of Jehoshaphat, when the tremendous trumpets of the Last Judgment ring out, and the naked corpses creep from their graves to await their doom. But the tormented violinist suddenly drew his bow so madly and desperately that his rattling fetters burst, and the diabolical ally with the mocking demons disappeared.

" At that instant my neighbor, the fur-dealer, said, ' Pity! pity! he has burst a string. That comes of his constant *pizzicato* ! '

" Had a string really burst on the violin ? I do not know. I only observed the transfiguration of the tones, and then it seemed to me as if Paganini and all his surroundings were again suddenly changed. I could hardly recognize him in the brown monk's dress, which rather disguised than clothed him. His wild and wasted face half-hidden by the hood, a rope round his waist, Paganini stood on a cliff overhanging the sea, and played his violin. It seemed to me to be twilight tide ; evening-flame flowed over the broad sea, which grew redder and redder, and rustled and roared more gaily and wildly in mysterious and perfect harmony with the violin. But the redder the sea became so much the more pallid grew the heaven, and when at last the waving water looked like bright scarlet blood, then the sky overhead became ghostly clear, all corpse-white, and out came the stars — and these stars were black, black as shining anthracite. But the tones of the violin grew more stormy and bolder, and in the eyes of the terrible player there sparkled such a mocking delight in destroying, and his thin lips moved with such appalling rapidity, that it was clear he was murmuring ancient forbidden witch-spells with which storms are called up and those evil spirits evoked who lie imprisoned in the sea's abyss. Many a time did he, when stretching forth his long, lean, bare arm, and sweeping the bow in the air, seem to be in sooth and truth a wizard who, with a magic staff, commanded the elements, for then there was a mad, delirious howling in the depths of the sea, and the furious waves of blood leaped up so furiously on high that they almost besprinkled the pale heaven and its black stars with their red foam.

" There was howling, crashing, cracking, as if the whole world was breaking to fragments, while the monk played more madly on his violin, as if he would, by the power of his raging will, burst the seven seals wherewith Solomon closed the iron jar in which he imprisoned the demons whom he had subdued. That jar the wise king cast into the sea, and it seemed as if I heard the voices of the demons when Paganini's violin growled out its angriest basso notes. But after a while I thought I heard the joyous cry of those set free, and I saw rising one by one out of the red waves of blood the heads of the unchained demons, monsters of incredible hideousness, crocodiles with bat's wings, serpents with stag's horns, monkeys capped with conch shells, seals with patriarchal long beards, women's faces with breasts instead of cheeks, green camels' heads, wild hybrids of inconceivable composition, all glaring greedily with cold crafty eyes, and grasping, with long webbed feet and fingers, at the fiddling monk. Then in the raging zeal of invocation his hood fell.back, and the ringlets flying in the wind curled round his head like black serpents.

" It was all so maddening, that not to utterly lose my mind I stopped my ears and closed my eyes. Then the enchantment disappeared, and when I looked again I saw the poor Genoese in his wonted form making his usual bows, while the public applauded rapturously.

" ' That is the celebrated performance on the G string,' remarked my neighbor. ' I play the violin myself, and know what it is to have such mastery over the instrument!'

"Fortunately the interval was not long, else my musical fur-dealer had certainly involved me in a tiresome talk on art. Paganini set his violin leisurely to his chin, and with the first touch of his bow, there began again the wondrous transfiguration of tones. But now they were neither so startling in color or so marked in form. They came forth calmly, majestically, waving and rising like those of an organ choral in a cathedral ; and all the surroundings seemed to have expanded to a colossal space, such as no bodily vision but only the eye of the spirit can grasp. In the midst of this space swept a burning ball, on which stood a man of giant stature and grand in pride, who played the violin. Was this sphere of light the sun ? I know not. But in the features of the man I recognised Paganini, ideally beautified, celestially refined, atoned for divinely, and smiling. This body was fresh and fair in vigorous manliness ; a light-blue garment was about his now far nobler limbs, the black hair flowed in shining locks on his shoulders, and as he stood there, firm and confidently, like the sublime statue of a god, and played the violin, it seemed as if all creation obeyed his tones. He was the man-planet round whom the universe moved, ringing with measured joy and in happy rhythm. Were those great lights which swept so calmly gleaming round him stars of heaven? Were those sweet-sounding harmonies which were caused by their motion, the music of the spheres, of which poets and seers have told so much that is bewildering and strange? Sometimes when with an effort I looked forth and far into the dim distance, I seemed to see white waving garments, in which colossal pilgrims wandered in disguise, with staves in their hands ; and, strange! the gold heads of their staves were those same great lights which I had taken for stars. These pilgrims went in a vast procession around the great player ; the heads of their staves flashed reflected light from the tones of his violin ; and the chorals which rang from their lips, and which I had taken for the noise of the spheres, were really only the rebounding echoes of his violin. An ineffable, nameless passion dwelt in these sounds, which often quivered almost inaudibly, like mysterious whispering on water, then again swelled up sweetly-terrible, like the tones of hunters' horns by moonlight, and then burst out into unbridled rejoicing, as though a thousand bards were sweeping the strings and raising their voices in a song of victory. That was the music which no ear has heard, only the heart can dream it when by night it rests against the heart of the beloved. But it may be that the heart comprehends it even in the clear, bright daylight, when it rejoicing loses itself in the lines of beauty and ovals of a Greek work of art."

" Or when a man had had a bottle too much of champagne," cried a laughing voice, which woke our narrator as if from a dream. As he turned he saw the doctor, who, with black Deborah, had softly entered the room to learn what effect his medicine had had on the invalid.

" I do not like this sleep," said the doctor, as he pointed to the sofa.

Maximilian, who, sunk in the fantasies of his own speech, had not observed that Maria had long been asleep, bit his lips as if vexed.

" This sleep," continued the doctor, " gives the face an appearance which has all the character of death. Does it not look like one of those white masks, or plaster casts, in which we try to preserve the traits of the departed?"

" And I would like," whispered Maximilian, " to have such a cast of our friend. She will be very beautiful, even in death."

" I advise you not to have it," replied the doctor. " Such masks lead astray our memories of the loved ones. We feel as if there was in them something of their lives still kept, while that which is really retained is actually death itself. Features which are regular and beautiful then become hard and frozen, satirical, or repulsive, by which they terrify us more than they please. But casts become complete caricatures when they are from faces whose charm was of a spiritual, refined nature, and whose features were less regular than interesting, for as soon as the graces of life are extinguished in them the actual departures from the ideal lines of beauty are no longer balanced by mental charms. One thing also is common to all these casts — it is a certain enigmatic expression which, the more we study them, the more it runs shivering like frost through the soul: they all look like people who intend to take a long journey."

"And whither?" asked Maximilian, as the doctor took his arm and led him forth.

Second Night

"AND WHY WILL YOU TORMENT ME WITH THIS HORRIBLE MEDICINE, since I must die so soon?"

Maria had just said this, as Maximilian had entered the room. The physician stood before her holding in one hand a vial of medicine, in the other a little cup, in which foamed a very unpleasant-looking brownish liquid.

"My dearest friend," he said to Maximilian, "your presence is very much needed just now. I beg you try to induce Signora to swallow these few drops. I am in a great hurry."

"I beg you, Maria!" said Maximilian, in the soft voice which was not often heard from him, and which seemed to come from a pained heart, so that the patient, deeply moved, almost forgetting her own suffering, took the cup. But ere she put it to her mouth she said, smiling: "To reward me you will tell the story of Laurence?"

"All that you desire shall be done," assented Maximilian.

The pale lady drank the contents of the cup, half smiling, half shuddering.

"I am in a hurry," said the doctor, as he drew on his black gloves. "Lie down calmly, Signora and move as little as possible. I am in a hurry."

He left the room accompanied by black Deborah, who lighted

125

him forth. When the two friends were alone they looked at one another for a long time in silence. There were thoughts in the souls of both which neither would express. Then the woman suddenly grasped the man's hand and covered it with burning kisses.

"For God's sake!" said Maximilian, "do not exert yourself so much, and lie calmly on the sofa."

As Maria obeyed him, he very carefully covered her feet with the shawl, which he first kissed. She must have seen this, for her eyes twinkled like those of a happy child.

"Was Mademoiselle Laurence very beautiful?"

"If you will not interrupt me, dear friend, and promise to be calm and quiet, I will tell you circumstantially all that you wish to hear."

Smiling at the assenting glance of Maria, Maximilian sat on the chair before the sofa, and thus began his story:—

"It is now eight years since I went to London to learn the language and people there. The devil take the people with their language! They take a dozen monosyllables in the mouth, chew them, crush them, and spit them out, and call that talking. But by good luck they are naturally tolerably taciturn, and though they always stare at us open-mouthed they at least spare us long conversations. But woe to him who meets a son of Albion who has made the grand tour, and learned to speak French. He will avail himself of the opportunity to practice the language, and overwhelm us with questions as to all subjects conceivable, and hardly is one answered before he begins with another either as to our age or home or how long we intend to remain where we are, and he believes that this incessant questioning is the best method to entertain us. One of my friends in Paris is perhaps right when he declares that the English learn to converse in French at the *Bureau des passeports*. Their conversation is most edifying at table when they carve their colossal roast beef, and with the most serious air ask us what part we prefer, rare or well done, from the middle or the brown outside, fat or lean? But roast beef and mutton are all they have which is good. Heaven keep every Christian from their gravies, which are made of one-third flour and two-thirds butter, or when

126

a change is needed, one-third butter and two-thirds flour. And Heaven guard every one from their naïve vegetables which, boiled away in water, are brought to the tables just as God made them! But more terrible than the cookery of the English are their toasts, with the obligatory standing speeches when the table-cloth is removed and the ladies departed, and so many bottles of port are in their place, which are supposed to be the best substitute for the fair sex ; but I may well say the *fair* sex, for English women deserve this name. They are beautiful, white, tall creatures, only the too great space between the mouth and nose, which is as common among them as with the men, often spoiled for me, in England, the most beautiful faces. This departure from the type of the beautiful impresses me more horribly when I see English people here in Italy, where their sparingly measured noses, and the broad space between them and the mouth, make a more startling contrast with the faces of the Italians, whose traits are of a more antique regularity, and whose noses, either aquiline like the Roman or straight like the Greek, often go into excess of length. It was very well remarked by a German that the English, when among Italians, look like statues with the noses knocked off.

" Yes, when we meet English people in a foreign country their defects first become striking by comparison. They are the gods of ennui, who, in shining, varnished coaches, drive post-haste through every country, and leave everywhere a grey dust-cloud of sadness behind them. Hence comes their curiosity without interest, their bedizened, over-dressed coarseness, their insolent bashfulness, their angular egotism, and their dismal delight in all melancholy things. For three weeks we have seen every day on the Piazza del gran Duca an Englishman who stands for hours gaping at the charlatan who, while seated on a horse, draws teeth. This spectacle is perhaps for the noble son of Albion an equivalent for the executions which he neglected to attend in his dear native land. For after boxing and cockfighting there is no sight so delightful to a Briton as the agony of a poor devil who has stolen a sheep or imitated a signature, and who is exhibited for an hour before the *façade* of the Old Bailey with a rope round his neck before he is hurled into eternity. It is no exaggeration to say that sheep-stealing and forgery in that abominably cruel country are punished not less severely than the most revolting crimes, such as parricide and incest. I myself happening to come that way by mere chance, saw a man hung in London for stealing a sheep, and from that time forth lost all relish for roast mutton—the fat always put me in mind of the white cap of the poor sinner. With him was hanged an Irishman, who had imitated the writing of a rich banker, and I think I can still see the naïve deathly agony of poor Paddy, who before the assizes could not understand why he was so severely punished for imitating other men's signatures, when he was quite willing to let any mortal man imitate his own! And these people talk always about Christianity, and go to church every Sunday, and flood the world with Bibles!

" I must own, Maria, that if nothing was to my taste in England, neither men nor meat, the fault lay partly in myself. I had brought a good stock of ill-temper and discontent with me from home, and I sought to be cheered up by a race which can only subdue its own ennui in the whirlpool of political and mercantile action. The perfection of machinery, which is there everywhere applied to some purpose, and which executes so many human tasks, had for me something mysterious and terrible ; the artificial headlong action of wheels, shafts, cylinders, with a thousand small hooks, cogs, and teeth, which whirl so madly, filled me with dread. The definiteness, the exactness, the meted out and measured punctuality of life, tormented me quite as much, for as the machines in England seem like men, so the men seem to me like mere machines. Yes, wood, iron, and brass, these seem to have usurped the spirit of humanity, and often to be raging with fullness of intelligence, while Man, with his soul gone, attends like a machine to his business and affairs ; eats at the appointed minute his beefsteak, delivers parliamentary speeches, brushes his nails, mounts the stage-coach, or — hangs himself.

" How my displeasure and discontent increased every day in this land, you may well imagine. But nothing could surpass the gloomy mood which once came over me as I, towards evening, stood on Waterloo Bridge and looked down into the Thames. It seemed to me as if my soul, with all its scars, was mirrored there, and looked up at me from the water. Then the most distressing memories vexed my mind. I thought of the rose daily sprinkled with vinegar, which thereby paid penance with its sweetest perfume, and prematurely died ; of the stray butterfly, whom a naturalist who once climbed Mont Blanc saw fluttering in solitude among blocks of ice ; of the tame she-monkey, who was so familiar with men that she played and ate with them ; but one day she recognised in the roast on the table her own little one, and, catching it up, rushed into the forest, and never came among mankind again. Ah! I was so wretched and sad that the hot tears leapt from my eyes ; they fell into the Thames, and swam forth into the great ocean, which has already swallowed so many without observing them.

" It happened at this instant that a strange music woke me from my dark dreams, and, looking round, I saw a group of people who seemed to form a ring round some entertaining show. I drew near, and saw a family of artists consisting of these four persons.

" Firstly, a little dumpy woman, dressed in black, who had a very little head, and before her a very big drum, on which she hammered away without mercy.

" Secondly, a dwarf, who wore an embroidered coat like that of an old French marquis, and had a great, powdered head, but very slender limbs, and who, while skipping, beat a triangle.

" Thirdly, a girl of perhaps fifteen years, who wore a short, close-fitting jacket of blue-striped silk, with full, wide trousers to match. It was an aerial and charming figure, the face of a perfectly beautiful Greek type. She had a noble, straight nose, beautifully curled lips, a dreamy, softly-rounded chin, her complexion sunny brown, with the shining black hair wound over the temples. Thus she stood, tall and serious, as it seemed out of tune or in ill-temper, and looked at the fourth member of the troupe, who was engaged in an artistic performance.

" This fourth person was a learned dog — a very promising poodle — who had, to the great delight of the English public, put together, from the wooden letters laid before him, the name of Lord Wellington, and added to it the very flattering word Hero. And as the dog, as one could easily see by his intelligent appearance, was no English brute, but had come with the other three performers from France, the sons of Albion rejoiced that their great general had, at least from the dogs of France, that recognition of his greatness which was so meanly denied to him by the other creatures of that country.

"This company was in fact French, and the dwarf, who announced himself as Monsieur Turlutu, began to bluster and boast in French with such passionate gestures that the poor English gaped with their mouths, and lifted their noses higher than ever. He often, after a long sentence, crowed like a cock, and these cock-a-doodle-doos, and the names of many emperors, kings, and princes which he scattered here and there, were all that the poor spectators understood. He boasted that these emperors, kings, and princes had been his patrons and friends. Even when only eight years of age he had, as he declared, held a long conversation with his late majesty Louis XVI., who subsequently frequently consulted him in most important affairs. He had, like many others, escaped the storms of the Revolution, nor was it till the Empire that he returned to his dear native land to take part in the glory of *la grande nation*. Napoleon, he declared, had never liked him, but he had been almost idolized by His Holiness Pope Pius the Seventh. The Emperor Alexander had given him bon-bons, and the Princess Wilhelm von Kyritz always took him on her lap. His Serene Highness, Duke Karl of Brunswick, had let him ride many a time on his dog, and His Majesty King Louis of Bavaria had read to him his sublime poems. The princes of Reuss Schleiz-Kreuz and of Schwarzburg-Sondershausen loved him like a brother, and always smoked from the same pipe with him. Yes, from childhood, he declared, he had always lived only among sovereigns ; the contemporary monarchs had grown up familiar with him, he regarded them as his equals, and always wore mourning when one of them passed away. After these words of weight he crowed again like a cock.

"Monsieur Turlutu was really one of the most curious dwarfs whom I had ever seen, for his wrinkled, ancient face formed such a comical contrast to his little, childlike body, and his whole person contrasted yet more funnily with his feats. For he next assumed the most defiant positions, and with an inhumanly long rapier stabbed the air right and left, while he incessantly swore on his honor that this *carte* or that *tierce* could not be parried by any one, that his *parade* was unassailable, and that he challenged any one present to compete with him in the noble art of fencing.

" After the dwarf had for some time amused the multitude in this manner, and found that no one would fight in public a duel with him, he bowed with old French grace, thanked his audience for the favor with which they had received him, and took the freedom to announce to the highly honorable public the most extraordinary exhibition which had ever been admired on English ground. ' You see this person,' he cried, as he drew on a dirty kid glove, and led the young girl of the troupe with respectful gallantry to the midst of the ring ; ' this lady is Mademoiselle Laurence, the only daughter of the noble and Christian lady whom you see there with the drum, and who now wears mourning on account of the recent death of her deeply-loved husband, who was the greatest ventriloquist in Europe. Mademoiselle Laurence will now dance ! Ladies and gentlemen will please to admire the dance of Mademoiselle Laurence !' After which he again crowed.

" The young girl did not seem to pay the slightest attention to this speech, nor to the gaze of those around. As if lost in troubled thought she waited till the dwarf had spread a carpet before her and began to play his triangle in accompaniment with the great drum. It was strange music, a mixture of awkward ill-temper and voluptuous tickling, and I noted in it a pathetic, fantastic, mournfully bold and bizarre melody, which was, however, of the strangest simplicity. But I forgot the music as soon as the young girl began to dance.

" Both dancer and dance attracted my whole attention. It was not the classic dancing such as we still see in great ballets, where, as in classic tragedy, only sprawling unities and artificial effects flourish. It was not those footed Alexandrines, those declamatory leaps, those antithetic *entrechats*, that noble passion which whirls in pirouettes so distractingly down on one foot that one sees nothing but heaven and *stockinette*—nothing but ideality and lies! There is really nothing so repulsive to me as the ballet in the great opera in Paris, where the traditions of ' classic ' dancing have been most perfectly preserved, while the French have overthrown the classic system in all other arts, poetry, music, and painting. But it will be hard for them to bring about a similar revolution in the art of dancing, unless it be that here, as in their political revolution, they fly to terrorism, and guillotine the legs of the obstinate male and female dancers of the old *régime*.

" Mademoiselle Laurence was no great *danseuse*, her toes were not very supple, her legs were not practised in all possible contortions ; she understood nothing of the art of dancing as Vestris teaches it, but she danced as Nature teaches ; her whole soul was in time with her steps ; not only did her feet dance, but her whole form and face. She often became pale, almost deadly pale ; her eyes opened spectrally wide, yearning and pain convulsed her lips, while her black hair, which in smooth ovals inclosed her temples, moved like two flapping ravens' wings. It was indeed no classic dance, but neither was it romantic in the sense in which a young Frenchman of the school of Eugene Renduel would explain the word. It had neither anything mediæval nor Venetian, nor distorted and deformed, nor macabre—there was in it neither moonshine nor incest. It was a dance which did not attempt to amuse by outward phases of motion, but by phases which seemed to be words of a strange language which would say strange things. But what did the dance say? I could not understand it, however passionately it pleaded. I only felt that here and there something terribly, shudderingly painful was meant. I who in other things grasp so readily the key of a mystery, could not solve this danced enigma, and that I sought in vain to find the sense was the fault of the music, which certainly sought to lead me astray, which cunningly tried to bewilder me and set me wrong. The triangle of Monsieur Turlutu tittered many a time mockingly, while Madame the mother beat so angrily on her great drum that her face beamed out of the cloud of black hood round her face like a blood-red Northern light.

" Long after the troupe had departed, I remained standing in the same place wondering what this dance could mean. Was it some national dance of the South of France or of Spain? These were recalled by the irrepressible energy with which the dancer threw her body to and fro, and the wildness with which she often threw her head backwards in the mad manner of the bold Bacchantæ whom we see with amazement on the reliefs of antique vases. Her dance had in it something of intoxicated unwillfulness, something gloomily inevitable or fatalistic, for she danced like destiny itself. Or was it a fragment of some primevally ancient, forgotten pantomime? Or a secret tale of life, set to motion? Very often the girl bent to the earth, with listening ear, as if she heard a voice calling up to her. Then she trembled like an aspen leaf, sprang quickly to the other side, and there indulged in her maddest gambols. Then she inclined her ear again to the earth, listened more anxiously than before, nodded with her head, grew sad and pale, shuddered, stood awhile straight as a taper, as if frozen, and finally made a motion *as if washing her hands!* Was it blood which she so carefully, with such terrible anxiety, washed away? While doing this she cast to one side a glance so pitifully imploring, so soul-melting — and this glance fell by chance on me.

" I thought all night long on this glance, on the dance, on the wild accompaniment, and as I, on the morrow, roamed as usual about the streets, I felt a deep longing to meet the beautiful dancer again, and I pricked up my ears to perceive if I could the sound of drum and triangle music. I had at last found in London something which interested me, and I no longer wandered aimlessly about in its gaping streets.

" I had just quitted the Tower, where I had carefully looked at the axe with which Anne Boleyn was beheaded, the diamonds of the British crown, and the lions, when I beheld again Madame the mother with the great drum, and heard Monsieur Turlutu crowing like a cock. The learned dog again raked together the heroism of Lord Wellington, the dwarf displayed his invincible *carte* and *tierce*, and Mademoiselle Laurence began once more her wonderful dance. And there were again the same enigmatical movements, the same language speaking what I could not understand, the same impetuous casting back of the beautiful head, the same listening at the ground, the terror which relieved itself by mad leaps, again the listening to the voice below, the trembling, the growing pale, the frozen silence, the frightfully mysterious washing of hands, and at last the side glance, imploring and beseeching, which she cast at me, lasting this time longer than before.

" Yes, women, girls as well as matrons, know at once when they have attracted the attention of a man. Although Mademoiselle Laurence, when not performing, always stood motionless and sad, and while she danced hardly looked at the public, from this time it was no longer by chance that her glance ever fell on me, and the oftener I saw her dance the more significantly she looked, but still more incomprehensible was her expression. I was as if bewitched by this glance, and for three weeks from morning till evening did I walk the streets of London, stopping wherever Mademoiselle Laurence danced. In spite of the great noise of the multitude I could catch at the greatest distance the sound of the drum and triangle, and Monsieur Turlutu as soon as he saw me coming, raised his most friendly crow. And without ever speaking a word to him or with Mademoiselle Laurence, with Madame Mère, or with the learned dog, I seemed in the end to belong entirely to the troupe. When Monsieur Turlutu took up his collections, he always behaved with the most refined tact, as soon as he drew near me, and always looked away when I threw into the three-cornered hat a small coin. He had really an aristocratic manner ; he recalled the exquisite politeness of the past. One could see in the little man that he had grown up among monarchs, and so much the stranger did it seem and quite below his dignity when he crowed like a cock.

" I cannot tell you how sad I felt when for three days I sought in vain for the little troupe in all the streets, and at last was certain they had left London. The blue devils held me once more in their leaden arms, and squeezed my heart. At last I could endure it no longer, and bade adieu to the mob, the blackguards, the gentlemen, and the fashionables of England — the Four Estates of the realm — and traveled back to the civilized world, where I knelt down, devoutly praying, before the white apron of the first cook whom I

134

met. For here I could once more dine like an intelligent human being, and refresh my soul by the contemplation of unselfish faces. But I could never forget Mademoiselle Laurence. She danced a long time in my memory, and in idle hours I often reflected on the enigmatic pantomime of the beautiful child, especially on the listening at the earth with inclined ear. It was long ere the uncanny triangle and drum melody faded away from my mind."

" And that is the whole story?" cried Maria, as she rose passionately excited.

But Maximilian gently pushed her back, laid his forefinger significantly on his mouth, and whispered, " Still — be still — speak not a word. Be good and calm, and I will tell you the tail of the story ; but, for life, do not interrupt me!"

Then as he lolled back somewhat more comfortably in his chair, he thus continued : —

" Five years after all this I came for the first time to Paris, and that at a very remarkable time. The French had put their Revolution of July on the stage, and the whole world applauded. This drama was not so terrible as the previous tragedies of the Republic and the Empire. Only a few thousand corpses remained on the showground, with which the political romanticists were not very well satisfied, and they announced a new piece in which more blood was to flow, and the executioner be much busier.

" Paris delighted me by the gaiety which is there manifested in everything, and which sheds its influence even on darkened souls. Strange, Paris is the stage where the greatest tragedies of the world's history are acted — tragedies of which the memory, even in most distant lands, makes hearts tremble and eyes weep — but to him who sees them here in Paris itself, it is as it once was with me when I saw the Tour de Nesle played at the Porte Saint Martin. For I was seated behind a lady who wore a hat of rose-red gauze, and this hat was so broad that it completely covered for me the whole stage-view, so that I only saw all that was being tragedied through the red gauze, and all the horrors of the Tour de Nesle appeared consequently in the gayest *couleur de rose*. Yes, there is such a roselight in Paris, which softens all tragedies for him who is

135

close by, so that his enjoyment of life shall not be diminished. Even the terrors or troubles which one has brought to Paris in his own heart lose their power to torment. There all sufferings are soothed. In the air of Paris all wounds heal more rapidly than elsewhere ; there is something in it as grandly elevating, as soothing, as charming as in the people themselves.

" What pleased me best in the Paris people was its polite manners and aristocratic mien. Sweet pineapple perfume of politeness, how beneficently didst thou refresh my sick and weary soul, which had imbibed in Germany so much tobacco nausea, smell of sauerkraut, and vulgarity ! The delightful and apt excuses of a Frenchman who, on the day of my arrival, had by accident run against me in the street, sounded to me like the melodies of Rossini. I was almost frightened at such sweet politeness, I who was accustomed to German boorish knocks in the ribs without a word of apology. During my first week in Paris I sought intentionally to be run against by people, that I might enjoy this apologetic music. But it is not merely from politeness, but owing to their language itself, the French people have a peculiar coating of eminent refinement. For, as you know, by us in the North the French language is an attribute of the higher nobility, and from childhood the idea of aristocracy was always associated in my mind with French. And so a French market-woman spoke better French than a German comtesse of sixty-four quarterings.

" On account of their language, which gives them an aristocratic air, the French people have to me something delightfully romantic in all their ways and words. This came from another reminiscence of my childhood. For the first book in which I learned to read French was the Fables of Lafontaine, in which the naively sensible phrases made such an ineffaceable impression on my memory that, when I came to Paris and heard French spoken everywhere, I continually recalled the old stories. It seemed to me that I heard the well-known voices of the animals ; now the lion spoke, then the wolf, then the lamb, or the stork, or the dove—ever and anon master fox, and in memory many a time I heard—

> 'Eh! bonjour, Monsieur du Corbeau!
> Que vous êtes joli! que vous me semblez beau!'

" Such reminiscences of fables awoke in my soul much oftener when I in Paris frequented the higher regions, which men called the world. For this was specially the world which supplied Lafontaine with the types of his animal characters. The winter season began soon after my arrival in Paris, and I took part in the salon life in which that world moves more or less merrily. What struck me as most interesting in this world was not the equality as regards refined politeness which prevails in it, so much as the difference in its elements. Very often, when I in a grand salon looked round on the people assembled there on the most friendly footing, it seemed as if I were in a curiosity-shop, where the relics of all ages are huddled higgledy-piggledy all together, a Greek Apollo by a Chinese pagoda, a Mexican Vizliputzli by a Gothic Ecce Homo, Egyptian idols with dogs' heads, holy horrors of wood, ivory, and metal, and so on. There I saw old *mousquetaires* who had once danced with Marie Antoinette, Republicans of mild observance who were regarded as gods in the Assemblée Nationale, Montagnards without money and without reproach, former members of the Directory who had been enthroned in the Luxembourg, bearers of great dignities under the Empire before whom all Europe had trembled, ruling Jesuits of the Restoration—in short, actual faded and mutilated divinities of all eras, in whom no one any longer believed. The names howl on coming into contact, but the men looked peaceably and stood together in peace, like the antiquities of which I have spoken in the bric-à-brac shops of the Quai Voltaire. In Germanic lands, where passions are less amenable to discipline, such a social assemblage of such heterogeneous persons would be simply impossible. Neither is the need of conversation so great with us in the cold North, as in warmer France, where the bitterest enemies, when they meet in a salon, cannot long maintain a gloomy silence. And the desire to please is there carried so far, that people strive earnestly to be agreeable not only

to their friends but even their enemies. Hence a constant disguise
and display of graces, so that women have their own time of it to
surpass men in their coquetry — but succeed in it all the same.

" I mean indeed nothing wrong by this comparison — and, on my
life! nothing in detraction of French women, and least of all the
Parisiennes. For I am their greatest adorer, and honor and admire
them more for their defects than for their virtues. I know nothing
so exquisitely to the point as a legend that the French women came
into the world with all possible faults, but that a beneficent fairy
took pity, and gave to every fault a magic by which it appeared as
a fresh charm. This enchanting fairy is grace. Are all French
women beautiful? Who can tell? Who hath seen through all the
intrigues of the toilet, into whose heart hath it entered to decipher
if that is real which the tulle betrays, or is that false which puffed-
out silk parades? And if it be given to the eye to penetrate the
shell even as we are intent to examine the kernel, lo it covers itself
in a new hull, and yet again in another, and by means of this
incessant metamorphosis of modes they mock mankind. Are their
faces beautiful? Even this is hard to determine. For all their features
are in constant motion ; every Parisienne has a thousand faces,
every one more laughing, more *spirituelle*, more charming than the
other, and he would be well bewildered who under it all could
detect the fairest, or the real face at all. Or are their eyes large?
What do I know? We do not long examine the calibre of a cannon
when its ball decapitates us. And even if they miss — these eyes —
at least they dazzle us by their fire, and he is glad enough who can
get out of shot-range. Is the space between the nose and mouth
broad or narrow? Very often broad, when they turn up the nose ;
very often small, when they scornfully curl their upper lips. Is her
mouth great or small? Who can tell where the lips leave off and
laughing begins? To form a correct judgment, the one judging and
the object judged must be in a condition of repose. But who can
rest by a Parisienne, and what Parisienne ever rests, herself? There
are people who believe they can see a butterfly quite accurately
when they have fastened it with a pin on paper, which is as foolish
as it is cruel, for a fixed and quiet insect is a butterfly no longer. It

must be seen while it flutters among the flowers, and the Parisienne must not be studied in her domestic life, where she is pinned down, but in the salon, at soirees and balls, where she flies freely with the wings of embroidered gauze and silk among the flashing crystal crowns of delight and gaiety! Then is revealed in her an eager rapture in life, a longing for sweet sensuous oblivion, a yearning for intoxication, by which she is made almost terribly beautiful, and gains a charm which at once enraptures and shocks our soul.

" This thirst to enjoy life, as if in another hour death would snatch them away from the sparkling fountain of enjoyment, or as if this fountain would be in another hour sealed for ever—this haste, this rage, this madness of the Parisiennes, especially as shown in balls, always reminds me of the legend of the dead dancing-girls who are called by us the Willis. These are young brides who died before the wedding-day, but who still have the unsatisfied mania for dancing so deeply in their hearts, that they rise by night from their graves and meet in crowds on the highways, where they at midnight abandon themselves to the wildest dances. In their bridal dresses, with wreaths of flowers on their heads, sparkling rings on their pale white hands, laughing fearfully, irresistibly beautiful, the Willis dance in the moonshine, and they dance the more impetuously and wildly the more they feel that the hour allowed them for dancing is drawing to an end, and they must again descend to the icy cold of the grave.

" It was at a soiree in the Chaussée d'Antin where this thought went deep into my soul. It was a brilliant reception, and nothing was wanting in all available ingredients of social enjoyment— enough lights to be seen by, enough mirrors to see one's self, enough people to squeeze among till one was warm, enough *eau sucré* and ices to cool one. It began with music. Franz Liszt had allowed himself to be forced to the pianoforte, threw his hair up above his genial brow, and played one of his most brilliant battle-pieces. The keys seemed to bleed. If I am not mistaken, he played a passage from the *Palingenesia* of Ballanche, whose ideas he translated into music, which was a great advantage for those who do not know the works of this celebrated author in the original. After this

he played the March to the Gallows — *la marche au supplice* — that
glorious composition of Berlioz which this young artist, if I do not
err, composed on the morning of his wedding-day.

" There were in the entire hall faces growing pale, heaving
bosoms, panting breaths during the pauses, and at last roaring
applause. Women always seem intoxicated when Liszt plays. With
wild joy these Willis of the salon threw themselves into the dance,
and I had trouble to escape from the crowd into a side-room. Here
play was going on, and a few ladies, reclining on great easy-chairs,
took, or feigned to take, an interest in the game. As I passed by one
of these dames, and her dress touched my arm, I felt a thrill pass
from my hand to my shoulder like a slight electric shock. And such
a shock, but with full strength, shook my heart when I saw the
lady's countenance. Was it *she* — or not? There was the same
countenance which in form and sunny hue was like an antique ;
only it was not so marbly-pure and marble smooth as before. A
closely observant eye could detect on brow and cheeks faint traces
as of small-pox, which exactly resembled the weather-marks which
one sees on statues which have been for some time exposed to the
rain. There were the same black locks which in smooth ovals
covered the temples like raven's wings. But as her eye met mine,
and that with the well-known side glance whose quick lightning
shot so enigmatically through my soul, I doubted no longer — it
was Mademoiselle Laurence.

" Leaning aristocratically, a bouquet in one hand, the other on
the chair arm, Mademoiselle Laurence sat near a table, and seemed
to give her whole attention to the cards. Her dress of white satin
was becoming and graceful, yet quite simple. With the exception
of bracelets and a brooch of pearls, she wore no ornaments. A
chemisette of lace covered her young bosom almost puritanically
to the neck, and in this simplicity and modesty of dress she formed
a touching, charming contrast with several older ladies, who, gaily
ornamented and flashing diamonds, sat by her, and exposed the
ruins of their former glory, the place where Troy once stood, in
melancholy wasted nakedness. She still seemed wondrously lovely
and charmingly sorrowful, and I felt irresistibly attracted to her,

and finally stood behind her chair, burning with impatience to speak to her, but restrained by aggravating scruples of delicacy.

" I had stood a little while behind her when she suddenly plucked a flower from her bouquet, and, without looking around, presented it to me over her shoulder. Strange was its perfume, and it exerted in me a strange enchantment. I felt myself freed from all social formalities ; I was as if in a dream, where one acts and speaks and wonders at one's self, and where our words have a childlike, confiding, and simple character. Calmly, indifferently, carelessly, as one speaks to an old friend, I inclined over the arm of the chair and softly said in her ear —

" ' Mademoiselle Laurence, where is your mother with the drum ?'

" ' She is dead,' she replied, in the same calm, indifferent tone.

" After a little pause I again bent over the arm of the chair and whispered —

" ' Mademoiselle Laurence, where is the learned dog ?'

" ' He has run away out into the wide world,' she answered, in the same calm tone.

" And again after a pause I leaned over the arm of the chair and whispered in her ear —

" ' Mademoiselle Laurence, where is Monsieur Turlutu, the dwarf ?'

" ' He is with the giants on the Boulevard du Temple.' These words were just uttered — in the same easy, indifferent tone — when a serious, elderly man of commanding military appearance approached her, and announced that the carriage was waiting. Slowly rising from her seat she took his arm, and, without casting a look at me, left the company.

" When I asked our hostess, who had stood during the whole evening at the door presenting her smiles to the coming and parting guests, for the name of the young lady who had just left with the elderly gentleman, she laughed gaily and said —

" ' Mon Dieu ! who can know everybody. I know as little who he is as '——

" She silenced suddenly, for she certainly was about to say ' You '

141

—for she saw me that evening for the first time.

"'Perhaps your husband,' I suggested, 'can give me some information. Where shall I look for him?'

"'Hunting at St. Germain,' replied Madame, with heartier laughter. 'He left this morning early, and will return tomorrow evening. But—wait—I know some one who has frequently conversed with the lady of whom you speak. I forget his name, but you can easily learn it if you will only inquire for the young gentleman who was kicked by M. Casimir Perier—I forget where.'

"Hard as it is to find a man who has been kicked out by a minister, I soon discovered mine, and begged him for some explanation of the marvelous being who so much interested me, and whom I depicted to him distinctly enough.

"'Yes,' said the young man; 'I know her well. I have conversed with her at several soirees.'

"And he repeated a lot of rubbish with which he had entertained the lady. What he had particularly remarked was her earnest look whenever he had said anything agreeable. And he marveled not a little that she always declined his invitation to take place in a quadrille, assuring him that she did not know how to dance. He knew nothing of her name or family. Nor could anybody, so far as I could ascertain, give me any closer information in this respect. I ran in vain through all possible soirees seeking for information; I could nowhere find Mademoiselle Laurence."

"And that is the whole story?" cried Maria, as she slowly turned and yawned as if sleepy. "That is your whole remarkable story! And you never saw again either Mademoiselle Laurence, nor the mother with the drum, nor the dwarf Turlutu, nor the learned dog?"

"Lie calm and still," replied Maximilian. "I saw them all again —even the learned dog. But he was in a sad case, the poor rogue, when I met him in Paris. It was in the Latin Quarter. I came by the Sorbonne as a dog rushed from its gate, and after him a dozen students with sticks, who were soon joined by two dozen old women, who all screamed in chorus, 'Mad dog!' The wretched animal looked almost human in his agony of death; tears ran like a stream from his eyes, and as he yelping rushed by me and his dimmed gaze fell on me, I recognised my old friend, the learned dog, the eulogist of Lord Wellington, who once caused the English people to wonder at his wisdom. Was he really mad, though? Had he overtaxed his intellect with sheer learning while pursuing his studies in the Latin Quarter? Or had he in the Sorbonne offended by his scraping and growling dissent at the puffy-cheeked charlatanery of some professor, who had got rid of his disapproving auditor by declaring that he was mad? Alas! youth does not investigate carefully whether it is irritated pedantry or professional envy which inspires the cry, 'The dog is mad!' but breaks away with thoughtless sticks — and of course all the old women are ready with their yells and howls, and they outscream the voice of innocence and of reason. My poor friend had to succumb — before my eyes he was pitiably struck dead amid jeers and curses, and at last cast on a dunghill — a wretched martyr to learning!

" Nor was the condition of the dwarf, Monsieur Turlutu, very much better when I rediscovered him on the Boulevard du Temple Mademoiselle Laurence had indeed said that he had gone thither, but whether I did not seriously attempt to seek him there, or the crowd of people was so great, it happened that some time passed before I observed the show place where the giants were found. Two tall knaves lay at ease on a bench, who jumped up and assumed the attitude of giants when I appeared. They were really not so large as their sign boasted, but only two overgrown rascals, clad in rose-coloured tricot, who had very black, and perhaps false, side-whiskers, and who swung immense but hollow wooden clubs over their heads. When I asked after the dwarf, who was also set forth on the sign, they replied that for four weeks he had been unable on account of increasing illness to appear in public, but that I might see him if I would pay an extra price of admission. How willingly one pays double to see an old friend! Alas! it was a friend whom I found on his deathbed! This deathbed was really a child's cradle, and in it lay the poor dwarf, with his sallow, wrinkled old man's face. A little girl of perhaps four years sat by him, rocking the cradle with her foot, and singing in a comical babbling tone —

"'Sleep, Turlututy — sleep!'

"As the little man saw me he opened his glazed blue eyes as wide as possible, and a melancholy smile twitched about his white lips; he seemed to recognize me at once, for he reached out his dried, withered little hand, and gasped softly, 'Old friend!'

"It was indeed in sad, troublous case that I found the man who, when eight years of age, had had a long conversation with Louis XVI., whom the Czar Alexander had fed with bonbons, whom the Princess of Kyritz had held on her lap, to whom the King of Bavaria had read his poems, who had smoked from the same pipe with German princes, whom the Pope had apotheosised, and whom Napoleon had never loved! This last fact troubled the wretched man even on his deathbed — I should say in his deathcradle — and he wept over the tragic destiny of the great Emperor who had never loved him, but who had ended his life in such lamentable circumstances at St. Helena — 'Even as I now die,' he added, 'rejected, neglected by all kings and princes, a mere mockery of former glory.'

"Though I could not quite understand how a dwarf who dies among giants could compare himself with a giant who dies among dwarfs, still the words of poor Turlutu and his neglected state in his dying hour moved me. I could not refrain from expressing my amazement that Mademoiselle Laurence, who had now become so grand, did not trouble herself about him. I had hardly mentioned her name when the dwarf was seized with agonising cramps, and wailed with white lips, 'Ungrateful child! She whom I brought up, and would have even made my wife, whom I taught how one should move and conduct one's self among the great people of this world — how one should smile and bow at court and act with elegance — thou hast turned my teaching to good account; now thou art a great lady, and hast a carriage and lackeys, and much money, and no heart! Thou leavest me to die here alone and miserable, like Napoleon at St. Helena. Oh, Napoleon, thou didst never love me!' What he then said I could not understand. He raised his head, made passes with his hand, as if fencing with some one, and defending himself against some one, it may have been Death. But the scythe of this adversary can be resisted by none, be he Napoleon or a Turlutu, for with him no parade or guard avails! Exhausted, as if overcome, the dwarf let his head sink, gazed at me with an indescribable spectral glare, crowed suddenly like a cock, and died!

" I confess that this death troubled me all the more because the sufferer had given me no more accurate information as to Mademoiselle Laurence. I was not in love with her, nor did I feel any specially great inclination towards her, and yet I was spurred by a mysterious, irresistible desire to seek her everywhere, and if I entered a salon and looked over those present and did not find her familiar face, then I became quite restless and felt impelled to depart.

" Reflecting on this feeling I stood once at midnight in a side entrance of the Grand Opera, waiting wearily for a coach, for it rained hard. But no coach came, or rather coaches only which belonged to other people, who got in gaily enough and departed, until little by little I was left alone.

" ' Well, then, you must ride with *me*!' said a lady who, closely wrapped in a black mantilla, had also stood waiting by me for some time, and who was now about to enter a carriage. The voice thrilled through my heart ; the well-known side-glance exerted once more its charm ; and I seemed to be in a dream, when I found myself in a softly-padded warm carriage by Mademoiselle Laurence. We spoke no word to one another, perhaps we could not have understood if we had spoken, since that vehicle rattled with a fearful droning noise through the streets of Paris for a long time, till it at last stopped before a vast gateway.

" Servants in brilliant livery lighted us up the steps through a suite of apartments. A lady's maid who with sleepy face approached us, stammered with many excuses that the red room was the only one with a fire lighted. As she gave the maid a sign to leave us, Laurence said laughing, ' Chance or luck has brought you far indeed today ; my bedroom is the only one which is warmed.'

" In this bedroom, where we were soon alone, blazed a beautiful fire, which was the more agreeable because the apartment was immensely large and high. This great chamber, which might better be called a great hall, had in it something strangely desolate or empty. Its furniture and decoration and architecture bore the impress of an age whose splendor is now so dusty, and whose dignity seems so sober and sad, that its relics awaken a feeling of discomfort, if not a subdued smile. I speak of the time of the Empire, of the days of golden eagles, high-flying plumes, Greek coiffures, the glory of grand drum-majors, military masses, official immortality decreed by the *Moniteur*, Continental coffee made from chicory, bad sugar from beetroot and princes and dukes manufactured out of nothing at all. Yet it had its charm, this age of pathetic materialism. Talma declaimed, Gros painted, Bigottini danced, Grassini sang, Maury preached, Rovigo had the police, the Emperor read Ossian, and Pauline Borghese had herself modelled as Venus, and stark naked at that, for the room was quite warm, like that in which I found myself with Mademoiselle Laurence.

" We sat by the fire conversing confidentially, and she told me sighing how she was married to a Buonaparte hero, who every evening before retiring entertained her with the history of his adventures. A few days before his late departure he had given her in full the battle of Jena ; but he was in very bad health, and would hardly survive the Russian campaign. When I asked how long it was since her father had departed this life, she laughed, and said she had never known one, and that her so-called mother had never been married.

" ' Not married !' I cried ; ' why, I myself saw her in London in deep mourning for her husband's death !'

" ' Oh !' replied Laurence, ' she wore mourning all the time for twelve years, to awaken compassion as a poor widow, and also to take in some simpleton who wanted a wife. She hoped that she would sail the sooner under the black flag into the port of matrimony. But death had pity on her, and she perished suddenly by bursting a vein. I never loved her, for she gave me many a beating and little food. I should have starved if Monsieur Turlutu had not many a time given me a piece of bread on the sly ; but for that the dwarf wanted me to marry him, and when his hopes were wrecked he allied himself to my mother—I say mother only from habit—and both tormented me cruelly. She was always saying I was a useless creature, and that the dog was worth a thousand times more than I with my wretched dancing. Then they praised the dog at my expense, fed him with cakes, and threw me the crumbs. The dog, she said, was her best support; he pleased the public, which did not take the least interest in me; that the dog must maintain me by his work, and that I lived on the charity and refuse of the dog. Damn the dog!'

"'Oh! you need not curse him again,' I interrupted the angry beauty. 'He is dead; I saw him die '——

"'Is the beast done for at last?' cried Laurence, as she sprang up with delight beaming in every feature.

"'The dwarf also is dead,' I added.

"'Monsieur Turlutu?' cried Laurence, also joyfully. But the expression faded from her face gradually, and with a milder, almost melancholy tone, she sighed, 'Poor Turlutu!'

"As I did not conceal from her that the dwarf in his dying moments had complained of her bitterly, she burst into passionate protestation that she had the fullest intention and desire to provide for the dwarf in the best manner, and that she had offered him an annual pension if he would live quietly and modestly, anywhere in the country. 'But with his habitual vanity and desire of distinction,' continued Laurence, 'he desired to remain in Paris and dwell in my hotel, for thus he thought he could through me again resume his former acquaintance in the Faubourg Saint Germain, and his old brilliant place in society. And when I flatly refused this he called me a cursed goblin-ghost, a vampire, and a child of death '——

"Laurence suddenly stopped and shuddering said, as she heaved a sigh from her very heart—

"'Ah! I wish he had left me lying with my mother in the grave!'

"When I prayed her to explain these mysterious words, a flood of tears burst from her eyes, and trembling and sobbing she con-

fessed that the drummer woman in mourning whom she called
' mother ' had once told her that a strange rumor current as to
her birth was not a mere fable. ' For in the town where we dwelt,'
continued Laurence, ' I was always called the Death Child. Old
women said I was really the daughter of a Count of that place, who
maltreated his wife terribly, and when she died gave her a magnificent funeral. But she was far gone with child, and not really
dead. Certain thieves, tempted by the richness of her funeral attire,
burst open the tomb and took out the Countess, whom they found
in the pangs of parturition. She died while giving birth to Laurence.
The thieves laid her body again in the tomb, closed it, and carried
the babe to the receiver of their stolen goods, who was the wife
of the great ventriloquist.

" ' This poor child, who was buried before she was born, was
everywhere called the Death Child. Ah! you cannot know how
much misery I had even as a little girl, when people called me
by this name. While the great ventriloquist was alive, and when
he was discontented with me — as often happened — he always
cried : " Cursed Death-Child, I wish I had never taken you from
the grave." As he was of great skill in his calling, he could so
modulate his voice as to make any one think that it came from the
ground, and so he would make me believe that it was the voice of
my dead mother who related her story. He knew the terrible tale
well enough, for he had once been a servant of the Count my
father. It was his greatest pleasure to torture me with the awful
terror which I, a mere infant, felt at hearing this. The words which
came in spectral tones from the ground told things so dreadful that
I could not altogether understand them, but all of which, when I
danced in after years, came vividly back into my mind. At such a
time strange memories seemed to possess me. I forgot myself, and
was another person tormented with all terrors and mysteries, but
so soon as I ceased to dance all vanished from my mind.'

" While Mademoiselle Laurence spoke, slowly and as if questioning, she stood before me by the fireplace, where the fire gleamed
ever more and more agreeably, and I sat in the great armchair,
which was probably the seat of her husband when he of evenings

related his battles before going to bed. Laurence looked at me with her great eyes, as if asking me for counsel, nodding her head in so mournfully reflective a manner that she inspired in me a deep sympathy. She was so delicate, so young, so beautiful, this slender lily sprung from the grave, this daughter of death, this ghost with the face of an angel and the body of a Hindu dancing girl.

" I know not how it happened — perhaps it was the influence of the arm-chair in which I sat ; but all at once it seemed to me as if I were the old general who the day before had been narrating the battle of Jena, and must continue my story, so I said—

" ' After the battle of Jena, within a few weeks, all the Prussian fortresses surrendered almost without a blow. First of these was Magdeburg, the strongest of all, and it had three hundred cannons. Was not that disgraceful ?'

" Mademoiselle Laurence let me proceed no further. All melancholy had fled from her beautiful face. She laughed like a child and said, ' Yes ; that was disgraceful, and more than disgraceful. If *I* were a fortress, and had three hundred cannon, I would never surrender.'

" But as Mademoiselle Laurence was no fortress, and had no three hundred cannons "——

Here Maximilian suddenly paused, and after a short pause asked softly—

" Maria, are you asleep?"

" Yes, I sleep," replied Maria.

. . . .

" I would say," added Maximilian, " that I sat by the fire in a red light, and it seemed to me as if I were the god Pluto amid the glowing flames of hell, holding the sleeping Proserpine in his arms. She slept, and I studied her charming face, and sought in its traits some explanation of that sympathy which my soul felt for her. What was the meaning of this woman? What significance lurked under the symbolism of this beautiful form? I held this winsome riddle now as my possession in my arms, yet could not discover its solution.

" Yet, is it not folly to endeavor to penetrate the inner meaning

149

of a strange appearance or phenomenon when we cannot as much as solve the problems of our own souls? Why, we are not even certain that these outer apparitions really *exist*. Many a time we cannot distinguish reality from faces seen in our dreams. Was it an image of my imagination, or was it a terrible reality, which I that night heard and saw? I do not know. I can only remember that while the wildest thoughts streamed through my heart, a rustling, ringing noise sounded in my ears. It was a crazy melody, singularly slow. It seemed to be very familiar, and at last I recognised in it the sound of a triangle and a drum. This music, tinkling and buzzing, seemed to approach from afar, and at last when I looked up I saw near me, in the centre of the room, a well-known show, for it was Monsieur Turlutu, the dwarf, who played the triangle, and Madame Mère, who beat the great drum, while the learned dog scratched round on the ground as if seeking for his wooden letters. The dog seemed to move with pain, and his hair was spotted with blood. Madame Mère still wore her black mourning, but she had no longer her old plump, comical figure, and her face was not now red but pale. The dwarf, who still wore the embroidered coat of an old French marquis, with a powdered wig, seemed to be somewhat taller, probably because he had become so fearfully thin. He displayed as before his skill in fencing, and seemed to be wheezing out his old boasts, but spoke so softly that I could not catch a word, and it was only by the movements of his lips that I could often observe that he was crowing like a cock.

" While these laughably horrible distorted images moved before my eyes with unseeming haste, I perceived that Laurence breathed more restlessly. A cold shudder ran like frost through all her body, and her beautiful limbs twitched convulsively, as if with intolerable pain. But at last, supple as an eel, she slid and slipped from my arms, stood in a second in the center of the room, and began to dance, while the mother with the drum and the dwarf with the triangle again raised their softly muffled music. She danced as she had done on the Waterloo Bridge and on the crossings of London. There was the same mysterious pantomime, the same passionate leaps, the same Bacchic casting back of the head, many times the same bending down to the earth, as if listening to what was being said below, then the old trembling, the growing pale, the frozen stillness, and yet again the listening with the ear inclined. And she also rubbed her hands as if washing them. At last she seemed to again cast her deep, painful, imploring glance at me, but it was only in the features of her deathly pale face that I recognised the glance, not in her eyes, for they were closed. The music sounded ever softer, the drum-mother and the dwarf growing paler, dimmer, and whirling away like mist, at last disappeared altogether, but Laurence remained as before, dancing with closed eyes. This dancing, as if blind, in the silent room by night, gave the beautiful creature such a ghostly air that I often shuddered, and was heartily glad when she ceased to dance, and glided and slipped, as softly as she had flown away, back into my arms.

" Certainly the sight of this scene was not agreeable. But man accustoms himself to everything, and it is possible that the unearthly mystery of this woman gave her a peculiar charm, which mingled with my feelings a terrible tenderness—enough that in a few weeks I was no longer amazed in the least when by night I heard the ring of the drum and triangle, and my dear Laurence suddenly leaped up and danced a solo with closed eyes. Her husband, the old Buonapartist, commanded near Paris, and his duties allowed him to pass only his days in the city. As a matter of course he became my most intimate friend, and he wept bright tears when the day came for him to bid me for a long time adieu. He traveled with his wife to Sicily, and I have never seen either of them since."

As Maximilian finished this story he quickly took his hat and slipped out of the room.

From the Memoirs of Herr von Schnabelewopski

CHAPTER I

MY FATHER WAS NAMED SCHNABELEWOPSKI, MY MOTHER SCHNA-
BELEWOPSKA. I was born as legitimate son of both, the 1st of April
1795, in Schnabelewops. My great aunt, the old lady von Pipitzka,
cared for me in my early childhood, and told me pretty tales, and
often sang me to sleep with a song of which I have forgotten both
the words and tune ; but I can never forget the strange, mysterious
way in which she nodded as she sang, and how mournfully her only
tooth, the solitary hermit of her mouth, peeped out. And I can
remember, too, much about the parrot, whose death she so bitterly
bewailed. My old great aunt is dead now herself, and I am the only
one in the world who still thinks of her parrot. Our cat was called
Mimi, and our dog Joli. He had a great knowledge of human nature,
and always got out of the way when I took down my whip. One
morning our servant said that the dog kept his tail rather close
between his legs and let his tongue hang out much more than
usual, for which reason poor Joli was thrown, with some stones
which were tied to his neck, into the water ; on which occasion
he was drowned. Our footman was called Prrschtzztwitsch. To pronounce this name properly one must sneeze at the same time. Our
maid was called Swurtszska, which indeed sounds rather roughly
in German, but which is musical to the last degree in Polish. She
was a stout, thick-set person, with white hair and blonde teeth.
Besides these there was a pair of beautiful black eyes running about
the house, which were called Seraphina. This was my beautiful,
beloved cousin, and we played together in the garden, and watched
the housekeeping of the ants, and caught butterflies and planted
flowers. She laughed once like mad when I planted my little stockings in the earth, believing that they would grow up into a great

pair of breeches for papa.

My father was the best soul in the world, and was long regarded as a very handsome man. He wore powdered hair, and behind a neatly braided little queue, which did not hang down, but was fastened with a little tortoise-shell comb to one side. His hands were of a dazzling whiteness, and I often kissed them. It seems as if I could still smell their sweet perfume, which made my eyes tingle. I loved my father dearly, and it never came into my mind that he could ever die.

My paternal grandfather was the old Herr von Schnabelewopski, and all I know of him is that he was a man, and my father was his son. My maternal grandfather was the old Herr von Wlrssrnski (sneeze again to pronounce this name correctly), and he is painted in a scarlet velvet coat, with a long sword, and my mother often told me that *he* had a friend who wore a green silk coat, rose-silk breeches, and white silk stockings, who swung his little chapeau-bas here and there in a rage when he spoke of the King of Prussia.

My mother, Lady von Schnabelewopska, gave me as I grew up a good education. She had read much: before my birth she read Plutarch almost exclusively, and was probably deeply impressed by one of his great men, perhaps one of the Gracchi. Hence my mystical yearning to realise the agrarian law in a modern form. My deep sympathy for freedom and equality is probably due to these maternal pre-lectures. Had she read the life of Cartouche I had possibly become a great banker. How often as a boy did I play truant from school to reflect on the beautiful meadows of Schnabelewopska how to benefit all mankind. For this I was often well scolded and punished as an idler, and so had to suffer with grief and pain for my schemes for benefiting the world. The neighborhood of Schnabelewops is, I may mention, very beautiful. There is a little river running there in which one can bathe in the summertime very agreeably, and there are the most delightful birds' nests in the copses along the banks. Old Gnesen, the former capital of Poland, is only three miles distant. There, in the cathedral, Saint Adalbert is buried. There is his silver sarcophagus, on which lies his very image, the size of life, with bishop's mitre and crosier, the hands piously folded—and all of molten silver! How often have I thought of thee, thou silver saint! Ah, how often my thoughts go back to Poland, and I stand once more in the cathedral of Gnesen, leaning on the column by the grave of Adalbert! Then the organ peals once more, as if the organist were trying a piece from Allegri's Miserere; a mass is being murmured in a distant chapel, the last rays of the sun shine through the many-colored glass windows, the church is empty, only there lies before the silver shrine a praying figure—a woman of wondrous beauty—who casts at me a sudden side glance, which she turns as suddenly again towards the saint, and murmurs with yearning, cunning lips, " I pray to *thee* !"

In the instant in which I heard those words, the sacristan rang his bell in the distance, the organ pealed as with extreme haste like a rising tide, the beautiful woman rose from the steps of the altar, cast her veil over her blushing face, and left the cathedral.

" I pray to thee !" Were these words addressed to me or to the silver Adalbert? Truly she had turned to him, but only her face. What was the meaning of that side-glance which she first threw at *me*, whose rays flashed over my soul like a long ray of light which the moon pours over a midnight sea when it breaks from a dark cloud, and in an instant is seen no more? In my soul, which was dark as such a sea, that gleam of light woke all the wild forms which lurk in the abyss, and the maddest sharks and sword-fish of passion darted upward and tumbled together, and bit one another in the tails for ecstasy, and over it all the organ roared and stormed more terribly, like a great tempest on the Northern Sea.

The next day I left Poland.

CHAPTER II

MY MOTHER PACKED MY TRUNK HERSELF. WITH EVERY SHIRT SHE put in a bit of moral advice. In after times the washerwomen got away with all my shirts, and morals too. My father was deeply moved, and gave me a long slip of paper, on which he had written out, precept by precept, how I was to behave in the world. The first article announced that I was to turn every ducat ten times before I spent it. I followed this advice at first ; after a while the constant turning became tiresome. With every item of advice I received a ducat. Then he took scissors, cut the queue from his dear head, and gave it to me for a souvenir. I have it yet, and never fail to weep when I see the powdered delicate hair.

The night before I left I had the following dream : —

I wandered alone in a cheerful, beautiful place by the sea-side. It was noon, and the sun shone on the water, which sparkled like diamonds. Here and there on the beach grew a great aloe, which lifted its green arms, as if imploring, to the sunny heaven. There stood a weeping willow with its long hanging tresses, which rose and fell as the waves came playing up, so that it looked like a young water-spirit letting down her green locks, or raising them to hear the better what the wooing sprites of the air were whispering to her. And, indeed, it often sounded like sighs and tender murmurs. The sea gleamed more beautifully and tenderly, the waves rang more musically, and on the rustling, glittering waves rose the holy Adalbert, as I had seen him in the Gnesen Cathedral, with the silver crosier in his silver hand, the silver mitre on his silver head, and he beckoned to me with his hand, and nodded to me with his head, and at last, as he stood before me, he cried with an unearthly silver voice——

Yes ; but I could not hear the words for the rustling of the waves. I believe, however, that my silver rival mocked me, for I stood a long time on the strand, and wept till the twilight came, and heaven and earth became sad and pale, and mournful beyond all measure. Then the flood rose — aloe and willow cracked and were wafted away by the waves, which ran back many times in haste, and came bursting up ever more wildly, rolling and embracing terribly in snow-white half rings. But then I began to perceive a noise in measured time, like the beat of oars, and there came a boat driven along by the waves. In it sat four white forms, with sallow, corpse faces, wrapped in shrouds, rowing with energy. In the midst stood a pale but infinitely beautiful woman, infinitely

155

lovely and delicate, as if made from lily-perfume, and she sprang ashore. The boat with its spectral rowmen shot like an arrow back into the rising sea, and in my arms lay Panna Jadviga, who wept and laughed, " I pray to thee!"

CHAPTER III

MY FIRST FLIGHT AFTER LEAVING SCHNABELEWOPS WAS TOWARDS Germany, and, indeed, to Hamburg, where I remained six months, instead of going directly to Leyden and applying myself, as my parents wished, to the study of theology. I must confess that during that half-year I was much more occupied with worldly than with heavenly affairs.

Hamburg is a good city, all of solid, respectable houses. It is not the infamous Macbeth who governs here, but Banko. The spirit of Banko rules and pervades this little free city, whose visible head is a high and very wise Senate. In fact it is a free state, and we find in it the greatest political freedom. The citizens can do what they please, and the high and very wise Senate acts as it likes. Every one is lord of his own deeds — it is a true republic. If Lafayette had not been so fortunate as to find Louis Philippe he would certainly have recommended the Senate and supervisors of Hamburg to his French fellow-citizens. Hamburg is the best republic. Its manners are English, and its cookery is heavenly. There are, in sober truth, between the Wandrahmen and the Dreckwall, dishes to be found of which our philosophers have no conception. The Hamburgers are good people who enjoy good eating. They are much divided as regards religion. politics, and science, but they are all beautifully agreed as to cooking. Their theologians may quarrel as much as they like over the Lord's Supper, but there is no difference as to the daily dinner. Though there be among the Jews there one division who give grace or the prayer at table in German, while others chant it in Hebrew, they both eat heartily and agree heartily as to what is on the table, and judge its merits with unfailing wisdom.

156

The lawyers, the turnspits of the law, who turn and twist it till at last they get a roast for themselves, may dispute as to whether feeing and pleading shall be publicly conducted or not, but they are all one as to the merits of feeding, and every one of them has his own favorite dish. The army is naturally of Spartan bravery, but it will not hear of black broth. The physicians vary much in treating disorders, and cure the national illness—indigestion—as Brownists, by giving still greater helpings of dried beef ; or, as homeopathists, by administering 1/10,000th of a drop of absinthe in a great tureen of mock-turtle soup—but all practise alike when it comes to discussing the soup and the smoked beef themselves. Of this last dish Hamburg is the paternal city, and boasts of it as Mainz boasts of John Faust, or Eisleben of Martin Luther. But what is the art of printing or the Reformation compared to smoked beef! There are two parties in Germany who are at variance as to whether the latter have done good or harm, but the most zealous Jesuits are united in declaring that smoked beef is a good invention, wholesome for humanity.

Hamburg was founded by Charlemagne and is inhabited by eighty thousand small people, none of whom would change with the great man who now lies buried in Aix la Chapelle. The population of the city may amount to one hundred thousand, I am not quite sure, though I walked whole days in its streets to look at the people. It is very possible that many men escaped my attention, as I was particularly occupied with looking at the women. The latter I found were by no means lean ; on the contrary, they were generally corpulent, and now and then charmingly beautiful—on the whole, of a flourishing, sensuous quality, which, by Venus! did not displease me. If they do not manifest much wild and dreamy idealism in romantic love, and have little conception of the grand passion of the heart, it is not so much their fault as that of Cupid, who often aims at them his sharpest arrows, but from mischief or unskilfulness shoots too low, and instead of the heart hits them in the stomach. As for the men, I saw among them mostly short figures, calmly reasoning cold glances, low foreheads, carelessly heavy hanging red cheeks, the eating apparatus being remarkably well developed, the hat as if nailed to the head, and the hands in both breeches' pockets, as though their owner would say, " How much must I pay, then?"

Among the lions of Hamburg we find —

1. The old Council House, or Town Hall, where the great Hamburg bankers are chiseled out of stone, and stand counterfeited with scepters and globes of empire in their hands.

2. The Exchange, where the sons of Hammonia assemble every day, as did the Romans of old in the Forum, and where there hangs overhead a black tablet of honor, with the names of distinguished fellow-citizens.

3. The Beautiful Marianne, an extremely handsome woman, on whom the tooth of Time has gnawed for twenty years. By the way, " tooth of time " is a bad metaphor, for Time is so old that by this time he cannot have a tooth left, while Marianne has all of hers, and hair on them at that.

4. That which was once the Central Treasury.

5. Altona.

6. The original manuscripts of Marr's Tragedies.

7. The owner of the Röding Museum.

8. The Borsenhalle or Stock Exchange.

9. The Bacchus Hall.

10. And, finally, the City Theater.

This last deserves to be specially praised. Its members are all good citizens, honorable fathers of families, who never let themselves be substituted or disguised, and never act so as to deceive anybody for an instant — men who make of the theater a church, since they convince the unhappy man who has lost faith in humanity, in the most actual manner possible, that all things in this world are not delusion and a counterfeit. In enumerating the remarkable things in Hamburg, I cannot refrain from mentioning that in my time the Hall of Apollo, on the Drehbahn, was a very brilliant place. Now it has very much come down, and philharmonic concerts, and shows by professors of legerdemain, are there given, and professors of natural history are fed. Once it was different. The trumpets pealed, the drums rattled and rolled loudly, ostrich feathers fluttered, and Heloise and Minka ran the races of the Oginski polonaise, and everything was so perfectly respectable! Sweet time it was for me when fortune smiled. And this *fortune* was called Heloise. She was a charming, loving, pleasure-giving treasure, with rosy lips, a little lily nose, warm, perfumed carnation lips, and eyes like blue mountain lakes, albeit there was something of stupidity on her brow, which hung there like a gloomy cloud over a brilliant spring landscape. She was slender as a poplar, lively as a dove, with a skin delicate as an infant's. Sweet time when Fortune ever smiled on me! Minka did not laugh so much, not having such beautiful teeth ; but her tears were all the lovelier when she wept, which she did on all occasions for suffering humanity ; and she was benevolent beyond belief. She gave the poor her last penny — yes, for charity's sake, I have known her to be reduced to the last shift. She was so good that she refused nothing to anybody, save that which was indeed beyond her gift. This soft and yielding character contrasted charmingly with her personal appearance, which was that of a brave Juno — a bold, white neck, shaded by wild black ringlets, like voluptuous snakes ; eyes which flashed forth as if ruling the world from under glooming arches of victory ; purple, proud, high-curving lips ; marble white commanding hands, somewhat freckled ; and she had on her right side a birthmark in the form of a small dagger.

If I have brought you into socalled bad company, dear reader, console yourself with the reflection that it does not cost you so much as it did me. However, there will be no want, further on in this book, of ideal women — and just here I will give you a specimen, just to cheer you up, of two highly decent dames, whom I learned in those days to know and honor. These were Mrs. Peiper and Mrs. Schnieper. The first was a handsome woman in full maturity, with great blackish eyes, a great white forehead, false black hair, a bold, old Roman nose, and a mouth which was a guillotine for every good name. Indeed there could be no contrivance equal to that mouth for the speedy execution and death of a reputation. There was no prolonged struggle, no long-delayed preparation, if the best of characters once got between her teeth she smiled, but that smile was the fall of the axe, and honor was decapitated and the head rolled into the bag. She was always a pattern of propriety, honor, piety, and virtue. The same may be said in celebration of Mrs. Schnieper. She was a tender woman, with a little anxious bosom, generally curtained with a mournful thin gauze or crape, light blonde hair, and clear blue eyes, which gleamed in a frightfully crafty manner out of her white face. People said you could never hear her footfall, and indeed ere you knew it she often stood close by, and then vanished as silently as she came. Her smile, too, was death to any decent reputation, but less like the fall of an axe than the poison wind of Africa, before whose breath all flowers perish ; so in the breath of this woman's voice every good name perished miserably as she smiled. Also a pattern of piety, propriety, honor, and virtue.

I shall not fail to exalt many of the sons of Hammonia, nor to praise in the highest certain men who are grandly esteemed — *videlicet*, those who are rated at several million marks *banco* — but just at present I will subdue my enthusiasm, that it may after a time flame up all the higher. For I have nothing less in my mind than to raise a temple of honor to Hamburg, according to the same plan which was sketched out some ten years ago by a celebrated man of letters, who with this intention requested every Hamburger to send him a specified inventory of his virtues and talents — with one dollar, specie — as soon as possible. I have never exactly understood why this temple of honor never appeared. Some say that the entrepreneur, or the man of honor who kept the temple, had hardly printed from — *Aaron* to *Abendroth* — and only got in his first quoins, before he broke down under the weight of copy or biography sent in ; others say that the very high and wise Senate, moved by excess of modesty, frustrated the project altogether, since they requested this architect of his own temple of honor to be out of Hamburg with all his virtues within twenty-four hours. Anyhow, from some cause or other, the work was never completed; and as I have an inborn yearning to do something great in this world, and have ever striven after the impossible, therefore I have revived this vast project, and will myself manufacture a great temple of honor to Hamburg, an immortal and colossal *book*, in

which I will describe without exception all its inhabitants—
wherein shall appear noble traits of secret charity which were
never mentioned in a newspaper, traits of such grandeur that
nobody will believe a word of them, to be preceded by a magnificent portrait of myself, as I appear when I sit on the Jungfernsteg
before the Swiss Pavilion, and muse over the magnificence of
Hamburg. This will be the vignette of my immortal work.

CHAPTER IV

FOR READERS WHO DO NOT KNOW HAMBURG—THERE ARE SUCH,
I suppose, in China or Upper Bavaria—I must remark that the most
beautiful promenade of the sons and daughters of Hammonia bears
the appropriate name of Jungfernsteg, and that it consists of an
avenue of lime-trees, which is bounded on one side by a row of
houses, and on the other by the Alster Basin, and that before the
latter, and built out into the water, are two tent-like pleasant cafés,
called pavilions. It is nice to sit, especially before one called the
Swiss Pavilion, of a summer day, when the afternoon sun is not
too hot, but only smiles gaily and pours its rays as in a fairy dream
over the lindens, the houses, the people, the Alster, and the swans,
who cradle themselves in it. Yes, it is nice to sit there ; and even
so I sat on many a summer afternoon and thought, as a young man
generally does, that is to say, about nothing at all, and looked at
what a young man generally looks at, that is, the girls—yes, there
they fluttered along, the charming things, with their winged caps,
and covered baskets, containing nothing ; there they tripped, the
gay Vierlander maids, who provide all Hamburg with strawberries
and their own milk, and whose petticoats are still much too long ;
there swept proudly along the beautiful merchants' daughters, with
whose love one gets just so much ready money ; there skipped a
nurse bearing on her arm a rosy boy, whom she constantly kissed
while thinking of her lover ; there wandered too the priestesses of
Venus Aphrodite, Hanseatic vestals, Dianas on the hunt, Naiads,

Dryads, Hamydryads, and similar clergymen's daughters ; and ah! there with them Minka and Heloise! How oft I sat in that pavilion fair and saw her wandering past in rose-striped gown — it cost four shillings and threepence a yard, and Mr. Seligmann gave me his word that even though washed the color would not fade. " What glorious girls!" exclaimed the virtuous youths who sat by me. I remember how a great insurance agent, who was always bedecked like a carnival ox, said, " I'd like to have one of them for breakfast, and the other for supper, just at will, and I don't think I should want any dinner that day." " She is an angel!" cried a sea-captain, so loudly that both the damsels at a glance looked jealously at one another. I myself said nothing, and thought my sweetest nothings, and looked at the girls and the pleasant gentle sky, and the tall Petri tower with its slender waist, and the calm blue Alster, on which the swans swam so proud, and beautiful, and secure. The swans! I could look at them for hours — the lovely creatures, with their soft, long necks, as they so voluptuously cradled themselves on the soft flood, diving in and out, and proudly splashing till the heaven grew dark and the golden stars came forth yearning, hope-giving, wondrously and beautifully tender and transformed. The stars! Are they golden flowers on the bridal bosom of heaven? Are they the eyes of enamored angels, who with yearning mirror themselves in the blue streams of earth below and vie with the swans?

Ah! that is all long, long ago. Then I was young and foolish. Now I am old and foolish. Many a flower has withered since that time, and many too been trodden into earth ; even the rose-striped stuff of Seligmann has lost the color warranted to wash. He has faded himself ; the firm is now Seligmann's blessed widow's. And Heloise, the gentle creature who seemed to be made to walk only on soft Indian flowered carpets and be fanned with peacock's feathers, went down among roaring sailors, punch, tobacco-smoke, and bad music. When I again saw Minka she had changed her name to Katinka, and dwelt between Hamburg and Altona ; she looked like the temple of Solomon after it had been destroyed by Nebu-chadnezzar, and smelt of Assyrian tobacco ; and as she told of

Heloise's death, she wept bitterly and tore her hair in despair, and fainted quite away ; nor did she recover till she had swallowed a great glass of spirits.

And how the town itself was changed! And the Jungfernsteg! Snow lay on the roofs, and it seemed as if the houses had grown old and had white hair. The lime trees of the Jungfernsteg were dead trees and dry boughs, which waved ghost-like in the cold wind. The sky was as a knife blue and soon grew dark. It was five o'clock on Sunday—the general hour for foddering—and the carriages rolled along. Gentlemen and ladies descended from them with frozen smiles upon their hungry lips. How horrible! At that instant I was thrilled with the awful thought that an unfathomable idiocy appeared in all these faces, and that all persons who passed by seemed bewildered in a strange delirium. Twelve years before, at the same hour, I had seen them with the same faces, like the puppets of a town-hall clock, with the same gestures ; and since then they had gone on in the same old way, reckoning and going on 'Change and assisting one another, and moving their jawbones, and paying their *pourboires*, and counting up again : twice two is four. Horrible! I cried. Suppose that it should suddenly occur to one of these people while he sat on the office stool *that twice two is five !* and that he consequently has been multiplying wrongly all his life, and so wasted that life in an awful error. All at once a foolish delirium seized me, and, as I regarded the passersby more nearly, it seemed to me as if they were themselves nothing but ciphers or Arabic numerals. There went a crook-footed Two by a fatal Three, his full-bosomed, encient spouse ; behind them came Mr. Four on crutches, waddling along came a fatal Five, then with round belly and a little hood a well-known little Six, and the still better known Evil Seven ; but as I looked more closely at the wretched Eight as it tottered past I recognised in it the insurance agent who once went adorned like a carnival ox, but who now looked like the leanest of Pharoah's lean kine—pale, hollow cheeks, like an empty soup-plate ; a cold, red nose, like a winter rose ; a shabby black coat, which had a pitiful white shine ; a hat into which Saturn with the scythe had cut air-holes ; but his boots were polished like looking-glasses, and he no longer seemed to think about devouring Heloise and Minka for breakfast and supper, but to be longing very much more for a good dinner of common beef. And I recognized many an old friend among the mere ciphers who rolled along. So these and the rest of the numerical folk drove by hurried and hungry, while more grimly droll a funeral passed not far off, past the houses of the Jungfernsteg. As a melancholy, masquerading show there walked on after the hearse, stilted on their little, thin, black silk legs, the well-known council-servants, the priviliged civic mourners, in a parodied old Burgundian costume, short black cloaks and black plumped breeches, white wigs, and cravats, out of which the red mercenary faces stared comically, short steel rapiers on their hips, with green umbrellas under their arms.

But more uncanny and bewildering than these figures which went silently by were the sounds which rang in my ears from the other side. They were shrill, harsh, creaking, metallic tones, a crazy screeching, a painful splashing and despairing gulping, a gasping and tumbling, and groaning and wailing bitterly — an indescribable ice-cold cry of pain. The basin of the Alster was frozen up, only that near the shore was a large square cut in the ice, and the terrible tones which I had heard came from the wind-pipes of the poor white creatures which swam round in it, and screeched in horrible agony ; and oh, they were the same swans who once had cheered my heart so softly and merrily. Ah! the beautiful white swans! Their wings had been broken to prevent them from flying in the autumn to the warm South, and now the North held them fast bound, fast banned in its dark, icy grave, and the waiter of the Pavilion said they were all right, in there, and that the cold was good for them. But it was not true ; it is not good for anybody to be imprisoned, powerless, in a cold pool almost frozen, with the wings broken so that one cannot fly away to the beautiful South, with its beautiful flowers, golden sunlight, and blue mountain lakes. Ah! with me it was little better, and I understood the suffering of these poor swans, and as it ever grew darker and the stars came out bright above, the same stars who once so

warm with love wooed the swans on fair summer nights, but who
now looked down with frosty brilliancy, and almost scornfully,
on them. Ah! I now perceive that the stars are no living, sympathetic beings, but only gleaming phantasms of night, eternal
delusions in a dreamed heaven—mere golden lies in dark blue
Nothingness.

CHAPTER V

WHILE WRITING THE FOREGOING CHAPTER I THOUGHT INVOLUN-
TARILY of something quite different. An old song was humming in
my memory, and forms and thoughts confused themselves most
intolerably, and, willy nilly, I must speak of it. Perhaps it really
belongs here, and is right in forcing itself into my scribbling. Ah,
yes! now I begin to understand it, and also to understand the
mysterious tone in which Klas Hinrichson sang it. He was a Jut-
lander, and served as our groom. He sang it the very evening before
he hung himself in our stable. At the refrain—

> Sir Vonved, look about thee!

he often laughed bitterly, the horses neighed in alarm, and the
great dog in the courtyard howled as though some one were dying.
It is the old Danish song of Sir Vonved, who rides out into the
world, and adventures about till all his riddles are answered, and
he in vexed mood returns home. The harp sings in it as refrain
from beginning to end. But what did he sing first and last? I have
often thought thereon. Klas Hinrichson's voice was many a time
subdued by tears when he began the ballad, and then became
gradually as rough and growling as the sea when a storm is rising.
It begins:

> Sir Vonved sits in his room alway,
> Well on his gold harp he can play;
> He hides the gold harp beneath his cloak,
> His mother entered, and thus she spoke:
> "Sir Vonved, look about thee!"

That was his mother Adeline the Queen. She said to him, " My son, let others play the harp. Gird on thy sword, mount thy horse, try thy courage, strive and strain, see the world ere thou turn again! Sir Vonved, look about thee!' "

Sir Vonved binds his sword to his side,
To battle with warriors he will ride ;
Strange was his journey and intent,
For no man knew the way he went.
    Sir Vonved, look about thee!

His helmet was blinking,
His spurs were clinking,
His horse was springing,
In saddle bow swinging!
    Sir Vonved, look about thee!

He rode one day and then days three,
Yet never a city could he see.
" Ha!" said the youth, " on either hand,
Is there no city in this land?"
    Sir Vonved, look about thee!

And as he went the road along,
There came to him Sir Thüle Väng,
Sir Thüle Väng, with many a son ;
They were good warriors every one.
    Sir Vonved, look about thee!

" My youngest son, hear what I say!
Our armor we must change to-day ;
My harness must be worn by thee,
Before we fight this hero free."
    Sir Vonved, look about thee!

Sir Vonved draws his sword from his side,
Against the warriors he will ride ;
Lord Thüle first of all he slew,
Then all of his twelve sons thereto.
    Sir Vonved, look about thee!

Sir Vonved binds his sword to his side, and rides on. Then he meets a hunter, and will have half his game. But the man refuses, and must fight, and is slain. And

166

Sir Vonved binds his sword to his side,
And onward ever he will ride;
O'er mountain high, and river deep,
To where a shepherd guards his sheep.
    Sir Vonved, look about thee!

And to the herd as he drew near,
Said, "Whose the flock thou drivest here?
And what is rounder than a wheel?
And where is the merriest Christmas meal?"
    Sir Vonved, look about thee!

"Say where the fish rests in the flood?
And where is the red bird so good?
Where is the best wine made or sold?
Where does Vidrich drink with his warriors bold?"
    Sir Vonved, look about thee!

The herd was silent as could be,
Of all of this no word knew he;
Then at a stroke the herd he slew,
Liver and lung he cleft in two.
    Sir Vonved, look about thee!

Then he came to another flock, and there sat another shepherd, whom he also questioned. This one answers wisely, and Sir Vonved takes a gold ring and puts it on the shepherd's arm. Then he rides further, and comes to Tyge Nold, and slays him with his twelve sons. And, further—

With his horse he rode and ran,
Sir Vonved, the young nobleman,
O'er rocks can ride and rivers swim,
But found no man to talk with him.
    Sir Vonved, look about thee!

He came unto the third, and there
Sat an old man with silver hair:
"List thou, good shepherd, with thy herd,
I deem thou'lt wisely speak a word."
    Sir Vonved, look about thee!

"Oh, what is rounder than a wheel?
Where is the merriest Christmas meal?
Where goes the sun across the sky?
And where do the feet of a dead man lie?"
    Sir Vonved, look about thee!

" What filleth up the valleys all?
What garb is best in royal hall?
What crieth louder than the crane?
And what is whiter than the swan?"
    Sir Vonved, look about thee!

" Who wears his beard on the back, or in?
Who bears his nose beneath his chin?
And what is blacker than a bolt?
Or faster than a frightened colt?"
    Sir Vonved, look about thee!

" Say where the broadest bridge may be,
And what do men most hate to see ;
Where is the highest road alone?
And where the coldest drink that's known?"
    Sir Vonved, look about thee!

" The sun is rounder than a wheel,
In heaven the merriest Christmas meal ;
The sun forever seeks the west,
Towards east the feet of a dead man rest."
    Sir Vonved, look about thee!

" The snow fills up the valleys all,
Courage beseems a royal hall ;
Thunder is louder than the crane,
And angels whiter than the swan."
    Sir Vonved, look about thee!

" The plover's beard on his neck hath grown,
The bear hath his nose 'neath his chin, alone ;
Sin is blacker than a bolt,
And thought flies faster than a colt."
    Sir Vonved, look about thee!

" No broader bridge than ice can be,
The toad is what man most hates to see ;
To heaven's the highest road I think,
And in hell they brew the coldest drink."
    Sir Vonved, look about thee!

" Thy answers are as shrewd, I see,
As the questions which I put to thee ;
I trust thee well, and will be bound
Thou knowest where heroes may be found."
    Sir Vonved, look about thee!

"The Sonderburg is over there,
Where knights drink mead withouten fear ;
There are many kempé and warriors known,
Who well in battle can hold their own."
    Sir Vonved, look about thee !

A golden armlet he unwound,
It weighed, I ween, full fifteen pound ;
He placed it in the shepherd's belt,
For showing him where the warriors dwelt.
    Sir Vonved, look about thee !

Then he rode unto the castle, and slew first Randulf and next Strandulf.

He slew strong Ege Under, another,
He slew the Ege Karl his brother ;
So right and left his sword blows fall,
To right and left he slew them all.
    Sir Vonved, look about thee !

Sir Vonved puts his sword in the sheath,
He rides afar o'er the gloomy heath ;
In the wild mark he found, ere long,
A warrior, and he was strong.
    Sir Vonved, look about thee !

"Tell me, thou noble rider good,
Where does the fish stay in the flood?
Where is the noblest wine of all?
Where does Vidrich drink with his lords in hall?"
    Sir Vonved, look about thee !

"In the east the fish stays in the flood,
In the north they drink the wine so good ;
In Holland thou findest Vidrich alone,
With knights and warriors many a one."
    Sir Vonved, look about thee !

From his breast he took an armlet bright,
And gave it to the other knight :
"Say that thou wert the very last man,
Who ever gold from Sir Vonved wan."
    Sir Vonved, look about thee !

Herr Vonved did to a castle ride,
And bid the porter open wide ;
He shut the gate, the bolt he drew,
Over the wall Sir Vonved flew.
    Sir Vonved, look about thee !

His good horse with a rope he bound,
His way to the castle-hall he found ;
He sat him at the table free ;
Never a word to man spake he.
    Sir Vonved, look about thee!

He ate, he drank, he broke his bread,
Unto the king no word he said :
"Never I heard before a king,
So much accursèd chattering!"
    Sir Vonved, look about thee!

The king said to his knights all round,
"The crazy fellow must be bound ;
Unless ye bind the stranger tight,
I ween your service is but slight."
    Sir Vonved, look about thee!

"Take five, take twenty, knights, I say,
Come thou thyself into the play ;
A whoreson name I give to thee,
Unless by force thou bindest me."
    Sir Vonved, look about thee!

"King Esmer, the father mine,
And my mother, proud Adeline,
Unto me have often told,
With a knave eat not thy gold."
    Sir Vonved, look about thee!

"Was Esmer father then of thine,
And thy mother proud Adeline,
Then thou'rt Vonved, the knight well known,
Also my own dear sister's son."
    Sir Vonved, look about thee!

"Sir Vonved, wilt thou stay with me?
Much honor shall be given thee ;
But if away thou will'st to ride,
Many a knight shall go beside."
    Sir Vonved, look about thee!

"All my gold to thee I give,
If thou here with me wilt live."
Sir Vonved would not have it so,
Back to his mother he will go.
    Sir Vonved, look about thee!

Sir Vonved rode along his way,
Grim he was in his soul that day ;
Ere he to the castle rode,
Witches twelve before him stood.
      Sir Vonved, look about thee !

With their rock and reel they came before,
And smote him on the knee full sore ;
He made his charger leap and spring,
He slew the twelve all in a ring.
      Sir Vonved, look about thee !

He slew the witches as they stood,
From him they got right little good ;
He slew his mother with them all,
Cut her in thousand pieces small.
      Sir Vonved, look about thee !

In his hall sits Vonved bold,
He drinks the wine so clear and cold ;
He played on his gold harp so long,
That all the strings asunder sprang.
      Sir Vonved, look about thee.

CHAPTER VI

IT WAS A CHARMING SPRING DAY WHEN I FIRST LEFT HAMBURG. I CAN still see how in the harbor the golden sunrays gleamed on the tarry bellies of the ships, and think I still hear the joyous, long-drawn *Ho-i-ho !* of the sailors. Such a port in spring-time has a pleasant similarity with the feelings of a youth who goes for the first time out into the world on the great ocean of life. All his thoughts are gaily variegated, pride swells every sail of his desires — *ho-i-ho !* But soon a storm rises, the horizon grows dark, the wind howls, the planks crack, the waves break the rudder, and the poor ship is wrecked on romantic rocks, or stranded on damp, prosaic sand-banks ; or perhaps, brittle and broken, with its masts gone, and without an anchor of hope, it returns to its old harbor, and there molders away, wretchedly unrigged, as a miserable wreck.

But there are men who cannot be compared to common ships, because they are like steamboats. They carry a gloomy fire within, and sail against wind and weather ; their smoky banner streams behind, like the black plume of the Wild Huntsman ; their zig-zagged wheels remind one of weighty spurs with which they prick the ribs of the waves, and the obstinate, resistant element must obey their will like a steed ; but sometimes the boiler bursts, and the internal fire burns us up !

But now I will escape from metaphor, and get on board a real ship bound from Hamburg to Amsterdam. It was a Swedish vessel, and besides the hero of these pages, was also loaded with iron, being destined probably to bring as a return freight a cargo of cod-fish to the aristocracy of Hamburg, or owls to Athens.

The banks of the Elbe are charming, especially so behind Altona, near Rainville. There Klopstock lies buried. I know of no place where a dead poet could more fitly rest. To exist there as a *living* poet is, of course, a much more difficult matter. How often have I sought thy grave, oh Singer of the Messiah, thou who hast sung with such touching truthfulness the sufferings of Jesus. But thou didst dwell long enough on the Königstrasse behind the Jungfern-steg to know how prophets are crucified.

On the second day we came to Cuxhaven, which is a colony from Hamburg. The inhabitants are subjects of the Republic, and have a good time of it. When they freeze in winter woolen blankets are sent to them, and when the summer is all too hot they are supplied with lemonade. A high or very wise senator resides there as pro-consul. He has an income of twenty thousand marks, and rules over five thousand subjects. There is also a sea-bath, which has the great advantage over all others, that it is at the same time an Elbe-bath. A great dam, on which one can walk, leads to Ritzebuttel, which also belongs to Cuxhaven. The term is derived from the Phœnician, as *Ritze* and *Buttel* signify in it the mouth of the Elbe. Many historians maintain that Charlemagne only enlarged Ham-burg, but that the Phœnicians founded it about the time that Sodom and Gomorrah were destroyed, and it is not unlikely that fugitives from these cities fled to the mouth of the Elbe. Between the

Fuhlentwiete and the coffee factory men have found old money, coined during the reign of Bera XVI. and Byrsa X. I believe that Hamburg is the old Tarsus whence Solomon received whole shiploads of gold, silver, ivory, peacocks, and monkeys. Solomon, that is, the king of Judah and Israel, always had a special fancy for gold and monkeys.

This my first voyage can never be forgotten. My old grand-aunt had told me many tales of the sea, which now rose to new life in my memory. I could sit for hours on the deck recalling the old stories, and when the waves murmured it seemed as if I heard my grand-aunt's voice. And when I closed my eyes I could see her before me, as she twitched her lips and told the legend of the Flying Dutchman.

I should have been glad to see some mermaids, such as sit on white rocks and comb their sea-green hair ; but I only heard them singing.

However earnestly I gazed many a time down into the transparent water, I could not behold the sunken cities, in which mortals enchanted into fishy forms lead a deep, a marvelous deep, and hidden ocean life. They say that salmon and old rays sit there, dressed like ladies, at their windows, and, fanning themselves, look down into the street, where cod-fish glide by in trim councilors' costume, and dandy young herrings look up at them through eye-glasses, and crabs, lobsters, and all kinds of such common crustaceans, swarm swimming about. I could never see so deep ; I only heard the faint bells of the sunken cities peal once more their old melodious chime.

Once by night I saw a great ship with outspread blood-red sails go by, so that it seemed like a dark giant in a scarlet cloak. Was that the *Flying Dutchman ?*

But in Amsterdam, where I soon arrived, I saw the grim Mynheer bodily, and that on the stage. On this occasion, in the theater of that city, I also had an opportunity to make the acquaintance of one of those fairies whom I had sought in vain in the sea. And to her, as she was particularly charming, I will devote a special chapter.

CHAPTER VII

YOU CERTAINLY KNOW THE FABLE OF THE *Flying Dutchman*. IT IS the story of an enchanted ship which can never arrive in port, and which since time immemorial has been sailing about at sea. When it meets a vessel, some of the unearthly sailors come in a boat and beg the others to take a packet of letters home for them. These letters must be nailed to the mast, else some misfortune will happen to the ship — above all if no Bible be on board, and no horse-shoe nailed to the foremast. The letters are always addressed to people whom no one knows, and who have long been dead, so that some late descendant gets a letter addressed to a far away great-great-grandmother, who has slept for centuries in her grave. That timber specter, that grim grey ship, is so called from the captain, a Hollander, who once swore by all the devils that he would get round a certain mountain, whose name has escaped me, in spite of a fearful storm, though he should sail till the Day of Judgement. The devil took him at his word, therefore he must sail for ever, until set free by a woman's truth. The devil in his stupidity has no faith in female truth, and allowed the enchanted captain to land once in seven years and get married, and so find opportunities to save his soul. Poor Dutchman! He is often only too glad to be saved from his marriage and his wife-savior, and get again on board.

The play which I saw in Amsterdam was based on this legend. Another seven years have passed ; the poor Hollander is more weary than ever of his endless wandering ; he lands, becomes intimate with a Scottish nobleman, to whom he sells diamonds for a mere song, and when he hears that his customer has a beautiful daughter, he asks that he may wed her. This bargain also is agreed to. Next we see the Scottish home ; the maiden with anxious heart awaits the bridegroom. She often looks with strange sorrow at a great, time-worn picture which hangs in the hall, and represents a handsome man in the Netherlandish-Spanish garb. It is an old heirloom, and according to a legend of her grandmother, is a true portrait of the Flying Dutchman as he was seen in Scotland a hundred years before, in the time of William of Orange. And with this has come down a warning that the women of the family must beware of the original. This has naturally enough had the result of deeply impressing the features of the picture on the heart of the romantic girl. Therefore, when the man himself makes his appearance, she is startled, but not with fear. He too is moved at beholding the portrait. But when he is informed whose likeness it is, he with tact and easy conversation turns aside all suspicion, jests at the legend, laughs at the Flying Dutchman, the Wandering Jew of the Ocean, and yet, as if moved by the thought, passed into a pathetic mood, depicting how terrible the life must be of one condemned to endure unheard-of tortures on a wild waste of waters — how his body itself is his living coffin, wherein his soul is terribly imprisoned — how life and death alike reject him, like an empty cask scornfully thrown by the sea on the shore, and as contemptuously repulsed again into the sea — how his agony is as deep as the sea on which he sails — his ship without anchor, and his heart without hope.

I believe that these were nearly the words with which the bridegroom ends. The bride regards him with deep earnestness, casting glances meanwhile at his portrait. It seems as if she had penetrated his secret ; and when he afterwards asks, " Katherine, wilt thou be true to me?" she answers, " True to death."

I remember that just then I heard a laugh, and that it came not from the pit but from the gallery of the gods above. As I glanced up I saw a wondrous lovely Eve in Paradise, who looked seductively at me, with great blue eyes. Her arm hung over the gallery, and in her hand she held an apple, or rather an orange. But instead of symbolically dividing it with me, she only metaphorically cast the peel on my head. Was it done intentionally or by accident? That I would know! But when I entered the Paradise to cultivate the acquaintance, I was not a little startled to find a white soft creature, a wonderfully womanly tender being, not languishing, yet delicately clear as crystal, a form of home-like propriety and fascinating amiability. Only that there was something on the left upper lip which curved or twined like the tail of a slippery gliding lizard. It was a mysterious trait, something such as is not found in pure angels, and just as little in mere devils. This expression comes not from evil, but from the *knowledge* of good and evil — it is a smile which has been poisoned or flavored by tasting the Apple of Eden. When I see this expression on soft, full, rosy, ladies' lips, then I feel in my own a cramp-like twitching — a convulsive yearning — to kiss those lips: it is our Affinity.

I whispered into the ear of the beauty : —

" *Yuffrou*, I will kiss thy mouth."

" *Bei Gott, Mynheer!* that is a good idea," was the hasty answer, which rang with bewitching sound from her heart.

But — no. I will here draw a veil over, and end the story or picture of which the Flying Dutchman was the frame. Thereby will I revenge myself on the prurient prudes who devour such narratives with delight, and are enraptured with them to their heart of hearts, *et plus ultra*, and then abuse the narrator, and turn up their noses at him in society, and decry him as immoral. It is a nice story, too, delicious as preserved pineapple or fresh caviar or truffles in Burgundy, and would be pleasant reading after prayers ; but out of spite, and to punish old offences, I will suppress it. Here I make a long dash ——————— which may be supposed to be a black sofa on which we sat as I wooed. But the innocent must suffer with the guilty, and I dare say that many a good soul looks bitterly and reproachfully at me. However, unto these of the better kind I will admit that I was never so wildly kissed as by this Dutch blonde, and that she most triumphantly destroyed the prejudice which I had hitherto held against blue eyes and fair hair. *Now* I understand why an English poet has compared such women to frozen champagne. In the icy crust lies hidden the strongest extract. There is nothing more piquant than the contrast between external cold and the inner fire which, Bacchante-like, flames up and irresistibly intoxicates the happy carouser. Ay, far more than in brunettes does the fire of passion burn in many a sham-calm holy image with golden-glory hair, and blue angel's eyes, and pious lily hands. I knew a blonde of one of the best families in Holland who at times left her beautiful chateau on the Zuyder-Zee and went incognito to Amsterdam, and there in the theater threw orange-peel on the head of any one who pleased her, and gave herself up to the wildest debauchery, like a Dutch Messalina! . . .

When I re-entered the theater, I came in time to see the last scene of the play, where the wife of the Flying Dutchman on a high cliff wrings her hands in despair, while her unhappy husband is seen on the deck of his unearthly ship, tossing on the waves. He loves her, and will leave her lest she be lost with him, and he tells her all his dreadful destiny, and the cruel curse which hangs above his head. But she cries aloud, " I was ever true to thee, and I know how to be ever true unto death!"

Saying this she throws herself into the waves, and then the enchantment is ended. The Flying Dutchman is saved, and we see the ghostly ship slowly sink into the abyss of the sea.

The moral of the play is that women should never marry a Flying Dutchman, while we men may learn from it that one can through women go down and perish — under favorable circumstances!

CHAPTER VIII

IT WAS NOT IN AMSTERDAM ALONE THAT THE GODS WERE SO KIND as to take pains to remove my prejudice against blondes. I had opportunities all over Holland to correct my errors in this respect. By my life! I will not exalt the ladies of Holland at the expense of those of other countries — heaven keep me from such injustice! — which would be in me rank ingratitude. Every country has its own kind of women and its own cookery, and in both it is all a matter of taste. One man likes roast chicken, another roast duck ; as for me, I love both, and roast goose too.

Regarded from the high idealistic standard, women the world over have a wonderful affinity with the *cuisine* or cookery of their country, wherever it be. Are not British beauties now — candidly confessed — just so wholesome, nourishing, solid, substantial, inartistic, and yet so admirable as old England's good and simple food : roast beef, roast mutton, pudding in flaming cognac, vegetables boiled once in water, with only two kinds of gravy, of which one is melted butter. There smiles no *fricassée*, there we are softly deceived by no flattering *vol-au-vent*, there sighs no refined *ragout*, there we are not flirted with and flattered by a thousand kinds of stuffed, boiled, puffed, roasted, sugared, piquant, sentimental, declamatory, declaratory dishes such as we find in a French restaurant, and which have a startling likeness to all beautiful Frenchwomen. Still we might often observe that by all these the real thing itself is only regarded as a secondary affair, that the roast is not worth so much as the gravy, and that here taste, grace, and elegance are the principal and principle.

Does not the golden fat, passionately spiced and flavored, humorously garnished and yet yearning ideal cookery of Italy, express to the life the whole character of Italian beauties? Oh, how I often long for the Lombard *stuffados* and *zampettis*, for the *fegatellis*, *tagliarinis*, and *broccolis* of blessed Tuscany. All swims in oil, delicate and tender, and trills the sweet melodies of Rossini, and weeps from onion perfume and desire. But macaroni must thou eat with thy fingers, and then it is called—Beatrice!

I often think of Italy, and oftenest by night. The day before yesterday. I dreamed that I was there—a checquered harlequin, and lay all lazy under a weeping willow. The hanging sprays of the tree were of macaroni, which fell, long and lovely, into my mouth, and in between, instead of sunrays, flowed sweet streams of golden butter, and at last a fair white rain of powdered Parmesan.

But from the macaroni of which one dreams no one grows fat— Beatrice!

Not a word about German cookery. It has every virtue and only one fault; and what that is I shall not tell. It has deeply feeling, susceptible pastry without decision, enamored eggdishes, admirable steamed dumplings, soul soup with barley, pancakes with apples and pork, virtuous homemade meat balls, and sour cabbage— lucky he who can digest it!

As for the Dutch cookery, it differs from the last, firstly in neatness, secondly by its peculiar relish. The preparation of fish is there indescribably delightful. A perfume of celery, which moves one to the very heart, and is yet deeply intellectual. A self-conscious *naïveté* and garlic.

But when I arrived in Leyden I found the food frightfully bad. The Republic of Hamburg had spoiled me—I must again extol the cookery there, and avail myself of the opportunity to praise the pretty girls and dames of that dear town. Oh, ye divinities! how for the first four weeks did I wish myself back among the smoked-meating houses, the butchers' flesh-world, and the deviltries and the mock turtle-doves of Hammonia! I yearned heart and stomach. If the landlady of the Red Cow had not at last fallen in love with me, I should have died of longing.

Hail to thee, landlady of that Red Cow!

She was a little woman, very plump, with a very little round head. Red little cheeks, little blue eyes, roses and violets. Many an hour we sat side by side in the garden, and drank tea out of real Chinese porcelain cups. It was a beautiful garden, with three and four cornered beds symmetrically strewed with gold sand, cinnabar, and little shining shells. The trunks of the trees were prettily painted red and blue. Copper cages full of canary birds. The most expensive bulbous flowers in variegated and glazed pots. Yew trees charmingly cut into various obelisks, pyramids, vases, and animal forms. Yes, there was a green ox cut from yew, who looked at me jealously when I embraced the lovely landlady of the Red Cow!

Hail to thee, landlady of the Red Cow!

When my frau had covered the upper part of her head with Frisian gold-plates, defended her person with an armor of many-colored stiff, hard, damask silk, and loaded her arms with the white abundance of her Brabant lace, she looked like a fabulous Chinese puppet—say the goddess of porcelain. And when I, enraptured and inspired, kissed her with a loving smack on both cheeks, she sat in porcelain stillness and sighed porce-languishly, "Mynheer!"— then all the tulips in the garden seemed to feel and wave and sigh in sympathy, "Mynheer!"

This delicate *liaison* procured me many delicacies. For every love-scene of the kind had an influence on the market-basket, which brought provisions to the house and to me. My table companions, six other students, could judge to a nicety by the roast veal or *filet-de-bœuf* how much I was loved by the landlady of the Red Cow. When the dinner was bad, then the word was, " Just see how miserably Schnabelewopski looks ! how yellow and wrinkled his face is ; what a cat's melancholy look there is in his eyes, as if they were coming out of his head ; why, it's no wonder that our land-lady is vexed with him and gives us poor food ! " Or else, " Lord help us ! Schnabelewopski is growing weaker and feebler every day, and by and by the landlady will love him no more, and then we shall have short commons every day like this ; we must feed him up well, so as to make him look nice and plump and rosy." And then they forced all the worst of everything there was on me, and compelled me to eat a great deal of celery. But when we had poor fare for several days in succession, then I was besieged with the most passionate prayers for better provender ; to inflame anew the heart of our landlady, to show greater tenderness towards her — in short, to sacrifice myself for the general welfare. It was set before me in long speeches how noble and glorious it was when any one gave himself up heroically for the good of his fellow-citizens, like Regulus, who let himself be put into a spiked barrel, or Theseus, who voluntarily entered the cave of the Minotaur, and then Livy and Plutarch were cited to give examples.

Yes, and I was also pictorially exhorted to rival these examples, by drawing these deeds on the wall, with grotesque variations, for the Minotaur was made to look like the Red Cow on the tavern sign, and the Carthaginian spiked tun like the landlady herself. And those ungrateful youths selected the personal appearance of that excellent woman as a constant butt for their wit. They imitated her round figure with apples, and rolled it up and kneaded its like-ness from breadcrumb. They took a large apple for the body, put a little rosy crabapple on this for the head, and into the former stuck two toothpricks for feet. Or, as I said, they made her from bread-crumb, and then a very little mannikin of the same, which they put on her lap, making the most scandalous remarks. Thus, one said that the smaller figure looked like Hannibal climbing the Alps, while another declared it was more like Marius sitting on the ruins of Carthage. All the same, if I had not climbed those Alps, or seated myself amid those ruins of Carthage, my table companions would have had but sorry fare.

CHAPTER IX

WHEN THE FOOD BECAME VERY BAD INDEED, THEN WE DISPUTED as to the existence of God. But the beneficent Deity always had the majority. Only three of the table society were atheistically inclined, and even they gave way if we had at least good cheese for dessert. The most zealous Theist was one little Simson, and when he disputed with tall Van Pitter as to whether there was a personal God, he became at times wildly excited, and ran up and down the hall crying constantly, "*Bei Gott!* that isn't fair!" Tall Van Pitter, a lean Frisian, whose soul was as calm as the water in a Dutch canal, and whose words followed one another as leisurely as one canal boat after another, drew his arguments from the German philosophy which was at that time very much studied in Leyden. He ridiculed the narrow-minded men who attribute to God a particular private existence ; he even accused them of blasphemy, because they endowed God with wisdom, justice, love, and other human qualities, which are utterly inappropriate, because these are relatively the negations or antithesis of human errors, such as stupidity, injustice, and hate. But when Van Pitter thus developed his own pantheistic views, there came forth against him the fat Fichtean, Dricksen of Utrecht, who stoutly confuted his vague conception of a God spread forth through all Nature — that is to say, existing only in space. Yes, he even declared it was blasphemy to so much as speak of the *existence* of God, since the very idea of existence involved that of space — in short, something substantial. Yes, it was blasphemy even to say of God *He is*, because the purest or most abstract Being could not be conceived without limitations of sense, whereas, if man would think of God, he must abstract Him from all substance, and not think of Him as a form

181

of extension, but as a series or order of developments, God not being an action *per se*, but only the principle of a cosmos beyond conception.

Hearing this little Simson fairly raved, and ran up and down the hall, and cried ever more loudly, " O God, O God! By God, that is not fair, O God!" I believe that he would, in honor of God, have beaten the fat Fichtean, had not his arms been too weak ; but as it was he often attacked him, when the big and burly one would grasp him by his little arms, hold him fast, and without taking the pipe from his mouth, blow his airy arguments, mixed with tobacco smoke, into Simson's face, so that the little man was almost stifled with fume and fret, and wailed more and more pitifully, " O God! O God!" but it availed him naught, though he defended His cause so valiantly.

Despite this divine indifference, despite this almost human unthankfulness, little Simson remained a staunch champion of Theism, as I believe from inborn inclination ; for his father belonged to God's chosen folk, a race which God once very specially protected, and which, in consequence, has maintained till this day a great dependence on him. Jews are ever the most devoted of Deists, especially those who, like little Simson, were born in the vicinity of Frankfort. These may be as republican as they please in political questions — yes, they may roll in the very mud of *sans culottéism* — but the instant that religious ideas are involved they become the humblest servants of their Jehovah, the old fetish, who, however, will know nothing of the entire company, and who has newly baptized himself to a divinely pure spirit.

I believe that this divinely pure spirit, this new ruler of heaven, who is now conceived as so moral, so cosmopolite and universal, takes it ill at heart that the poor Jews, who knew Him in his rude first form, remind him every day in their synagogues of his early and obscure national relations. Perhaps the ancient Lord would fain forget that he was of Palestine origin, and once the God of Abraham, Isaac, and Jacob, and was in those times called Jehovah.

CHAPTER X

WHILE I LIVED AT LEYDEN I SAW A GREAT DEAL OF LITTLE SIMSON,
and he will be often mentioned in these memoirs. Next to him I
met most frequently another of my table friends, young Van
Moeulen. I could look for hours at his perfectly symmetric face,
thinking what his sister, whom I had never seen, must be like. All
that I knew of her was that she was said to be the most beautiful
woman in Waterland. Van Moeulen was also a beautiful human
being, an Apollo, not of marble, but rather of cheese. He was a
strange mixture of force and indifference. Once in a café he so
enraged an Irish gentleman that the latter drew his pistol from his
pocket and fired. Instead of hitting him, he only knocked the clay
pipe from his mouth ; but Van Moeulen's features were as motionless as a cheese and in the calmest, most indifferent tone, he said,
" *Jan, e nüe piep !*" " John, a fresh pipe !" But his smile was intolerable to me, for then he showed a row of very small white teeth,
which looked like a fish spine. Nor did I like it that he wore great
gold ear-rings. He had the strange habit of rearranging every day
the furniture in his rooms, and when a visitor came he was generally found putting his bureau where the bed had been, or making
the study table change places with the sofa.

Little Simson was in this respect his most painfully earnest
antithesis. He could not endure that any one should disturb the
least thing in his room ; he even became restless and disturbed if
one so much as picked up the candle snuffers. Everything must lay
just as it was, for his goods and chattels served him as aids by
means of which, according to the principles of mnemonics, he
fixed all kinds of historical dates or philosophic principles in his
memory. Once when the housemaid carried away from his room
an old chest, and removed his shirts and stockings from the bureau
for the laundress, he was inconsolable when he returned, declaring
that he had lost his whole Assyrian History, and that all his proofs
of the immortality of the soul, which he had arranged so syste-
matically in the drawers, were gone to the wash.

Among the originals whom I learned to know in Leyden belongs

183

Mynheer van Bissen, a cousin of Van Moeulen, who introduced him to me. He was professor of theology at the university, and I attended his lectures on the Canticles of Solomon and the Apocalypse of St. John. He was a fine, flourishing, florid man, perhaps of fifty-five, and in his chair was very staid and serious. But once when I called on him and found no one in his study, I saw through the half-opened door of a side-room a very strange sight. This chamber was furnished in a half-Chinese, half-Pompadour style, with shot-gold damask hangings on the wall, on the ground the most costly Persian carpet, and everywhere marvelous Indian idols, bric-a-brac of mother-of-pearl, flowers, peacock's feathers, and gems, the sofa of red velvet with gold tassels ; and among it all a raised seat, which looked like a throne, on which sat a little girl, perhaps three years old, clad in a silver embroidered blue satin dress of very antiquated fashion. She held in one hand, like a sceptre, a many-colored peacock duster, and in the other a faded wreath of laurel. Before her Mynheer van Bissen was with his little negro page, his poodle, and his monkey, rolling over and over on the ground. They grappled with, tugged and bit one another, while the little girl and a green parrot sitting on its perch cried " Bravo!" At last Mynheer rose from the ground, kneeled before the child, and expressing in a long Latin speech the bravery with which he had fought and conquered his foes, let the little girl crown him with the laurel wreath, while she and the parrot cried " Bravo!" in which I joined as I entered the room.

Mynheer appeared to be somewhat taken aback as I surprised him in his performance. This, I was assured, was his daily amusement ; every day he fought and defeated the little negro, the poodle, and the monkey, and was then crowned by the little girl, who was not, however, his own child, but a foundling from the Orphans' Asylum of Amsterdam.

CHAPTER XI

THE HOUSE IN WHICH I LODGED IN LEYDEN WAS ONCE THE DWELLING of Jan Steen, the great Jan Steen, whom I regard as being as great as Raphael. And he was even his equal as a *religious* painter. That will be clearly seen when the religion of pain and suffering shall have ended, and the religion of joy tear the mournful veil from the rose-bushes of this earth, and the nightingales at last dare pour forth in rapture their long-suppressed notes of pleasure.

But really no nightingale will ever sing so gaily and rejoicingly as Jan Steen has painted. No one ever felt so deeply that, on this earth, life ought to be one endless Kermess. He knew that our life is only a colored kiss of God, and that the Holy Ghost reveals Himself most gloriously in light and laughter.

His eyes looked out into light, and the light mirrored itself in his laughing eyes.

And Jan was always a dear good fellow. When the harsh old preacher of Leyden sat beside him at the hearth, and gave him a long exhortation as to his jovial life, his laughing, un-Christian ways, his drunkenness and ill-regulated domestic life and reprobate merriment, Jan listened to him two long hours without betraying the least impatience at this preaching of punishment, until he at last interrupted him with the words, " Yes, Dominie, but the light would be much better — yes — I beg you, Dominie, just turn your stool a little round to the fire, so that your face may get a redder tone, while the rest of the body is in the shadow!"

The Dominie rose in a roaring rage and departed, but Jan caught up his palette and painted the stern old gentleman, just as he had sat in that punishment-sermon position for model without knowing it. The picture is admirable, and it hung in my bedroom in Leyden.

After having seen so many pictures of Jan Steen in Holland it seems to me as if I knew the man's whole life. Yes, I knew his whole kith and kin and acquaintance, wife and children, mother and cousins all, domestic foes, and other hangers on, absolutely face by face. They salute like friends from all his pictures, and a collection of them would be a biography of the painter. He has often set forth the deepest secrets of his soul with a few touches of his brush. I am very sure that his wife often scolded him for drinking, for in his picture of the Bean Feast, where Jan sits with his whole family at table, there we see his wife with a great wine jug in her hand, her eyes gleaming like those of a Bacchante. I am sure, however, that the good woman really drank very little, and the rogue wished to humbug us with the idea that it was his wife and not he who was given to toping. For this cause he himself laughs all the more joyfully from the painting. There he sits, perfectly happy ; his little son is the Bean-King, and stands on a stool wearing a tinsel crown ; his old mother, with the happiest wrinkled face, holds the youngest scion in her arms ; the musicians play their maddest, merriest dancing melodies, while the ever frugal thinking, economically grumbling good wife is set forth to all futurity as if she were tipsy !

How often in my lodgings in Leyden have I thought over the domestic life which this glorious Jan Steen must have experienced and endured. Many a time it seemed that I saw him in the body, sitting at his easel, now and then grasping the great pitcher, " reflecting and drinking, and drinking yet again without reflection." It is not a dreary Catholic specter, but a modern bright and merry spirit of joyousness, which, now that he is gone, haunts his studio, to paint jolly pictures and drink. Such will be the ghosts whom our descendants will see at times by bright daylight, while the sun shines through the clear white panes ; while it is not a black and doleful bell, but scarlet-swelling tones of trumpets, which, pealing from the tower, will announce the pleasant dinner-hour !

The memory of Jan Steen is, however, the best, or rather the only pleasant souvenir of my dwelling in Leyden. Had it not been for that, I should never have held out for eight days in that house. Its exterior was wretched, melancholy, and morbid, or altogether un-Dutch. The dark, moldy building stood close by the canal, and when one went to the other side it reminded one of an old witch looking at herself in a gleaming magic mirror. As on all Dutch roofs, there always stood on ours a couple of storks. Close by me lodged the cow whose milk I drank every morning, and there was a poultryroost under my window. My lady-poultry neighbors laid good eggs, but as they always, previous to publishing their works, preceded them by a long and wearisome prospectus of cackling, my enjoyment of their products was materially diminished. Among special annoyances was my landlord's playing the violin all day, and my landlady's playing the devil with him out of jealousy all night.

He who would know all about the mutual relations of this pair needed only to listen to them in a duet. The man performed on the violoncello and his wife on the viola d'amour, but they did not play in time, so that he was always a note behind, and there came withal such cutting cruel tones that when the 'cello growled and the viola gave grinding groans, one seemed to hear a matrimonial row without words. And after the husband stopped playing, the wife always kept on, as if determined to have the last word. She was a large but very thin woman, nothing but skin and bones, a mouth in which false teeth chattered, a low forehead, almost no chin, but a nose which made up for the deficiency, the tip of which curved like a beak, and with which she seemed, when playing, to muffle the sound of a string.

My landlord was about fifty years of age, and had slender legs, a worn away pale face, little green eyes, always blinking like those of a sentinel who has the sun shining in his face. He was by trade a bandage maker, and in religion an Anabaptist. He read the Bible so assiduously that it passed into his nightly dreams, and while his eyes kept winking he told his wife over their coffee how he had again been honored by converse with holiest dignitaries, how he had even met the highest Holy Jehovah, and how all the ladies of the Old Testament treated him in the friendliest and tenderest manner. This last occurrence was not at all to the liking of my landlady, and she not unfrequently manifested a jealous mood as to these meetings with the blessed damsels of the early days. " If he had only confined his acquaintance, now," she said, " to the pure mother Mary, or old Martha, or, for all I care, even Mary Magdalen, who reformed ; but to be meeting night after night those drinking hussies of Lot's daughters, and that precious Mrs. Judith and the vagabond Queen of Sheba, and similar dubious dames, could not be endured." But nothing could equal her rage when one morning her husband gave her an inspired account of how he had enjoyed an interview with the beautiful Esther, who had begged him to help in her toilet when enhancing her charms to fascinate Ahasuerus. In vain did the poor man protest that Mordecai himself had introduced him to his fair ward, that she was quite half-clad, and that his attentions had been confined to combing out her long black hair — the enraged wife beat the poor man with his own truss, poured hot coffee into his face, and would certainly have made away with him if he had not sworn, in the most solemn manner, in future to avoid all Old Testamental intercourse with ladies, and keep company in future only with the patriarchs and prophets.

The results of this ill-treatment were that from that time Mynheer said nothing about his nightly adventures ; he became a religious roué, and confessed to me that he had not only become ultra-intimate with the chaste Susanna, but that he had dreamed his way into Solomon's harem, and taken tea with his thousand wives.

CHAPTER XII

WRETCHED JEALOUSY! OWING TO IT ONE OF MY SWEETEST DREAMS — and perhaps the life of little Simson — were brought to a mournful end!

What is dreaming? What is death? Is it only an interruption of life or its full cessation? Yes, for people who only know the Past and the Future, and do not live an eternity in every moment of the Present, death must be terrible! When their two crutches, Space and Time, fall away, then they sink into the eternal Nothing.

And dreams? Why are we not more afraid before going to sleep than to be buried? Is it not terrible that the body can be as if dead all night, while the spirit in us leads the wildest life — a life full of all those terrors of that parting which we have established between life and soul! When in the future both shall be again united in our consciousness, then there will be perhaps no more dreams, or else only invalids, those whose harmony has been disturbed, will dream. The ancients dreamed only softly and seldom ; a strong and powerfully impressive dream was for them an event, and it was recorded in their histories.

Real dreaming began with the Jews, the people of the Spirit, and attained its highest development among the Christians, or the spiritual people. Our descendants will shudder when they read what a ghostly life we led, how Humanity was cloven in us and only one half had a real life. Our time — and it begins with the crucifixion of Christ — will be regarded as the great period of illness of Humanity.

And yet, what beautiful sweet dreams we have been able to dream! Our healthy descendants will hardly be able to understand them! All the splendors of the world disappeared from around us, and we found them again *in our own souls ;* yes, there the perfume of the trampled roses, and the sweetest songs of the frightened nightingales took refuge.

Thus I feel, and die of the unnatural anxieties and horrible dainties and sweet pains of our time. When I at night undress and lay me in bed, and stretch myself out at full length, and cover myself with the white sheets, I often shudder involuntarily, it seems so like being a corpse and burying myself. Then I close my eyes as quickly as I can to escape this fearful thought, and to save myself in the Land of Dreams.

It was a sweet, kind, sunshiny dream. The heaven was heavenly blue and cloudless, the sea sea-green and still. A boundless horizon ; and on the water sailed a gaily pennoned skiff, and on its deck I sat caressingly at the feet of Jadviga. I read to her strange and dreamy love songs, which I had written on strips of rose-colored paper, sighing yet joyful, and she listened with incredulous yet inclined ear and deeply loving smiles, and now and then hastily snatched the leaves from my hand and threw them in the sea. But the beautiful water fairies, with snow white breasts and arms, rose from the water and caught the fluttering lovelays as they fell. As I bent overboard I could see clearly far down into the depths of the sea, and there sat, as in a social circle, the beautiful water-maids, and among them was a young sprite who, with deeply sympathetic expression, declaimed my love songs. Wild enraptured applause rang out at every verse; the green-locked beauties applauded so passionately that necks and bosoms grew rosy red, and they praised cordially yet compassionately what they heard. " What strange beings these mortals are! How wonderful their lives, how dire their destinies! They love, and seldom dare express that love; and when they give it utterance at last, they rarely understand one another! And withal they do not lead eternal lives like ours; they are mortal. Only a little time is granted them to seek for happiness, they must grasp it quickly and press it hastily unto their hearts, ere it is gone; therefore their songs of love are so deeply tender, so sweetly painful and anxious, so despairingly gay, such strange blendings of joy and pain. The melancholy shadow of death falls on their happiest hours, and consoles them lovingly in adversity. They can weep. What poetry there is in mortal tears!"

" Dost thou hear," I said to Jadviga, " how they judge of us? Let us embrace, so that they may pity us no longer, and may envy us!" But she the beloved looked at me with infinite love, and without speaking a word. I had kissed her into silence. She grew pale, and a cold shiver thrilled her lovely form. She lay stiff as white marble in my arms, and I had deemed her dead if streams of tears had not poured from her eyes, and these tears flooded me while I held the loved image ever more firmly in my arms.

All at once I heard the keen shrill voice of my landlady, who wakened me from my dream. She stood before my bed with a dark lantern in her hand, and bade me rise quickly and follow her. She absolutely never looked so ugly before! Without knowing what she wanted, and still half asleep, I went after to where her husband lay, poor man, with night-cap over his eyes, apparently dreaming. He moved his limbs and his lips smiled as if with ineffable happiness, while he rattled and stammered, " Vashti! Queen Vashti! Your Majesty — fear not Ahasuerus — beloved Vashti!"

With eyes glowing with wrath the wife bent over her sleeping spouse, laid her ear to his head as if listening to his thoughts, and whispered to me, " Are you now convinced, Mynheer Schnabelewopski? He has now a love affair with Queen Esther — the scandalous wretch! I found out this horrid intrigue last night. Yes, he has preferred even a heathen to *me*! But I am wife and a Christian, and you shall see how I will revenge myself!"

Saying this she tore away the bedclothes, and grasping a truss of tough stag leather, laid it on horribly to the poor sinner. He, awakened so unpleasantly from his Biblical dream, screamed out as loudly as if the capital city of Susa were on fire and all Holland under water, and with his shrieks alarmed the whole neighborhood.

The next day it was all over Leyden that my landlord had raised this cry because he had caught me by night in company with his wife. This latter had been seen half-undressed through the window, and our housemaid, who was angry at me, and who had been questioned by the landlady of the Red Lion as to the occurrence, told how she herself had seen Myfrau make a nocturnal visit to my room.

Truly I cannot think of this affair without great pain, and what horrible results there were!

CHAPTER XIII

IF THE LANDLADY OF THE RED COW HAD BEEN AN ITALIAN SHE WOULD have poisoned my victuals, but as she was a Dutchwoman she only cooked them as badly as possible. In fact, we experienced the very next day the result of her feminine revenge. The first dish was *no soup*. That was awful, especially for a man brought up decently as I was, who from youth upwards had had soup every day, and who had hitherto never imagined that there was a world where the sun never shone and man soup never knew. The second course was beef, as cold and hard as Myron's iron cow. Then followed shell fish, which had the bad breath of a human, and which went untouched in silence as it came. Then came a great, old specter of a hen, which, far from satisfying our hunger, looked so wretchedly lean and hungry that we, out of sympathetic pity, could not touch it.

" And now, little Simson," cried the burly Dricksen, " dost thou still believe in God? *Is* this just? The Truss-brandisher visits Schna-belewopski in the dark watches of the night, and on that account we must starve by daylight!"

" O God, God!" sighed the little fellow, vilely vexed by such atheistic outbreak, and perhaps by such a miserable meal. And his irritability increased as the tall Van Pitter let fly his arrows of wit against Anthropomorphists and praised the Egyptians who of yore worshipped oxen and onions; the first because they tasted so well when roasted, and the latter when stuffed.

But little Simson under such mockery became furious, and at last he shot forth his defence of Deism.

" God is for man what the sun is for the flowers. When the rays of his heavenly countenance fall on the flowers, then they grow and open out their calyxes, and unfold their most varied colors. By night, when the sun is gone, they stand sorrowful with closed petals, and sleep or dream of the kisses of the golden rays of the past. Those which are ever in the shadow lose color and growth, shrink and grow pale, and wilt away miserable and unfortunate. But those which grow entirely in the dark, in old castle vaults, under ruined cloisters, become ugly and poisonous; they twine like snakes; their very smell is unhealthy, evilly benumbing, deadly."

" Oh, you need not spin out your Biblical parable any further," said burly Dricksen, as he poured unto himself a great glass of Schiedam gin. " Thou, little Simson, art a pious blossom who inhales in the sunshine of God the holy rays of virtue and love to such inspiration that thy soul blooms like a rainbow, while ours, turned away from God, fade colorless and hideous, if we don't indeed spread forth a poisonous stink."

" I once saw in Frankfort," said little Simson, " a watch which did not believe there was any watchmaker. It was of pinchbeck and went very badly."

" I'll show you anyhow that such a repeater knows how to strike," replied Dricksen, who suddenly became silent and teased Simson no more.

192

As the latter, notwithstanding his weak little arms, was an admirable fencer, it was determined that the two should duel that day
with rapiers. They went at it with great bitterness. The black eyes
of little Simson gleamed as if of fire and greatly magnified, and
contrasted the more strangely with his little arms, which came
forth so pitifully from his rolled-up shirt-sleeves. He became more
and more excited ; he fought for the existence of God, the old
Jehovah, the King of kings. But He aided not in the least His
champion, and in the sixth round the little man got a thrust in
the lungs.

" O God !" he cried, and fell to the ground.

CHAPTER XIV

THIS SCENE EXCITED ME TERRIBLY. BUT ALL THE FURY OF MY FEEL-
INGS turned against the woman who had directly caused such
disaster, and with a heart full of wrath and pain I stormed into the
Red Cow.

" Monster, why did you not serve us soup?" These were the
words with which I addressed the landlady, who became deadly
pale as I entered the kitchen. The porcelain on the chimneypiece
trembled at the tone of my voice. I was as desperate as only that
man can be who has had no soup, and whose best friend has just
had a rapier through his lungs.

" Monster, why did you not serve us soup?" I repeated these
words, while the consciously guilty woman stood as if frozen and
speechless before me. But at last, as if from opened sluices, the
tears poured from her eyes. They flooded her whole face, and ran
down into the canal of her bosom. But this sight did not soften me,
and with still greater bitterness I cried, " O ye women, I know
that ye can weep, but are tears *soup*? Ye are created for our misery.
Your looks are lies, and your breath is treason and deceit. Who first
ate the apple of sin? Geese saved the Capitol, but a woman ruined
Troy. O Troy, Troy! thou holy fortress of Priam, thou didst fall by

a woman! Who cast Marcus Aurelius into destruction? By whom was Marcus Tullius Cicero murdered? Who demanded the head of John the Baptist? Who was the cause of Abelard's mutilation? A woman. History is replete, yea unto repletion, with the terrible examples of man's ruin caused by you. All your deeds are folly, and all your thoughts are ingratitude. We give you the highest, the holiest flame of our hearts, our love — and what do we get for it? Beef that the devil would not eat, and worse poultry. Wretch and monster, why did you serve no soup?"

Myfrau began to stammer a series of excuses, and conjured me, by all the sweet memories of our love, to forgive her. She promised to provide better provender than before, and only charge six florins per head, though the Groote Dohlen landlord asked eight for his ordinary. She went so far as to promise oyster patties for the next day — yes, in the soft tone of her voice there was even a perfume as of truffles. But I remained firm. I was determined to break with her for ever, and left the kitchen with the tragic words, " Farewell ; between us two all is cooked out forever!"

In leaving I heard something fall. Was it a pot for cooking or Myfrau herself? I did not take the pains to look, and went straight to the Groote Dohlen to order six covers for the next day.

After this important business I hurried to little Simson's house and found him in a sad state. He lay in an immense old-fashioned bed which had no curtains, and at the corners of which were great marbled wooden pillars which supported a richly gilt canopy. The face of the little fellow was pale from pain, and in the glance which he cast at me was so much grief, kindness, and wretchedness, that I was touched to the heart. The doctor had just left him, saying that his wound was serious. Van Moeulen, who alone had remained to watch all night, sat before his bed, and was reading to him from the Bible.

" Schnabelewopski," sighed the sufferer, " it is good that you came. You may listen, and 'twill do you good. That is a dear, good book. My ancestors bore it all over the world with them, and much pain, misfortune, cursing and hatred, yes, death itself, did they endure for it. Every leaf in it cost tears and blood ; it is the written

194

fatherland of the children of God ; it is the holy inheritance of Jehovah."

" Don't talk so much ; it's bad for you," said Van Moeulen.

" And indeed," I added, " don't talk of Jehovah, the most ungrateful of gods, for whose existence you have fought to-day."

" O God!" sighed the little man, and tears fell from his eyes, " Thou help'st our enemies."

" Don't talk so much," said Van Moeulen again. " And thou, Schnabelewopski," he whispered to me, " excuse me if I bore thee ; the little man would have it that I should read to him the history of his namesake Samson. We are at the fourteenth chapter—listen !

" ' Samson went down to Timnath, and saw a woman in Timnath of the daughters of the Philistines.' "

" No," said the patient with closed eyes, " we are at the sixteenth chapter. It is to me as if I were living in all that which you read me, as if I heard the sheep bleating as they feed by Jordan, as if I myself had set fire to the tails of the foxes and chased them through the fields of the Philistines, and as if I had slain a thousand Philistines with the jawbone of an ass. Oh the Philistines ! they enslaved and mocked us, and made us pay toll like swine, and slung me out of doors from the ball-room on the Horse, and kicked me at Bockenheim—kicked me out of doors from the Horse !—oh, by God, that was not fair."

" He is feverish, and has wild fancies," softly said Van Moeulen, and began the sixteenth chapter.

" ' Then went Samson to Gaza, and saw there an harlot, and went in unto her.

" ' And it was told the Gazites, saying, Samson is come hither. And they compassed him in, and laid wait for him all night in the gate of the city, and were quiet all the night, saying, In the morning, when it is day, we shall kill him.

" ' And Samson lay till midnight, and arose at midnight, and took the doors of the gate of the city, and the two posts, and went away with them, bar and all, and put them upon his shoulders, and carried them up to the top of an hill that is before Hebron.

" ' And it came to pass afterward, that he loved a woman in the valley of Sorek whose name was Delilah.

" ' And the lords of the Philistines came up unto her and said unto her, Entice him and see wherein his great strength lieth, and by what means we may prevail against him, that we may bind him to afflict him : and we will give thee every one of us eleven hundred pieces of silver.

" ' And Delilah said to Samson, Tell me, I pray thee, wherein thy great strength lieth, and wherewith thou mightest be bound to afflict thee.

" ' And Samson said unto her, If they bind me with seven green withs that were never dried, then shall I be weak and be as another man.

" ' Then the lords of the Philistines brought up to her seven green withs which had not been dried, and she bound him with them.

" ' Now there were men lying in wait, abiding with her in the chamber. And she said, The Philistines be upon thee, Samson. And he brake the withs, as a thread of tow is broken when it toucheth the fire. So his strength was not known.' "

" Oh, the fools of Philistines!" cried the little man, and smiled well pleased ; " and they wanted to take me up and put me in the constable's guard."

Van Moeulen read on : —

" ' And Delilah said to Samson, Behold, thou hast mocked me, and told me lies: now tell me, I pray thee, wherewith thou mightest be bound.

" ' And he said unto her, If they bind me fast with new ropes that never were occupied, then shall I be weak, and be as another man.

" ' Delilah therefore took new ropes, and bound him therewith, and said unto him, The Philistines be upon thee, Samson. And there were liers in wait abiding in the chamber. And he brake them from off his arms like a thread.' "

" Fools of Philistines," cried the little man.

" ' And Delilah said unto Samson, Hitherto thou hast mocked

me, and told me lies : tell me wherewith thou mightest be bound?
And he said unto her, If thou weavest the seven locks of my head
with the web.

" ' And she fastened it with the pin, and said unto him, The
Philistines be upon thee, Samson. And he awaked out of his sleep,
and went away with the pin of the beam, and with the web.' "

The little man laughed. " That was in the Eschenheimer Lane."
But Van Moeulen continued : —

" ' And she said unto him, How canst thou say, I love thee, when
thine heart is not with me? thou hast mocked me these three
times, and hast not told me wherein thy great strength lieth.

" ' And it came to pass, when she pressed him daily with her
words, and urged him, so that his soul was vexed unto death ;

" ' That he told her all his heart, and said unto her, There hath
not come a razor upon mine head ; for I have been a Nazarite
unto God from my mother's womb ; if I be shaven, then my
strength will go from me, and I shall become weak, and be like any
other man.' "

" What folly ! " sighed the little man. Van Moeulen kept on : —

" ' And when Delilah saw that he had told her all his heart, she
sent and called for the lords of the Philistines, saying, Come up
this once, for he hath showed me all his heart. Then the lords of
the Philistines came up unto her and brought money in their hand.

" ' And she made him sleep upon her knees, and she called for a
man and caused him to shave off the seven locks of his head ; and
she began to afflict him, and his strength went from him.

" ' And she said, The Philistines be upon thee, Samson. And he
awoke out of his sleep, and said, I will go out as at other times
before, and shake myself. And he wist not that the Lord was
departed from him.

" ' But the Philistines took him, and put out his eyes, and brought
him down to Gaza, and bound him with fetters of brass ; and he
did grind in the prison house.' "

" O God ! God ! " wailed and wept the sick man. " Be quiet ! "
said Van Moeulen, and read on : —

" ' Howbeit the hair of his head began to grow again after he

197

was shaven.

" ' Then the lords of the Philistines gathered them together for to offer a great sacrifice unto Dagon their god, and to rejoice : for they said, Our God hath delivered Samson our enemy into our hand.

" ' And when the people saw him, they praised their god : for they said, Our God hath delivered into our hands our enemy, and the destroyer of our country, which slew many of us.

" ' And it came to pass, when their hearts were merry, that they said, Call for Samson, that he may make us sport : and they called for Samson out of the prison house ; and he made them sport : and they set him between the pillars.

" ' And Samson said unto the lad that held him by the hand, Suffer me that I may feel the pillars whereupon the house standeth, that I may lean upon them.

" ' Now the house was full of men and women ; and all the lords of the Philistines were there ; and there were upon the roof about three thousand men and women, that beheld while Samson made sport.

" ' And Samson called unto the Lord, and said, O Lord God, remember me, I pray thee, and strengthen me, I pray thee, only this once, O God, that I may be at once avenged of the Philistines for my two eyes.

" ' And Samson took hold of the two middle pillars upon which the house stood, and on which it was borne up, of the one with his right hand, and of the other with his left.

" ' And Samson said, Let me die with the Philistines. And he bowed himself with all his might ; and the house fell upon the lords, and upon all the people that were therein. So the dead which he slew at his death were more than they which he slew in his life.' "

At this little Simson opened his eyes ghostly wide, raised himself spasmodically, seized with his slender arms the two pillars at the foot of his bed, and shook them, crying out in wrath, " Let me die with the Philistines ! " The strong columns remained immovable ; but, exhausted and smiling sadly, the little man fell back on his pillow, while from his wound, the bandage of which was displaced, ran a red stream of blood.

The Rabbi of Bacherach

CHAPTER I

ON THE LOWER RHINE, WHERE ITS BANKS BEGIN TO LOSE THEIR smiling aspect, where hills and cliffs with romantic ruined castles rise more defiantly, and a wild and sterner dignity prevails, there lies, like a strange and fearful tale of the olden time, the gloomy and ancient town of Bacherach. But these walls, with their toothless battlements and blind turrets, in whose nooks and niches the winds blew and the sparrows nest, were not always so decayed and fallen, and in these poverty-stricken, repulsive muddy lanes which one sees through the ruined gate, there did not always reign that dreary silence which is only now and then broken by crying children, scolding women, and lowing cows. These walls were once proud and strong, and these lanes were alive with a fresh, free life, power and pride, joy and sorrow, much love and much hate. For Bacherach of old belonged to those municipalities which were founded by the Romans during their rule on the Rhine ; and its inhabitants, though the times which came after were sadly stormy, and though they had to submit first to the Hohenstaufen, and then to the Wittelsbach authority, managed, after the example of the other towns on the Rhine, to maintain a tolerably free commonwealth. This consisted of an alliance of different social elements, in which the patrician elder citizens and those of the guilds which were subdivided according to their different trades, mutually strove for power, so that while they were bound in union to keep ward and guard against the robber-barons, they nevertheless were obstinate in domestic dissensions waged for warring interests, the results of which were constant feuds, little neighborliness, much distrust, and not seldom actual outbursts of passion. The lord warden sat on the high tower of Sareck, and darted downwards like his falcon, whenever called for, swooping also many a time uncalled. The clergy ruled in darkness by darkening the souls of others. One of the most distracted and helpless of bodies, gradually ground down by local laws, was the little Jewish community. This was first formed in Bacherach in the days of the Romans, and during the later persecution of the people it had taken in many a flock of fugitive brothers in the faith.

The great oppression of the Jews began with the crusades, and raged most furiously about the middle of the fourteenth century, at the end of the great plague, which was, like all other great public disasters, attributed to the Jews, because people declared they had drawn down the wrath of God, and with the help of the lepers had poisoned the wells. The enraged rabble, especially the hordes of Flagellants, half naked men and women, who, lashing themselves for penance and singing a mad hymn to the Virgin, swept over South Germany and the Rhenish provinces, murdered in those days many thousand Jews, torturing others, or baptizing them by force. There was another accusation which had come down from earlier times, and which through all the Middle Ages, even to the beginning of the last century, cost much blood and suffering. This was the ridiculous story, repeated ad nauseam in chronicle and legend, that the Jews stole the consecrated wafer, and stabbed it through with knives till blood ran from it. And to this it was added that at the feast of the Passover the Jews slew Christian children to use their blood in the nightly service.

Therefore on this festival the Jews, hated for their wealth, their religion, and their ledgers, were entirely in the hands of their enemies, who could easily bring about their destruction by spreading the rumor of such a child-murder, and then secretly putting a bloody infant's corpse in the house of a Jew thus accused. Then there would be an attack by night on the Jews at their prayers, where there was murder, plunder, and baptism ; and great miracles wrought by the dead child aforesaid, whom the Church eventually canonised. Saint Werner is one of these holy beings, and in his honor the magnificent abbey of Oberwesel was founded. It is now one of the most beautiful ruins on the Rhine, and which, with the Gothic grandeur of its long ogival windows, proudly soaring pillars, and marvelous stone-carving, so strangely enchants us when we wander by it on some gay, green summer's day, and do not know its origin. In honor of this saint three other great churches were built on the Rhine, and innumerable Jews murdered or mal-treated. All this happened in the year 1287; and in Bacherach, where one of these Saint Werner's churches stood, the Jews suffered much misery and persecution. However, they remained for two centuries after, protected from such attacks of popular rage, though they were continually subject to enmity and threatening.

Yet the more hate oppressed them from without, the more earnestly and tenderly did the Jews of Bacherach cherish their domestic life within, and the deeper was the growth among them of piety and the fear of God. The ideal exemplar of a life given to God was seen in their Rabbi Abraham, who, though as yet a young man, was famed far and wide for his learning. Born in Bacherach, his father, who had been the rabbi there before him, had charged him in his last will never to leave the place unless for fear of life. This command, and a cabinet full of rare books, was all which his parent, who lived in poverty and learning, left him. However, Rabbi Abraham was a very rich man, for he had married the only daughter of his paternal uncle, who had been a great dealer in jewelry, and whose possessions he had inherited. A few mischief-makers in the community hinted now and then that the rabbi had married for money. But the women one and all denied this, declaring it was a well-known story that the rabbi, long ere he went to Spain, was in love with " Beautiful Sara," and how she waited for him seven years till he returned; he having already wedded her against the will of her father, and even her own inclination, by the betrothal-ring. For every Jew can make a Jewish girl his lawful wife, if he can put a ring on her finger, and say at the same time: " I take thee for my wife, according to the law of Moses and Israel." And when Spain was mentioned, the same gossips were wont to smile in the same significant manner, and all because of an obscure rumor that, though Rabbi Abraham had studied the holy law industriously enough at the academy of Toledo, yet that he had followed Christian customs and become imbued with habits of free thinking, like many Spanish Jews who had at that time attained a very remarkable degree of culture.

And yet in their hearts the tale-bearers put no faith in these reports ; for ever since his return from Spain the daily life of the Rabbi had been to the last degree pure, pious, and earnest. He carried out the most trivial details of all religious customs and ceremonies with painful conscientiousness ; he fasted every Monday and Thursday — only on Sabbaths and feast days did he indulge in meat or wine ; his time was passed in prayer and study ; by day he taught the Law to the students, whom his fame had drawn to Bacherach, and by night he gazed on the stars in heaven, or into the eyes of the beautiful Sara. His married life was childless, yet there was no lack of life or gaiety in the household. The great hall in his home, which stood near the synagogue, was open to the whole community, so that people went and came from it without ceremony, some offering short prayers, others exchanging news, or taking mutual counsel when in trouble. Here the children played of Sabbath mornings while the weekly portion was read ; here many met for wedding or funeral processions, and quarreled or were reconciled ; here, too, those who were cold found a warm stove, and the hungry a well-spread table. And, moreover, the Rabbi had a multitude of relatives, brothers and sisters, with their wives and children, as well as an endless array of uncles and cousins, in common with his wife, all of whom looked up to the Rabbi as the head of the family, and so made themselves at home in his house, and never failed to dine with him on all great festivals. Special among these grand gatherings in the Rabbi's house was the annual celebration of the Passover, a very ancient and remarkable feast which Jews still hold every year in the month Nissan, in eternal remembrance of their deliverance from Egyptian captivity.

Which takes place as follows : As soon as it is dark the mistress of the house lights the lamps, spreads the table-cloth, places in its midst three plates of unleavened bread, covers them with a napkin, and places on the pile six little dishes containing symbolical food, an egg, lettuce, horse-radish, the bone of a lamb, and a brown mixture of raisins, cinnamon, and nuts. At this table the father of the family sits among relations and friends, and reads to them from a very curious book called the *Haggadah*, whose contents are a strange mixture of legends of their forefathers, wondrous tales of Egypt, questions of theology, prayers and festival songs. During this feast there is a grand supper, and even during the reading there is tasting of the symbolical food and nibbling of Passover bread, while four cups of red wine are drunk. Mournfully merry, seriously gay, and mysteriously secret as a fairy tale is the character of this nocturnal festival, and the usual traditional sing-song with which the *Haggadah* is read by the father, and now and then re-echoed in chorus by the listeners at one time thrills the inmost soul as with a shudder, anon calms it as if it were a mother's lullaby, and anon startles it so suddenly into waking that even those Jews who have long fallen away from the faith of their fathers and run after strange joys and honors, are moved to their very hearts when by chance the old familiar tones of the Passover songs ring in their ears.

And so Rabbi Abraham once sat in his great hall surrounded by relations, disciples, and many other guests, to celebrate the great feast of the Passover. Everything was unusually sparkling ; over the table hung the gaily embroidered silk spread, whose gold fringes touched the floor ; the plate with the symbolic food shone in a comfortable home-like way, as did the tall wine goblets, adorned with embossed images of holy legends. The men sat in their black cloaks and black broad-brimmed hats, with white collars ; the women, in wonderful glittering garments of Lombard stuffs, wore on their heads and necks ornaments of gold and pearls, and the silver Sabbath lamps poured forth their pleasant light on the pleased faces of parents and children, happy in their piety. On the purple velvet cushions of a chair, higher than the others, and reclining as the Law enjoins, sat Rabbi Abraham, and read and sang the *Haggadah*, while the mixed assembly joined with him, or responded in the appropriate places. The Rabbi also wore the black festival garment, his nobly-formed but somewhat severe features wore a milder expression than usual, his lips smiled in the dark-brown beard as if they would fain tell something agreeable, while in his eyes there was an expression as of happy memories and anticipation. The beautiful Sara, who sat on the same high velvet cushion as her husband, wore, as hostess, none of her ornaments — only white linen enveloped her slender form and good and gentle face. This face was touchingly beautiful, even as all Jewish beauty is of a peculiarly moving kind ; for the consciousness of the deep wretchedness, the bitter scorn, and the evil chances amid which her kindred and friends dwelt, gave to her lovely features a depth of sorrow and an ever-watchful apprehension of love, such as most deeply touches our hearts. So on this evening the fair Sara sat looking into the eyes of her husband, yet glancing ever and anon at the beautiful parchment book of the *Haggadah* which lay before her, bound in gold and velvet. It was an old heirloom, with ancient wine stains on it, which had come down from the days of her grandfather, and in which were many boldly and brightly colored pictures, which she had often as a little girl looked at so eagerly on Passover evenings, and which represented all kinds of Bible stories — how Abraham broke asunder with a hammer the idols of his father, how the angels came to him, how Moses slew Mizri, how Pharaoh sat in state on his throne, how the frogs gave him no peace even at table, how he — the Lord be praised ! — was drowned, how the children of Israel went cautiously through the Red Sea ; how they stood open-mouthed, with their sheep, cows, and oxen, before Mount Sinai ; how pious King David played the harp ; and finally, how Jerusalem, with its towers and battlements, shone in the splendor of the setting sun.

The second wine-cup had been served, the faces and voices of the guests grew merrier, and the Rabbi, as he took a piece of unleavened bread and raised it, greeting gaily, read these words from the *Haggadah*: " Behold ! This is the food which our fathers ate in Egypt ! Let every one who is hungry come and enjoy it ! Let every one who is sorrowful come and share the joys of our Passover ! In this year we celebrate it here, but in years to come in the land of Israel. This year we celebrate it in servitude, but in the years to come as sons of freedom ! "

Then the hall-door opened, and there entered two tall, pale men, wrapped in very broad cloaks, who said : " Peace be with you.

We are men of your faith on a journey, and wish to share the Passover feast with you!" And the Rabbi replied promptly and kindly: " Peace be with you, sit ye down near me!" The two strangers sat down at the table, and the Rabbi read on. While the company conversed, he often cast a caressing word to his wife ; and playing on the old saying that on this evening a Hebrew father of a family regards himself as a king, said to her, " Rejoice, oh my Queen!" But she replied, smiling sadly, " The Prince is wanting," meaning by that a son, who, as a passage in the *Haggadah* requires, shall ask his father, with a certain formula of words, what is the meaning of the festival? The Rabbi said nothing, but only pointed with his finger to a picture on the opened leaves of the *Haggadah*. It was quaintly and touchingly drawn, showing how the three angels came to Abraham, announcing that he would have a son by his wife Sara, who, meanwhile, urged by feminine curiosity, is listening slyly to it all behind the tent-door. This little hit caused a threefold blush to rise to the cheeks of beautiful Sara, who looked down, and then glanced pleasantly at her husband, who went on chanting the wonderful story how Rabbi Jesua, Rabbi Eliezer, Rabbi Asaria, Rabbi Akiba, and Rabbi Tarphen sat reclining in B'ne Brak, and conversed all night long of the Exodus from Egypt till their disciples came to tell them it was daylight, and that the great morning prayer was being read in the synagogue.

As beautiful Sara listened with devotion while looking at her husband, she saw that in an instant his face assumed an expression as of agony or despair, his cheeks and lips were deadly pale, and his eyes bulged like balls of ice ; but almost immediately he became calm and cheerful as before, his cheeks and lips grew ruddy, he looked about him gaily — nay, it seemed as if a mad and merry mood, such as was foreign to his nature, had seized him. Beautiful Sara was frightened as she had never been in all her life, and a cold shudder came over her — less from the momentary mani- festation of dumb despair which she had seen in her husband's face, than from the joyousness which followed it and which passed into rollicking jollity. The Rabbi cocked his cap comically, first on one ear, then on the other, pulled and twisted his beard funnily, sang the *Haggadah* texts like tavern-songs ; and in the enumeration of the Egyptian plagues, where it is usual to dip the forefinger in the full wine-cup and cast the clinging drops to the ground, he sprinkled the young girls near him with the red wine, and there was great wailing over spoiled collars, and ringing laughter. At every instant beautiful Sara became more bewildered at this convulsive merriment of her husband, and oppressed with nameless fears she gazed on the buzzing swarm of gaily glittering guests who comfortably spread or rocked themselves to and fro, nibbling the thin Passover bread, drinking wine, gossiping, or singing aloud full of joy.

Then came the time for supper. All rose to wash, and beautiful Sara brought the great silver basin, richly adorned with embossed gold figures, which was presented to every guest, that he might wash his hands. As she held it to the Rabbi, he gave her a significant look, and quietly slipped out of the door. In obedience to the sign beautiful Sara followed him, when he grasped her hand, and in the greatest haste hurried her through the dark lanes of Bacherach, out of the town gate to the highway which leads to Bingen along the Rhine.

It was one of the nights in spring which are indeed softly warm and starry, yet which inspire the soul with strange uncanny feelings. There was something of the churchyard in the flowers, the birds sang peevishly and as if vexing themselves, the moon cast spiteful yellow stripes of light over the dark stream as it went murmuring away, the lofty masses of the Rhine cliffs looked dimly like quivering giants' heads, the watchman on the tower of Castle Strahleck blew a melancholy tune, and with it rang in jarring rivalry the funeral bell of Saint Werner's. Beautiful Sara carried the silver ewer in her right hand, while the Rabbi grasped her left, and she felt that his fingers were ice-cold, and that his arm trembled ; but still she went on with him in silence, perhaps because she was accustomed to obey blindly and unquestioning—perhaps, too, because her lips were mute with fear and anxiety.

Below Castle Sonneck, opposite Lorch, about the place where the hamlet of Nieder Rheinbach now stands, there rises a cliff which arches out over the Rhine bank. The Rabbi ascended it with his wife, looked around on every side, and gazed on the stars. Trembling and shivering, as with the pain of death, beautiful Sara looked at his pale face, which seemed specter-like in the moonlight, and seemed to express by turns pain, terror, piety, and rage. But when the Rabbi suddenly snatched from her hands the silver ewer and threw it far away into the Rhine, she could no longer endure her agony of uncertainty, and crying out, " *Shaddai*, full of mercy!" threw herself at his feet, and implored him to solve the dark enigma.

Unable at first to speak from excitement, the Rabbi moved his lips without uttering a sound, till at last he cried, " Dost thou see the Angel of Death? There below he sweeps over Bacherach. But we have escaped his sword. Praised be God!" And in a voice still trembling with fright he told her that while he was happily and comfortably singing the *Haggadah* he glanced by chance under the table, and saw at his feet the bloody corpse of a little child. " Then I knew," continued the Rabbi, " that our two guests were not of the community of Israel, but of the assembly of the godless, who had plotted to bring that corpse stealthily into the house so as to accuse us of child-murder, and incite the people to plunder and murder us. Had I given a sign that I saw through that work of darkness I should simply have brought destruction on the instant to me and mine, and only by craft did I preserve our lives. Praised be God! Grieve not, beautiful Sara. Our relations and friends will also be saved. It was only my blood which the wretches wanted. I have escaped them, and they will be satisfied with my silver and gold. Come with me, beautiful Sara, to another land. We will leave bad luck behind us, and that it may not follow us I have thrown to it the silver ewer, the last of my possessions, as an offering. The God of our fathers will not forsake us. Come down, thou art weary. There is Silent William standing by his boat ; he will row us up the Rhine."

Speechless, and as if every limb was broken, beautiful Sara sank into the arms of the Rabbi, who slowly bore her to the bank. There stood William, a deaf and dumb youth, but yet beautiful as a picture, who, to maintain his old fostermother, who was a neighbor of the Rabbi, was a fisherman, and kept his boat in this place. It seemed as if he had divined the intention of Abraham, and was waiting for him, for on his silent lips there was an expression as of sweet sympathy and pity, and his great blue eyes rested as with deep meaning on beautiful Sara, while he lifted her carefully into the boat.

The glance of the silent youth roused beautiful Sara from her lethargy, and she realised at once that all which her husband had told her was no mere dream, and a stream of bitter tears poured over her cheeks, which were as white as her garment. So she rested in the boat, a weeping image of white marble, while by her sat her husband and Silent William, rowing earnestly.

Whether it was owing to the measured beat of the oars, or the rocking of the boat, or the fresh perfume from the Rhine banks whereon joy grows, it always happens that even the most sorrowful being is marvelously calmed when on a night in spring he is lightly borne in a light boat on the dear, clear Rhine stream. For in truth old, kind-hearted Father Rhine cannot bear that his children shall weep, so, calming their crying, he rocks them on his trusty arm, and tells them his most beautiful stories, and promises them his most golden treasures, perhaps the old, old, long vanished Nibelungen hoard. Little by little the tears of beautiful Sara ceased to flow ; her worst sorrow seemed to be washed away by the eddying, whispering waves, while the hills about her home bade her the tenderest farewell. Most trustingly of all did the Kedrich, her favorite look-out, give her a farewell greeting ; and it seemed as if far up in the strange moonlight, resting on its summit, she saw a damsel with outstretched arms, while the daring dwarfs swarmed out of their caverns in the rocks, and a rider came rushing down the rocks at full gallop. And beautiful Sara felt as if she were a child again, sitting once more in the lap of her aunt from Lorch, who was telling her brave tales of the bold knight who freed the stolen damsel from the dwarfs, and many other true stories of the curious Wisperthal " over there," where the birds talk as sensibly as any mortals, and of Gingerbread Land, where good,

obedient children go, and of enchanted princesses, singing trees,
crystal castles, golden bridges, laughing waterfairies. . . . But all at
once among these pleasant tales which began to send forth sounds
of music and to gleam with lovely light, beautiful Sara heard the
voice of her father, who scolded the poor aunt for putting such
nonsense into the child's head. Then it seemed to her as if they
set her on the little stool before her father's velvet-covered chair,
with a soft hand he smoothed her long hair, and smiled as if well
pleased, and rocked himself comfortably in his full, Sabbath
dressing-gown of blue silk. Yes, it must be the Sabbath, for the
flowered cover was spread on the table, all the utensils in the room
gleamed like looking-glasses, the white-bearded sexton sat beside her
father, and ate raisins and talked in Hebrew ; even little Abraham
came in with an enormous book, and modestly begged permission
of his uncle to expound a portion of the Holy Scripture, that he
might prove that he had learned much during the past week, and
therefore deserved much praise — and a corresponding quantity of
cakes. . . . Then the lad laid the book on the broad arm of the
chair, and explained the history of Jacob and Rachel, and how
Jacob lifted up his voice and wept when he first saw his cousin
Rachel, how he talked so intimately with her by the well, how he
had to serve seven years for her, and how speedily they passed, and
how he at last married and loved her for ever and ever. . . . Then
all at once beautiful Sara remembered how her father cried with
merry voice, " Wilt thou not, like that also, marry thy cousin
Sara?" To which little Abraham seriously replied, " That I will,
and she shall wait seven years too." These memories stole like
twilight shadows through the soul of the young wife, and she saw
how she and her little cousin — now so great a man and her husband
— played like children together in the leafy tabernacle ; how they
were delighted with the gay hangings, flowers, mirrors, and gilded
apples ; how little Abraham petted her more tenderly, till he grew
to be little by little larger and less amiable, and at last of full
growth and altogether grim. . . . And now she sits in her room alone
of a Saturday evening ; the moon shines brightly in, and the door
flies open, and cousin Abraham, in traveling garb and pale as death,

comes in, and grasps her hand and puts a gold ring on her finger, and says solemnly, " I hereby take thee to be my wife, according to the laws of God and of Israel." " But now," he added, with a trembling voice, " now I must go to Spain. Farewell—for seven years thou must wait for me." So he hurried away, and Sara, weeping, told the tale to her father, who roared and raged. " Cut off thy hair, for now thou art a married woman," and he rode after Abraham to compel him to give her a letter of divorcement ; but he was over the hills and far away, and the father returned silently to his house. And when beautiful Sara helped to draw off his boots, and to soothe him said that Abraham would return in seven years, he cursed and cried, " Seven years shalt thou go begging," and he soon died.

And so old memories swept through her soul like a hurried shadow play, the images intermixing and blending strangely, while between them went and came unknown bearded faces, and great flowers with marvellous broad spreading foliage. Then the Rhine seemed to murmur the melodies of the *Haggadah*, and from its waters the pictures, large as life and in strange exaggerated guise, came forth one by one. There was the forefather Abraham fearfully breaking the idols, which put themselves together again quickly ; the Egyptian defending himself fiercely against the infuriated Moses ; Mount Sinai flashing and flaming ; King Pharaoh swimming in the Red Sea, holding his jagged gold crown tight in his teeth, frogs with men's faces swimming in between, and the waves foaming and roaring, while a dark giant hand rose threatening from the deep.

That was the Mouse Tower of Bishop Hatto, and the boat shot through the Binger Rapids. By this beautiful Sara was somewhat aroused from her dreams, and gazed at the hills on the shore, from whose summits the lights gleamed, and at whose feet the mist shimmering in moonlight began to rise. Suddenly she seemed to see in it her friends and relations, as they, with corpse-like faces and flowing shrouds, passed in awful procession along the Rhine. . . . All grew dark before her eyes, an icy current ran through her soul, and, as if in sleep, she only heard the Rabbi repeating the night-prayer slowly and painfully, as if at a deathbed, and dreamily she stammered the words, " Ten thousand to the right, ten thousand to the left, to protect the king from the terrors of the night."

Then all at once the oppressive gloom and grief passed away, the dark curtain was torn from heaven, and there appeared far above the holy city Jerusalem, with its towers and gates ; the Temple gleamed in golden splendor, and in its fore-court Sara saw her father in his yellow Sabbath dressing-gown, smiling as if well pleased. All her friends and relatives looked out from the round windows of the Temple, merrily greeting her ; in the Holy of Holies knelt pious King David, in his purple mantle and golden crown ; sweetly rang his song and harp-tones, and smiling happily beautiful Sara fell asleep.

CHAPTER II

AS BEAUTIFUL SARA OPENED HER EYES THEY WERE ALMOST BLINDED by the rays of the sun. The high towers of a great city rose before her, and Silent William stood with his boat-hook upright in the boat and pushed and guided it through the lively crowding of many vessels, gay with pennons and streamers, whose crews either looked leisurely at passers-by or were in groups busied in loading with chests, bales, and casks the lighters which should bear them to the shore, and with it all was a deafening noise, the constant halloos cry of steermen, the calling of traders from the shore, and the scolding of the customhouse officials who, in their red coats with white maces and white faces, jumped from boat to boat.

" Yes, beautiful Sara," said the Rabbi, cheerfully smiling to his wife, " this is the famous, free, imperial, and commercial city of Frankfort-on-the-Main, and we are now passing along that river. Do you see those pleasant looking houses up there, surrounded by green hillocks? That is Sachsenhausen, from which our lame Gumpert brings us the fine myrrh for the Feast of the Tabernacles. Here thou see'st the strong Main Bridge, with thirteen arches, over

which many men, wagons, and horses safely pass, and in the middle
stands a little house of which Aunty Täubchen says that a baptized
Jew lives there, who pays every man who brings him a dead rat
six farthings, on behalf of the Jewish community, who are obliged
to deliver annually to the State council five thousand rats' tails for
tribute."

At the thought of this war, which the Frankfort Jews were
obliged to keep up against the rats, beautiful Sara burst out laughing. The bright sunlight, and the new gay world now before her,
had driven all the terrors and horrors of the past night from her
soul, and as she was lifted to land from the boat by Silent William
and her husband, she felt inspired with a sense of joyful safety.
But Silent William looked long with his beautiful deep blue eyes
into hers, half sadly, half cheerfully, and then with a significant
glance at the Rabbi, sprang back into his boat and disappeared.

" Silent William much resembles my brother who died," said
beautiful Sara. " All the angels are alike," answered the Rabbi ; and
taking his wife by the hand he led her through the dense crowd
on the shore, where, as it was the time of the Easter Fair, stood
a great number of newly erected wooden booths. Then passing
through the gloomy Main Gate, they found themselves in quite as
noisy a multitude. Here in a narrow street one shop stood close by
another, every house, as was usual in Frankfort, being specially
adapted to trade. There were no windows on the ground floor, but
broad open arches, so that the passerby looking in, could see at a
glance all there was for sale. And how beautiful Sara was astonished
at the mass of magnificent wares, and the splendor, such as she
had never seen before! Here stood Venetians, who offered cheaply
all the elegancies and luxuries of the East and Italy, and beautiful
Sara seemed as if enchanted by the ornaments and jewels, the gay
and varied caps and bodices, the gold bangles and necklaces, and
the whole display of knick-knackery which women look at so
lovingly and wear even more endearingly. The richly embroidered
stuffs of velvet and silk seemed to speak to beautiful Sara, and
flash and sparkle back strange wonders into her memory, and it
really seemed to her as if she were again a little girl, and that

Aunty Täubchen had kept her promise and taken her to the Frankfort Fair, and that she now at last stood before the beautiful garments of which she had heard so much. With a secret joy she reflected what she should take back with her to Bacherach, and which of her two little cousins, Blossom and Birdie, would prefer that blue silk sash, and whether the green pants would suit little Gottschalk — when all at once it flashed on her, " Ah, Lord! they are all grown up now, and yesterday they were slain!" She shuddered and shrank into herself, and the shadows of the night seemed to settle again in her soul ; but the gold embroidered cloths glittered once more with a thousand roguish eyes, and coaxed dark thoughts from her mind, and as she looked into her husband's face it was free from clouds, and bore its habitual serious gentleness. " Shut your eyes, Sara!" said the Rabbi, and led his wife away through the crowd.

What a varied, variegated, struggling multitude! First were the tradesmen, who loudly outbid one another in offering bargains, or talked together, counting on their fingers, or, followed by porters bearing high-packed loads, who at a dogtrot led the way to their lodgings. By the faces of others one could see that they came from curiosity. The stout councilman was shown by his scarlet cloak and golden chain, while the black, prosperous swelling waistcoat betrayed the honorable and proud Altburger. The iron-peaked helmet, the yellow leather jerkin, and the rattling spurs, weighing one pound, indicated the heavy cavalryman, or squire. Under many a little black velvet cap, which came to a point over the brow, there hid a rosy girl face, and the young fellows who jumped after it, like hunting-dogs on the scent, showed they were finished dandies by their saucily feathered caps, their rattling peaked shoes, and their silk garments of separate colors, where one side was green and the other red, or the right striped like a rainbow, and the left in harlequin squares of many colors, so that the foolish youths looked as if they were split in two. Freeing themselves from the crowd, the Rabbi with his wife directed the way to the Römer. This is the great market-place of the city, surrounded by houses with high gables, and takes its name from one immense building, " the

Roman," which was bought by the municipality and dedicated as the town-hall. In it the German Emperor was elected, and before it tournaments were often held. King Maximilian, who was passionately fond of such sports, was then in Frankfort, and in his honor the day before there had been great tilting in the Römer ground. Many idle men still stood on or about the scaffolding, which was being removed by carpenters, and told how the Duke of Brunswick and the Margrave of Brandenburg had charged one another amid the sound of drums and of trumpets, and how Lord Walter the Blackguard had knocked the Knight of the Bear so soundly out of his saddle that the splinters of the lances flew high in the air, and the tall blonde King Max, standing upon the balcony among his courtiers, rubbed his hands for joy. The cloths of gold were still to be seen on the balconies and in the Gothic windows of the town-hall. The other houses of the market-place were also still bedecked and adorned with shields, especially the Limburg house, on whose banner was painted a maiden who bore a hawk on her hand, while a monkey held out to her a mirror. Many knights and ladies stood on the balcony engaged in gay conversation, while looking at the crowd below, which, in odd groups and as odd attire, shifted here and there. What a multitude of idlers and loiterers crowded together here to gratify curiosity! There was laughing, grumbling, stealing, naughty pinching, hurrahing, while ever and anon was heard in yelling, braying notes the trumpet of the mountebank quack, who, in a red cloak with his clown and monkey, stood on a high stand blowing bravely the horn of his own skill, and sounding the praises of his tinctures and marvelous salves, ere he solemnly regarded the glass of urine brought by some old woman, or applied himself to pull a poor peasant's tooth. Two fencing masters, fluttering about in gay ribbons, brandishing their rapiers, met as if by chance, and had a mock duel, with great apparent anger ; but after a long assault-at-arms each declared that the other was invincible, and took up a collection. Then the newly organized guild of archers marched by with drummers and pipers, and these were followed by the policeman, who carried a red flag, and led a disorderly mob of traveling adventuresses, who came from the

harlot house, known as " the Ass," in Würzburg, and were going to
Rosendale, where the highly honorable municipal authority had
assigned them their quarters for the fair. " Shut your eyes, Sara,"
said the Rabbi. For indeed the fantastic crowd of very lightly clad
girls, among whom were some who were really beautiful, behaved
in a most lewd manner, baring their bold white breasts, chaffing
those who went by with shameless words, and swinging their long
walking sticks. And as they came to the gate of Saint Katherine
they rode on them as children play at riding horses, and sang in
shrill tones the witch-song —

> " Where is the goat? the hellish beast ;
> Where is the goat? Oh bring him quick !
> And if there is no goat, at least
> We'll ride upon the stick."

This wild sing-song, which rang afar, was lost in the long drawn
solemn tones of a church procession. It was a mournful train of
bare headed and bare footed monks, who carried burning wax
tapers, banners with pictures of the saints, and great silver cruci-
fixes. Before it ran boys clad in red and white gowns, bearing
smoking censers of frankincense. In the midst, under a splendid
canopy, were priests in white robes, bedecked with costly lace or
in many colored stoles, and one of them held in his hand a sun like
golden vessel, which on arriving at a shrine by the market corner
he raised on high, while he half sang half spoke in Latin — when all
at once a little bell rang, and all round becoming silent fell on their
knees and made the sign of the Cross. " Shut your eyes, Sara !"
cried the Rabbi again, and hastily drew her away through a labyrinth of narrow and crooked streets, and at last over the desolate
empty place which separated the new Jewish quarter from the rest
of the city.

Before that time the Jews dwelt between the Cathedral and the
bank of the Main, that is, from the bridge to the Lumpenbrunnen,
and from the Mehlwage as far as Saint Bartholomew's. But the
Catholic priests obtained a Papal bull forbidding the Jews to live
so near the high church, for which reason the city fathers assigned
them a place on the Wollgraben, where they built their present

quarter. This was surrounded with high walls, and had iron chains across the gate to shut them in from the mob. Here they lived, crowded and oppressed, and with far more vivid memories of previous suffering than at present. In 1240 the raging populace had caused an awful " bath of blood " among them, which was remembered as the first Jewish massacre ; and in 1349, when the Flagellants, while passing through the town, set fire to it, and accused the Jews of the deed : the latter were nearly all murdered or burned alive in their own houses. This was called the second Jewish massacre. After this the Jews were oftener threatened with similar slaughter, and during the internal dissensions of Frankfort, especially during a dispute of the council with the guilds, the mob often meant to attack the Jewish quarter. This place had two doors, which on Catholic festivals were closed from without and on Jewish celebrations from within, and before each gate was a guard house with city soldiers.

As the Rabbi came with his wife to the entrance to the Jewish quarter, the soldiers lay, as one could see through the open windows, on the wooden bench of their guard-room, while out before the door sat the drummer playing small caprices on his great drum. He was a powerfully built, heavy fellow, wearing a jerkin and hose of fiery yellow, greatly puffed out on the arms and thighs, and profusely scattered with small red flowing tufts sewed on, which looked as if innumerable fiery tongues were licking him from head to foot. His breast and back were covered with cushions of black cloth, against which hung his drum ; he bore on his head a flat, round black cap, which was matched by his face in roundness and flatness, and which was in keeping with his dress, being also orange-yellow, spotted with red pimples, and contracted into a gaping smile. So the fellow sat and drummed the air of a song which the Flagellants had sung at the Jewish massacre, while he sang, in a rough, beery voice —

> "Our dear Lady true
> Walked in the morning dew,
>   Kyrie eleison !"

" Jack, that is a terrible tune," cried a voice from behind the

locked gate of the Jewish quarter. " Yes, Jack, and a bad song too
— don't suit the drum ; don't suit at all — by my soul — not the fair
on Easter morning — bad song — dangerous, Jack, Jacky, little drum-
Jacky boy — I'm a lone man — and if thou lovest me, the Star, the
tall Star, the tall Nose-Star — so stop it ! "

These words were forced out in fragments by the unseen speaker,
now as in hasty anxiety, anon in a sighing drawl, with a tone
which alternated from softness to harsh hoarseness, such as one
hears in consumptive people. The drummer was not moved, and
continued his song —

> " There came a little youth,
> His beard had run away, in truth,
> Halleluja !

" Jack," again cried the voice of the invisible speaker, " Jack,
I'm a lone man, and it is a dangerous song, and I don't like it ; and
I have my reasons for it, and if you love me sing something else,
and to-morrow we will drink together."

At the word " drink " Jack ceased his drumming and singing, and
said in gentler tone, " The devil take the Jews ! but thou, dear
Nose-Star, art my friend, I protect thee ; and if we should only
drink together often enough I will convert thee. Yea, I will be thy
godfather, and when baptized thou wilt be eternally happy ; and
if thou hast genius and wilt study industriously under me thou
mayest even become a drummer. Yes, Nose-Star, thou mayest yet
become something great. I will drum the whole catechism into
thee when we drink to-morrow together ; but now open the gate,
for here are two strangers who wish to enter."

" Open the gate ! " cried Nose-Star, and his voice almost deserted
him. " That can't be done in such a hurry, my dear Jack ; one can't
tell — don't know, you know — and I'm a lone man. Veitel Oxhead
has the key, and he is sitting now in the corner mumbling his
eighteen benedictions and he must not be interrupted. And Jäkel
the Fool is here too, but he is passing water ; I'm a lone man."

" The devil take the Jews ! " cried the drummer, and laughing
loudly at this, his own and only joke, he trundled himself to the
guard-room and laid down on the bench.

While the Rabbi waited with his wife before the great locked gate, there rose from behind it a strangely rasping, nasal, and somewhat mocking slow voice. " Starry—don't drone and groan so long. Take the keys from Oxheady's coat pockets, or else go stick your nose in the keyhole, and so unlock the gate. The people have been standing and waiting a long time."

" People!" cried the voice of Nose Star, as if frightened. " I thought there was only one ; and I beg you, Fool—dear Jäkel Fool— look out and see who are there."

A small, well grated window in the gate opened, and there appeared in it a yellow cap with two horns, and the drolly, wrinkled, and twisted jest-maker's face of Jäkel the Fool. At once the window was shut, and he cried angrily, " Open the gate— there is only a man and a woman."

" A man and a woman!" groaned Nose Star. " Yes, and when the gate's opened the woman will take her gown off, and become a man ; and there'll be two men, and we are only three!"

" Don't be a rabbit," replied Jäkel the Fool. " Pick up your heart and show courage!"

" Courage!" cried Nose Star, with mournful bitterness. " Rabbit! Rabbit is a bad comparison. The rabbit is an unclean beast. Courage! I am not put here to be courageous, but cautious. When too many come I am to call. But I alone cannot keep them back. My arm is weak, I have a fontanel, and I'm a lone man. Should one shoot me I should be slain. Then that rich man, Mendel Reiss, will sit on the Sabbath at his table, and wipe the raisin-sauce from his mouth, and rub his belly, and perhaps say, ' Tall Nose Star was a brave fellow after all ; if it had not been for him perhaps they would have burst the gate. He let himself be shot dead for us. He was a brave fellow ; pity that he's dead!' "

Here the voice became tender and tearful, but all at once it rose to a hasty and almost angry tone. " Courage! and because the rich Mendel Reiss wipes away the raisin-sauce from his mouth, and pats his belly, and calls me a brave fellow, I'm to let myself be shot dead! Courage! Be brave! Little Strauss was brave, and yesterday went to the Römer to see the tilting, and thought they would not know him because he wore a frock coat of violet velvet — three florins a yard — with fox-tails all embroidered with gold — quite magnificent ; and they dusted his violet coat for him till it lost its color, and his own back became violet and did not look human. Courage, indeed! The crooked, crippled Leser was courageous, and called our blackguardly chief magistrate a blackguard, and they hung him up by the feet between two dogs while Jack drummed. Courage! Don't be a rabbit! Among many dogs the rabbit is killed. I'm a lone man, and I am really afraid."

" That I'll swear to," cried Jäkel.

" Yes ; I *have* fear," replied Nose Star, sighing. " I know that it runs in my blood, and I had it from my mother "——

" Ay, ay," interrupted Jäkel, " and your mother had it from her father, and he from his, and so all thy ancestors one from the other, back to the forefather who marched with King Saul against the Philistines, and was the first to run away. But look! Oxhead is all ready — he has bowed his head for the fourth time ; now he is jumping like a flea at the Holy, Holy, Holy, and seeking cautiously in his pocket."

In fact the keys rattled, the gate grated and creaked as it opened, and the Rabbi and his wife entered the empty Judengasse. The man who opened was a little fellow with a good-natured grim face, who nodded absently, like one who did not like to be disturbed in his thoughts, and when he had carefully closed the portal, slipped without saying a word into a corner, murmuring his prayers. Less taciturn was Jäkel the Fool, a short fellow with bowed legs, a full blooming, red, and laughing face, and an enormous meaty hand, which he stretched out of the wide sleeve of his chequered jacket in welcome. Behind him a tall, lean figure showed or rather hid itself — the slender neck white feathered with a fine cambric ruff, and the thin pale face strangely adorned with an incredible long nose, which anxiously peered about in every direction.

" God's welcome to a pleasant feast-day!" cried Jäkel the Fool. " Do not be astonished that the street is so empty and silent just now. All our people are in the synagogue, and you are come just in the right time to hear the history of the sacrifice of Isaac. I know it — 'tis an interesting tale, and if I had not heard it before, thirty-three times, I would willingly hear it again this year. And — mind you! — 'tis an important story, for if Abraham had really killed Isaac and not the goat, then there would have been more goats in the world now — and fewer Jews." And then, with mad and merry grimaces, Jäkel began to sing the following song from the Haggadah: —

" A little kid, a little kid, which my father bought for two pieces of money. A little kid! a little kid!

" There came a little cat which ate the little kid, which my father bought for two pieces of money. A little kid!

" There came a little dog, who bit the little cat, who ate the little kid, which my father bought for two pieces of money. A little kid!

" There came a little stick, which beat the little dog, who bit the little cat, who ate the little kid, which my father bought for two pieces of money. A little kid! A little kid!

" There came a little fire, which burnt the little stick, which beat the little dog, who bit the little cat, who ate the little kid, which my father bought for two pieces of money. A little kid! A little kid!

" There came the little water, which quenched the little fire, which burnt the little stick, which beat the little dog, who bit the little cat, who ate the little kid, which my father bought for two pieces of money. A little kid! A little kid!

" There came a little ox, who drank the little water, which quenched the little fire, which burnt the little stick, which beat the little dog, who bit the little cat, who ate the little kid, which my father bought for two pieces of money. A little kid! A little kid!

" There came the little butcher, who slew the little ox, who drank the little water, which quenched the little fire, which burnt the little stick, which beat the little dog, who bit the little cat, that ate the little kid, which my father bought for two pieces of money. A little kid! A little kid!

" Then came the Angel of Death, who slew the little butcher, who killed the little ox, who drank the little water, which quenched the little fire, which burnt the little stick, which beat the little dog, who bit the little cat, who ate the little kid, which my father bought for two pieces of money. A little kid! little kid!"

" Yes, beautiful lady," added the singer, " and the day will come when the Angel of Death will slay the slayer, and all our blood come over Edom, for God is a God of vengeance."

But all at once, casting aside with violent effort the seriousness into which he had unconsciously fallen, Jäkel jumped again into his mad fancies, and kept on in his harsh jester tones, " Don't be afraid, beautiful lady, Nose Star will not harm you. He is only dangerous to the old Schnapper-Elle. She has fallen in love with his nose—and, it deserves it. Yea, for it is beautiful as the tower which looketh forth towards Damascus, and riseth like a cedar of Lebanon. Outwardly it gleameth like gold leaf and syrup, and inwardly it is all music and loveliness. It bloometh in summer and in winter it is frozen up—but in summer and winter it is petted and pulled by the white hands of Schnapper-Elle. Yes, she is madly in love with him. She cuddles him, she fodders him ; for her age he is young enough. When he is fat enough she means to marry him ; and whoever comes to Frankfort, three hundred years hence, will not be able to see the heavens for Nose Stars."

" Ah, you are Jäkel the Fool," exclaimed the Rabbi, laughing. " I mark it by your words, I have often heard of you."

" Yes—yes," replied Jäkel, with a comical air of modesty. " Yes, that comes of being famous. A man is often celebrated far and wide for being a bigger fool than he has any idea of. However, I take great pains and do my very best to be a fool, and jump and shake myself to make the bells ring ; other people manage it more easily. But tell me, Rabbi, why do ye journey on a feast-day ?"

" My justification," replied the Rabbi, " is in the Talmud, and it says, ' Danger drives away the Sabbath.' "

" Danger!" screamed the tall Nose Star, with an air of deadly terror. " Danger! danger! Drummer Jack!—drum, drum. Danger! danger! Drummer Jack!"

From outside resounded the deep beery voice of Drummer Jack, " *Tausend donner sacrament!* The devil take the Jews. That's the third time today that you've woke me out of a sound sleep, Nose Star! Don't make me mad! For when I am mad I'm the howling old devil himself ; and then as sure as I'm a Christian I'll up with my gun and shoot slap through the grated window of your tower —and then it'll be, old fellow, everybody look out for his nose!"

"Don't shoot! don't shoot! I'm a lone man," wailed Nose Star piteously, and pressed his face against the wall, and remained trembling and murmuring prayers in this position.

"But say, what has happened?" cried Jäkel the Fool, with all the impatient curiosity which was even then characteristic of the Frankfort Jews.

But the Rabbi impatiently broke loose from them, and went his way along the Jews' Street. "See, Sara!" he exclaimed, "how badly guarded is our Israel. False friends guard its gates without, and within its watchers are folly and fear."

They wandered slowly through the long and empty streets, where only here and there the head of some bright young girl looked out of a window, while the sun mirrored itself in the brilliant panes. In those days the houses in the Jewish quarter were still neat and new, and much lower than they now are, since it was only at a later time that the Jews, as their number greatly increased, although they could not enlarge their quarter, built one story over another, squeezed together like sardines, and so cramped themselves both in body and soul. That part of the Jewish quarter which remained after the great fire, and which is called the Old Lane—that series of high, grimly dark houses, where a strangely grimacing, damp race of people bargains, is a horrible relic of the Middle Ages. The older synagogue exists no more ; it was less capacious than the present one, built later, after the Nuremberger exiles came into the community. It lay more to the north. The Rabbi had no need to ask his way. He found it from afar by the buzz of many voices often raised aloud. In the court of the House of God he parted from his wife, and after washing his hands at the fountain there, entered the lower part of the synagogue where the men pray, while Sara went up a flight of stairs and came into the place reserved for women.

This upper portion was a kind of gallery with three rows of seats painted a reddish brown, whose backs were fitted in a manner very convenient for placing the prayer-books, with a hanging board. Here the women sat gossiping together or standing up in deep prayer. However, they often went and peered with curiosity through the large grating which was on the eastern side, through the thin green lattice of which one could look down into the lower portion of the synagogue. There, behind high praying-desks, stood the men in their black cloaks, their pointed beards shooting out over white ruffs, and their skullcapped heads more or less concealed by a fourcornered scarf of white wool or silk, furnished with the prescribed tassels, in some instances also adorned with gold lace. The walls of the synagogue were simply white-washed, and no other ornament was to be seen except the gilded iron grating on the square dais, where the extracts from the Law were recited, and the holy ark, a costly embossed chest, apparently upheld by marble columns with rich capitols, whose flower and leaf-work flourished charmingly, covered with a curtain of cornflower blue velvet, on which a pious inscription was worked in gold spangles, pearls, and many-colored gems. Here hung the silver memorial lamp, and there also rose a barred dais, on whose crossed iron bars were all kinds of sacred utensils, among the rest the seven-branched candlestick ; while before it, facing the ark, stood the cantor, whose song was accompanied as if instrumentally by the voices of his two assistants, the bass and soprano. The Jews have forbidden all instrumental music to be used in their Church, thinking that hymns to God are more true in spirit or edifying when they rise from the glowing breast of man, than from the cold pipes of an organ. Beautiful Sara was charmed like any child when the cantor, an admirable tenor, raised his voice, and the ancient, deep, and solemn melodies which she knew so well bloomed forth in a fresher loveliness than she had ever dreamed of, while the bass murmured in harmony the deep dark notes, while in the pauses the soprano trilled sweetly and daintily. Such singing beautiful Sara had never heard in the synagogue of Bacherach, where the head of the congregation, David Levi, was the cantor ; and when this elderly trembling man, with his broken baa-ing voice, would try to trill like a girl, and in his desperate effort to do so shook his weak and drooping arm feverishly, it rather inspired laughter than devotion.

A something of devotedness, not unmingled with feminine curiosity, drew beautiful Sara to the grating, where she could look down into the lower division, or the so-called men's school. She had never before seen so many of her faith together, and it cheered her heart to be in such a multitude of those so nearly allied by race, thought, and sufferings. And her soul was still more deeply moved when three old men reverentially approached the sacred repository, unlocked the chest, drew aside the glittering curtain, and very carefully brought forth the Book which God once wrote with His own hand, and to maintain which the Jews have suffered so much — so much misery and hate, disgrace and death — a thousand years' martyrdom. This Book — a great roll of parchment — was wrapped like a princely child in a gaily embroidered scarlet velvet cloak ; above, on both the wooden rollers, were two little silver cases, in which many pomegranates and small bells moved and rang prettily, while before, on a silver chain, hung gold shields with many colored gems. The cantor took the Book, and, as if it had been really a child — a child for whom one has greatly suffered, and whom we love all the more on that account — he rocked it in his arms, skipped with it here and there, pressed it to his breast, and, like one inspired by a holy touch, broke forth into such a devout hymn of praise and thanksgiving that it seemed to beautiful Sara as if the pillars of the holy shrine began to bloom, and the strange and lovely blossoms and leaves of the capitols shot ever higher, and the notes of the treble were changed to nightingales, while the arch of the synagogue was shattered by the tremendous tones of the bass singer, and the joy and splendor of God gleamed down and through from the blue heavens. Yes, it was a beautiful psalm. The congregation sang over as in chorus the concluding verse, and the cantor walked slowly to the raised platform in the middle of the synagogue bearing the holy Book, while men and boys crowded hastily about him to kiss its velvet covering or even to touch it. When on the platform, the velvet cover as well as the wrappings covered with illuminated letters were removed, and the cantor, in the peculiar intonation which in the Passover service is still more peculiarly sounded, read the edifying narrative of the temptation of Abraham.

Beautiful Sara had modestly withdrawn from the grating, and a stout, much ornamented woman of middle age, with a self asserting, forward, good natured aspect, had with a nod allowed her to read in company in her prayer book. This lady was evidently no great scholar, for as she read with a murmuring voice the prayers as the women do, not being allowed to take part in the singing, Sara observed that she made the best she could of many words, and omitted not a few good passages altogether. But after a while the watery blue eyes of the good woman were languidly raised, an insipid smile gleamed over her red and white porcelain-like face, and in a voice which she strove to make as genteel as possible, she said to beautiful Sara, " He sings very well. But I have heard far better singing in Holland. You are a stranger, and perhaps do not know that the cantor is from Worms, and that they will keep him here if he will be content with four hundred florins a year. He is a charming man, and his hands are as white as alabaster. I think a great deal of a handsome hand ; it makes one altogether hand-some " — saying which, the good lady laid her own hand, which was really a fine one, on the shelf before her, and with a polite bow which intimated that she did not care to be interrupted while speaking, she added, " The little singer is a mere child, and looks very much emaciated. The basso is too ugly for anything, and our Star once said — it was very witty of him — ' The bass singer is a bigger fool than even a basso is expected to be ! ' All three eat in my restaurant — perhaps you don't know that I'm Elle Schnapper ? "

Beautiful Sara expressed her thanks for the information, when Schnapper Elle proceeded to narrate in detail how she had once been in Amsterdam, how she had been subjected to base designs on account of her remarkable beauty, how she had come to Frank-fort three days before Pentecost and married Schnapper, how he had passed away, and what touching things he had said on his deathbed, and how hard it was to carry on the business of a cook-shop and keep one's hands nice. Several times she glanced aside with contemptuous looks, apparently directed at some giggling girls, who were apparently examining her clothes. Truly this dress was remarkable enough — a very much puffed gown of white satin, on which all the animals of Noah's Ark were embroidered in gaudy colors ; a jacket of cloth of gold like a cuirass, the sleeves of red velvet, yellow slashed ; an immensely high cap on her head, with a mighty ruff of stiff white linen round her neck, which also bore a silver chain, to which hung all kinds of coins, cameos, and curiosities, chief among which was a great image of the city of Amsterdam, which rested on her bosom.

But the dresses of the other women were not less remarkable. They consisted of a medley of fashions of different ages, and many a little woman there was so covered with gold and diamonds as to look like a wandering jeweler's shop. It is true that there was a fashion of dress prescribed by law to the Frankfort Jews, and to distinguish them from Christians the men must wear yellow rings on their cloaks, while the women bore very high standing, blue striped veils on their caps. However, in the Jewish quarter these laws were little looked after, and there, especially on Sundays, and in the synagogue, the women put on as much magnificent apparel as they could — partly to be envied by others, and partly to advertise the wealth and standing of their husbands.

Meanwhile, as passages from the laws of Moses were being read from the Book of Moses, the devotion somewhat lulled. Many made themselves comfortable and sat down, whispering perhaps business affairs with a friend, or went out into the court to get a little fresh air. Small boys took the liberty of visiting their mothers in the women's section ; and here worship was still more loosely observed, as there was gossiping, cluttering together or laughing, while, as will always happen, the young joke about the elder, while the latter blamed the lightheadedness of the girls and the general degeneracy of the age. And just as there was a head singer in the place below, so was there a head-cackler and gossip in the one above. This was Puppy Reiss, a shallow, flat woman, who had an inkling of every trouble, and always had a scandal on her tongue. The usual butt of her pointed sayings was the poor Schnapper Elle, and she could mock right well the affected genteel airs and languishing manner

226

with which the latter accepted the mocking compliments of young men.

" Do you know," cried Puppy Reiss, " that Schnapper Elle said yesterday, ' If I were not beautiful and clever, and beloved, I had rather not live.' "

Then there was a loud tittering, and Schnapper Elle, who was not far distant, noting that this was all at her expense, lifted her nose in scorn, and sailed away like a proud galleon to some further place. Then Birdie Ochs, a plump and somewhat awkward lady, remarked compassionately that Schnapper Elle might be a little vain and small of mind, but that she was an honest, generous soul, and did much good to many folk in need.

" Particularly to Nose Star," snapped Puppy Reiss. And all who knew of this tender tie laughed all the louder.

" Don't you know," added Puppy spitefully, " that Nose Star now sleeps in Schnapper Elle's house! But just look at Susy Flörsheim down there, wearing the necklace which Daniel Fläsch pawned to her husband! Fläsch's wife is vexed at it—*that* is plain. And now she is talking to Mrs. Flörsheim. *How* amiably they shake hands! — and hate one another like Midian and Moab! How sweetly they smile on one another! Oh, you dear souls, *don't* eat one another up out of pure tenderness! I'll just steal up and listen to them!"

And so, like a sneaking wild cat, Puppy Reiss stole along and heard the two women mutually bewailing to one another how they had worked all the past week to clean up the house and scour the kitchen things, and all they had to do before Passover, so that not a crumb of leavened bread stuck to anything. And such troubles as they had baking the unleavened bread! Mrs. Fläsch had bitter griefs over this — for she had no end of trouble over it in the public bakery, for according to the ticket which she drew she could not bake there till the afternoon of the very last day, just before Passover Eve ; and then old Hannah had kneaded the dough badly, and the maids had rolled it too thin, and half of it was scorched in baking, and worst of all, rain came pouring through the bakehouse roof, and so wet and weary they had to work till late in the night.

" And, my dear Mrs. Flörsheim," said Mrs. Fläsch, with gracious friendliness most insincere, " you were a little to blame for that, because you did not send your people to help me in baking."

" Ah! pardon," replied the other. " My servants were so busy — the goods for the fair had to be packed — my husband "——

" Yes. I know," said Mrs. Fläsch, with cutting irony in her speech. " I know that you have much to do — many pledges and a good business, and necklaces "——

And a bitter word was just about to glide from the lips of the speaker, and Dame Flörsheim had turned as red as a lobster, when Puppy Reiss cried out loudly, " For God's sake! — the strange lady lies dying — water! water!"

Beautiful Sara lay insensible, pale as death, while a swarm of women, busy and bewailing, crowded round her. One held her head, another her arm, some old women sprinkled her with the glasses of water which hung behind their prayer desks for washing the hands in case they should by accident touch their own bodies. Others held under her nose an old lemon stuck full of spices, which remained from the last fastday, when it had served for smelling and strengthening the nerves. Exhausted and sighing deeply, beautiful Sara at last opened her eyes, and with mute glances thanked them for their kind care. But now the eighteen benedictions, which no one dare neglect, was heard in thrilling sound below, and the busy women hurried back to their places and offered the prayer as the rite ordains, standing up with their faces turned towards the east, which is that part of the heavens where Jerusalem lies. Birdie Ochs, Schnapper Elle, and Puppy Reiss stayed to the last by beautiful Sara — the first two to aid her as much as possible, the latter to find out why it was that she fainted so suddenly.

Beautiful Sara had swooned from a singular cause. It is a custom in the synagogue that any one who has escaped a great danger shall, after the reading of the extracts from the Law, appear in public and return thanks for his Divine deliverance. As Rabbi Abraham rose in the multitude to make his prayer, and beautiful Sara recognized her husband's voice, she also observed how its accents gradually subsided into the mournful murmur of the prayer for the dead. She heard the names of her dear ones and relations, accompanied by the words which convey the blessing on the departed ; and the last hope vanished from her soul, for it was torn by the certainty that those dear ones had really been slain, that her little niece was dead, that her little cousins Blossom and Birdie were dead, that little Gottschalk was dead too. All murdered and dead. And she too would have died from the agony of this conviction, had not a kind swoon poured forgetfulness over her soul.

CHAPTER III

WHEN BEAUTIFUL SARA, AFTER SERVICE WAS ENDED, WENT DOWN into the courtyard of the synagogue, the Rabbi stood there waiting for her. He nodded to her with a cheerful expression, and accompanied her out into the street, where there was no longer silence but a noisy multitude. It was like a stream of ants, what with bearded men in black coats, women gleaming like gold-chafers, boys in new clothes carrying prayerbooks after their parents, young girls who, because they could not enter the synagogue, now came bounding to their parents, bowing their curly heads to receive their blessings—all gay and merry, and walking about with the happy anticipations of people expecting a good dinner, the lovely aroma of which—causing the mouth to water—rose from many black pots and covers carried by smiling girls from the great public oven.

In this multitude there was specially to be remarked the form of a Spanish cavalier, whose youthful features bore that fascinating pallor which ladies generally associate with an unfortunate—and men, on the contrary—with a very fortunate—love affair. His gait, naturally careless, had however in it a somewhat affected mincing daintiness ; the feathers of his cap were more agitated by the aristocratic waving of his head than by the wind ; and his golden spurs, and the jeweled guard of his sword, which he bore on his arm, rattled rather more than was needed. A white cavalier's cloak enveloped his slender limbs in an apparently careless manner, which, however, betrayed the most careful arrangement of the folds. Passing and repassing, partly with curiosity, partly with an air of a connoisseur, he approached the women walking by, looked calmly at them, paused when he thought a face was worth the trouble, gave to many a pretty girl a passing compliment, and went his way heedless as to its effect. He had met beautiful Sara more than once, but seemed to be repulsed every time by her commanding look, or the enigmatical smiling air of her husband, but at last, proudly subduing all diffidence, he boldly faced both, and with foppish confidence made in a tenderly gallant tone the following speech : —

" I swear, Senora! — list to me! — I swear — by the roses of both the kingdoms of Castile, by the Aragonese hyacinths and the pomegranate blossoms of Andalusia! by the sun which illumines all Spain, with all its flowers, onions, pea-soups, forests, mountains, mules, he-goats, and Old Christians! by the canopy of heaven, on which this sun is the golden tassel! and by the God who sits on the roof of heaven and meditates day and night over the creation of new forms of lovely women! — I swear that you, Senora, are the fairest dame whom I have seen in all the German realm, and if you please to accept my service, then I pray of you the favor, grace, and leave to call myself your knight and bear your colors henceforth in jest or earnest!"

A flush as of pain rose in the face of beautiful Sara, and with one of those glances which are the most cutting from the gentlest eyes, and with a tone such as is bitterest from a beautiful voice, the lady answered as one deeply hurt : —

" My noble lord, if you will be my knight you must fight whole nations, and in the battle there will be little thanks to win and less honor ; and if you will wear my colors, then you must sew yellow rings on your cloak, or bind you with a blue-striped scarf, for such are my colors — the colors of my house, the House of Israel, which is wretched indeed, one mocked in the streets by the sons of good fortune."

A sudden purple red shot into the cheeks of the Spaniard ; an inexpressible confusion seemed to seize him as he stammered —

" Senora, you misunderstood me. An innocent jest — but, by God, no mockery, no jest at Israel. I myself am sprung from that house ; my grandfather was a Jew, perhaps even my father."

" And it is very certain, Senor, that your uncle is one," suddenly exclaimed the Rabbi, who had calmly witnessed this scene ; and with a merry quizzical glance he added, " And I myself will be bound that Don Isaac Abarbanel, nephew of the great Rabbi, is sprung from the best blood of Israel, if not from the royal race of David!"

The chain of the sword rattled under the Spaniard's cloak, his cheeks became deadly white, his upper lip twitched as with scorn in which there was pain, and angry death grinned in his eyes as in an utterly changed, ice cold, sharp voice he said : —

" Senor Rabbi, you know me. Well, then, you know also who I am. And if the fox knows that I belong to the blood of the lion, let him beware and not bring his fox beard into danger of death, nor provoke my anger. Only he who feels like the lion can understand his weakness."

" Oh, I understand it well," answered the Rabbi, and a mournful seriousness came over his brow. " I understand it well, how the proud lion, out of pride, casts aside his princely hide and goes mumming in the scaly armor of a crocodile, because it is the fashion to be a grinning, cunning, greedy crocodile! What can you expect the lesser beasts to be when the lion denies his nature? But beware, Don Isaac, *thou* wert not made for the element of the crocodile. For water — thou knowest well what I mean — is thy evil fortune, and thou wilt go under. Water is not thy element ; the weakest trout can live in it better than the king of the forest. Hast thou forgotten how the eddy of the Tagus would swallow thee?"

Bursting into loud laughter, Don Isaac suddenly threw his arms round the Rabbi's neck, covered his mouth with kisses, leapt with jingling spurs high into the air, so that the Jews who were passing by shrank back in alarm, and in his own natural hearty and joyous voice cried—

" Truly thou art Abraham of Bacherach! And it was a good joke, and more than that, a friendly act, when thou — in Toledo — didst leap from the Alcantara bridge into the water, and grasp by the hair thy friend, who could drink better than he could swim, and drew him to dry land. I was very near making really deep research whether there is actually gold in the sands of the Tagus, and whether the Romans were right in calling it the golden river. I assure you that I shiver even now from only thinking of that water party."

Saying this the Spaniard made a gesture as if he were shaking water from his garments. The countenance of the Rabbi expressed great joy as he again and again pressed his friend's hand, saying every time—

" I am indeed glad."

" And so indeed am I," answered the other. " It is seven years now since we met, and when we parted I was as yet only a little downy bird, and thou — thou wert already so staid and serious. But whatever became of the beautiful Donna who in those days cost thee so many sighs, which thou didst accompany with the lute ? "

" Hush, hush ! the Donna hears us — she is my wife, and thou hast thyself given her today a proof of thy taste and poetic skill."

It was not without some trace of his former embarrassment that the Spaniard greeted the beautiful lady, who amiably regretted that she, by expressing herself so plainly, had pained a friend of her husband.

" Ah, Senora," replied Don Isaac, " he who grasps too clumsily at a rose must not complain that the thorns scratch. When the star of evening mirrors itself, gold gleaming, in the azure flood "——

" For God's sake ! " interrupted the Rabbi, " cease ! If we wait till the star of evening mirrors itself, gold gleaming in the azure flood, my wife will starve, for she has eaten nothing since yesterday, and suffered much meantime."

" Well, then, I will take you to the best cookshop of Israel," said Don Isaac, " to the house of my friend Schnapper Elle, which is not far away. I already smell the delightful fragrance of the kitchen ! Oh, didst thou but know, O Abraham, how this perfume woos and wins me. This it is which, since I have dwelt in this city,

232

has so often lured me to the tents of Jacob. Intimacy with God's people is not a weakness of mine, and truly it is not to pray but to eat that I visit the Jews' Street."

" Thou hast never loved us, Don Isaac."

" Well," continued the Spaniard, " I like your cookery much better than your creed — which lacks the right sauce. I really never could rightly digest you. Even in your best days, under the rule of my ancestor David, who was king over Judah and Israel, I never could have held out, and certainly I should some fine morning have run away from Mount Zion and emigrated to Phœnicia or Babylon, where the joys of life foamed in the temple of the gods."

" Thou blasphemest, Isaac, blasphemest the one God," murmured the Rabbi grimly. " Thou art much worse than a Christian — thou are a heathen, a servant of idols."

" Yes, I am a heathen, and the melancholy self-tormenting Nazarenes are quite as little to my taste as the dry and joyless Hebrews. May our dear Lady of Sidon, holy Astarte, forgive me, that I kneel before the many sorrowed Mother of the Crucified and pray. Only my knee and my tongue worship death — my heart remains true to life."

" But do not look so sourly," continued the Spaniard, as he saw how little gratification his speech seemed to give the Rabbi. " Do not look at me with disdain. My nose is not a renegade. When I once by chance came at dinner time into this street, and the well-known savory odors of the Jewish kitchen rose to my nose, I was seized by the same yearning which our fathers felt for the fleshpots of Egypt — pleasant tasting memories of youth came unto me. I saw again in spirit the carp with brown raisin sauce which my aunt prepared so sustainingly for Friday eve — I saw once more the steamed mutton with garlic and horse-radish which might raise the dead, and the soup with dreamily swimming dumplings — the Klösschen — and my soul melted like the notes of an enamored nightingale — and since then I eat in the cookshop of my friend Donna Schnapper Elle."

Meanwhile they had arrived at the place so highly praised, where Schnapper Elle stood at the door greeting in a friendly manner the

233

strangers come to the fair, who, led by hunger, streamed in. Behind, and putting forth his head over her shoulders, was the tall Nose Star, anxiously and inquisitively observing them. Don Isaac approached the landlady with exaggerated grand style, who returned his satirically deep reverences with endless curtseys, after which he drew the glove from his right hand, wound it about with the fold of his cloak, and grasping that of Schnapper Elle, drew it over his moustaches and said : —

"Senora! your eyes rival the glow of the sun! But as eggs the longer they are boiled the harder they become, so on the contrary my heart grows softer the longer it is cooked in the flaming flashes of your eyes. From the yolk of my heart flies up the winged god Amor and seeks a cosy nest in your bosom. And oh, Senora, wherewith shall I compare that bosom? For in all the world there is no flower, no fruit, which is like to it! This plant is only of its kind alone! Though the storm wind tears away the leaves from the tenderest rose, your bosom is still a winter rose which defies all storms. Though the sour lemon the older it grows becomes yellower and more wrinkled, your bosom rivals in color and softness the sweetest pineapple. Oh, Senora, if the city of Amsterdam be as beautiful as you told me yesterday, and the day before, and every day, yet is the ground on which it rests far lovelier still."

The cavalier spoke these last words with affected earnestness, and squinted as if yearning at the great picture which hung from Schnapper Elle's neck. Nose Star looked down with inquisitive eyes, and the much praised bosom heaved so that the whole city of Amsterdam rocked from side to side.

"Ah!" sighed Schnapper Elle, "virtue is worth more than beauty. What use is my beauty to me? My youth is passing away, and since Schnapper is gone — anyhow, he had handsome hands — what avails beauty."

With that she sighed again, and like an echo all but inaudible Nose Star sighed behind her.

"Of what avail is your beauty?" cried Don Isaac. "Oh, Donna Schnapper Elle, do not sin against the goodness of creative Nature! Do not scorn her most charming gifts. She will terribly revenge herself. Those blessing eyes will be fully glazed, those winsome lips grow flat and commonplace, that chaste and charming form be changed into a barrel of tallow hardly pleasing to any one, and the city of Amsterdam at last rest on a spongy bog."

So he sketched bit by bit the appearance of Schnapper Elle, so that the poor woman was bewildered, and sought to escape the uncanny compliments of the cavalier. She was delighted at this instant to see beautiful Sara appear, as it gave her an opportunity to inquire whether she had quite recovered from her swoon. Thereupon she rushed into lively chatter, in which she fully developed her sham gentility, mingled with real kindness of heart, and related with much more sensibility than common sense the awful story how she herself had almost fainted with horror when she, as innocent and inexperienced as could be, came in a canal boat to Amsterdam, and the rascally porter who carried her trunk led her — not to a respectable tavern, but oh, horrors! — to a bawdy house! She saw what it was the moment she entered, by the brandy-drinking ; and, oh! — the immorality that was going on! — and she would, as she said, " really have swooned, if it had not been that during the six weeks she stayed there she only once ventured to close her eyes."

" I dared not," she added, " on account of my virtue, And all that took place because of my beauty! But virtue will stay — when good looks pass away."

Don Isaac was beginning to go somewhat critically into the details of this story when, fortunately, Squinting Aaron Hirschkuh from Hamburg on the Lahn came, a white serviette in his teeth, and bitterly bewailed that the soup was already served, and that the boarders were seated at table, but that the hostess was missing.

(The conclusion and the chapters which follow are lost, not from any fault of the author.)

The Hartz Journey

"Nothing is permanent but change, nothing constant but death. Every pulsation of the heart inflicts a wound, and life would be an endless bleeding, were it not for Poetry. She secures to us what Nature would deny,—a golden age without rust, a spring which never fades, cloudless prosperity and eternal youth."—Börne.

Black dress coats and silken stockings,
　　Snowy ruffles frilled with art,
Gentle speeches and embraces—
　　Oh, if they but held a heart!

Held a heart within their bosom,
　　Warmed by love which truly glows;
Ah! I'm wearied with their chanting
　　Of imagined lovers' woes!

I will climb upon the mountains,
　　Where the quiet cabin stands,
Where the wind blows freely o'er us,
　　Where the heart at ease expands.

I will climb upon the mountains,
　　Where the dark-green fir-trees grow;
Brooks are rustling—birds are singing,
　　And the wild clouds headlong go.

Then farewell, ye polished ladies,
　　Polished men and polished hall!
I will climb upon the mountain,
　　Smiling down upon you all.

THE TOWN OF GÖTTINGEN, CELEBRATED FOR ITS SAUSAGES AND University, belongs to the King of Hanover, and contains nine hundred and ninety-nine dwellings, divers churches, a lying-in-hospital, an observatory, a university prison, a library, and a "rathskeller," where the beer is excellent. The stream which flows by the town is termed the *Leine*, and is used in summer for bathing, its waters being very cold, and in more than one place so broad, that LUDER was obliged to take quite a run ere he could leap across.

The town itself is beautiful, and pleases most when looked at —
backwards. It must be very ancient, for I well remember that five
years ago, when I matriculated there (and shortly after expelled),
it had already the same grey, wise look, and was fully furnished
with beggars, beadles, dissertations, tea-parties, with a little dancing, washerwomen, compendiums, roasted pigeons, Guelphic
orders, professors ordinary and extraordinary, pipe-heads, court-
counselors, law-counselors and dismissal-counselors. Many even
assert that at the time of the great migrations, every German tribe
left an unbound copy of its members in the town and that from
these descended all the Vandals, Frisians, Suabians, Teutons, Saxons,
Thuringians, and others, who at the present day abound in Göttingen, where, separately distinguished by the color of their caps and
pipe-tassels, they may be seen straying singly or in hordes along
the Weender Street. They still fight their battles on the bloody
arena of the *Rasenmill*, *Ritschenkrug*, and *Bovden*, still preserve
the mode of life peculiar to their savage ancestors, and are still
governed partly by their *Duces*, whom they call " chief cocks," and
partly by their ancient law book, known as the " Comment," which
fully deserves a place among the *legibus barbarorum*.

The inhabitants of Göttingen are generally and socially divided
into Students, Professors, Philistines, and Cattle, the points of
difference between these castes being by no means strictly defined.
The cattle class is the most important. I might be accused of
prolixity should I here enumerate the names of all the students
and of all the regular and irregular professors ; besides, I do not
just at present distinctly remember the appellations of all the
students ; while among the professors are many who as yet have
no name at all. The number of the Göttingen *Philistines* must be as
numerous as the sands (or, more correctly speaking, as the mud)
of the sea ; indeed, when I beheld them of a morning, with their
dirty faces and clean bills, planted before the gate of the collegiate
court of justice, I wondered greatly that such an innumerable pack
of rascals should ever have been created by God.

More accurate information of the town of Göttingen may be
very conveniently obtained from its " Topography," by K. F. H.

Marx. Though entertaining the most sacred regard for its author, who was my physician, and manifested for me much esteem, still I cannot pass by his work with altogether unconditional praise, inasmuch as he has not with sufficient zeal combatted the erroneous opinion that the ladies of Göttingen have enormous feet. On this point I speak authoritatively, having for many years been earnestly occupied with a refutation of this belief. To confirm my views, I I have not only studied comparative anatomy, and made copious extracts from the rarest works in the library, but have also watched for hours, in the Weender Street, the feet of the ladies as they walked by. In the fundamentally erudite treatise, which forms the result of these studies, I speak Firstly, of feet in general ; Secondly, of the feet of antiquity ; Thirdly, of elephants' feet ; Fourthly, of the feet of the Göttingen ladies ; Fifthly, I collect all that was ever said in Ulrich's Garden on the subject of female feet ; Sixthly, I regard feet in their connection with each other, availing myself of the opportunity to extend my observation to ankles, calves, knees, &c. ; and finally and Seventhly, if I can manage to hunt up sheets of paper of sufficient size, I will present my readers with some copperplate facsimiles of the feet of the fair dames of Göttingen.

It was as yet very early in the morning when I left Göttingen, and the learned * * *, beyond doubt still lay in bed, dreaming that he wandered in a fair garden, amid the beds of which grew innumerable white papers written over with citations. On these the sun shone cheerily, and he plucked them and planted them in new beds, while the sweetest songs of the nightingales rejoiced his old heart.

Before the Weender Gate, I met two native and diminutive schoolboys, one of whom was saying to the other, " I don't intend to keep company any more with Theodore ; he is a low little blackguard, for yesterday he didn't even know the genitive of *Mensa*." Insignificant as these words may appear, I still regard them as entitled to record — nay, I would even write them as town motto on the gate of Göttingen, for the young birds pipe as the old ones sing, and the expression accurately indicates the narrow minded academic pride so characteristic of the " highly learned " Georgia Augusta.

Fresh morning air blew over the road, the birds sang cheerily, and little by little, with the breeze and the birds, my mind also became fresh and cheerful. Such a refreshment was needed for one who had long been imprisoned in a stall of legal lore. Roman casuists had covered my mind with grey cobwebs ; my heart was cemented firmly between the iron paragraphs of selfish systems of jurisprudence ; there was an endless ringing in my ears of such sounds as " Tribonian, Justinian, Hermogenian, and Blockheadian," and a sentimental pair of lovers seated under a tree appeared to me like an edition of the Corpus Juris with closed clasps. The road began to wear a more lively appearance. Milkmaids occasionally passed, as did also donkey drivers with their grey charges. Beyond Weende, I met Schaefer and Doris. This is not the idyllic pair sung by Gessner, but the well installed University proctors, whose duty it is to keep watch and ward, so that no students fight duels in Bovden, and above all that no new ideas (such as are generally obliged to remain for several decades in quarantine before Göttin-gen) are smuggled in by speculative instructors. Schaefer greeted me very collegially and congenially, for he too is an author, who has frequently mentioned my name in his semi-annual writings. In addition to this, I may mention that when, as was frequently the case, he came to summon me before the university court and found me " not at home " ; he was always kind enough to write the citation with chalk upon my chamber door. Occasionally a one-horse vehicle rolled along, well packed with students, who traveled away for the vacation — or for ever. In such a university town there is an endless coming and going. Every three years beholds a new student generation, forming an incessant human tide, where one semester wave washes along its predecessor, and only the old professors remain upright in the general flood, immovable as the Pyramids of Egypt. Unlike their Oriental contemporaries, no tradition declares that in them treasures of wisdom are buried.

From amid the myrtle bowers near Rauschenwasser, I saw two hopeful youths appear. A wench, who there carried on her hori-

239

zontal business, accompanied them as far as the highway, clapped
with a practised hand the meagre legs of the horses, laughed aloud
as one of the cavaliers, inspired with a very peculiar spirit of gallantry, gave her a " cut behind " with his whip, and traveled off
for Bovden. The youths, however, rattled along towards *Nörten*,
trilling in a clever manner, and singing charmingly the Rossinian
lay of " Drink beer, pretty, pretty 'Liza!'" These sounds I continued
to hear when far in the distance, and after I had long lost sight of
the amiable vocalists, as their horses, which appeared to be gifted
with characters of extreme German deliberation, were spurred and
lashed in a most excruciating style. In no place is the mistreatment
of horses carried to such an extent as in Göttingen ; and often, when
I beheld some lame and sweating hack, who, to earn the scraps of
fodder which maintained his wretched life, was obliged to endure
the torment of some roaring blade, or draw a whole wagon load
of students, I reflected : " Unfortunate beast! most certainly thy
first ancestors, in some paradise, did eat of forbidden oats."

In the tavern at Nörten I again met my two vocalists. One
devoured a herring salad and the other amused himself with the
leathern complexioned maid, Fusia Canina, also known as Stepping-
Bird. He passed from compliments to caresses, until they became
finally " hand-in-glove " together. To lighten my knapsack, I extracted from it a pair of blue pantaloons, which were somewhat
remarkable in a historical point of view, and presented them to the
little waiter, whom we called Humming-Bird. The old landlady,
Bussenia, brought me bread and butter, and greatly lamented that
I so seldom visited her, for she loved me dearly.

Beyond Nörten the sun flashed high in heaven. It evidently
wished to treat me honorably, and warmed my heart until all the
unripe thoughts which it contained came to full growth. The
pleasant Sun Tavern in Nörten should not be passed over in silence,
for it was there that I lunched. All the dishes were excellent, and
suited me far better than the wearisome, academical courses of
saltness, leathery dried fish and cabbage *rechauffée*, which characterized both our physical and mental pabulum at Göttingen.
After I had somewhat appeased my appetite, I noticed in the same

room of the tavern a gentleman and two ladies, who appeared about to depart on their journey. The man was clad entirely in green, even to his eyes, over which a pair of green spectacles cast in turn a verdigris glow upon his copper red nose. His general appearance was that which we may presume King Nebuchadnezzar to have presented after having passed a few years out at grass. The Green One requested me to recommend him to a hotel in Göttingen, and I advised him when there to inquire of the first convenient student for the *Hotel de Brübach*. One lady was evidently his wife: an altogether extensively constructed dame, gifted with a red mile square countenance, with dimples in her cheeks, which looked like spittoons for cupids. A copious double chin appeared below, like an imperfect continuation of the face, while her high piled bosom, which was defended by stiff points of lace and a many cornered collar, as if by turrets and bastions, reminded one of a fortress. Still, it is by no means certain that this fortress would have resisted an ass laden with gold, any more than did that of which Philip of Macedon spoke. The other lady, her sister, seemed her extreme antithesis. If the one were descended from Pharaoh's fat kine, the other was as certainly derived from the lean. Her face was but a mouth between two ears; her breast was as inconsolably comfortless and dreary as the Lüneburger heath; while her altogether driedup figure reminded one of a charity table for poor students of theology. Both ladies asked me, in a breath, if respectable people lodged in the Hotel de Brübach? I assented to this question with certainty and a clear conscience, and as the charming trio drove away, I waved my hand to them once more from the window. The landlord of the Sun laughed, however, in his sleeve, being probably aware that the Hotel de Brübach was a name bestowed by the students of Göttingen upon their University prison.

Beyond *Nordheim* mountain ridges begin to appear, and the traveler occasionally meets with a picturesque eminence. The wayfarers whom I encountered were principally hucksters, traveling to the Brunswick fair, and also swarms of women, every one of whom bore on her back an incredibly large pack, covered with linen. In these packs were cages, containing every variety of singing birds, which continually chirped and sung, while their bearers merrily hopped along and sang together. It seemed droll to thus behold one bird carrying another to market.

The night was dark as pitch as I entered *Osterode.* I had no appetite for supper, and at once went to bed. I was as tired as a dog, and slept like a god. In my dreams I returned to Göttingen, even to its very library. I stood in a corner of the Hall of Jurisprudence, turning over old dissertations, lost myself in reading, and when I finally looked up, remarked to my astonishment that it was night, and that the hall was illuminated by innumerable overhanging crystal chandeliers. The bell of the neighboring church struck twelve, the hall doors slowly opened, and there entered a superb colossal female form, reverentially accompanied by the members and hangers-on of the legal faculty. The giantess, though advanced in years, retained in her countenance traces of severe beauty, and her every glance indicated the sublime Titaness, the mighty Themis. The sword and scale were carelessly grasped in her right hand, while with the left she held a roll of parchment. Two young *Doctores Juris* bore the train of her faded grey robe ; by her right side the lean Court Counselor Rusticus, the Lycurgus of Hanover, fluttered here and there like a zephyr, declaiming extracts from his last legal essay, while by her left, her *cavaliere servante*, the privy legal counselor Cajacius, hobbled gaily and gallantly along, constantly cracking legal jokes, laughing himself so heartily at his own wit, that even the grave goddess often smiled and bent over him, exclaiming as she tapped him on the shoulder with the great parchment roll, " Thou little scamp, who cuttest down the tree from the top!" All of the gentlemen who formed her escort now drew nigh in turn, each having something to remark or jest over, either a freshly worked up system, or a miserable little hypothesis, or some similar monster of their own brains. Through the open door of the hall now entered many strange gentlemen, who announced themselves as the remaining magnates of the illustrious order ; mostly angular suspicious looking fellows, who with extreme complacency blazed away with their definitions and hair-splittings, disputing over every scrap of a title to the title of a pandect. And other forms continually flocked in, the forms of those who were learned in law in the olden time,—men in antiquated costume, with long counselor's wigs and forgotten faces, who expressed themselves greatly astonished that they, the widely famed of the previous century, should not meet with especial consideration ; and these, after their manner, joined in the general chattering and screaming, which like ocean breakers became louder and madder around the mighty Goddess, until she, bursting from impatience, suddenly cried, in a tone of the most agonised Titanic pain, " Silence! Silence! I hear the voice of the loved Prometheus. Mocking cunning and brute force are chaining the Innocent One to the rock of martyrdom, and all your prattling and quarreling will not allay his wounds or break his fetters!" So cried the Goddess, and rivulets of tears sprang from her eyes, the entire assembly howled in mortal fear, the ceiling of the hall burst asunder, the books tumbled madly from their shelves, and in vain the portrait of old Münchausen called out " Order " from his frame, for all crashed and raged more wildly around. I sought refuge from this Bedlam broke loose in the Hall of History, near that gracious spot where the holy images of the Apollo Belvedere and the Venus de Medici stand near together, and I knelt at the feet of the Goddess of Beauty. In her glance I forgot all the wild turmoil which I had run from, my eyes drank in with intoxication the symmetry and immortal loveliness of her infinitely blessed form ; Hellenic calm swept through my soul, while above my head Phœbus Apollo poured forth like heavenly blessings the sweetest tones of his lyre.

Awaking, I continued to hear a pleasant musical ringing. The flocks were on their way to pasture, and their bells were tinkling. The blessed golden sunlight shone through the window, illuminating the pictures on the walls of my room. They were pictures showing us all as heroes from the War of Liberation and among them were placed representations of the execution of Louis XVI. on the guillotine, and other decapitations which no one could behold without thanking God that he lay quietly in bed drinking excellent coffee, and with his head comfortably adjusted upon neck and shoulders.

After I had drunk my coffee, dressed myself, read the inscriptions upon the window panes, and set everything straight in the inn, I left Osterode.

This town contains a certain quantity of houses and a number of inhabitants, among whom are divers and sundry souls, as may be ascertained in detail from " Gottschalk's Pocket-Book for Hartz Travelers." Ere I struck into the highway I ascended the ruins of the very ancient Osteroder Burg. They consisted of merely the half of a great, thick walled tower, which appeared to be fairly honey-combed by time. The road to *Clausthal* led me again uphill, and from one of the first eminences I looked back into the valley where Osterode with its red roofs peeps out from among the green fir woods, like a moss rose from amid its leaves. The pleasant sunlight inspired gentle, child-like feelings. From this spot the imposing rear of the remaining portion of the tower may be seen to advantage.

There are many other ruined castles in this vicinity. That of Hardenberg, near Nörten, is the most beautiful. When one has, as he should, his heart on the left, that is, the liberal side, he cannot banish all sad feeling on beholding the rocky nests of those privileged birds of prey, who left to their effete descendants only their fierce appetites. So it happened to me this morning. My heart thawed gradually as I departed from Göttingen ; I again became romantic, and as I went on I made this poem : —

> Rise again, ye dreams forgotten ;
>   Heart-gate, open to the sun !
> Joys of song and tears of sorrow
>   Sweetly strange from thee shall run.
>
> I will rove the fir-tree forest,
>   Where the merry fountain springs,
> Where the free proud stags are wandering,
>   Where the thrush, my darling, sings.
>
> I will climb upon the mountain,
>   On the steep and rocky height,
> Where the grey old castle ruins
>   Stand in rosy morning light.

I will sit awhile reflecting
    On the times long passed away,
Lineages which once were famous,
    Glories sunk in deep decay.

Grass now grows upon the tilt-yard,
    Where the proud and daring man
Overcame another champion,
    And the prize of battle wan.

O'er the balcony twines ivy,
    Where the fairest gave the prize,
Conquering the haughty warrior
    Who had conquered — with her eyes.

Knightly conqueror — lady victor,
    Both o'ercome by Death's cold hand ;
So the scythe-knight, dry and ghastly,
    Lays us all low in the sand.

After proceeding a little distance, I overtook and went along with a traveling journeyman, who came from Brunswick, and related to me, that it was generally believed in that city that their young Duke had been taken prisoner by the Turks on his way to the Holy Land, and could only be ransomed by an enormous sum. The extensive travels of the Duke probably originated this tale. The people at large still preserve that traditional fable-loving train of ideas which is so pleasantly shown in their " Duke Ernst." The narrator of this news was a tailor, a neat little youth, but so thin, that the stars might have shone through him as through Ossian's misty ghosts. Altogether, he formed an eccentric mixture of caprice and melancholy. This was peculiarly expressed in the droll and affecting manner in which he sang that extraordinary popular ballad, " A beetle sat upon the hedge, *zumm, zumm !*" That is a pleasant peculiarity of us Germans. No one is so crazy but that he may find a crazier comrade who will understand him. Only a German *can* appreciate that song, and in the same breath laugh and cry himself to death over it. On this occasion, I also remark the depth to which the words of Goethe have penetrated into the life of the people. My lean comrade trilled occasionally as he went along. "Joyful and sorrowful, thoughts are free !" Such a corruption of a text is usual among the multitude. He also sang a song in which " Lottie by the grave of Werther " wept. The tailor ran over with sentimentalism in the words, " Sadly by the rose beds now I weep, where the late moon found us oft alone! Moaning where the silver fountains sleep, which rippled once delight in every tone." But he soon became capricious and petulant, remarking, that " We have a Prussian in the tavern at Cassel, who makes exactly such songs himself. He can't sew a single decent stitch. When he has a penny in his pocket, he always has two-penny thirst with it ; and when he has a drop, he takes heaven to be a blue jacket, weeps like a roof-spout, and sings a song with double poetry." I desired an explanation of this last expression, but my tailoring friend hopped about on his walking-cane legs and cried incessantly, " Double poetry is double poetry, and nothing else." Finally, I ascertained that he meant doubly rhymed poems or stanzas. Meanwhile, owing to his extra exertion and an adverse wind, the Knight of the Needle became sadly weary. It is true that he still made a great pretense of advancing, and blustered, " Now I will take the road between my legs." But he immediately after explained that his feet were blistered, and that the world was by far too wide ; and finally sinking down at the foot of a tree, he wagged his delicate little head like the tail of a troubled lamb, and woefully smiling, murmured. " Here am I, poor vagabond, already again done-in!"

The hills here became steeper, the fir woods below like a green sea, and white clouds above sailed along over the blue sky. The wildness of the region was, however, tamed by its uniformity and the simplicity of its elements. Nature, like a true poet, abhors abrupt transitions. Clouds, however fantastically formed they may at times appear, still have a white, or at least a subdued hue, harmoniously corresponding with the blue heaven and the green earth ; so that all the colors of a landscape blend into each other like soft music, and every glimpse of nature tranquilizes and reassures the soul. The late Hoffman would have painted the clouds spotted and chequered. And like a great poet, Nature knows how to produce the greatest effects with the most limited means. She has only a sun, trees and flowers, water and love. Of course, if the latter be lacking in the heart of the observer, the whole will, in all probability, present but a poor appearance ; the sun will be so and so many miles in diameter, the trees are for fire-wood, the flowers are classified according to their stamens, and the water is wet.

A small boy who was gathering brushwood in the forest for his sick uncle pointed out to me the village of *Lerrbach*, whose little huts with grey roofs scatter along for two miles through the valley. " There," said he, " live idiots with goitres, and white negroes." By white negroes the people mean *albinos*. The little fellow lived on terms of peculiar understanding with the trees, addressing them like old acquaintances, while they in turn seemed by their waving and rustling to return his salutations. He chirped like a thistle-finch ; many birds around answered his call, and ere I was aware, he had disappeared with his little bare feet and his bundle of brush amid the thickets. " Children," thought I, " are younger than we ; they can perhaps remember when they were once trees or birds, and are consequently still able to understand them. We of large growth are, alas! too old for that, and carry about in our heads too much legal lore, and too many sorrows and bad verses." But the time when it was otherwise recurred vividly to me as I entered Clausthal. In this pretty little mountain village, which the traveler does not behold until he stands directly before it, I arrived just as the clock was striking twelve, and the children came tumbling merrily out of school. The little rogues, nearly all red cheeked, blue eyed, flaxen haired, sprang and shouted, and awoke in me wistful and cheerful memories — how I once myself, as a little boy, sat all the forenoon long in a gloomy Catholic cloister school in Düsseldorf, without so much as daring to stand up, enduring meanwhile such a terrible amount of Latin, whipping, and geography, and how I too hurrahed and rejoiced beyond all measure when the old Franciscan clock at last struck twelve. The children saw by my knapsack that I was a stranger, and greeted me in the most hospitable manner. One of the boys told me that they had just had a lesson in religion, and showed me the Royal Hanoverian Catechism, from which they were questioned on Christianity. This little book was very badly printed, so that I greatly feared that the doctrines of faith made thereby but an unpleasant blotting-paper sort of impression upon the children's minds. I was also shocked at observing that the multiplication table contrasted with the Holy Trinity on the last page of the catechism, as it at once occurred to me that by this means the minds of the children might, even in their earliest years, be led to the most sinful scepticism. We Prussians are more intelligent, and, in our zeal for converting those heathens who are familiar with arithmetic, take good care not to print the multiplication table behind the catechism.

I dined in the " Crown," at Clausthal. My repast consisted of spring-green parsley-soup, violet-blue cabbage, a pile of roast veal, which resembled Chimborazo in miniature, and a sort of smoked herrings, called *Bückings*, from their inventor, William Bücking, who died in 1447, and who, on account of the invention, was so greatly honored by Charles V. that the great monarch in 1556 made a journey from Middleburg to Bievlied in Zealand for the express purpose of visiting the grave of the great fish-drier. How exquisitely such dishes taste when we are familiar with their historical associations! Unfortunately, my after-dinner coffee was spoiled by a youth, who, in conversing with me ran on in such an outrageous strain of noise and vanity that the milk was soured. He was a counterjumper, wearing twentyfive variegated waistcoats, and as many gold seals, rings, breast-pins, &c. He seemed like a monkey, who, having put on a red coat, had resolved within himself that clothes make the man. This gentleman had by heart a vast amount of charades and anecdotes, which he continually repeated in the most inappropriate places. He asked for the news in Göttingen, and I informed him that a decree had been recently published there by the Academical Senate, forbidding any one under penalty of three dollars to dock puppies' tails, because during the dog-days mad dogs invariably ran with their tails between their legs, thus giving a warning indication of the existence of hydrophobia, which could not be perceived were the caudal appendage absent. After dinner I went forth to visit the mines, the mint, and the silver refineries.

In the silver refinery, as has frequently been my luck in life, I could get no glimpse of the precious metal. In the mint I succeeded better, and saw how money was made. Beyond this I have never been able to advance. On such occasions mine has invariably been the spectator's part, and I verily believe that if it should rain dollars from heaven, the coins would only knock holes in my head, while the children of Israel would merrily gather up the silver manna. With feelings in which reverence was blended comically with emotion, I beheld the new born shining dollars, took one as it came fresh from the stamp in my hand, and said to it, " Young Dollar! what a destiny awaits thee! what a cause wilt thou be of good and of evil! How thou wilt protect vice and patch up virtue! how thou wilt be beloved and accursed! how thou wilt aid in debauchery, pandering, lying, and murdering! how thou wilt restlessly roll along through clean and dirty hands for centuries, until, finally laden with trespasses and weary with sin, thou wilt be gathered again unto thine own, in the bosom of an Abraham, who will melt thee down and purify thee, and form thee into a new and better being."

I will narrate in detail my visit to " Dorothea " and " Caroline," the two principal Clausthaler mines, having found them very interesting.

Half a German mile from the town are situated two large dingy buildings. Here the traveler is transferred to the care of the miners. These men wear dark, and generally steel-blue colored jackets, of ample girth, descending to the hips, with pantaloons of a similar hue, a leather apron bound on behind, and a rimless green felt-hat, which resembles a decapitated nine-pin. In such a garb, with the exception of the " back-leather," the visitor is also clad, and a miner, his " leader," after lighting his mine-lamp, conducts him to a gloomy entrance, resembling a chimney-hole, descends as far as the chest, gives him a few directions relative to grasping the ladder, and requests him to follow without fear. The affair is entirely devoid of danger, though it at first appears quite otherwise to those unacquainted with the mysteries of mining. Even the putting on of the dark convict dress awakens very peculiar sensations. Then one must clamber down on all fours, the dark hole is so *very* dark, and Lord only knows how long the ladder may be! But we soon see that this is not a single ladder running into the black eternity, for there are many of from fifteen to twenty rungs apiece, each standing upon a board capable of supporting a man, and from which a new hole leads in turn to a new ladder. I first entered the *Caroline*, the dirtiest and most disagreeable of that name with whom I ever had the pleasure of becoming acquainted. The rungs of the ladders were covered with wet mud. And from one ladder we descended to another with the guide ever in advance, continually assuring us that there is no danger so long as we hold firmly to the rungs and do not look at our feet, and that we must not for our lives tread on the side plank, where the buzzing bucket rope runs, and where two weeks ago a careless man was knocked down, unfortunately breaking his neck by the fall. Far below is a confused rustling and humming, and we continually bump against beams and ropes which are in motion, winding up and raising buckets of broken ore or of water. Occasionally we pass galleries hewn in the rock, called " stollen," where the ore may be seen growing, and where some solitary miner sits the livelong day, wearily hammering pieces from the walls. I did not descend to those deepest depths where it is reported that the people on the other side of the world, in America, may be heard crying, " Hurrah for Lafayette!" Where I went seemed to me, however, deep enough in all conscience ; amid an endless roaring and rattling, the mysterious sounds of machinery, the rush of subterranean streams, the sickening clouds of ore dust continually rising, water dripping on all sides, and the miner's lamp gradually growing dimmer and dimmer. The effect was really benumbing, I breathed with difficulty, and held with trouble to the slippery rungs. It was not *fright* which overpowered me, but oddly enough, down there in the depths, I remembered that a year before, about the same time, I had been in a storm on the North Sea, and I now felt that it would be an agreeable change could I feel the rocking of the ship, hear the wind with its thunder-trumpet tones, while amid its lulls sounded the hearty cry of the sailors, and all above was freshly swept by God's own free air.

Yes, air! — Panting for air, I rapidly climbed several dozens of ladders, and my guide led me through a narrow and very long gallery towards the Dorothea mine. Here it is airier and fresher, and the ladders are cleaner, though at the same time longer and steeper, than in the Caroline. I felt revived and more cheerful, particularly as I observed indications of human beings. Far below I saw wandering, wavering lights ; miners with their lamps came one by one upwards, with the greeting, " Good luck to you! " and receiving the same salutation from us, went onwards and upwards. Something like a friendly and quiet, yet at the same time terrific and enigmatical, recollection flitted across my mind as I met the deep glances and earnest pale faces of these men, mysteriously illuminated by their lanterns, and thought how they had worked all day in lonely and secret places in the mines, and how they now longed for the blessed light of day, and for the glances of wives and children.

My guide himself was a thoroughly honest, honorable, blundering German being. With inward joy he pointed out to me the " stollen " where the Duke of Cambridge, when he visited the mines, dined with all his train, and where the long wooden table yet stands, with the accompanying great chair, made of ore, in which the Duke sat. " This is to remain as an eternal memorial," said the good miner, and he related with enthusiasm how many festivities had then taken place, how the entire " stollen " had been adorned with lamps, flowers, and decorations of leaves ; how a miner boy had played on the zither and sung ; how the dear, delighted fat Duke had drained many healths, and what a number of miners (himself especially) would cheerfully die for the dear, fat Duke, and for the whole house of Hanover. I am moved to my very heart when I see loyalty thus manifested in all its natural simplicity. It is such a beautiful sentiment! And such a purely *German* sentiment! Other people may be more intelligent and wittier, and more agreeable, but none are so faithful as the real German race. Did I not know that fidelity is as old as the world, I would believe that a German had invented it. German fidelity is no modern " yours very truly," or " I remain your humble servant."

In your courts, ye German princes, ye should cause to be sung, and sung again, the old ballad of *The trusty Eckhart and the base Burgund* who slew Eckhart's seven children, and still found him faithful. Ye have the truest people in the world, and ye err when ye deem that the old, intelligent, trusty hound has suddenly gone mad, and snaps at your sacred calves!

And like German fidelity, the little mine lamp has guided us quietly and securely, without much flickering or flaring, through the labyrinth of shafts and stollen. We jump from the gloomy mountain-night—sunlight flashes around: —" Luck to you!"

Most of the miners dwell in Clausthal, and in the adjoining small town of Zellerfeld. I visited several of these brave fellows, observed their little household arrangements, heard many of their songs, which they skilfully accompany with their favorite instrument, the zither, and listened to old mining legends, and to their prayers, which they are accustomed to daily offer in company ere they descend the gloomy shaft. And many a good prayer did I offer up with them. One old climber even thought that I ought to remain among them, and become a man of the mines; and as I, after all, departed, he gave me a message to his brother, who dwelt near Goslar, and many kisses for his darling niece.

Immovably tranquil as the life of these men may appear, it is, notwithstanding, a real and vivid life. That ancient trembling crone who sits before the great cupboard and behind a stove, may have been there for a quarter of a century, and all her thinking and feeling is, beyond a doubt, intimately blended with every corner of the stove and the carvings of the cupboard. And cupboard and stove *live*,—for a human being hath breathed into them a portion of its soul.

Only a life of this deep looking into phenomena and its " immediateness " could originate the German popular tale whose peculiarity consists in this,—that in it not only animals and plants, but also objects apparently inanimate, speak and act. To thinking, harmless folk, who dwelt in the quiet hominess of their lowly mountain cabins or forest huts, the inner life of these objects was gradually revealed; they acquired a necessary and consequential character, a sweet blending of fantasy and pure human reflection. This is the reason why, in such fables, we find the extreme of singularity allied to a spirit of matter-of-factness, as when the pin and the needle wander forth from the tailor's home and go astray in the dark ; when the straw and the coal seek to cross the brook and are destroyed ; when the dust-pan and broom quarrel and fight on the stairs ; when the interrogated mirror of " Snow-drop " shows the image of the fairest lady, and when even drops of blood begin to utter dark words of the deepest compassion. And this is the reason why our life in childhood is so infinitely significant, for then all things are of the same importance, nothing escapes our attention, there is equality in every impression ; while, when more advanced in years, we must act with design, busy ourselves more exclusively with particulars, carefully exchange the pure gold of observation for the paper currency of book definitions, and win in the breadth of life what we have lost in depth. Now, we are grown-up, respectable people, we often inhabit new dwellings ; the house-maid daily cleans them, and changes at her will the position of the furniture, which interests us but little, as it is either new, or may belong today to Jack, tomorrow to Isaac. Even our very clothes are strange to us, we hardly know how many buttons there are on the coat we wear, — for we change our garments as often as possible, and none of them remain deeply identified with our external or inner history. We can hardly remember how that brown vest once looked, which attracted so much laughter, and yet on the broad stripes of which the dear hand of the loved one so gently rested!

The old crone who sat before the cupboard and behind the stove wore a flowered dress of some old fashioned material, which had been the bridal robe of her long buried mother. Her great-grandson, a flashing eyed blonde boy, clad as a miner, knelt at her feet, and counted the flowers on her dress. It may be that she has narrated to him many a story connected with that dress ; seriously pretty stories, which the boy will not readily forget, which will often recur to him when he, a grown man, works alone in the midnight galleries of the Caroline, and which he in turn will narrate when the dear grandmother has long been dead, and he himself, a silver haired, extinguished old man, sits amid the circle of *his* grandchildren before the great cupboard and behind the oven.

I lodged that night in " The Crown," where I had the pleasure of meeting and paying my respects to the old Court Counselor B——, of Göttingen. Having inscribed my name in the book of arrivals, I found therein the honored autograph of Adalbert von Chamisso, the biographer of the immortal *Schlemihl*. The landlord remarked of Chamisso that the gentleman had arrived during one terrible storm and departed in another.

Finding the next morning that I must lighten my knapsack, I threw overboard the pair of boots, and arose and went forth unto Goslar. There I arrived without knowing how. This much alone do I remember, that I sauntered up and down hill, gazing upon many a lovely meadow vale. Silver waters rippled and rustled, sweet woodbirds sang, the bells of the flocks tinkled, the many shaded green trees were gilded by the sun, and over all the blue silk canopy of heaven was so transparent that I could look through the depths even to the Holy of Holies, where angels sat at the feet of God, studying sublime thoroughbass in the features of the eternal countenance. But I was all the time lost in a dream of the previous night, and which I could not banish. It was an echo of the old legend, how a knight descended into a deep well, beneath which the fairest princess of the world lay buried in a deathlike magic slumber. I myself was the knight, and the dark mine of Clausthal was the well. Suddenly innumerable lights gleamed around me, watchful dwarfs leapt from every cranny in the rocks, grimacing angrily, cutting at me with their short swords, blowing terribly on horns, which ever summoned more and more of their comrades, and frantically nodding their great heads. But as I hewed them down with my sword, and the blood flowed, I for the first time remarked that they were not really dwarfs, but the red-blooming long-bearded thistle-tops, which I had the day before hewed down on the highway with my stick. At last they all vanished, and I came to a splendid lighted hall, in the midst of which stood my heart's loved one, veiled in white, and immovable as a statue. I kissed her mouth, and then—O Heavens!—I felt the blessed breath of her soul and the sweet tremor of her lovely lips. It seemed that I heard the divine command, "Let there be light!" and a dazzling flash of eternal light shot down, but at the same instant it was again night, and all ran chaotically together into a wild desolate sea! A wild desolate sea, over whose foaming waves the ghosts of the departed madly chased each other, the white shrouds floating on the wind, while behind all, goading them on with cracking whip, ran a motley harlequin,—and I was the harlequin. Suddenly from the black waves the sea monsters raised their misshapen heads, and yawned towards me, with extended jaws, and I awoke in terror.

Alas! how the finest dreams may be spoiled! The knight, in fact, when he has found the lady, ought to cut a piece from her priceless veil, and after she has recovered from her magic sleep, and sits again in glory in her hall, he should approach her and say, "My fairest princess, dost thou not know me?" Then she will answer, "My bravest knight, I know thee not!" And then he shows her the piece cut from her veil, exactly fitting into it, and she knows that he is her deliverer, and both tenderly embrace, and the trumpets sound, and the marriage is celebrated!

It is really a very peculiar misfortune that my love dreams so seldom have so fine a conclusion.

The name of Goslar rings so pleasantly, and there are so many very ancient and imperial associations connected therewith, that I had hoped to find an imposing and stately town. But it is always the same old story when we examine celebrities too closely. I found a nest of houses, drilled in every direction with narrow streets of labyrinthine crookedness, and amid which a miserable stream, probably the Gose, winds its flat and melancholy way. The pavement of the town is as bumpy as Berlin hexameters. Only the antiquities which are imbedded in the frame or mounting of the city—that is to say, its remnants of walls, towers and battlements —give the place a piquant look. One of these towers, known as the *Zwinger*, or donjonkeep, has walls of such extraordinary thickness that entire rooms are excavated therein. The open place before the

255

town, where the world-renowned shooting matches are held, is a beautiful large plain surrounded by high mountains. The market is small, and in its midst is a fountain, the water from which pours into a great metallic basin. When an alarm of fire is raised, they strike strongly on this cupformed basin, which gives out a very loud vibration. Nothing is known of the origin of this work. Some say that the devil placed it once during the night on the spot where it stands. In those days people were as yet fools, nor was the devil any wiser, and they exchanged gifts.

The town hall of Goslar is a whitewashed police station. The Guildhall, hard by, has a somewhat better appearance. In this building, equidistant from roof and ceiling, stand the statues of the German emperors. Partly-gilded, and altogether of a smoke black hue, they look, with their scepters and globes of empire, like roasted college beadles. One of the emperors holds a sword instead of a scepter. I cannot imagine the reason of this variation from the established order, though it has doubtless some occult signification, as Germans have the remarkable peculiarity of meaning something in whatever they do.

In Gottschalk's "Handbook" I had read much of the very ancient cathedral, and of the far famed imperial throne at Goslar. But when I wished to see these curiosities, I was informed that the church had been torn down, and that the throne had been carried to Berlin. We live in deeply significant times, when millennial churches are shattered to fragments, and imperial thrones are tumbled into the lumber room.

A few memorials of the late cathedral of happy memory are still preserved in the church of St. Stephen. These consist of stained glass pictures of great beauty, a few indifferent paintings, including a Lucas Cranach, a wooden Christ crucified, and a heathen altar of some unknown metal. This latter resembles a long four-cornered chest, and is supported by four caryatids, which, in a bowed position, hold their hands over their heads, and make the most hideous grimaces. But far more hideous is the adjacent wooden crucifix of which I have just spoken. This head of Christ, with its real hair and thorns and bloodstained countenance, represents, in the most masterly manner, the death of a *man*,—but not of a divinely born Saviour. Nothing but physical suffering is portrayed in this image,—not the sublime poetry of pain. Such a work would be more appropriately placed in a hall of anatomy than in a house of the Lord.

The sacristan's wife—deeply artistic—who led me about, showed me a special rarity. This was a many cornered, well planed black board covered with white numerals, which hung like a lamp in the middle of the building. Oh, how brilliantly does the spirit of invention manifest itself in the Protestant Church! The numbers on this board are those of the Psalms for the day, which are generally chalked on a common black tablet, and have a very sobering effect on an æsthetic mind, but which in the form above described even ornament the church, and fully make up the want of pictures by Raphael. Such progress delights me infinitely, since I, as Protestant, and, in fact, Lutheran, am ever deeply annoyed when Catholic opponents ridicule the empty, God forsaken appearance of Protestant churches.

I lodged in a tavern near the market, where I should have enjoyed my dinner much better if the landlord, with his long super-fluous face, and his still longer questions, had not planted himself opposite to me. Fortunately I was soon relieved by the arrival of another stranger, who was obliged to run in turn the gauntlet of *quis? quid? ubi? quibus auxiliis? cur? quomodo? quando?* This stranger was an old, weary, worn out man, who, as it appeared from his conversation, had been all over the world, had resided very long in Batavia, had made much money, and lost it all, and who now, after thirty years' absence, was returning to Quedlinburg, his native city,—" for," said he, " our family has there its hered-itary tomb." The landlord here made the highly intelligent remark that it was all the same thing to the soul where the body was buried. " Have you scriptural authority for that?" retorted the stranger, while mysterious and crafty wrinkles circled around his pinched lips and faded eyes. " But," he added, as if nervously desirous of conciliating, " I mean no harm against graves in foreign lands,—oh, no! The Turks bury their dead more beautifully than we ours ; their churchyards are perfect gardens, and there they sit by their white turbaned gravestones under cypress trees, and stroke their grave beards and calmly smoke their Turkish tobacco from their long Turkish pipes ; and then among the Chinese it is a real pleasure to see how genteely they walk around, and pray and drink tea among the graves of their ancestors, and play the violin ; and how beautifully they bedeck the beloved tombs with all sorts of gilt lacquered work, porcelain images, bits of colored silk, fresh flowers and variegated lanterns — all very fine indeed. How far is it yet to Quedlinburg ?"

The churchyard at Goslar did not appeal very strongly to my feelings ; but a certain very pretty blonde ringletted head which peeped smilingly from a parterre window did. After dinner I again took an observation of this fascinating window, but instead of a maiden, I beheld a vase containing white bell-flowers. I clambered up, stole the flowers, put them neatly in my cap and descended, unheeding the gaping mouths, petrified noses, and goggle eyes with which the street population, and especially the old women, regarded this qualified theft. As I, an hour later, passed by the same house, the beauty stood by the window, and as she saw the flowers in my cap, she blushed like a ruby and started back. This time I had seen the beautiful face to better advantage ; it was a sweet transparent incarnation of summer evening air, moonshine, nightingale notes, and rose perfume. Later in the twilight hour, she was standing at the door. I came — I drew near — she slowly retreated into the dark entry. I followed, and seizing her hand, said, " I am a lover of beautiful flowers and of kisses, and when they are not given to me I steal them." Here I quickly snatched a kiss, and as she was about to fly, I whispered apologetically, " Tomorrow I leave this town, and never return again." Then I perceived a faint pressure of the lovely lips and of the little hand, and I — went smiling away. Yes, I must smile when I reflect that this was precisely the magic formula by which our red and blue coated cavaliers more frequently win female hearts than by their mustachioed attractiveness. " Tomorrow I leave, and never return again ! "

My chamber commanded a fine view towards Rammelsberg. It

258

was a lovely evening. Night was out hunting on her black steed, and the long cloud mane fluttered on the wind. I stood at my window watching the moon. Is there really a " man in the moon "? The Slavs assert that there is such a being named Clotar, and he causes the moon to grow by watering it. When I was little, they told me that the moon was a fruit, and that when it was ripe it was picked and laid away, amid a vast collection of old full moons, in a great bureau, which stood at the end of the world, where it is nailed up with boards. As I grew older, I remarked that the world was not by any means so limited as I had supposed it to be, and that human intelligence had broken up the wooden bureau, and with a terrible " Hand of Glory " had opened all the seven heavens. Immortality — dazzling idea! who first imagined thee? Was it some jolly burgher of Nuremburg, who with nightcap on his head and white clay pipe in mouth sat on some pleasant summer evening before his door, and reflected in all his comfort that it would be right pleasant if, with unextinguishable pipe and endless breath, he could thus vegetate onwards for a blessed eternity? Or was it a lover who in the arms of his loved one thought the immortality-thought, and that because he could think and feel naught beside? Love! Immortality! it speedily became so hot in my breast that I thought the geographers had misplaced the equator, and that it now ran directly through my heart. And from my heart poured out the feeling of love ;—it poured forth with wild longing into the broad night. The flowers in the garden beneath my window breathed a stronger perfume. Perfumes are the feelings of flowers, and as the human heart feels most powerful emotions in the night when it believes itself to be alone and unperceived, so also do the flowers, pensive, yet ashamed, appear to await for concealing darkness that they may give themselves wholly up to their feelings and breathe them out in sweet odors. Pour forth, ye perfumes of my heart, and seek beyond yon blue mountain for the loved one of my dreams! Now she lies in slumber ; at her feet kneel angels, and if she smiles in sleep, it is a prayer which angels repeat ; in her breast is heaven with all its raptures, and as she breathes, my heart, though afar, throbs responsively. Behind the silken lids of her eyes the sun has gone down, and when they are raised, the sun rises, the birds sing, and the bells of the flock tinkle, and I strap on my knapsack and depart.

During these philosophical reflections I was surprised by a visit from Court Counselor B., who had recently arrived in Goslar. I had never before felt so sensibly the benevolent good nature of this man. I honor him greatly for his remarkable and practically successful cleverness, and yet more for his modesty. I found him unusually cheerful, fresh, and active. That he is the last, he recently proved by his new book, " The Religion of the Future," a work which so much delighted the Rationalists, vexed the Mystics, and set the great public astir. I myself am just at present a Mystic, following the advice of my physician to avoid all stimulants to thought. Still I do not fail to appreciate the inestimable value of Paulus, Gurlitt, Krug, Eichhorn, Bouterwek, Wegscheider, and others. By chance it is greatly to my advantage that these people clear away so much ancient rubbish, particularly the old ecclesiastical ruins and refuse which shelter so many snakes and stinks. The air in Germany is too dense and sultry, and I often fear lest I smother or am strangled by my beloved fellow-mystics in their heat of love. Therefore I will have anything but ill feeling towards my good rationalists, even if they cool the air a little too much. Fundamentally, Nature has appointed limits even to rationalism itself ; man cannot exist under an air pump or at the North Pole.

During the night which I passed at Goslar, a remarkably curious occurrence befell me. Even now I cannot think of it without terror. I am not by nature cowardly, but I fear ghosts almost as much as the " Austrian Observer." What is fear? Does it come from the understanding or from the natural disposition? This was a point which I frequently disputed with Dr. Saul Ascher, when we accidentally met in the *Café Royal* in Berlin, where I for a long time dined. The Doctor invariably maintained that we feared anything, because we recognized it as fearful, owing to certain determinate conclusions of the reason. Only the reason was an active power, — not the disposition. While I ate and drank to my heart's content, the Doctor demonstrated to me the advantages of reason. Towards

the end of his dissertation, he was accustomed to look at his watch
and remark conclusively, "Reason is the highest principle!"
Reason! Never do I hear this word without recalling Dr. Saul
Ascher, with his abstract legs, his tight fitting transcendental grey
long coat, his immovably icy face, which resembled a confused
amalgam of geometrical problems. This man, deep in the fifties,
was a personified straight line. In his striving for the positive, the
poor man had philosophised everything beautiful out of existence,
and with it everything like sunshine, religion, and flowers, so that
there remained nothing for him but a cold positive grave. The
Apollo Belvedere and Christianity were the two especial objects
of his malice, and he had even published a pamphlet against the
latter, in which he had demonstrated its unreasonableness and
untenableness. In addition to this, he had, however, written a great
number of books, in all of which *Reason* shone forth in all its
peculiar excellence, and as the poor Doctor meant what he said in
all seriousness, they were, so far, deserving of respect. But the great
joke consisted precisely in this, that the Doctor invariably cut such
a seriously absurd figure in not comprehending that which every
child comprehends, simply because it is a child. I visited the Doctor
several times in his own house, where I found him in company
with very pretty girls; for Reason, it seems, however abstract,
does not prohibit the enjoyment of the things of this world. Once,
however, when I called, his servant told me that the "Herr Doctor"
had just died. I experienced as much emotion on this occasion as if
I had been told that the "Herr Doctor" had just stepped out.

To return to Goslar. "The highest principle is Reason," said I,
consolingly to myself as I slid into bed. But it availed me nothing.
I had just been reading in Varnhagen von Ense's "German Nar-
rations," which I had brought with me from Clausthal, that terrible
tale of a son, who was about to be murdered by his father, and
was warned in the night by the ghost of his mother. The wonderful
truthfulness with which this story is depicted, caused while reading
it a shudder of horror in all my veins. Ghost stories invariably thrill
us with additional horror when read during a journey, and by night
in a town, in a house, and in a chamber where we have never before

been. We involuntarily reflect, " How many horrors may have been perpetrated on this very spot where I now lie?" Meanwhile, the moon shone into my room in a doubtful, suspicious manner ; all kinds of uncalled for shapes quivered on the walls, and as I laid me down and glanced fearfully around, I beheld —

There is nothing so uncanny as when a man sees his own face by moonlight in a mirror. At the same instant there struck a deep booming, yawning bell, and that so slowly and wearily, that I firmly believed that it had been full twelve hours striking, and that it was now time to begin over again. Between the last and next to the last tones, there struck in very abruptly, as if irritated and scolding, another bell, who was apparently out of patience with the slowness of its friend. As the two iron tongues were silenced, and the stillness of death sank over the whole house, I suddenly seemed to hear, in the corridor before my chamber, something halting and waddling along, like the unsteady steps of an old man. At last the door slowly opened, and there entered deliberately the late departed Dr. Saul Ascher. A cold fever drizzled through marrow and vein — I trembled like an aspen leaf, and scarcely dared I gaze upon the ghost. He appeared as usual, with the same transcendental grey long coat, the same abstract legs, and the same mathematical face ; only this latter was a little yellower than usual, and the mouth, which formerly described two angles of $22\frac{1}{2}$ degrees, was pinched together, and the circles around the eyes had a somewhat greater radius. Tottering, and supporting himself as usual upon his Malacca cane, he approached me, and said, in his usual drawling dialect, but in a friendly manner, " Do not be afraid, nor believe that I am a ghost. It is a deception of your imagination, if you believe that you see me as a ghost. What is a ghost? Define one. Deduce for me the conditions of the possibility of a ghost. In what reasonable connection does such an apparition coincide with reason itself? Reason, I say, reason!" Here the ghost proceeded to analyse reason, cited from Kant's " Critic of Pure Reason," part 2, 1st sect., chap. 3, the distinction between phenomena and noumena, then proceeded to construct a hypothetical system of ghosts, piled one syllogism on another, and concluded with the logical proof that there are absolutely no ghosts. Meanwhile the cold sweat beaded over me, my teeth clattered like castanets, and from very agony of soul I nodded an unconditional assent to every assertion which the phantom doctor alleged against the absurdity of being afraid of ghosts, and which he demonstrated with such zeal, that finally, in a moment of abstraction, instead of his gold watch, he drew a handful of graveworms from his vest pocket, and remarking his error, replaced them with a ridiculous but terrified haste. " The reason is the highest——— ! " Here the clock struck one, and the ghost vanished.

I wandered forth from Goslar the next morning, half at random, and half intending to visit the brother of the Clausthaler miner. I climbed hill and mount, saw how the sun strove to drive afar the mists, and wandering merrily through the trembling woods, while around my dreaming head rang the bell flowers of Goslar. The mountains stood in their white night robes, the fir trees were shaking sleep out of their branching limbs, the fresh morning wind curled their down drooping green locks, the birds were at morning prayers, the meadow vale flashed like a golden surface sprinkled with diamonds, and the shepherd passed over it with his bleating flock. I had gone astray. Men are ever striking out short cuts and by-paths, hoping to abridge their journey. It is in life as in the Hartz. However, there are good souls everywhere to bring us again to the right way. This they do right willingly, appearing to take a particular satisfaction, to judge from their self-gratified air and benevolent tones, in pointing out to us the great wanderings which we have made from the right road, the abysses and morasses into which we might have sunk, and, finally, what a piece of good luck it was for us to encounter betimes people who knew the road as well as themselves. Such a guide-post I found not far from the Hartzburg, in the person of a well fed citizen of Goslar—a man of shining, double chinned, slow cunning countenance, who looked as if he had discovered the murrain. We went along for some distance together, and he narrated many ghost stories, which would have all been well enough if they had not all concluded with an explanation that there was no real ghost in the case, but that the

specter in white was a poacher, that the wailing sound was caused
by the new born farrow of a wild sow, and that the rapping and
scraping on the roof was caused by cats. " Only when a man is
sick," observed my guide, " does he ever believe that he sees
ghosts;" and to this he added the remark, that as for his own
humble self, he was but seldom sick, — only at times a little wrong
about the head, and that he invariably relieved this by dieting. He
then called my attention to the appropriateness and use of all things
in nature. Trees are green, because green is good for the eyes. I
assented to this, adding that the Lord had made cattle because beef
soup strengthened man ; that jackasses were created for the purpose of serving as comparisons, and that man existed that he might
eat beef soup, and realize that he was no jackass. My companion
was delighted to meet with one of sympathetic views ; his face
glowed with a greater joy, and on parting from me he appeared
to be sensibly moved.

As long as he was with me, Nature seemed benumbed, but when
he departed the trees began again to speak, the sun rays flashed,
the meadow flowers danced once more, and the blue heavens embraced the green earth. Yes, I know better. God hath created man
that he may admire the beauty and the glory of the world. Every
author, be he ever so great, desires that his work may be praised.
And in the Bible, that great memoir of God, it is distinctly written
that he hath made man for his own honor and praise.

After long wandering here and there, I came to the dwelling
of the brother of my Clausthaler friend. Here I staid all night and
experienced the following beautiful poem : —

I

On yon rock the hut is standing
Of the ancient mountaineer ;
There the dark-green fir-trees rustle,
And the moon is shining clear.

In the hut there stands an arm-chair,
Which quaint carvings beautify ;
He who sits therein is happy,
And that happy man am I.

On the footstool sits a maiden,
  On my lap her arms repose,
With her eyes like blue stars beaming,
  And her mouth a new-born rose.

And the dear blue stars shine on me,
  Full as heaven is their gaze,
And her little lily finger
  Archly on the rose she lays.

" Nay, thy mother cannot see us,
  For she spins the whole day long ;
And thy father plays the cithern
  As he sings a good old song."

And the maiden softly whispers,
  So that none around may hear ;
Many a solemn little secret
  Hath she murmured in my ear :

" Since I lost my aunt who loved me,
  Now we never more repair
To the shooting-ground at Goslar,
  And it is so pleasant there !

And up here it is so lonely,
  On the rocks where cold winds blow ;
And in winter we are ever
  Deeply buried in the snow.

And I'm such a timid creature,
  And I'm frightened like a child
At the evil mountain spirits,
  Who by night are raging wild."

At the thought the maid was silent,
  As if terror thrilled her breast,
And the small hands, white and dimpled,
  To her sweet blue eyes she pressed.

Loud without the fir-trees rustle,
  Loud the spinning-wheel still rings,
And the cithern sounds above them,
  While the father softly sings :

" Dearest child ! no evil spirits
  Should have power to cause thee dread ;
For good angels still are watching
  Night and day around thy head."

265

2

Fir-tree with his dark-green fingers
   Taps upon the window low,
And the moon, a yellow listener,
   Casts within her sweetest glow.

Father, mother, both are sleeping,
   Near at hand their rest they take ;
But we two, in pleasant gossip,
   Keep each other long awake.

" That thou prayest much too often,
   Seems unlikely, I declare ;
On thy lips there's a contraction
   Which was never born of prayer.

Ah ! that heartless, cold expression !
   Terrifies me as I gaze,
Though a solemn sorrow darkens
   In thine eyes their gentle rays.

And I doubt if thou believest
   What is held for truth by most ;
Hast thou faith in God the Father
   In the Son and Holy Ghost ?"

" Ah, my darling ! when an infant
   By my mother's knee I stood,
I believed in God the Father,
   He who ruleth great and good.

He who made the world so lovely,
   Gave man beauty, gave him force,
And to sun and moon and planets
   Pre-appointed each their course.

As I older grew, my darling,
   And my way in wisdom won,
I in reason comprehended,
   And believe now in the Son.

In the well-loved Son, who, loving,
   Oped the gates of Love so wide ;
And for thanks, — as is the custom, —
   By the world was crucified.

266

Now, at man's estate arriving,
  Full experience I boast ;
And with heart expanded, truly
  I believe in the Holy Ghost,

Who hath worked the greatest wonders,
  Greater still he'll work again ;
He hath broken tyrants' strongholds,
  And he breaks the vassal's chain.

Ancient deadly wounds he healeth,
  He renews man's ancient right ;
All to him, born free and equal,
  Are as nobles in his sight.

Clouds of evil flee before him,
  And those cobwebs of the brain
Which forbade us love and pleasure,
  Scowling grimly on our pain.

And a thousand knights well weaponed
  Hath he chosen, and required
To fulfil his holy bidding,
  All with noblest zeal inspired.

Lo! their precious swords are gleaming,
  And their banners wave in fight!
What! thou fain wouldst see, my darling,
  Such a proud and noble knight?

Well, then, gaze upon me, dearest ;
  I am of that lordly host.
Kiss me! I am an elected
  True knight of the Holy Ghost!"

3

Silently the moon goes hiding
  Down behind the dark-green trees,
And the lamp which lights our chamber
  Flickers in the evening breeze.

But the star-blue eyes are beaming
  Softly o'er the dimpled cheeks,
And the purple rose is gleaming,
  While the gentle maiden speaks.

267

" Little people — fairy goblins —
    Steal away our meat and bread ;
In the chest it lies at evening,
    In the morning it has fled.

From our milk the little people
    Steal the cream and all the best ;
Then they leave the dish uncovered,
    And our cat drinks up the rest.

And the cat's a witch, I'm certain,
    For by night, when storms arise,
Oft she glides to yonder ' Ghost-Rock,'
    Where the fallen tower lies.

There was once a splendid castle,
    Home of joy and weapons bright,
Where there swept in stately torch-dance
    Lady, page, and armed knight.

But a sorceress charmed the castle,
    With its lord and ladies fair ;
Now it is a lonely ruin,
    And the owls are nestling there.

But my aunt hath often told me,
    Could I speak the proper word,
In the proper place up yonder,
    When the proper hour occurred,

Then the walls would change by magic
    To a castle gleaming bright,
And I'd see in stately dances
    Dame and page and gallant knight.

He who speaks the word of power
    Wins the castle for his own,
And the knight with drum and trumpet
    Loud will hail him lord alone."

Thus sweet legendary pictures
    From the little rose-mouth bloom,
And the gentle eyes are shedding
    Star-blue lustre through the gloom.

Round my hand the little maiden
    Winds her gold locks as she will,
Gives a name to every finger,
    Kisses, smiles, and then is still.

The Hartz Journey

All things in the silent chamber
    Seem at once familiar grown,
As if e'en the chairs and clothes-press
    Well of old to me were known.

Now the clock talks kindly, gravely,
    And the cithern, as 'twould seem,
Of itself is faintly chiming,
    And I sit as in a dream.

Now the proper hour is o'er us,
    Here's the place where't should be heard ;
Child! how thou wouldst be astonished
    Should I speak the magic word!

If I spoke that word, then fading
    Night would thrill in fearful strife ;
Trees and streams would roar together
    As the castle woke to life.

Ringing lutes and goblin ditties
    From the clefted rock would sound,
Like a mad and merry spring-tide
    Flowers grow forest-high around.

Flowers — startling, wondrous flowers,
    Leaves of vast and fabled form,
Strangely perfumed, wildly quivering,
    As if thrilled with passion's storm.

Roses, wild as crimson flashes,
    O'er the busy tumult rise ;
Giant lilies, white as crystal,
    Shoot like columns to the skies.

Great as suns, the stars above us
    Gaze adown with burning glow ;
In the lilies' giant calyx
    All their floods of flashes flow.

We ourselves, my little maiden,
    Would be changed more than all ;
Torchlight gleams o'er gold and satin
    Round us merrily would fall.

> Thou thyself wouldst be the princess,
>   And this hut thy castle high ;
> Ladies, lords, and graceful pages
>   Would be dancing, singing by.
>
> I, however, I have conquered
>   Thee, and all things, with the word : —
> Serfs and castle : — lo ! with trumpet
>   Loud they hail me as their lord !

The sun rose. Clouds flitted away like phantoms at the third crow of the cock. Again I wandered up hill and down dale, while overhead swept the fair sun, ever lighting up new scenes of beauty. The Spirit of the Mountain evidently favored me, well knowing that a " poetical character " has it in his power to say many a fine thing of him, and on this morning he let me see his Hartz as it is not, most assuredly, seen by every one. But the Hartz also saw me as I am seen by few, and there were as costly pearls on my eyelashes as on the grass of the valley. The morning dew of love wetted my cheeks ; the rustling pines understood me ; their parting twigs waved up and down, as if, like mute mortals, they would express their joy with gestures of their hands, and from afar I heard beautiful and mysterious chimes, like the bell tones of some long lost forest church. People say that these sounds are caused by the cattle bells, which in the Hartz ring with remarkable clearness and purity.

It was noon, according to the position of the sun, as I chanced upon such a flock, and its herd, a friendly, blonde young fellow, told me that the great hill at whose base I stood was the old world renowned Brocken. For many leagues around there is no house, and I was glad enough when the young man invited me to share his meal. We sat down to a *déjeûner dinatoire*, consisting of bread and cheese. The sheep snatched up our crumbs, while pretty shining heifers jumped around, ringing their bells roguishly, and laughing at us with great merry eyes. We made a royal meal, my host appearing to me altogether a king ; and as he is the only monarch who has ever given me bread, I will sing him right royally.

Every shepherd is a monarch,
    And a hillock is his throne,
While the sun above him shining
    Is his heavy golden crown.

Sheep before his feet are lying,
    Softest flatterers, crossed with red,
And the calves are " cavalieros,"
    Round they strut with haughty head.

Court-players are the he-goats,
    And the wild bird and the cow,
With their piping and their herd-bell,
    Are the king's musicians now.

Ah ! they ring and sing so sweetly,
    And so sweetly chime around
Rustling waterfall and fir-trees,
    While the monarch slumbers sound.

As he sleeps, his trusty sheep-dog
    As prime minister must reign ;
How his snarling and his barking
    Echo over hill and plain.

Dozing still, the monarch murmurs,
    " Sure such work was never seen
As this reigning : I were happier
    Snug at home beside my queen !

There my royal head, when weary,
    In my queen's arms softly lies,
And my endless broad dominion
    In her deep and gentle eyes."

We took leave of each other in a friendly manner, and with a
light heart I began to ascend the mountain. I was soon welcomed
by a grove of stately firs, for whom I in every respect entertain the
most reverential regard ; for these trees in particular have not
found growing to be such an easy business, and during the days of
their youth it fared hard with them. The mountain is here sprinkled
with a great number of blocks of granite, and most of the trees are
obliged either to twine their roots over the stones, or split them in
two, that they may thus, with trouble, get at a little earth to

271

nourish them. Here and there stones lie on each other, forming, as it were, a gate, and over all rise the trees, their naked roots twining down over the wild portals, and first reaching the ground at its base, so that they appear to be growing in the air. And yet they have forced their way up to that startling height, and grown into one with the rocks, they stand more securely than their easy comrades, who are rooted in the tame forest soil of the level country. So it is in life with those great men who have strengthened and established themselves by resolutely subduing the obstacles which oppressed their youth. Squirrels climbed amid the fir twigs, while beneath yellow brown deer were quietly grazing. I cannot comprehend, when I see such a noble animal, how educated and refined people can take pleasure in its chase or death. Such a creature was once more merciful than man, and suckled the longing " Schmerzenreich " of the holy Genofeva.

Most beautiful were the golden sun rays shooting through the dark green of the firs. The roots of the trees formed a natural stairway, and everywhere my feet encountered swelling beds of moss, for the stones are here covered foot deep, as if with light green velvet cushions. Everywhere a pleasant freshness and the dreamy murmur of streams. Here and there we see water rippling silver clear amid the rocks, washing the bare roots and fibres of trees. Bend down to the current and listen, and you may hear at the same time the mysterious history of the growth of the plants, and the quiet pulsations of the heart of the mountain. In many places, the water jets strongly up amid rocks and roots, forming little cascades. It is pleasant to sit in such places. All murmurs and rustles so sweetly and strangely, the birds carol broken strains of love longing, the trees whisper like a thousand girls, odd flowers peep up like a thousand maidens' eyes, stretching out to us their curious, broad, droll pointed leaves ; the sun rays flash here and there in sport ; the thoughtful herbs are telling their green legends ; all seems enchanted, and becomes more secret and confidential ; an old, old dream is realized—the loved one appears. Alas that all so quickly vanishes!

The higher we ascend, so much the shorter and more dwarflike do the fir trees become, shrinking up, as it were, within themselves, until finally only whortle berries, bilberries, and mountain herbs remain. It is also sensibly colder. Here, for the first time, the granite boulders which are frequently of enormous size, become fully visible. These may well have been the balls which evil spirits cast at each other on the Walpurgis night, when the witches come riding hither on brooms and pitchforks, when the mad, unhallowed revelry begins, as our credulous nurses have told us, and as we may see it represented in the beautiful Faust pictures of Master Retsch. Yes, a young poet, who, in journeying from Berlin to Göttingen, on the first evening in May, passed the Brocken, remarked how certain belles-lettered ladies held their æsthetic tea-circle in a rocky corner, how they comfortably read the Evening Journal, how they praised as an universal genius their pet billy goat, who, bleating, hopped around their table, and how they passed a final judgment on all the manifestations of German literature. But when they at last fell upon " Ratcliff " and " Almansor," utterly denying to the author aught like piety or Christianity, the hair of the youth rose on end, terror seized him — I spurred my steed and rode onwards!

In fact, when we ascend the upper half of the Brocken, no one can well help thinking of the attractive legends of the Blocksberg, and especially of the great mystical German national tragedy of Doctor Faust. It ever seemed to me that I could hear the cloven foot scrambling along behind, and some one inhaling an atmosphere of humor. And I verily believe that " Mephisto " himself must breathe with difficulty when he climbs his favorite mountain, for it is a road which is to the last degree exhausting, and I was glad enough when I at last beheld the long desired Brocken house.

This house, as every one knows from numerous pictures, consists of a single story, and was erected in the year 1800 by Count Stollberg Wernigerode, for whose profit it is managed as a tavern. On account of the wind and cold in winter its walls are incredibly thick. The roof is low. From its midst rises a tower like observatory, and near the house lie two little outbuildings, one of which in earlier times served as shelter to the Brocken visitors.

On entering the Brocken house, I experienced a somewhat unusual and legend like sensation. After a long solitary journey amid rocks and pines, the traveler suddenly finds himself in a house amid the clouds. Far below lie towns, hills, and forests, while above he encounters a curiously blended circle of strangers, by whom he is received, as is usual in such assemblies, almost like an expected companion — half inquisitively and half indifferently. I found the house full of guests, and, as becomes a wise man, I first reflected on the night, and the discomfort of sleeping on straw. My part was at once determined on. With the voice of one dying I called for tea, and the Brocken landlord was reasonable enough to perceive that the sick gentleman must be provided with a decent bed. This he gave me in a narrow room, where a young merchant — a long emetic in a brown overcoat — had already established himself.

In the public room I found a full tide of bustle and animation. There were students from different universities. Some of the newly arrived were taking refreshments. Others, preparing for departure, buckled on their knapsacks, wrote their names in the album, and received Brocken bouquets from the housemaids. There was jesting, singing, springing, trilling, some questioning, some answering, fine weather, footpath, *prosit !* — luck be with you! Adieu! Some of those leaving were also partly drunk, and these derived a twofold pleasure from the beautiful scenery, for a tipsy man sees double.

After refreshing myself I ascended the observatory, and there found a little gentleman with two ladies, one of whom was young and the other elderly. The young lady was very beautiful — a superb figure, flowing locks, surmounted by a helmlike black satin *chapeau*, amid whose white plumes the wind played ; fine limbs, so closely enwrapped by a black silk mantle that their exquisite form was made manifest, and great free eyes, calmly looking down into the great free world.

When as yet a boy, I thought of naught save tales of magic and wonder, and every fair lady who had ostrich feathers on her head I regarded as an elfin queen. If I observed that the train of her dress was wet, I believed at once that she must be a water-fairy. Now I know better, having learned from natural history that those symbolical feathers are found on the most stupid of birds, and that the skirt of a lady's dress may be wetted in a very natural way. But if I had, with those boyish eyes, seen the aforesaid young lady in the aforesaid position on the Brocken, I would most assuredly have thought " that is the fairy of the mountain, and she has just uttered the charm which has caused all down there to appear so wonderful." Yes, at the first glance from the Brocken everything appears in a high degree marvelous. New impressions throng in on every side, and these, varied and often contradictory, unite in our soul to an overpowering and confusing sensation. If we succeed in grasping the idea of this sensation, we shall comprehend the character of the mountain. This character is entirely German as regards not only its advantages but also its defects. The Brocken is a German. With German thoroughness it points out to us — sharply and accurately defined as in a panorama — the hundreds of cities, towns, and villages, which are principally situated to the north, and all the mountains, forests, rivers, and plains which lie infinitely far around. But for this very cause everything appears like an accurately designed and perfectly colored map, and nowhere is the eye gratified by really beautiful landscapes — just as we German compilers, owing to the honorable exactness with which we attempt to give all and everything, never appear to think of giving integral parts in a beautiful manner. The mountain in consequence has a certain calm, German, intelligent, tolerant character, simply because it can see things so distant yet so distinctly. And when such a mountain opens its giant eyes, it may be that it sees somewhat more than we dwarfs, who with our weak eyes climb over it. Many indeed assert that the Blocksberg is very Philistine, and *Claudius* once sang " The Blocksberg is the lengthy Sir Philistine." But that was an error. On account of its bald head, which it occasionally covers with a cloud-cap, the Blocksberg has indeed something of a Philistine aspect, but this, as with many other great Germans, is the result of pure irony ; for it is notorious that it has its wild student and fantastic times, as for instance on the first night of May. Then it casts his cloud-cap uproariously and merrily on high, and becomes, like the rest of us, real German romantic mad.

275

I soon sought to entrap the beauty into a conversation, for we only begin to fully enjoy the beauties of nature when we talk about them on the spot. She was not *spirituelle*, but attentively intelligent. A perfect model of gentility. I do not mean that commonplace, stiff, negative respectability, which knows exactly what must *not* be done or said, but that rarer, independent, positive gentility, which inspires an accurate knowledge of what we may venture on, and which amid all our ease and abandon inspires the utmost social confidence. I developed, to my own amazement, much geographical knowledge, detailed to the curious beauty the names of all the towns which lay before us, and sought them out for her on the map, which with all the solemnity of a teacher I had spread out on the stone table which stands in the center of the tower. I could not find many of the towns, possibly because I sought them more with my fingers than with my eyes, which were scanning the face of the fair lady, and discovering in it fairer regions than those of " Schierke " and " Elend." This countenance was one of those which never excite, and seldom enrapture, but which always please. I love such faces, for they smile my agitated heart to rest.

The lady was as yet unmarried although in the full bloom so perfectly adapted to the wedded state. But it is a matter of daily occurrence that the most beautiful girls seem to be slowest in finding husbands. This was the case of yore—it is well known that the three Graces remained maids.

I could not divine the relation in which the little gentleman stood to the ladies whom he accompanied. He was a spare and remarkable figure. A head sprinkled with grey hair, which fell over his low forehead down to his dragon-fly eyes, and a round, broad nose, which projected boldly forwards, while his mouth and chin seemed retreating in terror back to his ears. His face looked as if formed of the soft yellowish clay with which sculptors mold their first models, and when the thin lips pinched together, thousands of semicircular and faint wrinkles appeared on his cheeks. The little man never spoke a word, only at times when the elder lady whispered something friendly in his ear, he smiled like a lapdog which has taken cold.

The elder lady was the mother of the younger, and she too was gifted with an air of extreme respectability and refinement. Her eyes betrayed a morbid, dreamy depth of thought, and about her mouth there was an expression of confirmed piety, yet withal it seemed to me that she had once been very beautiful, and often smiled, and taken and given many a kiss. Her countenance resembled a *codex palimpsestus*, in which, from beneath the recent black monkish writing of some text of a Church father, there peeped out the half obliterated verse of an old Greek love poet. Both ladies had been that year with their companion in Italy, and told me many things of the beauties of Rome, Florence, and Venice. The mother had much to say of the pictures of Raphael in St. Peter's, the daughter spoke more of the opera in La Fenice.

While we conversed, the sun sank lower and lower, the air grew colder, twilight stole over us, and the tower platform was filled with students, traveling mechanics, and a few honest citizens with their spouses and daughters, all of whom were desirous of witnessing the sunset. That is truly a sublime spectacle, which elevates the soul to prayer. For a full quarter of an hour all stood in solemn silence, gazing on the beautiful fire ball as it sank in the west ; faces were rosy in the evening red ; hands were involuntarily folded ; it seemed as if we, a silent congregation, stood in the nave of a giant church, that the priest raised the body of the Lord, and that Palestrina's everlasting choral song poured forth from the organ.

As I stood thus lost in piety, I heard some one near me exclaim, " Ah ! how beautiful Nature is, as a general thing ! " These words came from the full heart of my room-mate, the young merchant. This brought me back to my weekday state of mind, and I found myself in tune to say a few neat things to the ladies about the sunset, and to accompany them, as calmly as if nothing had happened, to their room. They permitted me to talk an hour longer with them. Our conversation, like the earth's course, was about the sun. The mother declared that the sun, as it sunk in the snowy clouds, seemed like a red glowing rose, which the gallant heaven had thrown upon the white and spreading bridal veil of his loved earth. The daughter smiled, and thought that a frequent observation of such phenomena weakened their impression. The mother corrected this error by a quotation from Goethe's " Letters of Travel," and asked me if I had read " Werther." I believe that we also spoke of Angora cats, Etruscan vases, Turkish shawls, macaroni, and Lord Byron, from whose poems the elder lady, while daintily lisping and sighing, recited several sunset quotations. To the younger lady, who did not understand English, and who wished to become familiar with those poems, I recommended the translation of my fair and gifted country woman, the Baroness Elise von Hohenhausen. On this occasion, as is my custom when talking with young ladies, I did not neglect to speak of Byron's impiety, heartlessness, cheerlessness, and heaven knows what beside.

After this business I took a walk on the Brocken, for there it is never quite dark. The mist was not heavy, and I could see the outlines of the two hills known as the Witch's Altar and the Devil's Pulpit. I fired my pistol, but there was no echo. But suddenly I heard familiar voices, and found myself embraced and kissed. The newcomers were fellow students from my own part of Germany, and had left Göttingen four days later than I. Great was their astonishment at finding me alone on the Blocksberg. Then came a floodtide of narrative, of astonishment, and of appointment making, of laughing, and of recollection, and in the spirit we found ourselves again in our learned Siberia, where refinement is carried to such an extent that bears are " bound by many ties " in the taverns, and sables wish the hunter good evening.

In the great room we had supper. There was a long table, with two rows of hungry students. At first we had only the usual subject of university conversation — duels, duels, and once again duels. The company consisted principally of Halle students, and Halle formed in consequence the nucleus of their discourse. The windowpanes of Court Counselor Schutz were exegetically lighted up. Then it was mentioned that the King of Cyprus's last levee had been very brilliant ; that the monarch had appointed a natural son ; that he had married — over the left — a princess of the house of Lichtenstein ; that the State mistress had been forced to resign, and that the entire ministry, greatly moved, had wept according to regulation. I need hardly explain that this all referred to certain beer dignitaries in Halle. Then the two Chinese, who two years before had been exhibited in Berlin, and who were now appointed professors of Chinese æsthetics in Halle, were discussed. Then jokes were made. Some one supposed a case in which a live German might be exhibited for money in China. Placards would be posted in which the Mandarins *Tsching-Tschang-Tschung* and *Hi-Ha-Ho* certified that the man was a genuine Teuton, including a list of his accomplishments, which consisted principally of philosophizing, smoking, and endless patience. Finally, visitors might be prohibited from bringing any dogs with them at twelve o'clock (the hour for feeding the captive), as these animals would be sure to snap from the poor German all his tit bits.

A young *Burschenschafter*, who had recently passed his period of purification in Berlin, spoke much, but very partially, of this city. He had been constant in his attendance on Wisotzki and the theater, but judged falsely of both. " For youth is ever ready with a word," &c. He spoke of wardrobe expenditures, theatrical scandal, and similar matters. The youth knew not that in Berlin, where outside show exerts the greatest influence (as is abundantly evidenced by the commonness of the phrase " so people do "), this apparent life must first of all flourish on the stage, and consequently that the especial care of the direction must be for " the color of the beard with which a part is played," and for the truthfulness of the dresses, which are designed by sworn historians, and sewed by scientifically instructed tailors. And this is indispensable. For if Maria Stuart wore an apron belonging to the time of Queen Anne, the banker, Christian Gumpel, would with justice complain that the anachronism destroyed the illusion ; and if Lord Burleigh in a moment of forgetfulness should don the hose of Henry the Fourth, then Madam, the War-Counselor Von Steinzopf's wife, *née* Lilienthau, would not get the error out of her head for the whole evening. And this delusive care on the part of the general direction extends itself not only to aprons and pantaloons, but also to the persons enclosed within. So in future Othello will be played by a real negro, for whom Professor Lichtenstein has already written to Africa ; in " Misanthropy and Remorse," the part of Eulalia is to be sustained by a lady who has really wandered from the paths of virtue ; Peter will be played by a real blockhead, and the Stranger by a genuine secret cuckold—for which last three characters it will not be necessary to send to Africa. In " The Power of Circumstances " there is to be a real author, who has had his face slapped, to play the part of the hero. In " The Ancestress " the artist who " gives " Jaromir must have robbed in earnest, or at least stolen something ; and Lady Macbeth be sustained by a lady who is, as Tieck required, naturally very charming, and yet to a certain degree familiar with the sanguinary sight of murderous stabbing ; and finally, to set forth in full force a shallow brained, senseless, vulgar fellow, the great Wurm should be engaged—he who enchants his like when he rises in his real greatness, high, high, " every inch a blackguard." But little as this young man had comprehended the relations of the Berlin drama, still less was he aware that the Spontini Janissary opera, with its kettle-drums, elephants, trumpets, and gongs, is a heroic means of inspiring with valor our sleeping race—a means once shrewdly recommended by Plato and Cicero. Least of all did the youth comprehend the diplomatic inner meaning of the ballet. It was with great trouble that I finally made him understand that there was really more political science in Hoguet's feet than in Buckholtz's head, that all his *tours de danse* signified diplomatic negotiations, and that his every movement hinted at state matters ; as, for instance, when he bent forward anxiously, widely grasping out with his hands, he meant our Cabinet ; that a hundred pirouettes on one toe without quitting the spot alluded to the Bundestag ; that he was thinking of the lesser princes when he tripped around with his legs tied ; that he described the European balance of power when he tottered hither and thither like a drunken man ; that he hinted at a Congress when he twisted his bended arms together like a skein ; and finally, that he sets forth our altogether too great friend in the East, when, very gradually unfolding himself, he rises on high, stands for a long time in this elevated position, and then all at once breaks out into the most terrifying leaps. The scales fell from the eyes of the young man, and he now saw how it was that dancers are better paid than great poets, and why the ballet forms in diplomatic circles an inexhaustible subject of conversation. By Apis! how great is the number of the exoteric, and how small the array of the esoteric frequenters of the theater! There sit the stupid audience, gaping and admiring leaps and attitudes, studying anatomy in the positions of Lemiere, and applauding the *entrechats* of Röhnisch, prattling of " grace," " harmony," and " limbs " — no one remarking meanwhile that he has before him in choregraphic ciphers the destiny of the German Fatherland.

While such observations flitted hither and thither, we did not lose sight of the practical, and the great dishes which were honorably piled up with meat, potatoes, *et cetera*, were industriously disposed of. The food, however, was bad. This I carelessly mentioned to my next neighbor at table, who, however, with an accent in which I recognized the Swiss, very impolitely replied that Germans knew as little of true frugality as of true liberty. I shrugged my shoulders, remarking that all the world over the humblest vassals of princes, as well as pastrycooks and confectioners, were Swiss, and known as a class by that name. I also took the liberty of stating that the Swiss heroes of liberty of the present day, who chatter so much that is politically daring to the public, reminded me of those tame hares which we see on market days in public places, where they fire off pistols to the great amazement of peasants and children, yet remain hares as before.

The son of the Alps had really meant nothing wicked ; " he was," as Cervantes says, " a plump man, and consequently a good man." But my neighbor on the other side, a Griefswalder, was deeply piqued by the assertion of the Swiss. Energetically did he assert that German ability and simplicity were not as yet extinguished, struck in a threatening manner on his breast, and gulped down a tremendous flagon of white beer. The Swiss said, " Nu! nu!" But the more appeasingly and apologetically he said this, so much the faster did the Greifswalder get on with his riot. He was a man of those days when haircutters came near dying of starvation. He wore long locks, a knightly cap, a black old German coat, a dirty shirt, which at the same time did duty as a waistcoat, and beneath it a medallion, with a tassel of the hair of Blücher's white horse. His appearance was that of a fullgrown fool. I am always ready for something lively at supper, and consequently held with him a patriotic strife. He was of the opinion that Germany should be divided into thirty-three districts. I asserted, on the contrary, that there should be forty-eight, because it would then be possible to write a more systematic guidebook for Germany, and because it is essential that life should be blended with science. My Greifswald friend was also a German bard, and, as he informed me in confidence, was occupied with a national heroic poem in honor of Hermann and the Hermann battle. Many an advantageous hint did I give him on this subject. I suggested to him that the morasses and crooked paths of the Teutobergian forest might be very onomatopœically indicated by means of watery and ragged verse, and that it would be a patriotic refinement should the Romans in his poem chatter the wildest nonsense. I hope that this bit of art will succeed in his works, as in those of other Berlin poets, even to the minutest particular.

The company around the table gradually became better acquainted and much noiser. Wine banished beer, punch bowls steamed, and drinking, toasting, and singing were the order of the night. The old " Landsfather " and the beautiful songs of W. Muller, Rückert, Uhland, and others rang around, with the exquisite airs of Methfessel. Best of all sounded our own Arndt's German words, " The Lord, who bade iron grow, wished for no slaves." And out of doors it roared as if the old mountain sang with us, and a few reeling friends even asserted that it merrily shook its bald head, which caused the great unsteadiness of our floor. The bottles became emptier and the heads of the company fuller. One bellowed like an ox, a second piped, a third declaimed from " The Guilt," a fourth spoke Latin, a fifth preached temperance, and a sixth, assuming the chair, learnedly lectured as follows : " Gentlemen, the world is a round cylinder, upon which human beings as individual pins are scattered apparently at random. But the cylinder revolves, the pins knock together and give out tones, some very frequently and others but seldom ; all of which causes a remarkably complicated sound, which is generally known as world history. We will, in consequence, speak first of music, then of the world, and finally of history, which latter we divide into positive and Spanish flies——" And so sense and nonsense went rattling on.

A jolly Mechlenburger, who held his nose to his punchglass, and, smiling with happiness, snuffed up the perfume, remarked that it caused in him a sensation as if he were standing again before the refreshment table in the Schwerin Theater! Another held his wine glass like a lorgnette before his eye, and appeared to be carefully studying the company, while the red wine trickled down over his cheek into his projecting mouth. The Greifswalder, suddenly inspired, cast himself upon my breast, and shouted wildly, " Oh, that thou couldst understand me, for I am a lover, a happy lover ; for I am loved again, and G—d d—n me, she's an educated girl, for she has a full bosom, wears a white gown, and plays the piano!" But the Swiss wept, and tenderly kissed my hand, and ever whimpered, " Oh, Molly dear! oh, Molly dear!"

During this crazy scene, in which plates learned to dance and glasses to fly, there sat opposite me two youths, beautiful and pale as statues, one resembling Adonis, the other Apollo. The faint rosy hue which the wine spread over their cheeks was scarcely visible. They gazed on each other with infinite affection, as if the one could read in the eyes of the other, and in those eyes there was a light as though drops of light had fallen therein from the cup of burning love, which an angel on high bears from one star to the other. They conversed softly with earnest, trembling voices, and narrated sad stories, through all of which ran a tone of strange sorrow. " Lora is also dead!" said one, and sighing, proceeded to tell of a maiden of Halle who had loved a student, and who, when the latter left Halle, spoke no more to any one, ate but little, wept day and night, gazing ever on the canary which her lover had given her. " The bird died, and Lora did not long survive it," was the conclusion, and both the youths sighed, as though their hearts would break. Finally, the other said, " My soul is sorrowful ; come forth with me into the dark night! Let me inhale the breath of the clouds and the moon rays. Partake of my sorrows! I love thee ; thy words are musical, like the rustling of reeds and the flow of rivulets ; they re-echo in my breast, but my soul is sorrowful!"

Both of the young men arose. One threw his arm around the neck of the other, and thus left the noisy room. I followed, and saw them enter a dark chamber, where the one by mistake, instead of the window, threw open the door of a large wardrobe, and that both, standing before it with outstretched arms, expressing poetic rapture, spoke alternately. "Ye breezes of darkening night," cried the first, "how ye cool and revive my cheeks! How sweetly ye play amid my fluttering locks! I stand on the cloudy peak of the mountain, far below me lie the sleeping cities of men, and blue waters gleam. List! far below in the valley rustle the fir trees! Far above yonder hills sweep in misty forms the spirits of my fathers. Oh, that I could hunt with ye on your cloud-steeds through the stormy night, over the rolling sea, upwards to the stars! Alas! I am laden with grief, and my soul is sad!" Meanwhile, the other had also stretched out his arms towards the wardrobe, while tears fell from his eyes as he cried to a broad pair of yellow pantaloons which he mistook for the moon, "Fair art thou, daughter of heaven! lovely and blessed is the calm of thy countenance. Thou walkest lonely in thy loveliness. The stars follow thy blue path in the east! At thy glance the clouds rejoice, and their dark brows gleam with light. Who is like unto thee in heaven, thou the nightborn? The stars are ashamed before thee, and turn away their green sparkling eyes. Whither, ah! whither, when morning pales thy face, dost thou flee from thy path? Hast thou, like me, thy hall? Dwellest thou amid shadows of sorrow? Have thy sisters fallen from heaven? Are they who joyfully rolled with thee through the night now no more? Yea, they fell adown, oh! lovely light, and thou hidest thyself to bewail them! Yet the night must at some time come when thou too must pass away, and leave thy blue path above in heaven. Then the stars, who were once ashamed in thy presence, will raise their green heads and rejoice. Now thou art clothed in thy starry splendor and gazest adown from the gate of

284

heaven. Tear aside the clouds, oh! ye winds, that the night-born may shine forth and the bushy hills gleam, and that the foaming waves of the sea may roll in light!"

A well-known and not remarkably thin friend, who had drunk more than he had eaten, though he had already at supper devoured a piece of beef which would have dined six lieutenants of the guard and one innocent child, here came rushing into the room in a very jovial manner, that is to say, *à la* swine, shoved the two elegiac friends one over the other into the wardrobe, stormed through the house door, and began to roar around outside, as if raising the devil in earnest. The noise in the hall grew more confused and duller ; the two moaning and weeping friends lay, as they thought, crushed at the foot of the mountain ; from their throats ran noble red wine, and the one said to the other, " Farewell! I feel that I bleed. Why dost thou waken me, oh! breath of spring? Thou caressest me, and sayst, ' I bedew thee with drops from heaven. But the time of my withering is at hand — at hand the storm which will break away my leaves. Tomorrow the Wanderer will come — come — he who saw me in my beauty — his eyes will glance, as of yore, around the field — in vain —— ' " But over all roared the well-known basso voice without, blasphemously complaining, amid oaths and whoops, that not a single lantern had been lighted along the entire Weender Street, and that one could not even see whose window panes he had smashed.

I can bear a tolerable quantity — modesty forbids me to say how many bottles — and I consequently retired to my chamber in tolerably good condition. The young merchant already lay in bed, enveloped in his chalk-white nightcap and yellow Welsh flannel. He was not asleep, and sought to enter into conversation with me. He was a Frankfort-on-Mainer, and consequently spoke at once of the Jews, declared that they had lost all feeling for the beautiful and noble, and that they sold English goods twenty-five per cent. under manufacturers' prices. A fancy to humbug him came over me, and I told him that I was a somnambulist, and must beforehand beg his parden should I unwittingly disturb his slumbers. This intelligence, as he confessed the following day, prevented him from sleeping a wink through the whole night, especially since the idea had entered his head that I, while in a somnambulistic crisis, might shoot him with the pistol which lay near my bed. But in truth I fared no better myself, for I slept very little. Dreary and terrifying fancies swept through my brain. A pianoforte extract from Dante's Hell. Finally I dreamed that I saw a law opera called the *Falcidia*, with libretto on the right of inheritance by Gans, and music by Spontini. A crazy dream! I saw the Roman Forum splendidly illuminated. In it Servius Asinius Göschenus sitting as *prœtor* on his chair, and throwing wide his toga in stately folds, burst out into raging recitative; Marcus Tullius Elversus, manifesting as *prima donna legataria* all the exquisite feminineness of his nature, sang the love-melting *bravura* of *Quicunque civis Romanus*; *Referees*, rouged red as sealing-wax, bellowed in chorus as *minors*; private tutors, dressed as genii, in flesh-colored tights, danced an anti-Justinian ballet, crowning with flowers the " Twelve Tables," while, amid thunder and lightning, rose from the ground the abused ghost of Roman Legislation, accompanied by trumpets, gongs, fiery rain, *cum omni causa*.

From this confusion I was rescued by the landlord of the Brocken, when he awoke me to see the sun rise. Above, on the tower, I found several already waiting, who rubbed their freezing hands ; others, with sleep still in their eyes, stumbled up to us, until finally the whole silent congregation of the previous evening was reassembled, and we saw how, above the horizon, there rose a little carmine red ball, spreading a dim, wintry illumination. Far around, amid the mists, rose the mountains, as if swimming in a white rolling sea, only their summits being visible, so that we could imagine ourselves standing on a little hill in the midst of an inundated plain, in which here and there rose dry clods of earth. To retain that which I saw and felt, I sketched the following poem :

> In the east 'tis ever brighter,
> Though the sun gleams cloudily ;
> Far and wide the mountain summits
> Swim above the misty sea.

Had I seven-mile boots for travel,
  Like the fleeting winds I'd rove,
Over valley, rock, and river,
  To the home of her I love.

From the bed where now she's sleeping,
  Soft the curtain I would slip ;
Softly kiss her child-like forehead,
  Soft the ruby of her lip.

And yet softer would I whisper
  In the little lily ear,
" Think in dreams we still are loving,
  Think I never lost thee, dear."

Meanwhile my desire for breakfast greatly increased, and after paying a few attentions to my ladies, I hastened down to drink coffee in the warm public room. It was high time, for all within me was as sober and as somber as in the St. Stephen's Church of Goslar. But with the Arabian beverage, the warm Orient thrilled through my limbs, Eastern roses breathed forth their perfumes, the students were changed into camels, the Brocken house maids, with their Congreve-rocket glances, became *houris*, the Philistine-noses, minarets. . . . . . .

But the book which lay near me, though full of nonsense, was not the Koran. It was the so-called *Brocken-book*, in which all travelers who ascend the mountain write their names — many inscribing their thoughts, or in default thereof their " feelings." Many even express themselves in verse. In this book one may observe the horrors which result when the great Philistine Pegasus at convenient opportunities, such as this on the Brocken, becomes poetic. The palace of the Prince of Pallagonia never contained such absurdities and insipidities as are to be found in this book. Those who shine in it with especial splendor are Messrs. the excise collectors, with their moldy " high inspirations ; " counter-jumpers, with their pathetic outgushings of the soul ; old German revolution dilettanti with their athletic club phrases, and Berlin schoolmasters with their unsuccessful efforts at enthusiasm. John Doe will also for once show himself as author. In one page the majestic

287

splendor of the sun is described, in another complaints occur of
bad weather, of disappointed hopes, and of the clouds which
obstruct the view. A Caroline writes that in climbing the mountain
her feet were wetted, to which a naïve Nanny, who was impressed
by this, adds, " I too got wet in this thing." " Went up wet without
and came down ' wet within,' " is a standing joke, repeated in the
book hundreds of times. The whole volume smells of beer, tobacco,
and cheese ; we might fancy it one of Clauren's romances.

While I drank the coffee aforesaid and turned over the Brocken-
book, the Swiss entered, his cheeks deeply glowing, and described
with enthusiasm the sublime view which he had just enjoyed in
the tower above, as the pure calm light of the sun, that symbol
of truth, fought with the night mists, and that it appeared like a
battle of spirits, in which raging giants brandished their long
swords, where armored knights on leaping steeds chased each other,
and war chariots, fluttering banners, and extravagant monster
forms emerged in the wildest confusion, till all finally entwined in
the maddest contortions, melted into dimness and vanished, leaving
no trace. This demagogical natural phenomenon I had missed and,
should the curious affair be ever made the subject of investigation,
I am ready to declare on oath that all I know of the matter is the
flavor of the good brown coffee.

Alas! this was the guilty cause of my neglecting my fair lady,
and now, with mother and friend, she stood before the door, about
to step into her carriage. I had scarcely time to hurry to her, and
assure her that it was cold. She seemed piqued at my not coming
sooner, but I soon drove the clouds from her fair brow by presenting to her a strange flower, which I had plucked the day before, at
the risk of my neck, from a steep precipice. The mother inquired
the name of the flower, as if it seemed to her not altogether correct
that her daughter should place a strange, unknown flower upon
her bosom — for this was, in fact, the enviable position which the
flower attained, and of which it could never have dreamed the day
before, on its lonely height. The silent friend here opened his
mouth, and after counting the stamens of the flower, dryly remarked that it belonged to the eighth class.

It vexes me every time when I remember that even the dear flowers which God hath made have been, like us, divided into castes, and, like us, are distinguished by those external names which indicate descent as in a family tree. If there *must* be such divisions, it were better to adopt those suggested by Theophrastus, who wished that flowers might be divided according to spirits, that is, their perfumes. As for myself, I have my own system of natural science, according to which all things are divided into those which may or may not be eaten!

The secret and mysterious nature of flowers was, however, anything but hidden to the elder lady, and she involuntarily remarked that she felt happy in her very soul when she saw flowers growing in the garden or in a room, while a faint, dreamy sense of pain invariably affected her on beholding a beautiful flower with broken stalk—that it was really a dead body, and that the withered head of such a flower-corpse hung down like that of a dead infant. The lady here became alarmed at the sorrowful impression which her remark caused, and I flew to the rescue with a few Voltairean verses. How quickly two or three French words bring us back into the conventional concert pitch of conversation. We laughed, hands were kissed, gracious smiles beamed, the horses neighed, and the wagon jolted heavily and slowly down the hill.

And now the students prepared to depart. Knapsacks were buckled, the bills, which were moderate beyond all expectation, were settled, the two susceptible housemaids, upon whose pretty countenances the traces of successful amours were plainly visible, brought, as is their custom, their Brocken-bouquets, and helped us to hasten them to our caps ; for all of which they were duly rewarded with either coppers or kisses. Thus we all went " downhill," albeit one party, among whom were the Swiss and Greifswalder, took the road towards Schierke, and the other, of about twenty men, among whom were my countrymen and I, led by a guide, went through the so-called " Snow Holes " down to Ilsenburg.

Such a head-over-heels, break-neck piece of business! Halle students travel quicker than the Austrian militia. Ere I knew where

I was, the bald summit of the mountain, with groups of stones strewed over it, was behind us, and we went through the fir wood which I had seen the day before. The sun poured down a cheerful light on the merry fellows, in gaily colored garb, as they cheerfully pressed onward through the wood, disappearing here, coming to light again there, running in marshy places, across on shaking trunks of trees, climbing over steep precipices by grasping the projecting tree-roots, while they yodelled all the time in the merriest manner, and were answered in as merry echoes by the invisibly plashing rivulets, and the resounding echo. When cheerful youth and beautiful nature meet, they mutually rejoice.

The lower we descended the more delightfully did subterranean waters ripple around us ; only here and there they peeped out amid rocks and bushes, appearing to be reconnoitering if they might yet come to light, until at last one little spring jumped forth boldly. Then followed the usual show — the bravest one makes a beginning, and then the great multitude of hesitators, suddenly inspired with courage, rush forth to join the first. A multitude of springs now leaped in haste from their ambush, united with the leader, and finally formed quite an important brook, which, with its innumerable waterfalls and beautiful windings, ripples adown the valley. This is now the Ilse — the sweet, pleasant Ilse. It flows through the blest Ilse vale, on whose sides the mountains gradually rise higher and higher, being clad even to their base with beech trees, oaks, and the usual shrubs, the firs and other evergreens having disappeared ; for that variety of trees prevails upon the " Lower Hartz, " as the east side of the Brocken is called in contradistinction to the west side or Upper Hartz, being really much higher and better adapted to the growth of evergreens.

No pen can describe the merriment, simplicity, and gentleness with which the Ilse leaps or glides amid the wildly piled rocks which rise in its path, so that the water strangely whizzes or foams in one place amid rifted rocks, and in another wells through a thousand crannies, as if from a giant watering-pot, and then in collected stream trips away over the pebbles like a merry maiden. Yes, the old legend is true ; the Ilse is a princess, who, laughing in beauty, runs down the mountain. How her white foam garment gleams in the sunshine! How her silvered scarf flutters in the breeze! How her diamonds flash! The tall beech tree gazes down on her like a grave father secretly smiling at the wanton play of a darling child; the white birch trees nod their heads around like delighted aunts, who are, however, anxious at such bold leaps; the proud oak looks on like a not overpleased uncle, as though he must pay for all the fine weather; the birds in the air sing their share in their joy; the flowers on the bank whisper, " Oh, take us with thee! take us with thee, dear sister!" but the wild maiden may not be restrained, and she leaps onward, and suddenly seizes the dreaming poet, and there streams over me a flower rain of ringing gleams and flashing tones, and all my senses are lost in beauty and splendor, as I hear only the voice, sweet pealing as a flute—

> I am the Princess Ilse,
> And dwell in Ilsenstein ;
> Come with me to my castle,
> Thou shalt be blest — and mine !

> With ever-flowing fountains
> I'll cool thy weary brow ;
> Thou'lt lose amid their rippling
> The cares which grieve thee now.

> In my white arms reposing,
> And on my snow-white breast,
> Thou'lt dream of old, old legends,
> And sink in joy to rest.

> I'll kiss thee and caress thee,
> As in the ancient day
> I kissed the Emperor Henry,
> Who long has passed away.

> The dead are dead and silent,
> Only the living love ;
> And I am, fair and blooming,
> — Dost feel my wild heart move ?

And as my heart is beating,
  My crystal castle rings,
Where many a knight and lady
  In merry measure springs.

Silk trains are softly rustling,
  Spurs ring from night to morn,
And dwarfs are gaily drumming,
  And blow the golden horn.

As round the Emperor Henry,
  My arms round thee shall fall ;
I held his ears — he heard not
  The trumpet's warning call.

We feel infinite happiness when the outer world blends with the world of our own soul, and green trees, thoughts, the song of birds, gentle melancholy, the blue of heaven, memory, and the perfume of flowers, run together in sweet arabesques. Women best understand this feeling, and this may be the cause that such a sweet, incredulous smile plays around their lips when we, with school-pride, boast of our logical deeds ; how we have classified everything so nicely into subjective and objective ; how our heads are provided, apothecary-like, with a thousand drawers, one of which contains reason, another understanding, a third wit, the fourth bad wit, and the fifth nothing at all, that is to say, the *idea*.

As if wandering in dreams, I scarcely observed that we had left the depths of the Ilse valley and were now again climbing up hill. This was steep and difficult work, and many of us lost our breath ; but, like our late lamented cousin, Till Eulenspiegel, we constantly kept in mind the ease with which we should descend, and were much the better off in consequence. Finally, we reached the Ilsenstein.

This is an enormous granite rock, which rises high and boldly from a glen. On three sides it is surrounded by woody hills, but from the fourth, the north, there is an open view, and we gaze upon the Ilsenburg and the Ilse lying far below, and our glances wander beyond into the lower land. On the towerlike summit of the rock stands a great iron cross, and in case of need there is also here a resting place for four human feet.

As Nature, through picturesque position and form, has adorned the Ilsenstein with strange and beautiful charms, so has also Legend poured over it her rosy light. According to Gottschalk, the people say that there once stood here an enchanted castle, in which dwelt the fair Princess Ilse, who still bathes every morning in the Ilse. He who is so fortunate as to hit upon the exact time and place, will be led by her into the rock where her castle lies, and receive a royal reward. Others narrate a pleasant legend of the loves of the Lady Ilse and of the Knight of Westenburg, which has been romantically sung by one of our most noted poets in the *Evening Journal*. Others again say that it was the old Saxon Emperor Henry who passed in pleasure his imperial hours with the water nymph Ilse in her enchanted castle. A later author, one Niemann, Esq., who has written a Hartz guide, in which the heights of the hills, variations of the compass, town finances, and similar matters are described with praiseworthy accuracy, asserts, however, that "what is narrated of the Princess Ilse belongs entirely to the realm of fable." So all men to whom a beautiful princess has never appeared assert ; but we who have been especially favored by fair ladies know better. And this the Emperor Henry knew too! It was not without cause that the old Saxon emperors held so firmly to their native Hartz. Let any one only turn over the leaves of the fair Lünenburg Chronicle, where the good old gentlemen are represented in wondrously faithful woodcuts as well weaponed, high on their mailed war steeds, the holy imperial crown on their blessed heads, scepter and sword in firm hands ; and then in their dear moustached and bearded faces he can plainly read how they often longed for the sweethearts of their Hartz princesses, and for the familiar rustling of the Hartz forests, when they lingered in distant lands. Yes, even when in the orange and poison rich Italy, whither they, with their followers, were often enticed by the desire to become Roman emperors, a genuine German lust for title, which finally destroyed emperor and realm.

I, however, advise every one who may hereafter stand on the summit of the Ilsenstein to think neither of emperor and crown nor of the fair Ilse, but simply of his own feet. For as I stood there, lost in thought, I suddenly heard the subterranean music of the enchanted castle, and saw the mountains around begin to stand on their heads, while the red tiled roofs of Ilsenburg were dancing, and green trees flew through the air, until all was green and blue before my eyes, and I, overcome by giddiness, would assuredly have fallen into the abyss, had I not, in the dire need of my soul, clung fast to the iron cross. No one who reflects on the critically ticklish situation in which I was then placed can possibly find fault with me for having done this.

The Hartz journey is and remains a fragment, and the variegated threads which were so neatly wound through it, with the intention to bind it into a harmonious whole, have been suddenly snapped asunder as if by the shears of the implacable destinies. It may be that I will one day weave them into new songs, and that that which is now stingily withheld will then be spoken in full. But when or what we have spoken will all come to one and the same thing at last, provided that we do but speak. The single works may ever remain fragments if they only form a whole by their union.

By such a connection the omissions may here and there be supplied, the rough be polished down, and that which is altogether too harsh be modified and softened. This is perhaps especially applicable to the first pages of the Hartz journey, and they would in all probability have caused a far less unfavorable impression could the reader in some other place have learned that the ill-humor which I entertain for Göttingen in general, although greater than I have here expressed it, is still far from being equal to the respect which I entertain for certain individuals there. And why should I conceal the fact that I here allude particularly to that estimable man who, in earlier years, received me so kindly, inspiring me even then with a deep love for the study of history; who strengthened my zeal for it later in life, and thus led my soul to calmer paths; who indicated to my peculiar disposition a healthier direction, and who finally gave me those historical consolations, without which I should never have been able to support the painful events of the present day. I speak of George Sartorius, the great investigator of history and of humanity, whose eye is a bright star in our dark times, and whose hospitable heart is ever open to all the griefs and joys of others—for the needs of the beggar or the king, and for the last sighs of nations perishing with their gods.

I cannot here refrain from remarking that the Upper Hartz, that portion of which I described as far as the beginning of the Ilse valley, did not by any means make so favorable an impression on me as the romantic and picturesque Lower Hartz, and in its wildly steep dark fir tree beauty contrasts strangely with the other, just as the three valleys formed by the Ilse, the Bode, and the Selke, beautifully contrast with each other, when we are able to personify the character of each. They are three beautiful women, of whom it is impossible to determine which is the fairest.

I have already spoken and sung of the fair sweet Ilse, and how sweetly and kindly she received me. The darker beauty, the Bode, was not so gracious in her reception, and as I first beheld her in the smithy dark, turnip land, she appeared to me to be altogether ill natured, and hid herself beneath a silver grey rain veil ; but with impatient love she suddenly threw it off ; as I ascended the summit of the Rosstrappe, her countenance gleamed upon me with the sunniest splendor, from every feature beamed the tenderness of a giantess, and from the agitated, rocky bosom there was a sound as of sighs of deep longing and melting tones of woe. Less tender but far merrier did I find the pretty Selke, an amiable lady, whose noble simplicity and calm repose held at a distance all sentimental familiarity, but who, by a half concealed smile, betrayed her mocking mood. It was perhaps to this secret merry spirit that I might have attributed the many " little miseries " which beset me in the Selkethal ; as, for instance, when I sought to spring over the rivulet, I plunged in exactly up to my middle ; how when I continued my wet campaign with slippers, one of them was soon " not at hand," or rather " not at foot," for I lost it ; how a puff of wind bore away my cap ; how thorns scratched me, and alas, *et cetera.* Yet do I forgive the fair lady all this, for she *is* fair. And even now she stands before the gates of Imagination, in all her silent loveliness, and seems to say, " Though I laugh, I mean no harm, and I pray you sing of me!" The magnificent Bode also sweeps into my memory, and her dark eye says, " Thou art like me in pride and in pain, and I will that thou lovest me." Also the fair Ilse comes merrily springing, delicate and fascinating in mien, form, and motion, in all things like the dear being who blesses my dreams, and like her she gazes on me with unconquerable indifference, and is withal so deeply, so eternally, so manifestly true. Well, I am Paris, and I award the apple to the fair Ilse.

It is the first of May, and spring is pouring like a sea of life over the earth, a foam of white blossoms covers the trees, the glass in the town windows flashes merrily, sparrows are again building on the roofs, people saunter along the street, wondering that the air affects them so much, and that they feel so cheerful ; the oddly dressed Vierlander girls are selling bouquets of violets ; foundling children, with their blue jackets and dear little illegitimate faces, run along the *Jungfernstieg* as happily as if they had all found their fathers ; the beggar on the bridge looks as jolly as though he had won the first lottery prize, and even on the grimy and as yet unhung pedlar, who scours about with his rascally " manufactured goods " countenance, the sun shines with his best natured rays. I will take a walk beyond the town gate.

It is the first of May, and I think of thee, thou fair Ilse ; or shall I call thee by the name which I better love, of Agnes? I think of thee, and would fain see once more how thou leapest in light adown thy hill. But best of all were it could I stand in the valley below and hold thee in my arms. It is a lovely day! Green, the color of hope, is everywhere around me. Everywhere flowers are blooming like beautiful miracles, and my heart will bloom again also. This heart is also a flower of strange and wondrous sort. It is no modest violet, no smiling rose, no pure lily, or similar flower, which with good gentle loveliness makes glad a maiden's soul, and may be fitly placed upon her pretty breast, and which withers today, and tomorrow blooms again. No, this heart rather resembles that strange, heavy flower from the woods of Brazil, which, according to the legend, blooms but once in a century. I remember well that I once, when a boy, saw such a flower. During the night we heard an explosion as of a pistol, and the next morning a neighbor's children told me that it was their " aloe " which had bloomed with the shot. They led me to their garden, where I saw to my astonishment that the low, hard plant, with ridiculously broad, sharp pointed leaves, which were capable of inflicting wounds, had shot high in the air, and bore aloft beautiful flowers, like a golden crown. We children could not see so high, and the old grinning Christian, who liked us all so well, built a wooden stair around the flower, upon which we scrambled like cats, and gazed curiously into the open calyx, from which yellow threads, like rays of light, and strange foreign odors pressed forth in unheard of splendor.

Yes, Agnes, this flower blooms not often, not without effort ; and according to my recollection it has as yet opened but once, and that must have been long ago — certainly at least a century since, and I believe that, gloriously as it then unfolded its blossoms, it must now miserably pine for want of sunshine and warmth, if it is not indeed shattered by some mighty wintry storm. But now it moves, and swells, and bursts in my bosom — dost thou hear the explosion ? Maiden, be not terrified ! I have not shot myself, but my love has burst its bud and shoots upwards in gleaming songs, in eternal dithyrambs, in the most joyful fulness of poesy !

But if this high love has grown too high, then, young lady, take it comfortably, climb the wooden steps, and look from them down into my blooming heart.

It is as yet early ; the sun has hardly left half his road behind him, and my heart already breathes forth so powerfully its perfumed vapor that it bewilders my brain, and I no longer know where irony ceases and heaven begins, or that I people the air with my sighs, and that I myself would fain dissolve into sweet atoms in the uncreated Divinity. How will it be when night comes on, and the stars shine out in heaven, the unlucky stars, who could tell thee——

It is the first of May, the lowest errand boy has today a right to be sentimental, and would you deny the privilege to a poet ?

297

Ideas—Book Le Grand

" She was worthy of love, and he loved her. He, however, was not lovable, and she did not love him."—*Old Play*.

MADAME, ARE YOU FAMILIAR WITH THAT OLD PLAY? IT IS AN altogether extraordinary performance—only a little too melancholy. I once played the leading part in it myself, so that all the ladies wept save one, who did not shed so much as a single tear, and in that consisted the *whole* point of the play—the real catastrophe.

Oh, that single tear! it still torments my thoughts. When the devil desires to ruin my soul, he hums in my ear a ballad of that tear which ne'er was wept, a deadly song with a more deadly tune. Ah! such a tune is only heard in hell!

You can readily form an idea, Madame, of what life is like in heaven—the more readily as you are married. There people amuse themselves altogether superbly, every sort of entertainment is provided, and one lives in mere desire and delight, or, as the saying is, " like the Lord in France." There they eat from morning to night, and the cookery is as good as Jagor's; roast geese fly around with gravy-boats in their bills, and feel flattered if any one condescends to eat them ; tarts gleaming with butter grow wild like sun-flowers ; everywhere there are rivulets of *bouillon* and champagne, everywhere trees on which clean napkins flutter wild in the wind, and you eat and wipe your lips and eat again without injury to your stomach. There, too, you sing psalms, or flirt and joke with the dear delicate little angels, or take a walk on the green Hallelujah Meadow, and your white flowing garments fit so comfortably, and nothing disturbs your feeling of perfect happiness—no pain, no vexation. Nay, when one accidentally treads on another's corns and exclaims, "*Excusez!*" he smiles as if enraptured, and insists, " Thy foot, brother, did not hurt in the least, quite *au contraire*—it only causes a deeper thrill of heavenly rapture to shoot through my heart!"

But of hell, Madame, you have not the faintest idea. Of all the devils in existence, you have probably made the acquaintance only of Amor, the nice little *croupier* of hell, who is the smallest Beelzebub of them all. And you know him only from "Don Juan," and doubtless think that for such a betrayer of female innocence hell can never be made hot enough, though our praiseworthy theater directors shower down upon him as much flame, fiery rain, squibs and colophonium as any Christian could desire to have emptied into hell itself.

However, things in hell look much worse than our theater directors imagine—or they would never permit such stuff to be played as they do. For in hell it is infernally hot, and when I was there, in the dog-days, it was past endurance. Madame, you can have no idea of hell! We have very few official returns from that place. Still, it is rank calumny to say that down there all the poor souls are compelled to read all day long all the dull sermons which were ever printed on earth. Bad as hell is, it has not *quite* come to that,—Satan will never invent such refinements of torture. On the other hand, Dante's description is too mild—I may say, on the whole, too poetic. Hell appeared to me like a great kitchen, with an endlessly long stove, on which were placed three rows of iron pots, and in these sat the damned and were cooked. In one row were placed Christian sinners, and, incredible as it may seem, their number was anything but small, and the devils poked the fire up under them with especial good-will. In the next row were Jews, who continually screamed and cried, and were occasionally mocked by the fiends, which sometimes seemed droll enough—as, for instance, when a fat, wheezy old pawnbroker complained of the heat, and a little devil poured several buckets of cold water on his head, that he might realize what a refreshing benefit baptism was. In the third row sat the heathen, who, like the Jews, could take no part in salvation, and must burn forever. I heard one of these, as a square-built, burly devil put fresh coals under his kettle, cry out from his pot, " Spare me! I was once Socrates, the wisest of mortals; I taught Truth and Justice, and sacrificed my life for Virtue." But the clumsy, stupid devil went on with his work, and grumbled, " Oh, shut up there! All heathens must burn, and we can't make an exception for the sake of a single man." I assure you, Madame, the heat was terrible, with such a screaming, sighing, groaning, croaking, crying, quacking, cracking, growling, grunting, yelling, squealing, wailing, trilling; and through all this terrible turmoil there rang distinctly the fatal melody of the Song of the Unwept Tear.

CHAPTER II

" She was worthy of his love, and he loved her. He, however, was not lovable, and she did not love him." — *Old Play.*

MADAME, THAT OLD PLAY IS A TRAGEDY, THOUGH THE HERO IN IT IS neither killed nor commits suicide. The eyes of the heroine are beautiful, very beautiful. Madame, do you scent the perfume of violets? Very beautiful, and yet so piercing that they struck like poignards of glass through my heart, and probably came out through my back, and yet I was not killed by those treacherous, murderous eyes. The voice of the heroine was also sweet. Madame, was it a nightingale you heard sing just as I spoke? — a soft, silken voice, a sweet web of the sunniest tones, and my soul was entangled in it, and choked and tormented itself. I myself — it is the Count of Ganges who now speaks, and, as the story goes on, in Venice — I myself soon had enough of those tortures, and had thoughts of putting an end to the play in the first act, and of shooting myself through the head, foolscap and all. Therefore I went to a fancy store in the Via Burstah, where I saw a pair of beautiful pistols in a case — I remember them perfectly well — near them stood many ornamental articles of mother-of-pearl and gold, steel hearts on gilt chains, porcelain cups with delicate devices, and snuff-boxes with pretty pictures, such as the divine history of Susannah, the

300

Swan Song of Leda, the Rape of the Sabines, Lucretia, a fat, virtuous creature, with naked bosom, in which she was lazily sticking a dagger ; the late Bethmann, *la belle Ferronière*, all enrapturing faces ; but I bought the pistols without much ado, and then I bought balls, then powder, and then I went to the restaurant of Signor Somebody, and ordered oysters and a glass of hock.

I could eat nothing, and still less could I drink. The warm tears fell in the glass, and in that glass I saw my dear home, the blue, holy Ganges, the ever-gleaming Himalaya, the giant banyan woods, amid whose broad arcades calmly wandered wise elephants and white-robed pilgrims ; strange dreamlike flowers gazed on me with meaning glance, wondrous golden birds sang softly, flashing sun-rays, and the droll, silly chatter of monkeys pleasantly mocked me ; from far pagodas sounded the pious prayers of priests, and amid them rang the melting, wailing voice of the Sultana of Delhi. She ran wildly around in her carpeted chamber, she tore her silver veil, she struck with her peacock fan the black slave to the ground ; she wept, she raged, she cried. I could not hear what she said ; the restaurant of Signor Somebody is three thousand miles distant from the harem of Delhi, besides the fair Sultana had been dead three thousand years ; and I quickly drank up the wine, the clear, joy-giving wine, and yet my soul grew darker and sadder. I was condemned to death.

As I left the restaurant I heard the " bell of poor sinners " ring ; a crowd of people swept by me ; but I placed myself at the corner of the *Strada San Giovanni* and recited the following monologue : —

> In ancient tales they tell of golden castles,
> Where harps are sounding, lovely ladies dance,
> And trim attendants serve, and jessamine,
> Myrtle, and roses spread their soft perfume,
> And yet a single word of disenchantment
> Sweeps all the glory of the scene to naught,
> And there remains but ruins old and grey,
> And screaming birds of night and foul morass.
> E'en so have I with a short single word
> Quite disenchanted nature's loveliness.

There lies she now, lifeless and cold and pale,
E'en like a monarch's corse laid out in state,
The royal deathly cheeks fresh stained with rouge,
And in his hand the kingly scepter laid ;
Yet still his lips are yellow and most changed,
For they forgot to dye them, as they should,
And mice are jumping o'er the monarch's nose,
And mock the golden scepter in his grasp.

It is everywhere agreed, Madame, that every one should deliver a soliloquy before shooting himself. Most men on such occasions use Hamlet's " To be or not to be." It is an excellent passage, and I would gladly have quoted it, but charity begins at home, and when a man has written tragedies himself, in which such farewell-to-life speeches occur, as, for instance, in my immortal " Almansor," it is very natural that one should prefer his own words even to Shakespeare's. At any rate the delivery of such speeches is an excellent custom, for thereby one gains at least a little time. And as it came to pass that I remained a long time standing on the corner of the Strada San Giovanni, and as I stood there like a condemned criminal awaiting death, I raised my eyes, and suddenly beheld HER.

She wore her blue silk dress and rose-red bonnet and her eyes looked at me so mildly, so death-conqueringly, so life-givingly. Madame, you well know that when the vestals in ancient Rome met on their way a malefactor condemned to death, they had the right to pardon him, and the poor rogue lived. With a single glance she saved my life, and I stood before her revived, and dazzled by the sunny gleaming of her beauty, and she passed on, and left me alive.

CHAPTER III

AND SHE SAVED MY LIFE, AND I LIVE, AND THAT IS THE MAIN POINT.

Others may, if they choose, enjoy the good fortune of having their lady-love adorn their graves with garlands, and water them with the tears of true love. Oh, women! hate me, laugh at me, jilt me, but let me live! Life is all too wondrously sweet, and the world is so beautifully bewildered ; it is the dream of an intoxicated god who has taken French leave of the carousing multitude of immortals, and has laid down to sleep in a solitary star, and knows not himself that he also creates all that which he dreams, and the dream images form themselves often so fantastically wildly, and often so harmoniously and reasonably. The Iliad, Plato, the battle of Marathon, Moses, the Medician Venus, the Cathedral of Strasburg, the French Revolution, Hegel, and steamboats, etc., etc., are other good thoughts in this divine dream ; but it will not last long, and the god awakes and rubs his sleepy eyes, and smiles ; and our world has run to nothing, yes, has never been.

No matter, I live! If I am but the shadowy image in a dream, still this is better than the cold black void annihilation of death. *Life* is the greatest of blessings and death the worst of evils. Berlin lieutenants of the guard may sneer, and call it cowardice, because the Prince of Homburg shudders when he beholds his open grave. Henry Kleist had, however, as much courage as his high-breasted, tightly-laced colleagues, and has, alas! proved it. But all strong men love life. Goethe's Egmont does not cheerfully take leave from " the cheerful wontedness of being and action." Immermann's Edwin clings to life " like a child upon the mother's breast." And though he finds it hard to live by stranger mercy, he still begs for mercy, " for life and breath are still the best of boons."

When Odysseus, in the lower world, regards Achilles as the leader of dead heroes, and extols his renown among the living, and his glory even among the dead, the latter replies—

> No more discourse of death, consolingly, noble Odysseus!
> Rather would I in the field as daily laborer be toiling,
> Slave to the meanest of men, a pauper and lacking possessions,
> Than 'mid the infinite host of long-vanished mortals be ruler.

Yes, when Major Duvent challenged the great Israel Lyon to fight with pistols, and said to him, " If you do not meet me, Mr. Lyon, you are a dog ; " the latter replied, " I would rather be a live dog than a dead lion!" and was right. I have fought often enough,

Madame, to dare to say this, God be praised, I live! Red life boils in my veins, earth yields beneath my feet, in the glow of love I embrace trees and statues, and they live in my embrace. Every woman is to me the gift of a world. I revel in the melody of her countenance, and with a single glance of my eye I can enjoy more than others with their every limb through all their lives. Every instant is to me an eternity ; I do not measure time with the ell of Brabant or of Hamburg, and I need no priest to promise me a second life, for I can live enough in this life, when I live backwards in the life of those who have gone before me, and win myself an eternity in the realm of the past.

And I live! The great pulsation of nature beats too in my breast ; and when I carol aloud, I am answered by a thousand-fold echo. I hear a thousand nightingales. Spring hath sent them to awaken earth from her morning slumber, and earth trembles with ecstacy, her flowers are hymns, which she sings in inspiration to the sun ; the sun moves far too slowly ; I would fain lash on his steeds that they might advance more rapidly. But when he sinks hissing in the sea, and the night rises with her great eyes, oh! then true pleasure first thrills through me like a new life, the evening breezes lie like flattering maidens on my wild heart, and the stars wink to me, and I rise and sweep over the little earth and the little thoughts of mankind.

CHAPTER IV

BUT A DAY MUST COME WHEN THE FIRE OF YOUTH WILL BE QUENCHED in my veins, when winter will dwell in my heart, when his snow-flakes will whiten my locks, and his mists will dim my eyes. Then my friends will lie in their weatherworn tombs, and I alone will remain like a solitary stalk forgotten by the reaper. A new race will have sprung up, with new desires and new ideas ; full of wonder, I hear new names and listen to new songs, for the old names are forgotten, and I myself am forgotten, perhaps honored by but few, scorned by many, and loved by none! And then the rosy-cheeked boys will spring around me and place the old harp in my trembling hand, and say, laughing, " Thou indolent grey-headed old man, sing us again songs of the dreams of thy youth."

Then I will grasp the harp, and my old joys and sorrows will awake, the clouds vanish, tears will again gleam on my pale cheeks. Spring will bloom once more in my breast, sweet tones of sorrow will tremble on the harp-string. I will see once more the blue stream and the marble palaces and the lovely faces of ladies and young girls, and I will sing a song of the flowers of Brenta.

It will be my last song, the stars will gaze on me as in the nights of my youth, the loving moonlight will once more kiss my cheeks, the spirit chorus of nightingales long dead will sound flutelike from afar, my eyes, intoxicated with sleep, will softly close, my soul will re-echo with the notes of my harp—perfume breathes from the flowers of the Brenta.

A tree will shadow my grave. I would gladly have it a palm, but that tree will not grow in the North. It will be a linden, and of a summer evening lovers will sit there caressing ; the greenfinches will be listening silently, and my linden will rustle protectingly over the heads of the happy ones, who will be so happy that they will have no time to read what is written on the white tombstone. But when, at a later day, the lover has lost his love, then he will come again to the well-known linden, and sigh and weep, and gaze long and often upon the stone where he reads the inscription, " He loved the flowers of the Brenta."

CHAPTER V

MADAME, I HAVE DECEIVED YOU. I AM NOT THE COUNT OF THE GANGES. Never in my life did I see the holy stream, nor the lotus flowers which are mirrored in its sacred waves. Never did I lie dreaming under Indian palms, nor in prayer before the diamond deity Juggernaut, who with his diamonds might have easily aided me out of my difficulties. I have no more been in Calcutta than the turkey of which I ate yesterday at dinner had ever been in the realms of the Grand Turk. Yet my ancestors came from Hindustan, and therefore I feel so much at my ease in the great forests of song of Valmiki. The heroic sorrows of the divine Ramo move my heart like familiar griefs, from the flower lays of Kalidasa the sweetest memories bloom ; and when a few years ago a gentle lady in Berlin showed me the beautiful pictures which her father, who had been Governor-General in India, had brought from thence, the delicately painted, holy, calm faces seemed as familiar to me as though I were gazing at my own family gallery.

Franz Bopp — Madame, you have of course read his " Nalus " and his " System of Sanskrit Conjugations " gave me much information relative to my ancestry, and I now know with certainty that I am descended from Brahma's head, and not from his corns. I have also good reason to believe that the entire *Mahabarata*, with its two-hundred thousand verses, is merely an allegorical love-letter which my first forefather wrote to my first foremother. Oh, they loved dearly ; their souls kissed, they kissed with their eyes, they were both but one single kiss !

An enchanted nightingale sits on a red coral bough in the silent sea, and sings a song of the love of my ancestors ; earnestly gaze the pearls from their shelly cells ; the wondrous water-flowers tremble with sad longing, the cunning sea snails, bearing on their backs many-colored porcelain towers, come creeping onwards ; the ocean-roses blush with shame ; the yellow, sharp-pointed starfish and the thousand-hued glassy jellyfish quiver and stretch, and all swarm and crowd and listen.

Unfortunately, Madame, this nightingale song is far too long to be set down here in translation ; it is as long as the world itself — even its dedication to Anangas, the god of love, is as long as all Sir Walter Scott's novels together, and there is a passage referring to it in Aristophanes, which in German reads thus : —

> " Tiotio, tiotio, tiotinx,
> Totototo, totototo, tototinx."
> — *Voss's Translation*

No, I was not born in India. I first beheld the light of the world on the shores of that beautiful stream, in whose green hills folly grows and is plucked in autumn, laid away in cellars, poured into barrels, and exported to foreign lands.

In fact, only yesterday I heard some one speaking a piece of folly which, in the year 1818, was imprisoned in a bunch of grapes, which I myself then saw growing on the Johannisburg. But much folly is also consumed at home, and men are the same there as everywhere ; they are born, eat, drink, sleep, laugh, cry, slander each other, are in great trouble and care about the continuation of their race ; try to seem what they are not and to do what they cannot ; never shave until they have a beard, and often have beards before they get discretion ; and when they at last have discretion, they drink it away in white and red folly.

Mon Dieu! if I had faith, so that I could remove mountains, the Johannisburg would be just the mountain which I would carry with me everywhere. But not having enough faith, fantasy must aid me, and she at once bears me to the beautiful Rhine.

Oh, *there* is a fair land, full of loveliness and sunshine. In its blue streams are mirrored the mountain shores, with their ruined towers, and woods, and ancient towns. There, before the house-door, sit the good people of a summer evening, and drink out of great cans, and gossip confidingly how the wine—the Lord be praised!—thrives, and how justice should be free from all secrecy, and how Marie Antoinette's being guillotined is none of our business, and how dear the tobacco-tax makes the tobacco, and how all mankind are equal, and what a glorious fellow Gœrres is.

I have never troubled myself much with such conversation, and greatly preferred sitting by the maidens in the arched window, and laughed at their laughter, and let them strike me in the face with flowers, and pretended ill-nature until they told me their secrets, or some other story of equal importance. Fair Gertrude was half wild with delight when I sat by her. She was a girl like a flaming rose, and once as she fell on my neck, I thought that she would burn away in perfumes in my arms. Fair Katherine melted in musical sweetness when she talked with me, and her eyes were of

that pure, perfect *internal blue*, which I have never seen in animated beings, and very seldom in flowers—one gazed so gladly
into them, and could then ever imagine the sweetest things. But the
beautiful Hedwiga loved me, for when I came to her she bowed
her head till her black locks fell down over her blushing face, and
her gleaming eyes shone forth like stars from a dark heaven. Her
diffident lips spoke not a word, and even I could say nothing to her.
I coughed and she trembled. She often begged me, through her
sisters, not to climb the rocks so eagerly, or to bathe in the Rhine
when I had exercised or drunk wine. Once I overheard her pious
prayer to the image of the Virgin Mary, which she had adorned
with leaf-gold and illuminated with a glowing lamp, and which
stood in a corner of the sitting-room. She prayed to the Mother of
God to keep me from climbing, drinking, and bathing! I should
certainly have been desperately in love with her had she had been
indifferent to me, and *I* was indifferent to her because I knew that
she loved me. Madame, if any one would win my love, they must
treat me *en canaille*.

Johanna was the cousin of the three sisters, and I was glad to be
with *her*. She knew the most beautiful old legends, and when she
pointed with the whitest hand in the world through the window
out to the mountains where all had happened which she narrated,
I became enchanted. The old knights rose visibly from the
ruined castles, and hewed away at each other's iron clothes, the
Lorely sat again on the mountain summit, singing adown her
sweet seductive song, and the Rhine rippled so intelligibly,
so calmingly, and yet at the same time so mockingly and
strangely, and the fair Johanna gazed at me so bewilderingly, so
mysteriously, so enigmatically confiding, as though she herself
were one with the legend which she told. She was a slender, pale
beauty, sickly and musing, her eyes were clear as truth itself, her
lips piously arched, in her features lay a great untold story, but it
was a sacred one, perhaps a love legend! I know not what it was,
nor had I ever courage to ask. When I gazed long upon her, I
became calm and cheerful; it seemed to me as though there were
a tranquil Sunday in my heart, and that the angels were holding

church service there.

In such happy hours I told her tales of my childhood, and she listened earnestly to me, and, strangely, when I could not think of this or that name, she remembered it. When I then asked her with wonder where she had learned the name, she would answer with a smile that she had learned it of a little bird which had built its nest on the sill of her window ; and she tried to make me believe that it was the same bird which I once bought with my pocket-money from a hard-hearted peasant boy, and then let fly away. But I believed that she knew everything because she was so pale, and really soon died. She also knew when she would die, and wished that I would leave Andernach the day before. When I bade her farewell, she gave me both her hands—they were white, sweet hands, and pure as the Host—and she said, " Thou art very good, and when thou art bad, then think of the little dead Veronica."

Did the chattering birds also tell her *this* name? Often in hours when desirous of recalling the past, I had wearied my brain in trying to think of that dear name, and could not.

And now that I have it again, my earliest infancy shall bloom into memory again ; and I am again a child, and play with other children in the castle court at Düsseldorf, on the Rhine.

CHAPTER VI

YES, MADAME, THERE WAS I BORN, AND I AM PARTICULAR IN CALLING attention to this fact, lest after my death seven cities—those of Schilda, Krähwinkel, Polwitz, Bockum, Dülken, Göttingen, and Schöppenstadt—should contend for the honor of being my birthplace. Düsseldorf is a town on the Rhine, where about sixteen thousand mortals live, and where many hundred thousands are buried, and among them are many of whom my mother says it were better if they were still alive—for example, my grandfather and my uncle, the old Herr von Geldern, and the young Herr von Geldern, who were both such celebrated doctors, and saved the lives of so many men, and yet at last must both die themselves. And good pious Ursula, who carried me as a child in her arms, also lies buried there, and a rose-bush grows over her grave; she loved rose-perfume so much in her life, and her heart was all rose perfume and goodness. And the shrewd old *Canonicus* also lies there buried. Lord, how miserable he looked when I last saw him! He consisted of nothing but soul and plasters, and yet he studied night and day as though he feared lest the worms might find a few ideas missing in his head. Little William also lies there, and that is my fault. We were schoolmates in the Franciscan cloister, and were one day playing on that side of the building where the Düssel flows between stone walls, and I said, " William, do get the kitten out, which has just fallen in!" and he cheerfully climbed out on the board which stretched over the brook and pulled the cat out of the water, but fell in himself, and when they took him out he was cold and dead. The kitten lived to a good old age.

The town of Düsseldorf is very beautiful, and if you think of it when in foreign lands, and happen at the same time to have been born there, strange feelings come over the soul. I was born there, and feel as if I must go directly home. And when I say *home* I mean the *Bolkerstrasse* and the house where I was born. This house will be some day very famous, and I have sent word to the old lady who owns it that she must not for her life sell it. For the whole house she would now hardly get as much as the present which the green-veiled English ladies will give the servant girl when she shows them the room where I was born, and the hen-house wherein my father generally locked me up for stealing grapes, and also the brown door on which my mother taught me to write with chalk — O Lord! Madame, should I ever become a famous author, it has cost my poor mother trouble enough.

But my renown as yet slumbers in the marble quarries of Carrara ; the paper laurel with which they have crowned my brow has not spread its perfume through the wide world, and when the green-veiled English ladies visit Düsseldorf, they leave the cele-brated house unvisited, and go directly to the Market-Place and there gaze on the colossal black equestrian statue which stands in its midst. This represents the Prince Elector, Jan Wilhelm. He wears black armor and a long hanging wig. When a boy, I was told that the artist who made this statue observed with terror while it was being cast that he had not metal enough to fill the mold, and then all the citizens of the town came running with all their silver spoons, and threw them in to make up the deficiency ; and I often stood for hours before the statue wondering how many spoons were concealed in it, and how many apple-tarts the silver would buy. Apple-tarts were then my passion—now it is love, truth, liberty and crab-soup—and not far from the statue of the Prince Elector, at the Theater corner, generally stood a curiously constructed sabre-legged rascal with a white apron, and a basket girt around him full of smoking apple-tarts, which he well knew how to praise with an irresistible voice, " Here you are! hot apple-tarts! just from the oven—see how they smoke—quite delicious!" Truly, whenever in my later years the Evil One sought to win me, he always cried in just such an enticing soprano voice, and I should certainly have never remained twelve hours by the Signora Guilietta, if she had not thrilled me with her sweet perfumed apple-tart tones. And in fact the apple-tarts would never have so sorely tempted me if the crooked Hermann had not covered them up so mysteriously with his white aprons ; and it is aprons, you know, which—but I wander from the subject. I was speaking of the equestrian statue which has so many silver spoons in it, and no soup, and which represents the Prince Elector, Jan Wilhelm.

He was a brave gentleman, 'tis reported, a lover of art and handy therein himself. He founded the picture-gallery in Düsseldorf ; and in the observatory there, they show a very artistic piece of wooden work, consisting of one box within another which he himself had carved in his leisure hours, of which latter he had every day four-and-twenty.

In those days princes were not the persecuted wretches which they now are. Their crowns grew firmly on their heads, and at night they drew their caps over them and slept in peace, and their people slumbered calmly at their feet, and when they awoke in the morning they said, " Good morning, father!" and he replied,

" Good morning, dear children ! "

But there came a sudden change over all this, for one morning when we awoke, and would say, " Good morning, father ! " the father had traveled away, and in the whole town there was nothing but dumb sorrow. Everywhere there was a funeral-like expression, and people slipped silently through the market and read the long paper placed on the door of the town-house. It was dark and lowering, yet the lean tailor Kilian stood in the nankeen jacket, which he generally wore only at home, and in his blue woolen stockings, so that his little bare legs peeped out as if in sorrow, and his thin lips quivered as he read, murmuringly, the handbill. An old invalid soldier from the Palatine read it in a somewhat louder tone, and little by little a transparent tear ran down his white, honorable old moustache. I stood near him, and asked why he wept? And he replied, " The Prince Elector has abdicated." And then he read further, and at the words " for the long-manifested fidelity of my subjects," " and hereby release you from allegiance," he wept still more. It is a strange sight to see, when so old a man, in faded uniform, with a scarred veteran's face, suddenly bursts into tears. While we read, the Princely Electoral coat-of-arms was being taken down from the Town-Hall, and everything began to appear as miserably dreary as though we were waiting for an eclipse of the sun. The town-councilors went about at an abdicating wearisome gait ; even the omnipotent beadle looked as though he had no more commands to give, and stood calmly indifferent, although the crazy Aloysius stood upon one leg and chattered the names of French generals, while the tipsy cripple Gumpertz rolled around in the gutter, singing *Ca ira! Ca ira!*

But I went home, weeping and lamenting because " the Prince Elector had *abducted!*" My mother had trouble enough to explain the word, but I would hear nothing. I knew what I knew, and went weeping to bed, and in the night dreamed that the world had come to an end — that all the fair flower gardens and green meadows of the world were taken up and rolled up, and put away like carpets from the floor ; that a beadle climbed up on a high ladder and took down the sun, and that the tailor Kilian stood by and said to himself, " I must go home and dress myself neatly, for I am dead and am to be buried this afternoon." And it grew darker and darker — a few stars glimmered sparely on high, and even these at length fell down like yellow leaves in autumn ; one by one all men vanished, and I, a poor child, wandered in anguish around, until, before the willow fence of a deserted farmhouse, I saw a man digging up the earth with a spade, and near him an ugly, spiteful-looking woman, who held something in her apron like a human head — but it was the moon, and she laid it carefully in the open grave — and behind me stood the Palatine invalid, sighing and spelling, " The Prince Elector has abducted."

When I awoke, the sun shone as usual through the window, there was a sound of drums in the street, and as I entered the sitting-room and wished my father, who was sitting in his white dressing-gown, a good morning, I heard the little light-footed barber, as he made up his hair, narrate very minutely that homage would that morning be offered at the Town-Hall to the Archduke Joachim. I heard, too, that the new ruler was of excellent family, that he had married the sister of the Emperor Napoleon, and was really a very respectacle man ; that he wore his beautiful black hair in flowing locks, that he would shortly enter the town, and in fine, that he must please all the ladies. Meanwhile the drumming in the streets continued, and I stood before the house-door and looked at the French troops marching in that joyful race of fame, who, singing and playing, swept over the world, the merry, serious faces of the grenadiers, the bear-skin shakoes, the tri-colored cockades, the glittering bayonets, the *voltigeurs*, full of vivacity and *point d'honneur*, and the omnipotent giant-like silver-laced tambour-major, who cast his *baton* with a gilded head as high as the first storey, and his eyes to the second, where pretty girls gazed from the windows. I was so glad that soldiers were to be quartered in our house, — in which my mother differed from me, — and I hastened to the market-place. There everything looked changed, somewhat as though the world had been new whitewashed. A new coat-of-arms was placed on the Town-Hall, its iron balconies were hung with embroidered velvet drapery. French grenadiers stood as sentinels ; the old town-councilors had put on new faces, and donned their Sunday-coats, and looked at each other Frenchily, and said " *Bon jour!*", ladies gazed from every window, inquisitive citizens and armed soldiers filled the square, and I, with other boys, climbed on the great bronze horse of the Prince Elector, and stared down on the motley crowd.

Our neighbors, Peter and tall Jack Short, nearly broke their necks in accomplishing this feat, and it would have been better if they had been killed outright, for the one afterwards ran away from his parents, enlisted as a soldier, deserted, and was finally shot in Mayence ; while the other, having made geographical researches in strange pockets, was on this account elected member of a public tread-mill institute. But having broken the iron bands which bound him to his fatherland, he passed safely beyond sea, and eventually died in London, in consequence of wearing a much too long cravat, one end of which happened to be firmly attached to something, just as a royal official removed a plank from beneath his feet.

Tall Jack told us that there was no school today on account of the homage. We had to wait a long time till this was over. Finally, the balcony of the Council-House was filled with gaily dressed gentlemen, with flags and trumpets, and our burgomaster, in his celebrated red coat, delivered an oration, which stretched out like india-rubber, or like a night-cap into which one has thrown a stone—only that it was not the stone of wisdom—and I could distinctly understand many of his phrases—for instance, that " we are now to be made happy ; " and at the last words the trumpets sounded, and the people cried *hurrah !* and as I myself cried hurrah, I held fast to the old Prince Elector. And it was really necessary that I should, for I began to grow giddy. It seemed to me as if the people were standing on their heads, because the world whizzed around while the old Prince Elector, with his long wig, nodded and whispered, " Hold fast to me !" and not till the cannon re-echoed along the wall did I become sobered, and climbed slowly down from the great bronze horse.

As I went home, I saw the crazy Aloysius again dancing on one

314

leg, while he chattered the names of French generals, and I also
beheld the crippled Gumpertz rolling in the gutter and growling
ça ira, ça ira, and I said to my mother that we were all to be made
happy, and so we had that day no school.

CHAPTER VII

THE NEXT DAY THE WORLD WAS AGAIN ALL IN ORDER, AND WE HAD
school as before, and things were got by heart as before—the
Roman emperors, chronology, the nouns in *im,* the irregular verbs,
Greek, Hebrew, geography, German, mental arithmetic—Lord! my
head is still giddy with it!—all must be thoroughly learned. And
much of it was eventually to my advantage. For had I not learned
the Roman emperors by heart, it would subsequently have been a
matter of perfect indifference to me whether Niebuhr had or had
not proved that they never really existed. And had I not learned
chronology, how could I ever, in later years, have found out any
one in Berlin, where one house is as like another as drops of water
or as grenadiers, and where it is impossible to find a friend unless
you have the number of his house in your head. Therefore I associated with every friend some historical event, which had happened
in a year corresponding to the number of his house, so that the
one recalled the other, and some curious point in history always
occurred to me whenever I met an acquaintance. For instance,
when I met my tailor, I at once thought of the battle of Marathon ;
if I saw the banker, Christian Gumpel, I remembered the destruction of Jerusalem ; if a Portuguese friend, deeply in debt, the flight
of Mahomet ; if the university judge, a man whose probity is well
known, the death of Haman ; and if Wadzeck, I was at once
reminded of Cleopatra. Ah, heaven ! the poor creature is dead
now ; our tears are dry, and we may say of her with Hamlet,
" Take her for all in all, she was a hag ; we oft shall look upon her
like again !" But as I said, chronology is necessary. I know men
who have nothing in their heads but a few years, yet who know

exactly where to look for the right houses, and are moreover regular professors. But oh! the trouble I had at school with dates ; and it went even worse with mathematics. I understood best of all *subtraction*, and for this I had a very practical rule, " four can't be taken from three, therefore I must borrow one ; " but I advise all in such a case to borrow a few extra dollars, for one never knows.

But oh! the Latin. Madame, you can really have no idea of what a mess it is. The Romans would never have found time to conquer the world if they had been obliged first to learn Latin. Lucky dogs! they already knew in their cradles the nouns ending in *im*. I, on the contrary, had to learn them by heart, in the sweat of my brow, but still it is well that I knew them. For if, for example, when I publicly disputed in Latin in the College Hall of Göttingen, on the 20th of July, 1825 — Madame, it was well worth while to hear it — if, I say, I had said *sinapem* instead of *sinapim*, the blunder would have been evident to the freshmen, and an endless shame for me. *Vis, buris, sitis, tussis, cucumis, amussis, cannabis, sinapis.* These words, which have attracted so much attention in the world, effected this, inasmuch as they belonged to a determined class, and yet were withal an exception. And the fact that I have them ready at my fingers' ends when I perhaps need them in a hurry, often affords me in life's darkened hours much internal tranquility and spiritual consolation. But, Madame, the *verba irregularia* — they are distinguished from the *verbis regularibus* by the fact that the boys in learning them got more whippings — are terribly difficult. In the arched way of the Franciscan cloister near our schoolroom there hung a large Christ-crucified of grey wood, a dismal image, that even yet at times rises in my dreams, and gazes sorrowfully on me with fixed bleeding eyes. Before this image I often stood and prayed, " Oh, Thou poor and also tormented God, I pray Thee, if it be possible, that I may get by heart the irregular verbs ! "

I will say nothing of *Greek*, otherwise I should vex myself too much. The monks of the Middle Ages were not so very much in the wrong when they asserted that Greek was an invention of the devil. Lord knows what I suffered through it. It went better with

Hebrew, for I always had a great predilection for the Jews, although they to this very hour have crucified my good name. But yet, I never could get so far in Hebrew as my watch, which had a much more intimate intercourse with pawnbrokers, and in consequence acquired many Jewish habits; for instance, it would not go on Saturday, and learned the holy language, and was subsequently occupied with its grammar, for often when sleepless in the night I have, to my amazement, heard it industriously repeating, *katal, katalta, katalki—kittel, kittalta, kittalti—pokat, pokadeti—pikat, pik, pik.*

Meanwhile I learned more of German than of any other tongue, though German itself is not such child's play, after all. For we poor Germans, who have already been sufficiently vexed with having soldiers quartered on us, military duties, poll-taxes, and a thousand other exactions, must needs, over and above all this, bag Mr. Adelung, and torment each other with accusatives and datives. I learned much German from the old Rector Schallmeyer, a good, clerical gentleman, whose protégé I was from childhood. Something of the matter I also learned from Professor Schramm, a man who had written a book on eternal peace, and in whose class my school-fellows quarreled and fought with especial vigor.

And while thus dashing on in a breath, and thinking of every thing, I have unexpectedly found myself back among old school stories, and I avail myself of this opportunity to mention, Madame, that it was not my fault if I learned so little of geography that later in life I could not make my way in the world. For in those days the French made an intricate mixture of all limits and boundaries; every day lands were recolored on the world's map; those which were once blue suddenly became green, many indeed were even dyed blood-red; the old established rules were so confused and confounded that the devil himself would never have remembered them. The products of the country were also changed; chickory and beets now grew where only hares and hunters running after them were once to be seen; even the character of different races changed; the Germans became pliant, the French paid compliments no longer; the English ceased making ducks and drakes of their money, and the Venetians were not subtle enough ; there was promotion among princes, old kings obtained new uniforms, new kingdoms were cooked up and sold like hot cakes ; many potentates were chased, on the other hand, from house and home, and had to find some new way of earning their bread, while others went at once at a trade, and manufactured, for instance, sealing-wax, or — Madame, this paragraph must be brought to an end, or I shall be out of breath — in fine, in such times it is impossible to advance far in geography.

I succeeded better in natural history, for there we find fewer changes, and we always have standard engravings of apes, kangaroos, zebras, rhinoceroses, etc., etc. And having many such pictures in my memory, it often happens that at first sight many mortals appear to me like old acquaintances.

I also did well in mythology, and took a real delight in the mob of gods and goddesses who ran so jolly naked about the world. I do not believe that there was a schoolboy in ancient Rome who knew the principal points of his catechism — that is, the loves of Venus — better than I. To tell the plain truth, it seems to me that if we must learn all the heathen gods by heart, we might as well have kept them from the first ; and we have not perhaps, made so much out of our New-Roman Trinity or our Jewish unity. Perhaps the old mythology was not in reality so immoral as we imagine, and it was, for example, a very decent idea of Homer to give to the much-loved Venus a husband.

But I succeeded best in the French class of the Abbé d'Aulnoi, a French *emigré* who had written a number of grammars, and wore a red wig, and jumped about very nervously when he recited his *Art poétique* and his German history. He was the only one in the whole gymnasium who taught German history. Still French has its difficulties, and to learn it there must be much quartering of troops, much drumming in, much *apprendre par cœur*, and above all, no one should be a *bête allemande*. From all this resulted many a cross word, and I can remember as though it happened but yesterday, that I got into many a scrape through *la réligion*. I was once asked at least six times in succession, " Henry,

what is the French for ' faith?' " And six times, ever more weep-
ingly, I replied, " It is called *le crédit.*" And after the seventh
question, with his cheeks of a deep red-cherry-rage color, my
furious examinator cried, " It is called *la réligion* "—and there was
a rain of blows and a thunder of laughter from all my schoolmates.
Madame! since that day I never hear the word *religion* without
having my back turn pale with terror, and my cheeks red with
shame. And to tell the honest truth, *le crédit* has during my life
stood me in better stead than *la réligion.* It occurs to me just at
this instant that I still owe the landlord of the Lion in Bologna five
dollars. And I pledge you my sacred word of honor that I would
willingly owe him five dollars more if I could only be certain that
I should never again hear that unlucky word, *la réligion.*

Parbleu, Madame! I have succeeded tolerably well in French ;
for I understand not only *pâtois*, but even aristocratic governess
French. Not long ago, when in noble society, I understood full
one-half of the conversation of two German countesses, one of
whom could count at least sixty-four years, and as many descents.
Yes, in the *Café Royal*, I once heard Monsieur Hans Michel Martens
talking French, and could understand every word he spoke, though
there was no understanding in anything he said. We must know the
spirit of a language, and this is best learned by *drumming. Parbleu !*
how much do I not owe to the French drummer who was so long
quartered in our house, who looked like the devil, and yet had the
good heart of an angel, and who above all this drummed so
divinely!

He was a little, nervous figure, with a terrible black moustache,
beneath which red lips came bounding suddenly outwards, while
his wild eyes shot fiery glances all round.

I, a young shaver, stuck to him like a burr, and helped him to
rule his military buttons till they shone like mirrors, and to pipe-
clay his vest—for Monsieur Le Grand liked to look well—and I
followed him to the watch, to the roll-call, to the parade—in those
times there was nothing but the gleam of weapons and merriment—
les jours de fête sont passées ! Monsieur Le Grand knew but a little
broken German, only the three principal words in every tongue—

" Bread," " Kiss," " Honor "—but he could make himself very intelligible with his drum. For instance, if I knew not what the word *liberté* meant, he drummed the *Marseillaise*—and I understood him. If I did not understand the word *egalité*, he drummed the march—

> " Ca ira, ça ira, ça ira,
> Les aristocrats à la lanterne!"

and I understood him. If I did not know what *bêtise* meant, he drummed the Dessauer March, which we Germans, as Goethe also declares, have drummed in Champagne—and I understood him. He once wanted to explain to me the word *l'Allemagne*, and he drummed the all too *simple* melody which on market-days is played to dancing-dogs—namely, *dum*—*dum*—*dum*! I was vexed, but I understood him!

In like manner he taught me modern history. I did not understand, it is true, the words which he spoke, but as he constantly drummed while speaking, I understood him. This is, fundamentally, the best method. The history of the storming of the Bastille, of the Tuileries, and the like, cannot be correctly understood until we know how *the drumming* was done on such occasions. In our school compendiums of history we merely read: " Their excellencies the Baron and Count, with the most noble spouses of the aforesaid, were beheaded." " Their highnesses the Dukes and Princes, with the most noble spouses of the aforesaid, were beheaded." " His Majesty the King, with his most sublime spouse, the Queen, was beheaded." But when you hear the red march of the guillotine *drummed*, you understand it correctly for the first time, and with it the how and the why. Madame, that is really a wonderful march! It thrilled through marrow and bone when I first heard it, and I was glad that I forgot it. People are apt to forget one thing and another as they grow older, and a young man has nowadays so much other knowledge to keep in his head—whist, Boston, genealogical tables, parliamentary data, dramaturgy, the liturgy, carving—and yet, I assure you that, despite all jogging up of my brain, I could not for a long time recall that tremendous tune! And only to think, Madame ; not long ago I sat at table with a whole menagerie of counts, princes, princesses, chamberlains, court-marshalesses, seneschals, upper court mistresses, court keepers of the royal plate, court hunters' wives, and whatever else these aristocratic domestics are termed, and *their* under-domestics ran about behind their chairs and shoved full plates before their mouths ; but I, who was passed by and neglected, sat at leisure without the least occupation for my jaws, and kneaded little bread-balls, and drummed with my fingers ; and, to my astonishment, I found myself suddenly drumming the red, long-forgotten guillotine march.

" And what happened?" Madame, the good people were not in the least disturbed, nor did they know that *other* people, when they can get nothing to eat, suddenly begin to drum, and that, too, very queer marches, which people have long forgotten.

Is drumming now an inborn talent, or was it early developed in me? Enough, it lies in my limbs, in my hands, in my feet, and often involuntarily manifests itself. I once sat at Berlin in the lecture-room of the Privy Councilor Schmaltz, a man who had saved the state by his book on the " Red and Black Coat Danger." You remember, perhaps, Madame, that in Pausanias we are told that by the braying of an ass an equally dangerous plot was once discovered, and you also know from Livy, or from " Becker's History of the World," that geese once saved the Capitol, and you must certainly know from Sallust that by the chattering of a loquacious *putain*, the Lady Livia, that the terrible conspiracy of Catiline came to light. But to return to our muttons. I listened to international law in the lecture-room of the Herr Privy Councilor Schmaltz, and it was a sleepy summer afternoon, and I sat on the bench, and little by little I listened less and less—my head had gone to sleep—when all at once I was wakened by the noise of my own feet, which had *not* gone to sleep, and had probably observed that anything but international law and constitutional tendencies was being preached, and my feet, which, with the little eyes of their corns, had seen more of how things go in the world than the Privy Councilor with his Juno eyes—these poor dumb feet, incapable of expressing their immeasurable meaning by words, strove

321

to make themselves intelligible by drumming, and they drummed
so loudly that I thereby came to grief.

Cursed, unreflecting feet! They once played me a similar trick,
when I on a time in Göttingen sponged, without subscribing, on
the lectures of Professor Saalfeld, and as this learned gentleman,
with his angular activity, jumped about here and there in his
pulpit, and heated himself in order to curse the Emperor Napoleon
in regular set style, right and left — no, my poor feet, I cannot
blame you for drumming *then* — indeed, I would not have blamed
you if in your dumb naïveté you had expressed yourselves by still
more energetic movements. How could *I*, the scholar of Le Grand,
hear the Emperor cursed? The Emperor! the Emperor! the great
Emperor!

When I think of the great Emperor, my thoughts again grow
summer-green and golden. A long avenue of lindens rises blooming
around, on the leafy twigs sit singing nightingales, the waterfall
rustles, flowers are growing from full round beds, dreamily nodding
their fair heads: I stood amidst them once in wondrous intimacy,
the rouged tulips, proud as beggars, condescendingly greeted me,
the nervous sick lilies nodded with woeful tenderness, the tipsy
red roses nodded at me at first sight from a distance, the night-
violets sighed; with the myrtle and laurel I was not then
acquainted, for they did not entice with a shining bloom, but the
mignonnette, with whom I am now on such bad terms, was my
very particular friend. I am speaking of the Court garden of
Düsseldorf, where I often lay upon the bank, and piously listened
there when Monsieur Le Grand told of the warlike feats of the
great Emperor, beating meanwhile the marches which were
drummed during the deeds, so that I saw and heard all to the life.
I saw the passage over the Simplon — the Emperor in advance and
his brave grenadiers climbing on behind him, while the scream of
frightened birds of prey sounded around, and the glaciers thundered
in the distance — I saw the Emperor with flag in hand on the bridge
of Lodi — I saw the Emperor in his grey cloak at Marengo — I saw
the Emperor mounted in the battle of the Pyramids, naught around
save powder, smoke, and Mamelukes — I saw the Emperor in the

battle of Austerlitz — ha! how the bullets whistled over the smooth, icy road! — I saw, I heard the battle of Jena — *dum, dum, dum* — I saw, I heard the battles of Eylau, of Wagram — no, I could hardly stand it! Monsieur Le Grand drummed so that I nearly burst my eardrums!

CHAPTER VIII

BUT WHAT WERE MY FEELINGS WHEN I FIRST SAW WITH HIGHLY blest eyes *him*, Hosannah! the Emperor!

It was exactly in the avenue of the Court garden at Düsseldorf. As I pressed through the gaping crowd, thinking of the doughty deeds and battles which Monsieur Le Grand had drummed to me, my heart beat the " general march " — yet at the same time I thought of the police regulation that no one should dare under penalty of five dollars fine ride through the avenue. And the Emperor with his *cortège* rode directly down the avenue. The trembling trees bowed towards him as he advanced, the sun-rays quivered, frightened, yet curiously through the green leaves, and in the blue heaven above there swam visibly a golden star. The Emperor wore his invisible-green uniform and the little world-renowned hat. He rode a white palfrey, which stepped with such calm pride, so confidently, so nobly — had I then been Crown Prince of Prussia I would have envied that horse. The Emperor sat carelessly, almost lazily, holding with one hand his rein, and with the other good-naturedly patting the neck of the horse. It was a sunny marble hand, a mighty hand — one of the pair which bound fast the many-headed monster of anarchy, and reduced to order the war of races — and it good-naturedly patted the neck of the horse. Even the face had that hue which we find in the marble Greek and Roman busts, the traits were as nobly proportioned as in the antiques, and on that face was plainly written, " Thou shalt have no gods before me!" A smile, which warmed and tranquilized every heart, flitted over the lips — and yet all knew that those lips needed but to whistle, *et la Prusse n'existait plus* — those lips needed

323

but to whistle, and the entire clergy would have stopped their ringing and singing — those lips needed but to whistle, and the entire Holy Roman realm would have danced. It was an eye clear as heaven ; it could read the hearts of men ; it saw at a glance all things at once, and as they were in this world, while we ordinary mortals see them only one by one and by their shaded hues. The brow was not so clear, the phantoms of future battles were nestling there, and there was a quiver which swept over that brow, and those were the creative thoughts, the great seven-mile-boot thoughts wherewith the spirit of the Emperor strode invisibly over the world ; and I believe that every one of those thoughts would have given to a German author full material wherewith to write all the days of his life.

The Emperor rode calmly straight through the avenue ; no policeman stopped him ; behind his *cortège* rode proudly, loaded with gold and ornaments, on panting horses ; the trumpets were sounded ; near me crazy Aloysius spun round and snarled the names of his generals ; not far off growled the tipsy Gumpert, and the multitude cried with a thousand voices, — Long live the Emperor !

CHAPTER IX

THE EMPEROR IS DEAD. ON A WASTE ISLAND IN THE INDIAN SEA LIES his lonely grave, and he for whom the world was too narrow lies silently under a little hillock, where five weeping willows hang their green heads, and a gentle little brook, murmuring sorrowfully, ripples by. There is no inscription on his tomb ; but Clio, with unerring pen, has written thereon invisible words, which will resound, like spirit-tones, through thousands of years.

Britannia ! the sea is thine. But the sea hath not water enough to wash away the shame with which the death of that mighty one hath covered thee. Not thy windy Sir Hudson — no, thou thyself wert the Sicilian bravo with whom perjured kings bargained, that they might revenge on the man of the people that which the people had once inflicted on one of themselves. And he was thy guest, and had seated himself by thy hearth.

Until the boys of France will for ages sing and tell of the terrible hospitality of the *Bellerophon*, and when those songs of mockery and tears resound across the Channel, there will be a blush on the cheeks of every honorable Briton. But a day will come when this song will ring thither, and Britannia will be no more—when the people of pride will be humbled to the earth, when Westminster's monuments will be broken, and when the royal dust which they enclosed forgotten. And St. Helena is the holy grave whither the races of the east and of the west will make their pilgrimage in ships, with flags of many a color, and their hearts will grow strong with great memories of the deeds of the worldly savior, who suffered and died under Sir Hudson Lowe, as it is written in the evangelists, Las Casas, O'Meara, and Autommarchi.

Strange! A terrible destiny has already overtaken the three greatest enemies of the Emperor. Londonderry has cut his throat, Louis XVIII. has rotted away on his throne, and Professor Saalfield is still professor in Göttingen.

CHAPTER X

IT WAS A CLEAR FROSTY MORNING IN AUTUMN AS A YOUNG MAN, whose appearance denoted the student, slowly loitered through the avenue of the Düsseldorf Court garden, often, with child-like pleasure, pushing aside with wayward feet the leaves which covered the ground, and often sorrowfully gazing towards the bare trees, on which a few golden-hued leaves still fluttered in the breeze. As he thus gazed up, he thought on the words of Glaucus:—

" Like the leaves in the forests, e'en so are the races of mortals ;
Leaves are blown down to the earth by the wind, while others are driven
Away by the green budding wood, when fresh up-liveth the spring-tide ;
So the races of man—this grows and the other departeth."

In earlier days the youth had gazed with far different eyes on the same trees. When he was a boy he had there sought birds' nests or summer insects, which delighted his very soul, as they merrily hummed around, and were glad in the beautiful world, and contented with a sap-green leaf and a drop of water, with a warm sun-ray and with the perfume of the grass. In those times the boy's heart was as gay as the fluttering insects. But now his heart had grown older, its little sun-rays were quenched, its flowers had faded, even its beautiful dream of love had grown dim ; in that poor heart was naught save pride and care, and to say the worst — it was my heart.

I had returned that day to my old father-town, but I would not remain there overnight, and I longed for Godesberg, that I might sit at the feet of my lady friend and tell of the little Veronica. I had visited the dear graves. Of all my living friends, I had found but an uncle and an aunt. Even when I met once known forms in the street, they knew me no more, and the town itself gazed on me with strange glances. Many houses were colored anew, strange faces gazed on me through the window-panes, worn-out old sparrows hopped on the old chimneys ; everything looked dead and yet fresh, like a salad growing in a graveyard. Where French was once spoken I now heard the Prussian dialect ; even a little Prussian court had taken up its retired dwelling there, and the people bore court titles. The hairdresser of my mother had now become the Court-hairdresser and there were Court-tailors, Court-shoemakers, Court-bedbug-destroyers, Court-grogshops — the whole town seemed to be a court-asylum for court-lunatics. Only the old Prince Elector knew me ; he still stood in the same old place ; but he seemed to have grown thinner. For just because he stood in the market-place, he had had a full view of all the miseries of the time, and people seldom grow fat on such sights. I was as if in a dream, and thought of the legend of the enchanted city, and hastened out of the gate, lest I should awake too soon. I missed many a tree in the Court garden, and many had grown crooked with age, and the four great poplars which once seemed to me like green giants had become smaller. Pretty girls were walking here and there, dressed as gaily as wandering tulips. And I had known these tulips when they were but little bulbs ; for ah ! they were the neighbor's children with whom I had once played " Princess in the Tower." But the fair maidens, whom I had once known as blooming roses were now faded roses, and in many a high brow whose pride had once filled my heart, Saturn had cut deep wrinkles with his scythe. And now for the first time, and alas ! too late, I understood what those glances meant, which they had once cast on the adolescent boy ; for I had meanwhile in other lands fathomed the meaning of similar passages in other lovely eyes. I was deeply moved by the humble bow of a man, whom I had once known as wealthy and respectable, and who had since become a beggar. Everywhere in the world, we see that men when they once begin to fall, do so according to Newton's theory, ever faster and faster in ratio as they descend to misery. One, however, who did not seem to be in the least changed was the little Baron, who tripped merrily as of old through the Court garden, holding with one hand his left coat-skirt on high, and with the other swinging hither and thither his light cane ; — he still had the same genial face as of old, its rosy bloom now somewhat concentrated towards the nose, but he wore the same comical hat, and the same old queue behind, only that the hairs which peeped from it were now white instead of black. But merry as the old Baron seemed, it was still evident that he had suffered much sorrow ; his face would fain conceal it, but the white hairs of his queue betrayed him behind his back ; yet the queue itself seemed striving to lie, so merrily yet sadly did it shake.

I was not weary, but a fancy seized me to sit once more on the wooden bench, on which I had once carved the name of my love. I could hardly discover it there among the many new names, which had since been cut around. Ah ! once I slept upon this bench, and dreamed of happiness and love. " Dreams are foam." And the old plays of childhood came again to my soul, and with them old and beautiful stories ; but a new treacherous game, and a new terrible tale ever resounded through them, and it was the story of two poor souls who were false to each other, and went so far in their untruth, that they were at last unfaithful to the good God himself.

327

It is a bad, sad story, and when one has nothing better to do, he can well weep over it. Oh, Lord! once the world was so beautiful, and the birds sang thy eternal praise, and little Veronica looked at me with silent eyes, and we sat by the marble statue before the castle court. On one side lies an old ruined castle, wherein ghosts wander, and at night a headless dame in long, trailing, black silken garments, sweeps around ; on the other side is a high, white dwelling in whose upper rooms gay pictures gleamed beautifully in their golden frames, while below stood thousands of mighty books which Veronica and I beheld with longing, when the good Ursula lifted us up to the window. In later years, when I became a great boy, I climbed every day to the very top of the library ladder, and brought down the topmost books, and read in them so long, that finally I feared nothing — least of all ladies without heads — and became so wise that I forgot all the old games and stories and pictures, and little Veronica, whose very name I also forgot.

But while I sat upon the bench in the Court garden and dreamed my way back into the past, there was a sound behind me of the confused voices of men lamenting the ill fortune of the poor French soldiers, who having been taken prisoners in the Russian war and sent to Siberia, had there been kept prisoners for many a long year, though peace had been re-established, and who now were returning home. As I looked up, I beheld in reality several of these orphan children of Fame. Through their tattered uniforms peeped naked misery, deep sorrowing eyes were couched in their desolate faces, and though mangled, weary, and mostly lame, something of the military manner was still visible in their mien. Singularly enough, they were preceded by a drummer who tottered along with a drum, and I shuddered as I recalled the old legend of soldiers who had fallen in battle, and who by night rising again from their graves on the battlefield, and with the drummer at their head, marched back to their native city. And of them the old ballad sings thus : —

328

" He beat on the drum with might and main ;
To their old night-quarters they go again ;
   Through the lighted street they come ;
   Trallerie — trallerei — trallera,
They march before Sweetheart's home.

Thus the dead return ere break of day,
Like tombstones white in their cold array,
   And the drummer he goes before ;
   Trallerie — trallerei — trallera,
And we see them come no more."

Truly the poor French drummer seemed to have risen but half repaired from the grave. He was but a little shadow in a dirty patched grey capote, a dead yellow countenance, with a great mustache which hung down sorrowfully over his faded lips, his eyes were like burnt-out tinder, in which but a few sparks still gleamed, and yet by one of those sparks I recognized Monsieur Le Grand.

He too recognized me, and drew me to the turf, and we sat down together as of old, when he taught me French and Modern History on the drum. He had still the well-known old drum, and I could not sufficiently wonder how he had preserved it from Russian plunderers. And he drummed again as of old, but without speaking a word. But though his lips were firmly pressed together, his eyes spoke all the more, flashing fiercely and victoriously, as he drummed the old marches. The poplars near us trembled as he again thundered forth the red march of the guillotine. And he drummed, as before, the old battles for freedom, the deeds of the Emperor, and it seemed as though the drum itself were a living creature which rejoiced to speak out its inner soul. I heard once more the cannon thunder, the whistling of balls, the riot of battle, the death-rage of the Guards — I saw once more the waving flags again, the Emperor on his steed ; — but little by little there fell a sad tone in amid the most stirring confusion ; sounds rang from the drum in which the wildest hurrahs and the most fearful grief were mysteriously mingled ; it seemed a march of victory and a march of death. Le Grand's eyes opened spirit-like and wide, and I

329

saw in them nothing but a broad white field of ice covered with corpses — it was the battle of Moscow.

I had never imagined that the hard old drum could give forth such wailing sounds as Monsieur Le Grand had drawn from it. They were tears which he drummed, and they sounded ever softer and softer, and like a troubled echo deep sighs broke from Le Grand's breast. And they became ever more languid and ghost-like ; his dry hands trembled as if from frost ; he sat as in a dream, and stirred with his drum-stick nothing but the air, and seemed listening to voices far away ; and at last he gazed on me with a deep — oh, so deep and entreating a glance. I understood him — and then his head sunk down on the drum.

In this life Monsieur Le Grand never drummed more. And his drum never gave forth another sound, for it was not destined to serve the enemies of liberty for their servile roll-calls. I had well understood the last entreating glance of Le Grand, and at once drew the rapier from my cane, and with it pierced the drum.

CHAPTER XI

DU SUBLIME AU RIDICULE IL N'Y A QU'UN PAS, MADAME!

But life is in reality so terribly serious that it would be insupportable were it not for these unions of the pathetic and the comic, as our poets well know. Aristophanes only exhibits the most harrowing forms of human madness in the laughing mirror of wit ; Goethe only presumes to set forth the fearful pain of thought comprehending its own nothingness in the doggerel of a puppet-show, and Shakespeare puts the most agonizing lamentations on the misery of the world in the mouth of a fool, who rattles his cap and bells in all the nervous suffering of pain.

They have all learned from the great First Poet, who, in his World Tragedy in thousands of acts, knows how to carry *humor* to the highest point, as we see every day : — after the departure of the heroes, the clowns and *graciosos* enter with their baubles and lashes, and after the bloody scenes of the Revolution there came waddling on the stage the fat Bourbons, with their stale jokes and tender "legitimate" *bon mots,* and the old noblesse with their starved laughter hopped merrily before them, while behind all swept the pious Capuchins with candles, cross, and banners of the Church. Yes, even in the highest pathos of the World Tragedy bits of fun slip in. It may be that the desperate republican, who, like a Brutus, plunged a knife to his heart, first smelt it to see whether some one had not split a herring with it—and on this great stage of the world all passes exactly the same as on our beggarly boards. On it, too, there are tipsy heroes, kings who forget their parts, scenes which obstinately stay up in the air, prompters' voices sounding above everything, *danseuses* who create astonishing effects with the poetry of their legs, and, *costumes,* which are and ever will be the main thing. And high in heaven, in the first row of the boxes, sit the lovely angels, and keep their *lorgnettes* on us poor comedians here down below, and the blessed Lord himself sits seriously in his splendid seat, and, perhaps, finds it dull, or calculates that this theatre cannot be kept up much longer because this one gets too high a salary, and that one too little, and that they altogether play far too badly.

Du sublime au ridicule il n'y a qu'un pas. Madame! As I ended the last chapter narrating to you how Monsieur Le Grand died, and how I conscientiously executed the *testamentum militare,* which lay in his last glance, some one knocked at my room-door, and there entered an old woman, who asked pleasantly if I were not a doctor. And as I assented, she asked me in a friendly, patronizing tone to go with her to her house, that I might there cut her husband's corns.

CHAPTER XII

THE GERMAN CENSORS OF THE PRESS —   ——   ——   ——
——   ——   ——   ——   ——   ——   ——
——   ——   ——   ——   ——   ——   ——
——   ——   ——   ——   ——   ——   ——
——   ——   blockheads   ——   ——
——   ——   ——   ——   ——   ——   ——
——   ——   ——   ——   ——   ——   ——
——   ——   ——   ——   ——   ——   ——

CHAPTER XIII

MADAME! UNDER LEDA'S PRODUCTIVE HEMISPHERES LAY IN EMBRYO
the whole Trojan world, and you could never understand the far-
famed tears of Priam if I did not first tell you of the ancient eggs
of the swan ; therefore, I pray you, do not complain of my digres-
sions. In all the previous chapters there is not a line which is irrel-
evant. I write in a condensed style ; I avoid all superfluity ; I even
neglect the necessary. For instance, I have not regularly cited, I do
not mean spirits, but, on the contrary, beings which are often
quite spiritless, that is to say, authors ; and yet the citation of old
and new books is the chief pleasure of a young author, and a few
fundamentally erudite quotations often adorn the whole man.
Never believe, Madame, that I am wanting in knowledge of titles
of books. Moreover, I have caught the knack of those great souls
who know how to pick the currants out of biscuits and quotations
from college lecture-books. In case of need, I can negotiate a loan
of quotations from my learned friends. My friend G——, in Berlin,
is, so to speak, a little Rothschild in quotations, and will gladly lend
me a few millions ; and if he does not happen to have them about
him, I can easily find some cosmopolite spiritual bankers who have.
Apropos, Madame, the three per cent. Böckhs are dull, but the five
per cent. Hegels have risen. But what need of loans have I, who am

a man who stands well with the world, and have my annual income of 10,000 quotations to spend at will? I have even discovered the art of passing off forged quotations for genuine. If any wealthy literary man — for instance, Michael Beer — would like to buy this secret, I will cheerfully sell it for 19,000 current dollars, or will trade with him. Another of my discoveries I will impart gratis for the benefit of literature.

I hold it to be an advisable thing when quoting from an obscure author to invariably give his address.

These " good men and bad musicians," as the orchestra is termed in *Ponce de Leon* — these unknown authors almost invariably still possess a copy of their long out-of-print works, and to hunt up this latter it is necessary to know the number of their houses. If I wanted, for example, to find " Spitta's Song Book for Traveling Journeymen Mechanics," my dear Madame, where would *you* look for the book? But if quoted —

" *Vide* Song Book for Traveling Journeymen Apprentices, by P. Spitta, Lüneburg, Lüner Street, No. 2, right hand, around the corner."

——Then you could, if it were worth your while, Madame, hunt up the book. But it is *not* worth the while.

Moreover, Madame, you can have no idea of the *facility* with which I quote. Everywhere do I discover opportunities to parade my profound pedantry. If I chance to mention eating, I at once remark in a note that the Greeks, Romans, and Hebrews also ate ; I quote all the costly dishes which were prepared by Lucullus's cook — woe me, that I was born fifteen hundred years too late. I also remark that these meals were called this, that, or the other by the Romans, and that the Spartans ate bad black broth. After all, it is well that I did not live in *those* days, for I can imagine nothing more terrible than if I, poor devil, had been a Spartan. Soup is my favorite dish. Madame, I have thought of going next year to London, but if it is really true that no soup is to be had there, a deep longing will soon drive me back to the soup and flesh-pots of the Fatherland. I could also dilate by the hour on the cookery of the ancient Hebrews, and also descend into the kitchen of the Jews of the present day. I may cite apropos of this the entire *Steinweg*. I might also allege the refined manner in which many Berlin *savants* have expressed themselves relative to Jewish eating, which would lead me to the other excellences and pre-eminences of the chosen people to which we are indebted — as, for instance, their invention of bills of exchange and Christianity. But hold! it will hardly do for me to praise ·the latter too highly, not having as yet made much use of it, and I believe that the Jews themselves have not profited so much by it as by their bills of exchange. While on the Jews I could appropriately quote Tacitus; he says that they honored asses in their temples, and what a field of rich erudition and quotation opens on us here! How many a noteworthy thing can be adduced on ancient asses as opposed to the modern! How intelligent were the former, and, ah! how stupid are the latter! How reasonably, for instance, spoke the ass of B. Balaam!

Vide Pentat. Lib. —   —   —   —   —

Madame, I have not the work just at hand, and will here leave a *hiatus* to be filled at a convenient opportunity. On the other hand, to confirm my assertion of the dullness, tameness, and stupidity of modern asses, I may allege.

Vide —   —   —   —   —

—   —   —   —   —   —

—   —   —   —   —   —

—   — No, I will leave these quotations also unquoted, otherwise I myself will be cited — namely, *injuriarum* or for *scan. mag.* The modern asses are great asses. The antique asses, who had reached such a pitch of refinement

Vide Gesneri *de antiqua honestate asinorum.*

(*In comment. Götting.* t. ii. p. 32).

— would turn in their graves could they hear how people talk about their descendants. Once " Ass " was an honorable title, signifying as much as " Court Councilor," " Baron," " Doctor of Philosophy." Jacob compared his son Issachar to one, Homer his hero Ajax, and now we compare Mr. von —— to the same.

Madame, while speaking of *such* asses I could sink deep into literary history, and mention all the great men who ever were in love—for example, Abelardus, Picus Mirandola, Borbonius, Curtesius, Angelus Politianus, Raymondus Lullius, and Henricus Heineus. While on *Love* I could mention all the great men who never smoked tobacco, as, for instance, Cicero, Justinian, Goethe, Hugo, I myself—by chance it happens that we all five have studied law. Mabillion could not for an instant endure anybody else's pipe, for in his *Itinere Germanico* he complains as regarded the German taverns, " *quod molestus ipsi fuerit tabaci grave olentis foetor.*" On the other hand, very great men have manifested an extraordinary partiality for tobacco. Raphael Thorus wrote a hymn in its praise. Madame, you may not perhaps be aware that Isaac Elzevir published it in 1628 at Leyden in quarto, and Ludovicus Kinschot wrote an oration in verses on the same subject. Grævius has even composed a sonnet on the soothing herb, and the great Boxhornius also loved tobacco. Bayle, in his *Dict. Hist. et Critiq.*, remarks of him that in smoking he wore a hat with a broad brim, in the forepart of which he had a hole, through which the pipe was stuck that it might not hinder his studies. Apropos of Boxhornius, I might cite all the great literati who were threatened with bucks' horns, and who ran away in terror. But I will only mention Joh. Georg Martius : *de fuga literatorum, et cetera, etc., etc*. If we go through history, Madame, we find that all great men have been obliged to run away once in their lives : Lot, Tarquin, Moses, Jupiter, Madame de Staël, Nebuchadnezzar, Benjowsky, Mahomet, the whole Prussian army, Gregory VII., Rabbi Jizchak Abarbanel, Rousseau—to which I could add very many other names, as, for instance, those whose names stand on the black board of the Exchange.

So, Madame, you see that I am not wanting in well-grounded erudition and profundity. Only in systematology am I a little behindhand. As a true German, I ought to have begun this book with a full explanation of its title, as is usual in the Holy Roman Empire, by custom and by prescription. Phidias, it is true, made no preface to his Jupiter, as little as to the Medicean Venus—I have regarded her from every point of view, without finding the slightest introduction ; but the old Greeks were Greeks, and when a man is an honest German, he cannot lay aside his German nature, and

The Sword and the Flame

I must accordingly " hold forth " in regular order on the title of my book.

Madame, I shall consequently proceed to speak

   I. Of ideas.

        A. Of ideas in general.

        a. Of reasonable ideas.

        B. Of unreasonable ideas.

        a. Of ordinary ideas.

        B. Of ideas covered with green leather.

These are again divided into   — — — but that we shall arrive at in due course.

CHAPTER XIV

MADAME, HAVE YOU, ON THE WHOLE, AN IDEA OF AN IDEA? WHAT IS an idea? " There are some good ideas in this coat," said my tailor to me, as he with earnest attention gazed on the overcoat which dates in its origin from my Berlin dandy days, and from which a respectable quiet dressing-gown is now to be manufactured. My washerwoman complains that the Reverend Mr. S—— has been putting " ideas " into the head of her daughter, which have made her foolish and unreasonable. The coachman, Pattensen, grumbles out on every occasion, " That's an idea! that's an idea!" Yesterday evening he was regularly vexed when I inquired what sort of a thing he imagined an idea to be? And vexedly did he growl, " *Nu, Nu*,—an idea is an idea! — an idea is any d——d nonsense that a man gets into his head." It is in this same sense that the word is used as the title of a book by the Court Councilor Heeren in Göttingen.

The coachman Pattensen is a man who can find his way through night and mist over the broad Lüneburger Heath ;—the Court Councilor Heeren is one who, with equally cunning instinct, can discover the ancient caravan road to the East, and plods on thither as safely and as patiently as any *camel* of antiquity. We can trust

336

such people and follow them without doubt, and therefore I have entitled this book " Ideas."

But the title of the book means, on that account, as little as the title of its author. It was chosen by him under any inspiration save that of pride, and should be interpreted to signify anything but vanity. Accept, Madame, my most sorrowful assurance that I am not vain. This remark — as you yourself were about to remark — is necessary. I am not vain — I would not become so if a forest of laurels grew on my head and a sea of incense were poured into my young heart, still I would not be vain. My friends, as well as divers more or less contemptible contemporaries, have fully taken care of *that* in advance of you. You know, Madame, that old women are accustomed to take children down a little when any one praised their beauty lest praise might hurt the little darlings. You remember, too, Madame, that in Rome when any one who had gained a military triumph and rode like a god, crowned with glory and arrayed in purple on his golden chariot with white horses from the *Campus Martius*, amid a festal train of lictors, musicians, dancers, priests, slaves, elephants, trophy-bearers, consuls, senators, soldiers : then behind him the vulgar mob sang all manner of mocking songs. And you know, Madame, that in our beloved Germany there are many old women and a very great vulgar mob.

As I intimated, Madame, the ideas here alluded to are as remote from those of Plato as Athens is from Göttingen, and you should no more form undue expectations as to the book than as to its author. In fact, how the latter could ever have excited anything of the sort is as incomprehensible to me as to my friends. The Countess Julia explains the matter by assuring us that when he says anything really witty and original, he only does it to humbug the world, and that he is in fact as stupid as any other mortal. That is false — I do not humbug at all ; I sing just as my bill grows. I write in all innocence and simplicity whatever comes into my head, and it is not my fault if that happens to be something dashed with genius. At any rate, I have better luck in writing than in the Altona Lottery — I wish that it was the other way — and there come from my pen many heart-stunners, many reams of thought, all of which is done by the Lord; for HE who has denied to the most devoted psalm-makers and moral poets all beautiful thoughts and all literary reputation, lest they should be praised too much by their earthly fellow-creatures, and thereby forget heaven, where the angels have already engaged board for them in advance — HE, I say, provides us other profane, sinful, heretical authors, for whom heaven is as good as nailed up, all the more with admirable ideas and earthly fame, and this indeed from divine grace and mercy, so that the poor souls, since they are really here, be not altogether wanting, and that they may at least enjoy upon earth some of that joy which is denied to them in heaven.

Vide Goethe and the writers of tracts.

You see, then, Madame, that you can, without distrust, read my writings, as they set forth the grace and mercy of God. I write in blind reliance on His omnipotence. I am in this respect a true Christian author, and, to speak like Gubitz, even in this present paragraph do not know exactly how I am going to bring it to an end, and to effect it I trust entirely to the aid of the Lord. And how could I write without this pious reliance? — for lo! even now there stands before me the printer's devil from Langhoff's printing-office, waiting for copy, and the new-born word wanders warm and wet to the press, and what I at this instant think and feel may tomorrow be waste paper.

It is all very fine, Madame, to remind me of the Horatian maxim, *nonum prematur in annum*. This rule, like many others, may be very pretty in theory, but is worth little in practice. When Horace gave to some author that celebrated precept, to let his works lie nine years in the desk, he should also have given with it a recipe for living nine years without food. While Horace was inventing this advice, he sat, in all probability, at the table of Mæcenas eating roast turkey with truffles, pheasant puddings with venison sauce, lark cutlets with mangled turnips, peacock's tongues, Indian bird's nests, and the Lord knows, what all, and everything *gratis* at that. But we, the unlucky ones, born too late, live in another sort of times. Our Mæcenases have an altogether different set of principles; they believe that authors, like medlars, are best after they have lain some time on straw; they believe that literary hounds are spoiled for hunting similies and thoughts if they are fed too well ; and when they do take it into their heads to give to some one a feed, it is generally the worst dog who gets the biggest piece,— some fawning spaniel who licks the hand, or tiny Italian greyhound who knows how to cuddle up into a lady's perfumed lap, or some patient pupply of a poodle, who has learned some bread-earning science, and who can fetch and carry, dance, and drum. While I write this, my little pug-dog behind me begins to bark. Be still there, *Ami !* I did not mean you, for you love me, and accompany your master about, in need and danger, and you would die on my grave, as true-heartedly as many other German dogs, who, turned away, lie before the gates of Germany, and hunger and whine. Excuse me, Madame, for digressing merely to vindicate the honor of my dog : —I now return to the Horatian rule and its inapplicability in the nineteenth century, when poets are compelled to make cupboard love to the Muse. *Ma foi*, Madame, I could never observe that rule for four-and-twenty hours, let alone nine years ; *my* belly has no appreciation of the beauties of immortality. I have thought the matter over, and concluded that it is better to be only half immortal and altogether fat ; and if Voltaire was willing to give three hundred years of his eternal fame for one good digestion, so would I give twice as much for the dinner itself. And oh! what lovely beautiful eating there is in this world! The philosopher Pangloss is right—this is the best world! But one must have money in this best of worlds—money in the pocket, not manuscripts in the desk. Mr. Marr, my landlord of " The King of England," is himself an author, and also knows the Horatian rule, but I do not believe that if I wished to put it into practice, he would feed me for nine years.

And why, in fact, should I practise it ? I have so much which is good to write of, that I have no occasion to fritter time away. So long as my heart is full of love, and the heads of my fellow-creatures full of folly, I shall never be hot pressed for writing material. And my heart will ever love so long as there are women ; should it cool over one, it will immediately fire up over another, and as the king never dies in France, so the queen never dies in my heart, where the word is *La reine est morte, vive la reine !* And in like manner the folly of my fellow-creatures will live forever. For there is but one wisdom, and it hath its fixed limits, but there are a thousand illimitable follies. The learned casuist and pastor, Schupp, even saith that in the world are more fools than human beings.

Vide Schupp's " Instructive Writings," p. 1121.

When we remember that the great Schuppius lived in Hamburg, we may find that his statistical return was not exaggerated. I live now in the same place, and may say that I really become cheerful, and when I reflect that all these fools whom I see here can be used in my writings ; they are cash down, ready money, I feel like a diamond in cotton. The Lord hath blessed me ; the crop of fools has turned out uncommonly well this year, and, like a good administrator, I consume only a few at a time, and lay up the best for the future. People see me out walking, and wonder that I am jolly and cheerful. Like a rich, plump merchant, who, rubbing his hands with genial joy, wanders here and there amid chests, bales, boxes, and casks, even so do I wander around among my people. Ye are all my mine own ! Ye are all equally dear to me, and I love ye, as ye yourselves love your own gold, and that is more than a little. Oh, how I laughed from my heart when I lately heard that one of my people had asserted with concern that he knew not how I could live, or what means I had ; and yet he himself is such a first-rate fool that I could live from him alone as on a capital. Many a fool is, however, to me not only ready money, but I have already determined in my own mind what is to be done with the cash which I intend to write out of him. Thus, for instance, from a certain well-lined plump millionaire I shall write me a certain well-lined plump arm-chair. From his fat millionairess I will buy me a horse. When I see the plump old gentleman — a camel will get into heaven before that man would ever go through the eye of a needle — when I see him waddling along on the Promenade, a strange feeling steals over me. I salute him involuntarily, though I have no acquaintance with him, and he greets me again so invitingly, that I would fain avail myself of his goodness on the spot and sit on him at once, and am only prevented by the sight of the many gaily dressed people passing by. His lady wife is not so bad-looking ; she has, it is true, only one eye, but that is all the greener on that account ; her nose is like the tower which looketh forth towards Damascus ; her bosom is broad as the billowy sea, and all sorts of ribbons flutter above it, like the flags of the ships which have long since sailed over this ocean bosom — it makes one sea-sick just to glance at it ; her neck is quite as fair and plumply rounded as — the comparison will be found further on — and on the violet blue curtain which covers this comparison, thousands on thousands of silkworms have spun away their lives. And I stand there, with folded arms, looking pleasedly on her as she goes, and reflect whether I shall ride my steed with a curb or on the snaffle. People who see me standing thus cannot conceive what there can be in the lady which so attracts me. Meddling scandal-bearing tongues have already tried to make her husband uneasy, and insinuated that I looked on his wife with the eye of a *roué*. But my honest, soft leather chair has answered that he regards me as an innocent, even somewhat bashful youth, who looks carefully, like one desirous of nearer acquaintance, but who is restrained by blushing bashfulness. My lady steed thinks, on the contrary, that I have a free, independent, chivalric air, and that my salutatory politeness only expresses a wish to be invited for once to dinner with her.

You see, Madame, that I can thus use everybody, and that the city directory is really the inventory of my property. And I can consequently never become bankrupt, for my creditors themselves are my profits, or will be changed to such. Moreover, as I before said, I live economically, — d———d economically ! For instance, while I write this, I sit in a dark, noisy room, on the " Dismal Street ; " but I cheerfully endure it, for I could, if I only chose, sit in the most beautiful garden, as well as my friends and my loves, for I only need to convert my boon companions into money. These, Madame, consist of decayed hairdressers, broken-down panders, bankrupt keepers of eating-houses who themselves can get nothing to eat — finished blackguards, who know where to seek me, and who, for a tip, furnish me with all the *chronique scandaleuses* of their quarter of the town. Madame, you wonder that I do not, once for all, kick such a pack out of doors? Why, Madame, what can you be thinking of? These people are my flowers. Some day I will write them all down in a beautiful book, with the proceeds from which I will buy me a garden, and their red, yellow, blue, and variegated countenances now appear to me like the flowers of that fair garden. What do I care if strange noses assert that these flowers smell of aniseed brandy, tobacco, cheese, and blasphemy! My own nose, the chimney of my head, wherein the chimney-sweep of my imagination climbs up and down, asserts the contrary, and smells in the fellows nothing but the perfume of roses, violets, pinks, and tuberoses. Oh, how gloriously will I some morning sit in my garden, listening to the song of the birds, and warm my limbs in the blessed sunshine, and inhale the fresh breath of the leaves, and, as I glance at the flowers, think of my old blackguards!

At present I sit near the dark " Dismal Street," in my darker room, and please myself by hanging up in it the greatest "obscurity" of the country, *" Mais est ce que vous verrez plus clair alors?"* Apparently, Madame, such is the case, but do not misunderstand me; I do not mean that I hang up the man himself, but the crystal lamp which I intend to buy with the money I mean to write out of him. Meanwhile, I believe that it would be clearer through all creation if we could hang up the Obscurantists, not in imagination, but in reality. But if they cannot be hung they must be branded — I again speak figuratively, referring to branding *en effigie*. It is true that Herr von White — he is white and innocent as a lily — tried to whitewash over my assertion in Berlin that he had really been branded. On account of this, the fool had himself inspected by the authorities, and obtained from them a certificate that his back bore no marks, and he was pleased to regard this negative certificate of arms as a diploma which would open to him the doors of the best society, and was astonished when they kicked him out — and now he screams death and murder at me, poor devil! and swears to shoot me wherever he finds me. And what do you suppose, Madame, that I intend doing? Madame, from this fool — that is, from the money which I intend to write out of him—I will buy me a good barrel of Rudesheimer Rhine wine. I mention this, that you may not think it is a malicious joy which lights up my face whenever I meet the Herr Von White in the street. In fact, I only see in him my blessed Rudesheimer ; the instant I set eyes on him, I become cheerful and genial-hearted, and begin to trill, in spite of myself, " Upon the Rhine, 'tis there our grapes are growing," " This picture is enchanting fair," " Oh, White Lady." Then my Rudesheimer looks horribly sour, enough to make one believe that he was compounded of nothing but poison and gall, but I assure you, Madame, it is a genuine vintage ; and though the inspector's mark be not branded on it, the connoisseur still knows how to appreciate it. I will merrily tap this cask, and should it chance to ferment and threaten to fly out dangerously, I will have it bound down with a few iron hoops by the proper authorities.

You see, therefore, Madame, that you need not trouble yourself on my account. I can look at ease on all in this world. The Lord has blessed me in earthly goods, and if he has not exactly stored the wine away for me in my cellar, he at least allows me to work in his vineyard. I only need gather my grapes, press them, barrel them, cellar them, and there I have my clear heavenly gift ; and if fools do not fly exactly roasted into my mouth, but run at me rather raw, and not even " half baked," still I know how to roast them, baste them, and " give them pepper," until they are tender and savory. Oh, Madame, but you will enjoy it when I some day give a grand fête ! Madame, you shall then praise my kitchen. You shall confess that I can entertain my satraps as pompously as once did the great Ahasuerus, when he was king from India even unto the Blacks, over one hundred and seven and twenty provinces. I will slaughter whole hecatombs of fools. That great Philoschnaps, who came as Jupiter in the form of an ox, and lusted for favor in the eyes of Europa, will supply the roast beef ; a tragical tragedian, who, on the stage, when it represented a tragical Persian kingdom, exhibited to us a tragical Alexander in whose education no Aristotle took part, will supply my table with a splendid pig's head, grinning, as usual, sourly sweet, with a slice of lemon in his mouth, and shrewdly decked by the artistic cook with laurel leaves ; while that singer of coral lips, swan necks, bounding, snowy, little hills, little things, little legs, little kisses, and little assessors, namely, H. Clauren, or, as the pious nuns cry after him on Frederick Street, " Father Clauren ! *our* Clauren ! " will supply me with all the dishes which he knows how to describe so juicily in his annual little pocket-brothels with all the imagination of a lusciously longing kitchen-maid. And he shall give us, over and above, an altogether extra little dish, with a little plate of celery, " for which the little heart bounds with love ! " A shrewd dried-up maid of honor will give us a similar dish, namely, asparagus, and there will be no want of Göttingen sausages, Hamburg smoked beef, Pomeranian geese-breasts, ox tongues, calves' brains, " cheek," salt-fish, steamed calves' brains, " small potatoes," and therewith all sorts of jellies, Berlin pancakes, Vienna tarts, comfits.

Madame, I have already, in imagination, over-eaten myself ! The devil take such guzzlings ! I cannot stand much, my digestion is bad ; the hog's head acts on me as on the rest of the German public. I must eat a Wilibald-Alexis salad on it — that purges and purifies. Oh, the wretched hog's head ! with the still wretcheder sauce, which has neither a Grecian nor a Persian flavor, but which tastes like tea and soft soap ! Bring me my plump millionaire !

CHAPTER XV

MADAME, I OBSERVE A FAINT CLOUD OF DISCONTENT ON YOUR LOVELY brow, and you seem to ask if it is not wrong that I should thus dress fools, stick them on the spit, carbonado them, lard them, and even butcher many which must lie untouched save by the sharp bills of the fowls of the air, while widows and orphans cry for want ?

Madame, *c'est la guerre !* But now I will solve you the whole riddle. I myself am by no means one of the wise, but I have joined their party, and now for five thousand five hundred and eighty-eight years we have been carrying on war with the fools. The fools believe that they have been wronged by us, inasmuch as they believe that there was once in the world but a limited quantity of reason, which was thievishly appropriated—the Lord only knows how—by the wise men, and it is a sin which cries to heaven to see how much sense one man often gets, while all his neighbors, and, indeed, the whole country for miles around, is fairly befogged with stupidity. This is the secret cause of war, and it is most truly a war of extermination. The intelligent show themselves, as usual, the calmest, most moderate, and most intelligent ; they sit firmly fortified behind their ancient Aristotelian works, have much ordnance, and also ammunition, in store—for they themselves were the inventors of powder—and now and then they shoot a well-aimed bomb among their foes. But, unfortunately, the latter are by far the most numerous, and their outcries are terrible, and day by day they do the most cruel deeds of torture—for, in fact, every folly is a torture to the wise. Their military stratagems are often very cunning indeed. Some of the chiefs of the great Fool Army take good care not to admit the secret origin of the war. They have heard that a well-known deceitful man, who advanced so far in the art of falsehood that he ended by writing false memoirs—I mean Fouché—once asserted that *les paroles sont faites pour nous cacher nos pensées ;* and therefore they talk a great deal in order to conceal their want of thought, and make long speeches and write big books ; and if any one is listening, they praise that only spring of true happiness, namely, wisdom ; and if any one is looking on at them, they work away at mathematics, logic, statistics, mechanical improvements, plain citizen-like common-sense, stable-fodder, and so forth ; and as a monkey is more ridiculous the more he resembles man, so are these fools more laughable the more reasonably they behave. Other chiefs of the great army are more open-hearted, and confess that their own share of wisdom is not remarkably great, and that perhaps they never had any, but they cannot refrain from asserting that wisdom is a very sour, bitter affair, and, in reality, of but little value. This may perhaps be true, but, unfortunately, they have not wisdom enough to prove it. They therefore jump at every means of vindication, discover new powers in themselves, explain that these are quite as effectual as reason, and, in some cases, much more so — for instance, feeling, faith, inspiration — and with this surrogate of wisdom, this beet-rooted reason, they console themselves. I, poor devil, am especially hated by them, as they assert that I originally belonged to their party, that I am a runaway, a fugitive, a bolter — a deserter, who has broken the holiest ties: — yes, that I am a spy, who secretly reveals their plans, in order to subsequently give point to the laughter of the enemy, and that I myself am so stupid as not to see that the wise at the same time laugh at me, and never regard me as an equal. And here the fools are perfectly right.

It is true that my party do not regard me as one of themselves, and often laugh at me in their sleeves. I know that right well, though I pretend not to observe it. But my heart bleeds in silence, and when I am alone, then my tears flow. I know right well that my position is abnormal, that all I do is folly to the wise and a torment to the fools. They hate me, and I feel the truth of the saying, " Stone is heavy and sand is a burden, but the wrath of a fool is heavier than both." And they do not hate me without reason. It is perfectly true, I have torn asunder the holiest bands, when I might have lived and died among the fools, in the way of the law and of God. And oh! I should have lived so comfortably had I remained among them! Even now, if I would repent, they would still receive me with open arms. They would see by my eyes if they could do anything to please me. They would invite me every day to dinner, and in the evening ask me to their tea-parties and clubs, and I could play whist with them, smoke, talk politics, and if I yawned from time to time, they would whisper behind my back, " What beautiful feelings!" " A soul inspired with such faith!" — permit me, Madame, that I hereby offer up a tear of emotion — ah! and I could drink punch with them, too, until the proper inspiration came, and then they would bring me in a hackney-coach to my house, anxiously concerned lest I might catch cold, and one would quickly bring me my slippers, another my silk dressing-gown, a third my white nightcap, and finally they would make me a " professor extraordinary," a president of a society for converting the heathen, or head calculator or director of Roman excavations ;—and then I would be just the man for all this, inasmuch as I can very accurately distinguish the Latin declensions from the conjugations, and am not so apt as other people to mistake a Prussian postillion's boot for an Etruscan vase. My sentiment, my faith, my inspiration, could, besides this, effect much good during religious exercises,—viz., for myself—and then my remarkable poetic genius would stand me in good stead on the birthdays and at the weddings of the great ; nor would it be a bad thought if I, in a great national epic, should sing of all those heroes, of whom we know with certainty that from their moldering bodies crept worms, who now give themselves out for their descendants.

Many men who are not born fools, and who were once gifted with reason, have on this account gone over to the fools, and live among them in a perfect fool's paradise life, and those follies which at first so pained them have now become second nature—yes, they are in fact no longer to be regarded as hypocrites, but as true converts. One of these, in whose head total darkness does not as yet prevail, really loves me ; and lately, when I was alone with him, he closed the door, and said, with an earnest voice, " Oh, Fool ! you who play the wise man and have not after all as much sense as an unborn child ; know you not that the great in the land only elevate those who abase themselves, and esteem their own blood less worthy than that of the great ? And now you would spoil your case with the pious ! Is it then such a difficult thing to roll up your eyes in a holy rapture, to hide your arms crossed in faith in your coat-sleeve, to let your head hang down like a lamb of God's, and to murmur Bible sayings got by heart. Believe me, no Gracious Highness will reward you for your godlessness ; the men of love will hate, abuse, and persecute you, and you will never make your way either in this world or in the next."

Ah, me ! it is all true enough. But I have unfortunately contracted this unlucky passion for Reason. I love her though her love I can't attain—I give her all, she gives me naught again. I cannot tear myself from her. And as once the Jewish King Solomon in his

347

canticles sang of the Christian Church, and that, too, under the form of a black, passionate maiden, so that his Jews might not suspect what he was driving at, so have I in countless lays sung just the contrary—that is to say, Reason, and that under the form of a pure, cold beauty, who attracts and repels me, who now smiles at me, then scorns me, and finally turns her back on me. This secret of my unfortunate love, which I reveal to none, gives you, Madame, some insight into my folly. You doubtless perceive that it is of an extraordinary description, and that it rises, magnificently rises over the ordinary follies of mankind. Read my Radcliffe, my Almanzor, my lyrical Intermezzo—reason, reason, nothing but reason—and you will be terrified at the immensity of my folly. In the words of Augur, I can say, " I am the most foolish of all mankind, and the wisdom of man is not in me."

High in the air rises the forest of oaks, high over the oaks soars the eagle, high over the eagle sweep the clouds, high over the clouds gleam the stars—Madame, is not that too high? *Eh bien!* high over the stars sweep the angels, high over the angels rises— no, Madame, my folly can bring it no higher than this. It soars high enough. It grows giddy before its own sublimity. It makes of me a giant in seven-mile boots. At noon I feel as though I could devour all the elephants of Hindostan, and then pick my teeth with the spire of Strasburg Cathedral ; in the evening I become so sentimental that I would fain drink up the Milky Way, without reflecting how indigestible I should find the little fixed stars, and by night there is the Devil himself broke loose in my head and no mistake. For then there assemble in my brain the Assyrians, Egyptians, Medes, Persians, Hebrews, Philistines, Frankforters, Babylonians, Carthaginians, Berliners, Romans, Spartans, Flatheads, and Chuckleheads. Madame, it would be too wearisome should I continue to enumerate all these people. Do you only read Herodotus, Livy, the Magazine of Haude and Spener, Curtius, Cornelius Nepos, the " Companion." Meanwhile, I will eat my breakfast. This morning I do not get along very well with my writing ; the blessed Lord leaves me in the lurch. Madame, I even fear—yes, yes, you remarked it before I did myself ; yes, I see—the right kind of divine

aid is today wanting. Madame, I will begin a new chapter, and tell
you how after the death of Le Grand I came to Godesberg.

CHAPTER XVI

WHEN I ARRIVED AT GODESBERG I SAT DOWN AGAIN AT THE FEET OF
my fair friend, and near me lay her brown hound, and we both
looked up into her lovely eyes.

Ah, Lord! in those eyes lay all the splendor of earth, and an
entire heaven besides. I could have died with rapture as I gazed
into them, and had I died at that instant, my soul would have
flown directly into *those eyes*. Oh, they are indescribable! I must
have some poet, who went mad for love brought from a lunatic
asylum here, that he may from the abyss of his madness fish up
some simile wherewith to compare those eyes, (Between you and
me, reader, I must be mad enough myself to want any help in such
a business.) "God damn!" said an English gentleman, "when she
looks at a man quietly from head to foot, she melts his coat
buttons and heart all into a lump!" "*F—e!*" said a Frenchman.
"Her eyes are of the largest calibre, and when she shoots one of
her forty-two pound glances—crack!—there you are in love!"
There was a red-headed lawyer from Mayence who said that her
eyes resembled two cups of coffee—without cream. He wished to
say something sweet, and thought that he had done it—because
he always sugared his coffee to death. Wretched comparisons! I
and the brown hound lay quietly at the feet of the fair lady and
gazed and listened. She sat near an old iron-grey soldier, a knightly
looking man with cross-barred scars on his terrible brow. They both
spoke of the Seven Mountains painted by the evening red, and the
blue Rhine which flooded its way along in sublime tranquility.
What did we care for the Seven Mountains and the blue Rhine, and
the snowy sail-boats which swam thereon, and the music which
rang from one boat, or the jackass of a student who, seated in it,
sang so meltingly and beautifully? I and the brown hound both

gazed into the eyes of our fair friend, and looked at the face which
came forth rosy pale from amid its black braids and locks, like the
moon from dark clouds. The features were of the noblest Grecian
type, the lips boldly arched, over which played melancholy, rapture, and child-like caprice, and when she spoke, the words were
breathed forth almost sighingly, and then again shot out impatiently
and rapidly ; and *when* she spoke, and her speech fell softly as
snow, yet like a warm genial flower shower from her lovely mouth
—oh! then the crimson of evening fell gently over my soul, and
through it flitted with ringing melody the memories of childhood ;
but above all, like a fairy bell there pealed within the voice of the
little Veronica, and I grasped the fair hand of my lady friend and
pressed it to my eyes till the ringing in my soul had passed away,
and then I leaped up and laughed, and the hound bayed, and the
brow of the old general wrinkled up sternly, and I sat down again
and clasped and kissed the beautiful hand, and spoke of little
Veronica.

CHAPTER XVII

MADAME, YOU WISH ME TO DESCRIBE THE APPEARANCE OF THE LITTLE
Veronica? But I will not. You, Madame, cannot be compelled to
read more than you please, and I, on the other hand, have the right
to write exactly what I choose. But I will now tell what the lovely
hand was like which I kissed in the previous chapter.

First of all, I must confess that I was not worthy to kiss that
hand. It was a lovely hand—so tender, so transparent, so perfumed,
brilliant, sweet, soft, beautiful—by my faith I must send to the
apothecary for twelve shillings' worth of adjectives.

On the middle finger there sat a ring with a pearl—I never saw
a pearl which played a more sorrowful part ; on the marriage
finger she wore a ring with a blue gem—I have studied archæology
in it for hours ; on the forefinger she wore a diamond—it was a
talisman ; as long as I looked at it I was happy, for wherever it
was, there too was the finger with its four friends—and she often

struck me on the mouth with all five of them. Since I was thus manipulated I believe fast and firm in animal magnetism. But she did not strike hard, and when she struck I always deserved it by some godless speech ; and as soon as she had struck me, she at once repented it, and took a cake, broke it in two, and gave me one half and the brown hound the other half, and smiled and said, " Neither of you have any religion and you will never be happy, and so you must be fed with cakes in this world for there will be no table spread for you in heaven." And she was more than half right, for in those days I was very irreligious, and read Thomas Paine, the *Système de la Nature*, the Westphalian Advertiser, and Schleiermacher, letting my beard and my reason grow together, and had thoughts of enrolling myself among the Rationalists. But when that soft hand swept over my brow, my " reason " stood still and sweet dreams came into my soul, and I again dreamed that I heard gentle songs of the Virgin Mother, and I thought of the little Veronica.

Madame, you can hardly imagine how beautiful little Veronica looked as she lay in her little coffin. The burning candles as they stood around cast a glow on the white smiling little face, and on the red silk roses and rustling gold spangles with which the head and the little shroud were decked. Good old Ursula had led me at evening into the silent chamber, and as I looked at the little corpse laid amid lights and flowers on the table, I at first believed that it was a pretty saint's image of wax. But I soon recognized the dear face, and asked, smilingly, why little Veronica laid so still? And Ursula said, " Because she is dead, dear ! "

And as she said, " Because she is dead ; "—but I will go no further today with this story, it would be too long ; besides I should first speak of the lame magpie which hopped about the castle courtyard, and was three hundred years old, and then I could become regularly melancholy. A fancy all at once seizes on me to tell another story, which is a merry one, and just suits this place, for it is really the history itself which I propose to narrate in this book.

CHAPTER XVIII

NIGHT AND STORM RAGED IN THE BOSOM OF THE KNIGHT. THE DAGGER thrusts of slander had struck to his heart, and as he advanced sternly along over the bridge of San Marco, the feeling stole over him as though that heart must burst and flow away in blood. His limbs trembled with weariness — the noble quarry had been fiercely hunted during the live-long summer day — sweat stood on his brow, and as he entered the gondola he sighed heavily. He sat unthinkingly in the black cabin of the gondola, unthinkingly the soft waves shook him and bore him along the well-known way to the Brenta ; and as he stepped out before the well-known palace he heard that the " Signora Laura was in the garden."

She stood leaning on the statue of the Laocoon, by the red rose-tree, at the end of the terrace, near the weeping willows, which hung down mournfully over the water. There she stood smiling, a pale image of love amid the perfume of roses. At the sight he suddenly awaked as from some terrible dream, and was at once changed to mildness and longing. " Signora Laura," said he, " I am wretched and tormented with hatred and oppression and false-hood," and here he suddenly paused and stammered, " but I love you," and then a tear of joy darted into his eye, and with palpitating heart he cried, " Be mine — and love me ! . . ."

There lies a veil of dark mystery over that hour ; no mortal has ever known what Signora Laura replied, and when they ask her guardian angel in heaven what took place, he hides his face and sighs, and is silent.

Solitary and alone stood the knight by the statue of the Laocoon ; his own face was not less convulsed and deathly pale ; unconsciously he tore away the roses from the rose-tree ; yes, he plucked even the young buds. *Since that hour the rose-tree never bore another flower ;* far in the dim distance sang a mad nightingale, the willows whispered in agony, mournfully murmured the cool waves of the Brenta ; night rose on high with her moon and stars, and one star, the loveliest of all, fell adown from heaven !

CHAPTER XIX

VOUS PLEUREZ, MADAME?

Oh, may the eyes which shed such lovely tears long light up the world with their rays, and may a warm and loving hand close them in the hour of death! A soft pillow, Madame, is also a very convenient thing when dying, and I trust that you will not be without it ; and when the fair, weary head sinks down, and the black locks fall in waves over the fast fading face, oh! then may God repay those tears which have fallen for me, for I myself am the knight for whom you wept ; yes, I am the erring errant-knight of love, the knight of the fallen star!

Vous pleurez, Madame!

Oh, I understand those tears! Why need I longer play a feigned part? You, Madame, you yourself are that fair lady who wept so softly in Godesberg when I told the sad story of my life. Like drops of pearly dew over roses, the beautiful tears ran over the beautiful face ; the hound was silent, the vesper chimes pealed far away in Königswinter, the Rhine murmured more gently, night covered the earth with her black mantle, and I sat at your feet, Madame, and looked on high into the starry heaven. At first I took your eyes also for two stars. But how could any one mistake such beautiful eyes for stars? Those cold lights of heaven cannot weep over the misery of a man who is so wretched that he can no longer weep.

And I had a particular reason for not mistaking those lovely eyes, for in them dwells the soul of little Veronica.

I have counted back, Madame ; you were born on the very day on which Veronica died. Johanna, in Andernach, told me that I would find little Veronica again in Godesberg, and I recognized you at once. That was a sad chance, Madame, that you should die just as the beautiful game was about to begin. Since pious Ursula said to me, " It is death, dear," I have gone about solitary and serious in great picture-galleries, but the pictures could not please me as they once did ; they seemed to have suddenly faded ; there was but a single work which retained its color and brilliancy ; you know, Madame, to which piece I refer—

It is the Sultan and Sultana of Delhi.

Do you remember, Madame, how we stood long hours before it, and how significantly good Ursula smiled when people remarked that the faces in that picture so much resembled our own? Madame, I find that your likeness is admirably taken in that picture, and it passes comprehension how the artist could have so accurately represented you, even to the very garments which you then wore. They say that he was mad and must have dreamed your form. Or was there perhaps a soul in the big, sacred ape who waited on you in those days like a page? In that case, he must certainly remember the silver-grey veil, on which he once spilled red wine and spoiled it. I was glad when you dismissed him ; he did not dress you remarkably well, and at any rate, the European dress is much more dressy than the Indian — not but that beautiful women are lovely in any dress. Do you remember, Madame, that a gallant Brahmin — he looked like Ganesa, the god with an elephant's trunk, who rides on a mouse — once paid you the compliment that the divine Maneka, as she came down from Indra's golden hill to the royal penitent Wiswamitra, was not fairer than you, Madame?

What, forgotten it already! Why it cannot be more than three thousand years since he said that, and beautiful women are not wont to so quickly forget delicate flattery.

However, for men, the Indian dress is far more becoming than the European. Oh, my rosy-red lotus-flowered pantaloons of Delhi! had I worn ye when I stood before Signora Laura and begged for love, the previous chapter would have rung to a different tune! Alas! alas! I wore straw-colored pantaloons, which some sober Chinese had woven in Nangking ; my ruin was woven with them — the threads of my destiny — and I was made miserable.

Often there sits in a quiet old German coffee-house a youth silently sipping his cup of Mocha ; and meanwhile there blooms and grows in far distant China his ruin, and there it is spun and woven, and, despite the high wall of China, it knows how to find its way to the youth who deems it but a pair of Nanking trousers, and all unheeding, in the gay buoyancy of youth, he pulls them on, and is lost for ever! And, Madame, in the small breast of a

354

mortal so much misery can hide itself, and keep itself so well hid there that the poor man himself for days together does not feel it, and is as jolly as a piper, and merily dances and whistles, and trolls—lalarallala, lalarallala——la——la——la.

CHAPTER XX

" She was lovable, and he loved her, but he was not worthy of love, and she did not love him." —*Old Play.*

AND FOR THIS NONSENSICAL AFFAIR YOU WERE ABOUT TO SHOOT yourself?

Madame, when a gentleman desires to shoot himself, he generally has ample reason for it—you may be certain of that. But whether he himself knows what these reasons are is another question. We mask even our miseries, and while we die of bosom wounds, we complain of the toothache.

Madame, you have, I know, a remedy for toothache?

Alas! I had the toothache in my heart. That is a wearying pain, and requires plugging—with lead and with the tooth-powder invented by Berthold Schwartz.

Misery gnawed at my heart like a worm, and gnawed—the poor devil of a Chinese was not to blame ; I brought the misery with me into the world. It lay with me in the cradle, and when my mother rocked me, she rocked it with me, and when she sang me to sleep, it slept with me, and it awoke when I opened my eyes. When I grew up, it grew with me, until it was altogether too great and burst my —— ——.

Now we will speak of other things—of virgins' wreaths, masked balls, of joy and bridal pleasure——lalarallala, lalarallala, lalaral ——la——la——la.

The Baths of Lucca

" I am as woman is to man."
— COUNT AUGUST VON PLATEN HALLERMUNDE.

" Would the Count like a dance?
Let him but say so,
I'll play him a tune." — FIGARO.

CHAPTER I

WHEN I SOUGHT MATILDA IN HER CHAMBER, SHE HAD JUST FASTENED the last button of her green riding-habit, and was putting on a chapeau with a white plume. She hastily cast it down as soon as she saw me, and ran to me with all her waving, golden locks. " Doctor of heaven and earth!" she cried, and, according to her old custom, she caught me by the ears and kissed me with the drollest cordiality.

" How are you? maddest of mortal men! How glad I am to see you again ; for never in this world shall I find a crazier soul. There are fools and blockheads in plenty, and people often do them the honor to consider them crazy, but real insanity is as scarce as real wisdom ; perhaps it is nothing but wisdom which is vexed to think that it knows everything — all the infamy of this world — and has consequently come to the wise conclusion to go mad. The Orientals are a shrewder race, they honor a maniac as a prophet, but we look upon prophets as maniacs."

" But, my lady, why have you not written to me?"

" Surely, Doctor, I wrote you a long letter, and directed it to ' New Bedlam.' But as you, contrary to all expectation, were not there, they sent it to St. Luke, and as you were not there either, it went to another establishment of the same sort, and so it went the rounds of all the lunatic asylums in England, Scotland, and Ireland, until they returned it to me with the remark that the gentleman to whom the letter was addressed was not as yet ' appre-

356

hended.' And how under the sun have you managed to keep at liberty?"

" Ah! I did it cunningly, my lady. Wherever I went, I contrived to slip away from the mad houses, and I think that I shall succeed in Italy too."

" Oh, friend, here you are safe enough, for, in the first place, there is no mad house in the neighborhood, and, secondly, we are here in the majority."

" *We?* my lady! You count yourself then as one of us? Permit me to imprint the kiss of brotherhood upon your brow."

" Ah! I mean we watering place guests, among whom I am really the most rational. And so you can easily imagine who the maddest must be, I mean Julia Maxfield, who always maintains that green eyes signify the spring of the soul ; and besides we have two young beauties——"

" English beauties, of course, my lady——"

" Doctor, what does this mocking tone mean? The yellow, greasy, maccaroni faces in Italy must suit your taste, if you have no fancy now for British——"

" Plum-puddings with raisin eyes, roast beef bosoms festooned with white strips of horse radish, proud pies——"

" There was a time, Doctor, when you were enchanted if a lovely English woman——"

" Yes, but that was *once!* I always have a proper reverence for your fellow-countrywomen ; they are bright as suns, but suns of ice ; they are white as marble, but are also marble cold ; on their bosoms are frozen the poor——"

" Oho! I know one who did not freeze there, but who jumped fresh and alive over the sea, and he was a great German impertinent——"

" At least he got such a cold on that British frosty heart that he still has a cold in his head in consequence."

My Lady seemed vexed at this answer, she grasped the riding whip which lay between the leaves of a novel as a bookmark, switched it around the ears of her great white hound, who slowly growled, hastily clapped her hat jauntily on her locks, looked once or twice with approbation at herself in the mirror, and said proudly, " I am still beautiful!" But then, all at once, as if penetrated by a gloomy thrill of pain, she remained silent, musing, slowly drew the long white riding glove from her hand, held the hand out to me, and, reading my thoughts like lightning, said, "This hand is not as beautiful as it was in Ramsgate. Ha! Since that time Matilda has suffered — much!"

Dear reader, we can seldom see a flaw in a bell ; we must hear its ring to know if it exists. Could you have heard the ring of the voice wherewith those words were spoken, you would have felt at once that my Lady's heart was a bell of the best metal, but that a secret flaw strangely mingled a discord with its sweetest tones, and gave it an air of strange sadness. Yet I love such bells ; they ever find a true echo in my own breast ; and I again kissed my Lady's hand, almost as earnestly as of old, though it was no longer in its first bloom, and the veins which rose from it, almost all *too* blue, seemed to repeat, " Since that time Matilda has suffered — much."

Her eyes gazed on me like sorrowful solitary stars in the autumnal heaven, and she said, softly and sadly, from her inmost soul, " You seem to love me less now, Doctor! for that was a tear of pity which you just wept on my hand. It seemed like an alms."

" Who taught you to interpret so unkindly the silent language of my tears? I'll bet that your white hound there, who fawns on you, understands me better. He looks first at me and then at you, and seems to be wondering that human beings, those proud lords of creation, are internally so wretched. Ah! my Lady, only a sympathetic sorrow draws forth such tears ; in reality we each weep for ourselves."

" Enough, enough, Doctor. It is good, at any rate, that we are contemporaries, and that we meet again with our foolish tears in the same corner of the earth. Oh, our bad luck! If you had only lived two centuries earlier, when I was getting on so well with my friend, Michael de Cervantes Saavedra, or rather if you had only been born a hundred years later, as another intimate friend of mine, whose name I don't just now happen to know, because his first birthday won't be celebrated until the year 1900. But tell me how you've been getting on since we parted."

" At the old business, my Lady, rolling the great stone. When I had shoved it to the top of the hill, then it rolled all at once down again, and I had to go at it once more ; and this up-and-down hill work lasted until at last I lie crouched beneath it, and Master Stonemason has carved on it with great letters, ' Here rests in the Lord———' "

" By my soul, Doctor, I'll bring you to life again. Don't you dare to be melancholy ! Laugh, or ———"

" No ; don't tickle me. I'd rather laugh of myself."

" That's right. Now you please me just as you did in Ramsgate, where we first became so intimate———"

" And finally a little more than intimate. Yes, I *will* be merry. It is fortunate that we have met, and the great German ——— will again find his greatest pleasure in risking his life near you."

My Lady's eyes laughed like sunshine after a soft rain, and her merry mood again flashed out as John entered, and, with the stiffest flunkey pathos, announced his Excellency the Marquis Christophero di Gumpelino.

" He's welcome ! And now, Doctor, you will become acquainted with a peer of the realm of fools. Don't be shocked at his personal appearance, particularly at his nose. The man has excellent qualities ; for instance, a great deal of money, common sense, and the desire to embody in himself all the follies of the age ; moreover, he is in love with my green eyed friend, Julia Maxfield, and calls her his Julia and himself her Romeo, and declaims and sighs ; and Lord Maxfield, the brother-in-law to whom the faithful Julia has been intrusted by her husband, is an Argus———"

I was just about to remark that Argus had charge of a cow, when the door opened, and, to my utmost amazement, in waddled my old friend, the banker Christian Gumpel, with his opulent smile and blessed belly. After his broad shining lips had sufficiently scoured my Lady's hand, and delivered themselves of the usual questions as to health, etc., he recognized me—and the friends sank into each other's arms.

CHAPTER II

MATILDA'S WARNING NOT TO BE STRUCK BY GUMPELINO'S NOSE HAD some foundation in fact, for he came within an ace of knocking out one of my eyes with it. I will say nothing against this nose ; on the contrary, it was one of the noblest form and seemed of itself to give my friend full right to claim, at least, the title of a Marquis. For it was evident from the nose that Gumpel was of high nobility, and descended from that very ancient world family into which the blessed Lord himself once married without fear of a mesalliance. Since those days, it is true that the family has come down a little, and in fact since the reign of Charlemagne they have been obliged to pick up a living by selling old pantaloons and Hamburg lottery tickets, but without diminishing in the least their pride of ancestry, or losing the hope that some day they will all come again into their long lost property, or at least obtain emigration damages, with interest, when their old legitimate sovereign keeps the promises made when restored to office — promises by which he has been leading them about by the nose for two thousand years. Perhaps this leading them about by the nose is the cause why the latter has been pulled out to such a length! Or it may be that these long noses are a sort of uniform whereby Jehovah recognizes his old bodyguards even when they have deserted. Such a deserter was the Marquis Gumpelino, but he always wore his uniform, and a brilliant one it was, sprinkled with crosses and stars of rubies, a Red Eagle order in miniature and other decorations.

" Look!" said my Lady, " that is my favorite nose, and I know of no more beautiful flower in all the world."

" This flower," grinned Gumpelino, " cannot be placed on your fair bosom, unless I lay my blooming face there also, and such an addition might trouble you in this warm weather. But I bring you an equally precious flower, which is here very rare."

Saying this, the Marquis opened a tissue paper cornet, which he had brought with him, and with great care slowly extracted from it a magnificent tulip.

Scarcely had my Lady seen the flower ere she screamed with all her might. " Murder! murder! would you murder me? Away with the horrible vision!" With this she acted as if about to be mur-dered, held her hands before her eyes, ran madly about the room, invoked maledictions on Gumpelino's nose and tulip, rang the bell, stamped on the ground, struck the hound with her riding switch till he bayed aloud, and as John entered she cried aloud, like Kean, in Richard III—

> " A horse! a horse!
> My kingdom for a horse!"

and stormed like a whirlwind from the room.

" A queer woman!" said Gumpelino, motionless with astonish-ment, and still holding the tulip in his hand, so that he looked like one of those lotus bearing fat idols carved on antique Indian temples. But I understood the lady and her idiosyncracy far better than he—this comedy delighted me beyond description, and open-ing the window, I cried, " My Lady, how you act! Is this sense—propriety—especially is it love?"

Up laughed the wild answer—

> " When I am o' horseback, I will swear
> I love thee infinitely."

CHAPTER III

" A CURIOUS WOMAN," REPEATED GUMPELINO, AS WE WENT OUR way to visit his two lady friends, Signora Letitia and Signora Francesca, whose acquaintance he promised me. As the dwelling of these ladies was situated on a somewhat distant eminence, I appre-ciated all the more this kindness of my corpulent friend, who found hill climbing somewhat difficult, and who stopped on every little mound to recover his breath, and sigh, " O Jesus!"

The dwellings at the baths of Lucca are situated either below, in a village surrounded by high hills, or are placed on one of these hills, which is not far from the principal spring, where a picturesque group of houses peeps down into the charming dale. But many are scattered here and there on the sides of the hill, and are attainable only by a wearisome climb through a wild paradise of vines, myrtle bushes, honeysuckles, laurels, oleanders, geraniums, and similar high born plants. I have never seen a lovelier valley, particularly when one looks from the terrace of the upper bath, where the solemn green cypresses stand, down into the village. We there see a bridge bending over a stream called the Lima, which cuts the village in two. At its either end there are waterfalls leaping over rocky fragments with a roar, as though they would fain utter the pleasantest things, but could not express themselves distinctly on account of the roaring echo.

The great charm of the valley is owing to the circumstance that it is neither too great nor too small, that the soul of the beholder is not forcibly elevated, but rather calmly and gradually inspired with the glorious view ; that the summits of the mountains themselves, true to their Apennine nature, are not magnificently misshapen in extravagant Gothic form, like rocky caricatures, just as the men in German lands on them are human caricatures ; but so that their nobly rounded, cheerful green forms seem of themselves inspired with the civilisation of art, and accord melodiously with the blue heaven.

" O Jesus!" sighed Gumpelino, as we, weary with climbing, and a little too well warmed with the morning sun, attained the above mentioned cypresses, and gazing down into the village, saw our English lady friend sweeping proudly along on her steed over the bridge, like the queen in a fairy legend, and then vanish, swift as a dream. " O Jesus! what a curious woman! In all my born days I never *did* see such a woman. Only in plays. Don't you think the actress Holzbecher could play her part well? There's something of the waterwitch about her — hey!"

" You're right, Gumpelino. When I went with her from London to Rotterdam, the captain compared her to a rose sprinkled with pepper. Out of gratitude for this spicy comparison she emptied a whole box of pepper in his hair as he lay asleep in the cabin. Nobody could come near the man without sneezing."

" A curious woman!" quoth Gumpelino once again. " Delicate

as white silk, but every bit as strong, and she rides horseback as well as I. I only hope she won't ride herself out of health. There, did you see that long lean Englishman on his lean horse, racing after her like a galloping consumption? Those English people ride too outrageously ; why, they'd spend all the money in the world on horses. Lady Maxfield's white horse cost three hundred golden real louis-d'ors ; ah! and louis-d'ors are at such a premium now, and keep rising every day!"

" Yes, the louis-d'ors will end by rising so high that a poor scholar like myself will never be able to reach them."

" You can't have an idea, Doctor, of how much money I have to spend, and yet I keep only one attendant, and only when I am in Rome hire a chaplain for my private chapel. Look, there comes my Hyacinth!"

The little figure who at this instant appeared approaching us from behind the turn of a hill, reminded me more of a " burning bush " than a hyacinth. It appeared like a waddling great scarlet coat overloaded with gold embroidery, which flashed in the sunlight, and above this red splendor sweated a little face well known to me of old, and which gaily nodded to me. And in fact, when I saw the sallow, cautious face and the busy, winking eyes, I recognized a face which I should sooner have expected to see on Mount Sinai than on the Apennines, and that was the face of Herr Hirsch, citizen of Hamburg, a man who was not only a very honorable lottery agent, but one who was also learned in hard and soft corns, and in jewels, inasmuch as he not only knew the difference between them, but had skill in cutting the former, and in putting a good round price on the latter.

" I do hope," he said, as he approached, " that you haven't forgot me, though my name ain't Hirsch now. I'm called Hyacinth, and I'm servant of Herr Gumpel."

" Hyacinth!" cried his master, in raging amazement at this indiscretion of his servant.

" Oh, be easy, Herr Gumpel, or Herr Gumpelino, or Herr Marquis, or your Excellency ; we needn't put ourselves out of the way with this here gentleman. He knows me ; he's bought lots of lottery tickets of me ; I'm not afraid to swear that he still owes me seven marks and nine shilling on the last drawing. I am really glad, Doctor, to meet you again. You're here, I s'pose, on pleasure-business. What else, of course, can a man be doing here when it's so hot, a-climbing up and down hill? I'm as used up every night as if I'd gone twenty times from the Altona Gate to the Stone Gate without earning a copper."

"O Jesus," cried the Marquis; "hold your tongue! I'll get another servant, I will."

"Why hold my tongue?" replied Hirsch Hyacinthus. "I do so love to get a chance to talk good German with a face whom I've known in Hamburg, and when I think of Hamburg——"

Here, at the memory of his bit of a step-fatherland, his eyes gleamed with tears, and he said, sighing as he spoke, "What is man? He goes walking with pleasure out of the Altona Gate and on the Hamburg Hill, and there he sees the sights, the lions, the birds, the poll-parrots, the monkeys, the great folks, and he takes a turn on the flying horses, or gets electrified, and then thinks how jolly he'd be if he was only in a place a thousand miles off, in Italy, where the oranges and lemons are a-growing! What is man? When he's before the Altona Gate he wants to be in Italy, and when he's in Italy he wants to be back again before the Altona Gate. Oh, I wish I was a-standing there now, looking at the Michael's steeple, and the big clock on it with the great gold figures—great gold figures—how often I've looked at 'em, when they were a-shining so jolly in the afternoon sun, till I felt like kissing 'em. Now I'm in Italy, where the lemons and oranges grow, and when I see 'em growing, it puts me in mind of the Steinweg in Hamburg, where there's lots of 'em lying in great heaping piles in the wheelbarrows, and where a man can eat and eat 'em to his heart's content, without all this trouble of going up hill and down, and getting so warm. As the Lord may have mercy on me, Herr Marquis, if it wasn't for the honor of the situation, and the genteel edecation I'm getting, cuss me if I'd a-come here. But I *will* say this for you, Marquis, that in your service there's both honor and genteel bringing up to be had, and *no* mistake."

364

" Hyacinth!" said Gumpelino, who had been somewhat mollified by this flattery, " Hyacinth, go to——"

" Yes, I know."

" I say you *don't* know, Hyacinth."

" And *I* say, Herr Gumpel, I *do* know. No use a-telling *me*. Your Excellency was a-going to say that I must go to Lady Maxfield. Sho! I know all your thoughts before you've thought them, and some maybe that you never will think in all your born days. Such a servant as I am isn't to be found easy, and I only do it for the honor and the genteel edecation, and it's a fact, I do get both by you." With these words, he wiped his face with a very clean white handkerchief.

" Hyacinth," said the Marquis, " go to Lady Julia Maxfield, to my Julia, and give her this tulip ; take good care of it, for it cost five paoli, and say to her——"

" Yes, I know——"

" You know nothing. Tell her that the tulip is among the flowers——"

" Yes, I know ; you want to say something to her with this here flower. I've made up such mottoes many a time for my lottery tickets."

" I don't want any of your lottery ticket notions. Go to Lady Maxfield, and say to her—

> 'The tulip is among the flowers
> Like among cheeses good Strachino,
> But more than cheese and more than flowers
> Thou'rt honored by thy Gumpelino.' "

" Now, as I hope to be saved, that's first rate," cried Hyacinth. " Oh, you needn't be a-nodding to me, Herr Marquis ; what you know, I know, and what I know, you know. And you, Doctor, good-bye! Never mind that little trifle you didn't settle with me." With these words he descended the mountain, and as he went I could hear him murmur, " Gumpelino, Strachino—Strachino Gumpelino."

" He's an honest fellow," said the Marquis, " or I should have

sent him off long ago, on account of his want of etiquette. However, before you it isn't of much consequence ; you understand
me. How do you like his livery ? There's thirty dollar's worth of
gold on it more than there is on that of Rothschild's servants. It is
my greatest delight to see how the man perfects himself. Now and
then I give him lessons in refinement and accomplishment myself.
I often say to him, ' What is money ? Money is round and rolls
away, but culture remains.' Yes, Doctor, if I — which the Lord forbid — should ever lose my money, I still have the comfort of knowing that I'm a great connoisseur in art — a connoisseur in painting,
music, and poetry. Yes, *sir*. Bind my eyes tight, and lead me all
around in the gallery of Florence, and before every picture I'll tell
you the name of the painter who painted it, or at least the school
to which he belongs. *Music !* Stop up my ears, and I can hear every
false note. *Poetry !* I know every actress in Germany, and have got
the poets all by heart. Yes, sir, and Nature, too. I'm great on
Nature. I traveled once two hundred miles in Scotland — two
hundred miles, just to see one single hill ! But Italy surpasses everything. How do you like this landscape here ? What creation ! Just
look at the trees, the hills, the heaven, and the water down yonder
there ; don't it all look as if it were painted ? Did you ever see
anything of the kind finer, even in the theater ? Why, a man gets
to be, as you might say, a poet ; verses come into your head, and
you don't know where they come from : —

> ' Silent, as the veil of twilight falls
> Rests the plain, the greenwood silent lies ;
> Save where near me, 'mid these moldering walls,
> The cricket's chirp in melancholy cries.' "

These sublime verses were declaimed by the Marquis with thrilling pathos, while he gazed as if transfigured down into the smiling
valley, which glowed with all the brightness of morning.

366

CHAPTER IV

AS I ONCE ONE FINE SPRING DAY, WALKED "UNDER THE LINDENS" IN Berlin, there strolled before me two females, who were for a long time silent, until one of them ecstatically exclaimed, "Ah! them green treeses!" To which the other, a young thing, answered, "Mother, what do you keer for them green treeses?"

I must observe, that the persons of whom I speak, though not clad in satin, still by no means belonged to the vulgar — who, by the way, are not to be found at all in Berlin, save in the highest circles. But as for that naïve question, I can never forget it. Wherever I meet with affected admiration of Nature, and similar verdant lies, it rises laughing in my soul. And during the declamation of the Marquis, it rang out loud within me ; and he, reading mockery on my lips, exclaimed as if vexed, "Don't disturb me now — you haven't any soul for pure simple nature ; you are a distorted being — a morbid soul, so to speak — a Byron."

Dear reader, do you perhaps belong to that flock of pious fowl who for the last ten years have been joining in that song of "Byronic dividedness," with all manner of whistling and twittering, and which had its echo in the skull of poor Gumpel? Ah! dear reader, if you would complain of dividedness and want of harmony, then as well complain that the world itself is divided. For as the heart of the poet is the central point of the world, it must, in times like these, be miserably divided and torn. He who boasts that his heart has remained whole, confesses that he has only a prosaic out-of-the-way corner heart. But the great world-rent passed through my own heart, and on that account I know that the gods have highly blessed me above many others, and held me to be worthy of a poet-martyrdom.

Once the world was whole and sound ; in its early ages and in its middle ages, despite many wild battles, it had still unity, and there were great whole poets. We may honor these poets and delight ourselves with them, but every imitation of their wholeness is a lie — a lie which every sound eye penetrates ; and which cannot escape scorn. Lately, with much trouble, I obtained in

Berlin the writings of one of these " perfect poets " who so bewailed my Byronic discordancy ; and by the affected verdancy, the delicate appreciation of Nature, which breathed like fresh hay from his poems, my own poor heart, which has been so long discordant, well nigh burst with laughter, and unthinkingly I cried, " My dear Herr Intendant Councilor William Neumann, what do you care for them green treeses ?"

" You are a discordant soul — so to speak, a Byron," quoth the Marquis, still gazing, as if enraptured, down into the valley, clucking at times his tongue against his gums in sighing admiration, and saying, " Lord ! Lord ! everything just as if it were painted !"

Poor Byron ! such a calm enjoyment was denied to thee. Was thy heart so ruined that thou couldst only see, yes, and even describe Nature, but wert incapable of being blessed by her? Or was Bysshe Shelley in the right when he said that thou hadst, Actæon-like, surprised Nature in her chaste nakedness, and wert on that account torn by her hounds?

Enough of all this. We are coming to pleasanter subjects, namely, to the dwelling of Signoras Letitia and Francesca, which itself seemed to be *en negligée*, and had in front two great round windows, about which grape-vines curled, so that they looked like a profusion of beautiful green ringlets falling about its eyes. And at a distance we heard ringing from within warbling trills guitar tones, and merry laughter.

CHAPTER V

Signora Letitia, a young rose of fifty summers, lay in bed, trilling and prattling with her two gallants, one of whom sat upon a foot-stool, while the other reclined in a great arm-chair and played the guitar. From an adjoining room rang scraps of a sweet song, or of a far sweeter laughter. With a certain cheap and easy irony, which he occasionally assumed, the Marquis presented me to the lady and to the two gentlemen, remarking that I was the Dr. Henry Heine so celebrated in German legal literature. Unfortunately one of the gentlemen was a professor in the University of Bologna, and a jurist at that, though his fat, round belly seemed rather to indicate that his forte was spherical trigonometry. Feeling as if I were rather in a scrape, I replied that I did not write under my own name, but under that of Jarke — a statement made from sheer modesty, as the name which came into my head was that of one of the most repulsive insects among our legal writers. The Bolognese regretted that he never had heard this distinguished name — which will probably be true of you, too, dear reader — but still entertained no doubt that its splendor would ere long irradiate the entire earth. With this he leaned back in the chair, touched a few chords on the guitar, and sang from " Axur "—

> " Oh, powerful Brama !
> Ah ! let the weak stammer
> Of innocence please thee,
> Its stammer and clamor !"

While a delicious mocking nightingale-echo warbled in the adjoining chamber the same air. Meanwhile Signora Letitia trilled in the most delicate soprano—

> " For thee alone these cheeks are glowing,
>   For thee alone these pulses beat ;
> With Love's sweet impulse overflowing,
>   This heart now throbs, and all for thee."

And with the commonest prose voice she added, " Bartolo, bring me the spittoon.".

Then from his lowly seat arose Bartolo, with his dry wooden legs, and presented, with all due respect, a spittoon of blue porcelain.

This second gallant, as Gumpelino whispered to me in German, was a far-famed poet, whose songs, though written twenty years ago, still ring through Italy, and intoxicate with their wild glow of love both old and young ; while the poet himself is now a poor elderly man, with dimmed eyes in a pale face, scanty white hair on his trembling head, and cold poverty in his care-worn heart. Such a poor old poet, with his bald dryness, resembles a vine which we see standing leafless in winter on the bleak hillside, trembling in the wind and covered with snow, while the sweet juice which once ran from it warms, in far distant lands, the heart of many a boon-companion, and inspires songs in its praise. Who knows but that when that wine-press of thought, the printing-press, has squeezed *me* dry, and the ancient tapped spirit is only to be found in the bookseller's vaults of Hoffman & Campe, I too may sit, as haggard and care-worn as old Bartolo, on a cricket near the bed of some old inamorata, and hand her, when called on — a spittoon.

Signora Letitia made excuses for lying in bed. She lay, in fact, in pretty much the attitude of a Sphinx, her head with its high coiffure supported on both arms.

" You are German ? " she inquired.

" I am too honest to deny it, Signora, " replied my Littleness.

" Ah! the Germans are honest enough! " she sighed, " but what does it avail that the Germans who rob us are honest! — they are ruining Italy. My best friends are imprisoned in Milan, and only slavery——"

" No, no, " cried the Marquis, " do not complain of the Germans ; we are conquered conquerors, vanquished victors, as soon as we come to Italy. To see you, Signora, and to fall at your feet, is one and the same thing. " And with this he spread his great yellow silk pocket handkerchief on the floor, and kneeling on it, exclaimed, " Here I kneel and honor you in the name of all Germany. "

" Christophoro di Gumpelino! " sighed the Signora, deeply moved, " arise and embrace me! "

But lest the beloved shepherd might disturb her curling locks and the rouge of her cheeks, she did not kiss him on the glowing lips, but on his noble brow, so that his face reached lower down, and its rudder, the nose, steered about in the Red Sea below.

" Signor Bartolo, " I cried, " permit me also to officiate with the spittoon! "

Sorrowfully smiled Signor Bartolo, but never a word spake he, though said to be, next to Mezzofanti, the best teacher of elocution in Bologna. We never converse willingly when talking is our profession. He served the Signora as a silent knight — only, from time

370

to time, he was called on to recite the poem, which he, twenty-five years before, had thrown on the stage when she first in Bologna made her debut in *Ariadne*. It may be that, in those days, he himself was in full bloom and full of fire enough—perhaps as much so as the holy Dionysios himself—while, beyond doubt, his Letitia-Ariadne leapt wildly, like a Bacchante, into his passionate arms—Evoe Bacche! In those days he wrote many poems, still living in Italian literature, while the poet himself, and the beloved one, have long since turned to waste paper.

For five-and-twenty years his devotion has endured, and I think that even until he dies he will sit on the footstool and recite his poem, or serve his lady as commanded. The professor of law has been entwined as long as the other in the love-chains of the Signora; he courts her still with as much ardour as at the beginning of the century, and must still pitilessly shorten his lectures when she requires his escort to any university place, and he is still burdened with all the servitude of a genuine admirer.

The constancy of these two adorers of a long ruined beauty may perhaps be mere habit, perhaps only a regard for an earlier feeling, and perhaps the feeling itself, which is now entirely independent of the present condition of its former object, and which now regards it with the eyes of memory. Thus in Catholic cities we often see, at some street corner, old people kneeling before an image of the Madonna, which is so faded that but few traces of it are visible—yes, it may be that it is entirely obliterated, nothing remaining but the niche wherein it was painted, and the lamp hanging over it; but the old people who so piously kneel there have done so since youth—habit sends them thither daily at the same hour—they have not noted the gradual disappearance of the picture, and at last they become so dim of sight with age that it makes no difference whether the object of adoration is visible or not. Those who believe without seeing are, at any rate, happier than the sharp-sighted, who at once perceive every little irregularity in the face of their Madonna. There is nothing so terrible as such observations! Once, I admit, I believed that infidelity in woman was the most dreadful of all possible things, and to give them the most dreadful name, once and for all, I called them serpents. But now, alas! the most terrible thing to me is that they are not altogether serpents, for then they would come out every year with a fresh skin, revived and rejuvenated!

Whether either of the ancient Celadons felt a thrill of envy because the Marquis — or rather his nose — swam in a sea of delight in the manner above described, is more than I know. Bartolo sat calmly on his low seat, his thin legs crossed, and played with the Signora's lap-dog, one of those pretty creatures peculiar to Bologna, and known among us by the familiar term of "Bolognese." The professor was not in the least put out in his song, which was occasionally interrupted by tittering sweet tones in the next room, which drowned it in a merry parody, and which he himself at times discontinued in order to illuminate me with legal questions. When we did agree in our opinions, he swept a few impatient chords and jingled quotations in proof. I, however, supported my views on those of my teacher, the illustrious Hugo, who is greatly celebrated in Bologna under the name of Ugone, and also of Ugolino.

"A great man!" cried the professor, and sang—

> "The gentle summons of his voice
> Still sounds so deeply in thy breast,
> Its very pain makes thee rejoice,
> And rapture brings thee heavenly rest."

Thibaut, whom the Italians call Tibaldo, is also much honored in Italy, though his writings are not so much known there as his principal opinions and their rebuttals. I found that only the *names* of Gans and Savigny were familiar to the professor, who was under the impression that the latter was a learned lady.

"Ah, indeed!" he remarked, as I corrected this very pardonable error ; " really no lady! I have been erroneously informed. Why, I was even told that once, at a ball, Signor Gans invited this lady to dance, but met with a refusal, and that from this originated a literary enmity."

"You have really been misinformed. Signor Gans does not dance, and for the philanthropic reason that he might cause an earthquake should he do so. The invitation to dance, of which you speak, is probably an allegory misunderstood. The historical and philosophical schools are regarded as dancers, and thus we may readily imagine a quadrille between Ugone, Tibaldo, Gans, and Savigny. And in this sense Signor Ugone, though he be the *diable boiteux* of jurisprudence, still dances as daintily as Lemiere, while Signor Gans has recently made some jumps which entitle him to be regarded as the Hoguet of the philosophical school."

"Signor Gans, then," amended the professor, "dances only allegorically, so to say, metaphorically." Then suddenly, without saying more, he again swept the strings of his guitar, and, amid the maddest playing, sang—

> "It is true, his well-loved name
> Is the joy of every bosom,
> Though the ocean waves be storming,
> And the clouds o'er heaven be swarming,
> Still we hear Tarar loud calling,
> As though heaven and earth were bowing
> To the mighty hero's name."

As for Herr Gœschen, the professor did not so much as know that he existed. But this was, however, natural enough, for the name of the great Göschen has not yet got so far as Bologna, but only to Poggio, which is four German miles distant, and where it will for amusement remain awhile. Göttingen itself is by no means so well known in Bologna as it ought to be, merely on the common principles of gratitude, since it calls itself the German Bologna. I will not inquire whether this name be appropriate or not ; suffice it to say, that the two universities are really distinguishable by the simple fact that in Bologna they have the smallest dogs and the greatest scholars, while in Göttingen, on the contrary, are the smallest scholars and the greatest dogs.

CHAPTER VI

WHEN THE MARQUIS CHRISTOPHORO DI GUMPELINO DREW HIS NOSE
from the red sea, wherein it had been wallowing like a very
Pharoah, his face gleamed with selfish delight. Deeply moved, he
promised the Signora that so soon as she should again be in a
condition to sit down, he would bring her in his coach to Bologna.
It was at once arranged that the professor should ride on ahead, but
that Bartolo should sit on the box, and hold the Signora's lap-dog,
and that they all would go in a fortnight to Florence, where
Signora Francesca, who intended traveling during the same time
with my Lady to Pisa, would finally meet us. While the Marquis
counted up the cost of all this on his fingers, he hummed *di tanti
palpiti*, Signora sang the clearest-toned trills, and the professor
stormed away on his guitar, caroling such burning words, that the
sweat ran down from his brow, and, mingled with tears from his
eyes, formed a perfect torrent. While all this ringing and singing
went merrily on, the door of the adjoining chamber was suddenly
opened and in sprang—a creature!

I adjure you, ye Muses of the Old and New World, and ye also,
oh! undiscovered Muses who are as yet to be honored by later races
—sprites of whom I have dreamed in the gay greenwood and by the
sounding sea—that ye give me colors wherewith to paint that being
which next to virtue is the most glorious of this world. Virtue, of
course, is the first among glories, and the Creator adorned her with
so many charms, that it would really seem that he could produce
naught beside to be compared to her. Yet in a happy hour he once
again concentrated all his energies and made Signora Francesca, the
fair *danseuse*, that great masterpiece, who was born after the
creation of Virtue, and in whom he did not in a single particular
repeat himself, as earthly artists are wont to do. No, Signora Francesca is perfectly original; she hath not the least resemblance to
Virtue, and there are critics and connoisseurs who even prefer her
to the latter, to whom they award only the precedence due to
superior antiquity. But is that much of a defect when a *danseuse* is
only some six thousand years too young?

374

Ah! methinks I see her again as she sprung from the open door to the midst of the room, and after an incredible pirouette, cast herself at full length on the sofa, hiding both eyes with her hands, and crying, " Ah! I am so tired from sleeping!" The Marquis now approached and entered into a long address, in which his ironical, broadly respectful manner enigmatically contrasted with his sudden pauses, when moved by common-sense business recollections, and his fluency when sentimentally inspired. Still this style was not unnatural. It was probably formed in him by his inability, through want of courage, to set forth successfully that supreme influence to which he believed himself to be entitled by his money and intelligence, and he therefore sought, coward-like, to conceal it in language of exaggerated humility. His broad laughter on such occasions was disagreeably delightful, as it inspired a doubt whether it was a matter of duty to reward him with kindness — or a kicking. In this wise he delivered his morning service to Signora Francesca, who, half-asleep, hardly listened to him. Finally he begged permission to kiss at least her left foot, and as he, preparing for the job, spread his yellow handkerchief again on the floor, she held it indifferently out to him. It was enveloped in an exquisitely neat red slipper, in contrast to that on the right, which was *blue*, a droll coquetry by which the dainty littleness of both became more apparent. As the Marquis with deep reverence kissed the small foot, he arose with a sighing " Oh, Jesus!" and begged permission to present me, which was also accorded in a gaping, sleepy manner, when my introducer delivered another oration, filled with praises of my excellence, not omitting the declaration, on his word of honor as a gentleman, that I had sung with great ability of unhappy love.

I also begged of the lady to be allowed to kiss her left foot, and at the instant in which I enjoyed my share of this honor, she awoke as if from a dim dream, bent smilingly down to me, gazed on me with great wondering eyes, leaped joyfully up to the center of the room, and pirouetted around on one foot. I felt strangely that my heart in my bosom spun around also, until it was well nigh dizzy. Then the professor merrily played on his guitar and sang—

375

" An Opera Signora
    Once loved and married me,
A step I soon regretted,
    And wished that I were free.

I sold her soon to pirates,
    They carried her afar,
E'er she could look around her ;
    Hey ! bravo ! Biscromà !"

Once more Signora Francesca measured me from head to foot
with a sharp glance, and then, as it fully contented, thanked the
Marquis, somewhat as if I were a present which he had been kind
enough to bring her. She found little to object to in me, save that
my hair was of too light a brown ; she could have wished that it
were darker, like that of the Abbate Cecco ; and my eyes were also
too small, and rather green than blue. In revenge, dear reader, I in
turn should also describe Signora Francesca as depreciatingly ; but
I have really no shadow of a defect to point out in her lovely form,
whose perfection was that of the Graces, and yet which was almost
frivolous in its lightness. Her face was entirely divine, such as we
see in Grecian statues, the brow and nose forming an almost
accurate straight line, while the lower line of the nose formed a
sweet right angle, which was wondrously short. As close, too, was
the distance from the nose to the mouth, whose lips at either end
seemed scarcely long enough, and which were extended by a soft
dreamy smile, while beneath them arched a dear round chin. And
the neck ! — ah ! my pious reader, I am getting along too far and
too fast, and, moreover, I have no right in this inaugural description
to speak of the two silent flowers which gleamed forth like white
poetry when the Signora loosened the silver neck-button of her
black silk dress. Dear reader, let us rather climb up again to a
portrayal of the face, of which I have yet to remark that it was
clear and gold-yellow, like amber ; that the black hair which framed
its temples in a bright oval gave it a childlike turn, and that it was
lighted up by two black abrupt eyes, as if with a magic light.

You see, dear reader, that I would gladly give you an accurate
description of my good fortune, and as other travelers are accustomed to give maps of the remarkable regions into which they have

penetrated, so would I gladly serve up Francesca on a plate—of copper. But, ah! what avails the dead copy of mere outline in forms whose divinest charm consists of living movement. Even the best painter cannot bring this before our eyes, for painting is but a flat lie. Of the two, a sculptor would be more successful, for, by a changing illumination, we can to a certain degree realize motion in forms, and the torches which light them from without appear to inspire a real life within. Yes, there is a statue, dear reader, which may give you some faint idea of Francesca's loveliness, and that is the Venus of the great Canova which stands in the last hall of the Palazzo Pitti at Florence. I often think of this statue. At times in dreams it slumbers in my arms, until little by little it awakens to warm life, and whispers with the accents of Francesca! But it was the tone of this voice which gave to every word the gentlest and most infinite significance, and should I attempt to give her phrases, it would be only a dry collection of flowers whose real charm was in their perfume. She often leaped up, dancing as she spoke, and it is possible that dancing was her most natural language. And my heart danced ever with her, executing the most difficult *pas* and exhibiting a capacity for Terpsichorean accomplishments which I had never suspected.

In this idiom Francesca narrated the history of the Abbate Cecco, a young blade who had loved her while she was still plaiting straw hats in the valley of the Arno, assuring me that I was so fortunate as to resemble him. During this description she indulged in the most delicate pantomime, pressing one over the other the points of her fingers on her heart, then seemed with cup-like hand to be scooping out the tenderest emotions, cast herself finally with heaving breasts on the sofa, hid her face in the cushions, raised her feet high in the air, and played with them as if they were puppets in a show. The blue foot represented the Abbate Cecco and the red his poor Francesca ; and while she parodied her own story, she made the two loving feet part from each other, and it was touchingly ludicrous to see them kiss with their tips, saying the tenderest things ; and the wild girl wept withal delightful tittering tears, which, however, came at times unconsciously from the soul with more depth than the part required. In her pride of pain she delivered for Cecco a long speech, in which he praised with pedantic metaphors the beauty of poor Francesca ; and the manner in which she replied in person, copying her own earlier sentimentalism, had in it something puppet-like and mournful, which strangely moved my heart. " Adieu, Cecco !" " Adieu, Francesca !" was the constant refrain ; and I was finally rejoiced when a pitiless destiny parted them far asunder, for a sweet foreboding whispered in my soul that it would be an unfortunate thing for me should the two lovers remain continually united.

The professor applauded with droll, shrill guitar tones, Signora trilled, the lap-dog barked, the Marquis and I clapped our hands as if mad, and Signora Francesca arose and gracefully curtsied her thanks. " It is really a pretty comedy," said she, " but it is now a long time since it was first brought out, and I am now so old — guess how old ?"

But without waiting for my answer, she sprang up and cried, " Eighteen years !" and spun round eighteen times on one foot. " And, Doctor, how old are you ?"

" I, Signora, was born on the New Year's night of the year eighteen hundred."

" I always said," quoth the Marquis, " that he was one of the *first* men of our century."

" And how old should you suppose I am ?" suddenly cried Signora Letitia, as she, forgetful of her Eve-costume, suddenly leaped up in great excitement. . . .

Startled at this cry I contrived to stammer out a few phrases as to the difficulty of answering such a question, " having as yet only half seen Signora," but as she pressed me all the more zealously for an answer, I confessed that in truth I had not as yet learned the proportion of the years in Italy to those of Germany.

" Is the difference so great ?" inquired Signora Letitia.

" Of course," I replied, " for since heat expands all bodies, it follows that the years in your warm Italy must be longer than those of our cold Germany."

The Marquis extricated me better from this embarrassment by

gallantly asserting that her beauty had now first begun to manifest itself in all its voluptuous maturity. " And, Signora," he added, " as the pomegranate, the older it is, the yellower it becomes, so will your beauty too become riper with age."

The lady seemed to be gratified with this comparison, and confessed that she really did feel much riper now than of old, when she was but a thin, little thing, and had made her debut in Bologna —and that, in fact, she could not comprehend how it was that with such a figure she could ever have made such a *furore*. And then she narrated all the particulars of this first appearance as Ariadne—a subject to which, as I subsequently ascertained, she frequently recurred, on which occasions Signor Bartolo was obliged to recite the poem which he had thrown upon the stage. It was a good poem, full of touching melancholy at the infidelity of Theseus, and of wild aspirations for Bacchus, and the glowing apotheosis of Ariadne, " *Bella cosa !* " cried Signora Letitia at every verse ; and I also praised the metaphors, the construction of the verse, and the entire treatment of the myth.

" Yes, it is very beautiful," said the professor, " and has beyond doubt a foundation in historical fact, for several writers distinctly state that Oeneus, a priest of Bacchus, married the mourning Ariadne when he found her abandoned on Naxos ; and, as often happens in the legend, the priest of the god eventually becomes the god himself."

I could by no means agree with him in this opinion, since in mythology I rather incline to historical interpretation, and consequently asserted, " I can see nothing in the whole fable that Ariadne, after being left by Theseus in the island of Naxos, submitted her person to the embraces of Bacchus, but an allegorical statement that she took to drinking—an hypothesis maintained by many learned men in my fatherland. You, Signor Marquis, are probably aware that, in accordance with this hypothesis, the late Banker Bethmann has so contrived to illuminate *his* Ariadne that she appears to have a red nose."

" Yes, yes, Bethmann in Frankfort was a great man ! " cried the Marquis. But at the same instant, some deep reflection seemed to flit across his brain, and with a sigh he said, " Lord! Lord! I have forgotten to write to Rothschild in Frankfort!" And with a serious business face, from which all parodising mockery seemed to have vanished, he departed somewhat abruptly, promising to return that evening.

When he had left, and I was about — as is usual in this world — to pass my comments on the man to whose kindness I was indebted for the most agreeable of introductions, I found, to my astonishment, that the whole party could not praise him sufficiently, and that, above all, his enthusiasm for the beautiful, his noble and refined deportment, and his utter want of selfishness, inspired in them the most exaggerated expressions of admiration. Even Signora Francesca joined in this hymn of praise, but naïvely confessed that his nose was rather alarming, and that its enormous size reminded her of the tower of Pisa.

When taking leave, I begged as a favor to be allowed to kiss her left foot once more, when she with smiling seriousness drew off not only the red shoe but her stocking also : and, as I knelt, held up to me the white, fresh, blooming, lily foot, which I pressed to my lips, more believingly, perhaps, than I would have done that of the Pope. Of course, I then performed the duties of ladies' maid, aiding her to draw on the stocking and shoe.

" I am contented with you," said Signora Francesca, after this act, and in accomplishing my share of which I had been by no means in a hurry, " I am contented ; and you shall often have an opportunity of pulling on my stockings. Today you have kissed my left foot, tomorrow the right shall be at your disposal. The next day you may kiss my left hand, and the day after the right. If you do your duty well, by and bye you will get to my mouth, and so on. You see that I'm inclined to help you along, and as you are still quite young, you may yet get along very well in the world."

I did, indeed, advance far into the world of which she spoke! Be my witnesses, ye Tuscan nights, thou clear blue heaven with great silver stars, ye wild laurels and secret myrtles, and ye, too, O nymphs of the Apennines, who swept around us in a bridal dance, and dreamed yourselves once more in those better days of the immortals, when there were no Gothic lies, which permit only blind, groping pleasures in secret, and hasten to stick before every free feeling their hypocritical fig-leaf.

There was, however, no need for any fig-leaves, since a whole fig-tree, with broad spreading branches, rustled over the heads of the happy pair!

CHAPTER VII

EVERY ONE KNOWS WHAT WHIPPINGS ARE, BUT NO ONE HAS AS YET made out what love is. Some natural philosophers have asserted that it is a sort of electricity, which is not impossible, for in certain rapturous periods of love we feel as though an electric flash from the eyes of the loved one had penetrated our heart. Ah! such lightnings are the most destructive of all; and I will honor above Franklin the man who will invent a conductor which will protect us against them. If there were only little lightning conductors running to the heart, to which lightning-rods were attached, which could divert the dreadful fire to some other quarter! But I fear that it is not so easy a matter to rob Cupid of his arrows as Jupiter of his lightning and tyrants of their scepters. Besides, every love does not work in the lightning style; many a time it is hidden like a snake amid roses, and looks for the first crevice in the heart wherein to nestle—often it is only a word, a glance, the light narration of some secret deed which falls like a seed into the heart, lies there through the long winter time until spring comes, when the little grain shoots up into a flaming flower, whose perfume benumbs the brain. The same sun which hatches forth crocodile's eggs in Egypt, may at the same time fully ripen the love-seed in a young heart in Potsdam—for in Potsdam, as in Egypt, there are tears—But tears are far from being explanations—what is love? Has no one penetrated its depths? has no one solved the riddle? Perhaps such a solution would cause greater pain than the riddle itself, and the heart would be by it stricken with horror, and petrified as at the sight of the Medusa. Serpents twine around the awful word which reveals this mystery. Oh, I will never know that word of solution, for the burning misery in my own heart is dearer to me than cold, marble-like death. Oh, utter it not, ye forms of the dead, which, painless as stone, but as feelingless, wander through the rose gardens of this world, and smile with pale lips on the foolish soul who praises the perfume of the roses and bewails their thorns.

But if I, dear reader, cannot tell thee what love really is, I can at least describe with the utmost accuracy how a man behaves, and how he feels when he falls in love in the Apennines. For he then behaves like a fool ; he dances on rocks and hills, believing that the whole world dances with him. He feels as if the earth had just been finished on that very day, and that he was the first man made. " Ah! how beautiful everything is !" I caroled, as I left Francesca's dwelling. " How fair and precious is this new world!" I felt as though I must give to all plants and animals a new name, and I called every one according to its inner nature and my own feelings, which blended so marvellously with all things without. My breast was a well-spring of revelation, and I understood all forms and figures, the perfume of plants, the song of birds, the piping of the wind, and the rustling of waterfalls. Often, too, I seemed to hear the divine voice, " Adam, where art thou ?" " Here am I, Francesca !" I replied. " I pray to thee, for well I know that thou hast created sun, moon, and stars, and the earth with all its creatures !" Then there was soft laughter among the myrtles, and I secretly sighed within myself, " Oh, delicious folly, do not forsake me !"

But it was when twilight stole over me that the delirious happiness of love first truly began. The trees danced on the rocks, while their heavy heads were ruddily flushed over by the setting sun as though intoxicated from their own embracing vines. Below them the brook darted more hurriedly along and murmured anxiously as though fearing to undermine and overthrow the enraptured quivering trees. And over all flashed the summer heat-lightning, rising and falling as charmingly as light kisses. " Yes," I cried, " the laughing heaven kisses laughing earth — O Francesca! lovely heaven, let me by thy earth ? I am all so earthly, and sigh for thee, my heaven!" So I cried, holding my hands in wild prayer up to heaven, and ran and struck my head against many a tree, which instead of scolding I embraced, and my whole soul cried out with joy in all the intoxication of love—when I suddenly beheld a gleaming scarlet form, which at once tore me violently from my dreams and brought me back to a sense of the coldest reality.

CHAPTER VIII

ON A MOSSY BANK, BENEATH A WIDE-BRANCHING LAUREL, SAT Hyacinthos, the Marquis's servant, and near him his dog Apollo. The latter, however, might rather be said to be standing, as he had both fore-paws on the scarlet knees of the little man, and inquisitively beheld how the latter, holding a tablet in his hand, wrote from time to time therein. At times, whilst thus employed, Hyacinthos smiled sorrowfully, then shook his head, and then handkerchiefed his face with an air of satisfaction.

"What the devil!" I cried, "Hirsch Hyacinth! are you composing poetry? Well the signs are favorable. Apollo is by your side and the laurel hangs over your head."

But I did the poor sinner injustice. He amiably answered, "Poems! no; I'm a lover of poems, but don't write 'em. What should I write? I hadn't anything to do just then, and so just for fun I was writing off a list of the names of those gentlemen who've played in my lottery—some of them are a little in debt to me yet— oh! don't suppose Doctor, I meant to hint anything!—plenty of time for that. I know that you're good. If you'd only taken ticket number 1365 last time, instead of 1364, you'd have been worth a hundred thousand marks banco now, and needn't have been running around here, and might be sitting cosy and easy in Hamburg, telling folks, as you laid off on the sofa, how things looked in Italy. As true as the Lord may help me, I wouldn't have come here if it hadn't been for Herr Gumpel! Oh, what heat and danger and getting tired I have to stand, and wherever there's anything out of the way or crazy, there's Herr Gumpel, and I must take my share in it. I'd have gone away long, long ago, if I thought he could do without me. For if I didn't, who could certify for him at home how much honor and cultivation he'd enjoyed when traveling? And to tell the truth, Doctor, I begin to set great store myself on cultivation and manners. In Hamburg, the Lord be praised! I don't need it, but a man never knows what he may want when he goes anywhere else. And folks are right, for a little accomplishment ornaments the whole man. And how much honor you get by it too. For instance, how Lady Maxfield received me this morning, and how handsome she ' came down,' just on a horizontal level with me. And she gave me a *francesconi* to drink her health, though the flower only cost five *paoli*. Besides, oh! isn't it a pleasure to hold the little, white naked foot of a pretty lady individual in your hand?"

I was startled by this last remark, and at once thought, " Is he making fun of *me?*" But how could the vagabond know of the good fortune which I had encountered at the same hour, when he was on the other side of the hill? Was there perhaps a similar scene, and was there perhaps displayed in it the irony of the great world-stage-poet, who has acted at the same instant a thousand similar scenes, each parodying the other for the amusement of the heavenly host? But my suspicions were unfounded, for after many and oft-repeated questions, ending with my solemn promise not to tell the Marquis, the poor fellow admitted that when he gave the flower to Lady Maxfield she was still abed, and that just at the instant in which he was about to deliver it, and with it a fine speech, one of her pretty naked feet was thrust out from beneath the counterpane. Observing a corn on it, he at once begged permission to extract the annoyance, which was readily granted, and for which, with the tulip, he was rewarded with a francesconi.

" Yet I only did it for the honor of the thing," added Hyacinth, " and that's just what I said to Baron Rothschild when I had the honor to cut his corns. It took place in his cabinet. He sat there in his green arm-chair like a king, with his courtiers standing around, and he all the while was a-sending expresses to all the kings.

And while I was cutting his corns I thought in my heart, ' Now, you've got in your hands the foot of the man who holds all the world in his hands, and you too are a man that's somebody, for if you cut too deep he'll be angry, and cut the kings himself more cruelly.' It was the happiest moment of my life ! ' "

" I can readily imagine your delightful feelings, Herr Hyacinth. But whom among the Rothschild dynasty did you thus amputate? Was it the high-hearted Briton, the man in Lombard Street, who has set up a pawnbroker's shop for emperors and kings?"

" Of course, Doctor, I mean the great Rothschild, the great Nathan Rothschild, to whom the Emperor of Brazil pawned his diamond crown. But I had the honor too to make the acquaintance of Baron Solomon Rothschild in Frankfort, and though I wasn't on exactly the same footing with him, and had not the same foot-hold as with the other, he still knew how to esteem me. When the Marquis said to him that I had once been a lottery agent, the Baron answered very wittily, ' I'm head agent of the Rothschild lottery myself, and a colleague of mine musn't eat among servants, he must sit alongside of me at the table.' And as true as God be good to me, Doctor, I sat by Solomon Rothschild, and he treated me just like one of his equals, quite famillionaire. I was with him too at the children's ball, which was in the newspapers. I shall never see such a grand show again in all my born days. I was once in Hamburg at a ball, which cost fifteen hundred marks and eight schillings ; but that was nothing but a hen-dirt compared to a dung-hill. What lots of gold and silver and diamonds I saw there ! Such stars and orders ! The falcon order, the golden fleece, a lion order, the eagle order, yes, even a child, a right down small child wore the whole order of the elephant. The children were masked very pretty, and played at pawns, and were dressed up like kings, with crowns on their heads ; but one of the biggest was dressed precisely like old Nathan Rothschild. He acted his part very well, kept both his hands in his breeches pockets, shook his money, shook his head, as if vexed when any of the little kings wanted to borrow anything, and only showed favor to the little one with the white coat and red pantaloons. This fellow he patted

385

on the cheeks and praised him, ' You're my boy, my pet, my pride ; but let your cousin Michael keep out of my way ; I'll not lend the goose a penny, he spends more men in a year than he has to eat ; he'll make some trouble yet in the world, and spoil my business.' As true as the Lord may help me the little fellow played his part very well, particularly when he helped a child to walk along, who was dressed in white satin with real silver lilies, and now and then said to him, ' Now, now, only take good care of yourself, get your living honestly, and look out that you're not driven away again, or I'll lose my money.' I tell you what, Doctor, it was a real pleasure to hear how the little chap and the other children—right nice children they were—played their parts very well till cakes were brought to them, and they begun to fight for the best pieces, and grabbed the crowns off one another's heads, and screamed and cried, and some of 'em even——"

CHAPTER IX

THERE IS NOTHING SO STUPID ON THE FACE OF THE EARTH, AS TO read a book of travels in Italy, unless it be to write one ; and the only way in which its author can make it in any degree palatable is to say as little in it as possible of Italy. But though I have availed myself of this artistic trick, I still cannot venture to promise the reader anything strikingly captivating in the coming chapter. And if you who read become tired of the stupid stuff in it, just think of what a dreary time I must have had writing it ! I would recommend you, on the whole, to once in a while skip half a dozen leaves, for in that way you will arrive much sooner at the end. Lord ! how I wish that I could follow the same plan. And do not believe that I am jesting, for if I were to speak out in saddest earnestness the real opinion of my very heart, I would advise you to at once close these pages, and read no more therein. By and bye I will improve ; and when we, in a book as yet unwritten, meet Matilda and Francesca together, the dear creatures shall delight you far more than anything in the present chapter, or even in the next.

The Lord be praised, I hear without, before my window, a hand-organ with merry tunes. My befogged head needed such a clearing up, particularly as I must now describe my visit to his Excellency the Marquis Christophero di Gumpelino. I will narrate this deeply moving history with the utmost accuracy, the most literal truth, and in all its filthy purity.

It was late as I reached the home of the Marquis. As I entered the room, Hyacinth stood alone, cleaning the golden spurs of his master, who, as I perceived through the half-opened door of his chamber, was on his knees before a Madonna and a great crucifix.

For you must know, dear reader, that this nobleman is now a good Catholic ; that he observes with the utmost strictness all the ceremonies of that Church which alone confers happiness ; and that when he is in Rome he even keeps his personal chaplain, on the same principle which induces to him keep in England the fastest horse, and in Paris the prettiest dancing girl.

" Herr Gumpel is just now doing his prayers," whispered Hyacinth with a significant smile, and, pointing to the cabinet of his master, added in a softer tone, " He lies that way every evening two hours on his knees before Our Lady with the child Jesus. It is a splendid work of art, and cost him six hundred francesconi."

" And you, Mr. Hyacinth, why don't you kneel behind him ? Or perhaps you are not inclined to the Catholic religion ?"

" I'm inclined, and again I'm not inclined," replied he, reflectively shaking his head. " It's a good religion for a Baron who can go about all day at his leisure, or for one who understands the fine arts, but it's no religion for a man from Hamburg, who has his business to mind, and no religion at all, any way you take it, for a lottery collector. I must write down fair and square every number that's drawn, and if I happen to think of — bum ! bum ! bum ! — the Catholic bells, or if my eyes swim like Catholic incense, and I make a mistake, and set down the wrong number, the worst sort of trouble may come out of it. Many a time have I said to Herr Gumpel, ' Your Excellency is a rich man, and can be as Catholic as you please, and may smoke up your wits with incense as much as you like, and may be as stupid as a Catholic bell, and still have victuals to eat ; but *I'm* a business man, and must keep my seven sense about me to earn something.' Herr Gumpel thinks, of course, that it's necessary for my accomplishment, and that if I don't become Catholic that I can't understand the pictures which accomplish people, such as John of Fizzley, the Verygreeno, the Correctshow, Caratshow, and Cravatshow ; but I've always held that all the Correctshows and Cravatshows wouldn't help much if nobody bought tickets of me, and then I should make a mighty poor show! And I must own, Doctor, that the Catholic religion don't amuse me ; and, as a reasonable man, you must allow that when it comes to that, I'm right. I don't see any fun in it—it's something such a religion as if the Lord (the Lord forbid it !) had just died, and everything smelt of burial incense, and with it all, they roll out such a melancholy funeral music as to give one the blues ; and the long and short of it is, that it's no religion for a Hamburger."

" Well, then, Mr. Hyacinth, how do you like the Protestant religion ?"

" That is altogether, on t'other hand, too commonsense like, and if the Protestant churches hadn't an organ, it wouldn't be a religion at all. Between you and me the religion does no harm, and is as pure as a glass of water — but it don't help any. I've tried it, sir, and the trial cost me four marks fourteen shilling."

" How so, my good Mr. Hyacinth ?"

" Well, do you see, Doctor, that I once came to the conclusion that it was a very enlightened religion, without any visionary notions or miracles, though, by the way, I still think that a church *must* have a few visionary notions and a trifle in the way of miracles to be one of the proper sort. ' But who'd ever work any miracle there ?' thought I one day in Hamburg, as I peeped into a Protestant church, one of the regular bald sort, with nothing but brown benches and white walls, and on the walls nothing but a blackboard with half a dozen white numbers on it. ' But,' thinks I, ' maybe you don't do justice to this religion. Who knows but what these numbers can work a miracle as well as the image of the Virgin Mary, or a bone of her husband, St. Joseph?' and, to settle the matter, I went straight to Altona and set these very numbers in the Altona lottery. The *deuce* I set with eight shilling, the *terne* with six, the *quaterne* with four, and the *quinterne* with two shilling. But I tell you, upon my honor, that not a single one of the Protestant numbers came out a prize. I very soon made up *my* mind what to think of the Protestant business. A great religion that, which can't so much as bring out the deuce!—and a nice goose I'd be to stake my salvation on a religion by which I've already lost four marks and fourteen shilling."

" I daresay that the old Jewish religion suits you much better, my friend."

" Doctor, the mischief take the old Jewish religion! I don't wish it on my worst enemy. It brings nothing but abuse and disgrace. I tell you it ain't a religion, but a misfortune. I keep out of the way of everything that puts me in mind of it, and because Hirsch is a Hebrew word, and means hyacinth, I've let the old Hirsch run, and now sign myself, ' Hyacinth, Collector, Operator, and Appraiser.' And then I have this advantage, that I've got an H on my seal ring, and my new name begins with an H, so that there's no need of having a new one cut. I tell you what—it amounts to a good deal in the long run, if you reckon up what a good name is worth to a man. Name's everything. When I write, ' Hyacinth, Collector, Operator, and Appraiser,' it has another sort of a sound from plain Hirsch. Nobody can treat me like a common blackguard then."

" My good Hyacinth, who would ever treat *you* in such a manner? You appear to have done so much towards accomplishing yourself, that it is easy to recognize a man of culture in you before you open your mouth."

" You're right, Doctor. I have gone ahead like a giant in improving myself. I really don't know who I ought to keep company with when I get back to Hamburg ; but I know what I'll do in the religion line. Just for the present I can get along with the New-Israelite temple, I mean the pure Mosaic-Lord's service, with

389

orthographic German hymns and moving sermons, and a few visionary notions, which are things no religion can do without. As true as the Lord may help me, I don't want any better religion, and it is worth keeping up. I mean to do my part for it any how, and every Saturday, when it isn't a day for drawing in the lottery, I'm going there. There are men, and more's the pity, who give this new faith a bad name, and say that it gives occasion for a schism ; but I give you my word, it's a good sound religion — perhaps a little too good for common folks, for whom the old Jewish religion is good enough. A common man must have something stupid to make him happy, and he *does* feel happier in something of the sort. A regular old Jew, with a long beard and a ragged coat, and who can't speak a word correct, perhaps feels better than I do, with all my accomplishment. There lives in Hamburg, in the Bæcker Breitengang by a gutter, a man named Moses Lump, — the folks call him Lumpy, for short, — and he runs around the whole week in wind and rain, with his pack on his back, to earn a few marks. Well, when Friday evening comes round, he goes home, and finds the seven-branched candlestick all lighted, a clean white cloth on the table, and he puts off his pack and all his sorrows, and sits down at the table with his crooked wife and crookeder daughter, and eats with them fish which have been cooked in nice white garlic sauce, and sings the finest songs of King David, and rejoices with all his heart at the Exodus of the children of Israel from Egypt. He feels glad, too, that all the bad people who did anything bad to them died at last ; that King Pharoah, Nebuchadnezzar, Haman, Antiochus, Titus, and such like, are all dead, but that Lumpy is still alive, and eats fish with his wife and child. And I tell you what, Doctor, the fish are delicate, and the man is happy ; he hasn't any cause to torment himself with any ' accomplishment ; ' he sits just as contented in his religion and in his green nightgown as Diogenes in his cask, and he looks with joy at the lights burning, which he hasn't even the trouble of tending. And I tell you that if the lights should happen to burn dim, and the Christian woman who ought to snuff them isn't at hand, and if Rothschild the Great should happen to come in, with all the brokers, discounters, forwarders, and head clerks with whom he overcomes the world, and if he should say, ' Moses Lump, ask what thou wilt, it shall be given thee,'—Doctor, I believe that Moses would say, quiet and easy, ' Trim the candles for me!' and Rothschild the Great would answer in wonder, ' If I wasn't Rothschild, I'd like to be such a Lump as this!' ' "

As Hyacinth, according to custom, thus developed his doctrines with epic copiousness, the Marquis rose from his cushions and came towards us, still mumbling a paternoster through his nose. Hyacinth then drew the green curtain over the image of the Madonna which hung over the bed, extinguished the two candles, took down the bronze crucifix, and approaching us, began to clean it with the same rag and with the same care with which he had just cleaned his master's spurs. But the Marquis was melting with heat and with soft sentiment ; instead of a coat he wore a full blue silk domino with silver fringe, and his nose shone sorrowfully, like an enamored louis-d'or. " Oh, Jesus!" he sighed, as he sank among the cushions of the sofa. " Don't you think, Doctor, that I have a very dreamy, visionary, poetical look this evening? I am very much moved ; my soul is melting ; I perceive from afar a higher world.

> ' My eye beholds the heaven open,
> My heart leaps up in wondrous bliss.' "

" Herr Gumpel, you must take something," interrupted Hyacinth. " The blood in your inside has got to going again. I know what is the matter with you."

" You *don't* know," sighed his master.

" I tell you I *do*," replied the man, nodding with his good-natured, going-to-work little face. " I know you in and out—I *know*. You are just my opposite ; when you're hungry I'm thirsty, and when I'm thirsty you're hungry. You are too corpulent, and I'm too lean. You have lots of imagination, and I've got all the more business capacity. I'm a *practicus*, and you're a *diarrheticus*—in short, you are altogether my *antipodex*."

" Ah, Julia!" sighed Gumpelino, " would that I were the yellow

391

glove upon thy hand, and kissed thy cheek. Doctor, did you ever see the actress Crelinger in Romeo and Juliet?"

"Of course, and my whole soul is still enraptured with the memory."

"Well, then," cried the Marquis with enthusiasm, and fire flashed from his eyes, illuminating his nose, "then you appreciate my feelings—then you know what I mean when I say *I love !* I will show myself to you, and expose everything. Hyacinth, just step out of the room!"

"I needn't go out," said his man, as if vexed; "you needn't stand on any ceremony with me, for I know what love is, too, and how it——"

"You *don't* know!" cried the Marquis.

"I'll prove that I know, Herr Marquis, by just speaking the name of Julia Maxfield. Oh, be easy! You're loved, too, but it's of no use. The brother-in-law of your lady never lets her go out of sight, and watches her night and day like a diamond."

"Ah! wretched that I am," moaned Gumpelino. "I love and am loved again; we secretly press each other's hands—we tread on each other's feet under the table—glance meaningly at each other—and yet can't find an opportunity to—— Ah! how often I stand in the moonlight on the balcony, and imagine that I am Julia and that my Romeo or my Gumpelino has promised me a rendez-vous—and then I declaim exactly like the Crelinger:—

> 'Come, night! come, Gumpelino!—come, day in night!
> For thou wilt lie upon the wings of night
>   Whiter than snow upon a raven's back—
> Come, gentle night; come, loving black-browed night,
> Give me my Romeo—or Gumpelino!'

But ah! Lord Maxfield watches us all the time, and we're both dying with intense desire. I shall never survive the day when either sets the blossom of youthful purity at stake, winning to lose. Ah! I'd rather enjoy one such hour with Julia than win the great prize in the Hamburg lottery!"

"What a crazy notion!" cried Hyacinth; "the great prize!—

392

one hundred thousand marks!"

" Yes, rather than the great prize," continued Gumpelino, " could I have one such hour — and she has promised me often that I should have such when the first opportunity occurs, and I've often thought that she would declaim to me — just like Crelinger —

> ' Wilt thou begone? it is not yet near day!
> It was the nightingale, and not the lark,
> That pierced the fearful hollow of thine ear ;
> Nightly she sings on yon pomegranate tree :
> Believe me, love, it was the nightingale.' "

" The great prize for only one night," repeated Hyacinth several times, as if he could never assent to such an assertion. " I have a very high opinion, Herr Marquis, of your accomplishments, but I never did think you'd have brought your visionary fancies up to such a pitch. That any man could ever prefer love to the great prize! Really, Herr Marquis, since I've waited on you I've got used to a great deal of accomplishment, but this much I know, I wouldn't give an eighth of the great prize for all the love afloat. The Lord keep me from it! Why, if I reckon off five hundred marks premium, there'd still remain twelve thousand marks. *Love !* Why, if I reckon up all together that I've ever paid out for love in all my life, it only comes to twelve marks and thirteen schilling. *Love !* Why, I've had lots of love, free, *gratis*, for nothing ; only once in a while, to please my woman, I've cut her corns for her. I never had a real senti-mental passionate love-scrape but once in my life, and that was for fat Sally of Dreckwall. She used to buy lottery tickets of me, and whenever I called on her to square accounts, she used to give me a piece of cake — very good cake indeed — and sometimes she'd make up a nice little fancy dish for me, with a drop of liquor to it ; and when I once told her that I was troubled with the blues, she gave me a recipe for the powder which her own husband used. I use the powder to this very day, it always works on me ; and that was the only consequence which our love ever had. I thought, Herr Marquis, that maybe you needed one of those powders. When I came to Italy they were the first thing I thought of, so I went to the apothecary and had 'em made up, and I always carry 'em about with me. Just wait a minute and I'll hunt for 'em ; and if I hunt for 'em, I'll find 'em ; and if I find 'em, your Excellency's got to take 'em."

It would require too much time to repeat all the comments with which Hyacinth accompanied his researches as he drew in succession each of the following articles from his pocket. These were : — I., half a wax candle ; II., a silver case, in which he kept his instruments for cutting corns ; III., a lemon ; IV., a pistol, which, though unloaded, was carefully wrapped in paper lest the sight of it might awaken apprehension ; V., a list of the last drawing of the Hamburg lottery ; VI., a black leather bound little book, containing the Psalms of David and the debts not as yet collected ; VII., a dry willow withe twined in a true-love knot ; VIII., a little packet covered with faded rose colored silk, and containing the receipt in full for a lottery prize which had once won fifty thousand marks ; IX., a flat piece of bread resembling ship's biscuit with a hole in the middle ; and X., the above mentioned powder, which the little man took out, not without a certain emotion and a sorrowful shaking of the head.

"When I think," he sighed, "that ten years ago fat Sally gave me this recipe, and that I'm in Italy now, and have the same recipe in my hands, and see the same words on it, ' *Sal mirable Glauberi* '—that means in German ' extra fine Glauber salt of the best quality '—ah! I feel as if I had already taken the salt and could feel it a-working inside. What is man! I'm in Italy a-thinking of fat Sally of Dreckwall! Who'd a thought it? I can think I see her now in the country in her garden, where the moon shines, and where there must be for certain a nightingale singing, or maybe a lark——"

"It is the nightingale, and not the lark!" sighed Gumpelino in parenthesis.

> "'Nightly she sings on yon pomegranate tree :
> Believe me, love, it was the nightingale.'"

"It's all one to me," continued Hyacinth ; "it may be a canary for all I care ; only wild birds in the garden don't cost so much.

The main thing is the hot house, and the carpet in the pavilion, and the statuaries all round it, and among 'em there's a naked General of the gods and the Venus Urinia ; both cost three hundred marks. And in the middle of the garden Sally's got a fontenelle, and may be she's a-standing there having make believe pleasures in her fancy, and thinking — of — me !''

After this sigh followed a rapt silence, which the Marquis finally broke with a languishing tone and question, '' Tell me, Hyacinth, on your honor, do you really believe that your medicine will have its effect ?''

'' Yes, upon honor, it will. Why shouldn't it work ? It works on *me*. And ain't I a living man just the same as you ? Glauber salts make all men alike, and when Rothschild takes Glauber salts, they operate on him just as they would on the smallest broker. And I'll just tell you now how it's all done. I shake the powder into a glass, pour some water on it, and as soon as you've swallowed it you twist up your face and say, ' Prr — phew ! — pooh !' Then you feel it a sort of quareling about inside of you, and you feel queer, and you lie down on the bed, and then I promise you, 'pon honor, that by and by you'll get up, then you'll lay down again and get up again, and so on and so forth, and the next morning you feel as light as an angel with white wings, and you'll dance about because you feel so well ; only you'll look a little pale, but I know you like to look pale, because its languishing-like, and that's interesting.''

While thus chattering, Hyacinth had prepared the powder ; but as for the Marquis, he would have taken this pains for nothing had not the passage suddenly flashed into his mind where Julia takes the draught which has such a dire effect on her destiny. '' What do you think, Doctor,'' he cried, '' of the actress Mueller in Vienna ? I have seen her as Julia, and Lord ! Lord ! how she *did* play ! I'm the greatest enthusiast for Crelinger living ; but Mueller, when she drank off the goblet, completely tore me down ! See !'' — this was his exclamation, as he took with a comic gesture the glass into which Hyacinth had poured the powder — '' See ! *this* was the way in which she took the cup, and shuddered, so that you could feel every thrill which *she* felt, as she said —

395

> ' There is a faint cold fear which thrills my veins,
> And almost freezes up the heat of life.'

And *so* she stood, just as I stand, and held the goblet to her lips, saying —

> ' Stay, Talbot, stay!
> Romeo, I come! this do I drink to thee.'

And with these words she swallowed the medicine."

" Much good may it do you, Herr Gumpel!" said Hyacinth in a joyful tone, for the Marquis had, in imitative inspiration, drained the entire dose, and sunk weary with declamation on the sofa.

He did not remain long in this position, for almost immediately there was a knock at the door, and there entered Lady Maxfield's little jockey, who gave to the Marquis, with a laugh and a bow, a note, and at once retired. Hastily did Gumpelino break the seal, and while he read, his eyes and nose gleamed with delight ; but suddenly a spectral paleness covered his face, emotion was apparent in every muscle, and he sprang about with gestures of despair, laughing grimly, and rushed about the chamber, exclaiming —

" Woe to me, fool of fortune!"

"What is it? what is it?" cried Hyacinth, with a trembling voice, as he distractedly cleaned away at the crucifix, which he had again taken up ; " are we going to make our attack tonight?"

" What is the matter, Herr Marquis?" I inquired, equally astonished.

" Read! read!" cried Gumpelino, as he threw towards us the note, and again rushed despairingly about the room, his blue domino streaming behind him like a storm cloud.

It was a note from Lady Maxfield, inviting him to call on her immediately, stating that she would leave on the following morning for England.

" Woe me, fool of fortune!" bewailed Gumpelino. " Love holds out to me his nectar cup, and I, alas! the Jack-fool of fortune, have already drained a goblet of Glauber salts! Who can get the accursed stuff out of me now? Help! help!"

" No earthly living man can help you now!" sighed Hyacinth.

" I pity you from my very heart," said I condolingly. " To drain a tumbler of Glauber salts instead of a goblet of nectar is bitter!"

" O Jesus! O Jesus!" cried the Marquis ; " I feel it thrill through my every vein. Oh, true apothecary, thy drugs are quick! but it shall not hinder me. I will hasten to her ; I will sink at her feet!"

" Don't be passionate!" replied Hyacinth. " Don't go off into rhapsodies."

" No, no! I will hasten to her, and in her arms——Oh, night! oh, night!"

" I tell you," continued Hyacinth, with philosophical indifference, " that you will find no repose in her arms. Don't be so passionate. Your mind plays into the hands of Nature. You must endure like a man what your fate has determined. Maybe it's good that it's come so, and perhaps it came so because it's good. Man is an earthly being, and doesn't understand the ways of Divinity. Folks often think they're going straight ahead to their happiness, and bad luck stands in the way with a stick ; and when a plain vulgar stick strikes a noble back, they feel it, Herr Marquis!"

" Woe me! a fool of fortune!" raved Gumpelino. But his servant calmly continued —

" A man often expects a cupful of nectar, and instead of it gets horse-whip soup — if the nectar is sweet, then the horsewhipping is all the bitterer ; and it is really lucky that the man who thrashes another must tire out sooner or later, or the fellow he whips could never stand it. But it is a great deal worse when bad luck with dagger and poison hides in a man's way to love, so that his life's in danger. Maybe, Herr Marquis, it is really all right that things have gone as they have, or perhaps, who knows, you might, while running in the heat of love, have been met on the way by a little Italian with a dirk six yards long, who would have gone slap at you, and have stuck you (not to put too fine a point upon it) through your calves. For a man can't holler for the watch here as in Hamburg, and there are no policemen among the Apennines. Or maybe," continued the pitiless consoler, without paying the slightest atten tion to the growing rage of his master, " maybe when you were sitting snug and warm by Lady Maxfield, the brother-in-law would

397

have come rushing back and clapped a pistol to your breast, and made you sign a bill of a hundred thousand marks. I don't want to make mischief or tell lies—but I say, suppose now—only suppose that you were a good-looking man, and Lady Maxfield was in despair for fear she should lose her beau, and was jealous—like all women—for fear some other woman might get you after she was gone, what would she do? Why, she'd just take an orange or a lemon and put a little white powder on it, and say, ' Here, dear, just suck this and cool yourself off a little ; you've got warm a-running so fast,' and the next day you'd be cooled down and no mistake. There was a man named Piper, who had a passional attraction for a female individual who was called Trumpet-Angel Jenny, and she lived in the Coffee-factory, and the man by the duck pond——"

" I wish, Hirsch," screamed the Marquis in a rage, " I wish that your Piper of the duck-pond, and his Trumpet-Angel of the coffee-mill, and you and your Sally, all had my Glauber's salts rammed down your throats!"

" What would you have, Herr Gumpel?" exclaimed Hyacinth, not without heat. " Was it my fault that Lady Maxfield's a-going away tomorrow and invited you to come tonight? Could I know *that* beforehand? Am I Aristotle? Have I got a situation in a prophecy office? I only said that the powder would work, and it *will* work, just as sure as I'm a-going to heaven, and if you go running about the room in such a disparaging and passionate way, it'll work all the sooner."

" Well, then, I'll sit down calmly on the sofa," groaned Gumpelino ; and, stamping on the ground, he rolled in a rage on the sofa, restrained his mood by a mighty effort, and both servant and master gazed long and silently at each other, until the latter said, with a deep sigh and in a whimpering tone—

" But, Hirsch, what will the lady say if I don't come? She waits for me, yes, lingers and trembles and burns with love."

" She has a beautiful foot," said Hyacinth to himself, and sorrowfully shook his little head. But there were mighty throbs of emotion at work in his heart, and a daring idea was working itself out under his scarlet coat.

" Herr Gumpel," said the words, as they came forth, " ——send me!"

And as he spoke, a deep blush stole over the sallow business countenance.

CHAPTER X

WHEN CANDIDE CAME TO EL DORADO, HE SAW SEVERAL BOYS IN THE street who were playing with nuggets of gold instead of stones. This extravagance made him think that they must be royal children, and he was not a little astonished to learn that in El Dorado nuggets of gold were as valueless as flint pebbles with us, so that the very schoolboys played with them. Something very similar happened to one of my friends, who, when he first came to Germany and read German books, was greatly amazed at the wealth of thought which he found in them, but soon observed that thoughts are as common in Germany as gold ingots in El Dorado, and that many a writer who seems to be an intellectual prince is, after all, a mere school-boy.

This reflection often occurs to me when I am about to write down the most admirable reflections on Art and Life. Then I laugh, and keep my thoughts in my pen, or scribble in their stead a picture or a carpet pattern on the paper, persuading myself that such carpets are more useful in Germany—that intellectual El Dorado—than the goldenest thoughts.

Dear reader, I shall bring on the carpet now, spreading out before thee, the familiar figures of Gumpelino and his Hirsch-Hyacinth ; and if the former be painted with less accurate traits, I trust that you will be sharp witted enough to appreciate a negative character, even if positive points be wanting in it. For he might bring a suit for libel against me, or something even more significant. For the Marquis is mighty with money and many friends. Besides, he is the natural ally of my enemies ; he upholds them with sub-sidies ; he is an aristocrat, an ultra-papist ; in fact, he only wants one thing as yet to be as bad as possible, and that one thing he must soon learn, having the book which teaches it already in his hands, as you will perceive from my picture-carpet.

It was again evening. On the table stood two candelabras with lighted wax candles, and their gleam flashed on the golden frames of the pictures of saints hanging on the wall, and which, in the flickering light and wavering shadow, seemed inspired with life. Without, before the window, the dark cypress trees stood strangely motionless in the silver moonlight, while far in the distance resounded a sad hymn to the Virgin, rising and falling in broken tones, apparently the voice of a sick child. The air within was close and warm, and the Marquis Christophoro di Gumpelino sat, or rather reclined, in aristocratic indolence on the cushions of the sofa, his noble though overheated figure being again clad in its blue silk domino, while in his hands he held a book bound in scarlet morocco-paper, heavily gilt, and from which he declaimed in a loud yet languishing tone. His eyes had that sticky-pasty luster peculiar to enamored tomcats, and his cheeks, including the nostrils, were pale as if from suffering. Still this pallor admits of a philosophically anthropological explanation if we remember that the Marquis had swallowed the night before a whole tumbler of Glauber salts.

Hirsch-Hyacinthus was down on all fours on the floor, and with a great piece of white chalk was busy in drawing on the brown tiles the following characters, or something like them: —

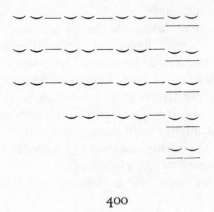

This business appeared to be anything but agreeable to the little man, for, puffing at every stoop, he growled vexedly, " Spondee, Trochee, Iambus, — I am bust ! — Pyrr-hic, Anapest — and the pest ! " For the sake of working more at his ease, he had taken off his red coat, and there now appeared two short modest looking legs in tight scarlet breeches, and somewhat longer arms in white loose sleeves.

" What curious figures are those ? " I inquired, after watching his work for a while.

" These are feet the size of life," he groaned for answer, " and I, wretched man, must keep these feet in my head, and my hands already ache with all the feet they've had to write. These are the real true feet of poetry, and if it wasn't for the accomplishments I'm getting, I'd let the poetry run with all its feet. Just now I have private lessons from the Marquis in the poetry business. The Marquis reads the poem and explains how many feet there are in it, and then I must note them down and reckon up whether the poem is all right."

" You find us," remarked the Marquis in didactically pathetic tone, " engaged in a truly poetic occupation. I well know, Doctor, that you belong to that body of poets who have ideas of their own, and do not perceive that in poetry the feet come first, and that *metre* is the main thing ; but a refined spirit can only express itself in refined forms, and these are only to be learned from the Greeks, and from those modern poets who strive to think like Greeks, *feel* like Greeks, and bring their feelings home in the Greek fashion to a man."

" To man, of course, and not to woman, as an unclassic, romantic poet is bound to do," replied my Insignificance.

" Herr Gumpel talks now and then like a book," whispered Hyacinth aside to me, as he contracted his thin lips, winked his little eyes with delighted pride, and significantly shook his small head, whose every motion was one of wondering amazement. " I tell you," he continued, in somewhat louder tones, " he talks sometimes like a book, and then he's what you might call no sort of a man at all, but a higher sort of being and I become dumb the more I listen."

" And what have you there in your hands?" I inquired of the Marquis.

" Gems," he replied laconically, holding out the book.

At the word " gems " Hyacinth leaped up, but, when he saw the book, smiled pityingly. The precious gem in question had on its title-page the following words:—

POEMS

OF

AUGUST, COUNT VON PLATEN.

STUTTGARD AND TUBINGEN :

PUBLISHED BY J. G. COTTA.

1828

On the blank leaf was neatly written, " A Gift of True Brotherly Friendship."

" I haven't slept a wink all night," he complained to me. " Fortunately, I had this glorious bit of reading by me, and I got from it not only poetical instruction, but also sound consolation for life. I swear, sir, by our blessed Lady of Loretto, and as true as I'm an honorable man, that these poems haven't their equal! You know that I was in a state of desperation yesterday evening—*au désespoir*, as one might say—because Fate forbade me to possess my Julia. Then I read these poems, one every time when I had to get up, and the result has been, that I feel so indifferent to women that my own passion became repulsive to me. And that is the beauty of this poet, that he only burns with friendship for men. Yes, he prefers us to women ; and for this very preference we ought to be grateful to him. How much greater he is in this than common poets! You do not find him flattering the everyday tastes of the masses ; he cures us of that passion for women which causes us so much suffering. O woman! woman! what a benefactor to his race is that man who frees us from your chains! It is an eternal shame that Shakespeare never applied his wonderful theatrical talent to this end, since he, as I have just found in these poems, was inspired by the same greatness of soul as the great Count Platen, who says, in his sonnets of Shakespeare :

> ' A maid's caprices never broke thy slumbers,
> And yet for friendship still we see thee yearning ;
> From female snares a friend thy steps is turning,
> His beauty is thy care, and fires thy numbers.' "

While the Marquis declaimed these verses with enthusiasm, and while the moisture gathered on his tongue, Hyacinth was making a series of grimaces which were evidently inspired by anything but assent, though they appeared partly to be those of vexation and partly of affirmation, until he at last exclaimed—

" Herr Marquis, you talk like a book, and the verses go out like a purge, but I don't like their contents. As a man, I feel flattered that Count Platen gives us the preference, but as a friend to women, I go against such men. Such is man ! One likes onions, and another has the feeling for warm friendship ; but I, as an honest man, must confess that I prefer onions, and that a cross-eyed scullery maid is more to my taste than any friend such as your poet talks about. And, in fact, I must say that I, for one, can't *begin* to see so much beauty in the male sex that one can fall in love with it."

Hyacinth spoke these last words while giving a side squint at his own reflection in the mirror as though he were the ideal pattern of manly perfection. But the Marquis, without suffering himself to be disturbed, read on—

> " ' Hope's foam-built palaces may fall together ;
> We strive, yet do not come at all together ;
> Melodious from thy mouth my name is ringing,
> And yet my verse thou wilt not call together.
> Like sun and moon must we be ever parted,
> That use and custom may be all together?
> Oh, lean thine head on mine, for sweet in union
> Thy dark locks and my light ones fall together ;
> But ah ! I dream, for lo I see thee parting
> Ere joy has found us in one thrall together ;
> Our souls are bleeding since our forms are parted,
> Would we were flowers, oft bound and all together !' "

" Queer poetry that !" exclaimed Hyacinth, as he re-echoed the rhymes : " ' Use and custom all together,' ' thrall together,' and

' fall together!' Queer poetry! I've got a brother-in-law who, when he reads poetry, often for fun puts ' from before ' and ' from behind ' in turn at the end of every other verse, but I declare I never knew that the poems he made up that way ought to be called ' gazelles.' I must try myself and see whether the verses which the Marquis has just declaimed won't be improved by putting ' from before ' and ' from behind ' in turn after the ' together.' Depend upon it they'll be twenty per cent. stronger!''

Without attending to this speech, the Marquis drove ahead in his declamation of ghazels and sonnets, in which the loving one sings his '' friend of beauty,'' praises him, wails over him, accuses him of indifference, devises plans to attain him, ogles him, is jealous of him, languishes for him, fondles through a whole scale of love tones with him, and that so meltingly, amorously, and lecherously, that the reader would suppose that the poet were a maiden suffering with nymphomania. One thing, however, must seem to him to a certain degree extraordinary, that this maiden is always complaining that her love is contrary to the usual manner or '' custom ; '' that she cherishes as intense a hatred of this '' custom which parts '' as a pickpocket could against the police ; that in her love she would fain embrace '' the limbs '' of her friend ; that she laments dolefully over envious wretches who cunningly part us, '' to hinder us and keep us ever parted ; '' that she bewails annoying personal afflictions on the part of her friend ; that she assures him that she will only casually glance at him ; that she protests that '' no single syllable shall shock thine ear,'' and finally confesses, that

> '' My wish in others but gave birth to strife ;
> Thou hast not granted it, but oh! as yet
> Thou hast not said me nay, oh my sweet life!''

I must do the Marquis the justice to admit, that he declaimed these verses well, sighed at full length in repeating them, and groaned while Hyacinth continued to babble the verses after him, not omitting to interweave with them his own original chatter. He honored the odes with the most attention. '' There's a heap more to be learned,'' quoth he, '' from this sort of poetry than from your sonnets and gazelles ; for in the odes the feet are set down all fair and square, and a man can count up every poem nice and easy. Every poet ought to do in his hardest poetry-verses like Count Platen — that is, set it down with the feet up, and say to folks, ' See here ! I'm an honorable man, one of the kind that don't cheat. The straight and crooked marks which I put before every poem are what you may call the *counter-feet* of it, and you may reckon up for yourself the trouble it all cost me. In fact, they're a kind of yardstick for every poem ; take it and measure 'em with it, and if you find I cheat you out of a single syllable, why then call me a d——d rascal — that's all !' But then the public may be taken in just by the honorable face he puts on it. When the feet are all set down so honest-looking and plain, the reader'll say, ' Well, I'm not going to be one of your suspicious sort ; what's the use of counting after the man. I daresay it's all right ; I ain't a-going to do it !' And he *don't* do it — and gets cheated. And who can always count 'em up ? Now we're in Italy, and I've got time to write the feet on the ground with chalk, and collationate every ode. But in Hamburg, where I've my business to attend to, I've no time for it, and must take Count Platen without calling him to account, just as a man takes the bags of money from the treasury with the number of the dollars they hold, written on 'em. They go about, sealed up, from one man to another, everybody takes it for granted that they hold as much as the number says ; and yet it *has* happened that a man who didn't have much to do has opened one and counted the specie, and found it ran short a few dollars. And there may be just the same sort of swindling in poetry. Particularly do I mistrust when I think of bags of money. For my own brother-in-law has told me that in the House of Correction at Odensee they've got a fellow who had some sort of a situation in the Post Office, and who opened the specie-bags that went through his hands, and then sewed 'em up again and forwarded 'em. When one hears of such rascality, he loses his trust in fellow mortals, and gets to be a mistrustful man. There's ever so much rascality in this world, and I suppose it's the same in the poetry business as in any other."

" Honesty," continued Hyacinth, while the Marquis declaimed

on, all absorbed in feeling and without attending to us,—" Honesty, Doctor, is the correct thing, and a man who isn't honest I consider a scamp, and when I consider a man as a scamp, I'll buy nothing from him, read nothing of his—in short, devil the bit of business of any sort will I do with him. I'm a man, Doctor, who don't set myself up on anything, but if there's anything I would set myself up on, it would be on doing the correct thing. If you've no objection, I'd like to tell you of a noble trait in my character, and you'll be astonished at it. I tell you you'll be astonished as sure as I'm an honorable man. There's a man lives in the Spear Place in Hamburg, and he's a greengrocer, and his name's Blocky—that is to say, I say that his name's Blocky, because we're good friends, for his real name is Block. And his wife of course is Madam Block, and she never could bear that her husband should buy lottery tickets of me, and when he did, I didn't dare to go to his house with 'em. So he used to tell me in the street, ' I want this or that number, and here's the money, Hirsch!' And I'd say, ' All right, Blocky!' And when I got home, I used to lay the number he'd taken apart for him under cover, and write on it in German hand, ' On account of Herr Christian Hinrich Block.' And now just listen and be astonished. It was a fine spring day, and the trees round the Exchange were all green, and the zephyr airs were nice, and the sun shone in the heaven, and I stood by the Bank of Hamburg. And then Blocky—my Blocky, you know—came walking along with fat Mrs. Blocky on his arm, and was the first to speak to me, and spoke of the Lord's splendid spring, and made some patriotic remarks on the town guard, and asked me how business was, and I told him that a little while before there'd been a chap in the pillory, and so as we talked he told me that the night before he'd dreamed that number 1538 had drawn the grand prize ; and just at that instant, while Madam Block was looking at the statutes of the Emperors before the town hall, he put thirteen louis-d'ors, full weight, into my hand. Lord! it seems to me that I can feel them now ; and before Madam could turn around I said, ' All right, Blocky!' and went away. And I went at once, without stopping, to the head office, and got number 1538, and covered it up as soon as

I was home, and wrote on the cover, ' On account of Herr Christian Hinrich Block.' And what did the Lord do? Fourteen days later, to try my honesty, he let number 1538 turn up a prize of fifty thousand marks. And what did Hirsch then do, the same Hirsch who now stands before you? This Hirsch put on a clean white shirt and a clean white cravat, and took a hackney-coach and went to the head office, and drew his fifty thousand marks and rode with 'em to the Spear Place. And when Blocky saw me he says, ' Hirsch, what are you dressed up so fine for today?' I, however, didn't answer a word, but set a great astonishing bag of gold on the table, and said, right cheerful and jolly, ' Herr Christian Hinrich Block! number 1538, which you were so kind as to order of me, has been so lucky as to draw fifty thousand marks. I have the honor to present you that same money in this bag, and take the liberty of begging a receipt for the amount.' When Blocky heard *that*, he began to cry ; when Madame Block heard it, *she* cried ; the fat red servant girl cried ; the crooked shop boy cried ; the children cried ; and I, a man of feelings as I am, couldn't cry at all, but fainted dead away, and it wasn't till I came to that the tears came into my eyes like a river, and I cried for three hours!"

The voice of the little man quivered as he told this story, and with an air of joy he drew from his pocket the packet I have already spoken of, unrolled the faded rose silk, and showed me the document in which Herr Christian Hinrich Block acknowledged the receipt of fifty thousand marks. " When I die," said Hyacinth with a tear in his eye, " this receipt must be buried with me, and on the judgment-day, when I must give an account of all my deeds, then I will go with this receipt in my hand before the throne of the Lord, and when my evil angel has read off the list of all the evil deeds I've been guilty of, and my good angel has read off in turn all my good deeds, I'll say, calm and easy, ' Be quiet! all I want to know is if this receipt is correct? — is that the handwriting of Herr Christian Hinrich Block?' Then a little angel will come flying up, and he'll say that he knows Block's hand perfectly well, and he'll tell the whole story of the honorable business I carried through. And the Creator of Eternity, the Almighty, who knows all things will remember it all, and he will praise me before the sun, moon, and stars, and reckon up at once in his head that if the value of my evil deeds be subtracted from fifty thousand marks, that there'll remain a balance to my account, and he'll say, ' Hirsch, you are appointed an angel of the first class, and may wear wings with white and red feathers.' "

CHAPTER XI

WHO IS, THEN, THE COUNT PLATEN, WHOM WE HAVE IN THE PRE-VIOUS chapter learned to know as a poet and warm friend? Ah! dear reader, I have been reading that very question for a long time in your countenance, and it is with a trembling heart that I set about answering it. The worst thing with German authors is, that whenever they show up a fool, they must beforehand set him forth in full by means of wearisome descriptions of character and personal peculiarities, firstly, that the reader may know of his existence, and secondly, that they may understand how, where, and when the lash cuts—before or behind. It was a different matter with the ancients, and it is still different with some modern nations, for instance, the English and French, who have a public life, and in consequence, public characters. We Germans, on the contrary, though we have a foolish enough public, have very few fools distinguished enough to be generally recognized as ' characters,' when used in prose or in verse. The few men of this mold whom we possess are perfectly justifiable in giving themselves airs of importance. They are of inestimable value, and are entitled to the highest claim to our consideration. For instance, the Herr Privy Counselor Schmaltz, professor at the University of Berlin, is a man worth his weight in gold ; a humorous writer could never do without him, and he himself is so perfectly conscious of his personal importance and needfulness that he loses no opportunity to supply such writers with material for satire. For this purpose, therefore, he labors night and day, either as statesman, civil villain, or civilian, deacon, anti-Hegelian, and patriot, to make himself as ridiculous as

408

possible, and thus advance that literature for which he sacrifices himself. And therefore the German universities deserve great praise, since they supply us with more fools than any other trade unions, especially Göttingen, which I have never failed to appreciate, so far as this point is concerned. This is the true and secret reason why I have always boldly advocated the maintenance of the universities, even while preaching freedom of exercising a trade, and recommending the abolition of the guilds. When fools of note are thus wanting, the world cannot be too grateful to me should I bring out a few new ones and render them available. For the advancement of literature, I will therefore now speak more in detail of Count August von Platen Hallermunde. I will so arrange it that he may be made well enough known to be useful, and to a certain degree celebrated, giving him, as it were, a literary fattening, as the Iroquois are said to do with prisoners who are subsequently devoured at their festivals. In this business I shall act with all due honor and courtesy, as a good citizen should, touching on the material or so-called personal interests only so far as they are needed to throw light upon spiritual phenomena, always giving the point of view from which I regarded him, and not unfrequently exhibiting the spectacles wherewith I took my peep.

The point of view from which I first beheld Count Platen was Munich, the scene of those efforts which rendered him very celebrated among his acquaintances, and where he will unquestionably be immortal, so long as he lives. The spectacles with which I saw him belonged to certain inhabitants of the city, who, in their merry moments, occasionally indulged in merry remarks relative to his personal appearance. I have never seen him myself, and when I have a fancy to imagine him, I recall the droll rage with which my friend Doctor Lautenbacher attacked poetic folly in general, and particularly that of a certain Count Platen, who, with a wreath of laurel on his brow, stood — in the way of passers-by — in an attitude of poetic inspiration on the public promenade at Erlangen, staring, with spectacled nose, up at heaven. Others have spoken better of the poor Count, lamenting only his straitened circumstances, which, as he was very ambitious of honor, compelled him to extraordinary industry, and thus at least gave him distinction as a poet. Such stories, of course, moved my pity to a certain extent, although I found that his failures in the art of pleasing were very natural.

In vain the poor Count declared that he was destined to become the greatest of poets ; that the shadow of the laurel was already visible on his brow, and that he could also make others immortal in poems which would live for ever. Alas ! even this celebrity was not acceptable to any one, nor was it, in fact, a thing to be particularly desired. So far as I am concerned, dear reader, I am not so malicious as you think ; I pity the poor Count, and when others mock him, I doubt whether he has ever practically revenged himself on the hated " custom " spoken of, although in his songs he sighs for such revenge ; no, I rather believe in the repulsive afflictions, injurious disregard, and rejections of which he sings so plaintively. I believe, in fact, that he acted towards morality in a far more laudable manner than he was desirous of doing, and it is possible that he can boast, with General Tilly, " I was never intoxicated, never touched a woman, and never lost a battle." It was, beyond question, for this that the poet says of himself—

" Thou art a sober and a modest youth."

The poor youth, or rather the poor old youth, for he had several lustrums behind him, once squatted, unless I err, at the University of Erlangen, where some sort of occupation had been allotted him, but as this was insufficient for his soaring spirit, since with his increasing lustrums he lusted with greater lustiness for illustrious luster, and as he day by day felt himself more inspired with his future glory, he gave up his business, being determined to live by writing, by gifts from heaven whenever they might turn up, and by similar earnings. For the county of the Count is unfortunately situated in the moon, and, owing to the bad state of the roads which communicate with Bavaria, will not (according to Gruithuisen's calculation) be attainable until 20,000 years have elapsed, after which time, when that planet approaches the earth, he will be able to draw from it his enormous revenues.

At an earlier period Don Platen de Colibrados Hallermunde had published by Brockhaus in Leipzig a collection of poems with the title of *Lyrical Leaves, No. I.*, which of course met with no success, although he assured us in the preface that the Seven Wise Men had lavished their praise on the author. At a later date he wrote, in Tieck's style, several dramatic legends and stories, which also had the fortune to remain hidden from the ignorant multitude, and were only read by the Seven Wise Men. In order to get a few more readers, the Count applied himself to controversy, and wrote a satire against eminent writers, especially against Müllner, who was already universally hated and morally overthrown, so that the Count came just in the nick of time to give the dead Court Counselor Oerindur another *coup de grâce* ; not gracefully, however, in the head, but very awkwardly, in the Falstaffian manner, in the thigh. A dislike of Müllner inspired every noble heart ; the attack of the Count " took," and " The Mysterious and Terrible Fork " met here and there with a kindly reception ; not from the public at large, but among literati and the regular school-people ; the latter being pleased with the satire because it was not an imitation of the romantic Tieck, but of the classic Aristophanes.

I believe that it was about this time that the Count traveled to Italy, no longer entertaining a doubt but that he would be able to live by his poetry. Cotta had indeed paid him the common prosaic honor to pay him money for his bill for poetry ; for Poetry, the nobly-born, never has any money herself, and when in difficulties always goes to Cotta. Now the Count versified day and night ; he no longer copied the patterns of Tieck and of Aristophanes, but imitated first Goethe in ballads, then Horace in odes, then Petrarch in sonnets, then Hafiz in Persian ghazels ; in short, he gave us, such as it was, a selection of flowers of the best poets, and with it his own lyrical leaves, under the title of " Poems of Count Platen, etc."

No one in Germany is so indulgent as I towards poetic productions, and I am willing from my very soul that a poor devil like Platen should enjoy his bit of celebrity which he has so bitterly earned by the sweat of his brow ; and no one is more willing to praise his industry, his efforts and his poetry, or to recognize his metrical merits. My own efforts enable me better than another to appreciate those merits. The bitter labor, the indescribable perseverance, the chattering of teeth through weary winter nights, the restrained anger at a fruitless straining for effect, is far more apparent to one of us than to the ordinary reader who supposes that the smoothness, neatness, and polish of the Count's verses are the effect of ease, and who thanklessly enjoys himself over the glittering play of words, just as spectators at the feats of circus *artistes*, when they behold the latter dancing on ropes, hopping among eggs, or standing on their heads, never reflect that the poor fellows have acquired this pliancy of limb and poetry of motion only by long years of hard work and bitter hunger. I, who have never worried myself so much in poetry, and who have always exercised it in company with good eating, esteem poor Platen all the more, since his experiences have been of such a sour and sober nature ; I will boast for him that no literary rope-dancer in Europe can balance so well as he on slack ghazels, that no one can perform so well as he such an egg-dance as

$$\smile \smile \text{——} \smile \smile \smile \text{————}$$

$$\smile \smile \text{——————} \smile \smile \smile \smile, \text{ etc.}$$

and that no one can stand so well on his head. If the Muses are not complaisant to him, he at least has the genius of our language in his power, or knows how to clothe it with power. As for winning the willing love of the genius, it is beyond his power ; he must perseveringly run after this youth as after others, and his utmost ability is to catch the outward form, which, despite its beautiful contour, never speaks to our soul. Never did the deep tones of Nature, as we find them in popular song among children and other true poets, burst from the soul of Platen, or bloom forth like an apocalypse from it, and the desperate effort which he is obliged to make in order to say something he calls a " great deed in words," for so utterly unfamiliar is he with the true spirit of poetry, that he does not know that the successful mastery of words can only be a great deed for the rhetorician ; for the true poet it should be a natural occurrence. Unlike the true poet, language was never yet his master. On the contrary, he has become master of it, playing on it as a virtuoso plays on an instrument. The more he advanced in this mechanical facility, the higher opinion did he form of his own powers of performance. He learned how to play in every manner and metre ; he versified even the most difficult passages, often poetising, so to speak, on the G string, and was vexed when the public did not applaud. Like all *virtuosi* who have developed this sort of single-string talent, he only exerted himself for applause, regarding with anger the celebrity of others. He envied his colleagues all that they gained, as, for instance, when he fired five-act pasquinades at Clauren at a time when he could not attract more than a mere poetic squib at himself ; he laid a strong hand on every review in which others were praised, and cried without ceasing, " I am not sufficiently praised, I am not sufficiently praised, for I am the poet, the poet of poets," etc. Such a hunger and thirst for praise and for alms was never yet shown by a true poet — by Klopstock or by Goethe, to whose companionship Count Platen has appointed himself, although any one can see that he justly forms a triumvirate only with Aug. Wilhelm von Schlegel, and perhaps with Ramler. " The great Ramler," as he was called in his own time, when he, without a laurel crown, it is true, but with all the greater cue and hair net, with his eyes raised to heaven, and with a canvas umbrella under his arm, wandered scanning about in the Berlin *Thiergarten*, believed himself to be the representative of poetry on earth. His verses were the most perfect in the German language, and his adorers, among whom even a Lessing went astray, believed that poetry could go no further. Such, at a late date, was almost the case with Aug. Wilhelm von Schlegel, whose poetical insufficiency became manifest as the language was more fully developed, so that many who once looked upon the singer of Arion as an Arion himself, now regard him merely as a schoolmaster of some ability. But whether Count Platen is as yet qualified to laugh at the otherwise really great Schlegel, as the latter once laughed at Ramler, I cannot take it on me to say. But this I do know, that they are all three on a par in poetry, and though Count Platen in his ghazels displays ever so exquisitely his juggling arts of balance, though he executes his egg-dance ever so admirably, and if in his plays even stands on his head, he is not for all that a poet. Severe critics, who wear first-class spectacles, add their voice to this verdict, or express themselves with more laconic significance.

Everywhere in Platen's poems we see the ostrich, which only hides its head, the vain, weak bird, which has the most beautiful plumage, and yet cannot fly ; and which, ever quarrelsome, stumbles along over the polemic sandy desert of literature. With his fine feathers, without the power to soar, with his fine verse, without poetic flight, he is the very opposite to that eagle of song who, with less brilliant wings, still rises to the sun. I must return to my old refrain ; Count Platen is no poet.

Two things are required of every poet : that there should be natural tones in his lyric poems, and characters in his epic or dramatic productions. If he cannot legitimately establish himself on these points, he must lose his title as poet, although all his other family papers and diplomas of nobility are in perfect order. I have no doubt that the last is the case with Count Platen, and I am convinced that he would only deign a smile of pitying sorrow to any one who should attempt to cast doubt on his title as Count. But dare to so much as level a couplet at his poetic title, and he will at once set himself down and publish five-act satires against you. For the more dubious and uncertain their title to an honor may be, the more earnestly do men hold to it. Perhaps Count Platen would have been a poet had he lived in another age, and had he been, moreover, somebody else. The want of natural chords in the poems of the Count is the more touching from the fact that he lives in an age when he dare not so much as name his real feelings, when the current morality which is so directly opposed to his love, even forbids him to openly express his sorrows, and when he must anxiously and painfully disguise every sentiment for fear of offending by so much as a single syllable the ear of the public as well as that of the " disdainful and beautiful one." This constant fear suppresses every natural chord in him — it condemns him to metrically labor away at the feelings of other poets which have already passed muster as acceptable, and which must of necessity be used to cloak his own conceptions. It may be that wrong is done him when those who understand such unfortunate situations assert that Count Platen is desirous of showing himself as Count in poetry and of holding in it to his nobility, and that he consequently only expresses the feelings of such well known families as have their sixty-four descents. Had he lived in the days of the Roman Pythagoras, it may be that he would have expressed these feelings more openly and perhaps have passed for a true poet. Then natural chords at least would not have been missed in his lyric poems — albeit the want of characters in his dramas must ever have remained, at least until he changed his physical nature and became an altogether different man. The forms of which I speak are those independent creatures which spring perfect and fully armed from the creative power of the poet, as Pallas Athene sprang from the head of Kronion — living dream-forms whose mystic birth stands, far more than is imagined, in active relation with the mental and moral nature of the poet — a spiritual production denied to the one who, a mere fruitless creature, vanishes gazelle-like in his windy weakness.

These are, however, after all, only the private opinions of a poet, and their importance depends on the degree of credit which is accorded them. But I cannot avoid mentioning that Count Platen has often assured the public that in days as yet to come he will compose the most remarkable poetry, of which no one has as yet even a presentiment ; yes, and that he will publish Iliads and Odysseys and classic tragedies, and similar immortally colossal poems, after he has toiled so and so many lustrums. Reader, you have perhaps read some of these outpourings of self-consciousness in his laboriously filed verses, and the promise of such a glorious future was probably the pleasanter to you when the Count at the same time represented all the contemporary German poets, with the exception of the aged Goethe, as a set of nasty wretches, who only stood in his way on the path to immortality, and who were so devoid of shame as to pluck the laurels and the praise which of right belonged to him alone.

I will pass over what I heard in Munich on this theme ; but for the sake of chronology I must mention that it was at this time that the King of Bavaria announced his intention of bestowing on some German poet a pension without any attendant official duties ; an unusual example, which might have the happiest result on the entire literature of Germany. I was told——

But I will not quit my theme. I spoke of the vain boasting of Count Platen, who continually cried, " I am the poet, the poet of poets! I shall yet write Iliads and Odysseys," etc., etc. I know not what the public thinks of such boasting, but I know right well what a poet thinks of them — that is to say, a true poet, who has felt the ashamed sweetness and the secret trembling of poetry, and who, like a happy page who enjoys the secret favors of a princess, most assuredly will not boast of them in the public market place.

Not unfrequently has the Count for thus puffing himself up been soundly taken down, yet, like Falstaff, he always knew how to excuse himself. He has for such excuses a useful talent, which is peculiarly his own, and one deserving special mention. It lies in this, that Count Platen, who is familiar with every failing in his own breast, is also quick at recognizing the faintest trace of kindred faults in any great man, and is not less prompt, on the strength of this elective affinity of vice, to institute a comparison between the other and himself. Thus, for instance, having observed that Shakespeare's sonnets have certain defects of his own, praises Shakespeare, compares himself with him — and that is all which he has to say of him. One might negatively write an apology for Count Platen, and assert that he has not as yet developed this or that failing because he has not as yet compared himself with this or that great man who has been reputed guilty of them. Most genial, however, and amazing did he show himself in the choice of one in whose life he discovered speeches void of modesty, and by whose example he fain would lend a color to his own boasting. In fact, the words of this man as establishing such a point have not been cited, for it was none other than Jesus Christ himself, who has hitherto always been taken for the pattern of meekness and humility. Christ

416

once boasted! the most humble of mankind, and the more humble since he was the divinest? Yes, what has escaped all theologians was discovered by Count Platen, for he insinuates that Christ, when he stood before Pilate, was not humble nor did he answer humbly, for when the latter asked him, " Art thou the king of the Jews?" he answered, " Thou sayest it." And so, says he, the Count Platen, " I am he ; I am the poet!" What the hate of one who scorned Christ never as yet effected was brought to pass by the exegesis of self-enamored vanity.

As we know what we should think when any one thus cries out without intermission, " I am the poet!" so we also understand the affinity which it has to the immensely remarkable poems which the Count, when he has attained due ripeness, intends to write, and which are to surpass in such an unheard-of manner all his previous performances. We know well enough that the later works of a true poet are no more superior to his first than the later children to which a woman gives birth are superior to her first-born, although the bearing them is easier. The lioness does not first bring forth a puppy, then a hare, then a hound, and finally a lion. Madame Goethe, at her first birth, brought forth her young lion, and he in turn, at the first throw, gave us his lion of Berlichingen. Even so did Schiller bring forth his " Robbers," whose claws at once showed the lion breed. At a later date came the polish and refinement and finish in the " Natural Daughter " and the " Bride of Messina." It was not thus with Count Platen, who began with anxious and elaborate art, and of whom the poet sings—

> " Thou who from naught so lightly didst advance,
> With thy smooth-licked and lacquered countenance,
> Like some toy-puppet neatly carved from cork."

Yet should I speak out the very thought of my soul, I would confess that I by no means regard Count Platen as the extraordinary fool which one would take him to be from his boasting and incessant burning of incense before his own shrine. A little folly, it is well known, always accompanies poetry ; but it would be terrible if Nature should burden a single man with such an incredible quantity of folly as would suffice for a hundred poets, and give him therewith such an insignificant dose of poetry. I have reason to suspect that the Count does not believe in his own boasting, and that he, poverty-stricken in life as in literature, is compelled in literature as in life by the needs of the instant to be his own self-praising pimp. Hence the phenomena of which one might say that they have rather a psychological than an æsthetic interest ; hence the coexistence of the most lamenting paralysis of the soul and affected excess of pride ; hence the talking down of approaching death and the overemphasis of immortality ; hence the high flashing beggarly pride, and the languishing slavish submissiveness ; hence the unceasing cry that " Cotta lets him starve," and again that " Cotta lets him starve," hence the paroxysms of Catholicism, etc., etc.

Whether the Count is in earnest with all his Catholicism is to me a matter of doubt. Nor do I know whether he has become specially Catholic, like certain of his high-born friends. That he intended to do so first came to my knowledge from the newspapers, wherein it was even stated that Count Platen was about to become a monk and retire to a monastery. Of course, when this news was heard in Munich, the pious chimes rang loudly in the hearts of his friends. His poems were praised with *Kyrie Eleison* and *Hallelujah* in the clerical papers. And quite as little was I astonished when the day before my departure for Italy I learned from my friend, Doctor Kolb, that Count Platen was very inimically disposed towards me, and that he had already prepared my utter annihilation in a comedy, entitled " King Œdipus," which in Augsburg had got into the hands of certain princes and counts, whose names I have either forgotten or shall forget. Others also told me that Count Platen hated me, assuming the position of an enemy towards me ; and I would much prefer having it reported that Count Platen hated me to my face, than that he loved me behind my back. As for the holy men whose holy hatred burst out at the same time against me, and which was inspired, not only by my anti-celibacy poems, but also by the " Political Annals " which I then published, it is evident enough that I could only gain when it became evident enough that I was not of their party. And when I here intimate that nothing good is said of them, it does not follow that I speak evil of them. I am even of the opinion that they, purely out of love for what is good, seek to weaken the words of the Evil One by pious deception and by slander pleasing to the Lord. Those good people who, in Munich, presented themselves publicly as a congregation, have been foolishly honored with the title of Jesuits. They are in faith no Jesuits, or they would have seen, for example, that of all men, I — one of the bad — least understand the literary alchemic art, by which, as in a mental mint, I strike ducats out of my enemies, and that in such a manner that I retain the ducats while my foes get the blows. They would have seen, too, that such blows, with their impressions, lose nothing of their value, even when the name of the mint-master is worn away, and that a wretched criminal does not feel the lash the less severely, though the executioner who lays it on be declared dishonorable. But — and this is the chief point — they would have seen that a slight prepossession for the anti-aristocratic Voss, and a few merry vergings towards jokes on the Virgin Mary, for which they pelted me with filth and stupidity, did not proceed from any anti-Catholic zeal. In truth they are no Jesuits, but only mixtures of filth and of stupidity, whom I am no more capable of hating, than I do a manure wagon and the oxen which draw it, and who, with all their efforts, only reach the very opposite of what they intended, and can only bring me to this point, that I show them how Protestant I am ; that I exercise my good Protestant right to its fullest extent, and swing around the good Protestant battle-axe with a right good will. To win over the multitude, they may have the old women's tales of my unbelief repeated by their poet laureate as much as they please, but by the well-known blows they shall recognize the fellow-believer with Luther, Lessing, and Voss. Of course I could not swing the old axe with the earnestness of these heroes, for I burst into laughter at the sight of such enemies, and I have a bit of the Eulenspiegel nature in me, and love a seasoning of jokes ; and yet I would not rap those manure oxen less soundly although I beforehand wreathe my axe with smiling flowers.

But I will not wander from my subject. I believe that it was about the time in question that the King of Bavaria, from the motives alluded to, gave to Count Platen an annual pension of six hundred florins, and that, indeed, not from the public treasury, but from his own royal private purse, this being requested by the Count as an especial favor. I mention this circumstance, trifling as it seems (since it characterises the caste of the Count), for the benefit of the investigator into the secrets of Nature, and who perhaps studies the aristocracy. Everything is of importance to science, and let him who would reproach me for devoting myself too seriously to Count Platen go to Paris, and see with what care the accurate, exquisite Cuvier, in his lectures, describes the filthiest insect even to the minutest particulars. I even regret that I cannot more accurately determine the date of those six hundred and forty florins ; but this much I know, that it was subsequent to the com-position of " King Œdipus," and that the play would not have been so biting if its author had had something more to bite.

It was in North Germany, where I was suddenly called by the death of my father, that I first received the monstrous creation which had finally crept from the great egg over which our beauti-fully-plumed ostrich had so long brooded, and which had been greeted long in advance by the night-owls of the congregation with pious croaking, and by the noble peacocks with joyful spreading of plumes. It was to be at least a destroying basilisk. Dear reader, do you know what the legend of the basilisk is ? People say that when a male bird lays an egg after the manner of the female, that a poisonous creature is hatched from it, whose breath poisons the air, and which can only be destroyed by holding a mirror before it, in which case it dies from terror at its own ugliness.

Sacred sorrows, which I would not profane, first permitted me, two months later, when visiting the watering place Heligoland, to read " King Œdipus," and there, raised to a lofty state of mind by the continual aspect of the great, bold sea, the petty, narrow thoughts, and the literary botching of the high-born writer were to me visible enough. I saw him at length in that master-work exactly as he is, with all his blooming decay, all his copiousness of

420

want of spirit, all his vain imaginings without imagination,—a writer, forced without force, piqued without being *piquant*, a dry, watery soul, a dismal debauchee. This troubadour of misery, weakened in body and in mind, sought to imitate the most powerful, the richest in fancy, and most brilliant poets of the young Grecian world! Nothing is really more repulsive than this cramped impotence, which would fain puff itself up into the likeness of bold strength, these painfully-collected invectives, foul with the moldiness of ancient spite, and this anxious imitation of delirious rapture, trembling throughout at syllables and trifles. As a matter of fact, there is nowhere in the Count's work the trace of a profound idea of world-annihilation such as lies darkling at the base of every Aristophanic comedy, and from which the latter shoots like a fantastic ironic magic tree, rich in the blooming garniture of flowers of thought, bearing amid its branches nests of singing nightingales and capering apes. Such an idea, with the death jubilation and the fireworks of destruction which it involves, cannot, of course, be expected from the poor Count. The central point, the first and last idea, ground, and aim of his so-called comedy, consists, as in the " Mysterious and Terrible Fork," of petty literary managing ; the poor Count indeed could only imitate a few of the external traits of Aristophanes—the dainty verses and the vulgar words. I say vulgar words, not wishing to use any vulgar expression myself. Like a brawling woman, he casts whole flower-pots of abuse on the heads of the German poets. I heartily forgive the Count his spite, but he should have guarded against a few oversights. But the indelicate wretch! he tells the public without reserve that we poets in North Germany have all " the itch, giving us cause, alas! to use a salve, in filthy scent peculiarly rich." The rhyme is good ; but he handles Immermann the most rudely. He did not even spare Houwald, that good soul, soft-hearted as a maiden ; ah! perhaps it is on account of this gentle woman-likeness that a Platen hates him. Müllner, whom he, as he says, " long since by real wit laid low, deprived of force," rises again like a dead man from the grave. Child and child's child are not spared in their rights. Raupach is a Jew—

"The small Jew canker-worm,
Who now as Raupach holds so high his nose."

" Who scrawls tragedy in sickly, drunken headaches." Far worse
does it fare with the " Baptized Heine." Yes, yes, reader, you are
not mistaken ; it is I of whom he speaks, and in " King Œdipus "
you may read how I am a real Jew ; how I, after writing love-songs
for a few hours, sit me down and circumcise ducats ; how I on the
Sabbath higgle and trade like some long-bearded Moses and sing
the Talmud ; how I on Passover eve slay a Christian youth, and out
of malice choose some unfortunate writer for the purpose. No,
dear reader, I will not tell you lies, such admirably painted pictures
are not to be found in " King Œdipus," and the fact that they are
not there is the very thing which I blame. Count Platen has sometimes the best subjects and does not know how to treat them. If
he had only been gifted with a little more imagination, he would
have shown me up at least as a secret pawnbroker, and what comic
scenes he might then have sketched ! It really vexes me when I see
how the poor Count suffers every opportunity to be witty to escape
him. How gloriously he could have represented Raupach as a
tragedy Rothschild, from whom the royal theaters get their loans !
By slightly modifying the plot of the fable, he might have made
far better use of Œdipus himself, the hero of his play. Again, I do
not find it politic in the Count that he assures us in his comedies
that he has " real wit." Or is he working to bring about the startling
and unprecedented effect as a *coup de theâtre* of making the public
continually expect wit, which after all will not appear ? Or does
he wish to encourage the public to look for the real secret wit in
the play, the whole affair being a game at blind-man's buff, in
which the Platenic wit is so shrewd as not to suffer itself to be
caught ? It is probably for this reason that the public, which is
accustomed to laugh at comedies, is so solemn and sad over the
Platen pieces ; in vain it hunts for the hidden wit and cannot find
it ; in vain the hidden wit squeaks out " Here I am," and again
more clearly, " Here I am, here I am indeed ! " — all is of no avail,
the public is dumb, and makes a solemn face. But I, who know
where the joke really lies, have laughed from my heart as I detected

the meaning of " the Count-like imperious poet, who veils himself in an aristocratic nimbus, who boasts that every breath which passes his teeth is a crushing to fragments," and who says to all the German poets—

> "Yes, like to Nero, I would ye had but one head,
>   That by one blow of wit I might decapitate it."

The verse is incorrect. But the hidden joke consists in this, that the Count really wishes that we were all out and out Neros, and he, on the contrary, our single dear friend, Pythagoras.

Perhaps I will, for the benefit of the Count, yet praise many a hidden jest of his up into notice ; but since he in his "King Œdipus" has touched me on my tenderest point—for what can be dearer to me than my Christianity?—it should not be blamed in me if I, yielding to human weakness, honor the Œdipus, this " great deed in words," less fervently than the earlier works of its composer.

Meanwhile, true merit never misses its reward, and the author of the Œdipus will prove to be no exception to the rule, though he has here, as everywhere, yielded entirely to the interest of his noble and spiritual liegemen. Ay, there is a very old tradition among the races of the East and of the West, that every good or bad deed has its direct consequences for the doer. And the day will come when they will come—get ready, I beg you, reader, for a flourish of the pathetic and the terrible combined—the day will come when they will rise from Tartarus, " the Eumenides," the terrible daughters of Night. By the Styx!—and by this oath we gods never swore falsely—the day will come when they will appear, the gloomy, primævally just sisters, and they will appear with countenances serpent-locked and glowing with rage, with the same scourges of snakes with which they once scourged Orestes, the unnatural sinner, who murdered his mother, the Tyndaridean Clytæmnestra. It may be that even now the Count hears the serpents' hiss ; I beg you, reader, just at this instant to think of the Wolf's Ravine and the Samiel music ; perhaps even now the secret shudder of the sinner seizes on the Count, heaven grows dark, night birds cry, distant thunders roll, lightning flashes, there is a smell of burning

423

rosin — woe! woe! the illustrious ancestors rise from their graves, they cry three and four times " Woe! woe!" over their wretched descendant, they adjure him to don their breeches of iron mail to protect himself from the terrible lashes — for the Eumenides intend slashing him with them — the serpents of the scourge will ironically solace themselves with him, and like lascivious King Rodrigo, when he was shut in the Tower of Serpents, the poor Count will at last whimper and wail—

> "Ah! they're biting ; ah! they're biting
> That with which I chiefly sinned!"

Be not alarmed, dear reader, 'tis all a joke! These terrible Eumenides are nothing but a merry comedy, which I, after a few lustrums, intend writing under this title, and the tragic verses which just now frightened you so much, are to be found in the jolliest book in the world, in " Don Quixote de la Mancha," where an old respectable lady in waiting recites them before all the court. I see that you're smiling again. Let us take leave of each other merry and laughing! If this last chapter is tiresome, it is owing to the subject ; besides, it was written rather for profit than for pleasure, and if I have succeeded in making a new fool fit for use in literature, the Fatherland owes me thanks. I have made a field capable of cultivation, on which more gifted authors will sow and harvest. The modest consciousness of this merit is my best reward. To such kings as are desirous of presenting me, over and above this, with snuff boxes for my deserts, I would remark that the book firm of " Hoffmann & Campe," in Hamburg, are authorized to receive anything of the sort on my account.

English Fragments

. . . . THE SALLOW MAN STOOD NEAR ME ON THE DECK, AS I gazed on the green shores of the Thames, while in every corner of my soul the nightingales awoke to life. "Land of Freedom!" I cried, "I greet thee! Hail to thee, Freedom, young sun of the renewed world! Those older suns, Love and Faith, are withered and cold, and can no longer light nor warm us. The ancient myrtle woods, which were once all too full, are now deserted, and only timid turtle-doves nestle amid the soft thickets. The old cathedrals, once piled in towering height by an arrogantly pious race, which fain would force its faith into heaven, are brittle, and their gods have ceased to believe in themselves. Those divinities are worn out, and our age lacks the imagination to shape new. Every power of the human breast now tends to a love of Liberty, and Liberty is, perhaps, the religion of the modern age. And it is a religion not preached to the rich, but to the poor, and it has in like manner its evangelists, its martyrs, and its Iscariots!"

"Young enthusiast," said the sallow man, "you will not find what you seek. You may be right in believing that Liberty is a new religion which will spread itself over all the world. But as every race of old, when it received Christianity, did so according to its requirements and its peculiar character, so, at present, every country adopts from the new religion of liberty only that which is in accordance with its local needs and national character.

"The English are a domestic race, living a limited, peaceable family life, and the Englishman seeks in the circle of those connected with and pertaining to him that easy state of mind which is denied to him through his innate social incapacity. The Englishman is, therefore, contented with that liberty which secures his most personal rights and guards his body, his property, and his conjugal relations, his religion, and even his whims, in the most unconditional manner. No one is freer in his home than an Englishman, and, to use a celebrated expression, he is king and bishop between his four stakes ; and there is much truth in the common saying, ' My house is my castle.'

" If the Englishman has the greatest need of personal freedom, the Frenchman, in case of need, can dispense with it, if we only grant him that portion of universal liberty known as equality. The French are not a domestic but a social race ; they do not like to sit together in silence, which they call *une conversation Anglaise ;* they run gossiping about from the *café* to the casino, and from the casino to the *salons ;* their light champagne-blood and inborn talent for company drives them to social life, whose first and last principle, yes, whose very soul is equality. The development of the social principle in France necessarily involved that of equality, and if the ground of the Revolution should be sought in the Budget, it is none the less true that its language and tone were drawn from those wits of low degree who lived in the *salons* of Paris, apparently on a footing of equality with the high *noblesse,* and who were now and then reminded, it may have been by a hardly perceptible, yet not on that account less aggravating, feudal smile, of the great and ignominious inequality which lay between them. And when the *canaille roturière* took the liberty of beheading that high nobility, it was done less to inherit their property than their ancestry, and to introduce a noble equality in place of a vulgar inequality. And we are the better authorized to believe that this striving for equality was the main principle of the Revolution, since the French speedily found themselves so happy and contented under the dominion of their great Emperor, who, fully appreciating that they were not yet of age, kept all their *freedom* within the limits of his powerful guardianship, permitting them only the pleasure of a perfect and admirable equality.

" Far more patient than the Frenchman, the Englishman easily bears the glances of a privileged aristocracy, consoling himself with the reflection that he has a right by which it is rendered impossible to the others to disturb his personal comfort or his daily requirements. Nor does the aristocracy here make a show of its privileges as on the Continent. In the streets and in places of public resort in London, colored ribbons are only seen on women's bonnets, and gold and silver signs of distinction on the dresses of lackeys. Even that beautiful colored livery which indicates with us military rank is in England anything but a sign of honor, and as an actor after a play hastens to wash off the rouge, so an English officer hastens, when the hours of active duty are over, to strip off his red coat and again appear like a gentleman, in the plain garb of a gentleman. Only at the theaters of St. James are those decorations and costumes, which were raked from the rubble of the Middle Ages, of any avail. There we may see the ribbons of orders of nobility ; there the stars glitter, silk knee-breeches and satin trains rustle, golden spurs and old-fashioned French styles of expression clatter ; there the knight struts and the lady spreads herself. But what does a free Englishman care for the Court comedy of St. James, so long as it does not trouble him, and so long as no one interferes when he plays comedy in like manner in his own house, making his lackeys kneel before him, or plays with the garter of a pretty cook? '*Honni soit qui mal y pense!*'

" As for the Germans, they need neither freedom nor equality. They are a speculative race, ideologists, prophets, and after-thinkers, dreamers who only live in the past and in the future, and who have no present. Englishmen and Frenchmen have a *present* ; with them every day has its field of action, its opposing element, its history. The German has nothing for which to battle, and when he began to realize that there might be things worth striving for, his philosophizing wiseacres taught him to doubt the existence of such things. It cannot be denied that the Germans love liberty. But it is in a different manner from other people. The Englishman loves liberty as his lawful wife, and if he does not treat her with remarkable tenderness, he is still ready in case of need to defend her like a man, and woe to the red-coated rascal who forces his way to her bedroom — let him do so as a gallant or as a constable. The Frenchman loves liberty as his bride. He burns for her ; he is a flame ; he casts himself at her feet with the most extravagant protestations ; he will fight for her to the death ; he commits for her sake a thou-

427

sand follies. The German loves liberty as though she were his old grandmother."

Men are strange beings! We grumble in our Fatherland ; every stupid thing, every contrary trifle, vexes us there ; like boys, we are always longing to rush forth into the wide world ; and when we finally find ourselves out in the wide world, we find it a world too wide, and often yearn in secret for the narrow stupidities and contrarieties of home. Yes, we would fain be again in the old chamber, sitting behind the familiar stove, making for ourselves, as it were, a " cubby-house " near it, and nestling there, read the *German General Advertiser*. So it was with me in my journey to England. Scarcely had I lost sight of the German shore ere there awoke in me a curious after-love for the German night-caps and forest-like wigs which I had just left in discontent, and when the Fatherland faded from my eyes I found it again in my heart.

And, therefore, it may be that my voice quivered in a somewhat lower key as I replied to the sallow man—" Dear sir, do not scold the Germans! If they are dreamers, still many of them have dreamed such beautiful dreams that I would hardly incline to change them for the waking realities of our neighbors. Since we all sleep and dream, we can perhaps dispense with freedom ; for our tyrants also sleep, and only dream their tyranny. We only awoke once—when the Catholic Romans robbed us of our dream-freedom; then we acted and conquered, and laid us down again and dreamed. O sir! do not mock our dreamers, for now and then they speak, like somnambulists, wondrous things in sleep, and their words become the seeds of freedom. No one can foresee the turn which things may take. The splenetic Briton, weary of his wife, may put a halter round her neck and sell her in Smithfield. The flattering Frenchman may perhaps be untrue to his beloved bride and abandon her, and, singing, dance after the Court dames of his royal palace. But the German will never turn his old grandmother quite out of doors ; he will always find a place for her by his fireside, where she can tell his listening children her legends. Should Freedom ever—which God forbid—vanish from the entire world, a German dreamer would discover her again in his dreams."

uniform as that of their houses.

On the opposite side of the town, which they call the West End —" *the west end of the town* "— and where the more aristocratic and less occupied world lives, the uniformity spoken of is still more dominant ; yet here there are very long and very broad streets, where all the houses are large as palaces, though anything but remarkable as regards their exterior, unless we except the fact that in these, as in all the better class of houses in London, the windows of the first *étage* (or second story) are adorned with iron-barred balconies, and also on the *rez de chaussée* there is a black railing protecting the entrance to certain subterranean apartments. In this part of the city there are also great " squares," where rows of houses like those already described form a quadrangle, in whose center there is a garden, enclosed by an iron railing and containing some statue or other. In all of these places and streets the eye is never shocked by the dilapidated huts of misery. Everywhere we are stared down on by wealth and respectability, while crammed away in retired lanes and dark, damp alleys Poverty dwells with her rags and her tears.

The stranger who wanders through the great streets of London, and does not chance right into the regular quarters of the multitude, sees little or nothing of the fearful misery existing there. Only here and there at the mouth of some dark alley stands a ragged woman with a suckling babe at her weak breast, and begs with her eyes. Perhaps, if those eyes are still beautiful, we glance into them, and are shocked at the world of wretchedness visible within. The common beggars are old people, generally blacks, who stand at the corners of the streets cleaning pathways — a very necessary thing in muddy London — and ask for " coppers " in reward. It is in the dusky twilight that Poverty with her mates Vice and Crime glide forth from their lairs. They shun daylight the more anxiously since their wretchedness there contrasts more cruelly with the pride of wealth which glitters everywhere ; only Hunger sometimes drives them at noonday from their dens, and then they stand with silent, speaking eyes, staring beseechingly at the rich merchant who hurries along, busy and jingling gold, or at the lazy lord who, like a surfeited god, rides by on his high horse, casting now and then an aristocratically indifferent glance at the mob below, as though they were swarming ants, or rather a mass of baser beings, whose joys and sorrows have nothing in common with his feelings. Yes—for over the vulgar multitude which sticks fast to the soil soar, like beings of a higher nature, England's nobility, to whom their little island is only a temporary resting-place, Italy their summer garden, Paris their social saloon, and the whole world their inheritance. They sweep along, knowing nothing of sorrow or suffering, and their gold is a talisman which conjures into fulfilment their wildest wish.

Poor Poverty! how agonizing must thy hunger be, where others swell in scornful superfluity! And when some one casts with indifferent hand a crust into thy lap, how bitter must the tears be wherewith thou moistenest it! Thou poisonest thyself with thine own tears. Well art thou in the right when thou alliest thyself to Vice and Crime. Outlawed criminals often bear more humanity in their hearts than those cool, reproachless town burghers of virtue, in whose white hearts the power of evil, it is true, is quenched— but with it, too, the power of good. And even vice is not always vice. I have seen women on whose cheeks red vice was painted, and in whose hearts dwelt heavenly purity. I have seen women— I would that I saw them again!——

III.   THE ENGLISH

UNDER THE ARCHWAYS OF THE LONDON EXCHANGE EVERY NATION has its allotted place, and on high tablets we read the names of Russians, Spaniard, Swedes, Germans, Maltese, Jews, Hanseatics, Turks, etc. Now, however, you would seek them there in vain, for the men have been jostled away; where Spaniards once stood Dutchmen now stand, the citizens of Hanse Towns have elbowed out the Jews, Russians are now where Turks once were, Italians are on the ground formerly held by Frenchmen; even the Germans have advanced a little.

As in the London Exchange, so in the rest of the world the ancient tablets have remained, and men have been moved away while other people appear in their place, whose new heads agree very indifferently with the old inscriptions. The old stereotyped characteristics of races, as we find them in learned compendiums and ale-houses, are no longer profitable, and can only lead us into dreary errors. As we during the last ten years have observed a striking change in the character of our Western neighbors, just so has there been, since the continent was thrown open, a corresponding metamorphosis on the other side of the canal. Stiff, taciturn Englishmen go pilgrimlike in hordes to France, there to learn to speak and move their limbs ; and on returning we observe with amazement that their tongues are loosened, they no longer have two left hands, and are no longer contented with beef-steak and plum-puddings. I myself have seen such an Englishman, who in Tavistock Tavern asked for some sugar with his cauliflower — a heresy against the stern laws of the English *cuisine*, which nearly caused the waiter to fall flat on his back ; for, certainly, since the days of the Roman invasion, cauliflower was never cooked otherwise than by simply boiling in water, nor was it ever eaten with sweet seasoning. It was the self-same Englishman who, although I had never seen him before, sat down opposite to me and began to converse so genially in French that I could not for my life help telling him how delighted I was to meet, for once, an Englishman who was not reserved towards strangers ; whereupon he, without smiling, quite as candidly remarked that he merely talked with me for the sake of practice in French.

It is amazing how the French, day by day, become more reflecting, deeper, and more serious, while the English, on the other hand, strive to assume a light, superficial, and cheerful manner, not merely in life, but in literature. The London presses are fully busied with fashionable works, with romances which move in the glittering sphere of " high life," or mirror it ; as, for instance, " Almacks," or " Vivian Grey," " Tremaine," " The Guards," and " Flirtation." This last romance bears a name which would be most appropriate for the whole species, since it indicates

that coquetry with foreign airs and phrases, that clumsy refinement, that heavy bumping lightness, that sour style of honeyed
compliment, that ornamented coarseness ; in a word, the entire
lifeless life of those wooden butterflies who flutter in the salons of
West London.

But, on the contrary, what a literature is at present offered us
by the French press—that real representative of French spirit and
volition! When their great Emperor undertook, in the leisure of his
captivity, to dictate his life, to reveal the most secret solutions of
the enigmas of his divine soul, and to change the rocks of St.
Helena to a chair of history, from whose height his cotemporaries
should be judged and latest posterity be taught, then the French
themselves began to employ the days of their adversity and the
period of their political inactivity as profitable as possible. They
also are now writing the history of their deeds, the hands which
once grasped the sword are again becoming a terror to their
enemies by wielding the pen, the whole nation is busied in publishing its memoirs, and if it will follow my advice it will prepare a
particular edition *ad usum Delphini*, with nicely colored engravings
of the taking of the Bastille and storming of the Tuileries.

If I have above remarked that the English of the present day are
seeking to become light and frivolous, and endeavoring to creep
into the monkey's skin which the French are gradually stripping
off, I must also add that the tendency in question proceeds rather
from the nobility and gentry, or aristocratic world, than from the
citizens. On the contrary, the trading and working portion of the
people, especially the merchants in the manufacturing towns, and
nearly all the Scotch, bear the external marks of pietism—yes, I
might almost say of Puritanism, so that this blessed portion of the
people contrast with the worldly-minded aristocrats, like the
cavaliers and Roundheads so truthfully set forth by Scott in his
novels.

Those readers honor the Scottish bard too highly who believe
that his genius imitated and penetrated the outer form and inner
manner of feeling of those two historical parties, and that it is an
indication of his poetic greatness that he, free from prejudice as a

god in his judgment, does justice to both and treats them with equal love. Let any one cast a glance into the prayer-meetings of Liverpool and Manchester, and then into the fashionable saloons of the West End, and he will plainly see that Walter Scott has simply described his own times, and clothed forms which are altogether modern in dresses of the olden time. And if we remember that he himself from one side, as a Scotchman, sucked in by education and national influence a Puritan spirit, while on the other side, as a Tory who even regarded himself as a scion of the Stuarts, he must have been right royally and aristocratically inclined, and that therefore his feelings and thoughts must have embraced either tendency with equal love, and must also have been neutralized by their opposition, we can very readily understand his impartiality in describing the democrats and aristocrats of Cromwell's time, an impartiality which might well lead us into error if we hoped to find in his " History of Napoleon " an equally " fair-play " description of the heroes of the French Revolution.

He who regards England attentively may now find daily opportunities of observing those two tendencies, the frivolous and the Puritanic, in their most repulsive vigor, and with them, of course, their mutual contest. Such an opportunity was recently manifested in the famous suit at law of Mr. Wakefield, a gay cavalier, who, in an off-hand manner eloped with the daughter of the rich Mr. Turner, a Liverpool merchant, and married her at Gretna Green, where a blacksmith lives who forges the strongest sort of fetters. The entire head-hanging community, the whole race of the elect of the Lord, screamed murder at such horrible conduct ; in the conventicles of Liverpool the vengeance of Heaven was evoked on Wakefield and his brother who assisted ; they prayed that the earth's abyss might swallow them as it once swallowed the host of Korah, Dathan, and Abiram ; while, to make celestial anger more certain, they brought the thunders of the King's Bench, of the Lord Chancelor, and even of the Upper House to bear on this profaner of the holy sacrament ; while in the fashionable salons people merely laughed merrily and jested in the most liberal manner at the bold damsel-stealer. But the contrast of the two states of thought or feeling was recently shown me in the most delightful manner as I sat in the Grand Opera near two fat Manchester ladies who visited this *rendezvous* of the aristocratic world for the first time in their lives, and who could not find words strong enough to express the utter detestation and abhorrence which filled their hearts as the ballet began, and the short-skirted beautiful dancing-girls exhibited their lasciviously graceful movements, and fell passionately, like burning Bacchantes, into the arms of the male dancers who leaped towards them. The inspiring music, the primitive clothing of flesh-colored stockinet, the bounds so like the exuberance of nature, all united to force the sweat of agony from the poor ladies ; their bosoms flushed with repugnance ; they continually heaved out in chorus, " *Shocking* ! *For shame* ! *for shame* !" and were so benumbed with horror that they could not for an instant take their opera-glasses from their eyes, and consequently remained in that situation to the last instant when the curtain fell.

Despite these diametrically opposed tendencies of mind and of life, we still find in the English people a unity in their way of thinking, which comes from the very fact that they are always realising that they are a people by themselves ; the modern cavaliers and Roundheads may hate and despise one another mutually and as much as they please ; they do not, for all that, cease to be English ; as such they are at union and together, like plants which have grown out of the same soil and are strangely interwoven with it. Hence the secret unity of the entire life and activity and intercourse of England, which at the first glance seems to us but a theater of confusion and of contradiction. Excessive wealth and misery, orthodoxy and infidelity, freedom and serfdom, cruelty and mildness, honor and deceit — all of these incongruities in their maddest extremes ; over all a grey misty heaven, on every side buzzing machines, reckoning, gas-lights, chimneys, pots of porter, closed mouths — all this hangs together in such-wise that we can hardly think of the one without the other ; and that which singly, really ought to excite our astonishment or laughter appears to be, when taken as a part of the whole, quite commonplace and serious.

But I imagine that such would be the case everywhere, even in countries of which we have much more eccentric conceptions, and where we anticipate a much richer booty of merriment or amazement. Our earnest longing to travel, our desire to see foreign lands, particularly as we feel it in early youth, generally results from an erroneous anticipation of extraordinary contrasts, and from that spiritual pleasure in masquerades which makes us involuntarily expect to find the men and manner of thought of our own home, and to a certain degree our nearest friends and acquaintances, disguised in foreign dress and manners. If we think, for example, of the Hottentots, at once the ladies of our native town dance around in our imaginations, but painted black and endowed with the proper *a posteriori* developments, while our *beaux esprits* climb the palm-trees as bush-beaters; and if we think of the North Polanders, we see there also the well-known faces ; our aunt glides in her dog-sleigh over the ice road ; the dry Herr Conrector lies lazily on the bearskin and calmly sips his morning train-oil ; Madame the inspector's wife, Madame the tax-gatherer's lady, and Madame the wife of the Councilor of Infibulation gossip together and munch candles. But when we are really in those countries, we at once observe that mankind has there grown up from infancy with its manners and modes ; that people's faces harmonize with their thoughts and clothes to their needs—yes, that plants, animals, human beings, and the land itself form a harmonious whole.

IV.   JOHN BULL

Translated from an English description of London

IT WOULD SEEM TO BE AN IMMUTABLE LAW OF THE NATURE OF THE Irish that they regard idleness as the characteristic of a gentleman, and as all of this race cannot cover their genteel backs, yet are all the same aristocrats, it comes to pass that comparatively few of the sprouts of Green Erin flourish among the merchants of the City. Those Irishmen who have had little or no education—and these are in the majority — are *gentlemen day-laborers*, and the rest gentlemen for and by themselves. If they could, by a bold stroke — *coup de main* — attain the enjoyment of mercantile wealth, they would gladly go into business ; but they cannot sit on the three-legged stools of a countinghouse or bend over desks and account-books so as to win treasure by long hard work.

On the other hand, this is just what suits a Scotchman. His desire to climb to the top of the tree is also pretty keen, but his hopes are not so sanguine as they are determined, and unwearied application with him takes the place of momentary fiery enthusiasm. The Irishman springs and jumps like a squirrel ; and when he, as often happens, does not keep firm hold of the twig or bough, down he goes into the mud, and finds himself defiled if not damaged. These numerous jumps and springs are the preparations for a fresh effort, which probably results in the same manner. The cautious Scotchman, on the contrary, chooses his tree with the greatest care ; examines if it be well grown, well rooted, and strong enough to bear him, so that it cannot be blown down by the storms of fortune or accident. And he takes good care that the lowest twigs are within his reach, and that there is a convenient series of knots or ridges in the bark to aid his climbing. He begins from the bottom, looks carefully at every twig before he trusts to it, and never advances one foot till he is sure that the other is firmly planted. Other people, more enthusiastic and less careful, climb over him, and ridicule the anxious slowness of his pace ; but he, patient and persevering, cares little for that ; and when they tumble and he is on the top, it is his turn to laugh, and he does so with all his heart.

This admirable ability of the Scotchman to make his way in business, his extraordinary docility and obedience to superiors, the invariable promptness with which he trims his sails to the winds, has had the result that we find in London firms not only an incredible number of Scottish clerks, but also Scottish partners. And yet, notwithstanding their number and their influence, the Scotch have not succeeded in impressing their national character on this sphere of London society. For the very gifts which enable them to become first the best of *employés*, and then the best of associates, cause them to adopt the manners and style or tastes of those around them.

For they soon find that those things to which they attached the utmost importance in their native land are of no account whatever in their new home. Their small feudal ties, their boasted relationship to some unshorn proprietor of two or three barren mountains, their legends of two or three wonderful men whose names were never heard of out of Scotland, the Puritanical temperance in which they were brought up, and the frugality which they have made their own — all is far from agreeing with the positive and lavish habits of John Bull.

The stamp of John Bull is as deeply impressed and as sharp as that on a Greek medal ; and wherever we find him, be it in London or in Calcutta, as master or man, he is always perfectly recognizable. He is everywhere a plump fact, very honorable, but cold and absolutely repelling. He has all the solidity of a material substance, and one cannot fail to remark that, wherever or with whom he may be, John Bull regards himself always as the chief person present ; also that he will accept no counsel or advice from any one, though he may have intimated that he required it. And be he where he may, we remark that his own comfort — comfort personal and peculiar — is the great subject of all his efforts and desires.

Should John Bull think there is an opening or opportunity to profit, he will fraternize with any one at the first interview. But to make an intimate friend of him he must be courted like a girl, and when his friendship is won it is generally found that it was not worth the trouble it cost. What he gave before he was sought was cold, correct politeness, and all that he gave afterwards was little more. We find in him a mechanical formality and an open avowal of that selfishness or egoism which other people perhaps possess just as much as he does, but which they conceal so carefully that the costliest banquet of an Englishman does not taste so pleasantly as a handful of dates from a Bedouin in the desert.

But while John Bull is the coldest friend, he is the surest of neighbors and the most straightforward and generous enemy. While he guards his own castle like a Pacha, he never seeks to penetrate

441

into another's. Comfort and independence are the essentials with him ; by the one he understands the right to buy whatever can contribute to his most convenient comfort, by the other to do whatever he pleases and say whatever he chooses — and this allowed, he troubles himself little with the chance and perhaps chimerical distinctions which cause so much plague and pain in the rest of the world. His pride — and he has it in full measure — is not that of Haman. Little would it trouble him that Mordecai the Jew sat full-spread before the door of his house ; all that he would guard against would be to keep Mordecai from entering without his special permission, which he would assuredly only grant under the condition that it should perfectly accord with his special comfort and be to his advantage.

His pride is an English growth, and though he boasts somewhat, his boasting is not that of other people. No one ever sees him take on airs because of his ancestors ; if John Bull has his pockets full of guineas, and has become one who is " warm," he cares not a mushroom whether his grandfather was a duke or a hand-carter. " Every man is himself, and not his father," is John's theory, and according to this he regulates his acts. He only boasts that " he is an Englishman ; " that he first saw the light of day somewhere between Lowestoft and Saint David's, between Penzance and Berwick, and he is more rejoiced at this than if he had been born on any other spot in this planet. For Old England belongs to him, and he belongs to Old England ; there is nothing like it in all the world, for it can support and teach all the world, and, if it should come to that, conquer it.

But this is only so generally speaking. For if we go to details and examine John closely, we find that, after all, in this so greatly praised England there is nothing with which he is really contented except himself.

Say anything to him, for example, about the king — the same king whose throne he bears with such pride on his shoulders — and lo ! at once he wails or rails at extravagance in the royal expenditure, venality and royal favoritism, the growing, threatening influence of the Crown, and declares that if serious and speedy action and restraint are not resorted to, England will soon be England no more. Mention Parliament, and he begins to grumble, and damns both Houses — the Upper because it is inspired with Court-patronage, and the Lower by faction and favor ; nay, he may declare, over and above all, that England would be better off if it had no Parliament at all. Say anything to him about the Church — he breaks out into a death-shriek at tithes and fattened parsons who have turned the Word of God into priestly property and devour at their leisure the hard-earned fruits of the labor of others. Speak of Public Opinion, and the great advantage of the rapid dissemination of information — he regrets that Error travels as quickly on these improved roads as Truth, and that the people abandon old follies only to embrace new. In short, there is not in all England an institution with which John is perfectly contented. Even the elements incur his blame, and he grumbles from the beginning of the year to the end at the climate, as much as at things which are of human cause.

He is discontented even with the property which he has acquired, as you will find on close examination. Though he may have amassed great riches, it is his endless refrain that he is going to the dogs ; and is poor as a beggar, while he sits between piles of gold in a palace ; and is dying of hunger, while he is fed so fat that he can hardly waddle from one end of the room to the other. One thing only does he praise with all his heart — even if you mention it — and that is the fleet, the ships of war, the wooden walls of Old England — and these he praises because perhaps he never sees them.

Yet we will not blame this passion for blaming almost everything, for it has contributed to make and keep England what it is. This instinct for grumbling of the rough and stiff-necked but honorable John Bull is perhaps the bulwark of British greatness abroad and of British freedom at home ; and though many of the British provinces do not properly esteem it, still the real prosperity which they enjoy is due far more to John Bull's endless grumbling than it ever could be to the docile, pliant philosophy of the Scotchman or the stormy fire of the Irishman. These two races in the present crisis do not seem to have the strength or endurance requisite to maintain their rights and achieve their own prosperity, and whenever there is to be resistance to attacks on popular liberty or a measure to be advanced for the common weal, then the records of Parliament, and petitions which are brought there, show that in most cases, be they of defence or reform, no other comes forward than John Bull — the grumbling, selfish, and growling, yet bold, manly, independent, unyielding, on and through-pushing John Bull.

V.   THE LIFE OF NAPOLEON BUONAPARTE

By Walter Scott

POOR WALTER SCOTT! HADST THOU BEEN RICH THOU WOULDST NOT have written that book, and so hadst not become a poor Walter Scott! But the trustees of the Constable estate met together, and reckoned up and ciphered, and after much subtraction and division, shook their heads, and there remained for poor Walter Scott nothing but laurels and debts. Then the most extraordinary of all came to pass, the singer of great deeds wished for once to try his hand at heroism, he made up his mind to a *cessio bonorum*, the laurels of the great unknown were taxed to cover great and well-known debts ; and so there came to life in hungry haste, in bankrupt inspiration, the " Life of Napoleon," a book to be roundly paid for by the wants of the English people in general, and of the English Ministry in particular.

Praise him, the brave citizen! praise him, ye united Philistines of all the earth! praise him, thou beautiful shopkeeper's virtue, which sacrificest everything to meet a note on the day when it is due! only do not ask of me that I praise him too.

Strange! the dead Emperor is, even in his grave, the bane of the Britons, and through him Britannia's greatest poet has lost his laurels!

He *was* Britannia's greatest poet, let people say and imagine

444

what they will. It is true that the critics of his romances carped
and cavilled at his greatness, and reproached him that he assumed
too much breadth in execution, that he went too much into details,
that his great characters were only formed by the combination of
a mass of minor traits, that he required an endless array of acces-
sories to bring out his bold effects ; but, to tell the truth, he
resembled in all this a millionaire, who keeps his whole property
in the form of small specie, and who must drive up three or four
wagons full of sacks of pence and farthings when he has a large
sum to pay. Should any one complain of the ill-manners of such a
style of liquidation, with its attendant troubles of heavy lifting and
hauling and endless counting, he can reply with perfect truth that,
no matter *how* he gives the money, he still gives it, and that he is
in reality just as well able to pay and quite as rich as another
who owns nothing but bullion in bars ; yes, that he even has an
advantage greater than that of mere facility of transport, since in
the vegetable market gold bars are useless, while every huckster
woman will grab with both hands at pence and farthings when they
are offered her. *Now* all this popular wealth of the British poet is
at an end, and he, whose change was so current that the duchess
and the cobbler's wife received it with the same interest, has at
last become a poor Walter Scott ! His destiny recalls the legend of
the mountain elves, who, mockingly benevolent, gave money to
poor people, which was bright and profitable so long as they spent
it wisely, but which turned to mere dust when applied to unworthy
purposes. Sack by sack we opened Walter Scott's new load, and lo !
instead of gleaming smiling pence, there was nothing but idle dust,
and dust again ! He was justly punished by those mountain elves
of Parnassus, the Muses, who, like all noble-minded women, are
enthusiastic Napoleonists, and who were consequently doubly
enraged at the misuse of the spirit-treasure which had been loaned.

The value and tendency of this work of Scott's have been shown
up in the journals of all Europe. Not only the embittered French,
but also the astonished fellow-countrymen of the author have
uttered sentence of condemnation against it. In such a world-wide
discontent the Germans must also have their share, and therefore

the Stuttgart *Literary Journal* spoke out with a fiery zeal difficult to restrain within due limit, while the Berlin *Annals of Scientific Criticism* expressed itself in tones of cold tranquility ; and the critic, who was the more readily swayed by that tranquility the less he admired the hero of the book, characterizes it with these admirably appropriate words : —

" In this narration we find neither substance nor color, harmony nor life. The mighty subject drags heavily along, entangled in superficial, not in profound perplexities, uncertain and changeable, without any manifestation of the characteristic ; no leading principle strikes us in its affected singularity, its violent points are nowhere visible, its connection is merely external, its subject-matter and significance are hardly appreciable. In such a manner of portrayal all the light of history must be quenched, and itself be reduced to, not wonderful, but commonplace stories. The unnecessary remarks and reflections which often intrude themselves on the subject under consideration are of a corresponding description. Such a watery, transparent preparation has long been out of date in our reading world. The scanty pattern of a moral, applicable only to certain particulars, is unsatisfactory." . . .

I would willingly pardon poor Scott for such, and even worse, things, to which the sharp-witted Berlin reviewer, Varnhagen von Ense, gives utterance. We are all mortal, and the best of us may once in a while write a bad book. People then say that the thing is below criticism, and that ends the matter. But it is really extraordinary that in this new work we do not find a trace of Scott's beautiful style. The colorless commonplace strain is sprinkled in vain with sundry red, green, and blue words ; in vain do glittering patches from the poets cover the prosaic nakedness ; in vain does the author rob all Noah's ark to find bestial comparisons ; and in vain is the Word of God itself cited to heighten the color of stupid thoughts. Stranger still is it that Walter Scott has not here succeeded in a single effort to bring into play his inborn talent of sketching characters, and of catching the traits of the outer Napoleon. Walter Scott learned nothing from those beautiful pictures which represent Napoleon surrounded by his generals and statesmen, though every one who regards them without prejudice must be deeply moved by the tragic tranquility and antique severity of those features, which contrast in such fearful sublimity with the modern, excitable, picturesque faces of the day, and which seem to announce something of the incarnate God. But if the Scottish poet could not comprehend the form, how much less capable must he have been of grasping the character of the Emperor! And I therefore willingly pardon his blasphemy of a divinity whom he never knew. And I must also forgive him that he regards his Wellington as a god, and in deifying him, falls into such excessive manifestations of piety, that, rich as he is in figures of beasts, he knows not wherewith to compare him. Everywhere on earth as men are so are their gods. Stupid black savages adore poisonous snakes ; cross-eyed Bash Kirs pray to ugly logs ; idiotic Laplanders reverence seals. Sir Walter Scott, in nothing behind them, worships his Wellington.

But if I am tolerant towards Walter Scott, and forgive him the emptiness, errors, slanders, and stupid things in his book — nay, if I even pardon him the weariness and *ennui* which its reading caused me, I cannot, for all that, forgive him its tendency. This is nothing less than the exculpation of the English Ministry as regards the crime of St. Helena. " In this case of equity between the English Ministry and public opinion," as the Berlin reviewer expresses it, " Walter Scott makes himself judge of its merits ; " he couples legal quibblings with his poetic talent, in order to distort both facts and history, and his clients, who are at the same time his patrons, may well afford, beside the regular fees, to privately press an extra *douceur* into his hand.

The English have merely murdered the Emperor — but Walter Scott sold him. It was a real Scotch trick, a regular specimen of Scottish national manners, and we see that Scotch avarice is still the same old dirty spirit as ever, and has not changed much since the days of Naseby, when the Scotch sold their own king, who had confided himself to their protection, for the sum of four hundred thousand pounds sterling. That king was the same Charles Stuart whom the bards of Caledonia now sing so gloriously — the Englishman murders, but the Scotchman sells and sings.

The English Ministry, to aid in the work, threw open the archives of the Foreign Office to their advocate, and he has, in the ninth volume of his work, scrupulously availed himself of every official document which could throw an advantageous light upon his own side, and a corresponding darkness upon that of his enemies. On this account the ninth volume in question still possesses a peculiar interest, despite all its æsthetic worthlessness, in which it is in no respect behind its predecessors. We expect in it important public papers, and since we find none, it is a proof that there were none in existence which spoke in favour of the English Ministers,—and this negative content of the book is an important result.

All the booty thus obtained from the English archives was limited to a few credible documents from the noble Sir Hudson Lowe and his myrmidons, and a few verbal expressions of General Gourgaud, who, if he really uttered them, deserves to be regarded as a shameless traitor to his imperial master and benefactor. I will not inquire into the authenticity of these expressions ; it even seems to be true that Baron Turner, one of the three mute supernumeraries of the great tragedy, has borne witness to them ; but I do not see to what favorable result they lead, save that Sir Hudson Lowe was not the only blackguard in St. Helena. With such assistance, and with pitiable suggestions of his own, Walter Scott treats the history of the imprisonment of Napoleon, and labors to convince us that the ex-Emperor—so the ex-poet terms him—could not have acted more wisely than to yield himself to the English, although he must have foreseen his banishment to St. Helena, and that he was there treated in the most charming manner, since he had plenty to eat and to drink ; and that he, finally, fresh and sound, and as a good Christian, died of a cancer in his stomach.

Walter Scott, by thus admitting, to a certain degree, that the Emperor foresaw how far the generosity of the English would extend, viz., to St. Helena, frees him at least from the common reproach : the tragic sublimity of his ill fortune so greatly inspired him that he regarded civilized Englishmen as Parisian barbarians, and looked upon the beef-steak kitchen of St. James as the fireside of a great monarch — and so committed a heroic blunder. Sir Walter Scott also makes of the Emperor the greatest poet who ever lived, since he very seriously insinuates that all the memorable writings which set forth his sufferings in St. Helena were collectively dictated by himself.

I cannot here refrain from the remark that this part of Walter Scott's book, with the writings themselves of which he speaks, especially the memoirs of O'Meara and the narrative of Captain Maitland, remind me sometimes so pointedly of the drollest story in the world, that the bitterest vexation of my soul suddenly bursts out in merry laughter. And the story of which I speak is none other than the " History of Lemuel Gulliver," a book over which I, as a boy, once had rare times, and in which much that is exquisitely delightful may be read — how the little Liliputians could not conceive what was to be done with their great prisoner ; how they climbed upon him by thousands, and bound him down with innumerable fine hairs ; how they, with preparations on a grand scale, built for him a great house, all to himself ; how they bewailed the vast amount of victuals with which they must daily provide him ; how they continually blackened his character in the State Council, always grieving that he was too great a cost to the country ; how they would gladly have destroyed him, but feared lest in death his corpse might bring forth a pestilence ; how they finally made up their minds to be most gloriously magnanimous and leave him his titles, only putting out his eyes, etc. Truly, Liliput is everywhere where a great man is subjected to little ones, who torment him incessantly in the most pitifully petty manner, and who in turn endure from him great suffering and dire extremity ; but had Dean Swift written his book in our day, the world would have seen, in his brilliantly polished mirror, only the history of the imprisonment of the Emperor, and have recognized even in the very color of the coats and countenances those dwarfs who tormented him.

Only, the conclusion of the story of St. Helena is somewhat different, for in it the Emperor dies of a cancer in the stomach, and Walter Scott assures us that it was the sole cause of his death.

In this I will not contradict him. The thing is not impossible. It is possible that a man who lies stretched on the rack may suddenly, and very naturally, die of an apoplexy. But the wicked world will say that the tormentor was the cause of his death. And the wicked world has taken it into its head to regard the affair in question in a very different light from our good Walter Scott. If this good man, who is in other respects so firm in his Bible, and who so readily quotes the Gospel, sees in that uproar of elements, and in that hurricane which burst forth at the death of Napoleon, nothing but an event which also took place at the death of Cromwell, the world will still have its own peculiar thoughts regarding it. It regards the death of Napoleon as a most terrible, tremendous, and revolting crime, and its wild burst of agonized feeling becomes adoration. In vain does Walter Scott play the *advocatus diaboli*—the canonisation of the dead Emperor flows from every noble heart; every noble heart of the great European fatherland despises his petty executioners, and with them the great bard who has sung himself into being their accomplice. The Muses will yet inspire better singers in honor of their favorite; and should men be dumb, then the stones will speak, and the martyr-cliffs of St. Helena will rise fearfully from the waves of the sea, and tell to thousands of years their terrible story.

VI.   OLD BAILEY

THE VERY NAME OF " OLD BAILEY " SENDS A SHUDDER THROUGH the soul. We at once think of a great, black, repulsive building — the palace of misery and of crime. The left wing, which forms the real Newgate, serves as a prison for criminals. In it we see nothing but a high wall of square, weather-blackened stones, in which are two niches with equally black, allegorical figures, one of which, unless I err, represents Justice, whose right hand, with the scales, is, as usual, broken off, so that nothing remains but a blind female figure with a sword. Not far off, and about the centre of the build-ing, is the altar of this goddess, that is to say, the window by which

450

the gallows is erected ; and, finally, to the right is the Criminal
Court, where the quarter-sessions are held. Here is a gate which,
like that of Dante's " Hell," should bear the inscription : —

> " Per me si va ne la citta dolente,
> Per me si va ne l'eterno dolore,
> Per me si va tra la perduta gente."

Through this gate we come to a small court, where the scum of the
people assemble to see criminals pass, and here their friends and
enemies also assemble — relations, beggar-children, weak-minded
people, and especially old women, who discuss the criminal cases
of the day, perhaps with more insight into their merits than judge
and jury possess, despite the time so pleasantly passed in ceremonies or so drearily lost in law. Why, I have seen, outside the
court door, an old woman who, amid her gossips, defended poor
Black William better than his very learned counsel did within ; and
as she wiped away her last tear with a ragged apron, it seemed to
me that with it vanished the last trace of William's guilt.

In the court-room itself, which is not very large, there is below —
beyond the so-called " bar " — little room for the public ; but in
the upper portion there are, on both sides, very spacious galleries,
with raised benches, where the spectators stand, their heads appearing as if piled in rows, step above step.

When I visited Old Bailey I obtained a place in one of these
galleries, for which I gave the old portress a shilling. I arrived just
at the instant in which the jury were about to determine whether
Black William was guilty or not guilty of the accusation.

Here, as in other courts of justice in London, the judges sit in
blue-black togas, which are trimmed with light-blue violet, and
wear white powdered wigs, with which black eyes and whiskers
frequently contrast in the drollest manner. They sit around a long
green table on high chairs at the upper end of the hall, just where
a Scripture text, warning against unjust judgments, is placed before
their eyes. On either side are benches for the jurymen, and places
where the prosecutors and witnesses stand. Directly opposite the
judges is the place for the accused, which latter do not sit on " the

poor sinners' bench," as in the criminal courts of France and Rhenish Germany, but must stand upright behind a singular plank, which is carved above like a narrow arched gate. In this an optic mirror is placed, by means of which 'the judge is enabled to accurately observe the countenance of the accused. Before the latter certain green leaves or herbs are placed to strengthen their nerves—and it may be that this is sometimes necessary, when a man is in danger of losing his life. On the judges' table I saw similar green leaves, and even a rose. I know not why it was, but the sight of that rose affected me strangely. A red blooming rose, the flower of love and of spring, upon the terrible judges' table of the Old Bailey! It was close, gloomy, and sultry in the hall. Everything seemed so fearfully vexatious, so insanely serious! The people present looked as though spiders were creeping over their shy and fearful faces. The iron scales rattled audibly over the head of poor Black William.

A jury had also formed itself in the gallery. A fat woman, above whose red, bloated cheeks two little eyes glittered like glowworms, made the remark that Black William was a very good-looking fellow. But her neighbor, a delicate, piping soul in a body of bad post-paper, declared that he wore his black hair too long and matted, and that his eyes gleamed like those of Kean in Othello; "while, on the other hand," she continued, "Thompson is a very different sort of a person, mem, I assure you, with light hair; and a very well-educated person, too, mem—for he plays the flute a little, and paints a little, and speaks French a little."

"And steals a little, too, hey?" added the fat woman.

"Fiddlesticks on stealing!" replied the lean body; "that isn't half so bad, mem, as forgery, you know; for a thief, if he's stolen nothing but a sheep, gets Botany Bay for it, but if a man counterfeits somebody's hand, why, he hangs for it, mem, as sure as fate, without pity or mercy."

"Without pity or mercy!" sighed a half-starved man in a widower-looking black coat. "Hang! why—why, no man has a right to put another to death, and Christians ought to be the last to think of it; for they ought to remember that Christ, our Lord

452

and Savior, who gave us our religion, was innocent when he was tried and executed!"

" Pshaw!" cried the lean woman, and smiled with her thin lips ; " if they didn't hang such a forger, no rich man would ever be sure of his money ; for instance, the fat Jew in Lombard Street, Saint Swithin's Lane, or our friend Mr. Scott, whose writing was imitated so well. And then Mr. Scott has worked so hard to get his money — trouble enough, mem, I assure you — and folks *do* say that he got rich by taking other people's diseases on himself. Yes, mem, they say the very children run after him in the street and cry, ' I'll give ye sixpence if you'll take my toothache!' or ' We'll give ye a shilling if you'll take Jimmy's hump-back!'"

" Well, that's odd!" interrupted the fat woman. " And it's odd, too, that Black William and Thompson used to be such cronies together, and lived and ate and drank together, and now James Thompson accuses his old friend of forgery! But why isn't Thompson's sister here? Why, she used to be a-running everywhere after her sweet William!"

A pretty girl, on whose lovely face lay a deep expression of grief, like a dark veil over a rose-bouquet, here whispered with tears a long, sad story, of which I could only understand that her friend, the pretty Mary, had been cruelly beaten by her brother, and lay sick to death in her bed.

" Pshaw! don't call her pretty Mary!" grumbled the fat woman discontentedly ; " she's too slim, too much like a stick, to be called pretty ; and if her William is hung——"

Just at this instant the jury appeared, and declared that the accused was guilty of forgery. As Black William was led from the hall he cast a long, long glance upon Edward Thompson.

There is an Eastern legend that Satan was once an angel, and lived in heaven with other angels, until he sought to seduce them from their allegiance, and therefore he was thrust down by Divinity into the endless night of hell. But as he sank from heaven he looked ever on high, ever at the angel who accused him ; the deeper he sank, more terrible and yet more terrible became his gaze. And it must have been a fearful glance, for the angel whom it met became pale — red was never again seen in his cheeks, and since that time he has been called the Angel of Death.

Pale as that Angel of Death grew Edward Thompson.

VII.   CORPORAL PUNISHMENT IN ENGLAND

I CANNOT DECLARE DECIDEDLY ENOUGH HOW MUCH OPPOSED I AM TO whipping in general, and how indignant I am whenever I see my fellow-creatures beaten. The proud lord of the earth, the lofty spirit who rules the sea and investigates the laws of the stars, is degraded by nothing so much as by corporal punishment. The gods, to quench the flaring pride of men, invented the lash. Then men, whose spirit of invention was sharpened by a brooding spirit of resistance, invented against it the *point d'honneur*. Frenchmen, Japanese, Indian Brahmins, have best developed this invention ; they have reduced the vengeance to blood to formal paragraphs, and duelling, though discouraged by religion, law, and even reason, is still a blossom of fair humanity.

But among the English, who have refined every other invention to highest perfection, the *point d'honneur* has not received its ultimate polish. The Briton by no means regards a beating as an evil bad as death, and while I was in England I was present at many a scene which suggested the reflection that blows in free England have by no means such evil effects on personal honor as in Germany. I have seen lords thrashed, and they seemed to suffer only from the bodily pain of the insult. In the races at Epsom and Brighton I saw jockeys who, to make room for the horses running, ran right and left with horse-whips, which they laid on liberally to the lords and gentlemen who were in the way. And what did the same so-disturbed gentlemen? They laughed sourly.

Though bodily punishment in England is not so dishonorable as with us, still the reproach of its cruelty is not by any means the milder for that. But this does not concern the English people, but the aristocracy, who by the welfare of England only understand

454

the safety of their own ruling position. Free men with an independent sense of honor would not trust this despotic gang ; it requires the blind obedience of whipped slaves. The English soldier must be a mere machine, a complete automaton which marches and fires by word of command. Therefore he requires no commander of imposing individual character. Free Frenchmen need, however, one who inspires enthusiasm, and it was under such a great leader they, as if drunken from his fiery soul, conquered the world. English soldiers need no marshal, not even a general, but only a corporal's stick, which carries out calmly and accurately the assigned Ministerial instructions, as a stick of wood is expected to do. And—ah me!—since I must praise him for once, a most admirable stick of this kind is—Wellington, this cowed puppet who moves entirely by the string by which the aristocracy pull him—this wooden vampire of the people, with a wooden loop, as Byron says, and I would add, with wooden heart. Verily old England may add him to the wooden walls of protection of which she for ever prates.

General Foy has, in his " History of the War in the Pyrenean Peninsula," admirably sketched the contrast between the French and English soldiery and their discipline, and this description shows us what a feeling of honor and what whipping make of soldiers.

It is to be hoped that the cruel system followed by the British aristocracy will not long endure, and that John Bull will break in twain his ruling corporal's cane. For John is a good Christian ; he is mild, and wishes well ; he sighs over the severity of his country's laws, and in his heart dwells Humanity. I could tell a pleasing tale of that—another time!

VIII.   THE NEW MINISTRY

LAST SUMMER I MADE IN BEDLAM THE ACQUAINTANCE OF A PHIL-OSOPHER, who, with mysterious looks and whispers, communicated to me many weighty conclusions as to the origin of evil. Like many of his colleagues, he held the opinion that it involved a history. So far as I was concerned, I also assented to what he assumed and declared, that the fundamental evil of the world arose from the fact that the blessed Lord had not created money enough.

" You're right," replied the philosopher ; " the blessed Lord was uncommonly short of funds when he created the world. He had to borrow money of the Devil, and mortgage the world to him as a pledge. But as the Lord, according to every law of God and of justice, is still in debt to him for the world, common politeness of course hindered him from preventing his creditor going about in the property and making all sorts of trouble and mischief. But the Devil, for his part, is deeply interested in the preservation of the world, lest he lose his pledge, so that he takes good care that things do not go altogether to the devil, and the blessed Lord, who is not stupid by any means, and who knows very well that he has his secret guarantee in the Devil's selfishness, often goes so far as to give over the whole government of the world to Old Nick — that is to say, tells him to form a Ministry. Then, as a matter of course, Samiel takes command of the armies of hell, Beelzebub becomes Chancelor, Vitzliputzli is Secretary of State, the old grandmother gets the Colonies, and so forth. These allies then carry on business according to their own evil will ; but as their own interests compel them to take good care of the world, they make up for this neces- sity by always employing the vilest means to bring about their good aims. Lately, they carried this to such an extent that God in heaven could no longer endure their rascality, and commissioned an angel to form a new Ministry. He of course gathered about him all the good spirits. A pleasant, joyful heat again ran through the world, there was light, and the evil spirits vanished. But they did not quietly fold their claws and kick their hoofs in idleness — no, they went to work in secret against all that was good, they poisoned the new springs of health, they spitefully snapped every rosebud of the fresh spring, they disturbed the tree of life with their amendments, a chaotic destruction threatened everything, and the blessed Lord will have, after all, to hand things over to the Devil, so that he, even by employing bad means, may at least keep things together. Just see, all that is the evil result of a debt."

This theory of my Bedlamite friend possibly explains the present change in the English Ministry. The friends of Canning are now subdued—those friends, whom I call the good spirits of England, because their opponents are devils, and, with the dumb devil, Wellington, at their head, now raise their cry of victory. Let no one scold poor George—he has been compelled to yield to circumstances. No one can deny that after Canning's death the Whigs were no longer in condition to maintain peace in England, since the measures which they were in consequence obliged to adopt were constantly nullified by the Tories. The King, to whom the maintenance of public tranquility—*i.e.*, the security of his crown— seemed the principal thing, was therefore obliged to transfer the government to the Tories. And oh! they will now again, as of old, govern all the fruits of the people's industry into their own pockets; like reigning corn-market Jews, they will be bulls themselves, and raise the price of bread-stuffs, while poor John Bull becomes lean with hunger, and finally must sell himself with body-service to the high gentlemen. And then they will yoke him to the plough, and lash him, and he will not so much as dare to low, for on one side the Duke of Wellington will threaten with the sword, and on the other the Archbishop of Canterbury will bang him on the head with the Bible—and there will be peace in the land.

The source of all the evil is the debt, the " national debt," or, as Cobbett says, " the King's debt." Cobbett remarks on this, and justly, that while the name of the King is prefixed to all institutions —as, for instance, the " King's army," " the King's navy," " the King's courts," " the King's prisons," etc.—the debt, which really sprang from these institutions, is never called the King's debt, and that it is the only case in which the nation has been so much honored as to have anything called after it.

The greatest evil is the debt. It cannot be denied that it upholds the English State, and that so firmly that the worst of devils cannot break it down ; but it has also resulted in making of all England one vast tread-mill, where the people must work day and night to fatten their creditors. It has made England old and grey with the cares of payment, and banished from her every cheerful and youthful feeling ; and, finally—as is the case with all deeply indebted men —has bowed the country down into the most abject resignation— though nine hundred thousand muskets, and as many sabres and bayonets, lie in the Tower of London, while those who guard them, the fat, red-coated beef-eaters, might be easily subdued.

IX. THE DEBT

WHEN I WAS A BOY THERE WERE THREE THINGS WHICH ESPECIALLY interested me in the newspapers. I first of all was accustomed to seek, under the head " Great Britain," whether Richard Martin had not presented a fresh petition to Parliament for the more humane treatment of poor horses, dogs, and asses. Then, under " Frankfort," I looked to see whether Dr. Schrieber had addressed the Diet on the subject of the Grand-Ducal purchasers of Hessian domains. Then I at once attacked " Turkey," and read through the long Constantinople, merely to find if a Grand Vizier had not been honored with the silken noose.

This last subject always supplied me with the most copious food for reflection. That a despot should strangle his servants without ceremony seemed to me to be natural enough ; for I had once seen, in a menagerie, how the king of beasts fell into such a majestic rage that he would, beyond question, have torn to pieces many an innocent spectator, had he not been caged in a secure constitution of iron bars. But what really astonished me was, that after the strangulation of the old Mr. Grand Vizier, there was always a new one willing to become Grand Vizier in turn.

Now that I am older grown, and busy myself more with the English than with their friends, the Turks, a like amazement seizes me when I see how, after the resignation of a Prime Minister, another at once forces himself into his place although the new one is always a man who has wherewithal to live, and who (with the exception of Wellington) is anything but a blockhead. This has been especially the case since the French Revolution ; care and trouble have multiplied themselves in Downing Street, and the burden of business is well-nigh unbearable.

Affairs of State, and their manifold relations, were much simpler in the olden time, when reflecting poets compared the Government to a ship and the Minister to a steersman. Now, however, all is more complicated and entangled ; the common ship of State has become a steamboat, and the Minister no longer has a mere helm to control, but must, as responsible engineer, take his place below, amid the immense machinery, and anxiously examine every little iron rivet, every wheel which could cause a stoppage — must look by day and by night into the blazing fire, and sweat with heat and vexation, since, through the slightest carelessness on his part, the boiler might burst and vessel and passengers be lost. Meanwhile the captain and passengers walk calmly on the deck — as calmly flutters the flag from its staff ; and he who sees the boat gliding so pleasantly along never thinks of the terrible machinery, or of the care and trouble hidden in its bowels.

They sink down to early graves, those poor, responsible engineers of the English ship of State! The early death of the great Pitt is touching ; still more so that of the yet greater Fox. Percival would have died of the usual ministerial malady, had he not been more promptly made away with by a stab from a dirk. It was the ministerial malady, too, which brought Castlereagh to such a state of desperation that he cut his throat at North Cray, in the county of Kent. Lord Liverpool in like manner sank into the death of madness. We saw the god-like Canning poisoned by High-Tory slanders, and fall like a sick Atlas under his world-burden. One after the other they are interred in Westminster, those poor Ministers, who must think day and night for England's kings ; while the latter, thoughtless and in good condition, have lived along to the greatest age of man.

But what is the name of the great care which preys by night and by day on the brains of the English Ministers, and kills them ? It is — the debt, the debt!

Debts, like patriotism, religion, honor, etc., belong, it is true, to the special distinctions of the humanity — for animals do not contract debts — but they are also a special torment to mankind, and as they ruin individuals, so do they also bring entire races to destruction, and appear to replace the old destiny, in the national tragedies of our day. And England cannot escape this destiny ; her Ministers see the dire catastrophe approach, and die in the swoon of despair.

Were I the royal Prussian head calculator, or a member of the corps of geniuses, then would I reckon in the usual manner the entire sum of the English debt in silver groschen, and tell you precisely how many times we could cover with them the great Frederick Street or the entire earth. But figures were never my forte, and I had rather leave to an Englishman the desperate business of counting his debts, and of calculating from them the resulting ministerial crisis. For this business no one is better than old Cobbett, and I accordingly communicate the following conclusions from the last number of his *Register*.

The condition of things is as follows : —

1. " This Government, or rather this aristocracy and Church ; but if you will have it so, this Government, borrowed a large sum of money, for which it has purchased many victories both by land and sea — a mass of victories of every sort and size.

2. " I must, however, remark by the way, on what occasions and for what purposes these victories were bought. The occasion was that of the French Revolution, which destroyed all aristocratic privileges and clerical tithes ; while the object was the prevention of a preliminary reform in England, which would probably have had, as its consequence, a similar destruction of all aristocratic privileges and clerical tithes.

3. " To prevent the example set by the French from being followed by the English, it was necessary to attack the French, to impede their progress, to render dangerous their newly obtained freedom, to drive them to desperate acts, and finally, to make such a scarecrow and bugbear of the Revolution to the people that the very name of liberty should suggest nothing but an aggregate of wickedness, cruelty, and blood ; while the English people, in the excitement of their terror, should go so far as to fairly fall in love

with the same despotic Government which once flourished in France, and which every Englishman has abhorred from the days of Alfred the Great down to those of George the Third.

4. " To execute these intentions the aid of divers foreign nations was needed, and these nations were consequently subsidised with English gold. French emigrants were sustained with English money ; in short, a war of twenty-two years was carried on, to subdue that people which had risen up against aristocratic privileges and clerical tithes.

5. " Our Government, therefore, gained ' numberless victories ' over the French, who, as it seems, were always conquered ; but these, our numberless victories, were bought—that is to say, they were fought by mercenaries, whom we hired for this purpose, and we had in our pay at one and the same time whole swarms of Frenchmen, Dutchmen, Swiss, Italians, Russians, Austrians, Bavarians, Hessians, Hanoverians, Prussians, Spaniards, Portuguese, Neapolitans, Maltese, and God knows how many nations besides.

6. " By thus seeking foreign service, and by using our own fleet and armies, we *bought* so many victories over the French (the poor devils being without money to do business in like manner) that we finally subdued their Revolution and restored their aristocracy to a certain degree, although all that could be done was of no avail to restore the clerical tithes.

7. " After we had successfully finished this great task, and had also by means of it put down every Parliamentary reform in England, our Government raised a roar of victory which strained their lungs not a little, and which was sustained as loudly as possible by every creature in this country who, in one way or another, lived by public taxes.

8. " This excessive intoxication of delight lasted nearly two years in this once so happy nation ; to celebrate our victories, they heaped together public feasts, theatrical shows, arches of triumph, mock battles, and similar pleasures, which cost more than a quarter of a million pounds sterling, and the House of Commons unanimously voted a vast sum (I believe three million pounds sterling) to

erect triumphal arches and other monuments to commemorate the glorious events of the war.

9. " Since the time of which I speak we have constantly had the fortune to live under the Government of the same persons who conducted our affairs during the aforesaid glorious war.

10. " Since that time we have been at profound peace with all the world ; we may indeed assume that such is still the case, despite our little difficulty with the Turks ; and therefore one might suppose that there is no reason in the world why we should not now be happy. We are at peace ; our soil brings forth its fruits abundantly ; and, as the philosophers and lawgivers of our time declare, we are the most enlightened nation on the face of the earth. We really have schools everywhere, to instruct the rising generation: we have not merely a rector, or vicar, or curate in every diocese in the kingdom, but we also have in each of these dioceses perhaps six more teachers of religion, of which each is of a different kind from his four colleagues, so that our country is abundantly supplied with instruction of every kind, in order that no human being of all this happy land shall live in ignorance — and consequently our astonishment must be all the greater that any one who will become Prime Minister of this happy land should regard the office as such a heavy and painful burden.

11. " Alas! we have one misfortune, and it is a real misfortune, viz., we have bought several victories ; they were splendid, and we got them at a bargain ; they were worth three or four times as much as we gave for them, as Lady Teazle says to her husband when she comes home from buying ; there was much inquiry and a great demand for victories ; in short, we could have done nothing more reasonable than to supply ourselves at such cheap rates with so great a quantity of reputation.

12. " But — I confess it with a heavy heart — we have, like many other people, *borrowed* the money with which we bought these victories as we wanted them, and now we can no more get rid of the debt than a man can of his wife, when he has once had the good luck to load himself with the lovely gift.

13. " Hence it comes that every Minister who undertakes our affairs must also undertake the payment of our victories, not a farthing of which has as yet been counted off.

14. " It is true that he is not obliged to see that the whole sum which we borrowed to pay for our victories is paid down in the lump, capital and interest ; but he must see — more's the pity ! — to the regular payment of the interest ; and this interest, reckoned up with the pay of the army, and other expenses coming from our *victories*, is so significant that a man must have pretty strong nerves if he will undertake the business of paying them.

15. " At an earlier date, before we took to buying victories and supplying ourselves too freely with glory, we already had a debt of rather more than two hundred millions, while all the poor-rates in England and Wales together did not annually amount to more than two millions, which was before we had any of that burden which, under the name of dead-weight, is now piled upon us, and which is entirely the result of our thirst for glory.

16. " In addition to this money which was borrowed from creditors who cheerfully lent it, our Government, in its thirst for victories, also indirectly raised a great loan from the poor ; that is to say, they raised the usual taxes to such a height that the poor were far more oppressed than ever, and so that the amount of poor and of poor-rates increased incredibly.

17. " The poor taxes annually increase from two to eight millions ; the poor have therefore, as it were, a mortgage or hypotheca on the land, and this causes, again, a debt of six millions, which must be added to those other debts caused by our passion for glory and by the purchase of our victories.

18. " The dead-weight consists of annuities, which we pay, under the name of pensions, to a multitude of men, women, and children, as a reward for the services which those men have rendered, or should have rendered, in gaining our victories.

19. " The capital of the debt which this Government has contracted in getting its victories consists of about the following sums : —

Sums added to the National Debt	£800,000,000
Sums added to the actual debt for Poor-rates	150,000,000
Dead-weight, reckoned as capital of a debt	175,000,000
	£1,125,000,000

That is to say, eleven hundred and twenty-five millions, at five per cent., is the sum-total of those annual fifty-six millions ; yes, this is about the present total, only that the Poor-rates Debt is not included in the accounts which were laid before Parliament, since the country pays them at once into the different parishes. If any one, therefore, will subtract that six millions from the forty-six millions, it follows that the creditors holding the State Debt, and the dead-weight people, really swallow up all the rest.

20. "The poor-rates are, however, just as much a *debt* as the debt held by the State's creditors, and apparently sprang from the same source. The poor are crushed to the earth by the terrible load of taxes ; every other person has borne, of course, some of the burden, but all, except the poor, contrived to shift it more or less from their shoulders, until it finally fell with a fearful weight entirely on the latter, and they lost their beer-barrels, their copper kettles, their pewter plates, their clocks, their beds, and even the tools of their trades ; they lost their clothes, and were obliged to dress in rags — yes, they lost the very flesh from their bones. It was impossible to go further ; and of that which had been taken from them, something was restored under the name of increased Poor-rates. These are, in consequence, a *real debt* — a real mortgage on the land. The interest of this debt may, it is true, be withheld ; but were this done, the people, who have a right to require it, would rise in a body and demand, no matter how, payment of the whole amount. This is consequently a *real debt*, and a debt which must be paid to the uttermost farthing ; and, as I distinctly declare, preference will be demanded for it before all other debts.

21. "It is therefore unnecessary to wonder at the hard case of those who undertake such duties. It would be rather a matter of astonishment if any one would attempt such a task, were it not

left to his free will to also undertake as he pleased a radical change in the whole system.

22. " To this add : The two first-mentioned debts, namely, the State debt and the dead-weight debts, were previously paid, or, to speak more correctly, the interest on them was paid in depreciated paper money, of which currency fifteen shillings were hardly worth a Winchester bushel of wheat. This was the manner in which those creditors were paid for many years ; but in the year 1819 a shrewd Minister, Peel, made the discovery that it would be better for the nation should their debts be paid in actual money (at par), of which five shillings instead of fifteen in paper money were worth a Winchester bushel of wheat.

23. " The *nominal sum* was not to be changed. This all remained the same ; nothing was done save that Mr. Peel and his Parliament *changed the value of the sum*, and required that the debt should be paid in a kind of money of which five shillings should be of such value that they realize so much work or so much property as fifteen shillings of that currency in which the debts were contracted, *and in which the interests of those debts were paid during many years*.

24. " From 1819 till today the nation lived in a most distressing condition, devoured by creditors, who are generally Jews, or, to speak more correctly, Christians who act like Jews, and who were not to be brought so easily to attack less eagerly their prey.

25. " Many attempts were made to moderate to a certain degree the change which was made in 1819 in the currency, but these efforts failed, and once came near exploding the whole system.

26. " Here there is no possibilty of relief should one undertake to lower the annual expenditure of the State creditors' debt, and of the dead-weight debt, and to expect such a diminution of the debt, or such a reduction from the country, or to hinder its causing great commotion, or to prevent half-a-million human beings, in or about London, from perishing of hunger, it is necessary that far more appropriate and proportional reductions be made *in other directions* before the reduction of those two debts or their interest be attempted.

27. " As we have already seen, these victories were purchased with the view of preventing a reform of Parliament in England, and to maintain aristocratic privileges and clerical tithes ; and it would be, in consequence, a deed of cruelty which would cry aloud to Heaven should we take their lawful dues from those persons who lent us the money, or if we withdrew payment from the people who hired us the hands with which we won the victories. It would be a deed of cruelty which would bring down the vengeance of God on us should we commit such things, while the profitable posts of honor of the aristocracy, their pensions, sinecures, royal gifts, military rewards, and, finally, the tithes of the clergy remained untouched.

28. " *Here, here*, therefore, lies the difficulty ; he who becomes Minister must be Minister of a country which has a great passion for victories, which is sufficiently supplied with them, and has obtained incomparable military glory ; but which, more's the pity, has not yet paid for these splendid things, and which now leaves it to the Minister to settle the bill, without his knowing where he is to get the money."

These be things which bear down a Minister to his grave, or at least make of him a madman. England owes more than she can pay. Let no one boast that she possesses India and rich colonies. As it appears from the last parliamentary debates, England does not draw a single farthing of income from her vast, immeasurable India ; nay, she must pay thither several millions from her own resources. This country only benefits England by the fact that certain Britons, who there grow rich, aid the industry and the circulation of money at home by their wealth, while a thousand others gain their bread from the East India Company. The Colonies, therefore, yield no income to the State, require supplies, and are of service simply to commerce, and to enrich an aristocracy, whose younger sons and nephews are sent thither as governors and subordinate officials. The payment of the National Debt falls, consequently, altogether upon Great Britain and Ireland. But here too the resources are not so great as the debt itself. Let us hear what Cobbett says of this :—

" There are people who, to suggest some sort of relief, speak of

466

the resources of the country. These are the scholars of the late Colquhoun, a thief-catcher, who wrote a great book to prove that our debt need not trouble us in the least, since it is so small in proportion to the resources of the nation ; and in order that his shrewd reader may get an accurate idea of the vastness of these resources, he makes an estimate of all that the land contains, down to the very rabbits, and really seems to regret that he could not, in addition to them, reckon up the rats and mice. He makes his estimate of the value of the horses, cows, sheep, sucking-pigs, poultry, game, rabbits, fish, the value of household stuff, clothes, fuel, sugar, groceries ; in short, of everything in the country ; and after he has assumed the whole, and added to them the value of the farms, trees, houses, mines, the yield of the grass, corn, turnips, and flax, and brought out of it a sum of God knows how many thousand millions, he struts and sneers in his sly, bragging, Scotch fashion, something like a turkey-cock, and laughing with scorn, asks people like me, ' How, with resources like these, can you fear a national bankruptcy ? '

" The man never reflects that all the houses are wanted to live in, the farms to yield fodder, the clothes to cover our nakedness, the cows to give milk to quench thirst, the horned cattle, sheep, swine, poultry, and rabbits to eat ; yes — the devil take the contrary, obstinate Scotchman ! — these things are not where they are to be *sold* so that people can pay the National Debt with the proceeds. In fact, he has actually reckoned up the daily wages of the working-men among the resources of the nation ! This stupid devil of a thief-catcher, whose brethren in Scotland made a doctor of him because he wrote such an excellent book, seems to have altogether forgotten that laborers want their daily hire themselves to buy with it something to eat and drink. He might as well have set a value upon the blood in our veins as if it were stuff to make blood-puddings of ! "

So far Cobbett. While I translate his words into German, he bursts forth, as if in person, in my memory as he appeared during last year at the noisy dinner in the Crown and Anchor tavern. I see him again with his scolding red face and his Radical laugh, in

467

which the most venomous, deathly hatred combined terribly with the scornful joy which sees beforehand in all certainty the downfall of his enemies.

Let no one blame me for quoting Cobbett! Accuse him as much as you please of unfairness, of a passion for reviling, and of an altogether too vulgar personality ; but no one can deny that he possesses much eloquence of spirit, and that he very often, as in the above assertions, is in the right. He is a chained dog, who attacks at once in a rage every one whom he does not know, who often bites the best friends of the family in the legs, who always barks, and who on that account is not minded even when he barks at a real thief. Therefore the aristocratic thieves who plunder England do not regard it as necessary to cast the snarling Cobbett a crust, and so stop his mouth. This aggravates him most bitterly, and he shows his hungry teeth.

Old Cobbett! dog of England! I do not love you, for every vulgar nature is hateful to me, but I pity you from my deepest soul, when I see that you cannot break loose from your chain, nor reach those thieves who, laughing, slip away their plunder before your eyes, and mock your fruitless leaps and unavailing howls.

X.   THE OPPOSITION PARTY

A FRIEND OF MINE HAS VERY APTLY COMPARED THE OPPOSITION IN Parliament to an opposition coach. Every one knows that this is a public stage-coach which some speculating company start at their own expense, and run at such low rates that the travelers give it the preference over the already established line. The latter must also put down their prices to keep passengers, but are soon outbid, or rather underbid, by the new opposition coach, ruin themselves by the competition, and are obliged eventually to give up the business. If the opposition coach has at last and after this fashion gained the day, and finds itself the only one on a certain route, it at once puts up the prices, often higher than those of the old coach, and the poor passengers, far from gaining, often lose by the change, and must curse and pay until a new opposition coach renews the old game, and then new hopes and new deceptions follow in turn.

How full of blood and pride were the Whigs when the Stuart party were defeated and the Protestant dynasty ascended the English throne! The Tories then formed the Opposition, and John Bull, the poor State passenger, had good cause to roar with joy when they got the upper hand. But his joy was of short duration. He was annually obliged to pay a higher and still higher fare ; there was dear paying and bad riding ; more than that, the coachmen were very rude, there was nothing but jolting and bumping, every cornerstone threatened an upset, and poor John Bull thanked the Lord, his Maker, when at last the reins of the State-coach were held by other and better hands.

Unfortunately the joy did not last long this time either ; the new Opposition coachman fell dead from the coach-box, others got off cautiously when the horses became restive, and the old drivers, the old courtly riders, with golden spurs, again took their old places, and cracked away with the old whips.

I will not run this figure of speech to the ground, and I therefore turn again to the words " Whigs " and " Tories," which I have already used to indicate the two opposition parties, and a discussion of the names will be all the better, since they have for a long time been a source of confusion of ideas.

As the names of Ghibellines and Guelfs acquired by mutations and new events, during the Middle Ages, the vaguest and most opposite significations, so also at a later date in England did those of Whigs and Tories, the origin of which is at present scarcely known. Some assert that they were formerly abusive terms which eventually became honest party names, which often happens ; as, for instance, when a party in Holland baptized themselves " beggars " from *les gueux*, as at a later date the Jacobins often called themselves *sans culottes*, and as perhaps the serviles and dark-lantern folks of our own time will perhaps, at some future day, bear these names as glorious epithets of honor — a thing which, it must be admitted, they cannot now do. The word *Whig* is said to have signified in Ireland something disagreeably sour, and was there used to ridicule the Presbyterians or new sects in general. The word *Tory*, which was used about the same time as a party name, signified in Ireland a sort of scabby thieves. Both nicknames became general in the time of the Stuarts, and during the disputes between the sects and the dominant Church.

The general view is, that the Tories incline altogether to the side of the throne, and fight for the crown's privileges ; while, on the other hand, the Whigs lean towards the people, and protect their rights. These explanations are, however, vague, and are rather bookish than practical. The terms may be regarded rather as coterie names. They indicate men who cling together on certain opposing questions, whose predecessors and friends held together on the same grounds, and who, through political storms, bore in common their joys, sorrows, and the enmity of the opposite party. Principles never enter into consideration ; they do not unite on certain ideas, but on certain rules of State government—on the abolition or maintenance of certain abuses—on certain bills, certain hereditary questions,—no matter from what point of view, generally from mere custom. The English do not, however, let themselves be led astray by these party names. When they speak of Whigs, they do not form in so doing a definite idea, as we do in speaking of Liberals, when we at once bring before us men who are, from their very souls, sincere as to certain privileges of freedom ; but they think of an external union of people, of whom each one, judged by his private manner of thought, would form a party by himself, and who, as I have already said, fight against the Tories through the impulse of extraneous causes, accidental interests, and the associations of enmity or friendship. In such a State as this we cannot imagine a strife against aristocracy in our sense of the term, since the Tories are really not more aristocratic than the Whigs, and often even not more so than the *bourgeoisie*, or middle class, themselves, who regard the aristocracy as something unchangeable as the sun, moon, and stars ; who see in the privileges of the nobility and clergy that which is not merely profitable to the State, but is actually a necessity of nature, and who would perhaps fight for these privileges with far more zeal than the aristocrats themselves, since they believe more implicitly in them, while the latter have very generally lost their faith. In this point of view, we must admit that the spirit of the English is still overclouded by the night of the Middle Ages — the holy idea of a citizen-like equality has not, as yet, enlightened them ; and many a citizen-statesman in England who has Tory tendencies ought not, by any means, to be regarded as servile, or be counted among those servile hounds who *could* be free, and still creep back into their old kennel and bay the sun of freedom.

The names of Whig and Tory are consequently utterly useless, so far as comprehending the British Opposition is concerned, and Francis Burdett, at the beginning of the session of last year, very correctly declared that these names have now lost all their significance. On this remark Thomas Lethbridge, a man who the Lord has not endowed with too much wit, made a very good joke — perhaps the only one of his life — which was as follows : — " He has un-toried the Tories and un-wigged the Whigs."

Far more significant are the names, " Reformers," or Radical Reformers, or, in short, " Radicals." They are generally regarded as one and the same, and they aim at the same defects in the State and suggest the same remedies, differing only in the moderation or intensity of their views. The defect alluded to is the well-known evil manner of popular representation, by which the so-called rotten-boroughs — obsolete, uninhabited places — or, to speak more correctly, the oligarchs to whom they belong, have the right to send representatives for the people to Parliament, while great and populous cities, among them many manufacturing towns, have not a single representative. The wholesome cure of this defect is naturally in the so-called Parliamentary Reform. This, of course, is not regarded as an ultimate aim, but as a means. It is hoped that by it the people will attain a better representation of its interests, and the abolition of aristocratic abuses, and help in their affliction. As may be supposed, the Reform — this just and moderate demand — has its champions among moderate men, who are anything but Jacobins ; and when they are called *Reformers*, it has a meaning differing, as widely as earth from heaven, from that of *Radicals*, which is pronounced in an altogether different tone — as, for instance, when Hunt or Cobbett is mentioned, or any of the impulsive, raging, revolutionary men, who cry for Parliamentary reform that they may bring about the overthrow of all forms, the victory of avarice, and complete mob-rule. The shades in the coryphæi of these parties are consequently innumerable. But, as before said, the English know their men very well ; names do not deceive the public, and the latter decides, with great accuracy, where the battle is in earnest and where it is mere show. Often, for years together, the strife in Parliament is little more than an idle game, a tournament, where the champions contend for a color chosen for a freak ; but when there is a real strife we see them all hasten, each man to the flag of his natural party. This we saw in the days of Canning. The most passionate opponents united when it came to a war of positive interests — Tories, Whigs, and Radicals formed a phalanx around the bold citizen-Minister who sought to diminish the pride of the oligarchy. But I still believe that many a high-born Whig who sat proudly behind Canning would have wheeled right-about-face to the old fox-hunting order had the question of abolishing all the privileges of the nobility been suddenly agitated. I believe (God forgive me the sin!) that Francis Burdett himself, who during his youth was one of the hottest Radicals, and is not as yet classed among the moderate reformers, would, in such a case, have very quickly have seated himself by Sir Thomas Lethbridge. The plebeian Radicals are perfectly aware of this, and they hate, therefore, the so-called Whigs who advocate Parliamentary reform — yes, almost more than the utterly hostile high Tories.

At present the English Opposition consists more of actual reformers than of Whigs. The leader of the Opposition in the Lower House belongs unquestionably to the latter. I allude to Brougham.

We daily read in the papers the reports of the speeches of this bold hero of Parliament. The personal peculiarities which are manifested in the delivery of these speeches are not so well known, and yet we must know them to duly appreciate the latter. The sketch which an intelligent Englishman has made of Brougham's appearance in Parliament may be appropriately given here : —

" On the first bench, at the left side of the Speaker, sits a figure, which appears to have cowered so long by the study-lamp, that not only the bloom of life, but even life's strength, seem to have begun to exhaust themselves ; and yet it is this apparently helpless form which attracts every eye in the House, and which, as it rises in a mechanical, automatic manner, excites all the reporters behind us into rapid movement, while every corner of the gallery is filled as though it were a massy stone value, and the mob of men without presses in through both the side-doors. In the House below, an equal interest seems to manifest itself ; for, as that form slowly unfolds itself in a vertical curve, or rather into a vertical zig-zag of stiff lines joined together, the two zealots on either side, who just before sought in crying out to check each other, have suddenly sunk back into their places, as though they had espied an air-gun hidden under the Speaker's robe.

" After this bustle of preparation, and during the breathless stillness which follows, Henry Brougham has slowly and with thoughtful step approached the table, and there stands' bent together — his shoulders elevated, his head inclined forward, his upper lip and nostrils quivering, as though he feared to utter a word. His external appearance, his manner, almost resembles that of one of those preachers who hold forth in the open air — not a modern man of the kind who attracts the indolent crowd on Sunday — but one of those preachers of the olden time who sought to uphold purity of faith, and to spread it forth in the wilderness, when it was banished from the city and even from the church. The tones of his voice are full and melodious, but they rise slowly, thoughtfully, and as we are tempted to believe, even with difficulty, so that we know not whether the intellectual strength of the man is incapable of mastering the subject, or whether his physical strength is incapable of mastering the subject, or whether his physical is inadequate to express it. His first sentence, or rather the first members of his sentence — for we soon find that with him every sentence goes further than the entire speeches of many other people — come forth very coldly and without confidence, and are especially so far from the real question under discussion that no one can comprehend how he will bring them to bear upon it. It is true that every one of these sentences is deep, clear, and satisfactory in itself, evidently drawn with artistic selection from the most chosen materials ; and let them come from what department of science they may, they still contain its purest essence. We feel that they will all be bent in a determined direction, and that, too, with wondrous force ; but the force is as yet invisible as the wind, and, like it, we know not whence it cometh or whither it goeth.

" But when a sufficient number of these beginning sentences have gone forth in advance ; when every lemma which human knowledge can supply to confirm a conclusion has been rendered serviceable ; when every exception has, by a single impulse, been successfully thrust forward ; and when the whole army of political and moral truth stands in battle-array, then it moves forwards to a determination, firmly closed as a Macedonian phalanx, and irresistible as Highlanders when they charge with fixed bayonets.

" When a leading point has been won with this apparent weakness and uncertainty, behind which, however, a real strength and firmness lies concealed, then the orator rises both physically and mentally, and with a bolder and shorter attack he conquers a second position. After the second he conquers a third, after a third a fourth, and so on until all the principles and the entire philosophy of the question in dispute are, as it were, conquered, and until every one in the House who has ears to hear and a heart to feel is as irresistibly convinced of the truths which he has just heard as of his own existence ; so that Brougham, if he would pause here, could pass unconditionally for the greatest logician of St. Stephen's Chapel. The intellectual resources of the man are really marvellous, and he almost recalls the old Northern legend of one who always slew the first masters of every branch of learning, and thereby became sole heir to all their united spiritual abilities. Let the subject be as it may, sublime or commonplace, abstruse or practical, Henry Brougham still understands it, and understands it fundamentally. Others may rival him — yes, one or the other may even surpass him in the knowledge of the external beauties of ancient literature, but

474

no one is more deeply penetrated than he by the spirit of the glorious and glowing philosophy which gleams like a precious gem from the caskets left us by antiquity. Brougham does not use the clear, faultless, and at the same time somewhat courtly language of Cicero, and his speeches are as little in the form of those of Demosthenes, though they have something of their color ; but he is not wanting either in the strongly logical conclusions of the Roman orator nor the terrible words of scorn of the Greek. Add to this that no one understands better than he how to use the knowledge of the day in his parliamentary speeches, so that they sometimes, apart from their political tendency and signification, merit our admiration merely as lectures on philosophy, literature, and art.

" It is, however, altogether impossible to analyze the character of the man while hearing him speak. When he, as already described, has laid the foundation of his speech on a good philosophical ground and in the depths of reason ; when he, again returned to the work, applies to it plummet and measure to see if all is in order, and seems to try with a giant's hand if all holds together securely ; when he has firmly bound together the thoughts of all hearers with arguments as with ropes which no one can rend asunder, then he springs in power on the edifice which he has built, he raises his form and his voice, he conjures the passions from their most secret hiding-place, and subdues and overwhelms his gaping parliamentary contemporaries and the whole murmuring House. That voice, which was at first so slow and unassuming, is now like the deafening roar and the endless billows of the sea ; that form, which before seemed sinking under its own weight, now looks as though it had nerves of steel and sinews of copper — yes, as though it were immortal and unchangeable as the truths which it has just spoken ; that face, which before was pale and cold as a stone, is now animated and gleaming, as though its inner spirit were still mightier than the words spoken ; and from those eyes, which at first looked so humbly at us, with their blue and tranquil rings, as thought they would beg our forbearance and forgiveness, there now shoots forth a meteoric fire which lights up every heart with admiration. In this manner he concludes the second, the passionate or declamatory part of his oration.

" When he has attained what might be regarded as the summit of eloquence, when he looks around as if to behold with a scornful laugh the admiration which he has excited, then his form again shrinks together and his voice sinks to the most singular whisper which ever came from human breast. This strange lowering, or rather letting fall, of expression, gesture, and voice, which Brougham possesses to a perfection such as was never found in any other orator, produces a wonderful effect, and those deep, solemn, almost murmured-out words, which are, however, fully audible, even to the breathing of every single syllable, bear with them a magic power which no one can resist, even when he hears them for the first time, and has not learned their real significance and effect. But let no one believe that the orator or the oration is exhausted. These subdued glances, these softened tones, signify nothing less than the beginning of a peroration, wherewith the orator, as though he feels that he has gone too far, will again soothe his opponent. On the contrary, this contraction of the body is no sign of weakness, and this lowering of the voice is no prelude to fear and exhaustion ; it is the loose, hanging inclination of the body in a wrestler who looks for an opportunity by which he can grasp his adversary the more powerfully ; it is the recoil of the tiger, who, an instant after, leaps with more certain claws upon his prey ; it is the indication that Henry Brougham puts on all his armor and grasps his mightiest weapons. He was clear and convincing in his arguments ; in conjuring up the passions he was, it is true, somewhat supercilious, yet powerful and triumphant ; now, however, he puts the last and longest arrow to his bow — he will be terrible in his invectives. Woe to the man on whom that eye, which was once so calm and blue, now flashes from the mysterious darkness of its contracted brows! Woe to the wight to whom these half-whispered words are a portent of the terrible fate which hangs over him!

" He who as a stranger visits today, perhaps for the first time, the Gallery of Parliament does not know what is coming. He merely sees a man who convinces him with his arguments, who has warmed him with his passion, and who now appears to arrive, with that strange whispering, at a weak and impotent conclusion. O stranger! wert thou acquainted with the phenomena of this House, and on a seat whence thou couldst see all the Members of Parliament, thou wouldst soon mark that they are by no means of thy opinion so far as concerns a lame and impotent conclusion. Thou wouldst see many a man whom party feeling or presumption has driven, without proper ballast or needful helm, into this stormy sea, and who now glances around as fearfully and anxiously as a sailor on the China Seas when he on one side of the horizon discovers the dark calm, which is a sure presage that on the other, ere a minute has passed away, the typhoon will blow with its destructive breath — thou wouldst perceive some shrewd man well-nigh groaning, and who trembles in body and soul like a small bird, which, yielding to the fascination of a rattlesnake, feels with terror its danger, yet cannot help itself, and which yields in a miserably foolish manner to destruction ; or thou wouldst observe some tall antagonist who clings with shaking legs to the benches, lest the approaching storm should drive him away ; or thou wouldst perhaps even see a stately, pursy representative of some fat county, who digs both fists into the cushions of his bench, fully determined, in case a man of his weight should be cast from the House, still to keep his seat and to bear it thence, beneath him. And now it comes — the words, which were so deeply whispered and murmured, swell out so loudly that they outsound even the rejoicing cry of his own party ; and after some unlucky opponent has been flayed to the bones, and his mutilated limbs have been stamped on through every figure of speech, then the body of the orator is as if broken down and shattered by the power of his own soul, he sinks back on his seat, and the assenting applause of the assembly bursts forth without restraint."

I was never so fortunate as to be able to see Brougham at my leisure during the delivery of such a speech in Parliament. I only heard him speak in fragments, or on unimportant subjects, and I seldom saw his face while so doing. But always, as I soon observed, whenever he began to speak an almost painful silence at once fol-

477

lowed. The sketch of him given above is most certainly not exaggerated. His figure, of ordinary stature, is very meager and in perfect keeping with his head, which is thinly covered with short black hair which lies smooth towards the temples. This causes the pale, long face to look even thinner ; its muscles are ever in strange, nervous movement, and he who observes them sees the orator's thoughts before they are spoken. This spoils his witty outbursts ; since jests, like borrowers, should, to succeed, surprise us unawares. Though his black dress is altogether gentlemanly, even to the very cut of the coat, it still gives him a certain clerical appearance. Perhaps this is owing more to his frequent bending of the back, and the lurking, ironic suppleness of his whole body. One of my friends first called my attention to this " clerical " appearance in Brougham's manner, and the above sketch fully confirms the accurateness of the remark. The " lawyer-like " in his general appearance was first suggested to me by the manner in which he continually demonstrates with his pointing finger, while he nods assentingly with his head.

The restless activity of the man is his most wonderful feature. These speeches in Parliament are delivered after he has been eight hours at his daily tasks, that is to say, practicing law in the courts, and when he perhaps has sat up half the night writing an article for the *Edinburgh Review*, or laboring on his improvements of Popular Education and Criminal Law. The last-mentioned work, that on Criminal Legislation, with which Brougham and Peel are now principally busied, is perhaps the most useful, certainly the most necessary ; for England's laws are even more cruel than her oligarchs. Brougham's celebrity was first founded by the suit against the Queen. He fought like a knight for this high dame, and, as any one might suppose, George IV. will never forget the service rendered to his wife. Therefore, when in April last the Opposition conquered, Brougham did not enter the Ministry ; althoungh, according to old custom, such an entry was due to him, as leader of the Opposition.

XI.   THE EMANCIPATION

TALK POLITICS WITH THE STUPIDEST ENGLISHMAN, AND HE WILL BE sure to say something sensible ; but so soon as the conversation turns on *religion*, the most intelligent Englishman utters nothing but silly speeches. Hence arises all that confusion of ideas, that mixture of wisdom and nonsense, whenever Catholic Emancipation is discussed in Parliament, a question in which politics and religion come into collision. It is seldom possible for the English, in their parliamentary discussions, to give utterance to a principle ; they discuss only the profit or loss of things, and bring forth *facts, pro* or *con*.

With mere *facts* there can, indeed, be much fighting, but no victory ; they induce nothing but blows on one or the other side ; and the spectacle of such a strife reminds us of the well-known *pro patria* conflicts of German students, the results of which are that so and so many lunges are exchanged, and so and so many carte and tierce thrusts made, and nothing gained with it all.

In the year 1827, as a matter of course, the Emancipationists again fought the Orangemen in Westminster, and, as another matter of course, nothing came of it. The best " hitters " of the Emancipation party were Burdett, Plunkett, Brougham, and Canning. Their opponents, with the exception of Peel, were the well-known, or, more correctly speaking, the not-at-all-known, fox-hunting squirearchy.

At all times the most intelligent and gifted statesmen of England have fought for the civil liberty of the Catholics, and this they did inspired as much by the deepest sense of right as by political shrewdness. Pitt himself, the discoverer of the firm system, held to the Catholic party. In like manner, Burke, the great renegade of freedom, could not so far suppress the voice of his heart as to act against Ireland. Even Canning, while yet a slave to Toryism, could not behold, without emotion, the misery of Ireland ; and at a time when he was accused of luke-warmness, he showed, in a naïvely touching manner, how dear its cause was to him. In fact, a great man can, to attain great aims, often act contrary to his convictions,

479

and go ambiguously from one party to another ; and, in such cases, we must be complacent enough to admit that he who will establish himself on a certain height must yield accordingly to circumstances, like the weathercock on a church-spire, which, though it be made of iron, would soon be broken and cast down by the storm-wind if it remained obstinately immovable, and did not understand the noble art of turning to every wind. But a great man will never so far contradict his own feelings as to see, or, it may be, increase, with cold-blooded indifference, the misfortunes of his fellow-countrymen. As we love our mother, so do we love the soil on which we were born ; and even so do we love the flowers, the perfume, the language, and the men peculiar to that soil. No religion is so bad, and no politics so good, that they can extinguish such a love in the bosoms of its devotees ; and Burke and Canning, though Protestants and Tories, could not, for all that, take part against poor, green Erin. Those Irishmen who spread terrible misery and unutterable wretchedness over their fatherland are men — like the late Castlereagh.

It is a regular matter of course that the great mass of the English people should be opposed to the Catholics, and daily beseige Parliament for the purpose of withholding privileges from the latter. There is a love of oppression in human nature, and when even we, as is constantly done, complain of civil inequality, our eyes are always directed upwards — we see only those who stand over us, and whose privileges abuse us. But we never look downwards when complaining thus — the idea never comes into our heads to raise to our level those who are placed by unjust custom below us ; yes, we are soundly vexed when they seek to ascend, and we rap them on the head. The Creole demands equality with the European, but oppresses the Mulatto, and flares up in a rage when the latter puts himself on an equality with him. Just so does the Mulatto treat the Mestizo, and he in turn the Negro. The small citizen of Frankfort worries himself over the privileges of the nobility, but he worries himself much more when any one suggests to him the emancipation of his Jews. I have a friend in Poland who is wild for freedom and equality, but who, to this hour, has never freed his peasants from their serfdom.

No explanation is requisite to show why the Catholics are persecuted, so far as the English clergy is concerned. Persecution of those who think differently is everywhere a clerical monopoly, and the Anglican Church strongly asserts her rights. Of course, tithes are the main thing with her ; by emancipating the Catholics she would lose a great part of her income, and the sacrifice of *self*-interest is a talent manifested as little by the priests of love as by sinful laymen. Hence it happened that that glorious revolution to which England owes most of her present liberty sprang from religious Protestant zeal ; a circumstance which imposes special duties of gratitude towards the dominant Church, and causes her to regard the latter as the main bulwark of her freedom. Many a fearful soul may at present really dread Catholicism and its restoration, and think of the flaming piles of Smithfield — and a burnt child dreads the fire ! There are also timid Members of Parliament who dread a new Gunpowder Plot — those fear powder most who have not discovered it — and so they often feel as if the green benches on which they sit in St. Stephen's Chapel became, little by little, warmer ; and when an orator, as very often happens, mentions the name of Guy Fawkes, they cry out " Hear, hear ! " as if in terror. As for the Rector of Göttingen, who has an appointment in London as King of England, he is fully familiar with his policy of moderation and forbearance ; he declares himself in favor of neither party ; he sees both mutually weaken themselves by combat ; he smiles in his hereditary manner when they peaceably court him ; he knows everything, does nothing, and in cases of difficulty leaves everything to his head catch-poll, Wellington.

I trust that I may be pardoned for treating in a flippant tone a question on whose solution depends the happiness of England, and with it, perhaps directly, that of all the world. But just the weightier the subject, so much the more merrily must we manage it ; the bloody butchery of battles, the fearful whetting of the sickle of death, would be beyond all bearing did there not ring out with it, and through it, deafening military music, with joy-inspiring drums and trumpets. This the English know right well, and therefore their Parliament displays a cheerful comedy of the most un-restrained wit, and of the wittiest unrestraint. In the most serious debates, where the lives of thousands and the welfare of whole countries is at stake, it never occurs to any one to make a stiff German district-representative face, or to declaim French pathetic-ally, and their minds, like their bodies, act freely and without restraint. Jest, self-quizzing, sarcasms, natural disposition and wis-dom, malice and good-nature, logic and verse, spray forth in the freshest variations of color, so that the annals of Parliament, years after, afford us a most glorious entertainment. How strongly do these debates contrast with the empty, bolstered-up, blotting-paper speeches of our South German Chambers, whose tiresomeness defies the patience of the most unwearied newspaper reader ; yes, whose very aroma suffices to scare away any living reader, so that we must believe that the tiresomeness in question is a secret and deliberate intention to frighten the public from reading their acts, and thereby to keep them secret, despite their publicity !

If the manner in which the English treat the Catholic question in Parliament is but little adapted to produce a result, it is not the less true that the reading of these debates is on that account all the more interesting, because facts are more entertaining than abstrac-tions, and they are especially amusing when a contemporary event is narrated in a story-telling form, which handles it with witty persiflage, and thereby illustrates it, it may be, in the best possible manner. In the debate on the Royal Speech, December 3, 1825, we had in the Upper House one of these parallel histories such as described, and which I here literally translate (*vide* " Parliamentary History and Review during the Session of 1825 - 1826," page 31) : —

" Lord King remarked that if England could be called flourishing and happy, there were, notwithstanding, six millions of Catholics in an altogether different condition on the other side of the Irish Channel, and that the bad government there was a shame to our age and to every Briton. The whole world, said he, is now too reasonable to excuse Governments which oppress their subjects, or rob them of a right, on account of differences in religion. Ireland and Turkey could be regarded as the only countries in Europe where whole classes of men were oppressed and made to suffer on account of their creeds. The Grand Sultan had endeavored to convert the Greeks in the same manner in which the English Government had attempted the conversion of the Catholics, but without result. When the unfortunate Greeks bewailed their sufferings, and begged in the humblest manner to be treated a little better than Mohammedan dogs, the Sultan summoned his Grand Vizier to give counsel. This Grand Vizier had been formerly a friend, and more recently an enemy, of the Sultana. He had thereby suffered considerably in the favor of his lord and was obliged to endure, in his own Divan, many contradictions from his own officers and servants. (Laughter.) He was an enemy of the Greeks. The second person in influence in the Divan was the Reis Effendi, who was favorably inclined to the just demands of that unlucky race. This officer, as was well known, was Minister of Foreign Affairs, and his policy merited and received general approbation. He manifested in this field extraordinary liberality and talent ; he did much good, and would have effected much more had he not been impeded in all his measures by his less enlightened colleagues. He was, in fact, the only man of real genius in the whole Divan—(laughter)—and he was esteemed as an ornament to the statesmen of Turkey, since he was also endowed with poetic talent. The Kiaya-Bey, or Minister of the Interior, and the Kapitan Pasha were also opposed to the Greeks ; the leader of the whole opposition to the demand for rights of this race was the Grand Mufti, or the head of the Mohammedan Faith. (Laughter.) This officer was an enemy to every change. He had regularly opposed every improvement in commerce, every improvement in justice, every improvement in foreign policy. (Laughter.) He declared and showed himself on every occasion to be the great champion of existing abuses. He was the most finished intriguer in the whole Divan. (Laughter.) At an earlier time he had declared for the Sultana, but he had turned against her so soon as he feared that he thereby might lose his seat in the Divan, and had even gone over to the party of her enemies. The proposition was once made to enlist some Greeks into the corps of regular troops or Janissaries, but the Head-Mufti raised against this such a terrible hue-and-cry — something like our No-Popery cry — that those who adopted the measure were obliged to quit the Divan. He gained the upper hand, and so soon as this was done he declared himself in favor of the very cause against which he previously displayed all his zeal. He took care of the Sultan's conscience and of his own ; but it had been remarked that his conscience was never in opposition to his interests. (Laughter.) Having studied the Turkish Constitution with the utmost accuracy, he had found in it that it was substantially Mohammedan — (laughter) — and consequently must be inimical to all the rights of the Greeks. He had therefore determined to adhere firmly to the cause of intolerance, and was soon surrounded by Mollahs, Imans, and Dervishes, who confirmed him in his noble determinations. To complete this picture of a perfect division in the Divan, it should also be mentioned that its members had agreed to unite on certain questions, and to oppose one another on others, without breaking up their union. After the evil arising from such a Divan had been seen, after it had been seen, too, how the Mussulman realm had been torn, and that by their intolerance to the Greeks and by their own want of harmony, we should pray Heaven to preserve the fatherland from such a division in the Cabinet."

It requires no remarkable acuteness to guess who the persons are here disguised in Turkish names ; still less is it necessary to set forth the moral of the tale in dry words. The cannon of Navarino have spoken it out loud enough ; and when the Sublime Porte shall be shattered — and shattered it will be, despite Pera's plenipotentiaried lackeys, who oppose the ill-will of the people — then John Bull may call to mind that, with changed names, the fable applies to him. England may already surmise something of the kind, since its best journalists have declared against the war of intervention and signified, naïvely enough, that the other nations of Europe might, with equal right, take up the part of Catholic Ireland, and compel the British Government to a better treatment of it. They think that they have thereby fully refuted the right of intervention, whereas they have simply illustrated it more perfectly and intelligibly. Of course, the nations of Europe would have the most sacred right to remedy, by force of arms, the sufferings of Ireland ; and this right would soon be realized were not injustice the stronger. It is no longer crowned heads, but the people themselves, who are the heroes of modern times, and these heroes have also formed their holy alliance. They hold together wherever there is a question of the common weal, or the popular rights of political and religious liberty ; they are connected by the *Idea ;* they have sworn themselves to it, and bleed for it — yes, they themselves have become an idea — and therefore it runs like a sharp pain through the hearts of all the people when the Idea is made to suffer, though it be in the uttermost corner of the earth.

But I wander from my topic. I meant to repeat old parliamentary jokes, and see! the spirit of the time turns my jest to earnest. But now I will give something merrier ; that is to say, an address which Spring Rice, on the 26th of May of the same year, delivered in the Lower House, and in which he jested most admirably at the Protestant terror at the possible supremacy of the Catholics.

" In the year 1753," he said, " there was brought before Parliament a Bill for the nationalization of Jews — a measure against which, today, in all this land, not so much as an old woman would have a word to say, but which in its time provoked the most violent opposition, resulting in a mass of petitions from London and other places, much like those which we now see presented against the Catholic Bill. In the one from the citizens of London it was declared that, should the Bill for the Jews receive legal sanction, it would terribly endanger the Christian religion and undermine the State and our holy Church. (Laughter.) Especially would it injure the interests of trade, and to an extraordinary degree those of the city of London. (Laughter.)

" However, notwithstanding this powerful denunciation, the next Chancellor of the Exchequer found that the dire results threatened had not taken place when the Jews were admitted to citizenship in London, and even to Downing Street. (Laughter.) At that time a newspaper called *The Artisan*, in denouncing the countless disasters to which such a measure would lead, expressed itself as follows : —
' I must beg leave to set forth separately the consequences of this

485

Bill. There is grace and mercy in God, but none in the Jews, and they have seventeen hundred years of oppression to revenge on us. Should this Bill pass we shall all become slaves of the Jews, and without hope of rescue, save by the goodness of God. The King will be subjected to Jews, and no longer look to the interests of the free landed proprietors. He will do away with our British soldiers, and establish a great army entirely of Jews, who will force us to renounce our Royal Family and be naturalized under a Jewish monarch. Therefore awake, my Christian and Protestant brothers! It is not Hannibal but the Jews who are before your gates, and they demand the keys of your church-doors.' (Long-continued laughter.)

" In the debates on this Bill in the House, a baron from the West — (laughter) — declared that if naturalization should be granted to the Jews we should be in danger of soon seeing them in Parliament. 'They will,' he said, 'divide our counties among their race, and sell our landed properties to the highest bidder.' (Laughter.) Another Member of Parliament was of the opinion that 'if the Bill should pass, the Jews will increase so rapidly that they will spread over the greatest part of England, and deprive the people of their land and of their power.' The Member for London, Sir John Bernard, regarded the matter from a deeper theological point of view, one which is repeated exactly in the late petition from Leicester, whose signers reproach the Catholics as being descendants of those who burned their ancestors. 'And, in like manner,' he cried, 'the Jews are the descendants of those who crucified the Savior, and for that are cursed by God unto their latest descendants.' He (Spring Rice) cited these instances to show that the old alarm-cry was as much founded in reason as the new outcry against the Catholics. (Hear, hear!) In the time of the Jewish Bill there was published a jesting mock Jewish journal, in which the following notice appeared: — 'Since our last number the post-coach from Jerusalem has arrived. The last week in the lying-in hospital, Brownlow Street, twenty-five boys were publicly circumcised. Yesterday evening the Bill for naturalizing Christians was unanimously rejected in the Sanhedrin. The report of a rising of the Christians in North Wales is without foundation. Last Friday the annual celebration of the Crucifixion was celebrated with great gaiety throughout the kingdom.'

" In this manner, and at all times, both as regards the Jewish and the Catholic Bills, the most laughable opposition was provoked by the most absurd means ; and if we seek for the causes of such alarms, we find that they were quite alike. If we investigate the causes of the opposition to the Jewish Bill in 1753, we find as leading authority Lord Chatham, who declared in Parliament that ' he, as well as most other gentlemen, was convinced that religion itself had nothing to do with this question, and that it was only *the old High Church's persecuting spirit* which had succeeded in persuading the people to the contrary.' (Hear, hear!) So it is in this case, and it is their love of exclusive power and precedence which now impels the old exalted Church to stir up the people against the Catholics ; and he (Spring Rice) was convinced that many who use such arts knew perfectly well how little religion was really involved in the last Catholic Bill—just as little as in a Bill for regulating weights and measures, or for determining the length of a pendulum according to the number of its swings. There had just then appeared in the *Hardwick Journal*, in reference to the Jewish Bill, a letter from Dr. Birch to Mr. Philip York, in which he declared that all this alarm was only intended to influence the next elections. (Hear! and laughter.) It had happened then, even as it has in this our time, that a reasonable, sensible Bishop of Norwich had come forward in favor of the Jewish Bill. Dr. Birch relates that the Bishop, on his return to his church district, was for this insulted. ' As he went to Ipswich to confirm certain boys, he was mocked by the way, people asking him to circumcise them, and it was also announced that the Lord Bishop would on the next Sabbath confirm the Jews, and the next day circumcise the Christians.' (Laughter.) In like manner the outcry against liberal measures in all ages was equally unreasonable and brutal. (Hear, hear!) Those fears as regarded the Jews could be compared with the alarm which had been excited in certain places by the Bill for the Catholics. The danger which men feared, should more power be granted to the Catholics, was just as absurd—the power to work mischief, should they be so inclined, could not be given them by law in even so high a degree as they now possessed simply by their oppression. For it is by this oppression that such men as Mr. O'Connell and Mr. Shiel have become so popular. These men were not named to make them suspicious characters ; on the contrary, one should respect them, and they have deserved well of their country ; but it would be better if power were in the laws instead of in the hands of individuals, no matter how deserving of respect they may be. The time will come when the resistance of Parliament to such concessions of justice will be regarded, not merely with amazement, but contempt. The religious wisdom of an earlier age was often the subject of contempt to the following generation." (Hear, hear!)

XII.   WELLINGTON

THIS MAN HAS THE BAD FORTUNE TO MEET WITH GOOD FORTUNE everywhere, and wherever the greatest men in the world were unfortunate ; and that excites us, and makes him hateful. We see in him only the victory of stupidity over genius — Arthur Wellington triumphant where Napoleon Bonaparte is overwhelmed! Never was a man more ironically gifted by Fortune, and it seems as though she would exhibit his empty littleness by raising him high on the shield of victory. Fortune is a woman, and perhaps in the way of woman she cherishes a secret grudge against the man who overthrew her former darling, though the very overthrow came from her own will. Now she lets him conquer again on the Catholic Emancipation question — yes, in the very fight in which George Canning was destroyed. It is possible that he might have been loved had the wretched Londonderry been his predecessor in the Ministry ; but it happens that he is the successor of the noble Canning — of the much-wept, adored, great Canning — and he conquers where Canning was overwhelmed. Without such an adversity of prosperity, Wellington would perhaps pass for a great man ; people would not hate him, would not measure him too accurately, at least not with the heroic measure with which a Napoleon and a

Canning is measured, and consequently it would never have been discovered how small he is as man.

He is a small man, and smaller than small at that. The French could say nothing more sarcastic of Polignac than that he was a Wellington without glory. In fact, what remains when we strip from a Wellington the field-marshal's uniform of glory?

I have here given the best apology for Lord Wellington—in the English sense of the word. My readers will be astonished when I honorably confess that I once praised this hero—and clapped on all sail in so doing. It is a good story, and I will tell it here:—

My barber in London was a Radical, named Mr. White—a poor little man in a shabby black coat, worn until it almost shone white again ; he was so lean that even his full face looked like a profile, and the sighs in his bosom were visible ere they rose. These sighs were caused by the misfortunes of Old England—by the impossibility of paying the National Debt.

" Ah!" I generally heard him sigh, " why need the English people trouble themselves as to who reigns in France, and what the French are a-doing at home? But the high nobility, sir, and the High Church were afraid of the principles of liberty of the French Revolution ; and to keep down these principles John Bull must give his gold and his blood, and make debts into the bargain. We've got all we wanted out of the war—the Revolution has been put down, the French eagles of liberty have had their wings cut, and the High Church may be cock-sure that none of them eagles will come a-flying over the Channel ; and now the high nobility and the High Church between 'em ought to pay, any way, for the debts which were made for their own good, and not for any good of the poor people. Ah! the poor people!"

Whenever Mr. White came to the " poor people " he always sighed more deeply than ever, and the refrain then was, that bread and porter were so dear that the poor people must starve to feed fat lords, stag-hounds, and priests, and that there was only one remedy. At these words he was wont to whet his razor, and as he drew it murderously up and down the strop, he murmured grimly to himself, " Lords, priests, hounds!"

But his Radical rage boiled most fiercely against the Duke of Wellington ; he spat gall and poison whenever he alluded to him, and as he lathered me he himself foamed with rage. Once I was fairly frightened when he, while barbering away at my neck, burst out in wonted wise against Wellington, murmuring all the while, " If I only had him *this* way under my razor, *I'd* save him the trouble of cutting his own throat, as his brother in office and fellow-countryman, Londonderry, did, who killed himself that-a-way at North Cray in Kent—God damn him!''

I felt that the man's hand trembled, and fearing lest he might imagine, in his excitement, that I really was the Duke of Wellington, I endeavored to allay his violence, and in an underhand manner, to soothe him, I called up his national pride, I represented to him that the Duke of Wellington had advanced the glory of the English, that he had always been an innocent tool in the hands of others, that he was fond of beefsteak, and that he finally — but the Lord only knows what fine things I said of Wellington as I felt that razor tickling around my throat!

What vexes me most is the reflection that Wellington will be as immortal as Napoleon Bonaparte. It is true that, in like manner, the name of Pontius Pilate will be as little likely to be forgotten as that of Christ. Wellington and Napoleon! It is a wonderful phenomenon that the human mind can at the same time think of both these names. There can be no greater contrast than the two, even in their external appearance. Wellington, the dumb ghost, with an ashy-grey soul in a buckram body, a wooden smile in his freezing face — and by the side of *that* think of the figure of Napoleon, every inch a god!

That image never disappears from my memory. I still see him, high on his steed, with eternal eyes in his marble-like, imperial face, glancing calm as destiny on the Guards defiling past — he was then sending them to Russia, and the old Grenadiers glanced up at him, so terribly devoted, so all-consciously serious, so proud in death—

" Te, Cæsar, morituri, salutant!"

There often steals over me a secret doubt whether I ever really saw him, if we were ever contemporaries, and then it seems to me as if his portrait, torn from the little frame of the present, vanished away more proudly and imperiously in the twilight of the past. His name even now sounds to us like a word of the early world, and as antique and as heroic as those of Alexander and Cæsar. It has already become a rallying word among races, and when the East and the West meet they fraternize on that single name.

I once felt in the deepest manner how significantly and magically that name can sound. It was in the harbor of London, at the India Docks, and on board an East Indiaman just arrived from Bengal. It was a giant-like ship, fully manned with Hindus. The grotesque forms and groups, the singularly variegated dresses, the enigmatical expressions of countenance, the strange gestures, the wild and foreign ring of their language, their shouts of joy and their laughter, with the seriousness ever rising and falling on certain soft yellow faces, their eyes like black flowers which looked at me as with wondrous woe — all of this awoke in me a feeling like that of enchantment. I was suddenly as if transported into Scheherezade's story, and I thought that broad leaved-palms, and long-necked camels, and gold-covered elephants, and other fabulous trees and animals must forthwith appear. The supercargo who was on the vessel, and who understood as little of the language as I myself, could not, in his truly English narrow-mindedness, narrate to me enough of what a ridiculous race they were, nearly all pure Mohammedans collected from every land of Asia, from the limits of China to the Arabian Sea, there being even some jet-black, woolly-haired Africans among them.

To one whose whole soul was weary of the spiritless West, and who was as sick of Europe as I then was, this fragment of the East which moved cheerfully and changingly before my eyes was a refreshing solace ; my heart enjoyed at least a few drops of that draught which I had so often tasted in gloomy Hanoverian or Royal Prussian winter nights, and it is very possible that the foreigners saw in me how agreeable the sight of them was to me, and how gladly I would have spoken a kind word to them. It was also plain from the very depths of their eyes how much I pleased them, and they would also have willingly said something pleasant to me, and it was a vexation that neither understood the other's language. At length a means occurred to me of expressing to them with a single word my friendly feelings, and stretching forth my hands reverentially as if in loving greeting, I cried the name, " Mohammed ! "

Joy suddenly flashed over the dark faces of the foreigners, and folding their arms as reverentially in turn, as a cheerful greeting they exclaimed, " Bonaparte ! "

XIII.   THE LIBERATION

SHOULD THE TIME FOR LEISURELY RESEARCH EVER RETURN, I WILL prove, in the most tiresomely fundamental manner, that it was not India but Egypt which originated that system of castes which has for two thousand years disguised itself in the garb of every country, and has deceived every age in its own language ; which is now perhaps dead, yet which, counterfeiting the appearance of life, wanders about among us, evil-eyed and mischief-making, poisoning our blooming life with its corpse vapor ; yes, which, like a vampire of the Middle Ages, sucks blood from the nations and light from their hearts. It was not merely crocodiles, who knew so well how to weep, who sprang from the mud of the Nile, but also priests who understand it far better, and that privileged hereditary race of warriors who, in their lust of murder and ravenous appetites, far surpass any crocodiles.

Two profound men of the German nation discovered the soundest and best counter-charm to the worst of all Egyptian plagues, and by the black art — by gunpowder and the art of printing — they broke the force of that clerical and laical hierarchy which had formed itself from an union of the priesthood and warrior caste ; that is to say, from the so-called Catholic Church and from the feudal nobility, and which enslaved all Europe both in body and in the spirit. The printing-press burst asunder the walls of the building of dogmas in which the high priest of Rome had imprisoned souls, and Northern Europe again breathed freely, freed from the nightmare of that clergy which had indeed abandoned the *form* of Egyptian inheritance of rank, but which remained all the truer to the Egyptian priestly spirit, since it presented itself with greater sternness and asperity, as a corporation of old bachelors, continued not by natural propagation, but by a Mameluke system of recruiting. In like manner we see how the warlike caste has lost its power since the old routine of the business is worth nothing in the modern methods of war. For the strongest castles are now thrown down by the trumpet-tones of the cannon, as the walls of Jericho were thrown down of old ; the iron harness of the knight is no better protection against the leaden rain than the linen blouse of the peasant ; powder makes men equal ; a citizen's musket fires as well as a nobleman's — the people are rising.

.   .   .   .

The earlier efforts of which we read in the history of the Lombard and Tuscan Republics, of the Spanish Communes, and of the free cities in Germany and other countries do not deserve the honor of being classed as a movement on the part of the people ; they were not efforts to attain liberty, but merely liberties ; not battles for right, but for municipal power ; corporations fought for privileges, and all remained fixed in the bonds of guilds and trades-unions.

Not until the days of the Reformation did the battle assume general and spiritual proportions, and then liberty was demanded, not as an imported but as an aboriginal, not as an inherited but as an inborn, right. Principles were brought forward instead of old parchments ; and the peasants in Germany and the Puritans in England fell back on the Gospel, whose texts then were of as high authority as our modern reasoning. Yes, and even higher, since they were regarded as the revealed reason of God himself. There it stood legibly written, that men are of equal birth, that the pride which exalts itself must be damned, that wealth is a sin, and that the poor also are summoned to enjoyment in the beautiful garden of God, the common Father of all.

With the Bible in one hand and with the sword in the other the peasants swept over South Germany, and announced to the proud and wealthy burgherhood of high-towered Nuremburg that in future no house should be left standing which seemed other than a peasant's house. So truly and so deeply had they comprehended the truth. Even at the present day in Franconia and in Suabia we see traces of this doctrine of equality, and a shuddering reverence of the Holy Spirit creeps over the wanderer when he sees in the moonshine the dark ruins of castles from the time of the peasants' war. It is well for him who in sober, waking mood sees naught besides ; but if one is a " Sunday child " — and every one familiar with history is that — he will also see the high hunt in which the German nobility, the rudest and sternest in the world, pursued their victims. He will see how unarmed men were slaughtered by thousands ; how they were racked, speared, and martyred ; and from the waving corn-fields he will see the bloody peasants' heads nodding mysteriously, while above a terrible lark is heard whistling, piping revenge, like the piper of Helfenstein.

Their brothers in England and Scotland were more fortunate ; their defeat was neither so disgraceful nor so unproductive, and to the present day we see there the results of their rule. But they did not effect a firm foundation of their principles ; the dainty cavaliers now rule again as before, and amuse themselves with merry tales of the stiff old Roundheads which a friendly bard has written so prettily to entertain their leisure hours. No social over-throw took place in Great Britain ; the framework of civil and political institutions remained undisturbed, the tyranny of castes and of trade-guilds has remained there till the present day, and though penetrated by the light and warmth of modern civilization, England is still congealed in a medieval condition, or rather in the condition of a fashionable Middle Age. The concessions which have there been made to liberal ideas have been with difficulty wrested from this medieval immovability, and all modern improvements have there proceeded, not from a principle but from actual neces-sity, and they all bear the curse of that half-way system which inevitably makes new exertion and new conflicts to the death, with all their attendant dangers, a matter of necessity. The religious reformation in England is consequently but half perfected, and one finds himself much worse off between the four bare prison-walls of the Episcopal Anglican Church than in the large beautifully painted and softly cushioned prison for the soul of Catholicism. Nor has it succeeded much better with the political reformation ; popular representation is in England as faulty as possible, and if ranks are no longer distinguished by their coats, they are at least divided by different courts of justice, patronage, rights of Court presentation, prerogatives, customary privileges, and similar fatalities ; and if the rights of person and property of the people depend no longer upon aristocratic caprice, but upon laws, still these laws are nothing but another sort of teeth with which the aristocratic brood seizes its prey, and another sort of daggers wherewith it treacherously murders the people. For in reality no tyrant upon the Continent squeezes, by his own arbitrary will, so many taxes out of his subjects as the English people are obliged to pay by law, and no tyrant was ever so cruel as England's criminal law, which daily commits murder for the amount of one shilling, and that with the coldest formality. Although many improvements have recently been made in this melancholy state of affairs in England, although limits have been placed to temporal and clerical avarice, and though the great falsehood of a popular representation is, to a certain degree, occasionally modified by transferring the perverted electoral voice of a rotten borough to a great manufacturing town, and although the harshest intolerance is here and there softened by giving certain rights to other sects, still it is all a miserable patching up which cannot last long, and the stupidest tailor in England can foresee that, sooner or later, the old garment of State will be rent asunder into the wretchedness of rags.

"No man putteth a piece of new cloth unto an old garment ; for that which is put in to fill it up taketh from the garment, and the rent is made worse. Neither do men put new wine into old bottles ; else the bottles break, and the wine runneth out, and the bottles perish ; but they put new wine into new bottles, and both are preserved."

The deepest truth blooms only from the deepest love, and hence comes the harmony of the views of the elder Preacher in the Mount, who spoke against the aristocracy of Jerusalem ; and those later preachers of the mountain, who from the summit of the Convention in Paris preached a tri-colored gospel, according to which not merely the form of the State but all social life should be, not patched, but formed anew, and be not only newly founded, but newly born.

I am speaking of the French Revolution, that epoch of the world in which the doctrines of freedom and of equality rose so triumphantly from those universal sources of knowledge which we call reason, and which must, as an unceasing revelation which repeats itself in every human head and founds a distinct branch of knowledge, be far preferable to that transmitted revelation which makes itself known only in a few of the elect, and which can only be *believed* in by the multitude. The privileged aristocracy, the caste-system, with their peculiar rights, were never able to combat this last-mentioned sort of revelation (which is itself of an aristocratic nature) so safely and surely as reason, which is democratic by nature, now does. The history of revolution is the military history of this strife, in which we have all taken a greater or lesser part ; it is the fight to the death with Egyptianism.

Though the swords of the enemies grow duller day by day, and though we have already conquered the best positions, still we cannot raise the song of victory until the work is perfected. We can only during the night, between battles, when there are armistices, go forth with the lantern on the field of death to bury the dead. Little avails the short burial-service! Calumny, the vile insolent specter, sits upon the noblest graves.

Oh that the battle were only with those hereditary foes of truth who so treacherously poison the good name of their enemies, and who even humiliated that first Preacher of the Mount, the purest hero of freedom ; since, when they could no longer deny that he was the greatest of men, they made of him the least of gods! He who fights with priests may make up his mind to have his poor good name torn and befouled by the most infamous lies and the most cutting slanders. But as these flags which are most rent, or blackened by powder-smoke in the battle, are more highly prized than the whitest and soundest recruiting banners, and as they are at last laid up as national relics in cathedrals, so at some future day the names of our heroes, the more they are torn and blackened, will be all the more enthusiastically honored in the holy Saint Genevieve Church of Freedom.

The Revolution itself has been slandered, like its heroes, and represented as a terror to princes, and as a popular scarecrow in libels of every description. All of the so-called " horrors of the Revolution " have been learned by heart by children in the schools, and at one time nothing was seen in the public fairs but harshly colored pictures of the guillotine. It cannot be denied that this machine, which was invented by Monsieur Guillotin, a French physician and a great world orthopedist, and with which the stupidest heads are easily separated from evil hearts, this most excellent and wholesome machine has indeed been applied rather frequently, but still only in incurable diseases ; in such cases, for example, as treachery, falsehood, and weakness ; and the patients were not for a long time tortured, racked, and broken on the wheel, as thousands upon thousands of *vilains*, citizens, and peasants were tortured or racked, and broken as *roturiers*, on the wheel, in the good old time. It is, of course, terrible that the French, with this machine, once even amputated the head of State, and no one knows whether they ought to be accused, on that account, of parricide or of suicide ; but, on more moderate and thorough reflection, we find that Louis of France was less a sacrifice to passion than to circumstances, and that those men who forced the people on to such a sacrifice, and who have themselves in every age poured forth princely blood far more abundantly, should not appear solely as accusers. Only two kings, both of them rather kings of the nobility than of the people, were sacrificed by the people, and that not in a time of peace, or to subserve petty interests, but in the extremest needs of war, when they saw themselves betrayed, and when they least spared their own blood. But certainly more than a thousand princes were treacherously slain, on account of avarice or frivolous interests, by the dagger, by the sword, and by the poison of nobility and priests. It really seems as though these castes regarded regicide as one of their privileges, and therefore bewail the more selfishly the death of Louis XVI. and of Charles I. Oh that kings at last would perceive that they could live more safely as kings of the people, and protected by the law, than under the guard of their noble body-assassins!

But not only have the heroes of our Revolution and the Revolution itself been slandered, but even our entire age has been parodied with unheard-of wickedness, and if one hears or reads our vile traducers and scorners, then he will learn that the people are the *canaille*—the vile mob—that liberty is license, and with heaven-bent eyes and pious sighs our enemies complain and bewail that we were frivolous, and had, alas! no religion. Hypocritical, dissembling souls, who creep about bent down beneath the burden of their secret vices, dare to vilify an age which is, perhaps, holier than any of its predecessors or successors—an age that sacrifices itself for the sins of the past and for the happiness of the future—a Messiah among centuries, which could hardly endure its bloody crown of thorns and heavy cross, did it not now and then trill a merry vaudeville and crack a joke at the modern Pharisees and Sadducees. Its colossal pains would be intolerable without such jesting and persiflage! Seriousness shows itself more majestically when laughter leads the way. And the age in this shows itself exactly like its children among the French, who have written frightfully frivolous books, and yet have been very strong and serious when strength and seriousness were necessary ; as, for instance, Laclos, and even Louvet de Couvray, who both, when it came home to them, fought for freedom with the boldness of martyrs and with self-sacrifices, yet who wrote very trivially and lasciviously, and alas! had no religion!

As if freedom were not as good a religion as any other! And since it is ours, we may, measuring with the same meter, declare its contemners to be themselves frivolous and irreligious.

Yes, I repeat the words with which I opened these pages — freedom is a new religion, the religion of our age. If Christ be no longer the God of this religion, he is, nevertheless, one of its high priests, and his name shines consolingly into the hearts of the younger believers. But the French are the chosen race of the new religion ; the first gospels and dogmas were penned in their language. Paris is the New Jerusalem, and the Rhine is the Jordan which separates the land of liberty from the country of the *Philistines*.

CONCLUSION

Written November 29, 1830

IT WAS IN DEPRESSED TIMES IN GERMANY — TIMES WHICH WERE under arrest — when I wrote the second volume of the " Pictures of Travel," and had it printed as I wrote. But before it appeared, something was whispered about it ; it was said that my book would encourage and awaken the cowed spirit of freedom, and that measures were being taken to suppress it. When such rumors were afloat it was advisable to bring out the book as quickly as possible, and to drive it through the press. As it was necessary that it should contain a certain number of leaves, to escape the requisitions of the eminently estimable censorship, I followed the example of Benvenuto Cellini, who, in founding his " Perseus," found himself 'short of bronze, and to supply the deficiency, and to fill up the mold, threw into the melted metal all the tin plates which he could find. It was, beyond question, easy enough to detect the difference between the tin — especially the tin termination of the book — and the better bronze, but any one who understood the business would not betray the secrets of the workman.

But as everything in this world is liable to turn up again, so it came to pass that, in this very volume, I found myself again in the same scrape, and I have been obliged to again throw some tin into the mold — let me hope that this renewed melting of baser metal will simply be attributed to the pressure of the times.

499

Alas! the whole book sprang from the pressure of the times, as did the similar tendency of earlier writings. The more intimate friends of the writer, who are acquainted with his private circumstances, know well how little his own vanity forced him to the tribune, and how great were the sacrifices which he was obliged to make for every independent word which he has spoken since then, and — if God will! — which he still means to speak. Nowadays a word is a deed whose consequences cannot be measured, and no one knows whether he may not eventually appear as blood-witness for every word.

For years I have waited in vain for the words of those bold orators who once in the meetings of the German Burschenschaft so often claimed a hearing, who so often overwhelmed me with their rhetorical talent, and spoke a language spoken so oft before ; they were then so forward in noise — they are now so backward in silence. How they then reviled the French and the Southern Babel, and the un-German frivolous betrayers of the Fatherland who praised Frenchdom. That praise verified itself in the great week!

The great week of Paris! The spirit of freedom, which was wafted thence over Germany, upset, of course, here and there, some night-lamps, so that the red curtains of sundry thrones took fire, and golden crowns grew hot under blazing night-caps ; but the old watchmen, in whom the royal police trusted, are already bringing out the fire-buckets, and now scent around all the more suspiciously and forge all the more firmly their secret chains, and I mark well that a far more impenetrable prison vault is being arched over the German people.

Poor imprisoned people! be not cast down in your need. Oh that I could speak catapults! Oh that I could shoot firebrands from my heart!

The aristocratic icy coat of reserve melts from my heart, a strange sorrow steals over me — is it love, and love for the German race? Or is it sickness? — my soul quivers and my eyes burn, and that is an unfortunate occurrence for a writer, who should command his material and remain nicely objective, as the schools of art require, and as Goethe himself did — he grew to be eighty years old in so doing, and a minister, and opulent at that—poor German race! that is thy greatest man!

I still have a few octavo pages to fill, and will do so with a story—it has been floating in my head since yesterday—a story from the life of Charles the Fifth. But it is now a long time since I heard it, and I no longer remember its details with accuracy. Such things are easily forgotten, if one does not receive a regular salary for reading them every half-year from his lecture books. But what does it matter if the names of places and historical dates are forgotten, so long as their inner significance or their moral remains in a man's memory? This it is which really stirs in my soul and mournfully moves me even to tears. I fear I am getting ill.

The poor Emperor was captive to his enemies, and lay in stern imprisonment. I believe that it was in Tyrol. There he sat in solitary sorrow, abandoned by all his knights and courtiers, and no one came to his aid. I know not if he already had in those days that pale complexion, like cheese, with which Holbein portrays him. But the misanthropically scornful under-lip protruded, beyond question, even more markedly then than in his pictures. He must have despised the people who fawned and wagged around him in the sunshine of prosperity, and who left him now in dark and bitter need. Suddenly the prison door opened, and there entered a man wrapped in a cloak, and when it was cast aside the Emperor recognized in the visitor his trusty Kunz von der Rosen, the court fool. This one brought him consolation and counsel—and it was the court fool.

O German Fatherland! dear German race! I am thy Kunz von der Rosen. The man whose real office was pastime, and who only made thee merry in better days, forces his way into thy prison in time of need; here, beneath my mantle, I bring thee thy strong scepter and the beautiful crown; dost thou not remember me, my emperor? If I cannot free thee, I will at least console thee, and thou shalt have some one by thee who will talk with thee about thy all too pressing oppressions, and will wake up thy courage, and who loves thee, and whose best jokes and best blood are ever at thy service. For thou, my people, art the true emperor, the true lord of the land ; thy will is sovereign and far more legitimate than that purple *Tel est notre plaisir*, who grounds his claim upon a divine right, without any better guarantee than the quackery of shaved and shorn jugglers ; thy will, my people, is the only righteous source of all power. Yet, even though thou liest down there in fetters, thine own good right must prevail at last, the day of freedom draws near, a new time begins — my emperor, the night is over, and the red light of morning gleams without.

" Kunz von der Rosen, my poor fool, thou errest. Thou hast mistaken the shining axe of the executioner for the sun, and the dawn is nothing but blood."

" No, no, my emperor, it is the sun, though it rises in the West — since six thousand years, we have always seen it rise in the East — it is high time that it for once made a change in its course."

" Kunz von der Rosen, my fool, thou hast lost the bells from thy red cap, and it now has such a strange look, that red cap!"

" Ah, my emperor, in your distress I have shaken my head in such mad earnest that the fool's bell fell from my cap ; but it is none the worse for that!"

" Kunz von der Rosen, my fool, what is it breaking and cracking without there?"

" Hush — silence! it is the saw and the carpenter's axe, and the doors of your prison will soon be broken in, and you will be free, my emperor!"

" Am I then really emperor? Ah, it is only the fool who tells me so!"

" Oh! do not sigh so, my dear lord ; it is the air of the dungeon which so dispirits you ; when you shall have regained your power, you will once more feel the bold imperial blood in your veins, and you will be proud as an emperor, and arrogant, and gracious, and unjust, and smiling, and ungrateful, as princes are."

" Kunz von der Rosen, my fool, when I am again free what wilt thou be doing?"

" I will sew new bells on my cap."

" And how shall I reward thy fidelity?"

" Ah! dear master — do not suffer me to be put to death!"

Doctor Faust

A Ballet Poem

INTRODUCTION

MR. LUMLEY, THE DIRECTOR OF HER MAJESTY'S THEATER IN LONDON, requested me to write a ballet, and in accordance with his wish I composed the following poem. I called it *Doctor Faust ein Tanz-poem* (" Dr. Faust a Ballet-poem "). However, it was not brought on the stage, partly because during " the season " for which it was announced the unexampled success of the so-called Swedish Nightingale, Jenny Lind, made any other exhibition superfluous, and partly because the *maître de ballet* (stage-manager), hindering and delaying, inspired by the *esprit de corps de ballet*, interposed with every manifestation of ill-will. This stage-manager of the ballet regarded it as a dangerous innovation that a poet should compose the libretto of a ballet, because such works had hitherto been contributed by the ballet monkeys of his kind, in collaboration with some miserable literary hack. Poor Faust! poor wizard! In this manner must thou renounce the honor of exhibiting thy black art before the great Victoria of England! Will it succeed any better for thee in thy native land? Should, contrary to all my expectation, any German stage display its good taste by producing my work, I beg the very praiseworthy management not to neglect on such occasion to send to the author the money due him to the care of the publishers, Hoffmann & Campe in Hamburg — that is, to me or to my legal heirs. I consider it a not superfluous remark that I, to secure my right of property in this ballet in France, have already published a French version of it, and sent the number of copies required by law to the proper places.

When I had the pleasure of giving my manuscript to Mr. Lumley, and we discussed over a fragrant cup of tea the spirit of the legend

of " Faust " and my treatment of it, the *impressario* requested me
to note down the principal details of our conversation, in order that
he might subsequently enrich with it the libretto which he proposed
to distribute to the audience on the night when the ballet should
be produced. In accordance with this friendly request, I wrote
the letter to Lumley which I give, somewhat abbreviated, at the end
of this little work, since it may be of some interest to the German
reader of these transitory pages.

As regards the historical Faust, I have in this letter to Lumley
said but little regarding the mythical character. Therefore I cannot
refrain from here giving briefly, as regards the origin and development of this legend, a fable of Faust, the result of my investigations.

It is not really the legend of Theophilus, major domo of the
Bishop of Adama in Sicily, but an old Anglo-Saxon dramatic form
of it, which must be considered as the foundation of " Faust." In
the still extant Low German pcem of Theophilus, there are old
Anglo-Saxon forms of speech, like petrified words or fossil phrases,
which show that this poem is only an imitation of an older original,
which was lost in the course of time. This Anglo-Saxon poem must
still have existed not long before the invasion of England by
the Norman French, since it was apparently imitated, and almost
literally imitated, by the Troubadour Rutebœuf, and was brought
out in France as a *Mystère* on the stage. For those to whom the
collection of Mommerque in which this mystery is printed is not
accessible, I would say that the learned Mangin spoke in detail
regarding it some seven years ago in the *Journal des Savants*. This
mystery of the Troubadour Rutebœuf was used by the English poet
Marlowe, when he wrote his " Faust." He had also the analogous
legend of the German sorcerer Faust, according to the old " Faust "
book, of which there was already an English translation, and put
it into dramatic form, suggested by the French *Mystère*, which was
also known in England. The work of Theophilus and the old *Volks-
buch*, a popular story of Faust, were therefore the two sources
from which the drama of Marlowe sprang. Its hero is, however,
not a reckless rebel against heaven, who, led astray by a sorcerer,
assigns his soul to the devil to gain earthly prosperity, but is finally

saved by the grace of the mother of God, who brings the compact out of hell, as in Theophilus. The hero of the play is here a sorcerer himself, in whom, as in the " Faust " book, all the legends of earlier magicians are united, and whose masterpieces he produces before eminent personages. This is done on Protestant ground, where the mother of God cannot appear, for which reason Faust is carried away by the devil without pardon or pity.

The puppet-show theatre, which flourished in London in Shakespeare's time, and which at once seized on every piece which succeeded in the great establishments, must certainly have given a " Faust " according to Marlowe's pattern, either parodying it more or less seriously, adapting it to local requisitions, or, as often happened, taking it from the author himself, who worked it up to suit their public. This " Faust " came over from England to the Continent, traveled through the Netherlands, visited our country in its fairs, and, translated into coarse German jawing, and bull-horned with German Jack-pudding ingredients, delighted the lower strata of German society. But however unlike the versions became in the course of time, especially from improvised additions, the play remained substantially the same, and it was such a puppet-play which Wolfgang Goethe saw in a side-show at Strasburg which supplied our great poet with the form and material of his masterwork. In the first fragment, or partial edition, of Goethe's " Faust," this is most perceptible, this has not the introduction taken from " Sakúntala," and the prologue imitated from Job ; it does not as yet vary from the simple form of the puppet-play, and there is no essential motive in it which indicates any knowledge of the older original books of Spiess and Widman.

That is the genesis of the legend of " Faust," from the poem of Theophilus to that of Goethe, who raised it to its present popularity. Abraham begat Isaac, Isaac begat Jacob, but Jacob begat Judah, in whose hands the scepter will remain forever. In literature, as well as in life, every son has a father, whom he certainly does not always know, or whom he would even fain deny.

HEINRICH HEINE

(Written in Paris, October 1, 1851)

Thou hast evoked me from the grave,
  All by thy magic will ;
Brought me to life by passion's glow,
  And that glow thou canst not still.

Oh, press thy mouth unto my mouth,
  Divine is human breath ;
I drink thy very soul from thee,
  Insatiable in death.

ACT I

A STUDY, LARGE AND ARCHED, IN GOTHIC STYLE. ON THE WALLS ARE
shelves of books, here and there astrological and alchemistic imple-
ments (celestial and terrestrial globes, schemes of the planets,
retorts and strangely-shaped glass vessels), anatomical preparations
(skeletons of men and animals), and similar requisites of nec-
romancy.

Midnight strikes. Doctor Faust sits reflecting in a high arm-chair
by a table, on which are piled books and scientific instruments. His
costume is that of a German scholar of the sixteenth century. He
rises at last and totters with unsteady steps to a book-case, where a
great folio is fastened with a chain. He unlocks it and bears with
difficulty the book (*Höllenzwang*, or the so-called " Hell-compul-
sion ") to his table. In his demeanor and whole personality there is
apparent a blending of helplessness and courage, of awkward
schoolmasterly manners and arrogant professional pride. After
lighting several candles and drawing magic circles on the ground
with a sword, he opens the great book, and his demeanor indicates
the mysterious awe of invocation. The study grows darker, there is
thunder and lighting, and from the ground, which opens with a
crackling, crashing sound, there rises a flaming red tiger. Faust does
not manifest the least fear ; he advances to the fiery beast with
contempt, and seems to command it to depart at once. It sinks into
the earth.

Faust begins anew his incantations, it again thunders and lightens terribly, and out of the opening earth darts a monstrous serpent, which, winding and twisting in the most terribly threatening manner, hisses out fire and flames. The Doctor also treats it with contempt ; he shrugs his shoulders, laughs and mocks it because the spirit of hell cannot appear in a far more terrible form, so that at last the snake creeps back into the earth. Faust renews his incantations with greater zeal. Then the darkness disappears, the room is suddenly lit with countless candles, instead of thunder there is heard the most exquisite dancing-music, and out from the opening earth, as if from a basket of flowers, leaps a lovely ballerina, dressed in the usual gauze and tricot costume, who capers about with the most frivolous pirouettes.

Faust seems to be at first astonished or somewhat displeased that the invoked devil Mephistopheles does not assume a more awful form than that of a ballet-dancer ; but at last he seems to be pleased with this smiling, graceful apparition, and pays her a courteous compliment. Mephistopheles, or rather Mephistophela, as we are now to call the womanized devil, returns the compliment in parody, and dances round him in the usual coquettish fashion. She holds in her hand a magic wand, and all she touches with it in the room becomes changed in the most amusing manner without losing shape : thus the dark planetary forms light up from within ; from the jars containing malformed creatures or abortions the most beautiful birds peep or fly ; owls bear brilliant nosegays in their bills ; from the walls come forth the most magnificent golden objects — Venetian mirrors, antique bas-reliefs, works of art ; all chaotic and unearthly, yet gleaming magnificently — a monstrous arabesque. The beautiful demon seems to glide into friendly relation with Faust, yet he will not sign the parchment — the terrible compact — which she offers him. He requires that she shall call up the other powers of hell, and these princes of darkness appear accordingly. They are monsters in grotesquely horrible forms of beasts, fabulous blendings of what is scurrilous, or comic and frightful, most of them wearing crowns, and bearing scepters in their claws. Faust is presented to them by Mephistophela, a ceremony in which the strictest court etiquette is observed.

Waddling along with much attempt at formality, their majesties begin a clumsy dance ; but as Mephistophela touches them with her wand, their ugly masks and garb fall off, and they are all changed into dainty ballet-dancers, who flutter about in gauze and tricot, with garlands of flowers. Faust amuses himself with this metamorphosis, yet does not seem to find among the pretty ballerinas one who quite pleases him. Mephistophela observing this again wields her wand, and in a large mirror, which appears by magic art upon the wall, there appears the form of a wonderfully beautiful woman in court dress, and with a ducal crown on her head. As soon as Faust beholds her he is carried away with admiration and rapture, and approaches the lovely form with every manifestation of desire and tenderness. But the lady in the looking-glass, who now acts as if living, repels him with the haughtiest turning up of her nose. He kneels before her, but she only redoubles her signs of contempt.

The poor Doctor turns his head with suppliant look towards Mephistophela, who only replies by roguishly shrugging her shoulders. Then she waves her magic wand. There rises from the ground, unto his hips, a hideous monkey, who at a sign from Mephistophela (who angrily shakes her head) disappears in an instant, and is succeeded by a young and handsome youth, a ballet-dancer, who executes the most commonplace *entrechats*. The dancer, approaches the lady in the looking-glass, and while he with the most commonplace impertinence makes love to her, she smiles again to him in the most charmed and charming manner, stretches out her arms to him, and exhausts herself in tenderest manifestations. At this sight Faust is in rage and despair, but Mephistophela takes pity on him, and touches with her wand the handsome youth. He lets fall his fine garments, appears as the hideous ape, and sinks into the ground. Mephistophela again offers the parchment to Faust, who, without ado or delay, opens a vein in his arm, and with his blood signs the contract by which for earthly enjoyment he resigns all heavenly happiness. He casts away his serious and honorable doctor's dress, and puts on the sinful, gaily-colored tinseled finery which the dancer has left lying on the ground. In this dressing, which he effects clumsily and comically, he is aided by the infernal *corps de ballet*.

Mephistophela now gives Faust a lesson in dancing and shows him all the handy, or rather footy, tricks of the trade or game. The awkwardness and stiffness of the sage, who attempts to perform the dainty and graceful *pas* of his teacher, form the most amusing effects and contrasts. The diabolical chorus of dancing-girls will also give their aid, and every one attempts to show how this or that is to be done. One throws the poor Doctor into the arms of another, who waltzes round with him ; he is pulled and hauled here and there, but by the power of love and of the magic wand, with which his rebellious limbs are constantly being touched, the pupil in choreography at last attains perfect dexterity. Then he dances a *pas de deux* with Mephistophela, and to the delight of all his devilish damsel fellow-artists, he flies about with her in the most marvelous figures. Having attained to this virtuosity he ventures to dance before the lovely lady of the looking-glass, who now responds to his pantomimic love-making with correspondingly passionate gestures. Faust thereon continues to dance with ever-increasing delirium, but Mephistophela tears him away from the mirror-form, who, touched by the magic wand, at once disappears, and the high-class dancing of the old-fashioned French classic school is resumed.

ACT II

A LARGE SPACE BEFORE A CASTLE WHICH IS SEEN TO THE RIGHT. ON the sloping terrace the Duke and his Duchess sit in high stately chairs, surrounded by their courtiers, knights, and ladies. The Duke is a stiff and formal elderly gentleman, his wife a young, voluptuous, and splendid beauty, remarkably similar to the lady of the looking-glass in the first act. It is noticeable that she wears a *gold shoe* on her left foot.

The scene is splendidly decorated for a court festival. A pastoral play is acted in the most old-fashioned rococo style, shallow

509

gracefulness and gallant innocence. This sweetly pretty Arcadian jigging is suddenly interrupted by the grand entrance of Faust and Mephistophela, who, in her dress as dancer, and with her troupe of diabolical ballerine makes a triumphal entry amid joyous trumpet peals. Faust and Mephistophela incline in bounding reverences before the ducal pair, but the former, as well as the Duchess, the more closely they regard one the other, are stirred as with delightful memories, and regard one another with mutually tender looks. The Duke seems to accept with peculiarly gracious acquiescence the courtesies of Mephistophela. In an impetuous *pas de deux* which the latter dances with Faust, both keep an eye on the ducal pair, and when the diabolical dancing-girls come and take their place, Mephistophela flirts with the Duke and Faust with the Duchess, the extreme passion of the latter being parodied by the ironic modesty with which Mephistophela repels the angular and starched gallantries of the Duke.

The Duke finally turns toward Faust and asks him to give a specimen of his magic art. He wishes to see King David as the latter danced before the Ark of the Covenant. In obedience to this august command, Faust takes the magic wand from Mephistophela, waves it in invocation, and the group called for appear. First comes the Ark drawn by Levites ; King David dances before it with the delight of a buffoon, and oddly dressed, like a king of cards ; while behind the holy ark, with spears in their hands, see-sawing about, hop the king's life-guards, dressed like Polish Jews, in long flapping black silk caftans, and with tall fur caps on their nodding heads, with pointed beards. After these caricatures have made the round of the stage, they sink into the earth amid stormy applause.

Faust and Mephistophela again leap forth in a brilliant *pas de deux*, in which one looks at the Duchess and the other at the Duke with such amorous piquancy that the illustrious pair can no longer resist, and, leaving their seats, join the dance. This is followed by a dramatic quadrille in which Faust attempts more earnestly than ever to entrap the Duchess. He has discovered a *Teufelsmal*, or the sign of a witch, on her neck, and as this reveals that she is a sorceress, he appoints a rendezvous with her at the next Sabbat. She is alarmed and denies it, but Faust points at her golden shoe, which is a sure sign that she is the *Domina* or chief mistress of Satan. With a bashful air she grants the rendezvous. The Duke and Mephistophela renew their affected love-scene, and the demon dancers take the place of the quartette, which gradually disappears behind them.

At the renewed request of the Duke to give another display of his magic art, Faust grasps the wand, and touches with it the whirling dancers. They change in an instant into the monsters of the first scene, and, instead of gracefully circling, go tumbling and stumbling among and on one another in the clumsiest manner, and amidst sputtering fires sink into the earth. Roaring applause, for which Faust and Mephistophela bow in thanks to the nobility and honorable public.

After each of these exhibitions of magic the gaiety increases, the four chief personages rush again to the dancing-place, and in the quadrille, which is renewed, passion becomes bolder and bolder. Faust kneels before the Duchess, who, in not less compromising action, admits her love ; the Duke, having pulled away by force the laughing Mephistophela, kneels before her like a lustful faun. But as he by chance turns round and sees his wife and Faust in such a compromising attitude, he jumps up in a rage, draws his sword, and will stab the insolent conjurer. Faust grasps his magic wand and taps the Duke on the head, from which spring two immense stag's horns, by the ends of which the Duchess holds him back. A general tumult among the courtiers, who attack Faust and Mephistophela. But as Faust waves his wand there is a warlike peal of trumpets, and from the back advances a procession of fully armored knights. While the courtiers turn as if to defend themselves, Faust and Mephistophela fly through the air on two black steeds. At the same instant the knights vanish like a phantasmagoria.

ACT III

NOCTURNAL MEETING-PLACE OF THE WITCHES' SABBAT. A BROAD plain on the summit of a mountain. Trees on either side, on whose branches hang strangely formed lamps, which illuminate the scene. In the midst is a stone pedestal, like an altar, on which stands a black goat with a black human face, and a burning candle between the horns. In the background rise, one above the other, the tops of mountains, as in an amphitheatre, on whose colossal steps sit as spectators the nobility of the Under-world—that is, those princes of hell whom we have seen in the previous acts, and who now appear giantlike. On the trees right and left sit musicians with faces like birds, holding eccentric stringed and wind instruments. The scene is animated with groups of dancers, whose dresses recall the most different lands and ages, so that the whole assembly seems like a fancy dress ball, the more so because many are really masked and mummed. But however baroque, bizarre, and startling many of these forms may be, they should not conflict with a sense of beauty, and the ugly impression of caricatured creatures is softened or extinguished by fairy-like splendor and positive horror. Before the goat's altar a man and woman walk up and down, each bearing a black candle ; they bow before the back-side of the goat, kneel down, and pay it the homage of a kiss. Meanwhile new guests come riding through the air on brooms, pitchforks, great spoons, or on wolves and cats. These arrivals find their lovers or sweethearts awaiting them. After a most joyful welcome they mix with the dancing groups. Also her Highness the Duchess comes flying on an immense bat ; she is as devoid of clothing as is possible, and wears on her left foot the golden shoe. She appears to seek with impatience for some one. Finally she beholds the desired one, namely, Faust, who comes with Mephistophela on a black horse to the festival. He wears splendid knightly clothing, and his companion is modestly clad in the chaste clothes of a noble German lady.

Faust and the Duchess rush into each other's arms, and their attachment shows itself in the most impassioned dancing. Mephistophela has meantime also found her expected sweetheart—a dry and slender gentleman in a black Spanish cloak, and with a blood-red cock's feather. But while Faust and the Duchess dance through all the steps of a progressive, passionate, wild love, the *duo* of Mephistophela and her partner is, as contrast, only the vulgar sensual expression of gallantry, or of the desire which makes sport of itself. All the four at last take black candles and pay homage to the goat in the manner already described, and end with a grand round, in which the whole assembly whirl about the altar. What is peculiar in the dance is this, that the performers turn their backs on one another, and do not see one another's faces, which are turned away.

Faust and the Duchess escaping from the round dance, having attained the acme of passionate love, disappear behind the trees to the right hand. The round dance ends. New guests come before the altar and renew the adoration of the he-goat ; among them are crowned heads, even the high dignitaries of the Church in their sacramental robes.

Meanwhile many monks and nuns appear in the front ground, whose extravagant polka-leaps delight the demons on the hills around, who applaud with their long stretched-out claws. Faust and the Duchess reappear, but all his expression is changed, and he turns with disgust from the woman who, with her hair flowing, pursues him with her voluptuous caresses. He shows her in most unmistakable manner that he feels satiety and aversion. In vain she throws herself imploringly before him, he repels her with disgust. At this instant three Negroes, clad in tabards of gold on which black goats are embroidered, come forward, ordering the Duchess to appear at once before her lord and master Satan, and the lady resisting is dragged away by force. In the background the goat is then seen to descend from his pedestal and, after making several very singular signs of courtesy, dances with her a minuet, in slow and ceremonious step. The face of the goat expresses the misery of a fallen angel and the profound ennui of a blasé prince, that of the Duchess desperate despair. The dance at an end the goat resumes his place on the pedestal, and the ladies who have been looking on approach the Duchess with courtesies and reverences, and then take her away. Faust meanwhile stands in the foreground, and while looking at the minuet Mephistophela appears by his side. Faust points at the Duchess with disgust and dislike, and seems to relate something horrible. He specially manifests his aversion for all the grotesque absurdities which he sees around, and all this Gothic rubbish, which only amounts to a stupid and despicable burlesque of ecclesiastical asceticism, and which is as disagreeable to him as the latter. He feels an infinite yearning for the purely beautiful, for Greek harmony, for the unselfish and noble forms of the Homeric world of spring. Mephistophela understands him, and touching the ground with her magic staff the image of Helen of Troy rises and at once disappears. This it was which the learned Doctor, with his heart yearning for the antique, had always desired. He manifests the greatest inspiration, and at a sign from Mephistophela the magical steeds again appear, on which both fly away.

At this instant the Duchess comes on the scene, sees Mephistophela and her lover disappearing, and falls fainting in despair to the ground. Eccentric monsters then raise and carry her round about as if in triumph, with laughter and coarse tricks. A renewal of the infernal round dance, which is interrupted all at once by the shrill ringing of a handbell and a choral of an organ, which is a wild sacrilegious parody of church-music. All press up to the altar, where the goat flames up crackling and burns away. After the curtain has fallen the grotesque and horrible sounds of the Satan's mass are still heard.

ACT IV

AN ISLAND IN THE ARCHIPELAGO, TO THE LEFT A VIEW OF THE SEA, of a pure emerald hue, contrasting charmingly with the turquoise blue of the sky, whose sunny daylight shines over an ideal landscape. Vegetation and Greek architecture as beautiful as once were dreamed by the poet of the Odyssey. Pines, laurel-bushes in whose shadows white statues repose, great marble vases with fabulous plants, trees wound with garlands of flowers, crystal waterfalls. To the right side a temple to Venus Aphrodite—whose statue gleams from among the pillars—all animated with a race of men in the prime of beauty, youths in white festival garments ; girls in lightly-girded dresses of nymphs, their heads crowned with roses or myrtle. Some amuse themselves in groups, others are engaged in religious ceremonies about the temple of the goddess. Everything breathes Greek joyousness, the ambrosial peace of the gods and classic repose. Nothing recalls the cloudy past, the mystical thrills of rapture and of agony, the supernatural ecstasy of a spirit which emancipates itself from the body. Here all is real, plastic happiness, without retrospective melancholy or any foreboding empty yearning. The Queen of this island is Helena of Troy, the most beautiful woman in poetry, and she dances as the leader of the ladies of her court before the temple of Venus. The dance and the attitudes are in keeping with the surroundings, all in measure chaste and solemn.

All at once Faust and Mephistophela break into this world. flying on their black steeds through the air. They seem to be suddenly freed from the gloomy pressure of a nightmare, from a horrible illness or a sad lunacy, and both are revived, and refresh themselves by this sight of the primevally beautiful and the truly noble. The Queen and her train dance hospitably toward them, offer them food and drink in richly embossed plate, and invite them to dwell in their peaceful, fortunate island. Faust and his companion accept the invitation by a joyous dance, and all forming a festive procession seek the temple of Venus, where Faust and Mephistophela exchange their romantic medieval garb for superb yet simple Greek dresses. Returning with Helena to the front scene, they execute a mythologic *pas de trois*.

Faust and Helena at last seat themselves on a throne at the right hand, while Mephistophela, seizing a tambourine, leaps about as a bacchante in wild attitudes. The maidens of Helena, seized with inspiration, tear the roses and myrtles from their heads, wind vine leaves into their loosened locks, and with flowing hair and swinging thyrses dance excitedly as Bacchante. Then the young men, arming themselves with shield and spear, take the place of the damsels, and dance in mock battle one of those warlike pantomimes which are so genially described by early authors.

Into this heroic pastoral there may be introduced an antique humorous byplay — that is, a swarm of Cupids riding on swans, who also begin with bows and spears a battle-dance. But this beautiful scene is suddenly interrupted by the entrance of the Duchess, who comes sweeping through the air on her enormous bat, and advances like a fury before the throne on which Faust and Helena are seated. The frightened Cupids leap hastily on their swans and fly away. The enraged Duchess appears to reproach Faust like a fury, and threatens Helena. Mephistophela, who regards the whole scene with malicious delight, begins anew the Bacchantic dance, in which the maids of the Queen also join, so that this joyous chorus contrasts mockingly with the rage of the Duchess. The latter can at last no longer contain her rage, she whirls the magic wand, and seems to accompany the action with the most terrible invocations. Then the heaven grows dark, there is thunder and lightning, the sea rises roaring and storming, and there is on the whole island a terrible change in persons and things. All seems struck by death. The trees stand leafless and barren, the temple falls into a ruin, the statues lie broken on the ground. Queen Helena sits as a dried-up corpse, almost a skeleton, in a white shroud by Faust's side ; the dancing maidens are also only bony specters, wrapped in white garments which, hanging over the head, only reach to their withered hips. These are the Lamiæ who are thus represented, and in this form they continue their gay dancing in the round as if nothing had taken place, nor do they appear to have observed any change. Then Faust, furious at seeing all his happiness wrecked by the revenge of a jealous sorceress, darts from the throne with drawn sword, and plunges it into the breast of the Duchess.

Mephistophela has meantime brought the two magic steeds. She anxiously urges Faust to mount one, and they ride away through the air. The sea continues to rise, it gradually covers men and monuments, only the dancing Lamiæ seem to take no notice of it, and they continue to dance to the merry sound of tambourines, till the waves reach their heads, and the whole island sinks. Far above the storm-lashed sea, high in the air, Faust and Mephistophela are seen racing away on their black steeds.

ACT V

A GREAT OPEN SPACE BEFORE A CATHEDRAL, WHOSE GOTHIC DOOR is seen in the background. On either side neatly trimmed lime trees, under which sit, eating and drinking, citizen folk dressed in the Netherlands style of the sixteenth century. Not far off, men with cross-bows, who in turn shoot at a bird on a pole. All about are amusements, as at a fair—booths, musicians, puppet-shows, jack-puddings, leaping, and merry groups. In the middle a strip of lawn, where the richer class are dancing.

The bird is at last shot down, and the victor, who is a great beer brewer, has his triumphal procession as archer-king, with an immense crown on his head, on which are many bells. On his back and before him are sheet-gold shields, with which he walks about proudly ringing and rattling. Before him march drummers and fifers, with a standard-bearer, a bandy-legged dwarf, who acts comically with an immense flag. The archer-procession follows gravely behind.

Before the fat burgomaster and his not less corpulent spouse, who sit with their daughter under the lime-tree, the flag is waved, and all passing bow in salutation. The burgomaster and wife return the compliment, and their daughter, a beautiful girl with blonde hair of the Flemish type, offers the cup of honor to the champion marksman.

Trumpet peals are heard, and the wise and learned Doctor Faust, in the scarlet and gold embroidered costume of an alchemist, appears on a high cart adorned with foliage. Mephistophela, who goes before the vehicle leading the horses, is also dressed in a "loud," highly-colored costume, as for one who cries in the market-place, extravagantly set off with ribbons and feathers. She bears a great trumpet, on which she sounds flourishes now and then, while she dances an attractive *réclame* to the mob. The people crowd round the wagon where the itinerant doctor sells all kinds of draughts and mixtures. Some bring him large flasks of water to examine. He draws the teeth of others. He works visible cures on crippled invalids, who leave him sound and well, dancing for joy. At last he leaves the cart, which is driven away, and distributes his phials containing a fluid, a few drops of which cure every ill, and excite in the taker an irresistible desire to dance. The king of the marksmen having tasted it, experiences its magic power ; he seizes Mephistophela, and hops with her a *pas de deux*. The drink has the same effect on the old burgomaster and his wife, and both hobble in an antiquated dance.

While all the public whirls in a mad waltz Faust has approached the burgomaster's daughter, and, enchanted by her unaffected naturalness, modesty, and beauty, declared his love, and with melancholy, and almost modest gestures, pointing to the church, begs for her hand. He renews his request to her parents, who sit gasping for breath on a bench. They are contented with the proposal, and the naïve beauty at last yields a modest assent. She is with Faust crowned with flowers, and they dance, as bride and bridegroom, a sober *bourgeois* nuptial round. The Doctor has found at last in a modest, sweet, and quiet life the domestic felicity which contents the soul. The doubt and extravagant and visionary raptures of suffering of a proud soul are forgotten, and he beams with inner happiness like the gilded cock on a church-spire.

The wedding procession is formed in becoming style, and it is on the way to church, when Mephistophela suddenly steps in the way, and with mocking laughter and gestures tears Faust from his idyllic sentiments, and seems to command him to instantly depart with her. Faust, in a rage, refuses, and the bystanders are startled at the scene. But far greater terror overcomes them when suddenly, at the invocation of Mephistophela, a midnight darkness and a terrible storm covers all. They fly in terror to the church near by, where a bell begins to toll, and the organ to peal—a sound suggesting religion and piety, which contrasts with the flashing and thundering infernal horrors of the stage. Faust, who would fain fly with the rest into the church for refuge, is kept back by a great black hand rising from the earth, while Mephistophela with bitter mockery draws from her bodice the parchment which Faust once signed with his blood, showing him that the time of the contract has expired, and that he now belongs, body and soul, to hell. He uses every argument in vain, and in vain has recourse to wailing and prayers for mercy — the female fiend dances round him with every grimace of scorn and mockery. The ground opens, and there come forth the horrible princes of hell, the crowned and sceptered monsters. In a round of rejoicing they also mock Faust, till Mephistophela, who has transformed herself into a horrible serpent, winds about and strangles him. The whole group sinks amid roaring flames into the earth, while the peal of the church-bells and the loud-ringing sound of the organ from the church, call pious Christian souls to prayer.

COMMENTS ON FAUST

To Lumley, Esq., Director of the Theater of Her Majesty the Queen

DEAR SIR, — I EXPERIENCED A HESITATION OR FEAR WHICH IS READILY understandable when I reflected that I had chosen for my ballet a subject which our great Wolfgang Goethe had already employed in his masterpiece. And if it was dangerous even with equal means of representation to compete with such a poet, how much more terribly perilous must the undertaking be when one provokes the combat with unequal weapons. In truth, Wolfgang Goethe had, to express his thoughts, the whole arsenal of the arts of speech ; he was the master of the German language, which is so rich in minted words of deep meaning, and ancient native sounds of the world of feeling, or magic formulas which, long vanished from life, still ring as echoes in the rhymes of Goethe's poems, and thrill so marvelously in our imagination. And how scant and poor are the means with which I, poor as I am, can express what I think and feel. I can work only with a slender libretto in which I must indicate as concisely as possible how male and female dancers are to act and make signs, and how I think the music and *mise en scène* should be arranged. Yet despite this I have dared to poetize a Doctor Faust in the form of a ballet, rivaling the great Wolfgang Goethe, who had before me taken all the freshness from the subject, and who to execute it could devote to it a long blooming life, like that of the gods, while to me, the afflicted invalid, only four weeks were allowed by you, my honored friend, in which to finish my work.

I could not go beyond the bounds prescribed, but within them I have done what a man with good heart and will may, and I have at least aimed at one excellence of which Goethe certainly cannot boast. What we entirely miss in his Faust-poem is fidelity to the original legend, a pious respect for its inner soul, a reverence which the sceptic of the eighteenth century (and such Goethe was to the end of his life) could neither feel nor understand. In this respect he was guilty of a certain arbitrary or original treatment, which was culpable from an aesthetic point, and which finally revenged itself on the poet. Yes, the faults of the poem came from this offence, since, in departing from the reverent symmetry according to which the legend lived in German popular familiarity with it, he could not execute the work according to the newly-conceived plan based on incredulity ; it was, in fact, never finished, unless we consider that lame or crippled second part of " Faust " which appeared forty years later as the completion of the whole poem. In this second part Goethe frees Faust the necromancer from the fangs of the devil ; he does not send him to hell, but permits him to enter heaven in triumph, accompanied by dancing angels and heavenly choirs, and the terrible compact with Satan, which caused such hair-on-end horror to our ancestors, ends like a frivolous farce — I had almost said like a ballet.

My ballet contains what is most important in the old legends of Doctor Faustus, and in combining their principal motives to a dramatic whole, I adhered conscientiously to the existing traditions as I found them in the popular chap-books, as they are sold in our market-places, and in puppet-shows as I saw them played in my youth.

The *Volksbücher*, or popular works referred to, are not by any means unanimous in their treatment of the tale. Most of them have been patched together, as the compiler pleased, from two much older and greater works on Faust, which, with the so-called *Höllenzwang*, are to be regarded as the chief sources of the legends. These works are in this relation too important to be passed over without special mention. The oldest of them was published in Frankfort in 1587 by Johann Spiess, who appears to have not only printed, but also to have written it, although in a dedication to his patrons he says that he received the MS. from a friend, a native of Speier. This old Frankfort Faust-book is far more poetic, profound, and with a deeper significance of symbolism than the second work on the same subject, written by George Rudolph Widman, and published in 1599, in Hamburg. The latter, however, became far more popular, perhaps because it is diluted with sermon - like remarks and grave erudition. By it the better book was crowded out of sight and sunk into oblivion. The third source of the Faust legend is to be found in the so-called *Höllenzwang* — " hell-compulsions " — which are written partly in Latin, partly in German, and which are attributed to Doctor Faust himself. They differ very oddly one from the other, and circulate under different titles. The most famous of them is the *Meergeist*, the Spirit of the Sea — the very name of which was whispered with trembling. The manuscript was long kept in a convent with chain and key. But by some bold indiscretion it was published by Holbek in the Kohlsteg in Amsterdam in 1692.

The popular works which were drawn from these sources also contributed to another remarkable book on Doctor Faust's servant, Christopher Wagner, who was also skilled in magic, and whose adventures and jests were frequently attributed to his celebrated master. Its author, who published his work in 1594, declared it was from a Spanish original, and called himself Tholeth Schotus. If it was really from the Spanish, which I doubt, there is here an indication by which the remarkable resemblance of the legend of "Faust" to that of " Don Juan " may be explained.

But did a Faust really ever exist? As with many other miracle workers, he has been declared to be a mere myth ; in fact, it went even worse with him, for the unfortunate Poles have claimed him for a fellow-countryman, declaring that he is known to them to this day under the name of Twardowski. It is true that, according to the most recent researches as to Faust, he studied magic at the University of Cracow, where it was publicly taught as one of the liberal arts, and that the Poles were then great conjurers, which they certainly are not today. But our Doctor Faust is of such a fundamentally honest nature, so yearning for the true inwardness of all things, and so learned, even in sensuality itself, that he must be either a German or a myth. But there is no reason to doubt of his existence; the most creditable authorities attest it: for example, Johannes Wierus, who wrote the celebrated book on witchcraft; then Philip Melancthon, the brother-in-arms of Luther, as well as the Abbot Tritheim, who was also addicted to mysteries, and who, by the way, perhaps decried Faust out of professional jealousy, and so represented him as a juggler of the market-place and fair. According to the witness of Wierus and Melancthon, Faust was born at Kündlingen, a little town in Suabia, and I may here remark that the above-mentioned principal authorities differed as to his birthplace. According to the older Frankfurt version, he was born as a peasant's son at Rod, near Weimar. In the Hamburg version by Widman, we are, however, told that " Faust was born in the County Anhalt, and his barents dwelt in the Mark of Soltwedel; they were pious peasants."

In a memoir of the admirable and honorable tapeworm doctor, Calmonius, with which I am now occupied, I have an opportunity to fully prove that the real historical Faust is no other than that Sabellicus whom the Abbot Tritheim sketched as a mountebank and arch-rogue, who had abandoned God and the world. The circumstance that he named himself Faustus junior on a visiting-card which he sent to Tritheim, induced the error that there was an elder magician who bore this name. But the word junior here means that Faust had a father or elder brother still living, who was so-called, which is a matter of no importance to us. Quite different would it be should I give our Calmonius of today such a title, since I should then connect him with an elder Calmonius, who lived in the middle of the last century, and who was by the way a great braggart and liar ; as, for instance, when he boasted that he enjoyed the intimate friendship of Friedrich the Great, and often related how the King with all his army marched past his house, and stopping before the window, called aloud to him " *Adies*, Calmonius ; I am going to the Seven Years' War, and I hope to see you again all well !"

It is a common error that our magician is the same Faust who invented the art of printing, and it is expressive and deeply significant. The multitude identified the two, because they surmised that the intellectual direction which the black-artist represented had found in printing its most terrible means of extension, and a union was thereby effected between the two. That intellectual direction is, however, Thought itself in opposition to the blind *credo* of the Middle Age ; to belief in all authorities of heaven and earth ; to a belief in recompense there for abstinence here, as the Church teaches the charcoal-burner who kneels before it. Faust begins to think ; his godless reason rises against the holy faith of his fathers ; he will no longer grope in darkness and idle about in want. He longs for knowledge, worldly power, earthly joys. He wants to know, have power and pleasure, and—to employ the symbolic language of the Middle Age—he becomes an apostate, renounces his heavenly happiness, and worships Satan and his earthly glory. This revolt and its doctrine were so mightily and magically aided by the art of printing, that in the course of time it inspired not only highly advanced and cultured minds, but whole masses of the people. Perhaps the legend of " Faust " exerts a mysterious charm on our contemporaries, because they here see so naïvely and comprehensively set forth the battle which we ourselves now fight, the modern strife between religion and science, between authority and reason, between faith and thought, between humble renunciation or submission to sorrow and daring luxury— a fight to the death, the end whereof will perhaps be that the devil will take us all, as he did the poor Doctor born of the Barony of Anhalt, or of Kundlingen in Suabia.

Yes, our necromancer in the legend oft appears as one with the first printer. This is specially the case in the puppet-plays, where we always find Faust in Mainz, while the popular chap-books invariably indicate Wittenberg as his abode. And it is very remarkable that Wittenberg, the home of Faust, was also the birthplace and laboratory of Protestantism.

The puppet-plays which I have mentioned were never printed, and it was only very recently that one of my friends published the manuscript text of such a work. This friend is Karl Simrock, who attended with me, at the University of Bonn, the lectures of Schlegel on German archæology and meters, and also measured out with me many a good pint of Rhine wine, and so to a degree perfected himself in the auxiliary studies which subsequently aided him when publishing the old puppet-play. He restored the missing passages with tact and genius, selecting from such variations as were available, while the treatment of comic characters shows that he had made deep study of the German Jack-puddings or clowns — probably in the lecture of August Wilhelm Schlegel in Bonn. How admirable is the beginning of the play where Faust sits alone in his study among his books and speaks this monologue:

> " And I have brought it now so far in learning,
> That everybody laughs when me discerning ;
> All books I have read over again and over,
> And yet the stone of Wisdom I can by no means discover.
> Jurisprudence and Medicine are of no use to me,
> There is no healing now — unless in Sorcery.
> The study of Theology did not avail a whit,
> Who'll pay me for the nights which I wasted over it?
> In this my only coat the rents are gaping wide,
> And from my creditors I know not where to hide.
> The hidden depths of hell perhaps may help me more,
> That I the hidden depths of Nature may explore ;
> But to call up its spirits by citation
> I must in magic get some further information."

The scene which follows contains several highly poetic and deeply moving motives, which would be well worthy of far greater tragic poems, and have indeed been taken from such. These are, firstly, the " Faust " of Marlowe, a genial masterpiece, which the puppet-plays imitate not only as regards plot but also in form. Marlowe's " Faust " may have served for model to other English poets of his time as regards treatment of material, and passages from such pieces have in fact passed into the puppet-plays. Such English Faust-comedies were probably at a later period translated into German and acted by the so-called English comedians, who also performed the best Shakespearean works on German stages. Only the names of the plays of these English companies have been kept ; the dramas themselves, which were never printed, have now perished, unless they possibly are preserved by some minor theater, or in strolling companies of the lowest class. I myself remember to have seen the life of Faust twice played by such art-vagabonds, and not as worked up by modern poets, but probably from fragments of old and long-perished plays. The first of these I saw twenty-five years ago, in a corner theater on the so-called Hamburger Berge, between Hamburg and Altona. I remember that the devils who were summoned were all deeply disguised in grey sheets or shrouds. To Faust's question, " Are ye men or women?" they replied, " We have no sex." Faust asked further, what they really looked like under their grey coverings, and they answered, " We have no form which we can call our own, but we will take according to thy will whatever shape you ask us to assume, for we shall ever seem like thine own thought." After the contract had been concluded, which assured him the knowledge and enjoyment of all things, he asked for information as to heaven and hell, which being given, he remarks that it seems to be too cool in heaven and too hot in hell, and that the most tolerable climate must be that of our own good earth. He wins the fairest women of this same good earth by the power of his magic ring, which confers on him the most blooming form of youth, beauty, and winsomeness, also the most magnificent knightly array. After many years of debauchery he has an intrigue with a Signora Lucretia, the most famous courtesan of Venice, but treacherously abandons her and sails for Athens, where the daughter of the Duke falls in love with, and will marry him. Lucretia in desperation seeks counsel of the infernal powers to be revenged on the faithless lover, and the devil confides to her that all the glory of Faust will vanish with the ring which he wears on his forefinger. Signora Lucretia travels in pilgrim garb to Athens, and arrives at court just as Faust, in wedding garments, holds out his hand to the beautiful Duchess to lead her to the altar. But the disguised pilgrim, the woman seeking vengeance, suddenly pulls the ring from his finger, when all at once the youthful features of Faust change to a wrinkled and aged face with toothless mouth ; instead of a wealth of golden curls, a few silver hairs cling to his poor skull ; his shining purple splendor of apparel falls like dry leaves from his bent and tottering form, which is now covered only with vile rags. But the disenchanted enchanter is not aware that he has changed, or rather that his body and clothes now reveal the real ruin which he had been twenty years before, and which has gone on while devilish glamor hid the sight from men ; he does not understand why the court-minions draw back from him in disgust, or why the Duchess cries : " Take the old beggar from my sight !" Then the disguised Lucretia vindictively holds a mirror before him, and he sees in it with shame his true form, and is cast out of doors by insolent servants like a mangy dog.

The other Faust-drama I saw during a horse-fair in a village in Hanover. A small theater had been carpentered up, and though the play was acted by broad daylight, still the evocation-scene was sufficiently effective. The demon who appeared did not call himself Mephistopheles but Astaroth, a name which is probably identical with that of Astarte, although the latter in the secret lore of the Magians was regarded as the spouse of Astaroth. This Astarte is in those writings represented with two horns on the head, which form a half-moon, as she was really once worshipped in Phœnicia as a moon-goddess, and was consequently regarded by the Jews, like all the deities of their neighbors, as a devil. King Solomon the Wise, however, prayed to her in secret, and Byron has celebrated her in his " Faust," which he called " Manfred." In the puppet-play published by Simrock, the book by which Faust is led astray is called *Clavis Astarti de Magica.*

In the play of which I speak, Faust prefaces his invocation with the complaint that he is so poor that he must always go on foot, that not even a cow-girl will give him a kiss, and that he would sell himself to the devil for a horse and a fair princess. The devil

when called appears at first in forms of different animals — of a
pig, an ox, an ape; but Faust rejects him every time with the
remark, " You must appear in a more frightful form to frighten
me!" Then the devil comes as a roaring lion — *quœrens quem
devoret* — but he is not impressive enough for the intrepid magician,
and must retreat with his tail between his legs behind the scenes,
whence he comes forth again as a giant serpent. " You are neither
hideous nor horrible enough!" exclaims Faust. The devil again put
to shame must pack off as before, and we see him reappear as a
magnificently handsome man, wrapped in a scarlet cloak. When
Faust expresses his astonishment at this, Red Cloak replies that,
" There is nothing more terrifying or horrible than man; there
grunt and bellow, bleat and hiss in him the natures of all other
beasts. He is as nasty as a pig, as brutal as a bull, as wrathful
as a lion, as venomous as a serpent — he is a combination of all
animality."

The extraordinary agreement of this old comedy tirade with one
of the chief doctrines of the new philosophy of nature, especially
as developed by Oken, struck me forcibly. After the diabolical
compact is signed Astaroth proposes to Faust several beautiful
women whom he commends — for instance, Judith. " I do not want
a she-executioner," replies the hero. " Cleopatra, then," suggested
the spirit. " No more than the other," answers Faust. " She is too
extravagant, too dissipated; she ruined Mark Antony — why, she
drinks pearls." " Well, then," remarks the mischievous fiend,
" what do you say to the beautiful Helen of Greece?" adding
ironically, " You can talk Greek to her."

The learned doctor is enraptured at the proposal, and then
requires that the devil shall bestow on him bodily beauty and
magnificent garments that he may successfully rival Paris, also a
horse on which to ride at once to Troy. Consent being obtained, he
departs with the demon, both reappearing directly, mounted on
high horses. They cast away their cloaks, and we see them in
gorgeous spangled finery, as English jockeys, perform the most
astonishing equestrian tricks, to the amazement of the assembled
grooms who stood round with their red Hanoverian faces, and in

rapture slapped their yellow leather breeches, so that there was such applause as I never heard before at any dramatic performance. Astaroth, who was a slender, very handsome girl, with the largest infernal black eyes, really rode most charmingly. Faust also was a smart young fellow in his gay jockey dress, and rode far better than all the German doctors whom I have ever seen. He galloped with Astaroth round the ring, at the further part of which we saw the city of Troy, with fair Helena looking from the battlements.

The appearance of Helen in the legend of "Faust" is of the utmost significance. She characterizes the time in which it appeared, and reveals its deepest sentiment. That ever flowering ideal of grace and beauty, fair Helena of Greece, who one fine morning makes her appearance in Wittenberg as Frau Doctor Faust, is that Greece and Hellenism itself which suddenly rose in the heart of Germany as if summoned by magic spell. The magic book, however, which contained the most powerful of those incantations was called Homer, the true and great *Höllenzwang*—Key or Compulsion of Hell—which allured and seduced Faust and so many of his contemporaries. Faust, whether the historical or literal, was one of those humanists who disseminated with zeal and enthusiasm in Germany Greek culture, learning and art. The capital of that propaganda was Rome, where the most distinguished prelates adhered to the cultus of the ancient gods, and where the Pope himself, like his predecessor Constantine, capped the office of a Pontifex Maximus of heathenism with the dignity of chief of the Christian Church. It was the so-called time of the Renaissance, that re-birth of the ancient view of all things. It was easier for it to flourish and rule in Italy than in Germany, where it was opposed by the contemporary appearance of the new translation of the Bible, and the new birth of the Jewish spirit, which we may call the Evangelical Renaissance, which attacked it with such iconoclastic fanaticism. Strange that the two great books of humanity, which had, a thousand years before, waged such fierce battle, and then rested during all the Middle Age as if weary of war—I mean Homer and the Bible—in the beginning of the sixteenth century again enter the lists. As I have already declared that the revolt of the

528

realistic sensual lust and love of life against the spiritual Catholic ascetism is the leading idea of the legend of " Faust," I will here remark in relation to it how that sensual realistic joy of life itself rose in the souls of thinkers suddenly as they became familiar with the monuments and records of Greek art and learning, and as they read the original works of Plato and Aristotle. And in both of these, as tradition expressly asserts, Faust had so deeply buried himself that he once declared that if those works should ever be lost he could restore them from his memory, as Ezra did of yore the Old Testament. How deeply Faust had penetrated into Homer appears by the legend that he once showed the students, who attended his lectures on the poet, all the heroes of the Trojan war in person. In the same manner he, at another time, to entertain his guests, called up the beautiful Helen, whom he subsequently obtained for himself of the devil, and whom he possessed even unto his unhappy end, as the older Faust-book informs us. The book of Widmann merely mentions these incidents as follows : —

" I will not keep from the Christian reader the fact that I found in this place certain stories of Dr. Johann Faust which I for very important Christian reasons would not describe, as, for instance, that the devil always kept him from marriage, and so drove him into his infernal and disgusting net of harlotry, giving him for concubine Helena from hell, who first had by him a horrible monster, and after that a son named Justus."

The two passages in the older work on Faust referring to the beautiful Helen are as follows : —

" On Whit-Sunday the above-mentioned students came unexpectedly again to supper in the house of Doctor Faustus, bringing with them their food and drink, and were agreeable guests. When the wine went round, conversation turned on beautiful women, and one said that there was no beauty whom he desired to see more than Helen of Græcia, through whom the fair town of Troy had perished, and that she must have been beautiful indeed, because she had been so often abducted, and caused such great disturbance. ' Since you are so desirous,' said Faust, ' of seeing the lovely form of Queen Helen, wife of Menelaus, or the daughter of Tyndarus and

Leda, sister of Castor and Pollux, she who was reputed to be the most beautiful in Græcia, I will bring her before you in form and figure as she was in life, as I also did to the Emperor Charles V., at his desire, the representation of the Emperor Alexander the Great and his spouse.' Thereupon Dr. Faustus forbade any one to speak or to rise from the table, or to venture to salute or embrace, and with this he left the room. When he returned, Queen Helena followed him on foot, so wondrous fair, that the students knew not whether they were themselves, so bewildered and burning with passion were they. This Helena appeared in a splendid dark purple dress ; her hair hung down beautiful and glorious as gold, and so long that it came unto the knee ; with coal-black eyes, a charming face with a small round head, her lips red as cherries with a dainty little mouth, a neck like that of a white swan, cheeks like roses, an extremely beautiful and shining face, with a tall and slender person. *In summa*, there was no fault to find in her, and she looked on all with such bold and coquettish glances, that the students were fired with love for her ; yet as they regarded her as a spirit, their passion passed away, as did Helena herself with Doctor Faust from the room. When the students had seen this, they begged Doctor Faust that he would do them the favor to let them see her again the next day, that they might bring an artist, who should take her portrait. But this Doctor Faust refused, saying that he could not evoke this spirit when he would ; yet did he promise them her picture, which they might have copied, which indeed was done, and painters spread it far and wide, for it was a truly magnificent picture of a woman. But who made the original for Faust no one ever knew. As for the students, when they went to rest none of them could sleep for thinking of the figure and form which they had so distinctly seen. From which we may see that the devil often inflames and bewilders men by means of love, so that they fall into lasciviousness, from which they cannot afterwards be drawn."

And we read further on in the old book : —

" And now it came to pass that this wretched Faust, to give full sweep unto his carnal lusts, thinking one midnight when he chanced to wake of Helena of Greece, whom he had shown unto the students upon Whit-Sunday, demanded of his spirit in the morn to bring her to him for a concubine, which was done, and this Helena was even the same form which had been called up for the students. And when Doctor Faustus saw her, she did so captivate his heart that he began at once to fornicate with her, and kept her for his bedfellow, and loved her so that he could not bear to be out of her sight. And in the last year she was with child by him, and bare him a son, at which Faustus rejoiced greatly, and called the babe Justus Faustus. This child revealed to his father many future things which should come to pass in all countries. But when Doctor Faustus afterwards lost his life, both mother and child vanished."

As most of the chap-books on Faust have been drawn from the work of Widmann, there is but scanty mention in them of the beautiful Helen, and its deep significance could therefore be easily passed over. Even Goethe at first missed it when he specially relied (in writing the first part of " Faust ") on these popular works, and did not avail himself specially of the puppet-plays. Not till four decades later, when he composed the second part of " Faust," did he bring Helen into his work ; but then, indeed, he treated her *con amore*. It is the best, or rather the only good thing in the said second part, in this allegoric and labyrinthine wilderness, in which, however, on a sublime pedestal, a marvelously perfect Greek marble statue rises before us, its white eyes gazing on us so heathenishly divine and fascinating in its loveliness that we are well nigh moved to sadness. It is the most precious statue which ever left the atelier of Goethe, and it is difficult to believe that it was cut by the hand of an aged man. It is, however, much more of a work of calm and deliberate execution than the result of inspired imagination, which latter seldom burst forth in great strength by Goethe any more than in his masters and elective affinities—I might almost say by his fellow-countrymen—the Greeks, for these themselves had more harmonious sense of form than excessive fulness of creation, more gift in giving shape than in imagination ; yes, I will plainly utter the heresy—more art than poetry.

You will, dearest friend, readily understand from the foregoing indications why I have given an entire act in my ballet to the beautiful Helen. The island to which I transferred her is, however, not one of my own discovery ; the Greeks found it out long ago, and according to the declaration of ancient authors, especially of Pausanius and Pliny, it was in the Euxine Sea, near the mouth of the Danube, and bore the name of Achillea, from the temple of Achilles, which was on it. It was said that the valiant Pelides himself, risen from the grave, there wandered about in company with the other celebrities of the Trojan war, among whom was the ever-blooming Helen of Sparta. Heroism and beauty must indeed perish prematurely, to the joy of the vulgar mob and of mediocrity ; but great poets raise them from the tomb, and bring them rescued to some isle of bliss, where flowers and hearts fade nevermore.

I have growled somewhat, it may be, over the second part of Goethe's " Faust," but I can in very truth not find words sufficient to set forth all my admiration of the art and poetry with which fair Helen is set forth in them. Here Goethe remained true to the spirit of the legend, which is, unfortunately, as I have already remarked, seldom the case with him, a stricture which I cannot repeat too often. As regards this, the devil has the most cause to complain of Goethe. His Mephistopheles has not the least inner relationship with the true " Mephistopheles," as the old chap-books call him. And here my opinion is strengthened that Goethe did not know the latter when he wrote the first part of " Faust." If he had, he would not have made him appear so hoggishly humorous, or in such a cynically scurrilous mask. For Mephistopheles is no common infernal blackguard ; he is " a subtle spirit," as he calls himself, very aristocratic and noble, and of high rank in the hierarchy of the lower regions, or in the diabolical diplomacy wherein he is a statesman, of whom an imperial chancellor may yet be made. Therefore I have given him a form corresponding to his dignity. The devil always delighted from the earliest time to take the form of a beautiful woman, and in the older Faust-book it was in such guise that Mephistopheles was wont to soothe and delude Faust when the poor soul was seized with scruples. On which the old book thus naïvely expresses itself : —

" When Faust, being alone, would meditate on the Word of God, the devil adorned himself as a fair woman for his pleasure, embraced and practised with him all lewdness and indecencies, so that he soon forgot the Holy Scripture, casting it to the wind, and going onward in his evil ways."

In representing the devil and his comrades as female dancers, I have been truer to tradition than you suppose. It was no fiction of your friend that there were *corps de ballet* of devils in the time of Faust, since it is a fact which I can prove by citations from the life of Christopher Wagner, who was Faust's pupil. In the sixteenth chapter of this old book we read that the evil sinner gave a banquet in Vienna, where devils in the form of women made with stringed instruments the sweetest and most enchanting music, while other devils performed strange and indecent dances. On which occasion they also danced as apes, since we are told, " Soon came twelve apes, who, making a circle, danced French ballets, as people now do in Italy, France, and Germany, leaping and hopping very well, so that many marveled thereat." The devil Auerhahn, who was the familiar spirit of Wagner, generally appeared as a monkey, especially as one which danced. The old book declares that when Wagner invoked him he became a monkey. " Then he sprang up and down, danced *gaillards* and other wanton dances, beat on the tambourine, and blew on the cross pipes and trumpet, as if he had been a hundred."

And here, dearest friend, I cannot resist the temptation to explain to you what the biographer of the necromancer means by the name " gaillard-dances," for I find in a still older book by Johann Prætorius, printed at Leipzig in 1668, and which contains information as to the Blocksberg, the remarkable information that the above-mentioned dance was invented by the devil, the honorable author saying expressly : —

" Of the new galliard-volta, an Italian dance in which the performers act in a most unseemly manner, and spin and reel round like tops when whipped, and which was brought by sorcerers from Italy to France, one may say that such a whirling is full of infamous and revolting gestures and indecent movements, and brings evil with it, since from it come murders and miscarriages. Which is

indeed, where there is a proper police, a thing to be looked
after and most severely prohibited. And while the city of Geneva
especially detests dancing. Satan taught a young daughter of that
place how she could make everybody there dance and spring as
much as she pleased, by touching them with an iron switch or rod
which he gave her. And she also mocked the judge, and said that
they could never bring her to be executed, and had for the evil
deed no remorse."

You see from this citation, dearest friend, firstly, what the galliard is, and secondly, that the devil encourages dancing to vex
the pious. Truly to force the holy city of Geneva, the Calvinistic
Jerusalem, to dance with an iron rod of magic was going far, even
to the pinnacle of insolent injury. Just imagine all these little
Genevese saints, all these God-fearing watchmakers, all these
chosen of the Lord, all of these virtuous female teachers, these firm,
stiff, angular preacher and pedagogue figures, all at once dancing
the galliard! The story must be true, for I remember to have read
it also in the *Dæmonomania* of Bodinus, and I had a great fancy to
work it up into a ballet, to be called Dancing Geneva.

The devil, as you see, is a great artist as to dancing, and therefore
no one should wonder when he presents himself as a *danseuse*
before a highly honorable public. Another metamorphosis which
is less natural, but of deep significance, is that in the oldest work
on Faust Mephistopheles changes to a winged horse, and carries
Faust to all lands and places wherever sense or sensuality desire
to go. The spirit here manifests not only the swiftness of thought,
but the power of poetry ; he is actually the Pegasus who bears
Faust to all the splendors and joys of life in the shortest time. He
brings him in a second to Constantinople, and there into the harem
of the Grand Turk, where Faust, who is believed by the odalisques
to be Mahomed, enjoys himself divinely. Again he is transported to
Rome, where in the Vatican, invisible to all, he steals from the
Pope his best food and wine ; and being merry, often laughs aloud,
so that the Pope, who believes himself to be alone, is terribly
frightened. Here, as everywhere in the " Faust " legend, we observe
sharp animosity to Papistry and the Catholic Church ; and in this

connection it is characteristic that Faust, after the first invocation, expressly orders him to appear in future when summoned, in the cowl of a Franciscan. The old chap-books, not the puppet-plays, show him in this monkish garb, when he disputes with Faust on religious subjects. Here breathes the air of the time of the Reformation.

Mephistopheles not only has no real form, but he has never become popular in any determined one, like other heroes of the chap-books — as, for instance, Tyll Eulenspiegel, that laughter personified in the rude and tough form of a German traveling journeyman ; or like the Wandering Jew, with long beard of eighteen hundred years' growth, whose white hairs have again become black at the tip, as if rejuvenated. Nor has Mephistopheles any peculiar shape in the books of magic, like other spirits — as, for example, Aziabel, who always appears as a little infant ; or the devil, Marbeul, who, as is expressly declared, invariably presents himself in the form of a boy of ten years.

And I would here remark, that I leave it entirely to your machinist whether Faust and his diabolical companion shall fly through the air on two horses, or both be wrapped in a great magic cloak. The magic cloak is the most common in popular legend.

As for the witches when flying to their festival, we must let them fly, no matter whether it be on household utensils or monsters. The German witch generally uses a broomstick on which she smears salve, such as she has previously rubbed all over her own naked body. When her infernal gallant comes in person to accompany her, then he sits before and she behind, during the journey. The French witches say, " *Emen-hetan ! Emen-hetan !* " while they are salving themselves. " *Oben hinaus und nirgends an*— " Out above and nowhere on " — is the cry of the German *chevalières* of the broom, when they fly out of the chimney. They know how to arrange it, so that they meet in the air, and fly in swarms to the Sabbath. As the witches, like the fairies, hate the Christian sound of church-bells from the depths of their hearts, they are accustomed when passing belfries to take the bells and throw them with horrible laughter into some morass. Accusations of this occur in witch trials, and the French proverb justly declares that a man should take to flight if he be accused of stealing the bells of Nôtre Dame.

As for the place of their meeting, which the witches call their *convent* or their Diet, there are widely differing opinions. But from the united testimony of a Remigius, a Godelmann, a Wierus, a Bodinus, and even of a Delancre, I have determined on the top of a mountain grown about with forest, as I have indicated in the third act of my ballet. In Germany, the witch-meeting was, or is usually held on the Blocksberg, which forms the central point of the Harz mountains. And it is not only witches of our native growth who assemble, for there are also many foreigners, and not only living, but also long dead sorceress-sinners, who have no rest in the grave, and who, like the Willis, are tormented in their graves by an irrepressible desire to dance. Therefore we see at the Sabbath a mixture of costumes of all countries and ages. Aristocratic ladies — *les dames de haut parage* — in order to be at their ease, are mostly masked. The wizards, who are also present in great numbers, are often men who, in ordinary life, affect the most honorable and Christian conduct. As for the fiends, who fulfil the functions of lovers, they are of all degrees, so that an old female cook or cow-girl must content herself with a very low-class, poor devil of a devil, while proud and stately patrician ladies or dames of high degree are proportionately accommodated or served with highly-refined and beautifully-tailed devils, and may solace themselves with the most gallant nobles of hell — *enfin les diables comme il faut*. These latter generally wear the old Spanish or Burgundian courtiers' dress, either all black, or else of some very " loud " light color, and on their cap waves the indispensable blood-red cock feather. Yet, however admirable in form and elegant of dress these cavaliers seem at first sight, it is always unpleasantly remarkable that a certain " finish " is wanting, and close consideration of their whole being reveals a want of harmony, or something out of keeping, which jars on eye and ear. They are always too fat or too lean ; their faces are too pale or too red ; the noses are a trifle too short or too long ; and now and then fingers like bird's claws, or even a horse's hoof, reveal themselves. They do *not* smell of brimstone, like the lovers of the lower-class witches, who have to content themselves with common snob-goblins, and with the stokers of hell — *les ramoneurs, fumistes et chauffeurs de l'enfer, et autre menu fretin*. But there is one sad infirmity common to all the devils of which all the witches of every rank complain bitterly, according to all the judicial investigations, which is the icy coldness of their embraces and their gush of love.

Lucifer, King of Darkness by the disgrace of God, presides at the witch meeting in the form of a black he-goat, with a human face and a candle between his two horns. In the center of the arena of the meeting, his majesty stands on a high pedestal, or stone table, and seems to be very serious and melancholy, like a man who is bored to death. All the assembled witches, magicians, devils, and other vassals worship him by passing in pairs, kneeling and then piously kissing his rear. But even this profession of loyalty seems to cheer him very little, still he is not happy, and he remains melancholy and serious while the whole very much mixed society dances in jubilation round him. This round is the famous Witches' Dance, the peculiarity of which consists in this, that the performers all turn their faces away so that they show their backs to one another, and none see each other's faces. This is certainly a rule of precaution, and instituted so that the witches in case of judicial investigation by torture might not be able to declare whom they had seen at the Sabbath. For fear of such betrayals the aristocratic dames came to the ball in masked faces. Many danced *en chemise*, other ladies dispensed with this garment. Many in dancing crossed their arms or held them akimbo, others stretched them widely out, numbers airing their brooms and shouting " *Har ! Har ! Sabbath ! Sabbath !"* It is a bad omen when any one while dancing slips and falls. And should a witch lose a shoe in the tumult of the dance it forbodes that she will be burned alive during the coming year.

The musicians who play for the dance are either infernal spirits of eccentric or hideous form, or else vagabond virtuosi, picked up on the public roads. Blind fiddlers and flutists are, however, preferred, so that they may not be terrified by the horrors of the

Sabbath, as would be the case if they could see. Among these horrors is the initiation of novices, or young witches, into the most fearful mysteries. Then they are officially wedded to hell, and the devil, their gloomy spouse, gives them a new name or *nom d'amour*, and brands them with a secret sign as souvenir of his tenderness. This mark is so well concealed that the judges at witch trials often had a hard time to discover it, for which reason they caused every hair to be shorn from the body of the accused witch by the beadle.

The prince of hell has among the witches of the meeting a chosen one, who is known by the title of *archi-sposa* or arch-betrothed, who is his special mistress. Her ball costume is simple, or more than simple, for it consists of only one shoe of gold, for which reason she is known as the Lady of the Golden Shoe. She is a beautiful and grand, yes, almost colossal lady, for the devil is not only a *connaisseur en belles formes*, like a true artist, but also a lover of flesh, and thinks that the more flesh the more sin. In his refinement of wickedness he seeks to increase his sin by never selecting a maid, but always a married woman, for his chief bride, thus adding adultery to simple immorality. This *archi-sposa* must also be a good dancer, and at an unusually brilliant Sabbath ball the illustrious Goat sometimes descends from his pedestal and in eminent person executes with his naked beauty a peculiar dance which I will not describe, " for reasons of Christian modesty," as old Widman would say. Only so much will I hint, that it is an old national dance of Gomorra, the tradition of which after the destruction of the Cities of the Plain was preserved by Lot's daughters, and is kept to the present day, as I myself often saw it executed in Paris at No. 359, Rue Saint Honoré, near the Church of the Holy Assumption. And when we consider that there is on the dancing-ground of the witches no armed morality in the uniform of municipal policemen, as in Paris, to check Bacchantic frenzy, one may easily imagine what wild goat capers are cut at the aforesaid *pas de deux*.

According to many authorities the great goat and bride-elect preside at the banquet after the dance. The table, furniture, and food at this meal are of extraordinary richness and delicacy ; but whoever carries aught of it secretly away, finds the next day that the golden goblet is only a coarse earthenware pipkin, and the fine cake, cow-dung. What is characteristic in the meal is the entire absence of salt. The songs which the guests sing are pure blasphemies, and they squall, bleat, or whine them to the airs of pious hymns. The most venerable religious ceremonies are aped by infamous buffooneries. Thus, for example, baptism is ridiculed by christening toads, hedgehogs, or rats exactly according to the rite of the Church ; and during this abominable deed the godfather and godmother act like devout Christians, and make the most hypocritical faces. The baptismal water is that of the devil himself. The witches also make the sign of the cross, but reversed, and with the left hand. Those who speak Latin languages pronounce meanwhile the words : " In nomine Patrica Aragneais, Petrica, agora, agora, Valentia, jouando goure gaits goustia," which means, "In the name of Patrike, of Petrike, of Aragonia, in this hour, Valentia, all our suffering is past." To mock the divine doctrine of love and forgiveness the infernal goat at last soars his most terribly thundering voice, " Revenge yourselves, revenge yourselves, else ye shall die!" These are the sacramental words with which the witch meeting closes, and to parody the sublimest act of the passion, the Anti-Christ sacrifices himself, but not for the good, but for the evil of mankind ; that is, the goat burns himself, flaming up with a great crackling sound, and every witch endeavors to obtain a handful of his ashes, to be used in subsequent sorceries. Then the ball and the banquet are at an end, the cock crows, the ladies begin to shiver, and as they came, so they go, but far faster ; and many a witch lies down in bed by her snoring spouse, who has not observed that it was only a log of wood, which, having assumed the form of his wife, had lain during her absence by his side.

I, too, my dear friend, will go to bed, for I have written deep into the night, to bring together all the items which you wished to have noted. I have in so doing thought less of the theatrical director who is to bring my ballet on the stage than of the *gentleman* of great culture, who is interested in everything relating to art and thought. You understand the most fleeting hit of the poet, and every word from you is of value to him. It is incomprehensible to me how you, the experienced and practical man of business, can be so gifted with that extraordinary sense of the beautiful ; and I am even more astonished how you, amid the many tribulations and trials of your professional activity, have been able to retain so much love and inspiration for poetry.

The Gods in Exile

PREFACE TO THE FRENCH EDITION

THE STUDY HERE PRESENTED IS THE LAST PRODUCT OF MY PEN ; only a few of its pages date from an earlier time. I make this remark that it may not seem as if I were treading in the footsteps of certain book-smiths who have often profited by my researches into legendary lore. I would gladly promise a continuation of this work, for which I have accumulated material in my memory, but the very critical state of health in which I now am does not permit me to contract any obligation for the future.

We are all passing away, men, gods, creeds, and legends. It is perhaps a pious work to preserve the latter from oblivion, so that they are embalmed, not by the hideous process of Gannal, but by employing secret means which are only to be found in the *apotheca* of the poet. Yes, creeds are fleeting and traditions too ; they are vanishing like burnt out tapers, not only in enlightened lands, but in the most midnight places of the world, where not long ago the most startling superstitions were in bloom. The missionaries who wander over these cold regions now complain of the incredulity of their inhabitants. In the report of a Danish clergyman of his journey in the North of Greenland, the writer tells us that he asked of an old man what was the present state of belief among them. To which the good man replied, " Once we believed in the moon, but now we believe in it no longer."

HEINRICH HEINE

PARIS, *March* 18, 1853

A QUEER THING IS THIS WRITING ! ONE MAN HAS LUCK IN THE practice thereof, and another none ; but the worst mischance in such work which could well befall any man happened to my poor friend, Heinrich Kitzler — Henry Tickler — *Magister Artium* in

Göttingen. There is not a man there so learned, so rich in ideas, so industrious as this friend ; and yet to this hour no book by him has ever appeared at the Leipzig Fair. Old Stiefel in the library always smiled when Heinrich Kitzler asked him for a book " which he needed for a work which he had ' under his pen.' " " It will be a long time under the pen!" murmured old Stiefel, while he went up the ladder. Even the cookmaids laughed when, having been sent for books, they cried for " something for the Kitzler!"

He was generally regarded as a goose, but in fact he was only an honest man. No one knew the real cause why no book by him was ever published, and it was only by chance that I discovered it, and thus it was. One midnight I went to his room to light my candle, for his apartments adjoined mine. He had just completed his great work on the " Magnificence of Christianity," but he seemed in nowise to rejoice thereover, and gazed with sorrow on his manuscript.

" And now," I remarked, " your name will figure at last in the catalogue of the Leipzig Fair among the books really published!"

" Ah, no!" he sighed from the depths. " This work too must be burned like the others."

Then he confided to me his terrible secret, and truly it appeared that whenever he wrote a book bad luck befell him in abundance ; for when he had fully developed for the subject in hand every point in its favor, he felt himself in duty bound to give every objection which an opponent might adduce. Therefore he sought out with care all the arguments on the other side of the question, and as these unconsciously took root and grew in his mind, it came to pass that his opinions changed, and in the end he was thoroughly convinced that his book was all wrong. But he was then honorable enough (as every French author would be, of course, under similar circumstances) to sacrifice the laurel of literary fame on the altar of truth—that is, to throw his manuscript into the fire. It was for this reason that he sighed from his very soul after having perfectly proved the magnificence of Christianity.

" I have," he said sorrowfully, " copied twenty basketfuls of quotations from the Church Fathers. I have bent for whole nights over my study table and read the *Acta Sanctorum,* while in your rooms punch was drunk and the *Landesvater* sung. Instead of buying a meerschaum pipe, which I deeply desired, I spent thirty-eight hard earned thalers, for recent theological works, on Vandenhoeck and Ruprecht the booksellers. I have worked like a dog for two years, two precious years of life, and all to make myself ridiculous, and to cast down my eyes like a baffled braggart when the church-counselor's wife, Madame Planck, asks me, ' When will your work on the Magnificence of Christianity appear?' Ah, the book is ready," sighed the poor man, " and it would please the public, for I have in it exalted the victory of Christianity over Heathenism ; and I have proved in it, too, that thereby Truth and Reason prevailed over Hypocrisy and Folly. But I, miserable man, feel in my heart of hearts that "——

" Silence!" I cried, with just indignation. " Do not dare, oh infatuated and blinded man, to blacken the sublime and pull the brilliant light down into dust. Even if thou wouldst deny the miracles of the New Testament, still thou canst not deny that the victory of that Evangel was in itself a miracle. A little troop of unprotected men pressed into the great Roman world, defying both its satellites and its sages, and triumphed by the Word alone. But what a Word! Dry and crumbling heathenism shook and was shattered by the words and voice of these foreign men and women, who announced a new kingdom of heaven, and feared nothing in the old world, not the claws of wild beasts, nor the wrath of wilder men, nor fire or sword—for they themselves were the fire and sword—sword and fire, of God. That sword, trimmed away the dead leaves and dry twigs from the tree of life, and thereby cured it of the rottenness which was eating in ; this flame warmed again to life the frozen trunk, so that fresh foliage and perfumed blossoms bloomed anew. It is the most terribly sublime manifestation in the history of the world, this first appearance of Christianity, its battles and its perfect victory."

I uttered these words all the more grandly as became the subject, because I had that evening drunk a great deal of Eimbecker beer, for which reason my voice resounded in its fullest tones.

543

Henry Tickler was in nowise touched by this discourse, nor was he disconcerted, and with ironic yet suffering smile he said, "Brotherly heart, give thyself no needless inconvenience! All which thou hast said I have stated in this manuscript, far better and far more fundamentally. In it I have depicted in the harshest colors the corrupt condition of the world during heathenism, and I dare to flatter myself that my bold touches with the brush recall the works of the best of the fathers of the Church. I have shown how debauched and debased the Greeks and Romans became from the bad examples of those gods who, to judge by the vices attributed to them, were hardly worthy to be classed with men. I have, without mincing the matter, boldly declared that even Jupiter, the chief of the gods, deserved, according to the criminal law of Hanover, a hundred times the penitentiary, if not the gallows ; while, on the other hand, I have appropriately paraphrased the moral axioms of the New Testament, and shown how, according to the example of their divine prototype, in spite of the scorn and persecution which they thereby incurred, taught and practised the most perfect moral purity. That is the most beautiful passage in any work where I depict, as if inspired, how youthful Christianity, like a little David, enters the lists with ancient heathenism and slays the great Goliath. But, ah me! since then this duel appears to me in a new and doubtful light! Alas! all love and joy for my apology disappeared when I vividly presented to myself how an opponent would represent the triumph of Christianity! There fell, unfortunately, into my hands the works of several later writers, such as that of Edward Gibbon, who did not speak so favorably of that victory, nor did they seem to be much edified by the fact that the Christians, when the spiritual sword and flame did not suffice, availed themselves of material weapons and material fire. Yes, I must confess that there at last stole over me a terrible pity for the remains of heathenism, for those beautiful temples and statues, for they no longer belonged to the religion which had been dead long, long before the birth of Christ, but to *Art*, which lives forever. And tears came to my eyes when I one day, by chance, read in the library the "Defence of the Temple," in which the old Greek

Libanius implored most touchingly the pious barbarians to spare those precious masterpieces with which the artistic genius of the Greeks had adorned the world. But all in vain! Those monuments of the spring-tide of mankind which could never return, and which could only bloom once, perished irrecoverably through the gloomy zeal for the destruction of the Christians. . . .

"No!" continued the master, "I will not by publishing this work contribute to such sacrilege. No, that will I never. And to you, ye shattered statues of beauty — to you, ye manes of the dead gods — to you who are now only lovely phantoms in the shadowy world of poetry — to you I sacrifice this book!"

Saying this, Henry Tickler threw his manuscript into the flames of the fireplace, and nothing remained of the "Magnificence of Christianity" save grey ashes.

This happened at Göttingen in the winter of 1820, a few days before that awful New Year's night when the University beadle, Doris, received the most terrible beating, and eighty-five duels were *contrahiert*, or arranged, between the Burchenschaft and Landsmannschaft. Those were fearful blows which fell like sudden showers of sticks on the broad back of the poor beadle. But he consoled himself, as a good Christian, with the conviction that we shall be recompensed at some time in heaven for the pains which we have undeservedly suffered here below. That was all long ago. Old Doris has since many years bid adieu to trouble, and sleeps in peaceful rest before the Weender Gate. The two great parties who once made the duelling grounds of Borden, Ritschenking, and Rasenmuhle ring with their crossing swords, have long since, in deep consciousness of their common worthlessness, drunk together with extreme tenderness to common brotherhood, and the law of time has made his mighty influence felt likewise on the author of those pages. In my brain less gay and wild caprice or fancy plays, and my heart has grown heavy, and where I once laughed I now weep, and I burn with vexation the altar pictures which I once worshipped.

There was a time when I in faith kissed the hand of every Capuchin whom I met in the street. I was a child, and my father

545

let me do so undisturbed, well knowing that my lips would not always be satisfied with Capuchin flesh. And I indeed grew up and kissed beautiful women. But they often gazed at me so pale and painfully that I was frightened in the arms of joy. Here was a hidden trouble which no one beheld, and with which every one suffered, and I often reflected on it. And also whether renunciation and abstinence are to be really preferred to all the joys of this life, and whether those who have, while here on earth below, contented themselves with thistles, will be on that account the more liberally treated with pineapples in the land above. No, he who ate thistles was an ass, and he who receives blows keeps them. Poor Doris!

However, it is not permitted to me to speak out plainly as to everything over which I have reflected, still less to impart the results of my reflection. Yet must I too go to the grave with closed lips, like so many others?

But I may be permitted to cite a few fleeting facts in order to impart some reason, or at least the appearance of it, to the fairy fables which I here compile. The facts refer to the victory of Christianity over heathenism. I am not at all of the opinion of my friend Kitzler that the iconoclasm of the early Christians was so bitterly to be blamed. They could not and dared not spare the old temples and statues, for in these still lived the old Greek joyousness which seemed to the Christian as devildom. In these temples he saw not merely the subjects of a strange cultus and a worthless and erroneous faith which wanted all reality, but the citadels of actual devils, while the gods whom the statues represented existed for him in reality, but as the devils themselves. When these Christians refused to kneel and sacrifice before the images of the gods, they always answered that they dared not worship demons. They preferred martyrdom to manifesting any act of adoration before the devil Juipter, the deviless Diana, or the arch-female fiend Venus.

Poor Greek philosophers! They could never understand this contradiction, just as they subsequently never understood that they, in their polemics with the Christians, had by no means to defend the old dead doctrines but far more living facts. What was wanted was not in reality to prove the deeper meaning of mythology by Neo-Platonic subtleties, to infuse new symbolic blood of life into the dead deities, and to terribly torment themselves by trying to refute the coarse and material abuse of the early Church fathers who ridiculed the moral character of the gods in a manner almost Voltarian — the point in question was to defend Hellenism itself or Greek methods of feeling and of thought, and to defeat the extension of Judaism or of Jewish ideas and sentiment. The real question was whether the dismal, meagre, over-spiritual, ascetic Judaism of the Nazarenes, or Hellenic joyousness, love of beauty, and fresh pleasure in life should rule the world? Those beautiful gods were not the essential part of the polemic ; no one believed any longer in the ambrosial dwellers on Olympus, but people amused themselves divinely in their temples at festivals and mysteries ; they crowned their heads with flowers ; there were charming religious dances ; they stretched themselves on couches in merry banquets, and perhaps for still sweeter pleasures.

All this joy and gay laughter has long been silent, and in the ruins of the ancient temples the old Greek deities still dwell ; but they have lost their majesty by the victory of Christ, and now they are sheer devils who hide by day in gloomy wreck and rubbish, but by night arise in charming loveliness to bewilder and allure some heedless wanderer or daring youth.

The most fascinating legends are based on this popular belief, and our more recent German poets drew from them the subjects of their most beautiful poems. Italy is generally the scene selected, and the hero some German knight who, on account of his youthful inexperience or his fine figure, is ensnared by the beautiful uncanny belles who seek him for their prey. He wanders forth on a fair autumn day with his solitary fancies, thinking perhaps of his native oak-forests, and the blonde maiden whom he left behind — the vain boy! But all at once he stands before a marble statue, at the sight of which he stops, startled. It may be the Goddess of Beauty, and he regards her face to face, and the heart of the young barbarian is secretly seized by the sorcery of the olden time. What can it mean? He never saw such graceful limbs before, and he strangely realizes that in this marble there is a livelier life than he ever found in the red cheeks and lips and all the rosy fleshiness of his fair countrywomen. Those white eyes gaze at him so voluptuously, yet with such suffering sorrow, that his breast swells with love and pity, pity and love. And now he often goes to walk among the old ruins, and the club of his fellow-countrymen is astonished that he is now so seldom seen at their convivial meetings and in their knightly sports. There are strange tales current as to his deeds among the ruins of heathen days. But one morning he bursts with pale distorted features into his inn, pays his reckoning, buckles his knapsack, and hastens over the Alps. What has happened to him?

Well, it happened that one day later than usual, he strolled, after the sun had set, to his beloved ruins, but owing to the growing darkness, could not find the place where he was accustomed to gaze for hours at the statue of the beautiful goddess. After wandering about for a long time at random, he suddenly found himself about midnight before a villa which he had never observed before, and was not a little astonished when servants with torches came forth and invited him in the name of their mistress to enter. What was his astonishment, on entering a vast and brilliantly lighted hall, to behold a lady who was walking to and fro alone, and who, in form and features, had the most startling resemblance to the beautiful statue of his love. And she was the more like that marble image from being clad in dazzling white garb, her countenance being also very pale. When the knight with a courtly reverence advanced to her, she gazed at him long and in silence, and at last asked him with a smile if he was hungry. And though the heart of the knight was leaping within him for love, he still had a German stomach ; in consequence of his wandering for hours he needed a bait, and so very gladly allowed himself to be led by the fair lady to the dining-hall. She took him graciously by the hand, and led him through vast and echoing apartments, which, in spite of all their splendor, seemed to be strangely desolate. The girandoles cast a pale spectral light on the walls, on which variegated frescoes represented all the legends of heathen love, such as those of Paris and

548

Helen, Diana and Endymion, Calypso and Ulysses. The great and strange flowers which stood in marble vases before the windows exhaled a corpse-like, bewildering odor, the wind sighed in the chimneys like a dying man. At last the beautiful lady sat in the dining-room opposite the knight, filled his cup with wine, and smiling, presented him with the choicest delicacies. And yet many things seemed significantly strange to the guest. When he asked for salt a convulsion which was almost hideous appeared on the face of the hostess, nor was it till the knight had several times repeated his request that she, visibly vexed, bade her servants bring the salt-cellar ; and as they placed it with trembling hands on the table, half of it spilled ! However, the good wine, which glowed like fire in the throat of the knight, soothed the secret terror which often thrilled him ; yes, he became confident, confiding, and amorous, and when the beautiful lady asked if he knew what love was, he answered with burning kisses, till at last, intoxicated with passion, and perhaps too with sweet wine, he slept on the bosom of his tender hostess. Yet wild and strange dreams whirred through his mind ; harsh and odd faces, such as we see in the delirium of fever, passed before him. Then he seemed to behold many times his old grandmother, as she sat at home in her great chair, praying with trembling lips. Anon he heard a mocking tittering which came from great bats, which fluttered around, bearing great candles in their claws ; but when he looked more closely, it seemed to him that they were the servants who had waited on him. At last he dreamt that his beautiful hostess had changed to a hideous monster, and that he, in reckless fear of death, had drawn his sword and cut her head off !

It was not until a late hour, when the sun was high in the heaven, that the knight awoke. But instead of the splendid villa in which he thought he had passed the night, he found himself amid the well-known ruins, and he saw that the beautiful statue, which he so dearly loved, had fallen from its pedestal, and its head, broken from the body, lay at his feet !

Of a similar character is the legend of the young knight who once, while playing at ball with some friends, finding that the ring on his finger was in the way, drew it off, and to keep it in safety, put it on the finger of a marble statue. But when the game was over, and he went to the statue, which was that of a heathen goddess, he saw with terror that the marble finger on which he had placed the ring was no longer straight as before, but bent so that he could not reclaim the ring without breaking the hand, from which a certain feeling of sympathy restrained him. He ran to his companions to tell the strange tale, bidding them come to see it with their own eyes, but when they were before it, the statue held out its fingers straight as before, and the ring was gone.

Some time after this occurrence, the knight determined to enter the holy state of matrimony, and the wedding was celebrated. But after the bridal, when he would retire to bed, a female form which was identical with that of the statue in face and form, came to him and claimed him for her own, declaring that as he had put his ring on her finger, he was thereby betrothed to her, and was her spouse by right. In vain did the knight resist this claim ; every time when he sought to approach his bride the heathen woman interposed herself between him and his wife, and this happened again and again, so that the knight became sad and troubled indeed. No one could help him, and the most pious people shrugged their shoulders at it. At last he heard of a priest named Palumnus, who had often shown himself potent in defeating heathenish delusions of the devil. But this man was very loath to aid him in this difficulty, declaring that he himself would incur the greatest danger by so doing. At last, however, he yielded to oft-repeated prayers, and wrote for the knight sundry strange characters on a parchment. Then he advised the latter to go at midnight to a certain cross-road near Rome, and wait. He would see pass by the strangest apparitions, but he must not be moved or terrified at anything, and when at last the woman should come who had taken his ring he must go to her and give her the parchment.

The knight did as he was bid, but it was not without a beating heart that he stood at the cross-roads and awaited the spectral procession. It came, and there were in it pale men and women, magnificently arrayed in festive garments of old Roman time, some bearing golden crowns, others laurel-wreaths on their heads, which, however, hung down in sorrow ; and there were also carried, as if in anxious haste, all kinds of silver cups, goblets, and such things as belong to the service of temples. Then in the crowd were seen great oxen with gilded horns, and hung with garlands, and at last, on a grand triumphal car, magnificent in purple and crowned with roses, appeared a tall and wonderfully beautiful goddess. To her the knight advanced and gave the parchment leaf of Palumnus, for he recognized in her the statue which kept his ring. And when the beautiful woman had read the writing on the parchment, she raised her hands, as if in agony, to heaven, burst into tears, and cried, " Cruel priest Palumnus! thou art not yet satisfied with the suffering which thou hast inflicted on us! But thy persecutions will soon come to an end, cruel priest Palumnus!" With these words she gave the knight again his ring, and on the following night there was no hindrance to his nuptials. But on the third day after this the priest Palumnus died.

I first read this story in the *Mons Veneris* of Kornmann, and more recently found it in the absurd book on magic by Del Rio, who took it from a work by a Spaniard. It is probably of Spanish origin. Baron von Eichendorff, a recent German writer, has availed himself of it most charmingly in a beautiful narrative, and Willibald Alexis has founded on it a novel which belongs to his most poetically inspired works.

The book by Kornmann, *Mons Veneris*, is the most important source for all the subject of which I treat. It is a long time since I saw it, and I can only speak of it from memory, but it always sweeps before me in memory, the little work of about 250 pages, with its charming old letters. It was probably printed about the middle of the seventeenth century.

The doctrine of elementary spirits is there most concisely set forth, and it is with this that the author concludes his strange information as to the Venusberg. After Kornmann's example, I must, as regards elementary spirits, also speak of the transformation of the old heathen divinities. And these are no specters, for they are not dead. As I have said full many a time and oft, they are uncreated immortal beings who, after the victory of Christ, were obliged to retire to under-earthly secrecy, where they in company with other elementary spirits carry on their dæmonic housekeeping. Among the German race rings most exquisitely romantic the legend of the goddess Venus, who, when her temple was destroyed, fled into the heart of a hidden mountain, where she leads the gayest, strangest life with a mad and merry mob of fairy, airy sprites, beautiful nymphs of forest and of stream, and many a famous hero who has suddenly vanished from the world. From afar, as you approach the mountain, you can hear the happy laughter and the sweet sounds of the cithern, which twine like invisible threads round the heart, and draw you to the hill. But, unfortunately, not far from the entrance, an old knight keeps watch and ward ; he is called the trusty Eckart. He stands leaning on his great battle-sword, motionless as a statue, save that his honorable and iron-grey head constantly shakes, warning the one approaching against the dangers which threaten him. Many take warning and are terrified, many more never heed the bleating voice of the ancient warner, and plunge blindly into the abyss of voluptuousness and of per-dition. For a while all goes well, but man is not made for laughter without end ; many a time he falls into silence and seriousness, and thinks back into the past, for the past is the true home of his soul, and he has home-sickness for the feelings of the old time, even though they should be of pain. And so it happened to the Tann-häuser according to the story of a song, which is one of the most remarkable records of language preserved among the German people. I read it first in the already-mentioned book of Kornmann. Prætorius has taken it from him almost verbatim, and the com-pilers of the *Wunderhorn* from the latter, and I must here communicate the ballad from a probably erroneous copy from it.

> " Now I again will raise my voice,
> Of Tannhäuser we'll sing ;
> And what he with Dame Venus did,
> It is a wondrous thing.

Tannhäuser was a noble knight,
    Great wonders he would see,
So went into the Venusberg,
    Where other fair ones be.

' Sir Tannhäuser, thou'rt dear to me,
    So lay it to thy heart ;
And thou likewise hast taken oath,
    From me thou'lt never part.'

' Dame Venus, that I never did,
    And firmly I deny't ;
If no one says the same save you,
    God help me to the right !'

' Sir Tannhäuser, how speak you so,
    You'll stay here all your life ;
I'll give you of my playfellows
    The fairest for a wife.'

' And if unto another wife
    At any time I turn,
So must I in the flame of hell
    Ever in torment burn.'

' Thou speakest much of the fire of hell,
    Yet ne'er hast felt its power ;
O think upon my rosy mouth,
    Which smiles in every hour !'

' What care I for your rosy mouth?
    'Tis naught to me, I trow ;
For the honor of all women-kind
    I pray you let me go !'

' Sir Tannhäuser, would you take leave?
    To you no leave I'll give ;
Oh, stay by me, Tannhäuser dear,
    And merrily let us live !'

' My life is sick, I must be gone,
    No longer can I stay ;
Your face is fair, and proud your form,
    But let me haste away !'

' Tannhäuser, speak not so to me,
    You are no more the same ;
Come with me to a chamber, dear,
    And play our secret game.'

' Thy tender love is lost on me,
　　I have it in my heart ;
O noble Venus, beautiful,
　　That thou a devil art !'

' How darest thou speak so to me?
　　None could save thou alone ;
And should'st thou longer stay by us,
　　These words thou would'st atone.

' Sir Tannhäuser, the leave you ask
　　You must of our elders seek ;
But see where'er abroad you roam
　　You still my praises speak.'

Tannhäuser from the hill has gone
　　With rue and pain in soul ;
To holy Rome I'll wend my way,
　　And tell the Pope the whole.

' I'll go full gaily on the road—
　　God governs it all, I'm sure—
Unto the Pope who's called Urban,
　　He'll find me certain cure !

' Lord Pope, spiritual father mine,
　　My sins are dire distress,
And all I ever did commit
　　I will to you confess !

' I have lived a year with Venus fair,
　　That sin I now deplore ;
No prayer or penance will I spare
　　To be with God once more.'

The Pope he held a wand so white,
　　Broke from a barren tree :
Not till this rod bears leaves again
　　Shall thy sins forgiven be !'

' And I live but a year on earth,
　　One year in bitter pain,
'Twill pass in prayer and penitence,
　　To win God's grace again.'

So from the town he went his way
　　In grief and misery ;
' O Mary Mother, purest maid !
　　Must I then part from thee?

554

' So I will seek the hill again,
    And there for ever stay
By Venus, my own lady dear,
    Since God points out that way.'

' Now welcome, my good Tannhäuser,
    I've missed you since you're gone ;
Be welcome now, my dearest lord,
    My hero, my own true one.'

'Twas on the third day after this,
    The rod bore leaves so green ;
And men went far and wide to find
    Where Tannhäuser had been.

But he was in the hill again,
    And there he now must stay,
Till God shall judge him as he may,
    Upon the final day.

No priest shall ever here on earth
    Deny man's hope of heaven,
For by his penitence and prayer
    His sins shall be forgiven."

I remember when I first read this song in Kornmann's book how I was struck by the contrast of its language with that of the pedantic, be-Latinized, unrefreshing style of the seventeenth century. I felt like one who, in the gloomy shaft of a mine, has suddenly discovered a great vein of gold ; and the proudly-simple, original, and strong words flashed up so brightly that my heart was well nigh dazzled at the sudden gleam. It seemed as if from this song there spoke to me a well-known joyous voice. I heard in it the notes of those heretical or suspected nightingales who during the Passion season of the Middle Age must needs hide themselves in silence, and only now and then, when it was least expected, perhaps even behind some cloister grating, pipe forth a few joyous tones. Knowest thou the letters of Heloise to Abelard ? Next to the high song of the great king (I mean King Solomon), I know of no more burning or flaming song of tenderness than the dialogue between Venus and the Tannhäuser. This song is like a battle of love, and in it runs the reddest heart's blood.

Ah, how magnificent is this poem ! Even in its beginning we

strike on a startling passage. The poet gives us the reply of Lady Venus without having set forth the question of Tannhäuser which called for it. By this ellipsis our imagination gains room in which to play, and permits us to fancy what Tannhäuser might have said, what perhaps would have been difficult to express in a few words. Despite his medieval poverty and piety, the old poet has admirably depicted the unholy arts of seduction and shameless love-tricks of Lady Venus. Even a vicious and sinful modern writer could not have better described the form of this enchanting witch — *cette diablesse de femme* — who with all her *morgue Olympienne* — celestial pride and splendid passion — still shows the *femme galante* or fast woman. Yes, she is a heavenly courtesan perfumed with ambrosia, a camelia goddess, and, so to speak, *une déesse entre-tenue* — a kept divinity. When I turn over my memories it seems as if I must have met her some day on the Place Bréda, walking with a divinely light and graceful step. She wore a *petite capote grise* — a little grey head-covering of deliberate simplicity, and was wrapped from chin to heels in a magnificent cashmere shawl, whose fringe swept the pavement. " What is that woman?" I asked of De Balzac, who was with me. " A kept woman," was his reply. I indeed was much more inclined to believe that she was a duchess. And from a third friend, who just then stepped up, I learned that we were both quite in the right.

The old poet of the ballad has sketched with a skill equal to his character of Venus that of Tannhäuser, who is the Chevalier des Grieux of the Middle Age. What a fine touch is that when Tann-häuser, in the midst of the ballad, suddenly speaks in his own name to the public, and relates what the poet should really tell — that is, how he goes as a pilgrim in despair. Herein we see the want of skill of a poet poor in invention, but such tones produce by their naïveté wonderful and winsome effects.

The real age of the Tannhäuser ballad would be difficult to determine. It existed in flying leaves, or broadsides, of the earliest age of printing. A young German poet, Mr. Bechstein, who kindly remembered in Germany that when in Paris he had met me at the house of our mutual friend Wolf, when the Tannhäuser had formed the subject of our conversation, has recently sent me one of those broadsides, entitled *Das Lied von den Danheüser*. It was only the greater antiquity of the language which prevented me from giving this older version. It contains many variations, and is, to my mind, of a far more poetic character.

And by accident I also received not long ago a version of the same song, in which there is hardly the outer form of the old version, while the inner motives are most strangely changed. In its older form the poem is unquestionably more beautiful, simple, and grand. All that the younger version has in common with it is a certain truth of feeling, and as I certainly possess the only copy of it, it shall here find place : —

"Good Christians, be not led astray
    By 'lurements of the devil,
I sing you the Tannhäuser song,
    To warn your souls from evil.

The Tannhäuser, a noble knight,
    Would win him love and pleasure,
And so he lived in the Venusberg,
    Just seven years full measure.

'Dame Venus, lovely lady mine,
    No longer I'll deceive thee,
By thee I can no longer stay,
    Oh, give me leave to leave thee.'

'Tannhäuser dear, my chevalier,
    Today we've had no kissing ;
Come, kiss me quick, and let me know
    What it can be that's missing.

'Have I not poured the sweetest wine
    For thee, my darling, daily?
And hast thou not with roses red
    Been crowned, and that right gaily?'

'Your too sweet wine, fair lady mine,
    And kisses give me twitters ;
My very soul is sick in me,
    Because I long for bitters.

557

' Until this day we've joked and smiled,
   I long for tears tomorrow ;
Instead of roses, I would fain
   Be crowned with thorns of sorrow.'

' Tannhäuser brave, my chevalier,
   Why wilt thou be unruly?
For thou has sworn a thousand times
   To never leave me—truly.

' Come to my room—let's conjugate
   Of love all the moods and tenses ;
My beautiful form, so lily-white,
   I am sure will revive your senses.'

' Dame Venus, lovely lady mine,
   Thy beauty is eternal ;
But many have read those pages before,
   And many will read thy journal.

' And when I think of the heroes and gods
   Who have browsed in that field before me,
A certain unpleasant *je ne sais quoi*
   For your beautiful form comes o'er me.

' That beautiful form, so lily-white,
   Gives me the horrors—heed me—
When I think how many gentlemen
   Are destined to succeed me.'

' Tannhäuser, noble chevalier !
   With that thou shalt not twit me ;
I'd rather by far thou would'st hit me again,
   As thou often before hast hit me.

' I had rather by far be beaten outright,
   Than told that others will win me ;
How canst thou, ungrateful Christian knight,
   Break the pride of my heart within me ?

' Because I loved you far too well,
   All love for you now I banish ;
Adieu ! you have full permission to go—
   And the door is open—now vanish !' "

———————

" At Rome, at Rome, in the holy town,
    There is ringing and singing and fiddle ;
A grand procession is going about,
    And the Pope he walks in the middle.

That is the pious Pope Urbán,
    With a triple tiara, like Aaron's ;
He wears a red-purple mantle grand,
    Its train is held up by barons.

' O holy father, Pope Urbán,
    By thy power o'er things eternal !
Thou shalt not go till thou hear'st me confess,
    And sav'st me from pains infernal.'

Then all the crowd around draw back,
    Silence o'er all is stealing ;
Who is the pilgrim so wasted and pale
    Before His Holiness kneeling?

' O holy father, Pope Urbán,
    With power o'er good and evil ;
Oh, save me from the terrors of hell,
    And the fearful might of the devil !

' I am called the noble Tannhäuser,
    With loving and sinning wearied ;
For I have been in the Venusberg,
    Where for seven long years I tarried.

' Dame Venus is a lady fair,
    So winsome and enchanting ;
Like sunlight and the scent of flowers
    Is her voice my senses haunting.

' As the butterfly flits about a flower
    And drinks the dew of posies,
So my soul once fluttered every hour
    Around her lips like roses.

' And clustering, blooming, deep black hair
    Round her noble face is wreathing ;
And should once at you her great eyes stare,
    'Twould certainly stop your breathing.

' If her grand black eyes should stare at you,
    You would certainly be enraptured ;
'Twas with greatest trouble I escaped
    From the hill where she held me captured.

559

' It was with trouble that I escaped,
    Yet I'm still possessed by that fairest
Of women, whose glances seem to say,
    " Come back—oh, return to me, dearest."

' I am but a wretched ghost by day,
    But by night in dreams beguiling,
I am ever with that lady fair,
    Who sits by me sweetly smiling.

' Her laugh is so real, so gay, so wild,
    With beautiful teeth in keeping ;
Oh, when I think how once she smiled,
    Oh, then I burst out weeping.

' My love is like a wild spring flood,
    All things before it jamming ;
It is a roaring waterfall,
    Whose course defies all damming.

' It springs adown from cliff to cliff,
    With terrible roar and foaming ;
Though it broke its head a thousand times,
    It would still keep rushing and roaming.

' If all the heaven above were mine
    (In confidence between us),
I would give it with the sun and moon,
    And also the stars to Venus.

' I love her with almighty power,
    Fire clothes my soul like a raiment ;
Is that a touch of the fire of hell,
    Which I get in advance for payment ?

' O holy father, Pope Urbán,
    With power o'er good and evil,
Oh, rescue me from the pains of hell,
    And from the might of the devil.'

The Pope in sorrow upraised his hand,
    When all of these words were spoken :
' Tannhäuser, most unfortunate man,
    This charm can never be broken !

' The devil Venus is worst of all,
    Without any respect or reverence ;
When a man is once in her beautiful claws
    He has not a chance of deliv'rance.

'For lust of the flesh thou hast utterly lost
   All chances of salvation,
And now for ever thou must burn
   In the depths of all damnation.'

Tannhäuser returned so rapidly
   That his feet were sore with piking,
He came again to the Venusberg
   As the midnight hour was striking.

Lady Venus awoke, and hearing his voice,
   Out of her bed came springing ;
And in an instant, with snow-white arms,
   To the dear good fellow was clinging.

Sir Tannhäuser tumbled dead weary to bed,
   O'er his ears she drew the cover ;
Then went into the kitchen below
   To warm a bouillon for her lover.

She gave him bouillon, she gave him a roll,
   She washed his sore feet so neatly ;
She combed his awfully tousled hair,
   And laughed so divinely sweetly.

'Tannhäuser dear, sweet chevalier,
   How long you've been gone — oh gracious !
Pray tell me now, wherever on earth
   Have you traveled about, my precious !'

'Dear Venus, beautiful lady mine,
   I have been to Rome a rover ;
I had business there — but now, I think,
   That job is pretty well over.

'There's a river called Tiber near, and the town
   Is in seven hills dismembered ;
I saw the Pope — he mentioned you —
   And begs to be remembered.

'I stopped at Florence on my way,
   And also looked in at Milan ;
And went as a traveler through Switzerland —
   The Swiss were perfectly willin'.

' And as I crossed the Alpine pass,
 The sun was flying and falling ;
But the fair blue lakes smiled far below,
 And eagles were croaking and calling.

' And as I on the Gotthardt stood,
 Where the snow and ice are coolers,
I heard a snoring — 'twas Germany,
 With its six-and-thirty rulers.

' In Suabia I saw the poet-school
 Of ninnies — past all bearing ;
They sat in a circle, each on a stool,
 With guards round their heads all wearing.

' To Frankfort I came on the *Schabbes* day,
 Where I ate *schalet* and *klösse* ;
Ye have the best religion, I own,
 I am fond too of geese *gekröse*.

' In Dresden, too, I saw a dog
 Once among better numbered,
But now his teeth are falling out,
 He only barked or slumbered.

' In Weimar, the widowed muses' seat,
 To grief full utterance giving ;
Men wept and wailed that Goethe was dead,
 And that Eckermann still was living.

' In Potsdam I heard a mighty shout.
 " What's the matter?" I cried, while speeding ;
" Oh, that is Professor Gans in Berlin,
 On the eighteenth century reading."

' In Göttingen still much learning blooms,
 But produces no fruit for dining ;
I passed through the town in stock dark night,
 For never a light was shining.

' In the workhouse in Celle I only saw
 Hanoverians — O German nation !
Ye need a national workhouse for all,
 And one whip — for your salvation !

' In Hamburg I asked them why it was
 The streets all stunk so sadly,
And Jews and Christians declared it came
 From the gutters, which ran so badly.

' In Hamburg, which is a right good town,
　　Lives many a right bad fellow ;
But when I came upon the Exchange
　　I thought I was still in Celle.

' In Hamburg, in that right good town,
　　The people will see me never,
For now I will live in the Venusberg
　　With my beautiful lady for ever.' "

I will not impose upon the public, be it in verse or prose, and I publicly confess that this poem is by myself, and does not belong to any minnesinger of the Middle Age. I felt myself, however, tempted to follow the original song in which the old poet used the same material. Comparison of the two will be most interesting and edifying for the critic, who would fain see how differently two poets of entirely opposed epochs would handle one and the same theme, should they retain the same subject, measure, and almost the same mold. The spirit of the two ages must become more manifest from such juxtaposition ; it is, so to speak, a specimen of comparative anatomy in the field of literature. In fact, when one reads the two together, he cannot fail to perceive how the ancient faith inspired the older poet ; while in the modern, who was born at the beginning of the nineteenth century, the scepticism of his age reveals itself. One sees how the latter, limited by no authority, gives his imagination full flight, and has no other aim than to properly and well express, *bien exprimer*, in his verse, purely human feelings. The older poet, however, is under the yoke of ecclesiastical authority, he has a didactic aim, he will exalt a religious doctrine, he preaches the virtue of Christian love, and his last words indicate the gracious power of repentance for forgiveness of all sins. The Pope himself is reproved because he forgot this sublime Christian truth, and the dry rod which burgeons in his hands teaches him, unfortunately too late, the infinite depths of divine mercy.

The previously given original Tannhäuser ballad was probably composed just before the Reformation. The legend itself does not go much further back ; it is probably hardly one hundred years older.

Lady Venus also appears at a very late period in German legend, while other divinities, as, for instance, Diana, were known all through the Middle Ages. The latter appears even in the seventh and eighth centuries as an evil demon, decried in the decrees of the bishops. She appears since then generally as riding, she who of yore in Greece ran so lightly shod through the forests. During fifteen hundred years she had to flit about in varied forms, and her character underwent strange transformations. I shall in another place set forth the legends relating to them.

And here a remark suggests itself, the development of which suggests material for most interesting researches. I again speak of the metamorphoses into demons which the Græco-Roman gods underwent when Christianity gained the upper hand in the world. Popular opinion assigned to those deities a real but banned or exorcised existence, agreeing in this with the doctrine of the Church, which by no means explained the ancient deities, as the philosophers had done, as mere chimeras or births from falsehood and error, but regarded them as evil spirts who, by the triumph of Christ, had been thrown from the shining pinnacle of power, and who now lead a gloomy secret life on earth in the darkness of old ruined temples or enchanted forests, where they allure weak Christian souls, who have therein lost their way by seductive devilish arts, lust, and beauty, specially by dances and song, to their ruin. All which refers to this theme — the transformation of the early worship of Nature into devil-worship, and of heathen priesthood into sorcery or witchcraft, or the diabolisation of deity — I have freely discussed in my contributions to the History of Religion and Philosophy in Germany, as well as in the Elementary Spirits ; and I may hold myself to be the more excused from further following up of the subject since many other authors, following in my track, and inspired by the hints which I had given as to the importance of the subject, have treated it far more extensively, comprehensively, and thoroughly than I have done. If they in so doing did not mention the name of the author who had the merit of taking the initiative or being first in the field, this was of course mere forgetfulness, of but little consequence.

I myself will not set a very high value on the claim. It is true that the theme which I brought forward was no novelty, but it had with such vulgarization of old ideas the same relation as with the egg of Columbus. Everybody knew the fact, but no one expressed it. Yes, what I said was no novelty, and was long since to be found printed in the honorable folios and quartos of compilers and antiquarians ; in those catacombs of erudition where, duly arranged with a terrible symmetry, which is far more terrible than wild freewill or fancy, the most heterogeneous bones of thought are piled together. And I also admit that modern scholars have handled the same themes ; but they have, so to speak, coffined them in the wooden mummy-chests of their confused and abstract scientific language, which the public cannot decipher and takes to be Egyptian hieroglyphs. Out of such vaults and catacombs I have evoked these thoughts to real life by the magic power of generally intelligent language, by the black-art of a sound, clear, popular style.

But I return to my theme, whose leading idea, as I have already intimated, shall not be further elaborated here. I will only with a few words call the reader's attention to the fact that the poor old gods above-mentioned were, at the time of the definite victory of Christianity — that is to say, in the third century — in sad difficulties, which bore the greatest resemblance to those in which they had been involved at a much earlier period. They found themselves in the alarming and dire need which they had suffered in the primevally early time, at that revolutionary epoch when the Titans, bursting the bounds of Orcus and piling Pelion on Ossa, stormed Olympus. The unfortunate gods were compelled to take to ignominious flight, and hid themselves in all disguises among us here on earth. Most of them fled to Egypt, where for greater safety they, as is generally known, assumed the forms of animals. In the same manner the poor heathen gods were again driven to flight, and to seek under all kinds of disguises in remote retreats a refuge, when the true lord of the world planted his crusading banner on the castle of heaven, and those iconoclastic zealots, the black bands of monks, destroyed the temples and hunted down the gods with fire and malediction. Many of these poor emigrants, who were without shelter or ambrosia, were obliged to take to some everyday trade, to earn at least their daily bread. In such circumstances, many whose holy groves had been confiscated were obliged, among us in Germany, to work by the day as hewers of wood, and to drink beer instead of nectar. Apollo seems to have taken kindly to his tasks, and entered the service of cattle raisers ; and as he once took care of the cows of Admetus, so he now lived as shepherd in Lower Austria. But there he, having become suspected on account of his beautiful singing, was recognized by a learned monk as an old magical god of the heathens, and handed over to the spiritual court. He confessed on the scaffold that he was the god Apollo. But before his execution he begged that he might be allowed to play on the cithern, and to sing one more song. And his playing was so exquisitely charming, and his song so enchanting, and he was so beautiful in face and form, that all the women wept, and many of them from their emotion fell ill. After his death they sought to take his body from the tomb, to drive a pole through it, thinking that he must have been a vampire, and that the women who had suffered would be cured by such a well-proved remedy. But the grave was empty.

I have not much to relate of the destiny of Mars, the ancient god of war, since the Christians won their victory. I am inclined to think that during the feudal times he exercised the *Faustrecht*, or law of the strong hand. The tall Westphalian Schimmelpfennig, nephew of the executioner of Münster, met him in Bologna, where he had with him a long conversation, which I will relate anon. Some time before he served under Frundsberg as a Landknecht or mercenary soldier, and was at the storming of Rome, where he must have suffered bitterly in seeing the merciless ruin of his favorite ancient city, and of the temple in which he had been worshipped, as well as the shrines of all his relations.

It went better with the god Bacchus than it did with Mars and Apollo ; and a legend relates the following: "There are in the Tyrol large lakes surrounded by forests whose trees rise to heaven, and which are mirrored in the blue depths below. Trees and waters rustle so strangely and uncannily, that a wondrous feeling steals over him who wanders there in solitude. By the shore of such a lake stood the hut of a young fisher, who also acted as ferryman when any one wished to be carried over the water. He had a great boat which was bound to a tree, not far from the house in which he lived alone. Once during the autumnal equinox, towards midnight, he heard a knocking at the window, and going to the door met three monks, whose heads were deeply hidden in their cowls, and who seemed to be in great haste. One of them begged him hurriedly to lend them his boat, and promised to return it in a few hours. The fisherman had no cause to hesitate, and so untied the boat ; and while the monks entered it and rowed away, he returned to his bed and slept. After a few hours he was awakened by their return. One of them gave him a piece of silver, and all three departed. The youth went to look at his boat, and found it tied fast : then he shivered, but it was not the night-air. When the monk paid him the money, he had touched his fingers, which were icy cold, and a frosty shudder ran through all his limbs. He could not for several days forget this ; but youth soon dismisses what is uncanny, and he thought no more of it when the following year at the same time, and towards midnight, there was again a tapping at the window, the three monks again appeared, and again in great haste asked for the boat. This time he let them have it with less care and when they returned a few hours after, and he was again paid, he again felt with a shudder the icy cold fingers.

The same thing happened again and again, till on the seventh year the fisherman began to long — cost what it might — to find out the mystery which was hidden under those three cowls. So he put into the boat a pile of nets, which formed for him a hiding-place, into which he crept, while the monks went on board. They came at the usual time, and he concealed himself unseen by them. To his great amazement the passage across the lake, which always required an hour, was executed in a few minutes ; but what was his amazement when he, who knew the whole country so well, found that the boat had arrived at a vast open space in the woods, which he had never before seen, which was grown about with trees of a kind all unknown to him. Many lamps hung on the branches of these trees, while here and there, on pedestals, were vases full of blazing pitch, and the moon also shone so brightly, that he could perceive all the many persons who were present, as if it had been daylight. Of these there were hundreds, young men and young women, nearly all beautiful, though their faces were white as marble, and this, with their clothing, which consisted of white tunics, girt up very high, with purple borders, gave them the appearance of walking statues. The ladies wore on their heads garlands of grape leaves, which were either real or made of gold and silver thread, while their hair was partly woven from the parting in a kind of crown, and partly flowed wildly from this crown in tresses to the neck. The young men were also crowned with grape-leaves. But men and women all, flourishing golden wands bound with similar leaves, came bounding joyously to welcome the three newly arrived. One of these threw off his cowl and frock, and appeared as an impudent fellow of middle age, who had a repulsive, lascivious, yes, lewd face, with pointed he-goat's ears, and a laughably exaggerated stupendous virile organ. The second, laying aside his garments, revealed an enormously fat paunch, and a bald head, on which the wanton women placed a wreath of roses. But the faces of both monks were white as marble, as was that of the third, who stripped off his disguise with a hearty laugh. As he unbound the rope round his waist, and threw away the pious dirty dress, cross, and rosary with every sign of disgust, he appeared as a young man of extraordinary beauty, clad in a tunic glittering with diamonds, and who was of perfect form, only that his supple rounded haunch and slender waist seemed feminine. And his delicately arched lips and soft features gave him a maiden air, though his face had a bold and almost haughty and heroic expression. The women caressed him with wild inspiration, placed a garland of ivy-leaves on his head, and threw a magnificent leopard's skin over his shoulders. At the same time there came a two-wheeled golden triumphal chariot drawn by two lions, on which the young man, with the dignity of a conqueror, yet with joyous smile, leaped. He drove the wild span with purple reins. On one side of his chariot walked one of his unfrocked companions, whose lustful gestures and indecent extravagance amused the multitude, while his companion with the mighty paunch, whom the merry wives had lifted up on an ass, rode along holding a golden goblet, which was constantly filled for him with wine. Slowly went the chariot, and behind it whirled in wild eddies the reckless troop of vine-clad revellers, while before it advanced the court-choir of the victor. Beautiful full-cheeked youths blowing the double flute, then high-girt maidens with their tambourines, drumming with knuckles on ringing skin ; then other beauties beating triangles ; then horn-players, he-goat footed-fellows with fair but lascivious faces, who blew flourishes on strange horns of animals or sea-shells, and then the lute-players.

But, dear reader, I forget that you are very well educated and informed, who have long observed that all this is a description of a Bacchanalian orgie or festival of Dionysius. You have seen often enough old bas-reliefs, or in the engravings of archæological works, the triumphal processions which glorify the god, and in faith with your classic and refined sense you would be but little alarmed, I trow, should you even at midnight, in the darkest solitude of the forest, encounter the beautiful apparition of such a Bacchic train, even if all its gloriously tipsy crew were to dance on before your very eyes. At the utmost you would only feel a slightly licentious thrill, an æsthetic shiver, at seeing this assembly of delightful phantoms, risen from the sarcophagi of their monuments or their lairs in ruined temples, to again renew their ancient gay and festive rites, to once more celebrate with games and dance the triumph of the divine liberator, of the savior of sensuality, to revive the joyous dance of heathendom, the cancan of the merry world of yore, without any of the policemen of spiritual morality to hinder — all revelling, rioting, hurrahing, Evoe Bacche ! But, dear reader, the poor fisherman of our story was not, like you, familiar with mythology ; he had not studied archæology, and he was terrified and agonized at the sight of that beautiful *triumphator* with his two strange acolytes, when they leaped from their monk's dress ; he shuddered at the immodest gestures and leaping of the bacchantæ, the fauns, the satyrs, who, from their he-goat's feet and horns, seemed to him to be devils, so that he regarded the whole society as a congress of specters and demons, who sought by their sorceries to bring destruction to human beings. The hair stood on his head as he saw the neck-breaking impossible postures of a mœnad, who with flowing locks cast her head back, and only kept her balance with the thyrsus. His brain reeled at beholding Corybantes, who wounded themselves with short swords, madly seeking for ecstasy in pain. The soft, sweet, and yet terrible tones of the music flowed through his soul like flames — flashing, shuddering, awful! But when the poor mortal saw that abominable Egyptian symbol which, of enormously exaggerated size, and crowned with flowers, was carried by a shameless beauty on a long pole, he fairly lost his senses, and, rushing back to the boat, crept under the nets, shivering with clattering teeth, as though the devil already held him by one foot. Soon after the three monks returned and pushed forth. And when they reached the opposite shore, the fisherman contrived to slip away so quietly, that the monks thought he had waited for them behind the willows ; and so, when one of them had pressed with icy-cold fingers into his hand the usual fee, they went their way.

For his own salvation's sake, which he deemed endangered, as well as to preserve all other good Christians from perdition, the fisherman believed it was his duty to denounce the unholy and strange events to a spiritual tribunal ; and as the superior or prior of a Franciscan convent not far off was president of such a court, and was in great repute as a learned exorcist, he determined to seek him without delay. Therefore the early morning sun saw him on his way to the cloister, and it was with his eyes humbly cast down that he found himself before his reverence the prior, who sat with his capuchin drawn deep over his eyes in a high armchair, remaining in this reflective attitude while the fisherman narrated the terrible tale. But when the young man had ended, the prior suddenly raised his head, and the visitor was startled at recognizing in his reverence one of the three monks who went annually over the lake, and he was indeed the very one whom he had seen the night before seated as a heathen deity on the triumphal chariot with the yoke of lions. There was the same marble, pale countenance, the same regular and beautiful features, the same mouth with its delicately arched lips, and over those lips played a pleasant smile, and from that mouth flowed the soft-ringing and sanctimonious words : —

" Beloved son in Christ ! we truly believe that you have passed this night in company with the god Bacchus, as your fantastic ghost-story perfectly proves, and we would not for our life say aught unloving of this god. Many a time doth he break the sorrows and soothe the heart of man ; but he is also very dangerous unto those who cannot bear much, and verily you seem to me to be one of those weak mortals. We therefore counsel you to enjoy in future with great moderation the golden juice of the grape, and to trouble no further in future the spiritual authorities with the imaginary tipsy fancies of your brain, and also to be silent as regards this last vision — that is, to hold your jaw altogether, else the secular arm of the beadle shall count off on you five and twenty stripes with a cart-whip. But now, dearly beloved son in Christ, go to the cloister-kitchen, where the brother butler and brother cook shall serve you with a luncheon."

With this the reverent father gave the fisherman his blessing ; but when the latter, quite bluffed and abashed, packed away to the kitchen, and saw the *pater* cellarer and the *pater* cook, he nearly fell flat with terror, for they were the two very nocturnal companions of the prior, the two monks who had rowed with him over the lake ; for right well did the visitor know the great paunch and bald head of the one, and the grinning, lustful face and goat's ears of the other. But he held his tongue, and spoke thereof word to none till many years after.

Old chronicles which relate similar tales transfer the scene to Spires on the Rhine.

There are similar traditions of the East Frisian coast in which the ancient heathen description of the voyage of the dead to the realm of shadows is most significantly set forth. Nothing indeed is said in them of a Charon who steers, though this old cock — *alter Kawz* — has not kept his place in legends, but in puppet-shows. But we recognize a far more important mythological personage in the so-called *Spediteur*, or forwarding agent, who attends to the passage of the dead, and the ferryman who performs Charon's duties, and who, as a common fisherman, receives the due payment. Yet, despite his *baroque* disguise, we can readily divine his true name, and I will therefore give the tradition as accurately as possible.

In East Friesland, on the North sea-coast, are many coves, which are also small harbors, known as *siehle*. On the jutting headland of one of these stands the lonely house of a fisherman, who lived with his family, peaceful and contented. Nature is sad here, not a bird is heard save the sea-mews, who often fly with evil cry from their nests in the sand announcing a storm. The monotonous splashing of the surging sea agrees well with the gloomy flying clouds. Even man never sings, and on this melancholy coast there is never heard a verse of any popular song. The people here are serious, honest, more reasonable than religious, and very proud of the bold common sense and freedom of their ancestors. They are not imaginative, and speculate but little. The main object of the fisherman who dwelt on his lonely *siehl* was fishing, and now and then the fare of the travellers who wished to be ferried over to some neighboring island of the North Sea.

At a certain time of the year, it is said, just at noon, when the fisher and his family sat at their meal, a stranger appeared in the great family room, and begged the master of the house to speak with him apart for a few minutes, on business. The fisherman, having in vain endeavored to induce the visitor to take part in the meal, complied with his request, and both retired to a bow-window. I will not describe the appearance of the stranger in the leisurely manner of modern novelists, a simply accurate account must suffice. He is a man somewhat advanced in years, but still fresh ; in short, an old boy, well rounded but not fat, his cheeks as red as Borsdorfer apples, and with merry eyes glancing everywhere, while on his powdered head is a three-cornered hat. Under an overcoat of clear yellow, garnished with innumerable small capes, the man wears the old-fashioned dress which we see in old portraits of Dutch merchants, and which denotes a certain ease — a silk parrot-green coat, a flower-embroidered waistcoat, short black breeches, striped stockings, and buckled shoes, the latter so bright and shining that it seemed strange that he could have come through the mud of the Siehl with such clean feet. His voice is asthmatic, wiry, and sometimes passing into a whine or treble ; but the demeanor and manner are grave and measured, as becomes a Dutch merchant. This gravity seems, however, to be more assumed than natural, and often contrasts oddly with the searching glances of the eyes here and there, as well as the indifferently suppressed and nervous activity of his limbs. That the stranger is a Dutch merchant is shown, not only by his clothing, but by the mercantile accuracy and caution with which he conducts a negotiation to the advantage of his employers. He is, as he says, a forwarding agent, and has received from one of his business friends an order to have conveyed a certain number of souls, or as many as may find room in an ordinary boat, from the East Frisian coast to the White Island. On this account, he continued, he would like to know whether the fisherman could carry such a cargo on that very night, in which case he would pay the money down in advance, but hoped that in conscience he would put the price as low as became a Christian. The Dutch merchant—albeit the word is a pleonasm, since every Dutchman is a merchant—made this proposition as if it was concerning carrying so many cheeses, and not the souls of the departed. The fisherman was startled indeed somewhat by the word " souls," and he felt a shiver in the back, and observed at once that he had before him the spectral Dutchman who had so often given a similar commission to his colleagues, who had been well paid for it. But, as I have before remarked, these East Frisian coast dwellers are courageous, healthy, and sober ; they are wanting in that morbid, sickly imagination which renders us so susceptible to the ghostly and supernatural, therefore the secret shudder of our fisherman lasted but an instant, he soon became himself, and with an air of perfect indifference began to bargain the ferry-money up to the highest possible figure. After some chaffering and higgling the two came to an understanding, shook hands over it, and the Dutchman drew out a soiled leather purse, full of small silver pennies, the smallest which had ever been coined in Holland, and paid down all the sum in this Lilliputian money. After having instructed the fisherman that he must be ready about midnight, at the time when the full moon would appear from the clouds with his boat at a certain place on the shore to receive his cargo, he took leave of the family, who again repeated in vain their invitation to share their meal, and the ever dignified figure tripped away with strange agility.

At the appointed time the skipper found himself at the proper place with his barque, which, being empty and light of ballast, rocked lightly on the waves ; but as the moon rose he observed that it became steadier, and gradually sank deeper, till the water was within a hand's-breadth of the gunwale. By this he knew that his passengers, the souls, were now all on board, so he pushed forth with his freight. But however he strained his eyes he could see nothing in his boat but something like trails of mist moving about, but which assumed no certain form, and which seemed to whirl into one another. Nor could he hear anything save a soft chirping and whisper-like sound. Now and then a sea-gull shot with shrill cry overhead, or some fish lifted its head from the water with a strange glare. The night wore on and the air grew cold ; everywhere all was water, moonshine, and silence ; and silent as his surroundings, the fisherman came to the White Island, where he moored his boat. He saw no one on the strand, but heard a sharp asthmatic gasping and whining voice, which he recognized as that of the Dutchman. He seemed to be reading a list of proper names monotonously, as if verifying them, and among them were those of many whom the fisher had known, but who had died during the past year. During this calling off the boat was lightened, so that while at first it had lain deep in the sand, it now swam lightly on the waves when the reading was over, and the skipper, perceiving that his cargo was duly delivered, sailed quietly back to wife and child, and his dear home on the Siehl.

So it passes every year as regards the transport of souls to the White Island. A skipper once remarked as a peculiar circumstance that the invisible controller, while reading the names, suddenly paused and said, " But where is Pitter Jansen? That is not Pitter Jansen." Whereupon a piping, wailing little voice replied, " I am Pitter Jansen's Mieke, and have had my name inscribed in his place."

I have already ventured, despite their crafty disguises, to surmise the names of the important mythological characters who appear in these traditions. This one is nothing less than the god Mercury, the ancient leader of souls, Hermes Psychopompos. Yes, under that shabby overcoat, and in that sober shopman's form, the most brilliant and youthful of the heathen deities, the crafty son of Maia, is disguised. On that three-cornered hat there is not the least sign of a feather which could recall the wings of his divine head-covering, and the heavy shoes with steel buckles do not at all suggest pinioned sandals ; this heavy Dutch lead is different from the mobile quicksilver to which the god gave a name, but the very contrast betrays the identity, and the god chose this disguise to be the more securely concealed. Yet it may be that he in nowise chose it from mere caprice. Mercury was, as you know, at the same time the god of thieves as well as merchants, and it was natural that in choosing a garb which rendered him incognito, and a calling by which he could live, he had in mind his antecedents and talents. Therein he was experienced, he had discovered the tortoise-shell lyre and the helioscope, he robbed men and gods, and even as a babe he was a little Calmonius, who slipped from his cradle to steal a yoke of oxen. He had to choose between the two occupations, which are in reality not very different, since in both the aim is to obtain the property of others as cheaply as possible ; but the shrewd god reflected that thievery does not stand so high in public opinion as trade, that the former is interdicted by the police while the latter is even protected by law, that merchants reach the top-rung on the ladder of honor while those of the thieving fraternity must climb a ladder of a much less agreeable description, that the latter stake liberty and life while the merchant only risks his capital or that of his friends ; and so the cunningest of gods became a merchant, and to be as perfect a one as possible, Dutch at that. His long practice as Theopompos, or leader of the shades, specially adapted him

575

for forwarding souls, the transport of which to the White Island is by him carried on.

The White Island is sometimes called Brea or Britinia. Does this allude to white Albion and to the chalk cliffs on its coast? It would be a droll idea to set forth England as a land of the dead, as the realm of Pluto or hell. Great Britain does, in fact, appear to many strangers in such a light.

In my discussion of the legend of " Faust " I have entered fully into the subject of the realm of Pluto and of himself. I have there shown how the ancient realm of shadows became a complete hell, and how its gloomy and ancient ruler was altogether diabolized. But it is only in the formal official style of the Church that the matter sounds so harsh, for in spite of the Christian anathema the position of Pluto remained much the same as it was. Neither he, the god of the world below, nor his brother Neptune, ruler of the ocean, emigrated like their mates, and even after the prevalence of Christianity they ruled on in their domains or in their elements. Though the wildest and most absurd fables were circulated on earth concerning him, old Pluto sat down below, warm by his Proserpine. Neptune suffered even less from calumny than did his brother Pluto, and neither church-bells nor the peals of organs offended his ears far below in the ocean depths, by his white-bosomed Amphitrite and his dripping courtiers, the Nereids and Tritons. Only now and then, when some young sailor for the first time crossed the Equator, did he rise from the flood, holding the trident, his head crowned with seeds, with a silver beard hanging down to below his waist. Then he bestowed on the neophyte the terrible baptism of the sea, delivering on these occasions a long address full of unction and pathos, also abounding in hard old salt-water jokes, rather spit forth than spoken in company with tobacco-juice, to the great delight of the jolly tars. A friend who described to me in detail how such a water mystery-play was acted by sailors on ships, assured me that those very sailors who laughed the most insanely at the droll burlesque of Neptune, never doubted for an instant of the existence of such a marine god, and often prayed to him when in peril.

576

Neptune, therefore, remained ruler of the waves, as Pluto, despite his metamorphosis, continued to govern the lower regions. It went better with them than with their brother Jupiter, the third son of Saturn, who after the fall of his father attained the sovereignty of heaven, and led, free from care, an ambrosial *régime* of joyousness with the splendid retinue of laughing gods, goddesses, and nymphs of honor. When the sad catastrophe took place, and the rule of the cross, of suffering and sorrow, was proclaimed, the great Chronidas also fled and disappeared in the migration of races. All traces of him were lost, and I have questioned in vain old chronicles and old women — no one could give me tidings of his fate. With the same view I have rummaged and hunted through many libraries, where I had shown me the most magnificent manuscripts, adorned with gold and jewels — true odalisques in the harems of learning ; and I thank with all my heart the literary eunuchs who guard them for the affability, with which they unlocked for me their shining treasures. But it seemed as if no popular tradition as to a medieval Jupiter had been preserved, and all which I forked up consists of a story which my friend Niels Andersen told me. This was a man whose droll delightful figure rises in life before me as I write. To him I here devote a few lines, for I willingly indicate the sources whence my tales are derived, and set forth their peculiarities, that the kind reader may himself judge how far they deserve his confidence. Therefore a few words as to this particular source.

Niels Andersen, born at Drontheim in Norway, was one of the greatest whale-fishers whom I ever knew. I am deeply indebted to him for all my knowledge relating to his craft. He told me of all the tricks which the cunning animal employs to escape the fisherman, and confided to me the secrets of war by which those tricks are defeated. He taught me the trick of handling the harpoon ; how one must push with the right knee against the forward edge of the boat when throwing the harpoon, and at the same time give a good kick to the sailor whose duty it is to pay out the harpoon rope, should he not let it go fast enough. All this I owe to him, and if I never become a great whaler myself the fault is neither Andersen's nor mine, but that of my evil destiny, which never allowed me in all my life to come across a whale with which I could have a conflict worthy of me. I have met hitherto only common dun-fish and — ill or well — red herrings. But what is the use of a harpoon against a herring? And now I must abandon all hopes of all fishery whatever, on account of my stiff leg. But when I first made the acquaintance of Niels at Ritzebuttel near Cuxhaven, he himself was not in best condition as to his feet, inasmuch as one of them was gone. A young shark by Senegal, who perhaps mistook his right leg for a stick of sugar-candy, had bitten it off, and poor Niels ever after had to hobble about on a wooden leg. His great delight was to sit on a hogshead and drum thereon with that wooden leg. Many a time did I help him to climb, and many a time too I refused to help him down until he had told me one of his marvelous salt-yarns.

As Mahomet Eln Mansur began all his poems by praising the horse, Niels Anderson prefaced his tales with an eulogy of the whale. Therefore the story which I here repeat commences with such exaltation.

" The whale," exclaimed Niels Andersen, " is not only the greatest but also the handsomest of animals. From his two nostrils spring great streams of water, which look like wonderful fountains, and which in the night, by moonshine, seem like magic. He is also good-natured, peaceable, and very fond of family life. It is a touching sight when father whale with his folk are gathered together on an enormous ice-flake, and young and old frolic and contend in loving and harmless games. Very often they all jump together into the water to play at blind man's bluff among the floating blocks of ice. The purity of manners and chastity of the whale are far more due to the ice-water in which they continually paddle their fins than to any moral principles. Nor can it be denied that they have no sense of religion, nay, are utterly wanting in it."

" I believe," I said, interrupting my friend, " that *that* is a mistake." I lately read a narrative by a Dutch missionary in which he describes the glory of creation as revealed in the high polar regions, when the sun rises and day shines on the stupendous and strange masses of ice. " These," he says, " which remind us of fairy-palaces of diamonds, afford such striking proofs of the power

578

of God, that not only man but even the coarse natures of fish are so moved at the sight as to adore their Creator." " Yea," declares the *dominie*, " I have with my own eyes seen many whales who, leaning against a wall of ice, stood up and moved the upper part of their bodies after the fashion of people who pray."

Niels Andersen shook his head doubtfully. " He had himself seen," he said, " whales leaning against upright ice-blocks, making movements like such as we behold in the religious exercises of many sects, but he could not attribute such acts to piety." He explained the phenomenon physiologically, remarking that the whale — the Chimborazo of animals — has under his skin such an enormous layer of fat (blubber) that a single individual often yields from one hundred to a hundred and fifty barrels of tallow. And this tallow is so thick that many hundred water-rats make their nests in him, while the great animal sleeps on a flake of ice ; and these creatures, which are infinitely larger and more voracious than our land-rats. lead a joyous life under the skin of the whale, where they by day and night eat the best of fat without leaving their nests. This reveling becomes at last somewhat annoying or intolerably painful to the unwilling host, who, not having hands like man wherewith to scratch himself when tickled, seeks to allay his pain by placing himself on the sharp edge of an ice-floe, and rubbing his back up and down against it, as dogs do when they scrape themselves against any board when they are afflicted with fleas. The honest Dominie mistook these movements for those of prayer and so ascribed them to piety, while they were merely caused by the orgies of rats. " The whale," said Niels Andersen, in concluding his proeme, " though he holds so much oil, is utterly wanting in the least sense of religion." It is indeed only among the middle-sized animals that one finds it, vast creatures like the whale are not endowed with this quality. What can be the cause of this? Is it because they cannot find a church sufficiently roomy or " broad " enough to receive them in its bosom ? This monster honors neither the law nor the prophets ; even the little prophet Jonas, whom he once heedlessly swallowed, went against his stomach, and after three days he spat him out. This magnificent animal no more adores the Lord our God than does the false heathen deity, who lives on Rabbit Island near the North Pole, and whom he sometimes goes to visit.

" What place is that — the Rabbit Island?" I asked Niels Andersen. He drummed awhile with his wooden leg on the hogshead, and answered : —

" Well, it was the island on which the thing happened which I am going to tell you. But I can't tell you exactly where it is. Nobody has ever been able to find it again since it was first discovered. Perhaps the great icebergs which float everywhere round it, and don't allow many approaches to it, have prevented ships from getting there. However, it may be a hundred years ago, the crew of a Russian whaler, driven there by storms, landed on it. Going ashore with a boat they found it a very desolate place. Broom plants waved sadly along the quicksands ; only here and there grew a dwarf fir, or there were some worthless dwarf bushes. But they saw many rabbits jumping about, from which they called it Rabbit Island.

" At last they saw a poor hut, which showed that some human being dwelt there. Going into it they found a very old man, who, badly clothed in rabbit skins sewed together, sat on a stone bench by the fire-place warming his lean hands and tottering knees by a few burning twigs. By him at his right hand stood an immense bird, which seemed to be an eagle, but which time had gnawed so cruelly that only the long bristly quills of his wings remained, giving him a comic and yet horribly ugly look. On the left side of the old man cowered on the ground a very large hairless she-goat, which also seemed to be very old, though full udders with fresh and rosy nipples were on her belly.

" There were among these Russian sailors several Greeks, and one of them, not supposing that he would be understood by the old man, said to a comrade in Greek : —

" ' This old fellow is either a ghost or an evil spirit.'

" But on hearing this the old man rose from his seat, and to their astonishment the sailors saw a tall and stately figure, who in spite of his age appeared to be of majestic or royal dignity, whose head almost touched the timbers of the roof—a man whose features, though wasted and worn, indicated that he had once been very handsome, for they were noble and strongly outlined. A few silvery locks hung over his forehead, which was stern with age and pride ; his eyes gleamed sharply, though pale and staring, and from his high-curling mouth came forth in ancient Greek the sonorous and mournful words : —

" ' You are wrong, young man. I am neither a ghost nor an evil spirit, but only an unfortunate being who has seen better days. But who are ye?'

" The sailors told him of the disaster which had befallen them, and asked for information concerning the place, but obtained very little. The old man said that he had lived since time immemorial on the island, whose bulwarks of ice protected him securely against bitter enemies. He lived chiefly by catching rabbits, and once a year when the icebergs were solidly frozen there came to him on sledges certain savages, to whom he sold his rabbit-skins, and who gave him in exchange the articles which he most needed. The whales, which often swam about the shore, were his favorite companions. But it gave him pleasure then to talk with them, for he was a Greek by birth, and therefore begged his fellow-countrymen to tell him something about the present condition of Greece. He seemed spitefully pleased to learn that the Cross had been torn from the battlement of the Greek cities, but less glad to know that the Crescent had taken its place. And it was very strange that none of the sailors knew the names of the cities of which the old man inquired, and which he said were flourishing in his time, nor did he recognize the names of the towns and villages of Greece of which they spoke. On this account he often shook his head sorrowfully, and they gazed at one another in amazement. But they observed that he knew the situation of every place in detail ; the bays, the promontories, the cliffs, often even the smallest hills and little groups of rocks, so that his ignorance of the chief places caused the greatest wonder. Then he inquired of them with great interest, indeed with some anxiety, as to a certain great temple, which he declared had been in his time the most beautiful building in all Greece. Yet none of his listeners knew the name which the old man pronounced with tenderness, till at last, when he described its situation closely, a young sailor recognized the place.

" The young man said that the village where he was born stood on that very spot, and that he had in it long tended the swine of his father. There, as he declared, were really the ruins of very ancient buildings, which indicated a magnificent grandeur of the past. Only here and there stood a few great marble pillars, either singly or connected by the blocks of a pediment, from the fissures in which hung down blooming masses of honeysuckles and red bell-flowers, like tresses of hair. Other columns, among them several of rose-marble, lay broken on the ground, and the grass grew exuberantly on the magnificent capitals, which were carved in leaves and flowers. And there too were great four-cornered or triangular slabs of marble, which had covered the roof, lying here and there, half sunken in the ground, overshadowed by an immense wild fig-tree, which had grown from among the fragments. The youth related that he had often passed hours under the shadow of that tree, looking at the wondrous figures in high relief on the sculptured stones, which represented all kinds of games and conflicts, but which were full sadly worn, as if by time, or overgrown with moss and ivy wild. His father, whom he had questioned as to the meaning of all these columns and images, had replied that they were the remains of an ancient temple, in which a heathen god of evil fame had dwelt in days of yore, who was given, not only to the most naked and shameless debauchery, but who also practised unnatural crime and incest ; yet the blind heathen ever held him in such reverence that they often sacrificed to him hundreds of oxen at once. And that the hollowed marble block into which the blood of the victims ran was there before his eyes, and it was that very stone trough in which he fed his pigs with offal or gave them drink.

" When the young man had said this the greybeard sighed bitterly, and then manifesting the greatest grief sank, as if heartbroken, on his stone seat, covered his face with both hands, and wept like a child. The great bird screamed horribly, and flapping his monstrous wings threatened the strangers with beak and claws.

But the old goat licked the hand of her master, and bleated sorrowfully, as if to soothe him.

"An uncanny dread seized the sailors, they hastened from the hut, and felt relieved when they no longer heard the sobs of the old grey man, the screams of the bird, and the bleating of the she-goat. When returned to the ship they told the tale. Among others on board was a learned Russian, professor of the philosophical faculty at the University of Kasan, and he declared, placing his forefinger knowingly on his nose, that the discovery was of great import, for the old man on the Island of Rabbits could be none other than the ancient deity, Jupiter, son of Saturn and Rhea, once the king of all the gods. The bird at his right side was probably the eagle who once bore the terrible lightnings in his talons. And the old she-goat could be no other person than Amalthea, the old nurse who had suckled the god long since in Crete, and which now in exile again fed him with her milk."

Such was the story of Neils Andersen, and I confess that it filled my soul with sorrow. I will not deny that what he had already told me of the secret sufferings of the whales had greatly excited my sympathy. Poor colossal beast! There is no help for thee against the despicable rabble of rats which have nested in thee and gnaw thee continually, and whom thou must bear about with thee for life, though thou shouldst flee in despair from the northern to the southern pole, and rub thee on the icy corners of the bergs! It is all of no avail, and withal thou hast not the consolation of religion! And such rats gnaw at every great being on this earth, and the gods themselves must at last go in shame to sorrow and a lowly end. Such is the will of the iron law of fate, and unto it the grandest and highest of immortals must bow in suffering. He whom Homer sung and Phidias did counterfeit in gold and ivory, he who had but to wink to crush the world, he who had folded in his passionate arms Leda, Alcmena, Semele, Danae, Kallisto, Io, Leto, Europa—he must after all hide at the North Pole behind icebergs, and trade in rabbit-skins like a beggarly Savoyard!

I do not doubt that there are many people who would take spiteful pleasure in such a spectacle. Such folk are possibly the descendants of the unfortunate oxen who were slaughtered in hecatombs on the altars of Jupiter. Rejoice, ye children of cattle, for the blood of your ancestors, the sacrifice unto superstition is avenged! But we who have no hereditary grudge rankling in us are shocked at the sight of fallen grandeur, and devote to it the deepest pity of our hearts. This susceptibility hinders us perhaps from imparting to the narrative that air of seriousness which is the charm of history ; only in a degree can we master that gravity which is only to be attained in France. Modestly, therefore, do we commend ourselves to the kind indulgence of the reader, for whom we ever manifest the utmost respect, and therewith we conclude the first part of our history of " The Gods in Exile."